Praise for *Network Programmability and Automation*

I highly recommend this new edition of the book to anyone looking to improve their network automation skills. The authors do an outstanding job of explaining complex topics in a clear and concise way. They also provide a comprehensive overview of current technology trends in the field, as well as architectural design options and methodologies that you can use to achieve positive results for your organization. I found the book to be very helpful and informative, and I am confident that you will too.

—*Nicolas Leiva (Staff Solutions Architect at Red Hat and author of* Network Automation with Go*)*

Networking infrastructures have undergone significant evolution in various aspects of cloud computing, as well as cloud-native eras, including scale, complexity, functionalities, and virtualization depths. As a result, traditional network operation fashions are rapidly becoming obsolete. This book offers a comprehensive guide to addressing the challenge through network automation, covering fundamental programming languages, common automation tools, and the development of user-facing systems. By leveraging the techniques presented in this book, readers can establish a robust, flexible, and evolving automation platform using cutting-edge tools.

—*Arthur (Yanan Zhao), Senior Architect in Cloud Department, Trip.com*

This book helps networking professionals and developers write clear, easily extensible network automation playbooks. It covers almost everything that you need to be at the helm of network automation.

—*Akhil Behl, Partner Manager, Red Hat*

SECOND EDITION

Network Programmability and Automation

Skills for the Next-Generation Network Engineer

Matt Oswalt, Christian Adell,
Scott S. Lowe, and Jason Edelman

Beijing · Boston · Farnham · Sebastopol · Tokyo

Network Programmability and Automation

by Matt Oswalt, Christian Adell, Scott S. Lowe, and Jason Edelman

Published by O'Reilly Media, Inc., 1005 Gravenstein Highway North, Sebastopol, CA 95472.

O'Reilly books may be purchased for educational, business, or sales promotional use. Online editions are also available for most titles (*https://oreilly.com*). For more information, contact our corporate/institutional sales department: 800-998-9938 or *corporate@oreilly.com*.

Acquisitions Editors: Simina Calin and Jennifer Pollock	**Proofreader:** Stephanie English
Development Editor: Melissa Potter	**Indexer:** WordCo Indexing Services, Inc.
Production Editor: Kristen Brown	**Interior Designer:** David Futato
Copyeditor: Sharon Wilkey	**Cover Designer:** Karen Montgomery
	Illustrator: Kate Dullea

February 2018:   First Edition
August 2023:   Second Edition

Revision History for the Second Edition
2023-08-16:   First Release

See *https://oreilly.com/catalog/errata.csp?isbn=9781098110833* for release details.

The O'Reilly logo is a registered trademark of O'Reilly Media, Inc. *Network Programmability and Automation*, the cover image, and related trade dress are trademarks of O'Reilly Media, Inc.

978-1-098-11083-3

[LSI]

Table of Contents

Preface

Welcome to *Network Programmability and Automation*!

The networking industry is changing dramatically. The drive for organizations and networking professionals to embrace the ideas and concepts of network programmability and automation is greater now than perhaps it has ever been, fueled by a revolution in new protocols, new technologies, new delivery models, and a need for businesses to be more agile and more flexible in order to compete. But what *is* network programmability and automation? Let's start this book by answering that question.

What This Book Covers

As its title indicates, this book is focused on network programmability and automation. At its core, network programmability and automation is about simplifying the tasks involved in configuring, managing, and operating network equipment, network topologies, network services, and network connectivity.

Many, many components are involved—including operating systems that are now seeing far broader use in networking than in the past, new methodologies like continuous integration, and tools that formerly might have fallen only in the realm of the system administrator (tools like source code control and configuration management systems). Because all of these play a part in the core definition of network programmability and automation, we cover all these topics. Our goal for this book is to enable you to establish a foundation of knowledge around network programmability and automation.

What's New in This Edition

This edition of the book has been updated from the original to include four totally new chapters:

- Chapter 4, "Cloud"
- Chapter 5, "Network Developer Environments"
- Chapter 7, "Go"
- Chapter 14, "Network Automation Architecture"

We've also updated the existing chapters to include newer concepts such as these:

- Google Protocol Buffers
- gRPC/gNMI
- Terraform
- Nornir

On top of all these new additions, we've refreshed and extended every chapter to reflect the advances and industry changes that have taken place since the first edition was published.

We're thrilled to have the opportunity to add these new, exciting topics to the book. Because of size constraints, some content from the first edition was not carried over into this one. However, rather than simply removing this content, we've made it freely available at *https://oreilly-npa-book.github.io*.

How This Book Is Organized

This book isn't necessarily intended to be read from start to end; instead, we've broken up the topics so that you can easily find the content that most interests you. You may find it useful to start out sequentially reading the first three chapters, as they provide background information and set the stage for the rest of the book. From there, you're welcome to jump to whatever topics are most useful or interesting to you.

We've tried to keep the chapters relatively standalone, but—as with any technology—that's not always possible. Wherever we can, we provide cross-references to help you find the information you need.

Here's a quick look at how we've organized the topics:

Chapter 1, *"Network Industry Trends"*
Provides an overview of the major events and trends that launched software-defined networking (SDN). As you'll see, SDN was the genesis for an increased focus on network programmability and automation.

Chapter 2, *"Network Automation"*
Takes the SDN discussion from Chapter 1 and focuses specifically on network automation—the history of network automation, types of automation, tools and technologies involved in automation, and how automation affects operational models (and how operational models affect automation).

Chapter 3, *"Linux"*
Provides an overview of the Linux operating system. By no means a comprehensive discussion of Linux, this chapter aims to get networking professionals up to speed on Linux, basic Linux commands, and Linux networking concepts.

Chapter 4, *"Cloud"*
Introduces cloud computing from a networking perspective, and provides a jumping-off point for many relevant topics like containers and Kubernetes networking. We also discuss how network engineers' existing skills translate to a cloud-based environment.

Chapter 5, *"Network Developer Environments"*
Explores the tools and techniques for maintaining a network developer environment. This is a crucial part of any network automation project, and it allows teams to collaborate on solutions more effectively, as well as efficiently move from development to testing, all the way to production.

Chapter 6, *"Python"*
Introduces networking professionals to Python (*https://python.org*). This programming language is frequently used in network programmability and automation contexts, and this chapter covers many of the basics of programming with Python: data types, conditionals, loops, working with files, functions, classes, and modules.

Chapter 7, *"Go"*
Adds a second option to the network automation professional's programming language repertoire, by exploring Go. Having recently grown in popularity—in large part because of the cloud native ecosystem—Go is a valuable asset even for those just starting on their automation journey.

Chapter 8, "Data Formats and Models"

Digs into the formats and methods for transmitting, storing, and modeling network automation data. The ability to understand and work with data is a fundamental skill for any network automation professional, and in this chapter, we build a solid foundation for the chapters to follow.

Chapter 9, "Templates"

Looks at the use of templating languages to create network device configurations. While the primary focus of this chapter is on the Jinja templating language, as it integrates natively with Python, we also explore Go templates and Extensible Stylesheet Language Transformations (XSLT).

Chapter 10, "Working with Network APIs"

Covers the role of APIs in network programmability and automation. We explore key terms and technologies pertaining to APIs including HTTP, NETCONF, RESTCONF, and gNMI as examples to show how they can be used for network programmability and automation. We use both Python and Go libraries to automate network devices using these APIs.

Chapter 11, "Source Control with Git"

Introduces Git (*https://git-scm.com*), a popular and widely used tool for source code control. We talk about why source code control is important, how it is used in a network programmability and automation context, and how to work with popular online services such as GitHub (*https://github.com*).

Chapter 12, "Automation Tools"

Explores the use of open source automation tools such as Ansible (*https://www.ansible.com*), Nornir (*https://oreil.ly/L7rFo*) with NAPALM (*https://oreil.ly/MngGc*), and Terraform (*https://www.terraform.io*). You'll learn how these tools can be used specifically for network programmability and automation, using the imperative and declarative approaches.

Chapter 13, "Continuous Integration"

Examines continuous integration (CI) and the key tools and technologies that are involved. We discuss the use of test-driven development (TDD), explore tools and frameworks like GitLab and Jenkins, and take a look at a sample network automation workflow that incorporates all these CI elements.

Chapter 14, "Network Automation Architecture"

Unifies all the concepts covered in prior chapters by proposing a reference architecture for a holistic network automation solution. Brings together automation and orchestration, explores the idea of a source of truth, and shows how user interactions might work in such a system.

Who Should Read This Book

As we mentioned previously, the goal of this book is to equip you with foundational knowledge and a set of baseline skills in the areas of network programmability and automation. We believe that members of several IT disciplines will benefit from reading this book.

Network Engineers

Given the focus on network programmability and automation, it's natural that one audience for this book is the "traditional" network engineer, someone who is reasonably fluent in network protocols, configuring network devices, and operating and managing a network. You'll learn how to use automation for configuration management, troubleshooting, observability, and more. This book will enable network engineers to be more efficient and to build more reliable infrastructure through automation and programmability.

Prerequisites

Network engineers interested in learning more about network programmability and automation don't need any previous knowledge in software development, programming, automation, or DevOps-related tools. The only prerequisite is an open mind and a willingness to learn about new technologies and how they will affect you—the networking professional—and the greater networking industry as a whole.

Systems Administrators

Systems administrators, who are primarily responsible for managing the systems that connect to the network, may already have previous experience with some of the tools discussed in this book (notably, Linux, source code control, and configuration management systems). This book, then, could serve as a mechanism to help systems administrators expand their knowledge and understanding of such tools by presenting them in a different context (for example, using Ansible to configure a network switch as opposed to using Ansible to configure a server running a distribution of Linux).

Prerequisites

This book *doesn't* provide any coverage or explanation of core networking protocols or concepts. However, as a result of managing network-connected systems, we anticipate that many systems administrators also have a basic knowledge of core networking protocols. So most experienced systems administrators should be fine. If you're a bit weak on your networking knowledge, we recommend supplementing this book with one that focuses on core networking concepts and ideas. For example,

Packet Guide to Core Network Protocols by Bruce Hartpence (O'Reilly) may be a good choice.

Software Developers

Software developers may also benefit from reading this book. Many developers will have prior experience with some of the programming languages and developer tools we discuss (such as Python and/or Git). Like systems administrators, developers may find it useful to see developer tools and languages used in a networking-centric context (for example, seeing how Python could be used to retrieve and store networking-specific data).

Prerequisites

We do assume that you have a basic understanding of core network protocols and concepts, and all the examples we provide are networking-centric examples. As with systems administrators, software developers who are new to networking will probably find it necessary to supplement the material in this book with a book that focuses on core networking concepts.

Tools Used in This Book

As with any field of technology, the technologies and tools found in the network programmability and automation space have many versions and variations. Therefore, we standardized on a set of tools in this book that we feel best represents those you will find in the field. For example, Linux has many distributions, but we focus on only Debian, Ubuntu (which is itself a derivative of Debian), and CentOS (a derivative of Red Hat Enterprise Linux or RHEL). To help make it easy for you, we call out the specific version of the various tools in each tool's specific chapter.

Online Resources

We can't possibly cover *all* the material we'd like to regarding network automation and network programmability. Therefore, throughout the book we reference additional online resources that you may find helpful in understanding the concepts and skills being presented.

Conventions Used in This Book

The following typographical conventions are used in this book:

Italic
    Indicates new terms, URLs, email addresses, filenames, and file extensions.

Constant width

> Used for program listings, as well as within paragraphs to refer to program elements such as variable or function names, databases, data types, environment variables, statements, and keywords.

Constant width bold

> Shows commands or other text that should be typed literally by the user.

Constant width italic

> Shows text that should be replaced with user-supplied values or by values determined by context.

 This element signifies a tip or suggestion.

 This element signifies a general note.

 This element indicates a warning or caution.

Using Code Examples

Supplemental material (code examples, exercises, etc.) is available for download at *https://github.com/oreilly-npa-book/examples/tree/v2*.

If you have a technical question or a problem using the code examples, please send email to *support@oreilly.com*.

This book is here to help you get your job done. In general, if example code is offered with this book, you may use it in your programs and documentation. You do not need to contact us for permission unless you're reproducing a significant portion of the code. For example, writing a program that uses several chunks of code from this book does not require permission. Selling or distributing examples from O'Reilly books does require permission. Answering a question by citing this book and quoting example code does not require permission. Incorporating a significant amount of example code from this book into your product's documentation does require permission.

We appreciate, but do not require, attribution. An attribution usually includes the title, author, publisher, and ISBN. For example: "*Network Programmability and Automation*, 2nd Edition, by Matt Oswalt, Christian Adell, Scott S. Lowe, and Jason Edelman (O'Reilly). Copyright 2023 Matt Oswalt, Scott S. Lowe, and Christian Adell, 978-1-098-11083-3."

If you feel your use of code examples falls outside fair use or the permission given above, feel free to contact us at *permissions@oreilly.com*.

O'Reilly Online Learning

 For more than 40 years, *O'Reilly Media* has provided technology and business training, knowledge, and insight to help companies succeed.

Our unique network of experts and innovators share their knowledge and expertise through books, articles, and our online learning platform. O'Reilly's online learning platform gives you on-demand access to live training courses, in-depth learning paths, interactive coding environments, and a vast collection of text and video from O'Reilly and 200+ other publishers. For more information, visit *https://oreilly.com*.

How to Contact Us

Please address comments and questions concerning this book to the publisher:

O'Reilly Media, Inc.
1005 Gravenstein Highway North
Sebastopol, CA 95472
800-889-8969 (in the United States or Canada)
707-829-7019 (international or local)
707-829-0104 (fax)
support@oreilly.com
https://www.oreilly.com/about/contact.html

We have a web page for this book, where we list errata, examples, and any additional information. You can access this page at *https://oreil.ly/NPA_2e*.

For news and information about our books and courses, visit *https://oreilly.com*.

Find us on LinkedIn: *https://linkedin.com/company/oreilly-media*

Follow us on Twitter: *https://twitter.com/oreillymedia*

Watch us on YouTube: *https://youtube.com/oreillymedia*

Acknowledgments

This book would not have been possible without the help and support of a large community of people.

First, we'd like to extend our thanks to the vibrant network automation community. There are too many folks to name directly, but these are the people who have created open source projects like NAPALM, Netmiko, Nornir, and Containerlab, who have helped lead the charge in educating the industry about network automation, and who have tirelessly contributed their knowledge and experience for the benefit of others. Thank you all for your efforts and your contributions.

Our technical reviewers were critical in ensuring that the content is both technically accurate and easily consumable by readers. We'd like to extend our thanks to Patrick Ogenstad, Akhil Behl, Eric Chou, Sreenivas Makam, Michael Kehoe, and Arthur Chiao. Thanks for helping make sure this book is the best it could be!

Finally, our thanks would not be complete without including the staff of O'Reilly Media: our editors Simina Calin, Jennifer Pollock, and Melissa Potter; production editor Kristen Brown; copyeditor Sharon Wilkey; proofreader Stephanie English; and indexer Bill Morrison.

## CHAPTER 1

Network Industry Trends

More than a decade has passed since the term *software-defined networking* (SDN) was coined, representing one of the biggest revolutions in the networking industry since the 1990s, and likely the term is still confusing you. Whether you are new to SDN or have been hung up in its craze for the past several years, don't worry. This book will walk you through foundational topics to start your journey of understanding how software, the cloud, and open source have completely transformed the way we architect and manage networking in the modern era.

This chapter provides insight into trends in the network industry focused on SDN, its relevance, and its impact in today's world of networking. We'll get started by reviewing how SDN made it into the mainstream and ultimately led to network programmability and automation practices.

The Rise of Software-Defined Networking

If one person could be credited with all the change occurring in the network industry, it would be Martin Casado, a general partner in the venture capitalist company Andreessen Horowitz. Previously, Casado was a VMware fellow, senior vice president, and general manager in the Networking and Security Business Unit at VMware. He has had a profound impact on the industry, not just from his direct contributions (including OpenFlow and Nicira), but by opening the eyes of large network incumbents and showing that network operations, agility, and manageability must change. Let's take a look at this history in a little more detail.

The Advent of OpenFlow

For better or worse, *OpenFlow* served as the first major protocol of the SDN movement. Casado worked on OpenFlow while earning his PhD at Stanford University, under the supervision of Nick McKeown. The OpenFlow protocol allows for the decoupling of a network device's control plane from the data plane (see Figure 1-1). In simplest terms, the control plane can be thought of as the *brains* of a network device, and the data plane can be thought of as the *hardware* or *application-specific integrated circuits* (ASICs) that perform packet forwarding.

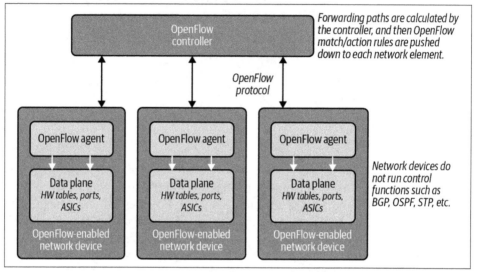

Figure 1-1. Decoupling the control plane and data plane with OpenFlow

 Figure 1-1 depicts the network devices having no control plane. This represents a pure OpenFlow-only deployment. Many devices also support running OpenFlow in a hybrid mode, meaning Open-Flow can be deployed on a given port, virtual local area network (VLAN), or even within a normal packet-forwarding pipeline. Then, there is no match in the *OpenFlow table*, the existing forwarding tables—media access control (MAC) routing, etc.—are used, making packet forwarding more analogous to policy-based routing (PBR).

This means OpenFlow is a low-level protocol used to directly interface with the hardware tables (e.g., forwarding information base, or FIB) that instruct a network device on how to forward traffic (for example, "traffic to destination 192.168.0.100 should egress port 48").

 OpenFlow is a low-level protocol that manipulates flow tables, thus directly impacting packet forwarding. OpenFlow is not intended to interact with management plane attributes like authentication or Simple Network Management Protocol (SNMP) parameters.

Because the tables OpenFlow uses support more than the destination address as compared to traditional routing protocols, OpenFlow offers more granularity (matching fields in the packet) to determine the forwarding path. This is not unlike the granularity offered by PBR to decide the next routing hop by taking into account the source address. As OpenFlow would do many years later, PBR allows network administrators to forward traffic based on "nontraditional" attributes, like a packet's source address. However, it took quite some time for network vendors to offer equivalent performance for traffic that was forwarded via PBR, and the final result was still very vendor specific.

The advent of OpenFlow meant that we could achieve the same granularity with traffic-forwarding decisions but in a vendor-neutral way. It became possible to enhance the capabilities of the network infrastructure without waiting for the next version of hardware from the manufacturer.

History of Programmable Networks

OpenFlow was not the first protocol or technology used to decouple control functions and intelligence from network devices. A long history of technology and research predates OpenFlow, although OpenFlow is the technology that started the SDN revolution. A few of the earlier technologies include Forwarding and Control Element Separation (ForCES), active networks, routing control platform (RCP), and path computation element (PCE). For a more in-depth look at this history, take a look at the paper "The Road to SDN: An Intellectual History of Programmable Networks" (*https://oreil.ly/o-pq0*) by Nick Feamster et al.

Why OpenFlow?

While it's important to understand what OpenFlow is, it's even more important to understand the reasoning behind the research and development effort of the original OpenFlow spec that led to the rise of SDN.

Casado had a job working for the United States government while he was attending Stanford. At that time, the government needed to react to security attacks on its IT systems (after all, this is the US government). Casado quickly realized that he was able to program and manipulate the computers and servers as needed. The actual use cases were never publicized, but it was this type of control over endpoints that made it possible to react, analyze, and potentially reprogram a host or group of hosts when and if needed.

When it came to the network, it was nearly impossible to do this cleanly and programmatically. After all, each network device was *closed* (locked from installing third-party software, for example) and had only a command-line interface (CLI). Although the CLI was and is still well known and even preferred by network administrators, it was clear to Casado that it did not offer the flexibility required to truly manage, operate, and secure a network.

In reality, the way networks were managed had *never* changed in more than 20 years except for the addition of CLI commands for new features. The biggest change was the migration from the Telnet to the Secure Shell (SSH) protocol, which was a joke often used by the SDN company Big Switch Networks in its slides, as you can see in Figure 1-2.

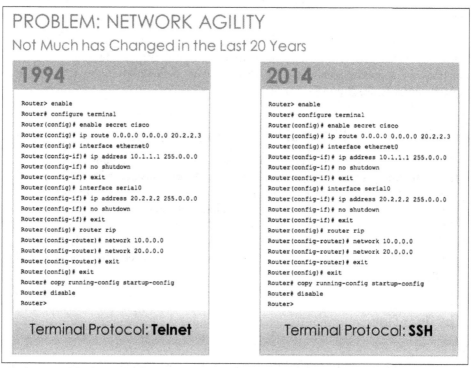

Figure 1-2. What's changed? From Telnet to SSH (image source: Big Switch Networks, acquired by Arista Networks)

All joking aside, the management of networks has lagged behind other technologies quite drastically, and this is what Casado eventually set out to change over the next several years. This lack of manageability is often better understood when other technologies are examined. Other technologies almost always have more modern ways of managing many devices for both configuration management and data gathering and analysis—for example, hypervisor managers, wireless controllers, IP PBXs (i.e., private IP telephony exchange), PowerShell, DevOps tools, and the list goes on. Some of these are tightly coupled to vendors as commercial software, but others are more loosely aligned to allow for multiplatform management, operations, and agility.

If we go back to the scenario Casado encountered while working for the government, what sort of questions came up when looking for answers? Was it possible to redirect traffic based on the application? Did network devices have an application programming interface (API)? Was there a single point of communication to the network? The answers were largely *no* across the board. How could it be possible to *program* the network to dynamically control packet forwarding, policy, and configuration as easily as it was to write a program and have it on an end host machine?

The initial OpenFlow spec was the result of Casado experiencing these types of problems firsthand. While the hype around OpenFlow has died down since the industry started to finally focus more on use cases and solutions than low-level protocols, this initial work was the catalyst for the entire industry to rethink the way networks are built, managed, and operated. Thank you, Martin.

This also means if it weren't for Casado, this book may never have been written!

What Is Software-Defined Networking?

We've introduced OpenFlow, but what is software-defined networking? Are they the same thing, different things, or neither? To be honest, SDN is just like the cloud was more than a decade ago, before we knew about different types of cloud, such as infrastructure as a service (IaaS), platform as a service (PaaS), and software as a service (SaaS).

Having reference examples and designs streamlines our understanding of the cloud over time, but even before these terms existed, it could be debated that when you saw the cloud, you knew it. That's kind of where we are with SDN. Some definitions state that white-box networking is SDN or that having an API on a network device is SDN. Are they *really* SDN? Not really.

Rather than attempt to define SDN, this chapter covers the following technologies and trends that are often thought of as SDN and included in the SDN conversation:

- Opening up the data plane
- Network functions virtualization
- Virtual switching
- Network virtualization
- Device APIs
- Network automation
- Bare-metal switching
- Data center network fabrics
- Software-defined WAN
- Controller networking
- Cloud native networking

We are intentionally not defining SDN in this book. While SDN is mentioned in this chapter, our primary focus is on general trends that are often categorized as SDN to ensure that you're aware of each trend more specifically.

Of these trends, the rest of the book focuses on network automation, APIs, and peripheral technologies that are critical in understanding how all the pieces come together in network devices that expose programmatic interfaces with modern automation tools and instrumentation.

Aside from the previous list, other technologies and patterns not directly related to networking will continue to have a big impact on the way networks are built and operated. For instance, artificial intelligence/machine learning (AI/ML) solutions will bring new capabilities to help make educated decisions when designing a new network, proposing an optimization change, or learning about normal traffic patterns to detect outliers. Keep your mind open to all the new opportunities that will appear in tech, and consider how they can be used in the networking field.

Opening Up the Data Plane

OpenFlow was the main disruptor to expose the benefits of opening up the data plane and allowing its control by external control planes. This separation enabled the independence of the software controller and the underlying network. To make this possible, OpenFlow came up with its abstract *standard* modeling that was not able to support vendors' extensions, and with predefined packet-processing pipelines (i.e., how a packet traverses the ASICs) and predefined data structures, both to allow OpenFlow to change the forwarding path in *runtime*. These limitations, and others, made evident OpenFlow was not capable of solving the decoupling of control and data plane because of the challenges of a centralized control plane at scale.

No changes in OpenFlow standard development have been published since release 1.5.1 in 2017 (*https://oreil.ly/y-7s9*), and its adoption is limited to specific use cases.

Understanding some of the limitations in OpenFlow raises new questions:

- Why must these packet-processing *pipelines* be fixed?
- Why can't we define new data structures?

Barefoot Networks (*https://oreil.ly/dnbzi*), acquired by Intel, answered that call, creating a new family of high-performing chips (Tofino (*https://oreil.ly/J2OXk*)) with

---

a *full programmable execution pipeline*, along with a new programming language, Programming Protocol-Independent Packet Processors, or P4 (*https://p4.org*).

> P4 and OpenFlow protocol specifications are driven by the same organization, the Open Networking Foundation, or ONF (*https://oreil.ly/H2r3_*).

This new disruptive approach challenged the status quo of the silicon switch market. Broadcom, the biggest player in the game, launched Network Programming Language, or NPL (*https://nplang.org*), as an alternative programmable solution (with a limited set of configurable options) and also made a significant move to offer an easier way to program its chips by opening its OpenBCM SDK (*https://oreil.ly/ajk2X*) in 2020. Other players have also adopted some level of programmability. For instance, Cisco Silicon One and Juniper Trio/Penta solutions support P4 programmability.

> Traditionally, ASICs have been programmed (with the constraints of a fixed-processing pipeline) via chip vendors' SDKs, which expose the pre-created data structures and methods to define how the packet forwarding will be executed (taking into account the forwarding state data).
>
> A few years ago, chip vendors started to open their SDKs that were previously shared by request and under nondisclosure agreements (NDAs), to facilitate the third-party programmability of their solutions. This change was likely motivated by the industry to push toward the low-level programmability of ASICs.

These highly customizable ASICs have a limited market today because of the higher cost and some technical constraints; some market forecasts show a significant increase in adoption in the coming years. Time will tell how this market evolves (for example, Intel announced the halt of Tofino chip development in 2023) and which use cases will benefit the most from the flexibility that these programmable pipelines offer.

In Figure 1-3, you can see how the networking control and data planes are decoupled, exposing two new interfaces, the northbound and southbound APIs. The *northbound API* allows external applications to interact with the network controllers, and the *southbound API* is used by the network controller to define the packet forwarding in the data plane. Then, in the data plane, you can see one forwarding implementation that has a fixed ASIC integrated with an OpenFlow agent, and a programmable ASIC that can be programmed via P4.

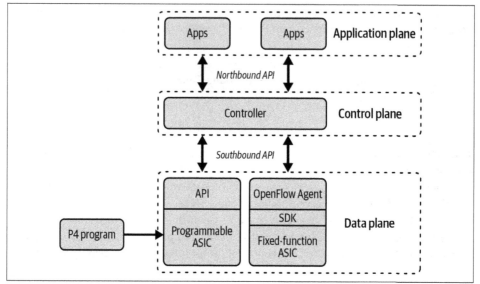

Figure 1-3. Programmable ASICs

Programming the data plane enables us to more granularly define the way traffic traverses the network, but this flexibility comes with extra complexity. This is great if you have a team of developers (in big corporations such as Google or Amazon) or if programming the data plane is your core business (networking vendors and integrators). But, for most organizations, the use of OpenFlow, P4, or any other given protocol will be less important than what an overall solution offers to the business being supported.

Network Functions Virtualization

Network functions virtualization (*NFV*) isn't a complex concept. It refers to taking functions that have traditionally been deployed as hardware and instead deploying them as software. The most common examples are virtual machines (VMs) that operate as routers, firewalls, load balancers, intrusion detection systems and intrusion prevention systems (IDS/IPS), virtual private networks (VPNs), application firewalls, and any other service/function.

 Don't confuse our description of the NFV concept with the concrete ETSI NFV specification (*https://oreil.ly/w5MeD*) for the telecom industry (ETSI is the European Telecommunications Standards Institute, focused on telecommunications, broadcasting and other electronic communications networks and services). Here, we approach NFV from an abstract point of view, without concrete implementation details.

With NFV, it becomes possible to break down a monolithic piece of hardware that may have cost tens or hundreds of thousands of dollars and that has hundreds to thousands of lines of commands, in order to configure it into *N* pieces of software—namely, virtual appliances. These smaller devices become much more manageable from an individual device perspective.

The preceding scenario uses virtual appliances as the form factor for NFV-enabled devices. This is merely an example. Deploying network functions as software could come in many forms, including embedded in a hypervisor (known as virtual network function, VNF), as a container (known as container network function, CNF), or as an application running atop an x86 server.

It's common to deploy hardware that *may* be needed in three to five years, just in case, because gradual upgrades would be too complicated and even more expensive. So hardware is not only an intensive capital cost but also used for the what-if scenarios *only if* growth occurs. Deploying software-based, or NFV, solutions offers a better way to scale out and minimize the failure domain of a network or particular application while using a *pay-as-you-grow model*. For example, rather than purchasing a single large Cisco ASA (*https://oreil.ly/XY7S3*), you can gradually deploy Cisco ASAv appliances and pay as you grow. You can also easily scale out load balancers with newer technologies from a company like Avi Networks, now part of VMware.

Even though NFV offered so many benefits, the industry—mostly telcos and managed service providers (MSPs)—took a while to adopt these solutions in production. There were a few reasons. First, the change required rethinking how the network is architected. In a single monolithic firewall (as an example), everything goes through that firewall—meaning all applications and all users, or if not all, a defined set that you are aware of. In the NFV paradigm, many virtual firewalls could be deployed, with a firewall per application or tenant as opposed to a single big-box firewall. This makes the failure domain per firewall, or any other service appliances, fairly small, and if a change is being made or a new application is being rolled out, no change is required for the other per-application (per-tenant) firewalls.

On the other hand, in the more traditional world of monolithic devices, a single pane of management existed for security—a single CLI or graphical user interface (GUI). This could make the failure domain immense, but it does offer administrators streamlined policy management since only a single device is being managed. For some teams or staff supporting these devices, this reason could lead them to keep the monolithic approach.

However, recently, with the accelerated IT transition to cloud-based environments, private and public, the customers' demand for more dynamic architectures has motivated networking teams to build hybrid networks requiring different types of NFV solutions. In this journey, the appearance of new tooling to consume and manage software-centric solutions and the answer to the call from vendors (traditional and new), has popularized the use of NFV solutions.

 In the beginning, a factor that delayed the adoption of NFV was that some vendors were not selling their *virtual appliance* edition with the same determination as the rest of their portfolio. We're not saying they didn't have virtual options, but they were usually not the preferred choice of many traditional equipment manufacturers. If a vendor had a hardware business for a while, it was a drastic shift to a software-led model from a sales and compensation perspective. On the contrary, nowadays vendors are investing in evolving their hardware and software solutions in parallel.

As will be seen in many of these technology areas, a major value of NFV is in agility too. Eliminating hardware decreases the time to provision new services by removing the time needed to rack, stack, cable, and integrate into an existing environment. Leveraging a software approach, it becomes as fast as deploying a new VM into the environment, and an inherent benefit of this approach is being able to clone and back up the virtual appliance for further testing—for example in disaster recovery (DR) environments or emulating virtual labs, as you will see in Chapter 5. Moreover, this flexibility plays a key role in supporting new technologies, such as edge computing or 5G networks.

Finally, when NFV is deployed, it eliminates the need to route traffic through a specific physical device to get the required service, multiplying the flexibility to change the network architecture depending on the specific service and creating *service chains* (concatenating multiple NFVs that a network packet has to traverse through), such as the ones that segment routing (*https://www.segment-routing.net*) enables.

Virtual Switching

The more common virtual switches on the market include the VMware vSwitch, Microsoft Hyper-V Virtual Switch, a Linux bridge, and Open vSwitch (OVS).

These switches every so often get wrapped into the SDN discussion, but in reality, they are software-based switches that reside in the hypervisor kernel and provide network connectivity between VMs/containers and the node itself, which connects to the external network. They provide functions such as MAC learning and features like link aggregation, SPAN, and sFlow, just like their physical switch counterparts have been doing for years. While these virtual switches are often found in more comprehensive SDN and network virtualization solutions, by themselves they are switches that just happen to be running in software.

While virtual switches are not a solution on their own, they are extremely important as we move forward as an industry. They've created a new access layer, or new edge, within the data center. No longer is the network edge the physical top-of-rack (ToR) switch that is hardware defined with limited flexibility (in terms of feature/function development). Since the new edge is software based through the use of virtual switches, it offers the ability to rapidly create new network functions in software, and thus, it is possible to distribute policy more easily throughout the network. As an example, the security policy can be deployed to the virtual switch port nearest to the actual endpoint, be it a VM or container, to further enhance the security of the network.

Network Virtualization

Solutions categorized as network virtualization have become synonymous with SDN solutions. For the purposes of this section, *network virtualization* refers to software-only overlay-based solutions. Some popular solutions that fall into this category are VMware NSX, Nokia's Nuage Networks Virtualized Services Platform (VSP), and Juniper's Contrail.

A key characteristic of these solutions is that an overlay-based protocol such as Virtual Extensible LAN (VXLAN) is used to build connectivity between hypervisor-based virtual switches. This connectivity and tunneling approach provides Layer 2 adjacency between VMs that exist on different physical hosts independent of the physical network, meaning the physical network could be Layer 2, Layer 3, or a combination of both. The result is a virtual network that is decoupled from the physical network and that is meant to provide choice and agility.

 The term *overlay network* is often used in conjunction with *underlay network*. For clarity, the *underlay* is the underlying physical network that you physically cable up. The *overlay* network is built using a network virtualization solution that dynamically creates tunnels between virtual switches within a data center. Again, this is in the context of a software-based network virtualization solution. Also, note that many hardware-only solutions are now being deployed with VXLAN as the overlay protocol to establish Layer 2 tunnels between ToR devices within a Layer 3 data center.

While the overlay is an implementation detail of network virtualization solutions, these solutions are much more than just virtual switches being stitched together by overlays. These solutions are usually comprehensive, offering security, load balancing, and integrations back into the physical network, all with a single point of management (the controller). Often these solutions offer integrations with the best-of-breed Layer 4–7 services companies as well, offering choice as to which technology could be deployed within network virtualization platforms.

These solutions use a centralized control plane to distribute the mapping information between the overlay and underlay networks. However, this centralized approach introduces limitations in terms of scalability, interoperability, and flexibility. An alternative approach appeared in the form of a distributed protocol, Ethernet VPN (EVPN). In EVPN, every network device distributes the mapping information (via Border Gateway Protocol, or BGP) to the rest of the network to establish the VXLAN tunnels. It is also known as the *controller-less* VXLAN solution.

 A good reference for VXLAN and EVPN is *Cloud Native Data Center Networking* by Dinesh G. Dutt (O'Reilly).

Device APIs

Over the past several years, vendors have begun to realize that just offering a standard CLI is not going to cut it anymore and that using a CLI has severely held back operations. If you've ever worked with any programming or scripting language, you can probably understand that. For those who haven't, we'll talk more about this in Chapter 10.

The major pain point is that scripting with legacy or CLI-based network devices does not return structured data. Data would be returned from the device to a script in a raw text format (the output of show version), and then the person writing the script would need to parse that text to extract attributes such as uptime or operating system (OS) version. When the output of show commands changed even slightly, the scripts would break because of incorrect parsing rules. While this approach is all administrators have had, automation was technically possible, but now vendors are gradually migrating to API-driven network devices.

Offering an API eliminates the need to parse raw text, as structured data is returned from a network device, significantly reducing the time required to write a script. Rather than parsing through text to find the uptime or any other attribute, an object is returned, providing exactly what is needed. Not only does it reduce the time to write a script, lowering the barrier to entry for network engineers (and other non-programmers), but it also provides a cleaner interface such that professional software developers can rapidly develop and test code, much like they operate using APIs on non-network devices. "Test code" could mean testing new topologies, certifying new network features, validating particular network configurations, and more. These are all done manually today and are time-consuming and error prone.

However, this isn't a new idea; the Network Configuration Protocol (NETCONF) was published via RFC 4741 (*https://oreil.ly/KZNU2*) in 2006 and remained one of the relatively few options for some time, Juniper Networks being the primary vendor promoting it. More recently, other vendors started creating their own APIs such as Arista's eAPI (*https://oreil.ly/CG82P*) or Cisco Nexus NX API, and later, they adopted open interfaces such as NETCONF, Representational State Transfer Configuration Protocol (RESTCONF), and gRPC Network Management Interface (gNMI). Nearly every vendor out there has some sort of API these days (and its documentation), and consumer demand has driven part of this transformation. We cover APIs in more detail in Chapter 10, and the data formats used by them in Chapter 8.

 Even though Juniper with NETCONF and Arista Networks with eAPI were API-first, they also provided a CLI (on top of those APIs) because network operators were (and are still) used to operating with this kind of interface.

Hyper-scale networks, like the ones supporting the big public cloud providers, can't be operated manually (and match the required operational excellence). Therefore, the presence of APIs (i.e., gNMI or NETCONF) for managing network infrastructure has long been a hard requirement for these companies. It is well-known that large network operators like these can shape network vendors' roadmaps with requests like: "If model *XYZ* doesn't support the management interface *ABC*, I am not going to consider it" or "If this feature is available only via CLI, it is not a feature for us." You can realize how influential these sentences can be when we are talking about large potential purchases; this is a big reason vendors have ramped up their support for programmability in recent years.

Network Automation

As APIs in the network world continue to evolve, more interesting use cases for taking advantage of them will also continue to emerge. In the near term, *network automation* is a prime candidate for taking advantage of the programmatic interfaces being exposed by modern network devices that offer an API.

To put it in a greater context, network automation is *not* just about automating the configuration of network devices. Although that's the most common perception of network automation, using APIs and programmatic interfaces can automate and offer much more than pushing configuration parameters.

Leveraging an API streamlines access to all the data bottled up in network devices. Think about data such as flow-level data, routing tables, FIB tables, interface statistics, MAC tables, VLAN tables, and serial numbers—the list can go on and on. Using modern automation techniques that in turn leverage an API can quickly aid in the day-to-day operations of managing networks for data gathering and automated diagnostics and remediation. On top of that, since an API is being used that returns structured data, as an administrator, you will have the ability to display and analyze the exact data set you want and need, even coming from various show commands, ultimately reducing the time it takes to debug and troubleshoot issues on the network. Rather than connecting to *N* routers running BGP trying to validate a configuration or troubleshoot an issue, you can use automation techniques to simplify this process, or even better, run it periodically while you sleep.

Additionally, leveraging automation techniques leads to a more predictable and uniform network as a whole. You can see this by automating the creation of configuration files, automating the distribution of firewall rules, or automating the process of troubleshooting. It streamlines the process for all users supporting a given environment instead of having each network administrator have *their own* best practices.

Within the context of network automation, another buzzword is *intent-based networking* (*IBN*), which we could summarize as the ability to manage the network via a *business* language (the *intent*) without focusing on the low-level details, and enabling autonomous automation, leveraging closed-loop orchestration, capable of reacting to events (also known as *event-driven automation*).

The overall strategy to build a network automation solution is summarized in Figure 1-4. It starts (1) by translating the user intention into the data that codifies the intent into structured data (*the source of truth*). Then (2), using this data, an automation engine will update the state of the network. Continuously, the network *operational* state is observed (3), and if some drift from the intended state occurs (e.g., a packet loss spike on a network circuit, breaking the expected service-level agreement, or SLA), the automation engine will try to *mitigate* the drift accordingly (4) to the intent (e.g., shifting traffic from the impacted circuit to a healthy one).

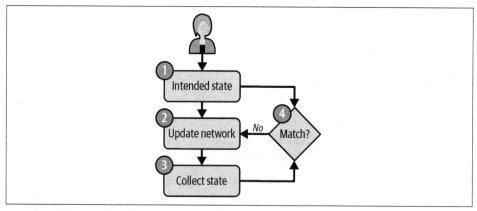

Figure 1-4. Intent-based automation

IBN solutions can be complex to implement, proportionally to the network complexity. Proprietary platforms are available (commonly in the form of a controller). For example, Cisco offers a group of IBN solutions (*https://oreil.ly/0Pztl*) for various areas: access, data center, software-defined wide area network (SD-WAN), and security. However, in most cases, some extensibility and customization will be required to cover specific use cases. One solution rarely suffices, so you will likely end up assembling different components to create your own automation system. In Chapter 14, we recommended an approach to building complete network automation solutions.

The various types of network automation are covered in Chapter 2 in much greater depth. Throughout the rest of the book, you will learn the concepts and tools to implement them.

Bare-Metal Switching

Bare-metal switching is also often thought of as SDN, but it's not. Really, it isn't! That said, in our effort to introduce the various technology trends that are *perceived* as SDN, the topic needs to be covered. If we rewind to 2014 (and even earlier), the term used to describe bare-metal switching was *white-box*, or *commodity switching*. The term has changed, and not without good reason.

Before we cover the change from white box to bare metal, it's important to understand what this means at a high level since it's a massive change in the way network devices are thought of. Network devices for the last 20 years were always bought as physical devices—these physical devices came as hardware appliances, an operating system, and features/applications to use on the system. These components all came from the same vendor.

Both white-box and bare-metal switching use commodity-based switches, which look more like x86 servers (see Figure 1-5). This allows the user to disaggregate each of the required components, making it possible to purchase hardware from one vendor, purchase an operating system from another, and then load features/apps from other vendors or even the open source community.

White-box switching was a hot topic for a while during the OpenFlow hype, since the intent was to commoditize hardware and centralize the brains of the network in an OpenFlow controller (now known as an SDN controller). And in 2013, Google announced it had built its own switches and was controlling them with OpenFlow! This was the topic of a lot of industry conversations at the time, but in reality, not every end user is Google, so not every user will be building their own hardware and software platforms.

Parallel to these efforts, we saw the emergence of a few companies solely focused on providing solutions around white-box switching. They included Big Switch Networks (now part of Arista Networks), Cumulus Networks (now part of NVIDIA), and Pica8. Each offered software-only solutions, so they still needed hardware for their software to run on to provide an end-to-end solution. Initially, these white-box hardware platforms came from original design manufacturers (ODMs) such as Quanta Networks (*https://oreil.ly/LBG-A*), Supermicro (*https://oreil.ly/XqVU3*), Alpha Networks (*https://oreil.ly/IUotv*), and Accton Technology Corporation (*https://oreil.ly/IAACA*). Even if you've been in the network industry, more than likely you've never even heard of those vendors.

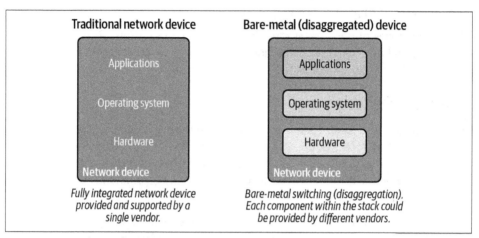

Figure 1-5. Traditional and bare-metal switching stacks

It wasn't until Cumulus and Big Switch announced partnerships with companies including HP and Dell Technologies that the industry started to shift from calling this trend white-box to bare-metal, since now name-brand vendors were supporting third-party operating systems from the likes of Big Switch and Cumulus on their hardware platforms. So, in *bare-metal switches*, you combine switches from ODMs with third-party network operating systems (NOSs) like the ones mentioned. The same switches from ODMs (using merchant silicon ASICs) have also been incorporated into traditional network vendor catalogs, becoming the norm for the mass market.

Confusion may still remain on why bare-metal is technically not SDN because of solutions like the one Big Switch played in both worlds. The answer is simple. If a controller integrated with the solution is using a protocol such as OpenFlow (it does not *have* to be OpenFlow), and it is programmatically communicating with the network devices, that gives the approach the flavor of SDN. This is what Big Switch did—it loaded software on the bare-metal hardware running an OpenFlow agent that then communicates with the controller as part of the solution.

On the other hand, an NOS such as NVIDIA Cumulus Linux provides a Linux distribution purpose-built for network switches. This distribution, or operating system, runs traditional protocols such as Link Layer Discovery Protocol (LLDP), Open Shortest Path First (OSPF), and BGP, with no controller requirement at all, making it more comparable, and compatible, with non-SDN-based network architectures.

With this description, it should be evident that Cumulus Linux is an NOS that runs on bare-metal switches, while Big Switch was a bare-metal-based SDN solution requiring the use of its SDN controller, but also leveraging third-party, bare-metal switching infrastructure.

Nowadays, almost every NOS relies on Linux as its base OS. This has promoted innovation in this space, and a lot of new solutions have appeared. However, not all the NOSs are implemented the same. For instance, some NOSs are implemented solely on the Linux user space with an independent network stack. In this group, you find solutions based on the Data Plane Development Kit (DPDK), such as FD.io (*https://fd.io*) or Cisco NX-OS. Notice that using a totally independent network stack means having to reimplement all the Linux kernel network features.

On the other side, following the path of Cumulus, most Linux-based NOSs are partially or totally leveraging the Linux kernel stack. In this group, aside from Cumulus, you can find vendor solutions—e.g., Arista Extensible Operating System (EOS) and Dell OS10; you can also find open source ones—e.g., SONiC (*https://sonic-net.git hub.io/SONiC*), VyOS (*https://vyos.io*), and OpenWrt (*https://openwrt.org*). Some of these solutions (special mention to SONiC) have gained a lot of adoption because of the flexibility to run on different hardware (bare-metal or traditional vendors) and virtual platforms, and are being adopted in cloud-scale environments.

These solutions allow plugging in other network applications—for instance, adding a routing daemon like FRRouting (*https://frrouting.org*) from the Quagga project to extend the routing capabilities, as done by Cumulus Linux and VyOS. Another benefit of software disaggregation is the capability to run the solution's control plane as a VM or even container, allowing easier development and testing strategies, as we explain in Chapter 5. In the previously referenced *Cloud Native Data Center Networking* book, you can find a more detailed explanation of the various options.

In short, bare-metal switching is about disaggregation and having the ability to purchase network hardware from one vendor and load software from another, should you choose to do so. In this case, administrators are offered the flexibility to change designs, architectures, and software, without swapping out hardware, just the underlying operating system.

Data Center Network Fabrics

Have you ever faced a situation where you could not easily interchange the various devices in a network even if they were all running standard protocols such as the Spanning Tree Protocol or OSPF? If you have, you are not alone. Imagine having a data center network with a collapsed core and individual switches at the top of each rack. Now think about the process that needs to happen when it's time for an upgrade.

We can upgrade networks like this in many ways, but what if only the ToR switches need to be upgraded, and in the evaluation process for new ToR switches, it's decided that a new vendor or platform will be used? This is 100% normal and has been done time and time again. The process is simple: interconnect the new switches to the existing core (of course, we are assuming that the core has available ports) and properly configure 802.1Q trunking if it's a Layer 2 interconnect or configure your favorite routing protocol if it's a Layer 3 interconnect.

Enter *data center network fabrics*. Data center network fabrics aim to change the mindset of network operators from managing individual boxes one at a time to managing a system in its entirety. If we use the earlier scenario, it would not be possible to swap out a ToR switch for another vendor, which is just a single component of a data center network. Rather, when the network is deployed and managed as a system, it needs to be thought of as a system. This means the upgrade process would be to migrate from system to system, or fabric to fabric.

In the world of fabrics, fabrics can be swapped out when it's time for an upgrade, but the individual components within the fabric cannot be—at least most of the time. It *may* be possible when a specific vendor is providing a migration or upgrade path and when bare-metal switching (replacing only hardware) is being used. A few examples of data center network fabrics are Cisco's Application Centric Infrastructure (ACI); Arista's Converged Cloud Fabric (CCF), formerly Big Switch Big Cloud Fabric (BCF); or Aruba Fabric Composer (formerly Plexxi).

In addition to treating the network as a system, data center networking fabrics also commonly do the following:

- Offer a single interface to manage or configure the fabric, including policy management
- Offer distributed default gateways across the fabric
- Offer multipathing capabilities
- Use some form of SDN controller to manage the system

SD-WAN

One of the hottest trends in SDN over the past years has been software-defined wide area networking (SD-WAN). Over the past years, a growing number of companies have been launched to tackle the problem of wide area networking.

 A lot of SD-WAN startups have been acquired by dominant networking and security vendors—for instance, Viptela by Cisco, CloudGenix by Palo Alto Networks, VeloCloud by VMware, Silver Peak by Aruba, and 128 Technology by Juniper—showing the relevant importance of these solutions in the portfolio of all vendors.

The WAN had not seen a radical shift in technology since the migration from Frame Relay to Multiprotocol Label Switching (MPLS). With broadband and internet costs being a fraction of costs for equivalent private-line circuits, the use of site-to-site VPN tunnels has increased over the years, laying the groundwork for the next big thing in WAN.

Common designs for remote offices typically include a private (MPLS) circuit and/or a public internet connection. When both exist, the internet is usually used as backup only, specifically for guest traffic, or for general data riding back over a VPN to corporate while the MPLS circuit is used for low-latency applications such as voice or video communications. When traffic starts to get divided between circuits, this increases the complexity of the routing protocol configuration and also limits the granularity of how to route to the destination address. The source address, application, and real-time performance of the network are usually not taken into consideration in decisions about the best path to take.

A common SD-WAN architecture used by many of the modern solutions is similar to that of network virtualization used in the data center, in that an overlay protocol interconnects the SD-WAN edge devices. Since overlays are used, the solution is agnostic to the underlying physical transport, making SD-WAN functional over the internet or a private WAN. These solutions often ride over two or more internet circuits at branch sites, fully encrypting traffic by using Internet Protocol Security (IPSec). Additionally, many of these solutions constantly measure the performance of each circuit in use and are able to rapidly fail over between circuits for specific applications even during brownouts. Since application layer visibility exists, administrators can also easily pick and choose which application should take a particular route. These types of features are often not found in WAN architectures that rely solely on destination-based routing using a traditional routing protocol such as OSPF or BGP.

From an architecture standpoint, the SD-WAN solutions from the vendors mentioned earlier also typically offer some form of zero-touch provisioning (i.e., installing new network devices without manual intervention), and centralized management with a portal that exists on premises or in the cloud as a SaaS-based application, drastically simplifying management and operations of the WAN going forward.

A valuable by-product of using SD-WAN technology is that it offers more *choice* for end users since any carrier or type of connection can be used on the WAN and across the internet. This flexibility simplifies the configuration and complexity of carrier networks, which in turn will allow carriers to simplify their internal design and architecture, hopefully reducing their costs. Going one step further from a technical perspective, all logical network constructs such as virtual routing and forwarding (VRF) would be managed via the controller platform user interface (UI) that the SD-WAN vendor provides, again eliminating the need to wait weeks for carriers to respond to you when changes are required.

Controller Networking

When it comes to several of these trends, some overlap occurs, as you may have realized. That is one of the confusing points when you are trying to understand all the new technology and trends that have emerged over the last few years.

For example, popular network virtualization platforms use a controller, as do several solutions that fall into the data center network fabric, SD-WAN, and bare-metal switch categories too. Confusing? You may be wondering why controller-based networking has been broken out by itself. In reality, it often is just a mechanism for delivering modern solutions, but not all the previous trends cover all of what controllers can deliver from a technology perspective.

For example, a popular open source SDN controller is OpenDaylight, or ODL (*https://oreil.ly/WRpzm*) by the Linux Foundation, as shown in Figure 1-6. ODL, as with many other controllers, is a platform, not a product. This platform can offer specialized applications such as network virtualization, but can also be used for network monitoring, visibility, tap aggregation, or any other function in conjunction with applications that sit on top of the controller platform. This is the core reason it's important to understand what controllers can offer above and beyond being used for more traditional applications such as fabrics, network virtualization, and SD-WAN.

ODL is not the only open source controller. Others include Open Network Operating System, or ONOS (*https://oreil.ly/0Lkjy*), by the Open Network Foundation, and Tera-Flow (*https://oreil.ly/xnSSg*) by ETSI. Each comes with a different focus and feature set that must be evaluated depending on the use case to address.

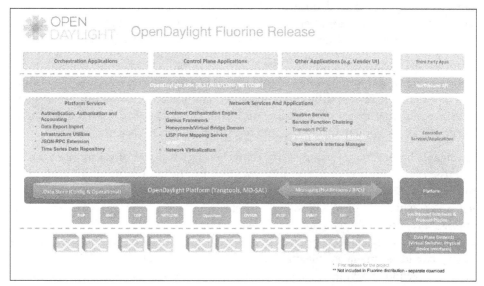

Figure 1-6. OpenDaylight architecture

Cloud Native Networking

The way to run applications has changed notably since the rise of public cloud services and container runtime environments. Naturally, networking has embraced this trend, and today's networking landscape has become hybrid, including container networking technologies and cloud network services. In Chapter 4, we review both in more detail.

Containers are lightweight, portable, and easily deployable units of software that can run on any platform. They run as a process, without all the overhead of a VM, leveraging a few Linux features. Docker (*https://www.docker.com*) is the most popular one, but there are other alternatives, including Podman (*https://podman.io*) and LXC (*https://linuxcontainers.org*). Moreover, an NOS can also run as a container (with some limitations) facilitating the creation of network lab scenarios, as we will show in Chapter 5 using Containerlab.

The popularity of containers came with the appearance of runtime platforms (the Kubernetes project being the most popular one), which allow deploying these containers consistently over diverse infrastructure using the standard Container Network Interface (CNI).

Cloud networking, on the other side, includes several networking services with different levels of abstraction. Platforms like Amazon Web Services (AWS), Microsoft Azure, Google Cloud Platform (GCP), DigitalOcean, and others offer network services that *emulate* network functionalities without having to use complex configuration artifacts. For example, with some differences, all cloud providers allow the creation of *virtual* regional networks where other IT infrastructure services can attach and interconnect, and other networking services can connect to the on-premises data centers (e.g., VPN connections). Many network services exist, but all have some characteristics in common: the customization settings are more limited than usual and not so granular, and management is done via HTTP APIs.

Cloud platforms offer *dynamic infrastructure*, provisioned on demand when requested. This dynamism offers higher flexibility and a shorter delivery time than the traditional approach of buying and installing physical devices. Moreover, it aligns perfectly with the DevOps culture of developing the application, provisioning the infrastructure, and running it, everything defined by code.

This approach is known as *infrastructure as code* (*IaC*) and consists of describing the desired state of the infrastructure in text files that will then be *interpreted* to bring them to life. Managing IaC has many solutions, including Terraform (*https://www.terraform.io*) by HashiCorp (more about it in Chapter 12), Pulumi (*https://www.pulumi.com*), and cloud-provider-specific ones (e.g., AWS CloudFormation and Google Cloud Deployment Manager).

Managing these container and cloud environments may seem intimidating in the beginning. Take it easy. It is still networking, so your network engineer skills are valid and needed. Certainly, it requires specific domain knowledge and other skills such as programming languages, domain-specific languages, and tools. This book will help you get started with all of them.

Summary

There you have it: an introduction to the trends and technologies that are most often categorized as SDN, paving the path into better network operations through network programmability and automation. Dozens of SDN startups have been created over the past seven years, millions in venture capital money invested, and billions spent on acquisitions of these companies. The evolution has been unreal, and if we break it down one step further, we can see the common goal of leveraging software principles and technology to offer greater power, control, agility, and choice to the users while increasing operational efficiencies.

In Chapter 2, we take a look at network automation and dive deeper into its various types. You'll learn about some common protocols and APIs, and how automation has started to evolve in the last several years.

## CHAPTER 2

Network Automation

In this chapter, we're focused on providing a baseline of high-level network automation concepts so that you are better equipped to get the most out of each chapter going forward. To accomplish this, the following topics are included in this chapter:

Why network automation?
Examines various reasons to adopt automation and increase the efficiencies of network operations while proving there is much more to automation than delivering configurations faster to network devices.

Types of network automation
Explores various types of automation, from traditional configuration management to automating network diagnostics and troubleshooting, proving once again that there is more to automation than decreasing the time it takes to make a change.

Evolving the management plane from SNMP to device APIs
Briefly introduces a few API types found on network devices of the past and present.

Network automation in the SDN era
Provides a short synopsis of why network automation tooling is still valuable when SDN solutions, specifically referring to controller-based architectures, are deployed.

 This chapter is not meant to provide deep technical content but rather an introduction to the concepts of network automation. This chapter simply lays the foundation and provides context for the chapters that follow.

Why Network Automation?

Network automation, like most types of automation, is considered a means of doing things faster. While accomplishing tasks more quickly is nice, reducing the time for deployments and configuration changes isn't always a problem that needs solving for many IT organizations.

In this section, we take a look at a few reasons, including speed, that IT organizations of all shapes and sizes should be looking at gradually adopting network automation. You should note that the same principles apply to other types of automation as well (application, systems, storage, telephony, etc.).

Simplified Architectures

It is still common today that network devices are configured as unique snowflakes (having many one-off, nonstandard configurations), and network engineers take pride in solving transport and application issues with one-off network changes that ultimately make the network not only harder to maintain and manage but also harder to automate.

Instead of network automation and management being treated as a secondary project or an add-on, it needs to be included from the outset as new architectures are being created. This includes ensuring a proper budget for personnel and tooling. Unfortunately, tooling is often the first item cut in budget shortage.

The end-to-end architecture and associated day 2 operations need to be one and the same. You need to think about the following questions as architectures are created:

- Which features work across vendors?
- Which extensions work across platforms?
- What type of API or automation tooling works with particular network device platforms?
- Is there solid API documentation?
- What libraries exist for a given product?

When these questions get answered early in the design process, the resulting architecture becomes simpler, repeatable, and easier to maintain *and* automate, all with fewer vendor-proprietary extensions enabled throughout the network.

Even after the simplified architecture gets deployed with the right management and automation tooling, remember that minimizing one-off changes is still a necessity, to ensure that the network configurations don't become snowflakes again.

Deterministic Outcomes

In an enterprise organization, change review meetings take place to examine upcoming changes on the network, their impact on external systems, and rollback plans. In a world where a human is touching the CLI to make those upcoming changes, the impact of typing the wrong command can be catastrophic. Imagine a team with 3, 4, 5, or 50 engineers. Every engineer may have their own way of making that particular upcoming change. Moreover, the ability to use a CLI and even a GUI does not eliminate or reduce the chance of error during the control window for the change.

Using proven and tested network automation to make changes helps achieve *more predictable* behavior than making changes manually, and gives the executive team a *better chance* at achieving deterministic outcomes, moving one step closer to ensuring that the task at hand will get done right the first time, without human error. This task could be anything from a VLAN change to onboarding a new customer that requires several changes throughout the network.

Moreover, these deterministic outcomes imply lower operating expenses (OpEx) because less manual labor is involved in executing network changes, increasing the efficiency of the overall network operations (e.g., automating time-consuming processes like upgrading the operating system on a network device). The operating time saved by network engineers can be used to focus on more strategic projects, to keep improving the process.

Business Agility

Since the advent of server virtualization, systems administrators could deploy new applications almost instantaneously. And the faster applications are deployed, the more questions are raised as to why it takes so long to configure network resources such as VLANs, routes, firewall policies, load-balancing policies, or all of the above if deploying a new three-tier application.

It should be fairly obvious that by adopting network automation, the network engineering and operations teams can react faster to their IT counterparts for deploying applications. More importantly, automation helps the business be more agile. From an adoption perspective, it's critical to understand the existing, and often manual, workflows before attempting to adopt automation of any kind, no matter how good your intentions are for making the business more agile.

If you don't know what you want to automate, that lack of knowledge will complicate and prolong the process. Our *number one* recommendation as you start your network automation journey is to always understand existing manual workflows, document them (e.g., average time to complete, the number of times each step occurs), and understand the impact they have on the business. Then, the implementation of an automation solution becomes simpler and more effective.

Enhanced Security and Risk Reduction

Describing the networking-related workflows as code brings an implicit benefit of automation: the code captures and documents the step-by-step process definition and analysis, making it available for everyone, at any time. This exposure allows the introduction of peer review in the workflow (as other engineers share responsibility for the changes) as well as the automated processing to discover potential security issues or configuration errors before actually deploying the changes to the network. And, when the automation is in place, it will make sure that the network keeps operating as defined, remediating any deviations as needed.

In traditional network operations, the outcome of a task depends heavily on the network engineers' experience performing it, and the available documentation, which is always hard to keep up-to-date. However, when the same task is automated, every time the workflow is executed, it will apply all the knowledge from all the engineers who have contributed to it.

Automation enables sharing of responsibility across the team and makes the process more effective and less prone to introducing problems because it enforces extra human review. Automation also enables processing by tools that can enforce rules, such as security policies, or even connecting with artificial analysis tools to *recommend* improvements from the context.

Furthermore, network automation is not a one-time effort. Unexpected issues or missing points will likely be detected, and every time this happens, the workflow code will need to be adjusted, becoming better than before. This continuously improving approach, over time, will merge all the contributions, from former and current team members, in an incremental improvement process.

From simplified architectures to continuous improvement, this section introduced some of the high-level reasons you should consider network automation. In the next section, we take a look at types of network automation.

Types of Network Automation

Automation is commonly equated with speed, and considering that some network tasks don't require speed, it's easy to see why some IT teams don't see the value in automation. VLAN configuration is a great example; you may be thinking, "How *fast* does a VLAN really need to be created? Just how many VLANs are being added on a daily basis? Do *I* really need automation?" These are all valid questions.

This section focuses on several other tasks for which automation makes sense: device provisioning, data collection and enrichment, migrations, configuration management, configuration compliance, state validation, troubleshooting, and reporting. But remember, as we stated previously, automation is much more than speed and agility; it also offers you, your team, and your business more predictable and more deterministic outcomes while reducing risk and increasing security.

Device Provisioning

One of the easiest and fastest ways to get started with network automation is to automate creating the device configuration files used for initial device provisioning and pushing them to network devices.

If we break this process into two steps, the first is creating the configuration file, and the second is pushing the configuration onto the device.

To automate the creation of configuration files (or configuration data in general), we first need to decouple the *inputs* (configuration parameters) from the underlying vendor-proprietary syntax (CLI) of the configuration. We'll end up with separate files: one file with values for the configuration parameters such as VLANs, domain information, interfaces, routing, and everything else; and another file that is the configuration template.

For now, think of the configuration template as the equivalent of a standard golden template that's used for all devices getting deployed. By using *network configuration templating*, you can quickly produce consistent network configuration files specifically for your network. You'll never have to use Notepad ever again, copying and pasting configs from file to file—isn't it about time for that?

Two tools that streamline using configuration templates with variables (data inputs) are Ansible and Nornir. In less than a few seconds, these tools can generate hundreds of configuration files predictably and reliably.

> Building and generating configuration files from templates are covered in much more detail in Chapter 9, while performing the templating process with Ansible and Nornir is covered in Chapter 12. This section is merely showing a high-level basic example.

Let's look at an example of taking a current configuration and decomposing it into template and variable (input) files to articulate the point we're making. In Example 2-1, you can observe a CLI configuration from a random vendor.

Example 2-1. Configuration file snippet

```
hostname leaf1
ip domain-name ntc.com
!
vlan 10
  name web
!
```

```
vlan 20
  name app
!
vlan 30
  name db
!
```

If we decouple the data from the CLI commands, this file is transformed into two files: a template and a data (variables) file. First, let's look at the YAML definition in the variables file in Example 2-2 (we cover YAML in depth in Chapter 8).

Example 2-2. YAML data

```
---
hostname: leaf1
domain_name: ntc.com
vlans:
  - id: 10
    name: web
  - id: 20
    name: app
  - id: 30
    name: db
```

Note that the YAML file contains only our *data*.

The resulting template that is rendered with the data file looks like Example 2-3 and is given the filename *leaf.j2*.

Example 2-3. Jinja template

```
!
hostname {{ inventory_hostname }}
ip domain-name {{ domain_name }}
!
{% for vlan in vlans %}
vlan {{ vlan.id }}
  name {{ vlan.name }}
{% endfor %}
!
```

 In Example 2-3, we're showing the Python-based Jinja templating language (*https://jinja.palletsprojects.com*). Jinja is covered in detail in Chapter 9.

In this example, the *double curly braces* denote a Jinja variable. This is where the data variables get inserted when a template is rendered with data. Since the double curly braces denote variables, and we see those values are not in the template, they need to be stored somewhere. Again, we stored them in a YAML file. Rather than use flat YAML files, you could also use a script to fetch this type of information from an external system such as a network management system (NMS) or IP address management (IPAM) system.

In this example, if the team members who control VLANs want to add a VLAN to the network devices, no problem. They just need to change it in the variables file and regenerate a new configuration file by using Ansible or the rendering engine of their choice (e.g., Salt, pure Python, etc.).

At this point in our example, once the configuration is generated, it needs to be *pushed* to the network device. The *push* and *execution* process is not covered here, as there are plenty of ways to do this, including vendor-proprietary provisioning solutions as well as a few other methods that we present in Chapters 10 and 12.

Additionally, this is only a high-level introduction to templates; don't worry if the details are not 100% clear yet. As we've said, working with templates is covered in far greater detail in Chapter 9.

Aside from building configurations and pushing them to devices, something that is arguably more important is data collection, which happens to be our next topic.

Data Collection and Enrichment

Monitoring tools typically use SNMP to poll certain management information bases (MIBs) for data. The data returned may be more or less than you actually need. What if interface stats are being polled? You may get back every counter displayed in a show interface command, but what if you need only interface resets and not cycling redundancy check (CRC) errors, jumbo frames, or output errors? Moreover, what if you want to see the interface resets correlated to the interfaces that have Cisco Discovery Protocol (CDP) or LLDP neighbors on them, and you want to see them *now*, not on the next polling cycle? How does network automation help with this?

Given that our focus is on providing you more power and control, you can leverage open source tools and technology to customize exactly what you get, when you get it, how it's formatted, and how the data is used after it's collected. This automated approach ensures that you get the most value from the data.

Example 2-4 is a *very* basic illustration of collecting data from a Cisco Internetwork Operating System (IOS) device via the Python library Netmiko, which we cover in more detail in Chapter 10.

Example 2-4. Netmiko script

```
from netmiko import ConnectHandler

device = ConnectHandler(
  device_type='cisco_ios',
  host='csr1',
  username='ntc',
  password='ntc123'
)

output = device.send_command('show version')
print(output)
```

The great part is that `output` contains the `show version` response, and you can parse it as you see fit based on your requirements. But the code also has a not-so-pretty part: the output of this CLI command is unstructured data, so you would end up implementing custom screen-scraping logic, which is difficult to maintain. Small output changes could break the whole parsing. As you will see in Chapter 8, most platforms nowadays are offering structured data formats that enable more robust automation, and screen scraping is used only as a *last resort*.

In the preceding example, we are describing *pulling* data off the devices, which may not be ideal for all environments (but still suitable for many). Be aware that newer devices are starting to support a *push* model, often referred to as *streaming telemetry*: the device itself streams real-time data such as interface stats to an application server of your choice. You'll see more details in Chapters 10 and 14.

Of course, any data collection may require some up-front custom work but is totally worth it in the end—because the data being gathered is what you need, not what a given tool or vendor is providing you. Plus, isn't that why you're reading this book?

Network devices have an enormous amount of static and ephemeral data buried inside, and using open source tools or building your own gets you access to this data. Examples of this type of data include active entries in the BGP table, OSPF adjacencies, active neighbors, interface statistics, specific counters and resets, and even counters from ASICs themselves on newer platforms. Additionally, general facts and characteristics of devices can be collected too, such as serial number, hostname, uptime, OS version, and hardware platform, just to name a few. The list is endless.

Always consider these questions as you start an automation project: "Does it make sense to build, buy, or customize?" and "Does it make sense to consume or operate?"

But not least important in data collection is *how* we get the best of this data. As you will learn in Chapter 14, after we collect the network state (metrics, logs, or flows), we can enrich it with metadata—such as adding a *tag* for the site an interface counter metric comes from. Then, in the analysis or visualization tooling, we could correlate all this data to get more educated outcomes. To make this happen, we need to get this information from someplace where a relationship exists between the device (owner of the interface) and the site where it is installed. This is the role of the *source of truth*, covered in the same chapter.

Migrations

Migrating from one platform to the next is never an easy task. This may involve platforms from the same vendor or from different vendors. Vendors may offer a script or a tool to help with migrations to *their* platform, but you can use various forms of automation to build out configuration templates, just as in our example earlier, for all types of network devices and operating systems. You could then generate a configuration file for all vendors, given a defined and common set of inputs (common data model).

Of course, if you are using vendor-proprietary extensions, they'll need to be accounted for too. The beautiful thing is that a migration tool such as this is much simpler to build on your own than having a vendor do it: whereas the vendor needs to account for all features the device supports, an individual organization needs only a finite number of features. In reality, this is something vendors don't care much about; they are concerned with their equipment, not making it easier for you, the network operator, to manage a multivendor environment.

Having this type of flexibility helps with not only migrations, but also DR, as it's common to have different switch models in the production and DR data centers, and even different vendors. If a device fails for any reason and its replacement has to be a different platform, you'd be able to quickly leverage your common data model (think parameter inputs) and generate a new configuration immediately. We're starting to use the term *data model* loosely, but rest assured, we spend more time describing data models in Chapter 8.

Thus, if you are performing a migration, think about it at a more abstract level and think through the tasks necessary to go from one platform to the next. Then, see what can be done to automate those tasks, because only you, not the large networking vendors, have the motivation to make multivendor automation a reality. For example, think about adding a VLAN as an abstract step—then you can worry about the lower-level commands per platform. The point is, as you start adopting automation, it's extremely important to think about tasks and document them in a human-readable format that is vendor neutral, before putting your hands to the keyboard to type in CLI commands or write code (per platform).

Configuration Management

As we've stated, configuration management is the most common type of automation, so we aren't going to spend too much time on it here. We define *configuration management* as deploying, pushing, and managing the configuration state of a device. This includes anything as basic as interfaces' descriptions to more complex workflows that configure ToR switches, firewalls, load balancers, and advanced security infrastructure, to deploy three-tier applications.

As you can see already through the forms of automation that are *read-only*, you do not need to start your automation journey by pushing configurations. That said, if you are spending countless hours pushing the same change across a given number of routers or switches, you may want to!

The reality is that there are so many ways to start a network automation journey, but when you start automating configuration management, remember, with great power comes great responsibility. More importantly, don't forget to test new automation tools before rolling them out to production environments. You have several options to test your automation logic via emulation network platforms, as you will see in Chapter 5.

Lessons Learned from a Network Automation Outage

In October 2021, one of the largest automated networks in the world went down. Facebook, now Meta, provided an outage report (*https://oreil.ly/0jUqD*) explaining that despite having an *audit control* for its configuration management system to prevent pushing harmful configurations, a BGP configuration change caused a global outage.

We shouldn't forget that automation amplifies everything—the good and the bad. Thus, it is crucial to understand the importance of testing a network automation system with a *continuous integration* (CI) process (as it has been adopted in software development) before deploying to production. We explain how CI works in Chapter 13. The Facebook outage is an example of how complex it is to get CI right.

Nowadays, tools such as Batfish can perform analytical network verification; from given configurations, these tools create a network model to simulate the state of the network—but this is only an approximation. Simulating *all* the options configured in a network is extremely complex (do you remember when we mentioned the importance of simplicity for automation?). As we stated before, network emulation tools can help us run network devices in on-demand environments. All these tools can be used in CI pipelines to verify how the network automation tooling interacts with the network devices before going into production, anticipating potential issues and unexpected collateral effects.

As expected, Facebook had its own homegrown audit control tool to validate changes via CI, but the chance of hitting an unexpected bug always remains. To mitigate this, we recommend you embrace uncertainty and adopt software development approaches, such as *canary deployments*, which progressively roll out changes to the fleet. This allows us to validate the outcome of a small subset of devices, and then, incrementally, continue releasing to the rest of the network.

The next few types of network automation we cover stem from automating the process of data collection. We've broken out a few of them to provide more context, and the first up is automating compliance checks.

Configuration Compliance

As with many forms of automation, making configuration changes with any type of automation tool is seen as a risk. While making manual changes could arguably be riskier, as you've read and may have experienced firsthand, you have the option to start with data collection, monitoring, and configuration building, which are all *read-only* and *low-risk* actions.

One low-risk use case that uses the data being gathered is configuration compliance checks and configuration validation. Does the deployed configuration meet security requirements? Are the required networks configured? Is protocol *XYZ* disabled? When you have control over the tools being deployed, it is more than possible to determine whether something is True or False. It's easy enough to start small with one compliance check and then gradually add more as needed.

Based on the compliance of what you are checking, it's up to you to determine what happens next—maybe the data just gets logged, or maybe a complex operation is performed, making your application capable of auto-remediation. These are forms of event-driven automation that we also touch upon when we cover Ansible in Chapter 12.

Our recommendation is that it's always best to start simple with network automation, but being aware of what's possible adds significant value as well. For example, if you just log or print messages to see what an interface maximum transmission unit (MTU) is, you're already prepared should you want to automatically reconfigure any undesirable MTU to the right value. You'd need just a few more lines underneath your existing log/print messages. Again, the point is to start small but think through what else you may need in the future.

State Validation

A step further than configuration compliance—still read-only and low risk—is to validate the *result* of the configuration, the actual operational state of the network (also known as network assurance). Obviously, this requires the definition of the *intended* operational state alongside the configuration one. For instance, regarding a BGP neighbor configuration, configuration compliance would validate the configuration state, syntax, and data for the neighbor IP address, autonomous system number (ASN), and MD5 authentication key. In addition, the state validation checks the state of these sessions, expecting an `Established` status. The configuration could be right, but a network outage or a misconfiguration on the other end could rise a validation issue.

The state validation adds an extra control layer on top of the automation process. This validation can be used to verify that the rollout of a desired configuration change is not breaking the desired operational state, or to constantly verify the network state. The outcome, for example, could be raising warnings with relevant state data or triggering a mitigation process. Following the BGP example, when an unexpected BGP session state is detected, the automation will retrieve and attach the related BGP logs, and stats, into a notification to the network team.

 A common state validation type is the *pre/post change validation*. In this case, there is no predefined intended operational state. The intended state is simply taken from a snapshot collected before performing a future action. For instance, during an OS upgrade workflow, the operational state is collected before the upgrade and defines the desired state. After the upgrade, this state is validated against the actual state. If the final state is not successful, a rollback process could be triggered to use the previous OS version.

Reporting

Once you start automating data collection, you may want to start building out custom and dynamic reports too. Maybe the data being returned becomes the input to other configuration management tasks (event-driven again or more basic conditional configuration), or maybe you just want to create reports.

Reports can also be easily generated from templates combined with the actual ephemeral data from the device that'll be inserted into the template. Creating and using reporting templates follows the same process as for configuration templates that we touched upon earlier in the chapter (remember, we explore templates in much more depth in Chapter 9).

Because of the simple nature of using text-based templates, you can produce reports in any format you wish, including, but not limited to, the following:

- Simple text files
- Markdown files that can be easily viewed on GitHub or another Markdown viewer
- HTML reports that are deployed to a web server for easy viewing

Your format choice depends on your requirements. The great thing is that the *network automator* has the power to create the exact type of report needed. In fact, you can use one set of data to generate different types of reports, maybe some technical and some higher level for management, and then select the best UI to send them, maybe via email or instant messaging.

Next up, we take a look at the value of automated troubleshooting.

Troubleshooting

Who enjoys getting consistently pulled into break/fix problems, especially when you should be sleeping or focused on other things? Once you have access to real-time data and don't need to do any manual parsing on that data, automated troubleshooting becomes a reality.

Think about *how* you troubleshoot. Do you have a personal methodology? Is that methodology consistent across all members of your team? Does everyone check Layer 2 before troubleshooting Layer 3? What steps do you take to troubleshoot a given problem?

Let's take troubleshooting OSPF as an example:

- Do you know what it takes to form an OSPF adjacency between two devices?
- Can you rattle off the same answers at 2 a.m. or while on vacation at the beach?
- Do you remember that some devices need to be on the same subnet, have the same MTU, and have consistent timers, but forget that they need to be the same OSPF network type?
- Do we really need to remember all of this and the associated commands to run on the CLI to get back each piece of data?

And these questions are only a *few* of the things that need to match for OSPF.

In any given environment, these types of compatibility checks need to be performed. Can you fathom running a script or using a tool for OSPF neighbor validation versus performing that process manually? Which would you prefer?

Again, OSPF is only the tip of the iceberg. Think about these other questions, still just being the tip:

- Can you correlate particular log messages to known conditions on the network?
- What about BGP neighbor adjacencies? How is a neighbor formed?
- Are you seeing all of the routes you think you should in the routing table?
- What about port channels? Are there any inconsistencies?
- Do neighbors match the port-channel configuration (going down to the vSwitch)?
- What about cabling? Are all of the cables plugged in properly?

Even with these questions, we are just scratching the surface of the possibilities when it comes to automated diagnostics and troubleshooting.

 As you start to consider all the types of automation possible, start to imagine a closed-loop system: data is collected in an automated fashion, the data is then processed and analyzed in an automated fashion, and then you use advanced analytics to troubleshoot in an automated fashion. As these start to happen together and uniformly, the system becomes a closed loop, fully changing the way operations are managed within an organization.

If you are the rock star network engineer on your team, you may want to think about partnering up with a developer, or at the very least, start documenting your workflows so it's easier to share your knowledge and it becomes easier to *codify*. Better yet, start your own personal automation journey so you can sleep in every so often and empower everyone else to troubleshoot by using some of your automated diagnostic workflows.

As you can see, network automation is much more than deploying configurations faster. After looking at several types of automation, we are going to shift topics now and look at a few ways automation tools and applications communicate with network devices.

Evolving the Management Plane from SNMP to APIs

If you want to improve the way networks are managed and operated day-to-day, you must begin with the way you interface with the underlying devices being managed. This interface is how you and, more importantly, automation tools communicate with devices to perform the various types of network automation, such as data collection and configuration management.

In this section, we provide an overview of the methods available to connect to the management plane of network devices—starting with SNMP and then moving on to more modern ways such as NETCONF, RESTful APIs, RESTCONF, and gNMI. We then look at the impact of the *open networking* movement as it pertains to network operations and automation.

Application Programming Interfaces

As a network engineer, you need to embrace APIs going forward and not fear them. Remember that an API is just a mechanism used for computer software on one device to talk to computer software on another device. APIs are used nearly everywhere on the internet today—they just happen to finally be getting the focus they deserve from network vendors. Today we are seeing that APIs are becoming the primary means of managing new network devices.

While we cover specific network APIs in more detail in Chapter 10, this section provides a high-level overview of a few types of APIs that you'll find on network devices today.

SNMP

SNMP has been widely deployed for over 25 years on network devices. It shouldn't be new to anyone reading this book, but SNMP is a protocol that is used quite commonly for polling network devices for information such as up/down status and CPU, memory, and interface utilization.

To use SNMP, there must be an SNMP agent on a managed device and a network management station, which is the device that functions as a *server* that monitors and/or controls the managed devices.

Each network device being managed exposes a set of data that can be collected and configured via the SNMP agent. This set of data that is managed through SNMP is described and modeled through MIBs. Only if an MIB is exposing a certain feature can it be monitored or managed. This includes making configuration changes through SNMP. Often overlooked, SNMP not only supports GetRequests for monitoring but also supports SetRequests for manipulating objects and variables exposed through MIBs. The issue is that not many vendors offer full support for configuration management via SNMP; when they do, they often use custom MIBs, slowing the integration process to network management platforms.

As mentioned, SNMP has been around for decades, but it was not built to be a real-time programmatic interface to network devices. We are already seeing vendors claim the gradual death of SNMP as it pertains to next-generation management and automation tooling. That said, SNMP does exist on nearly every network device, and

Python libraries for SNMP also exist—so, if you need to collect basic information from a vast number of device types, using SNMP may still make sense.

Just as SNMP has been used for years to perform network monitoring, SSH/Telnet and the CLI have been used for configuration management (and for retrieving state). Let's take a look now at SSH/Telnet and the CLI.

SSH/Telnet and the CLI

If you've ever managed a network device, you've definitely used the CLI to issue commands to perform an action on a device. You probably entered commands through the console and over Telnet and SSH sessions. As we stated in Chapter 1, the reality is that the migration from Telnet to SSH is arguably the biggest shift we've had in network operations over the past decade, and that shift wasn't about operations; it was about security ensuring that communications to network devices were encrypted.

The most important point to realize as it pertains to managing devices via the CLI is that the CLI was built for humans. It was put on devices to improve usability for human operators. The CLI was *not* meant to be used for machine-to-machine communication (network scripting and automation).

If you issue a show command on the CLI of a device, you get raw text back. This output has no structure. The best options to *parse* the response are to use the *pipe* (|) and keywords such as grep, include, and begin to look for particular lines of configuration. You might check the description of an interface with the command show interface Eth1 | include description, for example. If you needed to know how many CRC errors were on an interface after issuing a show interface in a script, you'd be forced to use some type of regular expression or manual parsing to figure it out. This is unacceptable.

However, when all we have is the CLI, the CLI gets used. This is why plenty of network management platforms and custom scripts have been built over the past two decades that perform management and automated operations by using the CLI over SSH to deal with expect scripts and manual parsing. It's not that SSH/CLI makes it impossible to automate; rather, it makes automation extremely error prone and tedious.

The network vendors started to realize this, and now most newer device platforms have some type of API that simplifies machine-to-machine communication (many are incomplete, so be sure to test your favorite device's API). This change has yielded a much simpler approach to automation that is also more in line with general software development principles.

Now that we've introduced common protocols such as SSH and SNMP, let's look at NETCONF, an API that is becoming quite popular as it pertains to network automation.

NETCONF

Like SNMP, NETCONF is a network management layer protocol defined by the Internet Engineering Task Force (IETF). At the highest level, NETCONF can be compared to SNMP, as both are protocols used to make configuration changes and retrieve data from networking devices. The differences come in the details, of course. We cover a few high-level points here but spend more time on NETCONF in Chapter 10.

NETCONF is a connection-oriented protocol that commonly leverages SSH as its transport; the data transferred is encoded with XML. NETCONF supports remote procedure calls (RPCs) to send prearranged operations to the devices (i.e., the edit-config operation). Also, it uses data models represented in YANG to define the data structures supported. Don't worry if you aren't familiar with XML or YANG; we cover both in Chapter 8.

NETCONF devices expose the supported data models and operations via their *capabilities*, which differ from one platform to another. Just because two device platforms support NETCONF (or any common transport method) does not mean they are compatible from a tooling and developer's perspective. Even with the assumption that both devices support the same NETCONF features and capabilities, the way the data is modeled is, more often than not, vendor specific.

Additionally, NETCONF offers value in that it supports transaction-based changes. If you are making more than one change in a given NETCONF session or single XML document, and one of those changes fails, the complete change is *not* applied to the device (of course, these types of settings can usually be overridden too). This is in contrast to sending CLI commands sequentially and ending up with a partial configuration due to a typo or invalid command.

RESTful APIs

REST, which stands for *Representational State Transfer*, is a style used to design and develop networked applications. Thus, systems that implement and adhere to a REST-based architecture are said to be *RESTful*.

In the context of a network, the most common devices that expose APIs and adhere to the REST architectural style are network controllers. That said, network devices expose RESTful and general HTTP-based APIs too, including a derivative from NETCONF called RESTCONF. We cover HTTP-based APIs in Chapter 10.

While the terms *REST* and *RESTful APIs* are new from a network standpoint, you're already interacting with many RESTful systems on a daily basis as you browse the internet via a web browser. We said that REST is a style used to develop networked applications. That style relies on a stateless client-server model in which the client keeps track of the session and no client state or context is held on the server. And best yet, the underlying transport protocol used is most commonly HTTP. Doesn't this sound like most systems found on the internet?

This means that RESTful APIs operate just like HTTP-based systems. First, you need a web server accessible via a URL (i.e., *SDN controller* or *network device* to communicate with), and second, you need to send the associated HTTP request to that URL. For example, if you need to retrieve a list of devices from an SDN controller, you just need to send an HTTP GET to the given URL of the device, which could look something like this: `http://192.0.2.1/v1/devices`. The response that comes back would be some type of structured data like XML or JSON (which we cover in Chapter 8).

gNMI

Traditionally, network interfaces and protocols have been driven by standardization entities, such as NETCONF defined by the IETF. However, in 2017 the OpenConfig consortium (*https://www.openconfig.net*), led by Google, released the gNMI (*https://oreil.ly/TuI43*), a gRPC-based protocol to handle configuration management and state data collection via telemetry streams as a community open source project that could benefit from a faster development pace due to its simpler consensus process.

OpenConfig was created in 2014 to develop programmatic interfaces and tools for managing networks in a dynamic and vendor-neutral way. Since then, more and more participants (*https://oreil.ly/islad*) have joined, representing some of the biggest networking organizations in the world. Their initial focus was on compiling a set of vendor-neutral data models based on actual operational needs to solve the use cases and requirements of their members.

gNMI supports RPC operations (e.g., `set` or `get`) and uses YANG data models like NETCONF. So, how do both protocols/interfaces differ? They have a few technical differences such as the transport (i.e., gRPC) or the encoding (i.e., protobuf). You'll learn more about gNMI in Chapter 10. The main difference is in the development strategy, with its own feature roadmap. For instance, gNMI supported streaming telemetry via subscription from the beginning because it was a top priority for the OpenConfig consortium.

Next up is a short look at the impact *open networking* is having on the overall management of network devices.

Impact of Open Networking

We're seeing a growing trend of all things *open*—open source, open networking, open APIs, OpenFlow, Open Compute, Open vSwitch, OpenDaylight, OpenConfig, and the list goes on. While the definition of *open* can be debated, one thing is certain: the *open networking* movement is expanding what is possible when it comes to network operations and automation. With this movement, we are seeing drastic changes in network devices, and this is the primary reason for writing this book.

First, many devices now support running Python directly in them. This means that you can drop into the Python dynamic interpreter and execute Python scripts locally on each network device. We cover Python in much more detail in Chapter 6, and you'll see what we mean firsthand.

Second, many devices now support a more robust API other than SNMP and SSH. For example, we just looked at NETCONF, gNMI, and RESTful HTTP-based APIs. One or more of those APIs are supported on many of the newer device operating systems that have emerged in recent years. Remember, we cover device APIs in more detail in Chapter 10.

Finally, network devices are exposing more of the Linux internals that have been hidden from network operators in the past. You can now drop into a *bash* shell on network devices and issue commands such as `ifconfig`, write bash scripts, and install monitoring and configuration management tools via package managers such as `apt` and `yum`. You'll learn about all of these things in Chapter 3. And with Linux, you can also run applications packaged as containers (covered in Chapter 4), changing the understanding of what we can achieve on network devices.

While *open networking* doesn't always mean interoperability, network devices and controllers are opening themselves up to be operated in a much more programmatic manner that's better suited for enhanced network automation. The net result, for you as an operator, is that you can take control of your networks and reduce the number of operational inefficiencies that exist today as you start using these APIs.

Network Automation in the SDN Era

We'll now take a look at the continued importance of network automation even when controller solutions such as OpenDaylight or even commercial offerings like Cisco ACI or VMware NSX are being deployed. The operations that the controllers perform on the network, such as acting as the control plane or managing policy and configuration, are irrelevant to this section.

The fact is that controllers are becoming common in next-generation architectures. Vendors such as Cisco, Juniper, VMware, Arista Networks, NVIDIA, and many others all offer controller platforms for their next-gen solutions, not to mention open source controllers such as OpenDaylight, ONOS, and TeraFlow.

Almost every controller on the market exposes northbound RESTful APIs, making controllers extremely easy to automate. While controllers themselves inherently simplify management and visibility through a single pane of glass, you can still end up making manual and error-prone changes through the GUI of a controller. If several pods or controllers are deployed, from the same or different vendors, the problems of manual changes, troubleshooting, and data collection are still relevant.

As we start to wrap up this chapter, it's important to note that even in the new era of SDN architectures and controller-based network solutions, the need for automation, better operations, and more predictable outcomes does not go away.

Summary

This chapter provided an overview of the value of network automation and various types of network automation; an introduction to common device APIs including SNMP, CLI/SSH, and more importantly, NETCONF, RESTful APIs, and gNMI (Chapter 10 takes a deep dive on them); and a brief mention of YANG, a data modeling language that we cover in more detail in Chapter 8.

The chapter closed with a brief look at the impact that the open networking movement is having on network operations and automation. Finally, we touched on the value of network automation even when SDN controllers are deployed.

In each subsequent chapter, we dive deeper into each technology, providing hands-on practical examples whenever possible, but at the same time reviewing the importance of the people, process, and culture required to adopt comprehensive automation frameworks and pipelines.

## CHAPTER 3

Linux

This chapter aims to help you become familiar with the basics of Linux, an operating system that is becoming increasingly common in networking circles. You might wonder why we've included a chapter about Linux in this book. After all, what in the world does Linux, a Unix-like operating system, have to do with network automation and programmability?

Examining Linux in a Network Automation Context

In looking at Linux from a network automation perspective, we feel this content is important for several reasons.

First, several modern network operating systems (NOSs) are based on Linux, although some use a custom CLI that means they don't look or act like Linux. Others, however, do expose the Linux internals and/or use a Linux shell such as *bash*.

Second, some new companies and organizations are bringing to market full Linux distributions that are targeted at network equipment. For example, the OpenCompute Project (OCP) uses Open Network Linux (ONL) as a base upon which to build Linux-powered NOSs (Big Switch, now part of Arista, built Switch Light on ONL, and the DENT Project built dentOS on ONL as well). Cumulus Networks (now part of NVIDIA) is another example, offering its Debian-based Cumulus Linux as a NOS for supported hardware platforms. SONiC—an acronym that stands for *Software for Open Networking in the Cloud*—is yet another example, supported by organizations like Microsoft, Intel, NVIDIA, Broadcom, Dell, and others. As a network engineer, you're increasingly likely to need to know Linux in order to configure your network.

Third, and finally, many of the tools that we discuss in this book have their origins in Linux, or require that you run them from a Linux system. For example, Ansible (a tool we discuss in Chapter 12) requires Python (a topic we discuss in Chapter 6).

For a few reasons we cover in Chapter 12, when automating network equipment with Ansible, you'll typically run Ansible from a network-attached system running Linux and *not* directly on the network equipment. Similarly, when you're using Python to gather and/or manipulate data from network equipment, you'll often do so from a system running Linux.

Finally, relatively recent developments such as eBPF and XDP are increasing Linux's influence in the networking world overall. These interrelated topics are important enough to warrant their own section at the end of this chapter ("Evolving the Linux Kernel with eBPF and XDP" on page 93). We define these two technologies, explain their importance, and discuss some use cases in that section. At this point, suffice it to say that eBPF is transforming multiple aspects of Linux, including (but not limited to) networking, security, and observability.

For these reasons, we feel it is important to include a chapter that seeks to accomplish the following goals:

- Provide a bit of background on the history of Linux
- Briefly explain the concept of Linux distributions
- Introduce you to bash, one of the most popular Linux shells available
- Discuss Linux networking basics
- Dive into some advanced Linux networking functionality
- Furnish a short discussion of bash scripting for automation

Keep in mind that this chapter is not intended to be a comprehensive treatise on Linux or the bash shell; rather, it is intended to get you up and running with Linux in the context of network automation and programmability. Having said that, let's start our discussion of Linux with a brief look at its history and origins.

Exploring a Brief History of Linux

The history of Linux is a story with a couple of threads.

One thread started out in the early 1980s, when Richard Stallman launched the GNU Project as an effort to provide a free Unix-like operating system. GNU, by the way, stands for GNU's Not Unix, a recursive acronym Stallman created to describe the free Unix-like OS he was attempting to create. Stallman's GNU General Public License (GPL) came out of the GNU Project's efforts. Although the GNU Project was able to create free versions of a wide collection of Unix utilities and applications, the kernel—known as GNU Hurd—for the GNU Project's new OS never gained momentum.

A second thread is found in Linus Torvalds's efforts to create a MINIX clone in 1991 as the start of Linux. Driven by the lack of a free OS kernel, his initial work rapidly gained support, and in 1992 was licensed under the GNU GPL with the release of version 0.99. Since that time, the kernel he wrote (named Linux) has been the default OS kernel for the software collection created by the GNU Project.

Because Linux originally referred only to the OS kernel and needed the GNU Project's software collection to form a full operating system, some people suggested that the full OS should be called GNU/Linux, and some organizations still use that designation today (Debian, for example). By and large, however, most people just refer to the entire OS as Linux, so that's the convention that we follow in this book.

Understanding Linux Distributions

As you saw in the previous section, the Linux operating system is made up of the Linux kernel plus a large collection of open source tools primarily developed as part of the GNU Project. The bundling together of the kernel plus a collection of open source software led to the creation of Linux *distributions* (also known as Linux *distros*).

A distribution is the combination of the Linux kernel plus a selection of open source utilities, applications, and software packages that are bundled together and distributed together (hence the name *distribution*). Over the course of Linux's history, multiple Linux distributions have risen and fallen in popularity (anyone remember Slackware?), but as of this writing there are two major branches of Linux distributions: the Red Hat/CentOS branch and the Debian and Debian-derivative branch.

Red Hat Enterprise Linux, Fedora, CentOS, and Amazon Linux

Red Hat was an early Linux distributor that became a significant influencer and commercial success in the Linux market, so it's perfectly natural that one major branch of Linux distributions is based on Red Hat.

Red Hat offers a commercial distribution, known as *Red Hat Enterprise Linux* (*RHEL*), in addition to offering technical support contracts for RHEL. Many organizations today use RHEL because it is backed by Red Hat, focuses on stability and reliability, offers comprehensive technical support options, and is widely supported by other software vendors.

However, the fast-moving pace of Linux development and the Linux open source community is often at odds with the slower and more methodical pace required to maintain stability and reliability in the RHEL product. To help address this dichotomy, Red Hat has an upstream distribution known as *Fedora*. We refer to Fedora as an *upstream distribution* because much of the development of RHEL and RHEL-based distributions occurs in Fedora, then flows "down" to these other products. In coordination with the broader open source community, Fedora sees new kernel versions, new kernel features, new package management tools, and other new developments first; these new things are tested and vetted in Fedora before being migrated to the more enterprise-focused RHEL distribution at a later date. For this reason, you may see Fedora used by developers and other individuals who need the "latest and greatest," but you won't often see Fedora used in production environments.

Although RHEL and its variants are available only from Red Hat through a commercial arrangement, the open source license (the GNU GPL) under which Linux is developed and distributed *requires* that the source of Red Hat's distribution be made publicly available. A group of individuals who wanted the stability and reliability of RHEL but without the corresponding costs imposed by Red Hat took the RHEL sources and created *CentOS* (which stands for *Community Enterprise OS.*) Originally, CentOS was essentially a clone of RHEL, built from the same sources and freely available without cost, but—like many open source software packages—it did not come with any form of technical support.

In late 2020, the purpose of CentOS shifted away from being a RHEL clone and into being a "midstream" distribution, sitting halfway between Fedora and RHEL. This led to the rise of RHEL-compatible distributions branding themselves as CentOS replacements, like AlmaLinux and Rocky Linux. For many organizations and many use cases, the support available from the open source community is sufficient, so it's common to see these RHEL-compatible distributions used in a variety of environments, including enterprise environments.

In September 2011, AWS introduced its own Linux distribution named *Amazon Linux*, optimized for AWS and built to be largely compatible with RHEL. Amazon Linux was replaced by Amazon Linux 2 in 2018. The successor to Amazon Linux 2, named Amazon Linux 2022, was announced in preview in late 2021. At the time of this writing, it had not yet been released for general availability. Amazon Linux 2022 is largely based on Fedora, but also incorporates components from CentOS Stream and the RHEL sources.

One aspect shared by all these distributions (RHEL, Fedora, CentOS/RHEL clones, and Amazon Linux) is a common *package format*. When Linux distributions first started emerging, one key challenge that had to be addressed was the way in which software was packaged with the Linux kernel. Because of the breadth of free software available for Linux, shipping *all* of it in a distribution wasn't really effective, nor would users necessarily *want* all of the various pieces of software installed.

If not all of the software was installed, though, how would the Linux community address dependencies? A *dependency* is a piece of software required to run another piece of software on a computer. For example, some software might be written in Python, which of course would require Python to be installed. Installing Python, however, might require other pieces of software to be installed, and so on.

As an early distributor, Red Hat came up with a way to combine the files needed to run a piece of software along with additional information about that software's dependencies into a single package—a *package format*. That package format is known as an RPM, perhaps so named after the tool originally used to work with said packages: RPM Manager (formerly Red Hat Package Manager), whose executable name was simply `rpm`. All the Linux distributions we've discussed so far—RHEL, CentOS, Fedora, and Amazon Linux—leverage RPM packages as their default package format, although the specific tool used to work with these packages has evolved over time.

We mentioned that RPM originally referred to the actual package manager itself, which was used to work with RPM packages. Most RPM-based distributions have since replaced the `rpm` utility with newer package managers that do a better job of understanding dependencies, resolving conflicts, and installing (or removing) software from a Linux installation. For example, RHEL/CentOS/ Fedora moved first to a tool called `yum` (short for *Yellowdog Updater, Modified*) and are now migrating again to a tool called `dnf` (which stands for *Dandified YUM*).

Other distributions also leverage the RPM package format, such as Oracle Linux, Scientific Linux, and various SUSE Linux derivatives.

You might think that, because multiple Linux distributions all leverage the same package format (RPM), RPM packages are portable across these Linux distributions. In theory, this is possible, but in practice it rarely works. This is usually because of slight variations in package names and package versions across the distributions, which makes resolving dependencies and conflicts practically impossible.

Debian, Ubuntu, and Other Derivatives

Debian GNU/Linux is a distribution produced and maintained by the Debian Project. The Debian Project was officially founded by Ian Murdock in 1993, and the creation of Debian GNU/Linux was funded by the Free Software Foundation's GNU Project from November 1994 through November 1995. To this day, Debian remains the only major distribution of Linux that is not backed by a commercial entity.

All Debian GNU/Linux releases since version 1.1 have used a code name taken from a character in one of the *Toy Story* movies. Debian GNU/Linux 1.1, released in June 1996, was code-named *Buzz*. The most recent stable version of Debian GNU/Linux, version 11.0, was released in August 2021 and is code-named *Bullseye*.

Debian GNU/Linux offers three branches: stable, testing, and unstable. The testing and unstable branches are rolling releases that will, eventually, become the next stable branch. This approach results in a typically very high-quality release, and could be one of the reasons that other distributions are based on (*derived* from) Debian GNU/Linux.

One of the more well-known Debian derivatives is *Ubuntu Linux*, started in April 2004 and funded in large part by Canonical, a company founded by Mark Shuttleworth. The first Ubuntu, released in October 2004 as version 4.10 (the "4" denotes the year, and the "10" denotes the month of release), was code-named Warty Warthog. All Ubuntu codenames are composed of an adjective and an animal with the same first letter (Warty Warthog, Hoary Hedgehog, Breezy Badger, etc.). Ubuntu was initially targeted as a usable desktop Linux distribution, but now offers both desktop-, server-, and mobile-focused versions.

Ubuntu uses time-based releases, releasing a new version every six months and a long-term support (LTS) release every two years. LTS releases are supported by Canonical and the Ubuntu community for a total of five years after release. All releases of Ubuntu are based on packages taken from Debian's unstable branch, which is why we refer to Ubuntu as a Debian derivative.

Speaking of packages: like RPM-based distributions, the common thread across the Debian and Debian derivatives—probably made clear by the term *Debian derivatives* used to describe them—is that they share a common package format, known as the Debian package format (and denoted by a *.deb* file extension). The founders of the Debian Project created the DEB package format and the dpkg tool to solve the same problems that Red Hat attempted to solve with the RPM package format. Also like RPM-based distributions, Debian-based distributions evolved past the use of the dpkg tool directly, first using a tool called dselect and then moving on to the use of the apt tool (and programs like apt-get and aptitude).

 Just as with RPM packages, the fact that multiple distributions leverage the Debian package format doesn't mean that Debian packages are necessarily portable among distributions. Slight variations in package names, package versions, filepaths, and other details will typically make portability difficult, if not impossible.

A key feature of the apt-based tools is the ability to retrieve packages from one or more remote *repositories*, which are online storehouses of Debian packages. The apt tools also feature dependency determination, conflict resolution, and package installation (or removal).

Other Linux Distributions

Although other distributions exist in the market, these two branches—the Red Hat/Fedora/CentOS/clones/Amazon Linux branch and the Debian/Ubuntu branch—cover the majority of Linux instances found in organizations today. For this reason, we focus on only these two branches throughout the rest of this chapter. (Specifically, we'll be using Debian, Amazon Linux, AlmaLinux, and Ubuntu.) If you're using a distribution not from one of these two major branches—perhaps you're working with SUSE Enterprise Linux, for example—keep in mind there may be slight differences between the information contained here and your specific distribution. You should refer to your distribution's documentation for details.

Now that we've provided an overview of the history of Linux and Linux distributions, let's shift our focus to interacting with Linux, primarily via the shell.

Interacting with Linux

As a popular server OS, Linux can be used in a variety of ways across the network. For example, you could receive IP addresses via a Linux-based Dynamic Host Configuration Protocol (DHCP) server, access a Linux-powered web server running the Apache HTTP server or NGINX, or utilize a Domain Name System (DNS) server running Linux in order to resolve domain names to IP addresses. There are, of course, *many* more examples; these are just a few. In the context of our discussion of Linux, though, we're going to focus primarily on interacting with Linux via the shell.

The *shell* provides the CLI used by most users to interact with a Linux system. Linux offers several shells, but the most common shell is *bash*, the Bourne Again Shell (a play on the name of one of the original Unix shells, the Bourne Shell). In the vast majority of cases, unless you've specifically configured your system to use a different shell, you're using bash when you're interacting with Linux.

In this section, we're going to provide you with enough basic information to get started interacting with a Linux system's console, and we'll assume that you're using bash as your shell. If you are using a different shell, keep in mind that some of the commands and behaviors we describe might be slightly different.

 An entire book could be written about bash. In fact, one already has—and is now in its third edition. If you want to learn more about bash than we have room to talk about here, we *highly* recommend *Learning the bash Shell*, third edition, by Cameron Newham and Bill Rosenblatt (O'Reilly).

We've broken our discussion of interacting with Linux into four major areas:

- Navigating the filesystem
- Manipulating files and directories
- Running programs
- Working with background services, known as *daemons*

 This section is primarily targeting users who are new to Linux (a lot of network engineers and IT professionals are mostly familiar with Microsoft Windows). If you're familiar with Linux, feel free to skip ahead.

Let's start with navigating the filesystem.

Navigating the Filesystem

Linux uses a *single-root* filesystem: all the drives, directories, and files in a Linux installation fall into a single namespace, referred to quite simply as /. (When you see / by itself, say "root" in your head.) This is in stark contrast to an OS like Microsoft Windows, where each drive typically has its own root (the drive letter, like *C:* or *D:*). Note that it *is* possible to mount a drive in a folder under Windows, but the practice isn't as common.

 Linux follows in Unix's footsteps in treating everything like a file. This includes storage devices (which are treated as block devices), ports on the computer (like serial ports), or even I/O devices. Thus, the importance of a single-root filesystem—which encompasses devices as well as storage—becomes even greater.

Like most other OSs, Linux uses *directories* (known as *folders* in some other OSs) to group files in the filesystem. Every file resides in a directory, and therefore every file has a unique *path* to its location. To denote the path of a file, you start at the root and list all the directories it takes to get to that file, separating the directories with a forward slash. For example, the command `ping` is often found in the *bin* directory inside the *usr* directory off the root directory. The path, therefore, to `ping` would be noted like this: */usr/bin/ping*.

In other words, start at the root directory (/), enter the *usr/* directory, continue into the *bin/* directory, and find the file named *ping*. Similarly, on Debian Linux 11, the `ip` utility (which is a replacement for many older utilities like `arp`, `ifconfig`, `iwconfig`, and `route`) is found at (in other words, its *path* is) */usr/bin/ip*.

This concept of a path becomes important when we start considering that bash allows you to navigate, or move around, within the filesystem. The *prompt*, or the text that bash displays when waiting for you to input a command, will indicate your location in the filesystem. Here's the default prompt for Debian 11 running on an Amazon Elastic Compute Cloud (EC2) instance (a cloud computing service we discuss in much more detail in Chapter 4):

```
admin@ip-172-31-26-181:~$
```

Do you see it? Unless you're familiar with Linux, you may have missed the tilde (~) following admin@ip-172-31-26-181: in this example prompt. In the bash shell, the tilde is a shortcut that refers to the user's *home directory*. Each user has a home directory that is their personal location for storing files, programs, and other content for only that user. To make it easy to refer to one's home directory, bash uses the tilde as a shortcut. So, looking back at the sample prompt, you can see that this particular prompt tells you a few facts:

1. The first part of the prompt, before the @ symbol, tells you the current user (in this case, admin).

2. The second part of the prompt, directly after the @ symbol, tells you the current hostname of the system on which you are currently operating (in this case, ip-172-31-26-181 is the automatically generated hostname provided by AWS).

3. Following the colon is the current directory, noted in this case as ~, meaning that this user (admin) is currently in their home directory.

4. Finally, even the $ at the end has meaning—in this particular case, it means that the current user (admin) does not have root permissions. The $ will change to a hash sign (the # character, also known as an octothorpe) if the user has root permissions. This is analogous to the way that the prompt for a network device, such as a router or switch, may change depending on the user's privilege level.

The default prompt on an Amazon Linux 2 system looks like this:

```
[ec2-user@ip-172-31-5-69 ~]$
```

As you can see, it's similar, and it conveys the same information as the preceding example prompt, albeit in a slightly different format. Like the earlier example, this prompt shows us the current user (ec2-user), the hostname of the current system (ip-172-31-5-69), the current directory (~), and the effective permissions of the logged-in user ($).

Throughout this chapter, you'll see various Linux prompts similar to ones we just showed you. As we mentioned earlier, we're using four Linux distributions in this chapter: Debian 11, Amazon Linux 2, AlmaLinux 9, and Ubuntu 20.04. For the first part of the chapter, we'll be running these on AWS, which means normally the prompts would look similar to what we've shown you so far. Later, we'll be running them as VMs on a hypervisor on our local network. Regardless, we've taken the liberty of customizing these prompts to show the username and a user-friendly distribution name. Keep in mind that the appearance of the prompt on your own Linux systems may look different depending on where and how you are running them.

The use of the tilde is helpful in keeping the prompt short when you're in your home directory, but what if you don't know the path to your home directory? In other words, what if you don't know where on the system your home directory is located? When you need to determine the full path to your current location, bash offers the pwd (print working directory) command, which produces output something like this:

```
admin@debian11:~$ pwd
/home/admin
```

The pwd command simply returns the directory where you're currently located in the filesystem (the working directory).

Now that you know where you are located in the filesystem, you can begin to move around the filesystem by using the cd (change directory) command along with a path to a destination. For example, if you were in your home directory and wanted to change into the *bin* subdirectory, you'd simply type **cd bin** and press Enter (or Return).

Note the lack of the leading slash here. This is because /bin and bin might indicate two *very* different locations in the filesystem:

- Using bin (no leading slash) tells bash to change into the *bin* subdirectory of the current working directory.

- Using /bin (with a leading slash) tells bash to change into the *bin* subdirectory of the root (/) directory.

See how, therefore, bin and /bin might indicate very different locations? This is why understanding the concept of a single-root filesystem and the path to a file or directory is important. Otherwise, you might end up performing an action on a different file or directory than you intended! This is particularly important when it comes to manipulating files and directories, which we discuss in the next section.

Before moving on, though, we need to discuss a few more navigational commands.

To move up one level in the filesystem (for example, to move from *usr/local/bin/* to */usr/local/*), you can use the .. shortcut. Every directory contains a special entry, named .. (two periods), that is a shortcut entry for that directory's parent directory (the directory one level above it). So, if your current working directory is *usr/local/ bin*, you can simply type **cd** .. and press Enter (or Return) to move up one directory:

```
admin@debian11:/usr/local/bin$ cd ..
admin@debian11:/usr/local$
```

You can combine the .. shortcut with a directory name to move laterally between directories. For example, if you're currently in */usr/local* and need to move to */usr/ share*, you can type **cd ../share** and press Enter. This moves you to the directory whose path is up one level (..) and is named *share*:

```
admin@debian11:/usr/local$ cd ../share
admin@debian11:/usr/share$
```

You can also combine multiple levels of the .. shortcut to move up more than one level. For example, if you are currently in */usr/share* and need to move to / (the root directory), you could type **cd ../../** and press Enter. This would put you into the root directory:

```
admin@debian11:/usr/share$ cd ../..
admin@debian11:/$
```

All these examples are using *relative paths*—paths that are relative to your current location. You can, of course, also use *absolute paths*—paths that are anchored to the root directory. As we mentioned earlier, the distinction is the use of the forward slash (/) to denote an absolute path starting at the root versus a path relative to the current location.

For example, if you are currently located in the root directory (/) and need to move to */media/cdrom*, you don't need the leading slash (because *media* is a subdirectory of /). You can type **cd media/cdrom** and press Enter. This will move you to */media/ cdrom* because you used a relative path to your destination:

```
admin@debian11:/$ cd media/cdrom
admin@debian11:/media/cdrom$
```

From here, though, if you needed to move to */usr/local/bin*, you'd want to use an absolute path. Why? Because there is no (easy) relative path between these two locations that doesn't involve moving through the root. Using an absolute path, anchored with the leading slash, is the quickest and easiest approach:

```
admin@debian11:/media/cdrom$ cd /usr/local/bin
admin@debian11:/usr/local/bin$
```

If you're thinking that you could have also used the command cd ../../usr/local/bin to move from *media/cdrom* to */usr/local/bin*, you've mastered the relationship between relative paths and absolute paths on a Linux system.

Finally, we want to share one final navigation trick. Suppose you're in */usr/local/bin*, but you need to switch over to */media/cdrom*. So you enter **cd /media/cdrom**, but after switching directories realize you needed to be in */usr/local/bin* after all. Fortunately, you can use a quick fix. The notation cd - (using a hyphen after the cd command) tells bash to switch back to the last directory you were in before you switched to the current directory. (If you need a shortcut to get back to your home directory, just enter cd with no parameters.) Here's an example:

```
admin@debian11:/usr/local/bin$ cd /media/cdrom
admin@debian11:/media/cdrom$ cd -
/usr/local/bin
admin@debian11:/usr/local/bin$ cd -
/media/cdrom
admin@debian11:/media/cdrom$ cd -
/usr/local/bin
admin@debian11:/usr/local/bin$
```

Here are all of these filesystem navigation techniques in action:

```
admin@debian11:/usr/local/bin$ cd ..
admin@debian11:/usr/local$ cd ../share
admin@debian11:/usr/share$ cd ../..
admin@debian11:/$ cd media/cdrom
admin@debian11:/media/cdrom$ cd /usr/local/bin
admin@debian11:/usr/local/bin$ cd -
/media/cdrom
admin@debian11:/media/cdrom$ cd -
/usr/local/bin
admin@debian11:/usr/local/bin$
```

Now you should have a pretty good grasp on how to navigate around the Linux filesystem. Let's build on that knowledge with some information on manipulating files and directories.

Manipulating Files and Directories

Armed with a basic understanding of the Linux filesystem, paths within the filesystem, and how to move around the filesystem, let's take a quick look at manipulating files and directories. We'll cover four basic tasks:

- Creating files and directories
- Deleting files and directories
- Moving, copying, and renaming files and directories
- Changing permissions

Let's start with creating files and directories.

Creating files and directories

To create files or directories, you'll work with one of two basic commands: touch, which is used to create files, and mkdir (make directory), which is used—not surprisingly—to create directories.

 You can create files in other ways, such as echoing command output to a file or using an application (like a text editor, for example). Rather than trying to cover all the possible ways to do something, we want to focus on getting you enough information to get started.

The touch command creates a new file with no content (it's up to you to use a text editor or appropriate application to add content to the file after it is created). Let's look at a few examples:

```
[ec2-user@amazonlinux2 ~]$ touch config.txt
```

Here's an equivalent command:

```
[ec2-user@amazonlinux2 ~]$ touch ./config.txt
```

The reason this command is equivalent to the earlier example may not be immediately obvious. In the previous section, we talked about the .. shortcut for moving to the parent directory of the current directory. Every directory also has an entry noted by a single period (.) that refers to the *current directory*. Therefore, the commands touch config.txt and touch ./config.txt will *both* create a file named *config.txt* in the current working directory.

If both syntaxes are correct, why are there two ways of doing it? In this case, both commands produce the same result—but *this isn't the case for all commands*. When you want to be sure that the file you're referencing is the file in the current working directory, use ./ to tell bash you want the file in the current directory:

```
[ec2-user@amazonlinux2 ~]$ touch /config.txt
```

In this case, we're using an absolute path, so this command creates a file named *config.txt* in the root directory, assuming your user account has permission. (We talk about permissions in "Changing permissions" on page 58.)

We haven't discussed in detail yet bash's *search paths*, which are paths (locations) in the filesystem that bash will automatically search when you type in a command. In a typical configuration, paths such as */usr/bin*, */usr/sbin*, and similar locations are included in the search path. Thus, if you specify a filename from a file in one of those directories without using the full path, bash will find it for you by searching these paths. This is one of the times when being specific about a file's location (by including ./ or the absolute path) might be a good idea, so that you can be sure which file is the one being found and used by bash.

The mkdir command is simple: it creates the directory specified by the user. Let's look at a quick example:

```
[ec2-user@amazonlinux2 ~]$ mkdir bin
```

This command creates a directory named *bin* in the current working directory. It's different from this command (relative versus absolute paths!):

```
[ec2-user@amazonlinux2 ~]$ mkdir /bin
```

Like most other Linux commands, mkdir has a lot of options that modify its behavior, but one you'll use frequently is the -p parameter. When used with -p, mkdir will not report an error if the directory already exists, and will create parent directories along the path as needed.

For example, let's say you have some files you need to store, and you want to store them in */opt/sw/network*. If you are in the */opt* directory and enter mkdir sw/network and the *sw* directory doesn't already exist, the mkdir command will report an error. However, if you simply add the -p option, mkdir will create the *sw* directory if needed, and then create *network* under *sw*. This is a *great* way to create an entire path all at once without failing because of errors if a directory along the way already exists.

Creating files and directories is half of the picture; let's look at the other half (deleting files and directories).

Deleting files and directories

Just as Linux has two commands for creating files and directories, it has two commands for deleting files and directories. Generally, you'll use the rm command to delete (remove) files, and you'll use the rmdir command to delete directories. You can also use rm to delete directories, as we'll show you in this section.

To remove a file, you simply use rm *filename*. For example, to remove a file named *config.txt* in the current working directory, you'd use one of the two following commands (do you understand why?):

```
ubuntu@ubuntu2004:~$ rm config.txt
ubuntu@ubuntu2004:~$ rm ./config.txt
```

You can, of course, use absolute paths (/home/ubuntu/config.txt) as well as relative paths (./config.txt).

To remove a directory, you use rmdir *directory*. Note, however, that the directory has to be empty; if you attempt to delete a directory containing files, you'll get this error message:

```
rmdir: failed to remove 'src': Directory not empty
```

In this case, you'll need to first empty the directory, then use rmdir. Alternately, you can use the -r parameter to the rm command. Normally, if you try to use the rm command on a directory but fail to use the -r parameter, bash will respond like this (in this example, we tried to remove a directory named *bin* in the current working directory):

```
rm: cannot remove 'bin': Is a directory
```

When you use rm -r *directory*, though, bash will remove the entire directory tree. Note that, by default, rm *isn't* going to prompt for confirmation; it's simply going to delete the whole directory tree. No Recycle Bin, no Trash Can—it's gone. (If you want a prompt, you can add the -i parameter.)

> The mv and cp commands that we discuss in the next section also will simply overwrite files in the destination without any prompt, unless you use the -i parameter. Be sure to exercise the appropriate level of caution when using these commands.

Creating and deleting files and directories aren't the only tasks you might need to do, though, so let's take a quick look at moving (or copying) files and directories.

Moving, copying, and renaming files and directories

When it comes to moving, copying, and renaming files and directories, the two commands you'll need to use are cp (for copying files or directories) and mv (for moving and renaming files and directories).

> The basic use of all the Linux commands we've shown you so far is relatively easy to understand, but—as the saying goes—the devil is in the details. If you need more information on any of the options, parameters, or the advanced usage of just about any command in Linux, use the man (manual) command. For example, to view the manual page for the cp command, type **man cp**. The manual pages show a more detailed explanation of how to use the various commands.

To copy a file, it's just cp *source destination*. Similarly, to move a file, you would use mv *source destination*. Renaming a file, by the way, is considered moving it from one name to a new name (typically in the same directory).

Moving a directory is much the same; use mv *source-dir destination-dir*. This is true whether the directory is flat (containing only files) or a tree (containing both files as well as subdirectories).

Copying directories is only a bit more complicated. Just add the -r option, like cp -r *source-dir destination-dir*. This will handle most use cases for copying directories, although some less common use cases may require additional options. We recommend you read and refer to the man (manual) page for cp for additional details (see the preceding tip).

The final topic we'd like to tackle in our discussion of manipulating files and directories is permissions.

Changing permissions

Taking a cue from its Unix predecessors (keeping in mind that Linux rose out of efforts to create a free Unix-like operating system), Linux is a multiuser OS that incorporates the use of permissions on files and directories. To be considered a multiuser OS, Linux had to have a way to make sure one user couldn't view/see/ modify/remove other users' files, and so file- and directory-level permissions were a necessity.

Linux permissions are built around a couple of key ideas:

- Permissions are assigned based on the user (the user who owns the file), group (other users in the file's group), and others (other users not in the file's group).
- Permissions are based on the action (read, write, and execute).

Here's how these two ideas come together. Each action (read, write, and execute) is assigned a value; specifically, read is set to 4, write is set to 2, and execute is set to 1. (Note that these values correspond exactly to binary values.) To allow multiple actions, add the values for each underlying action. For example, if you want to allow both read and write, the value you assign is 6 (read = 4, write = 2, so read + write = 6).

These values are then assigned to user, group, and others. For example, to allow the file's owner to read and write to a file, you assign the value 6 to the user's permissions. To allow the file's owner to read, write, and execute a file, you assign the value 7 to the user's permissions.

Similarly, if you want to allow users in the file's group to read the file but not write or execute it, you assign the value 4 to the group's permissions. User, group, and other permissions are listed as an octal number, like this:

644 (user = read + write, group = read, others = read)
755 (user = read + write + execute, group = read + execute, others = read + execute)
600 (user = read + write, group = none, others = none)
620 (user = read + write, group = write, others = none)

You may also see these permissions listed as a string of characters, like rwxr-xr-x. This indicates the read (r), write (w), and execute (x) permissions for each of the three entities (user, group, and others). Here are the same examples as earlier, but written in alternate format:

644 = rw-r--r--
755 = rwxr-xr-x
600 = rw-------
620 = rw--w----

The read and write permissions are self-explanatory, but execute is a bit different. For a file, it means just what it says: the ability to execute the file as a program (something we discuss in more detail in "Running Programs" on page 61). For a directory, though, it means the ability to look into and list the contents of the directory. Therefore, if you want members of a directory's group to see the contents of that directory, you need to grant the execute permission.

A couple of Linux tools are used to view and modify permissions. The ls utility, used for listing the contents of a directory, will show permissions when used with the -l option and is most likely the primary tool you'll use to view permissions. Figure 3-1 contains the output of ls -l /usr/bin on a Debian 11 system and clearly shows permissions assigned to the files in the listing.

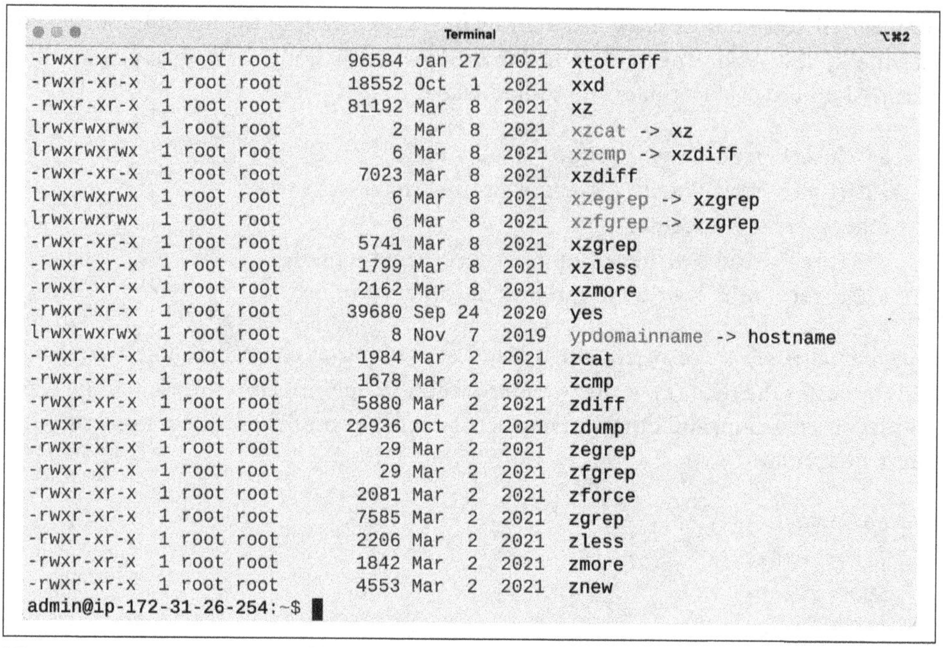

```
●  ●  ●                              Terminal                                    ⌥⌘2
-rwxr-xr-x  1 root root    96584 Jan 27  2021  xtotroff
-rwxr-xr-x  1 root root    18552 Oct  1  2021  xxd
-rwxr-xr-x  1 root root    81192 Mar  8  2021  xz
lrwxrwxrwx  1 root root        2 Mar  8  2021  xzcat -> xz
lrwxrwxrwx  1 root root        6 Mar  8  2021  xzcmp -> xzdiff
-rwxr-xr-x  1 root root     7023 Mar  8  2021  xzdiff
lrwxrwxrwx  1 root root        6 Mar  8  2021  xzegrep -> xzgrep
lrwxrwxrwx  1 root root        6 Mar  8  2021  xzfgrep -> xzgrep
-rwxr-xr-x  1 root root     5741 Mar  8  2021  xzgrep
-rwxr-xr-x  1 root root     1799 Mar  8  2021  xzless
-rwxr-xr-x  1 root root     2162 Mar  8  2021  xzmore
-rwxr-xr-x  1 root root    39680 Sep 24  2020  yes
lrwxrwxrwx  1 root root        8 Nov  7  2019  ypdomainname -> hostname
-rwxr-xr-x  1 root root     1984 Mar  2  2021  zcat
-rwxr-xr-x  1 root root     1678 Mar  2  2021  zcmp
-rwxr-xr-x  1 root root     5880 Mar  2  2021  zdiff
-rwxr-xr-x  1 root root    22936 Oct  2  2021  zdump
-rwxr-xr-x  1 root root       29 Mar  2  2021  zegrep
-rwxr-xr-x  1 root root       29 Mar  2  2021  zfgrep
-rwxr-xr-x  1 root root     2081 Mar  2  2021  zforce
-rwxr-xr-x  1 root root     7585 Mar  2  2021  zgrep
-rwxr-xr-x  1 root root     2206 Mar  2  2021  zless
-rwxr-xr-x  1 root root     1842 Mar  2  2021  zmore
-rwxr-xr-x  1 root root     4553 Mar  2  2021  znew
admin@ip-172-31-26-254:~$ ▋
```

Figure 3-1. Permissions in a file listing

To change or modify permissions, you need to use the chmod utility. This is where the explanation of octal values (755, 600, 644, etc.) and the rwxr-xr-x notation (typically referred to as *symbolic notation*) comes in handy, because that's how chmod expects the user to enter permissions. As with relative paths versus absolute paths, the use of octal values versus symbolic notation is really a matter of what you're trying to accomplish:

- If you need (or are willing) to set all the permissions at the same time, use octal values. Even if you omit some of the digits, you'll still be changing the permissions because chmod assumes missing digits are leading zeros (and thus you're setting permissions to none).

- If you need to set only one part (user, group, or others) of the permissions while leaving the rest intact, use symbolic notation. This will allow you to modify only one part of the permissions (for example, only the user permissions or only the group permissions).

Here are a few quick examples of using chmod. First, let's set the *bin* directory in the current working directory to mode 755 (owner = read/write/execute, all others = read/execute):

```
[ec2-user@amazonlinux2 ~]$ chmod 755 bin
```

Next, let's use symbolic notation to add read/write permissions to the user who owns the file *config.txt* in the current working directory, while leaving all other permissions intact:

```
[ec2-user@amazonlinux2 ~]$ chmod u+rw config.txt
```

Here's an even more complex example—this adds read/write permissions for the file owner, but removes write permission for the file group:

```
[ec2-user@amazonlinux2 ~]$ chmod u+rw,g-w /opt/share/config.txt
```

The chmod command also supports the use of the -R option to act *recursively*, meaning the permission changes will be propagated to files and subdirectories (obviously, this works only when you're using chmod against a directory).

 Given that file ownership and file group play an integral role in file permissions, it's natural that Linux also provides tools to modify file ownership and file group (the ls command is used to view ownership and group, as shown earlier in Figure 3-1). You'll use the chown command to change ownership and the chgrp command to change the file group. Both commands support the same -R option as chmod to act recursively.

We're now ready to move on from file and directory manipulation to our next major topic in interacting with Linux, which is running programs.

Running Programs

Running programs is pretty simple, given the material we've already covered. To run a program, here's what's needed:

- A file that is executable (you can use the file utility to help determine whether a file is executable)
- Execute permissions (either as the file owner, as a member of the file's group, or with the execute permission given to others)

We discussed the second requirement (execute permissions) in the previous section on permissions, so we don't need to cover that again here. If you don't have execute permissions on the file, use the chmod, chown, and/or chgrp commands as needed to address it. The first requirement (an executable file) deserves a bit more discussion, though.

What makes up an executable file? It could be a binary file, compiled from a programming language such C or C++. However, it could also be an executable text file, such as a bash shell script (a series of bash shell commands) or a script written in a language like Python or Ruby. (We cover Python extensively in Chapter 6.) The file utility can help here (`file` may or may not be installed by default; use your Linux distribution's package management tool to install it if it isn't already installed).

Here's the output of the `file` command against various types of executable files:

```
admin@debian11:~$ file /bin/bash
/bin/bash: ELF 64-bit LSB executable, x86-64, version 1 (SYSV), dynamically
linked, interpreter /lib64/ld-linux-x86-64.so.2, BuildID[sha1]=3313b4cb119dcce
16927a9b6cc61dcd97dfc4d59, for GNU/Linux 3.2.0, stripped
admin@debian11:~$ file /usr/local/bin/kubectl
/usr/local/bin/kubectl: ELF 64-bit LSB executable, x86-64, version 1 (SYSV),
statically linked, Go BuildID=udvEuh-txVq1kB1pCAyG/K_fqce2JzNpLs4j8aaW9/fKnl1Z
SWXEi1VKww0UrK/rUvBWXXhKqBjdb_5dTXI, stripped
admin@debian11:~$ file shellscript.sh
script.sh: Bourne-Again shell script, ASCII text executable
admin@debian11:~$ file testscript.py
script.py: Python script, ASCII text executable
admin@debian11:~$ file testscript-2.rb
script.rb: Ruby script, ASCII text executable
```

 The `file` command can identify text files as a Python script, a Ruby script, or a shell (bash) script. This might sound like magic, but in reality it's relying upon a Linux construct known as the *shebang*. This first line in a text-based script starts with the characters #!, followed by the path to the interpreter to the script (the *interpreter* executes the commands in the script). For example, on a Debian 11 system, the Python interpreter is found at */usr/bin/ python3*, and so the shebang for a Python script would look like #!/usr/bin/python3. A Ruby script would have a similar shebang, but pointing to the Ruby interpreter. A bash shell script's shebang would point to bash itself, of course.

Once you've satisfied both requirements—you have an executable file and you have execute permissions on the executable file—running a program is as simple as entering the program name on the command line. *That's it.* Each program may, of course, have certain options and parameters that need to be supplied. The only real "gotcha" here might be around the use of absolute paths; for example, if multiple programs named `testnet` exist on your Linux system and you simply enter `testnet` at the shell prompt, which one will it run? This is where an understanding of bash search paths (which we discuss next) and/or the use of absolute paths can help ensure that you're running the intended program.

Let's expand on this potential gotcha just a bit. In "Navigating the Filesystem" on page 50, we covered relative paths and absolute paths. We're going to add to this discussion by introducing the concept of a *search path*. Every Linux system has a search path, which is a list of directories on the system that it will search when the user enters a filename. You can see the current search path by entering echo $PATH at your shell prompt, and on an Amazon Linux 2 system you'd see something like this:

```
[ec2-user@amazonlinux2 ~]$ echo $PATH
/usr/local/bin:/usr/bin:/usr/local/sbin:/usr/sbin:/home/ec2-user/.local/bin:
/home/ec2-user/bin
```

This means that if you have a script named *testscript.py* stored in */usr/local/bin*, you can be in *any* directory on the system and simply enter the script's name (*testscript.py*) to execute the script. The system will search the directories in the search path (in order) for the filename you enter and execute the first one it finds (which, in this case, will typically be the one in */usr/local/bin* because that's the first directory in the search path).

You'll note, by the way, that the search path does *not* include the current directory. Let's say you create a *scripts* directory in your home directory, and in that directory you have a shell script you've written called *shellscript.sh*. Take a look at the behavior from the following set of commands:

```
[ec2-user@amazonlinux2 ~]$ pwd
/home/ec2-user/scripts
[ec2-user@amazonlinux2 ~]$ ls
shellscript.sh
[ec2-user@amazonlinux2 ~]$ shellscript.sh
-bash: /home/ec2-user/bin/shellscript.sh: No such file or directory
[ec2-user@amazonlinux2 ~]$ ./shellscript.sh
This is a shell script.
```

Because the shell script isn't in the search path, we have to use an absolute path—in this case, the absolute path is telling bash (via the ./ notation) to look in the current directory.

Therefore, the gotcha is that any program you run—be it a compiled binary or an ASCII text script that will be interpreted by bash, Python, Ruby, or another interpreter—needs to be in the search path, or you'll have to explicitly specify the absolute path (which may include the current directory) to the program. In the case of multiple programs with the same name in different directories, the program that bash finds *first* will be the program that gets executed, and the search order is determined by the search path.

To help with this potential gotcha when you have multiple programs with the same name, you can use the which command. For example, suppose you have a Python script named uptime that gathers uptime statistics from your network devices. Most Linux distributions also ship with a command called uptime (it displays information about how long the Linux system has been up and running). By typing **which uptime**, you can ask the Linux system to tell you the full path to the first uptime executable it finds when searching the search path. (This is the one that will be executed if you just type **uptime** at the prompt.) Based on this information, you can either specify a full path to your Python script or modify the search path (if needed).

 You can, of course, change and customize the search path. The search path is controlled by an *environment variable* whose name is PATH. (By convention, all environment variables are specified in uppercase letters.) Modifying this environment variable will modify the search order that bash uses to locate programs.

We're going to cover one more topic before moving on to a discussion of networking in Linux, and that's working with background programs, also known as daemons.

Working with Daemons

In the Linux world, we use the term *daemon* to refer to a process that runs in the background. (You may also see the term *service* used to describe these types of background processes.) Daemons are most often encountered when you're using Linux to provide network-based functionality. Examples—some of which we discussed earlier when we first introduced interacting with Linux—might include a DHCP server, an HTTP server, a DNS server, or an FTP server. On a Linux system, each of these network services is provided by a corresponding daemon (or service). In this section, we cover how to work with daemons: start daemons, stop daemons, restart a daemon, or check on a daemon's status.

It used to be that working with daemons on a Linux system varied pretty widely among distributions. Startup scripts, referred to as *init scripts*, were used to start, stop, or restart a daemon. Some distributions offered utilities—often nothing more than bash shell scripts—such as the service command to help simplify working with daemons. For example, on Ubuntu 14.04 LTS and CentOS 7.1 systems, the service command (found in */usr/sbin*) allowed you to start, stop, or restart a daemon. Behind the scenes, these utilities are calling distribution-specific commands (such as initctl on Ubuntu or systemctl on CentOS) to actually perform their actions.

In recent years, though, virtually all the major Linux distributions have converged on the use of systemd as their init system: RHEL/CentOS 7.x, Debian 8.0 and later, and Ubuntu 15.04 and later all use systemd. While this brings a great deal of consistency to working with daemons across different Linux distributions, keep in mind that slight variations may occur in the implementation of systemd among different distributions.

Prior to version 8.0, Debian did not use systemd. Instead, Debian used an older init system known as *System V init* (or *sysv-rc*). Similarly, Ubuntu 14.04 used a Canonical-developed system called Upstart, but switched to systemd with the next major LTS release (16.04).

There's a great deal more to systemd than we have room to discuss here. When we provide examples on how to start, stop, or restart a background service using systemd, we assume that the systemd *unit* has already been installed and enabled, and that it is recognized by systemd. We encourage you to review the man pages for the systemd commands shared in this section for more details.

If you are interested in more details on systemd, we recommend having a look at the systemd website (*https://oreil.ly/R7Lqc*).

Let's start by looking at starting background services.

Starting, stopping, and restarting background services

For distributions using systemd as the init system, the primary means by which you'll work with background services is via the `systemctl` utility (found on the system as */usr/bin/systemctl*). Some distributions have "wrapper" scripts that call `systemctl` on the backend, but we won't discuss those here. Instead, we'll show you how to work with `systemctl` directly.

To start a daemon using systemd, you call `systemctl` with the `start` subcommand (by the way, we're using *subcommand* here to refer to the parameter supplied to `systemctl` that provides the action it should take—we also use this nomenclature later in this chapter when working with Linux networking):

```
admin@debian11:~$ systemctl start service-name
```

The *service-name* referenced in the preceding command is the name of a systemd *unit*. If you don't know the name of the service, `systemctl` offers the `list-units` subcommand, which will give you a paged list of all the loaded and active units.

To stop a daemon using systemd, replace the `start` subcommand with `stop`, like this:

```
[ec2-user@amazonlinux2]:~$ systemctl stop service-name
```

Similarly, use the `restart` subcommand to stop and then start a daemon:

```
ubuntu@ubuntu2004:~$ systemctl restart service-name
```

Note that `systemctl` also supports a `reload` subcommand, which will cause a daemon to reload its configuration. This may be less disruptive than restarting a daemon (via `systemctl restart`, which will almost always be disruptive), but the exact way a daemon will respond to reloading its configuration will vary (in other words, not all daemons will apply the new configuration automatically or behave in the same fashion).

Checking the status or configuration of a background service

In addition to starting, stopping, and restarting daemons, `systemctl` offers other functionality to help manage background services. For example, you can use the `status` subcommand to `systemctl` to check the current status of a daemon. Figure 3-2 shows the output of running `systemctl status`.

```
  ● ● ●                              Terminal                              ⌥⌘2
ubuntu@ip-172-31-47-187:~$ sudo systemctl status ssh.service
● ssh.service - OpenBSD Secure Shell server
     Loaded: loaded (/lib/systemd/system/ssh.service; enabled; vendor preset: e
    Drop-In: /usr/lib/systemd/system/ssh.service.d
             └─ec2-instance-connect.conf
     Active: active (running) since Thu 2023-04-27 21:34:34 UTC; 5min ago
       Docs: man:sshd(8)
             man:sshd_config(5)
    Process: 1257 ExecStartPre=/usr/sbin/sshd -t (code=exited, status=0/SUCCESS)
   Main PID: 1258 (sshd)
      Tasks: 1 (limit: 9399)
     Memory: 4.4M
     CGroup: /system.slice/ssh.service
             └─1258 sshd: /usr/sbin/sshd -D -o AuthorizedKeysCommand /usr/share

Apr 27 21:34:34 ip-172-31-47-187 systemd[1]: Starting OpenBSD Secure Shell serv
Apr 27 21:34:34 ip-172-31-47-187 sshd[1258]: Server listening on 0.0.0.0 port 2
Apr 27 21:34:34 ip-172-31-47-187 sshd[1258]: Server listening on :: port 22.
Apr 27 21:34:34 ip-172-31-47-187 systemd[1]: Started OpenBSD Secure Shell serve
Apr 27 21:40:18 ip-172-31-47-187 sshd[1305]: Accepted publickey for ubuntu from
Apr 27 21:40:18 ip-172-31-47-187 sshd[1305]: pam_unix(sshd:session): session op
lines 1-20/20 (END)
```

Figure 3-2. Output of the `systemctl status` command

We've mentioned the idea of a systemd unit a couple of times so far; a systemd *unit* can be considered any resource that systemd knows how to operate and/or manage. Systemd knows how to operate or manage resources via configuration files known as *unit files*. While a full explanation of systemd unit files is beyond the scope of this book, you can use `systemctl` to show you a unit's configuration file via the `systemctl cat` command, as shown in Figure 3-3.

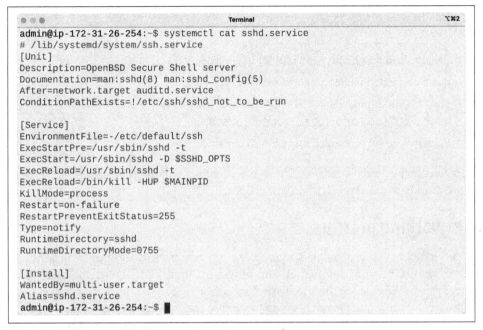

```
• • •                          Terminal                          ⌥⌘2
admin@ip-172-31-26-254:~$ systemctl cat sshd.service
# /lib/systemd/system/ssh.service
[Unit]
Description=OpenBSD Secure Shell server
Documentation=man:sshd(8) man:sshd_config(5)
After=network.target auditd.service
ConditionPathExists=!/etc/ssh/sshd_not_to_be_run

[Service]
EnvironmentFile=-/etc/default/ssh
ExecStartPre=/usr/sbin/sshd -t
ExecStart=/usr/sbin/sshd -D $SSHD_OPTS
ExecReload=/usr/sbin/sshd -t
ExecReload=/bin/kill -HUP $MAINPID
KillMode=process
Restart=on-failure
RestartPreventExitStatus=255
Type=notify
RuntimeDirectory=sshd
RuntimeDirectoryMode=0755

[Install]
WantedBy=multi-user.target
Alias=sshd.service
admin@ip-172-31-26-254:~$ ▮
```

Figure 3-3. Output of the systemctl cat *command*

To change the configuration of a systemd unit, you need to perform a daemon reload of systemctl so that it reads in the new configuration:

```
[ec2-user@amazonlinux2 ~]$ systemctl daemon-reload
```

Before we wrap up this section on working with daemons and move into a discussion of Linux networking, let's explore a few final commands you might find helpful.

Other daemon-related commands

When working with daemons, you might find a few other commands useful. For full details on all the various parameters for these commands, we encourage you to read the man pages (use man *command* at a bash prompt):

- To show network connections to a daemon, you can use ss. One particularly helpful use of this command is to show listening network sockets, which is one way to ensure that the networking configuration for a particular daemon (background service) is working properly. Use ss -lnt to show listening TCP sockets, and use ss -lnu to show listening UDP sockets. Note that this syntax replaces the use of the now-deprecated netstat command.

- The ps command is useful for presenting information on the currently running processes.

Before we move on to the next section, let's take a quick moment and review what we've covered so far:

- Background and history for Linux
- Basic filesystem navigation and paths
- Basic file manipulations (creating files and directories, moving/copying files and directories, and removing files and directories)
- Background services, also known as daemons

Our next major topic is networking in Linux, which will build on many of the areas we've already touched on so far in this chapter.

Networking in Linux

We've stated that this chapter is intended to get you up and running with Linux in the context of network automation and programmability. You'll likely be using tools like Python, Ansible, or Jinja (covered in Chapters 6, 12, and 9, respectively) on Linux, and your Linux system is going to need to communicate across the network to various devices. Naturally, therefore, our discussion of Linux would not be complete without also discussing networking in Linux. This is, after all, a networking-centric book!

 Because networking in public cloud environments can, at times, work a bit differently than typical on-premises networks, in this section we'll be using Linux running in VMs on a local hypervisor. As a result, we're switching out Amazon Linux 2 for AlmaLinux 9. AlmaLinux 9 is one of several successors to CentOS after the transition to CentOS Stream, and describes itself as 1:1 binary compatible with RHEL.

Working with Interfaces

The basic building block of Linux networking is the *interface*. Linux supports several types of interfaces; the most common are physical interfaces, VLAN interfaces, and bridge interfaces. As with most other things in Linux, you configure these various types of interfaces by executing command-line utilities from the bash shell or using certain plain-text configuration files. Making interface configuration changes persistent across a reboot typically requires modifying a configuration file. Let's look first at using the command-line utilities, and then we'll discuss persistent changes using interface configuration files.

Interface configuration via the command line

Just as the Linux distributions have converged on systemd as the primary init system, most of the major Linux distributions have converged on a single set of command-line utilities for working with network interfaces. These commands are part of the `iproute2` set of utilities, available in the major Linux distributions as either `iproute` or `iproute2`. This set of utilities uses the `ip` command to replace the functionality of earlier (and now deprecated) commands such as `ifconfig` and `route`.

If you're interested in more information on `iproute2`, visit the "iproute2" Wikipedia page (*https://oreil.ly/q5tJj*).

For interface configuration, two subcommands to the `ip` command will be used: `ip link`, to view or set interface link status, and `ip addr`, to view or set IP addressing configuration on interfaces. (We present other forms of the `ip` command later in this section.)

Let's look at a few task-oriented examples of using the `ip` commands to perform interface configuration.

Listing interfaces. You can use either `ip link` or `ip addr` to list all the interfaces on a system, although the output will be slightly different for each command.

If you want a listing of the interfaces along with the interface status, use `ip link list`, like this:

```
[almalinux@alma9 ~]$ ip link list
1: lo: <LOOPBACK,UP,LOWER_UP> mtu 65536 qdisc noqueue state UNKNOWN mode DEFAULT
 group default qlen 1000
    link/loopback 00:00:00:00:00:00 brd 00:00:00:00:00:00
2: eth0: <BROADCAST,MULTICAST,UP,LOWER_UP> mtu 1500 qdisc fq_codel state UP mode
 DEFAULT group default qlen 1000
    link/ether 52:54:00:d2:c5:f4 brd ff:ff:ff:ff:ff:ff
    altname enp0s3
    altname ens3
```

The default action, so to speak, for most (if not all) of the `ip` commands is to list the items with which you're working. Thus, if you want to list all the interfaces, you can just use `ip link` instead of `ip link list`, or if you want to list all the routes, you can just use `ip route` instead of `ip route list`. We specify the full commands here for clarity.

As you can tell from the prompt, this output was taken from an AlmaLinux 9 VM (which, as we described earlier in this section, is considered to be 1:1 binary compatible with RHEL). The command syntax is the same across the three major distributions we're discussing in this chapter, and the output is largely identical (with the exception of interface names).

This output shows you the current list of interfaces (throughout this section, note that the different Linux distributions may use different naming conventions for network interfaces), the current MTU, the current administrative state (UP), and the ethernet MAC address, among other things.

The output of this command also tells you the current state of the interface (note the information in angle brackets immediately following the interface name):

UP
>   The interface is enabled.

LOWER_UP
>   The interface link is up.

NO_CARRIER *(not shown)*
>   The interface is enabled, but there is no link.

If you're accustomed to working with network equipment, you're probably familiar with an interface being "down" versus being "administratively down." If an interface is down because there is no link, you'll see NO_CARRIER in the brackets immediately after the interface name; if the interface is administratively down, then you won't see UP, LOWER_UP, or NO_CARRIER, and the state will be listed as DOWN. In the next section, we'll show you how to use the ip link command to disable an interface (set an interface as administratively down).

You can also list interfaces by using the ip addr list command, like this (this output is taken from Ubuntu 20.04 LTS):

```
ubuntu@ubuntu2004:~$ ip addr list
1: lo: <LOOPBACK,UP,LOWER_UP> mtu 65536 qdisc noqueue state UNKNOWN group default
qlen 1000
    link/loopback 00:00:00:00:00:00 brd 00:00:00:00:00:00
    inet 127.0.0.1/8 scope host lo
       valid_lft forever preferred_lft forever
    inet6 ::1/128 scope host
       valid_lft forever preferred_lft forever
2: ens3: <BROADCAST,MULTICAST,UP,LOWER_UP> mtu 1500 qdisc fq_codel state UP group
default qlen 1000
    link/ether 52:54:00:8d:04:a3 brd ff:ff:ff:ff:ff:ff
    inet 192.168.122.215/24 brd 192.168.122.255 scope global dynamic ens3
       valid_lft 2581sec preferred_lft 2581sec
    inet6 fe80::5054:ff:fe8d:4a3/64 scope link
       valid_lft forever preferred_lft forever
```

As you can see, `ip addr list` also lists the interfaces on the system, along with some link status information and the IPv4/IPv6 addresses assigned to the interface.

For both `ip link list` and `ip addr list`, you can filter the list to only a specific interface by adding the interface name. The final command then becomes `ip link list interface` or `ip addr list interface`, like this:

```
debian@debian11:~$ ip addr list ens5
2: ens3: <BROADCAST,MULTICAST,UP,LOWER_UP> mtu 1500 qdisc pfifo_fast state UP
group default qlen 1000
    link/ether 52:54:00:7d:2b:d1 brd ff:ff:ff:ff:ff:ff
    altname enp0s3
    inet 192.168.122.104/24 brd 192.168.122.255 scope global dynamic ens3
       valid_lft 2856sec preferred_lft 2856sec
    inet6 fe80::5054:ff:fe7d:2bd1/64 scope link
       valid_lft forever preferred_lft forever
```

Listing interfaces is useful, of course, but perhaps even more useful is actually modifying the configuration of an interface. In the next section, we'll show you how to enable or disable an interface.

Enabling/disabling an interface. In addition to listing interfaces, you also use the `ip link` command to manage an interface's status. To disable an interface, for example, you set the interface's status to down by using the `ip link set` command:

```
[almalinux@alma9 ~]$ ip link set eth0 down
[almalinux@alma9 ~]$ ip link list eth0
2: eth0: <BROADCAST,MULTICAST> mtu 1500 qdisc fq_codel state DOWN mode DEFAULT
group default qlen 1000
    link/ether 52:54:00:d2:c5:f4 brd ff:ff:ff:ff:ff:ff
    altname enp0s3
    altname ens3
```

Note `state DOWN` and the lack of `NO_CARRIER`, which tells you the interface is administratively down (disabled) and not just down because of a link failure. (We've bolded the `state DOWN` in the preceding output to make it easier to spot.)

To enable (or re-enable) the eth0 interface, you simply use `ip link set` again, this time setting the status to up:

```
[almalinux@alma9 ~]$ ip link set eth0 up
[almalinux@alma9 ~]$ ip link list eth0
2: eth0: <BROADCAST,MULTICAST,UP,LOWER_UP> mtu 1500 qdisc fq_codel state UP mode
 DEFAULT group default qlen 1000
    link/ether 52:54:00:d2:c5:f4 brd ff:ff:ff:ff:ff:ff
    altname enp0s3
    altname ens3
```

Setting the MTU of an interface. If you need to set the MTU of an interface, you once again turn to the `ip link` command, using the `set` subcommand. The full syntax is `ip link set mtu MTU interface`.

As a specific example, let's say you want to run jumbo frames on the eth0 interface on your Linux system. Here's the command:

```
[almalinux@alma9 ~]$ ip link set mtu 9000 eth0
```

As with all the other ip commands we've looked it, this change is immediate but not persistent—you'll have to edit the interface's configuration file to make the change persistent. We discuss configuring interfaces via configuration files in "Interface configuration via configuration files" on page 73.

Assigning an IP address to an interface.   To assign (or remove) an IP address to an interface, you use the ip addr command. We've already shown you how to use ip addr list to see a list of the interfaces and their assigned IP address(es); now we'll expand the use of ip addr to add and remove IP addresses.

 The commands and configurations shown in this section may change or behave differently when you are running Linux as an instance on a public cloud provider. For example, managing IP addresses in a public cloud environment is typically handled via the cloud provider's APIs instead of the commands presented in this section. We discuss networking in the cloud, including these sorts of considerations, in Chapter 4.

To assign (add) an IP address to an interface, you use the command ip addr add *address* dev *interface*. For example, to assign the address 172.31.254.100/24 to the ens3 interface on a Debian system, run this command:

```
debian@debian11:~$ ip addr add 172.31.254.100/24 dev ens3
```

If an interface already has an IP address assigned, ip addr add simply *adds* the new address, leaving the original address intact. So, in this example, if the ens3 interface already has an address of 192.168.122.104/24, running the previous command will result in this configuration:

```
debian@debian11:~$ ip addr list ens3
2: ens3: <BROADCAST,MULTICAST,UP,LOWER_UP> mtu 1500 qdisc pfifo_fast state UP
group default qlen 1000
    link/ether 52:54:00:7d:2b:d1 brd ff:ff:ff:ff:ff:ff
    altname enp0s3
    inet 192.168.122.104/24 brd 192.168.122.255 scope global dynamic ens3
       valid_lft 3523sec preferred_lft 3523sec
    inet 172.31.254.100/24 scope global ens3
       valid_lft forever preferred_lft forever
    inet6 fe80::5054:ff:fe7d:2bd1/64 scope link
       valid_lft forever preferred_lft forever
```

To remove an IP address from an interface, use `ip addr del` *address* dev *interface*. Here we are removing the 172.31.254.100/24 address we assigned earlier to the ens3 interface:

```
debian@debian11:~$ ip addr del 172.31.254.100/24 dev ens3
debian@debian11:~$ ip addr list ens3
2: ens3: <BROADCAST,MULTICAST,UP,LOWER_UP> mtu 1500 qdisc pfifo_fast state UP
group default qlen 1000
    link/ether 52:54:00:7d:2b:d1 brd ff:ff:ff:ff:ff:ff
    altname enp0s3
    inet 192.168.122.104/24 brd 192.168.122.255 scope global dynamic ens3
       valid_lft 3412sec preferred_lft 3412sec
    inet6 fe80::5054:ff:fe7d:2bd1/64 scope link
       valid_lft forever preferred_lft forever
```

As with the `ip link` command, the syntax for `ip addr add` and `ip addr del` is the same across the three major Linux distributions we're discussing in this chapter. The output is also largely identical, although variations may exist in interface names.

So far, we've shown you how to use the `ip` commands only to modify the configuration of an interface. If you're familiar with configuring network devices (and since you're reading this book, you probably are), this could be considered analogous to modifying the running configuration of a network device. However, we haven't yet made these configuration changes permanent. In other words, we haven't changed the startup configuration. To do that, we need to look at how Linux uses interface configuration files.

Interface configuration via configuration files

To make changes to an interface persistent across system restarts, using the `ip` commands alone isn't enough. You need to edit the interface configuration files that Linux uses on startup to perform those same configurations for you automatically. Unfortunately, while the `ip` commands are pretty consistent across Linux distributions, interface configuration files across Linux distributions can be quite different.

For example, on RHEL/CentOS/Fedora and derivatives, interface configuration files are found in separate files located in */etc/sysconfig/network-scripts*. The interface configuration files are named `ifcfg-`*interface*, where the name of the interface (such as eth0 or enp0s3) is embedded in the name of the file. An interface configuration file might look something like this (this example is taken from an older CentOS 7.1 distribution but is equally applicable to more modern distributions like AlmaLinux or Rocky Linux):

```
NAME="ens33"
DEVICE="ens33"
ONBOOT=yes
NETBOOT=yes
IPV6INIT=yes
```

```
BOOTPROTO=dhcp
TYPE=Ethernet
```

Some of the most commonly used directives in RHEL/Fedora/Amazon Linux interface configuration files are as follows:

NAME
> A friendly name for users to see, typically used only in GUIs (this name wouldn't show up in the output of ip commands).

DEVICE
> The name of the physical device being configured.

IPADDR
> The IP address to be assigned to this interface (if you're not using DHCP or Bootstrap Protocol).

PREFIX
> If you're statically assigning the IP address, this setting specifies the network prefix to be used with the assigned IP address. (You can use NETMASK instead, but the use of PREFIX is recommended.)

BOOTPROTO
> This directive specifies how the interface will have its IP address assigned. A value of dhcp, as shown in the preceding example, means the address will be provided via DHCP. The other value typically used here is none, which means the address is statically defined in the interface configuration file.

ONBOOT
> Setting this directive to yes activates the interface at boot time; setting it to no means the interface will not be activated at boot time.

MTU
> The default MTU for this interface.

GATEWAY
> The gateway to be used for this interface.

Many more settings are available, but these are the ones you're likely to see most often. For full details, see the documentation for your RHEL/Fedora/Amazon Linux system.

For Debian and Debian derivatives (including older versions of Ubuntu), on the other hand, interface configuration is handled by the file *etc/network/interfaces*. Here's an example network interface configuration file from an older Ubuntu 14.04 LTS system:

```
# This file describes the network interfaces available on your system
# and how to activate them. For more information, see interfaces(5).

# The loopback network interface
auto lo
iface lo inet loopback

# The primary network interface
auto eth0
iface eth0 inet dhcp

auto eth1
iface eth1 inet static
        address 192.168.100.11
        netmask 255.255.255.0
```

Debian and older Ubuntu versions can use a single file to configure all the network interfaces; each interface is separated by a configuration stanza starting with `auto` *interface* (to view all the options for configuring interfaces on a Debian or Ubuntu system, run **man 5 interfaces**). In each configuration stanza, the most common configuration options are as follows:

- You'll typically use either `inet dhcp` or `inet static` to assign IP addresses to interfaces. In the preceding example, the eth0 interface is set to use DHCP, while eth1 is assigned statically.

- The `netmask` option provides the network mask for the assigned IP address (when the address is being assigned statically via `inet static`). However, you can also use the prefix format (like `192.168.100.10/24`) when assigning the IP address, which makes the use of the `netmask` directive unnecessary.

- The `gateway` directive in the configuration stanza assigns a default gateway when the IP address is being assigned statically (via `inet static`).

If you prefer using separate files for interface configuration, similar to the way RHEL/ AlmaLinux/Amazon Linux handle it, you can include a line like this in the */etc/ network/interfaces* file:

```
source-directory /etc/network/interfaces.d/*
```

This line instructs Linux to look in the */etc/network/interfaces.d/* directory for per-interface configuration files and to process them as if they were directly incorporated into the main network configuration file. When using per-interface configuration files, it's possible that this might be the *only* line found in the */etc/network/interfaces* file. Note that cloud instances may also source interface configurations from other directories, such as */run/network/interfaces.d*.

Per-interface configuration files may give you additional flexibility when using a configuration management tool such as Chef, Puppet, Ansible, or Salt. These are important tools of the trade for managing systems, including Linux systems, and when using these tools, generating per-interface configuration files may be easier than managing different sections within a single file. We discuss using these tools for network automation in more detail in Chapter 12.

Newer versions of Ubuntu, however—starting with Ubuntu 17.10—use an extension to systemd called *systemd-networkd*. Systemd-networkd uses files ending in *.network* to configure network connectivity. These files are sourced by systemd-networkd to configure interfaces. Here is an example of a *.network* file from Ubuntu 20.04:

```
[Match]
Name=ens3

[Network]
DHCP=ipv4
LinkLocalAddressing=ipv6

[DHCP]
RouteMetric=100
UseMTU=true
```

Those of you who have worked with systemd unit files will immediately recognize the syntax; the same INI-style syntax is used by systemd-network as the rest of systemd. For the full list of options supported within systemd-networkd's *.network* files, run **man 5 systemd.network**.

Regardless of the Linux distribution, when you make a change to a network interface's configuration file, the configuration changes are *not* immediately applied. (If you want an immediate change, use the ip commands we described earlier in addition to making changes to the configuration files.) To put the changes into effect, you need to restart the network interface.

The easiest way to do this is to simply use ip link set to administratively disable the interface, and then re-enable it again. This was described in "Enabling/disabling an interface" on page 71.

There are other ways, but they vary from distribution to distribution. For example, on Debian 11, you can use systemctl to restart the networking systemd unit:

```
debian@debian11:~$ systemctl restart networking
```

On Amazon Linux 2, there is a network systemd unit:

```
[ec2-user@amazonlinux2 ~]$ systemctl restart network
```

AlmaLinux 9, however, has no such network systemd unit.

On Ubuntu 20.04, systemd-networkd drives the networking subsystem, and users should use the `networkctl` command to interact with interfaces managed by systemd-networkd. For example, use the `networkctl reconfigure` command to reconfigure a network interface according to its *.network* configuration file:

```
ubuntu@ubuntu2004:~$ networkctl reconfigure ens3
```

The output of `networkctl status` will show interface reconfiguration events, as shown in Figure 3-4.

```
●  ●  ●                          Terminal                                 ⌥⌘2
ubuntu@ip-172-31-47-187:~$ sudo networkctl status --no-pager -l
●          State: routable
         Address: 172.31.47.187 on ens5
                  fe80::c4e:13ff:fe77:123a on ens5
         Gateway: 172.31.32.1 on ens5
             DNS: 172.31.0.2
  Search Domains: ca-central-1.compute.internal

Apr 27 21:34:20 ip-172-31-47-187 systemd-networkd[439]: ens5: Link UP
Apr 27 21:34:20 ip-172-31-47-187 systemd-networkd[439]: ens5: Gained carrier
Apr 27 21:34:20 ip-172-31-47-187 systemd-networkd[439]: ens5: Link DOWN
Apr 27 21:34:20 ip-172-31-47-187 systemd-networkd[439]: ens5: Lost carrier
Apr 27 21:34:20 ip-172-31-47-187 systemd-networkd[439]: ens5: IPv6 successfully
enabled
Apr 27 21:34:20 ip-172-31-47-187 systemd-networkd[439]: ens5: Link UP
Apr 27 21:34:20 ip-172-31-47-187 systemd-networkd[439]: ens5: Gained carrier
Apr 27 21:34:20 ip-172-31-47-187 systemd-networkd[439]: ens5: DHCPv4 address 172
.31.47.187/20 via 172.31.32.1
Apr 27 21:34:22 ip-172-31-47-187 systemd-networkd[439]: ens5: Gained IPv6LL
Apr 27 21:34:22 ip-172-31-47-187 systemd[1]: Finished Wait for Network to be Con
figured.
ubuntu@ip-172-31-47-187:~$ ▮
```

Figure 3-4. Output of the `networkctl status` *command*

More information on using `networkctl` is—you guessed it—available via its man page, accessed with **man networkctl**.

Once the interface is restarted or reconfigured, the configuration changes are applied and in effect (and you can verify this via the appropriate `ip` commands).

Everything we've shown you so far has involved physical interfaces, like eth0 or ens32. However, in much the same way that Linux treats many things as files, Linux networking also treats many things as interfaces. One such example is the way Linux interacts with VLANs, a topic we explore in more detail in the following section.

Using VLAN interfaces

We mentioned in "Working with Daemons" on page 64 that the interface is the basic building block of Linux networking. In this section, we discuss *VLAN interfaces*, which are logical interfaces that allow an instance of Linux to communicate on multiple VLANs simultaneously without needing a dedicated physical interface for each VLAN. Instead, Linux uses logical VLAN interfaces that are associated with both a physical interface and a corresponding 802.1Q VLAN ID.

Chances are that you're already familiar with VLANs, so we won't bother covering this concept in any great detail. If you need a good reference to VLANs (or many other networking concepts), one to consider is *Packet Guide to Routing and Switching* by Bruce Hartpence (O'Reilly).

Creating, configuring, and deleting VLAN interfaces. To create a VLAN interface, you use the command `ip link add link` *parent-device vlan-device* `type vlan id` *vlan-id*. As you can see, this is simply an extension to the `ip link` command we've been discussing throughout the last several sections of this chapter.

This command has a few pieces, so let's break it down a bit:

- The *parent-device* is the physical adapter with which the logical VLAN interface is associated. This would be something like eth1 or ens33.
- The *vlan-device* is the name to be given to the logical VLAN interface; the common convention is to use the name of the parent device, a dot (period), and then the VLAN ID. For a VLAN interface associated with eth1 and using VLAN ID 100, the name would be eth1.100.
- Finally, *vlan-id* is exactly that—the 802.1Q VLAN ID value assigned to this logical interface.

Let's look at an example. Suppose you want to create a logical VLAN interface on a Debian system. This logical interface is to be associated with the physical interface named ens3 and should use 802.1Q VLAN ID 150. The command looks like this:

```
debian@debian11:~$ ip link add link ens3 ens3.150 type vlan id 150
```

You can now verify that the logical VLAN interface was added by using `ip link list` (note the ens3.150@eth2 as the name of the interface; you need to use only the portion before the @ symbol when working with the interface):

```
debian@debian11:~$ ip link list ens3.150
3: ens3.150@ens3: <BROADCAST,MULTICAST> mtu 1500 qdisc noop state DOWN mode
DEFAULT group default qlen 1000
    link/ether 52:54:00:7d:2b:d1 brd ff:ff:ff:ff:ff:ff
```

To verify (aside from the name) that the interface is a VLAN interface, add the -d parameter to the `ip link list` command, like this:

```
debian@debian11:~$ ip -d link list ens3.150
3: ens3.150@ens3: <BROADCAST,MULTICAST> mtu 1500 qdisc noop state DOWN mode
DEFAULT group default qlen 1000
    link/ether 52:54:00:7d:2b:d1 brd ff:ff:ff:ff:ff:ff promiscuity 0 minmtu 0
    maxmtu 65535
    vlan protocol 802.1Q id 150 <REORDER_HDR> addrgenmode eui64 numtxqueues 1
    numrxqueues 1 gso_max_size 65536 gso_max_segs 65535
```

For the VLAN interface to be fully functional, though, you must also enable the interface and assign an IP address:

```
debian@debian11:~$ ip link set ens3.150 up
debian@debian11:~$ ip addr add 192.168.150.10/24 dev ens3.150
```

Naturally, this means you must also have a matching configuration on the physical switches to which this system is connected; specifically, the switch port must be configured as a VLAN trunk and configured to pass VLAN 150. The commands for this will vary depending on the upstream switch model and manufacturer.

Just like physical interfaces, a logical VLAN interface that is enabled and has an IP address assigned will add a route to the host's routing table:

```
debian@debian11:~$ ip route list
default via 192.168.122.1 dev ens3
192.168.122.0/24 dev ens3 proto kernel scope link src 192.168.122.104
192.168.150.0/24 dev ens3.150 proto kernel scope link src 192.168.150.10
```

To delete a VLAN interface, we recommend that you first disable the interface (set its status to down) and then remove the interface:

```
debian@debian11:~$ ip link set ens3.150 down
debian@debian11:~$ ip link delete ens3.150
```

As we discussed earlier in this chapter, the `ip` commands change the current (running) configuration but don't persist the changes—on a reboot, any VLAN interfaces you've created and configured will disappear. To make the changes persistent, you need to edit the interface configuration files.

On a Debian system (or an Ubuntu system prior to 17.10), it's a matter of simply adding a stanza to */etc/network/interfaces* or adding a per-interface configuration file to */etc/network/interfaces.d* (and ensuring that the file is sourced from */etc/network/interfaces*). The configuration stanza should look something like this:

```
auto ens3.150
iface ens3.150 inet static
   address 192.168.150.10/24
```

For RHEL/Fedora/AlmaLinux systems, you create a per-interface configuration file in */etc/sysconfig/network-scripts* with a name like *ifcfg-eth2.150*. The contents need to look something like this:

```
VLAN=yes
DEVICE=eth2.150
BOOTPROTO=static
ONBOOT=yes
TYPE=Ethernet
IPADDR=192.168.150.10
NETMASK=255.255.255.0
```

For Ubuntu systems running systemd-networkd, the process is a bit more complicated:

1. Create a NetDev file (ending with a *.netdev* extension) referencing the VLAN ID, with Kind=vlan.

2. Map the NetDev onto a physical interface by referencing the VLAN NetDev in the systemd-networkd network file.

3. Create a systemd-networkd network file for the VLAN interface itself; this will allow you to assign an IP address to the VLAN interface.

The Debian man pages for systemd-network (*https://oreil.ly/xI00w*) are useful for additional information, even if the Debian 11 release (the latest as of this writing) doesn't use systemd-networkd by default.

Use cases for VLAN interfaces. VLAN interfaces will be tremendously useful anytime you have a Linux host that needs to communicate on multiple VLANs at the same time *and* you wish to minimize the number of switch ports and physical interfaces required. For example, if you have a Linux host that needs to communicate on one VLAN to web servers, as well as communicate on another VLAN to database servers, using a single physical interface with two logical VLAN interfaces is an ideal solution (assuming you have enough bandwidth on a single physical interface).

In addition to configuring and managing interfaces, another important aspect of Linux networking is configuring and managing the Linux host's IP routing tables. The next section provides more details on what's involved.

Routing as an End Host

Interface and routing configuration go hand in hand, naturally, but sometimes some tasks for IP routing need to be configured separately from interface configuration. First, though, let's look at how interface configurations affect host routing configuration.

Although the ip route command is your primary means of viewing and modifying the routing table for a Linux host, the ip link and ip addr commands may also affect the host's routing table.

First, if you want to view the current routing table, you can simply run `ip route list`:

```
ubuntu@ubuntu2004:~$ ip route list
default via 192.168.122.1 dev ens3 proto dhcp src 192.168.122.215 metric 100
192.168.100.0/24 dev ens8  proto kernel  scope link  src 192.168.100.11
192.168.122.0/24 dev ens3 proto kernel scope link src 192.168.122.215
192.168.122.1 dev ens3 proto dhcp scope link src 192.168.122.215 metric 100
```

The output of this command tells us a few things:

- The default gateway is 192.168.122.1. The ens3 device will be used to communicate with all unknown networks via the default gateway. (Recall from the previous section that this would be set via DHCP or via a configuration directive such as `GATEWAY` on a RHEL/CentOS/Fedora system or `gateway` on a Debian/Ubuntu system.)
- The IP address assigned to ens3 is 192.168.122.215, and this is the interface that will be used to communicate with the 192.168.122.0/24 network.
- The IP address assigned to ens8 is 192.168.100.11/24, and this is the interface that will be used to communicate with the 192.168.100.0/24 network.

If we disable the ens8 interface by using `ip link set ens8 down`, the host's routing table changes automatically:

```
ubuntu@ubuntu2004:~$ ip link set ens8 down
ubuntu@ubuntu2004:~$ ip route list
default via 192.168.122.1 dev ens3 proto dhcp src 192.168.122.215 metric 100
192.168.122.0/24 dev ens3 proto kernel scope link src 192.168.122.215
192.168.122.1 dev ens3 proto dhcp scope link src 192.168.122.215 metric 100
```

Now that ens8 is down, the system no longer has a route to the 192.168.100.0/24 network, and the routing table updates automatically. This is all fully expected, but we want to show you this interaction so you can see how the `ip link` and `ip addr` commands affect the host's routing table.

For less automatic changes to the routing table, you use the `ip route` command. What do we mean by "less automatic changes"? Here are a few use cases:

- Adding a static route to a network over a particular interface
- Removing a static route to a network
- Changing the default gateway

Here are some concrete examples of these use cases.

Let's assume the same configuration we've been showing off so far—the ens3 interface has an IPv4 address from the 192.168.122.0/24 network, and the ens8 interface has an

IPv4 address from the 192.168.100.0/24 network. In this configuration, the output of ip route list looks something like this:

```
ubuntu@ubuntu2004:~$ ip route list
default via 192.168.122.1 dev ens3 proto dhcp src 192.168.122.215 metric 100
192.168.100.0/24 dev ens8 proto kernel scope link src 192.168.100.11
192.168.122.0/24 dev ens3 proto kernel scope link src 192.168.122.215
192.168.122.1 dev ens3 proto dhcp scope link src 192.168.122.215 metric 100
```

If we model this configuration as a network diagram, it looks something like Figure 3-5.

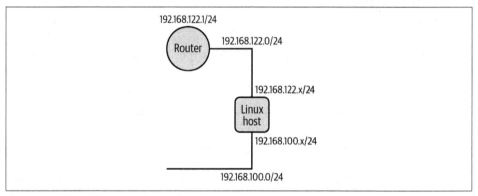

Figure 3-5. Sample network topology

Now let's say that a new router is added to the 192.168.100.0/24 network, and a network with which this host needs to communicate (using the subnet address 192.168.101.0/24) is placed beyond that router. Figure 3-6 shows the new network topology.

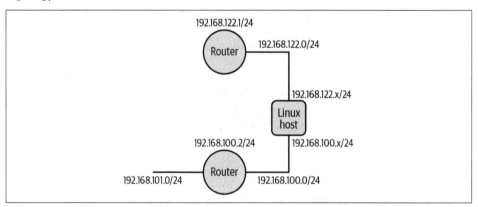

Figure 3-6. Updated network topology

The host's existing routing table won't allow it to communicate with this new network. Since the host doesn't have a route to the new network, Linux will direct traffic to the default gateway, which doesn't have a connection to the new network. To fix this, we add a route to the new network over the host's ens8 interface like this:

```
debian@debian11:~$ ip route add 192.168.101.0/24 via 192.168.100.2 dev ens8
debian@debian11:~$ ip route list
default via 192.168.122.1 dev ens3 proto dhcp src 192.168.122.215 metric 100
192.168.100.0/24 dev ens8 proto kernel scope link src 192.168.100.11
192.168.101.0/24 via 192.168.100.2 dev ens8
192.168.122.0/24 dev ens3 proto kernel scope link src 192.168.122.215
192.168.122.1 dev ens3 proto dhcp scope link src 192.168.122.215 metric 100
```

The generic form for this command is ip route add *destination-net* via *gateway-address* dev *interface*.

This command tells the Linux host (a Debian system, in this example) that it can communicate with the 192.168.101.0/24 network via the IP address 192.168.100.2 over the ens8 interface. Now the host has a route to the new network via the appropriate router and is able to communicate with systems on that network. If the network topology is updated again with another router and another new network, as shown in Figure 3-7, we'll need to add yet another route.

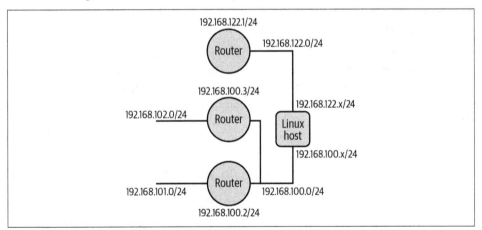

Figure 3-7. Final network topology

To address this final topology, you run this command:

```
debian@debian11:~$ ip route add 192.168.102.0/24 via 192.168.100.3 dev ens8
debian@debian11:~$ ip route list
default via 192.168.122.1 dev ens3 proto dhcp src 192.168.122.215 metric 100
192.168.100.0/24 dev ens8 proto kernel scope link src 192.168.100.11
192.168.101.0/24 via 192.168.100.2 dev ens8
192.168.102.0/24 via 192.168.100.3 dev ens8
192.168.122.0/24 dev ens3 proto kernel scope link src 192.168.122.215
192.168.122.1 dev ens3 proto dhcp scope link src 192.168.122.215 metric 100
```

To make these routes persistent (remember that the `ip` commands *don't* typically make configuration changes persistent), you add these commands to the configuration stanza in */etc/network/interfaces* for the eth1 device, like this (or, if you are on a RHEL/Fedora/CentOS system, you edit */etc/sysconfig/network-scripts/ifcfg-eth1*):

```
auto eth1
iface eth1 inet static
      address 192.168.100.11
      netmask 255.255.255.0
      up ip route add 192.168.101.0/24 via 192.168.100.2 dev $IFACE
      up ip route add 192.168.102.0/24 via 192.168.100.3 dev $IFACE
```

The `$IFACE` listed on the commands in this configuration stanza refers to the specific interface being configured, and the up directive instructs Debian/Ubuntu systems to run these commands after the interface comes up. With these lines in place, the routes will automatically be added to the routing table every time the system is started.

If, for whatever reason, you need to *remove* routes from a routing table, you can use the `ip route` command for that as well, this time using the `delete` subcommand:

```
[almalinux@alma9 ~]$ ip route del 192.168.103.0/24 via 192.168.100.3
```

The generic form of the command to remove (delete) a route is `ip route del` *destination-net* via *gateway-address*.

Finally, changing the default gateway is also something you might need to do using the `ip route` command. (We note, however, that you can also change the default gateway—and make it persistent—by editing the interface configuration files. Using `ip route` will change the gateway immediately, but the change will not be persistent.) To change the default gateway, you use a command somewhat like this (this assumes that a default gateway is already present):

```
ubuntu@ubuntu2004:~$ ip route del default via 192.168.122.1 dev ens3
ubuntu@ubuntu2004:~$ ip route add default via 192.168.122.2 dev ens3
```

The `default` keyword is used in these commands to refer to the destination 0.0.0.0/0.

Linux also offers *policy routing*, which is the capability to support multiple routing tables via rules that instruct Linux to use a specific routing table. For example, perhaps you'd like to use a different default gateway for each interface in the system. Using policy routing, you could configure Linux to use one routing table (and thus one particular gateway) for ens3, but use a different routing table (and a different default gateway) for ens8. Policy routing is a bit of an advanced topic, so we don't cover it here, but if you're interested in seeing how this works, read the man pages or help screens for the `ip rule` and `ip route` commands for more details (in other words, run **man ip rule** and **man ip route**).

The focus so far in this section has been on IP routing from a host perspective, but you can also use Linux as a full-fledged IP router. As with policy routing, this is a bit of an advanced topic; however, we are going to cover the basic elements in the next section.

Routing as a Router

By default, virtually all modern Linux distributions have IP forwarding *disabled*, since most Linux users don't need this feature. However, Linux can perform IP forwarding in order to act as a *router*, connecting multiple IP subnets together and passing (routing) traffic among multiple subnets. To enable this functionality, you must first enable IP forwarding.

To verify whether IP forwarding is enabled or disabled, you run this command (it works on pretty much all Linux distributions, although the command might be found at different paths on different systems):

```
ubuntu@ubuntu2004:~$ /usr/sbin/sysctl net.ipv4.ip_forward
net.ipv4.ip_forward = 0
ubuntu@ubuntu2004:~$ /usr/sbin/sysctl net.ipv6.conf.all.forwarding
net.ipv6.conf.all.forwarding = 0
```

 If a command's filesystem location differs across Linux distributions, the `which` command mentioned earlier in this chapter can be helpful. You can use `which` to tell you where a particular command is located (assuming it is in the search path).

In both cases, the command output indicates that the value is set to 0, which means it is disabled. You can enable IP forwarding on the fly without a reboot—but nonpersistently, meaning it will disappear after a reboot—by using this command:

```
[almalinux@alma9 ~]$ systcl -w net.ipv4.ip_forward=1
```

This is like the `ip` commands we discussed earlier in that the change takes effect immediately, but the setting will not survive a reboot of the Linux system. To make the change permanent, you must edit */etc/sysctl.conf* or put a configuration file into the */etc/sysctl.d* directory. Either way, add this value to either */etc/sysctl.conf* or to a configuration file in */etc/sysctl.d*:

```
net.ipv4.ip_forward = 1
```

Or, to enable IPv6 forwarding, add this value:

```
net.ipv6.conf.all.forwarding = 1
```

You can then either reboot the Linux host to make the changes effective, or you can run `sysctl -p` *path to file with new setting.*

We've mentioned a couple of times that in some cases Linux distributions can make use of separate configuration files in a directory (as with */etc/network/interfaces.d* or */etc/sysctl.d*). Which approach is better? This is the subject of some debate with Linux sysadmins, and each approach has advantages and disadvantages. Using separate configuration files may be more advantageous when you're using a configuration management tool (as the tool can help manage those files and their contents), but either approach will work just fine.

Once IP forwarding is enabled, the Linux system will act as a router. At this point, the Linux system is capable of performing only static routing, so you need to use the `ip route` command to provide all the necessary routing instructions so that traffic can be routed appropriately. However, dynamic routing protocol daemons do exist for Linux that would allow a Linux router to participate in dynamic routing protocols such as BGP or OSPF. Two popular options for integrating Linux into dynamic routing environments are Quagga (*https://oreil.ly/TB06q*) and BIRD (*https://oreil.ly/M1J8o*).

Using features like iptables or its successor, nftables (*https://oreil.ly/YRYXe*), you can also add functionality like network address translation (NAT) and access control lists (ACLs).

In addition to being able to route traffic at Layer 3, Linux can *bridge* traffic—that is, connect multiple Ethernet segments together at Layer 2. The next section covers the basics of Linux bridging.

Bridging (Switching)

The Linux bridge enables you to connect multiple network segments together in a protocol-independent way; that is, a bridge operates at Layer 2 of the OSI model instead of at Layer 3 or higher. Bridging—specifically, multiport transparent bridging—is widely used in data centers today in the form of network switches, but most uses of bridging in Linux are centered on various forms of virtualization—either via the Kernel-Based Virtual Machine (KVM) hypervisor or via other means like Linux containers. For this reason, we only briefly cover the basics of bridging here, and only in the context of virtualization.

Practical use case for bridging

Before we get into the details of creating and configuring bridges, let's look at a practical example of using a Linux bridge.

Let's assume that you have a Linux host with two physical interfaces (we'll use ens3 and ens8 as their names). Immediately after you create a bridge (a process we describe in the following section), your Linux host looks something like Figure 3-8.

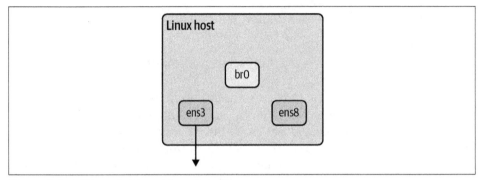

Figure 3-8. A Linux bridge with no interfaces

The bridge has been created, but it can't really *do* anything yet. Recall that a bridge is designed to join network segments—without any segments attached to the bridge, there's nothing it can (or will) do. You need to add some interfaces to the bridge.

Let's say you add the interface named ens3 to the bridge named br0. Now your configuration looks something like Figure 3-9.

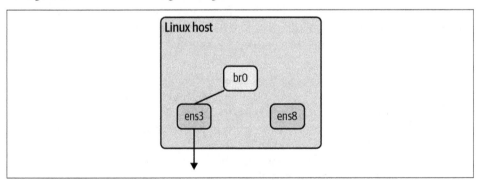

Figure 3-9. A Linux bridge with a physical interface

Next, you attach a VM to this bridge—this is typically accomplished via the use of KVM (*https://oreil.ly/dwbrL*) and libvirt (*https://libvirt.org*). Your configuration now looks something like Figure 3-10.

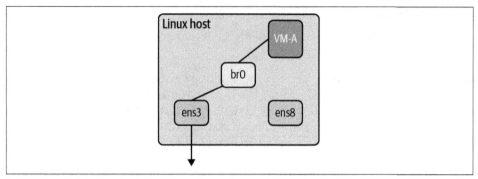

Figure 3-10. A Linux bridge with a physical interface and a VM

In this final configuration, the bridge named br0 connects (or *bridges*, if you prefer that term) the network segment to the VM and the physical interface, providing a single Layer 2 broadcast domain from the VM to the network interface card (NIC)—and then on to the physical network. Providing network connectivity for VMs is a common use case for Linux bridges, but not the only use case. You might also use a Linux bridge to join a wireless network (via a wireless interface on the Linux host) to an Ethernet network (connected via a traditional NIC).

Now that you have an idea of what a Linux bridge can do, let's take a look at creating and configuring Linux bridges.

Creating and configuring Linux bridges

To configure Linux bridges, you'll use the same ip utility you've been using to configure and manage interfaces. Recall from "Working with Interfaces" on page 68 that interfaces are the basic building block of Linux networking. That statement holds true here, as bridges are treated as a type of interface by Linux.

 You may be familiar with an older command for working with Linux bridges—specifically, brctl. Much in the same way that the ip command has superseded the older ifconfig command, ip also supersedes the older brctl. That being said, brctl is still available for most modern Linux distributions and can still be used to manipulate Linux bridges. In this section, we focus on the newer commands that are part of the iproute2 packages.

To create a bridge, you use ip link with the add subcommand, like this:

```
debian@debian11:~$ ip link add name bridge-name type bridge
```

This creates a bridge that contains no interfaces (a configuration similar to Figure 3-7). You can verify this by using the ip link list command. For example, if you had used the name br0 for *bridge-name* when you added the bridge, your command would look something like this:

```
debian@debian11:~$ ip link list br0
4: br0: <BROADCAST,MULTICAST> mtu 1500 qdisc noop state DOWN mode DEFAULT
group default qlen 1000
    link/ether ba:98:99:d8:0d:5e brd ff:ff:ff:ff:ff:ff
```

Note that the new bridge interface is marked as DOWN; you'll need to use ip link set *bridge-name* up in order to bring the bridge interface up.

Once you've created the bridge, you can again use the ip link command to add a physical interface to the bridge. The general syntax for the command is ip link set *interface-name* set master *bridge-name*. So, if you want to add the ens3 interface to a bridge named br0, the command looks like this:

```
debian@debian11:~$ ip link set ens3 master br0
```

Your configuration now looks similar to Figure 3-8.

When you add a physical interface to a bridge, Linux stops treating it like a network interface and starts treating it like a bridged port. As such, protocols—like TCP, UDP, and IP—are ignored by the kernel. Practically, this has two notable impacts. First, when you add a physical interface to a bridge, you will lose IP-based connectivity via that network interface. Second, any IP addresses assigned to physical interfaces that are part of a bridge should be removed, or they could negatively impact the routing table and cause connectivity issues.

So how do you tell which interfaces are part of a bridge? Your good friend the ip command is here to help:

```
[almalinux@alma9 ~]$ ip link list master br0
2: eth0: <BROADCAST,MULTICAST,UP,LOWER_UP> mtu 1500 qdisc fq_codel master
br0 state UP mode DEFAULT group default qlen 1000
    link/ether 52:54:00:d2:c5:f4 brd ff:ff:ff:ff:ff:ff
    altname enp0s3
    altname ens3
```

The ip link list master *bridge-name* command will show the interfaces that are considered part of the specified bridge.

To remove an interface from a bridge, you again use ip link, like this:

```
[almalinux@alma9 ~]$ ip link set interface-name nomaster
```

Finally, to remove a bridge, the command is ip link del along with the name of the bridge to be removed. If you want to remove a bridge named br0, the command looks like this:

```
[almalinux@alma9 ~]$ ip link del br0
```

Note that you don't need to remove interfaces from a bridge before removing the bridge itself.

All the commands we've shown you so far create nonpersistent configurations. To make these configurations persistent, you need to go back to "Interface configuration via the command line" on page 69. Why? Because Linux treats a bridge as a type of interface—in this case, a *logical* interface as opposed to a *physical* interface.

Because Linux treats bridges as interfaces, you use the same types of configuration files we discussed earlier: in RHEL/CentOS/Fedora, you use a file in */etc/sysconfig/network-scripts*, while in Debian you use a configuration stanza in the file */etc/network/interfaces* (or a standalone configuration file in the */etc/network/interfaces.d* directory). In recent versions of Ubuntu running systemd-networkd, you use a network device (a *.netdev* file) and a network unit (a *.network* file).

Let's take a quick look at what a bridge configuration looks like in Debian. When setting up a bridge on Debian, you typically add a configuration stanza to the */etc/network/interfaces* file to configure the bridge itself, like this:

```
iface br0 inet manual
  up ip link set $IFACE up
  down ip link set $IFACE down
  bridge-ports ens3
```

This creates a bridge named br0 with the ens3 interface as a member of the bridge. Note that no configuration is needed in the configuration stanzas for the interfaces that are named as members of the bridge.

In this configuration, neither br0 nor ens3 has an IP address assigned. It's best, perhaps, to reason about this in the following way: on a typical network switch, a standard switch port configured for only Layer 2 isn't addressable via an IP address. That's the configuration we've replicated here: br0 is the switch, and ens3 is the Layer 2–only port that is part of the switch.

If you *do* want an IP address assigned (perhaps for management purposes, or because you also want to leverage Layer 3 functionality in Linux), then you can assign an IP address to the *bridge*, but *not* to the member interfaces in the bridge. (Remember that physical interfaces won't process IP-based traffic when they are part of a bridge.) Again, you can make an analogy to traditional network hardware here—it's like giving the switch a management IP address, but the individual Layer 2–only switch ports still aren't addressable by IP.

To assign an IP address to the bridge interface, simply change inet manual to inet dhcp (for DHCP) or inet static (for static address assignment). When using static address assignment, you also need to include the appropriate configuration lines to assign the IP address (specifically, the address, netmask, and optionally the gateway directives). Why assign an IP address to the bridge interface? The primary reason is to avoid the connectivity issue that occurs when physical interfaces are added to a bridge.

Once you have configuration files in place for the Linux bridge, the bridging configuration will be restored when the system boots, making it persistent. (You can verify this by using `ip link list`.)

Before we close out this chapter, two additional topics are important to address. First, we want to look briefly at scripting in the bash shell, which is one way—among many—to automate tasks in Linux.

Automating Linux with bash Scripting

We mentioned previously that our goal for this chapter is not to provide comprehensive coverage of all things Linux; rather, we want to get you up and running with Linux in the context of networking, automation, and network automation. We've given you the networking context, and now it's time to add some automation context with a brief description of bash scripting. This is a high-level overview only; for more detailed information, we again recommend *Learning the bash Shell*, which offers several chapters specifically focused on bash scripting.

Thus far, our focus on interacting with bash has been *manual* and *interactive*, meaning the user is manually interacting with the shell to execute commands and receive the output of those commands. What if you want to combine a series of these commands to be executed in sequence, without further interaction from the user? That is the essence of a shell script and the focus on this section of the chapter.

Every bash script starts with the *shebang*, as we described previously. For a bash script, the shebang points to bash itself. On most systems—definitely on the distributions we've discussed in this chapter—bash is found at */usr/bin/bash*, and so the shebang would be `#!/usr/bin/bash`. From there, you simply add the commands you want to execute.

Let's look at a networking-centric example here, since this is a book on networking and automation. Suppose you need to create a bridge and add a physical interface to that bridge. In general, the process looks like this:

1. Create the bridge.
2. Move the IP address from the physical interface to the bridge (recall that physical interfaces that are part of a bridge won't participate in IP-based traffic).
3. Add the physical interface to the bridge.

We've already shown you all the commands to do this:

- `ip addr` to list, add, and remove IP addresses from interfaces
- `ip link` to create bridges and add physical interfaces to a bridge

Building only upon what we've shown you so far, a rudimentary script to do what we're seeking here looks something like this:

```
#!/usr/bin/bash

# Create the bridge interface
ip link add name br0 type bridge

# Remove the route and IP address from the physical interface
ip addr del 192.168.100.10/24 dev eth0

# Add the IP address to the bridge
ip addr add 192.168.100.10/24 dev br0

# Add the physical interface to the bridge
ip link set eth0 master br0
```

This script works, but it's not ideal because it hardcodes certain values into the script. If we introduce some new concepts and features we haven't discussed already—like piping the output of one command into another command, and storing the output of a command in a variable—then we can make this script a tad more flexible:

```
# First, get the first IP address from the physical interface
IP_ADDR=$(ip --brief addr list eth0 | awk '{print $3}')

# Create the bridge interface
ip link add name br0 type bridge

# Remove the route and IP address from the physical interface
ip addr del $IP_ADDR dev eth0

# Add the IP address to the bridge
ip addr add $IP_ADDR dev br0

# Add the physical interface to the bridge
ip link set eth0 master br0
```

The use of the | character tells bash to use the output of one command as the input of the next command, and so here we are showing you how to take the output of `ip --brief addr list eth0` and *pipe* it to the `awk` command. This `awk` command returns only the IP address, and that value is then stored as the variable `IP_ADDR`. Later in the script we reference that variable with a leading $ sign; bash knows to substitute the *value* of the variable in the command where it is referenced.

Wondering how you might then run (or execute) this script? We covered this early in this chapter (see "Running Programs" on page 61)! This file needs to be marked as executable—you can use the `chmod` utility for this—and then you invoke the script directly. For example, if this script is stored in a file named *conv-to-br* in the */usr/*

local/bin directory and marked as executable, then—assuming */usr/local/bin* is in your PATH, which it normally is—you can enter conv-to-br as a command at the shell prompt, and the script will execute. (Refer back to our discussion on how to invoke programs that are not in the search path for more details on how you might invoke this script if it were stored in another filesystem location.)

We could show you *far* more regarding bash scripting, but we'll wrap up with some practical use cases where this might be useful:

Distribution of network interface files
You could use a bash script to securely copy files from a central location (using scp, for example) and then move them (with mv) into the correct filesystem location (such as */etc/network/interfaces.d* on a Debian system).

Mass updates of routes
You could automate the updating of a Linux system's routing table with a bash script. (At a certain scale, though, you're better off just using a dynamic routing protocol—yes, implementations do exist for Linux!)

Complex network configuration changes
Similar to the previous example of moving a physical interface into a bridge, bash scripts could be used to perform network configuration changes (or any set of changes, really) that involve multiple steps.

However, bash scripts have drawbacks that are mitigated by more advanced automation tools (many of which are discussed in Chapter 12). The most notable drawback is that bash scripts are *imperative*: they'll execute a command whether it needs to be executed or not. Thus, a bash script will attempt to add an interface regardless of whether the interface has already been added. This is in contrast to *declarative* systems, in which changes are made only if necessary.

Despite the drawbacks, bash scripts can be enormously useful in automating changes to Linux systems, and they certainly have a place in your automation toolkit. Think also about the usefulness of being able to write imperative scripts to configure network equipment that is running Linux and exposes a Linux shell—it would be pretty straightforward to write a script to configure a bunch of different interfaces, assign IP addresses, set up bridges, etc.

Having now discussed bash scripting, we can move on to this chapter's final topic. We mentioned this subject at the start of the chapter: using eBPF and XDP.

Evolving the Linux Kernel with eBPF and XDP

We brought up eBPF at the beginning of this chapter as one of the reasons we feel it is important to provide readers of a book on network automation and programmability an entire chapter on Linux. However, we've held off on discussing eBPF until now.

Why? eBPF is rapidly gaining adoption across open source and commercial products, but it's still a relatively early-stage technology.

So what is eBPF? eBPF, which originally stood for *extended Berkeley Packet Filter* and was an evolution of "classic" BPF (Berkeley Packet Filter, used to capture network traffic with tools like `tcpdump`), is considered a safe and efficient way to extend the functionality of the Linux kernel without needing to change the kernel source code or load kernel modules.

This is an important point, because prior to eBPF *any* changes to kernel functionality came only through loadable kernel modules (or changes to the kernel source code itself, but this is far less common). Kernel modules, which have existed since the 1.*x* versions of the Linux kernel, are the primary way by which support is added to Linux for new hardware—like a storage controller, a network card, or a GPU—or new filesystems like ext4 or Btrfs. Although loadable kernel modules can be dynamically loaded and unloaded while the kernel is running (no reboot needed), they are considered part of the kernel. As part of the kernel, they have free run of the system and can easily crash the kernel. A buggy or unreliable loadable kernel module can have significant negative ramifications on system uptime and reliability.

eBPF programs, on the other hand, are held to strict requirements. All eBPF programs must pass a verification process by the kernel before they are allowed to execute; this process ensures that the program does not harm or crash the system and that it runs to completion (doesn't hang in a loop). eBPF programs are also *sandboxed*, meaning they are restricted to only a limited set of functions. However, eBPF code is just as efficient as "native" kernel code. We could say that eBPF takes the best part of loadable kernel modules—being part of the kernel itself and the performance that comes as a result—without the drawbacks of loadable kernel modules (such as the ability to crash the kernel).

Finally, it's important to note that eBPF programs are *event-driven*. An eBPF program is run when triggered by an event, which is generated when the kernel or an application passes a certain hook point. Examples of hook points include system calls, function entry/exit, kernel tracepoints, and network events. This has important ramifications on certain use cases, as we'll illustrate shortly.

eBPF is finding success in the following use cases:

Observability
 eBPF's ability to hook into system calls and network events gives it access to wide range of sources, often without the overhead that can come with sampling-based approaches. For example, the eBPF-based `tcplife` utility (part of `bcc-tools`, a collection of eBPF-based tools and utilities) needs to use only kernel probes to detect state transitions in order to do its job. There's no need for packet capture or processing millions of packets to get the necessary information.

Security

> eBPF allows for more context in making security decisions, giving security engines packet- and socket-level visibility to all network operations along with seeing and understanding all system calls.

Networking

> It is probably obvious by now, but eBPF allows for such things as reading and writing packet data and metadata, looking up sockets and routes, setting socket options, and even redirecting packets. Given this level of access and control, it is clear to see how useful eBPF can be for networking applications. This is one reason eBPF is seeing wide use in containers and Kubernetes environments. We discuss this more in Chapter 4.

Where does XDP fit into all of this? XDP is an "attachment" point for an eBPF program that allows for eBPF code to be attached directly to a network driver at the very earliest point in packet processing, or—in some cases—even have the eBPF code offloaded to a hardware device such as a smart NIC. This allows for packet processing to occur before even reaching the kernel level. The primary reason for this is performance—doing packet processing before even reaching the kernel, or offloading packet processing to a smart NIC—can offer notable performance benefits.

 This section can't cover all aspects of eBPF and XDP. For more in-depth information, we encourage you to review the eBPF.io website (*https://ebpf.io*).

Summary

In this chapter, we've provided a brief history of Linux, and why it's important to understand a little bit of this operating system as you progress down the path of network automation and programmability. We've also supplied some basic information on interacting with Linux, working with Linux daemons, and configuring Linux networking. We discussed using Linux as a router and explored the functionality of the Linux bridge. Finally, we provided a brief discussion of bash scripting for rudimentary automation and then wrapped up with a look at eBPF and XDP.

In the next chapter, we tackle a topic that has had and continues to have a significant impact on networking and automation: the cloud.

## CHAPTER 4

Cloud

Few technology trends have had the impact that cloud computing has had on the IT industry—save perhaps virtualization, which is a foundational technology for cloud computing. As a network engineer, you may be asking yourself, "What does cloud computing have to do with me?" Some network engineers may dismiss cloud computing, feeling like their skills aren't needed for cloud-based environments. Others, including the authors, feel quite differently.

Networking is every bit as important "in the cloud" as it is for an on-premises environment. In fact, some might say that networking is *even more* important in the cloud. Additionally, to truly reap the benefits of cloud computing—easy scale-in/ scale-out, on-demand resources, and ephemeral environments, among others—you really need to embrace automation. It's only natural, then, that a book on network automation and programmability discusses the role of cloud computing in the context of network automation.

Entire tomes have been written and will probably continue to be written about the various cloud providers, the services these cloud providers offer, how to architect solutions for the cloud providers, and more. With that in mind, this chapter aims to be a bit more compact and provide only the key essentials you need as a network engineer to add cloud computing to your arsenal of tools for solving the problems you encounter on a daily basis.

The best place to start is by establishing a baseline definition of cloud computing.

Brief Definition of Cloud Computing

While many definitions of cloud computing exist (one need only perform a web search for "what is cloud computing"), one of the quintessential definitions comes from the United States Department of Commerce—specifically, from the National

Institute of Standards and Technology (NIST). NIST's definition of cloud computing, as contained in Special Publication 800-145 (*https://oreil.ly/t1KZb*), is a multifaceted definition that tackles key characteristics of cloud computing as well as service and deployment models. The NIST definition describes all these things in a vendor-agnostic manner.

NIST defines five essential characteristics of cloud computing:

On-demand self-service
Users (NIST refers to "consumers") should be able to provision their own resources from the cloud provider as needed, without needing to involve human interaction (in other words, without having to file a service ticket!).

Broad network access
Cloud environments are inherently networked environments, accessible over the network. This is where the statement that networking is just as important in the cloud originates—without ubiquitous network access, it's not cloud computing.

Resource pooling
Cloud provider resources are pooled and served to multiple tenants automatically. This includes physical and virtual resources and applies not only to computing capacity but also to storage and networking.

Rapid elasticity
Cloud resources should be able to scale "infinitely" (from the user's perspective, they appear to be unlimited). Scaling up or scaling down, based on demand, should be possible—even automatic, in some cases.

Measured service
Cloud resources are metered, and users are charged for what they use. Usage can be monitored, controlled, and reported.

The NIST definition also defines three service models:

Software as a service (SaaS)
The "service" supplied here is access to a provider's applications, likely running on a cloud infrastructure. However, the cloud infrastructure is *not* exposed to the users; only the application and application interface(s) are exposed to the users. Examples of SaaS offerings include Salesforce, Okta, and Microsoft 365.

Platform as a service (PaaS)
In the case of PaaS, users have access to a platform—comprising "programming languages, libraries, services, and tools supported by the provider" (to use NIST's wording)—onto which they can deploy applications. These applications may be acquired by the user (purchased or licensed) or created by the user. The users do *not* have access to the cloud infrastructure under this platform; only the

platform's interface(s) are exposed to the users. Examples of PaaS offerings are Heroku and AWS Elastic Beanstalk.

Infrastructure as a service (IaaS)

The last service model is IaaS, in which users have access to provision compute, storage, networking, security, and other fundamental resources in order to deploy arbitrary software, up to and including OS instances and applications. The users do *not* have access to the cloud infrastructure directly, but have access to control the way fundamental resources are provisioned. For example, users don't have access to the underlying components that make an Amazon Virtual Private Cloud (VPC) work, but users do have the ability to create and configure VPCs. Real-world examples of IaaS offerings include many aspects of AWS, many services provided by Microsoft Azure, and multiple services offered by Google Cloud.

The wording we use in our examples of IaaS—"many aspects of" or "many services provided by"—is intentional. All, or nearly all, cloud providers offer a variety of services that fall into different service models. Some offerings are squarely IaaS, while others may be classified as PaaS or even SaaS.

Finally, the NIST definition discusses deployment models:

Private cloud

For a private cloud, the cloud infrastructure—defined by NIST as the collection of hardware and software that enables the five essential characteristics of cloud computing—is provisioned for use by a single entity, like a corporation. This infrastructure may be on premises or off premises; the location doesn't matter. Similarly, it may be operated by the organization or someone else. The key distinction here is the intended audience, which is *only* the organization or entity.

Community cloud

A community cloud is provisioned for use by a shared community of users—a group of companies with shared regulatory requirements, perhaps, or organizations that share a common cause. It may be owned by one or more of the organizations in the community or a third party. Likewise, it may be operated by one or more members of the community or by a third party and does not distinguish between on premises and off premises.

Public cloud

The cloud infrastructure of a public cloud is provisioned for use by the general public. Ownership, management, and operation of the public cloud may be by a business, a government organization, an academic entity, or a combination of these. A public cloud exists on the premises of the provider (the organization that owns, manages, and operates the cloud infrastructure).

Hybrid cloud
A hybrid cloud is simply a composition of two or more distinct cloud infrastructures that are joined in some fashion, either by standardized or proprietary technology that enables some level of data and application portability among the cloud infrastructures.

As you can see from these three aspects—the essential characteristics of cloud computing, the service models by which it is offered to users, and the deployment models by which it is provisioned for an audience—cloud computing is multifaceted.

In this chapter, we focus primarily on public cloud deployment models that typically fall within the IaaS service model.

We say "typically fall within the IaaS service model" because some service offerings can't be cleanly categorized as IaaS or PaaS. The industry has even coined new terms, like *functions as a service* (*FaaS*) or *database as a service* (*DBaaS*), to describe offerings that don't cleanly fall into one of the categories defined by NIST.

It's now appropriate, having defined the various forms of cloud computing, to shift your attention to the fundamentals of networking in the cloud.

Networking Fundamentals in the Cloud

Although networking operates a bit differently in cloud environments, in the end, cloud networking is just networking. Many (most?) of the skills you've developed as a network engineer continue to apply when dealing with networking in cloud environments, and the hard-won knowledge and experience you've gathered won't go to waste.

In particular, you'll no longer need to worry much about low-level details (i.e., you don't need to know how the network constructs, such as virtual networks, are implemented—just use the abstractions), but things like routing protocols, routing topologies, network topology design, and IP address planning remain very much needed. Let's start with a look at some of the key building blocks for cloud networking.

Cloud Networking Building Blocks

Although the specific details vary among cloud providers, all the major ones offer some basic (generic) features and functionalities:

Logical network isolation

Much in the same way that encapsulation protocols like VXLAN, Generic Routing Encapsulation (GRE), and others create *overlay networks* that isolate logical network traffic from the physical network, all the major cloud providers offer network isolation mechanisms. On AWS, this is a Virtual Private Cloud (VPC), which we better explain in "A small cloud network topology" on page 103; on Azure, it's a Virtual Network (also known as a VNet); and on Google Cloud, it's just called a Network. Regardless of the name, the basic purpose is the same: to provide a means whereby logical networks can be isolated and segregated from one another. These logical networks provide complete segregation from all other logical networks, but—as you'll see in a moment—can still be connected in various ways to achieve the desired results.

Public and private addressing

Workloads can be assigned public (routable) addresses or private (nonroutable) addresses. See RFC 1918 (*https://oreil.ly/D755i*) and RFC 6598 (*https://oreil.ly/iI4Dp*). The cloud provider supplies mechanisms for providing internet connectivity to both public and private workloads. All of this is typically done at the logical network layer, meaning that each logical network can have its own IP address assignments. Overlapping IP address spaces are permitted among multiple logical networks.

Persistent addressing

Network addresses can be allocated to a cloud provider customer's account, and then assigned to a workload. Later, that same address can be unassigned from the workload and assigned to a different workload, but the address remains constant and persistent until it is released from the customer's account back to the cloud provider. Elastic IP addresses (EIPs) on AWS or public IP addresses on Azure are examples.

Complex topologies

The logical network isolation building blocks (VPCs on AWS, VNets on Azure, Networks on Google Cloud) can be combined in complex ways, and network engineers have control over how traffic is routed among these building blocks. Large companies with significant cloud resources in use may end up with multiple hundreds of logical networks, along with site-to-site VPN connections and connections back to on-premises (self-managed) networks. The level of complexity here can easily rival or surpass even the most comprehensive on-premises networks, and the need for skilled network engineers who know how to design these networks and automate their implementation is great.

Load balancing

Cloud providers offer load-balancing solutions that are provisioned on demand and provide Layer 4 (TCP/UDP) load balancing, Layer 7 (HTTP) load balancing (with or without TLS termination), internal load balancing (internal to a customer's private/nonroutable address space within a VPC or VNet), or external load balancing (for traffic originating from internet-based sources).

 For network engineers who are just getting accustomed to cloud networking, Timothy McConnaughy's *The Hybrid Cloud Handbook for AWS* (Carpe DMVPN) is a good introduction to the basics of AWS networking.

Numerous other network services are available from the major cloud providers that aren't discussed here—including API gateways, network-level access controls, instance-level access controls, and even support for third-party network appliances to perform additional functions. Further, all of these network services are available on demand. Users need only log into their cloud management console, use the cloud provider's CLI tool, interact with the cloud provider's APIs, or even use one of any number of cloud automation tools to instantiate one or more of these network services (we discuss these tools in more detail in Chapter 12). Our goal in this chapter isn't to try to explain all of them but rather to help you see how these pieces fit into the overall picture of network programmability and automation.

With this high-level understanding of the cloud networking building blocks in place, let's shift our attention to a few examples of how you would go about assembling these building blocks.

Cloud Network Topologies

To help solidify the concepts behind the relatively generic constructs described in the previous section, this section narrows the discussion to the actual offerings from one specific public cloud provider: AWS. AWS is the largest of the public cloud providers, both in terms of the breadth of services offered as well as in terms of market adoption (according to a June 2022 Gartner report, AWS had 38.9% of the total cloud market). Therefore, it's a good place to start. However, similar concepts apply to other cloud providers, including Microsoft Azure, Google Cloud Platform, Alibaba Cloud, Oracle Cloud, DigitalOcean, and others.

 Plenty of great resources online can help you learn about cloud providers' best design practices. For AWS, you can get started with the AWS Well-Architected framework (*https://oreil.ly/fgEfZ*).

This section discusses four scenarios:

- A small environment involving only a single logical network
- A medium-sized environment involving a few to several logical networks
- A larger environment dealing with multiple dozens of logical networks
- A hybrid environment involving both on-premises and cloud-based networks

A small cloud network topology

Our small cloud network topology leverages only a single VPC. At first, this might seem limiting—will a single VPC be able to scale enough? Is this sort of topology valid for only the very smallest of customers, those who have only a few workloads in the public cloud?

 The *virtual network* construct, like AWS VPC, is the key building block for cloud networking. Even though each cloud provider implements this construct a bit differently, the basic idea is the same: a virtual network is a logical network (with *some* Layer 2 and 3 features) that can be used to isolate workloads from one another. All the cloud services are attached to a virtual network so they can communicate with one another (assuming the appropriate network access controls are in place).

In thinking about scalability, consider these dimensions:

IP addressing
When you create a VPC, you must specify a Classless Inter-Domain Routing (CIDR) block. It's recommended to use blocks from the ranges specified in RFC 1918 and RFC 6598. The block can range in size from a /16 (supplying up to 65,536 IP addresses) all the way to a /28 (supplying only 16 IP addresses). Further, you can add CIDR blocks—up to four additional, nonoverlapping blocks for a total of five CIDR blocks in a VPC—to provide even more available IP addresses. Five /16 CIDR blocks would provide over 300,000 IP addresses.

Bandwidth
AWS supplies two mechanisms for connecting workloads to the internet. For workloads on a public subnet, you use an *internet gateway*. AWS describes this component as "a horizontally scaled, redundant, and highly available VPC component" that "does not cause availability risks or bandwidth constraints"; see the Amazon VPC documentation (*https://oreil.ly/M602C*). For workloads on a private subnet, you typically use a NAT gateway, which according to AWS (*https://oreil.ly/MfMVh*) scales up to 100 Gbps. *NAT* stands for *network address*

translation, which is the name given to the process of mapping private (nonroutable) IP addresses to public (routable) IP addresses.

 For the purposes of this book, a *public subnet* is defined as a subnet that is connected to or has a default route to an internet gateway. Typically, a public subnet is also configured to assign a routable IP address to resources. A *private subnet* is defined as a subnet that is connected to or has a default route to a NAT gateway (or a self-managed NAT instance). A private subnet is also typically configured to use only nonroutable (RFC 1918/6598) IP addresses.

Availability

A single VPC can span multiple availability zones but cannot span multiple regions. A *region* in AWS parlance is a grouping of data centers. An *availability zone (AZ)* within a region is a physically separate, isolated logical cluster of data centers. Each availability zone has independent power, cooling, and redundant network connectivity. AZs within a region have high-speed, low-latency connections among them. The idea behind spanning multiple AZs is that a failure in one AZ of a region will generally not affect other AZs in a region, thus giving you the ability to withstand failures in a more resilient way. A subnet is limited to a single AZ and cannot span AZs.

Security

AWS offers network-level traffic-filtering mechanisms (called *network access control lists*) and host-level traffic-filtering mechanisms (called *security groups*). Network access control lists (network ACLs, or NACLs) are stateless and operate at the network level (specifically, the subnet level). NACL rules are processed in order, according to the rule's assigned number (think of the number as a priority: the lowest-numbered rule decides first or has the highest priority). Security groups, on the other hand, are stateful, operate at the instance level, and evaluate all the rules before deciding whether to allow traffic. NACLs and security groups can—and should be—used together to help provide the strongest level of control over the types of traffic that are or are not allowed between workloads within a VPC.

None of these areas presents any significant limitation or constraint, proving that even a cloud network design leveraging a single VPC can scale to thousands of workloads, providing sufficient bandwidth, availability, and security to the workloads it houses.

In Figure 4-1, we bring all of these concepts together to create a typical single VPC design in AWS.

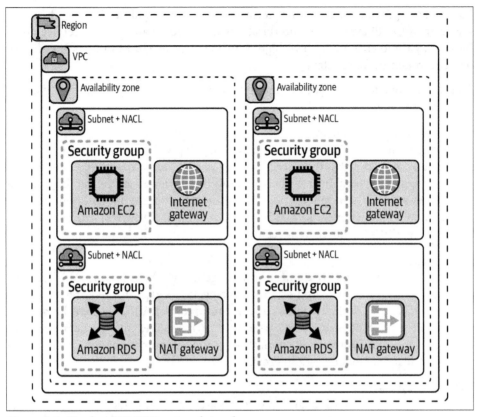

Figure 4-1. Single AWS VPC network topology

All of these things could be created manually and linked together using the AWS Management Console, but the opportunity for the network engineer here is to automate this process by using IaC tooling and processes. In "Network Automation in the Cloud" on page 108, we discuss the available programmable options for managing cloud resources.

A medium cloud network topology

Although a single VPC is very scalable, there are reasons to use multiple VPCs. The most obvious reason is that a VPC cannot span an AWS region; each VPC is limited to the region in which it was created. If you need to architect a network topology that can accommodate workloads in multiple regions, you're looking at a multi-VPC topology. There are also other reasons for using multiple VPCs; just because you *can* put thousands of workloads in a single VPC doesn't necessarily mean you *should*.

Public cloud providers design their infrastructure to be highly resilient and express this in the form of availability and durability SLAs. To go above these service offerings, you have to create your own high-availability architectures in the same way we do in on-premises data centers.

As soon as your topology goes to multiple VPCs, new challenges arise for the network engineer:

Managing the IP address space
> While each VPC can have identical, overlapping CIDR blocks, as soon as you want to connect VPCs together, you need to have nonoverlapping CIDR blocks. It's necessary to architect a plan for how IP addresses will be carved out and allocated to VPCs in multiple regions while still planning for future growth (in terms of future subnets in existing VPCs, additional VPCs in current regions, and new VPCs in entirely new regions).

Connectivity
> AWS provides a way to connect VPCs together via *VPC peering*. VPC peering provides nontransitive connectivity between two VPCs and requires that VPC route tables are explicitly updated with routes to peer VPCs. When the number of VPCs is small, using VPC peering is manageable, but as the number of VPCs grows, the number of connections—and the number of route tables to be updated and maintained—also grows.

Usage-based pricing
> Although as a network engineer you can architect a topology that will provide the necessary connectivity among all the workloads in all the VPCs in all the regions, will your topology provide that connectivity in the most cost-effective way when usage increases? This means considering cross-AZ traffic charges, cross-region traffic charges, and egress charges to internet-based destinations (just to name a few).

All of these considerations layer on top of what's already needed for smaller (single VPC) cloud network topologies.

A large cloud network topology

In a *large cloud network topology*, you're looking at multiple dozens of VPCs in multiple regions worldwide. VPC peering is no longer a serviceable option; there are simply too many peering connections to manage, and nontransitive connectivity is introducing even more complexity.

A new set of design considerations emerge:

Centralized connectivity
> Using tools like transit VPCs and transit gateways, you can move away from the nontransitive VPC peering connectivity to a *fully routed* solution. These tools also allow you to integrate additional options like AWS Direct Connect (for dedicated connectivity back to on-premises networks) or VPN capabilities. Implementing centralized egress—where "spoke" VPCs use NAT gateways in the "hub" VPC for internet connectivity—is also possible. In all these cases, you need to define a routing strategy such as static routing or a dynamic routing protocol like BGP.

Multi-account architectures
> In topologies this large, you're far more likely to encounter situations where entire VPCs belong to different AWS accounts. Your network topology now needs to address how to provide connectivity securely among resources that are owned by different entities.

Using the mentioned centralized connectivity tools, we can expand cloud networks to reach other cloud providers and on-premises networks.

A hybrid cloud network topology

With the increase in cloud service adoption, new interconnection scenarios are becoming more and more common. These scenarios include connecting different cloud providers (public or private) and connecting these cloud providers to on-premises networks; Flexera's 2023 State of the Cloud Report (*https://oreil.ly/wQbwt*) says that 87% of the organizations surveyed use more than one cloud provider. Also, the boundaries between these environments are getting fuzzier, because cloud services can be running on their client's on-premise data centers (for instance, AWS Outposts service). The industry uses the term *hybrid cloud* to describe these scenarios.

Aside from the challenges of managing and orchestrating various infrastructure services (and the applications on top), the first obvious challenge is how to connect all these environments together.

Hybrid cloud connectivity has no one-size-fits-all solution. All the public cloud service providers offer mechanisms to connect their services to on-premises networks. These mechanisms are usually based on VPN connections or dedicated connectivity services (e.g., AWS Direct Connect or Azure ExpressRoute). Figure 4-2 shows an example of a hybrid cloud network topology: an on-premises network is connected to AWS and Azure clouds via dedicated transport services, and the routing information is exchanged via BGP. Notice that you could also connect both cloud providers via the on-premises network.

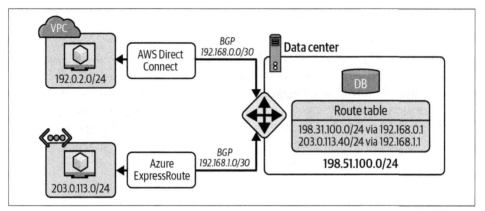

Figure 4-2. Hybrid network topology

When you connect your network to a cloud provider, you can reach your own cloud workloads (e.g., your databases and VMs) but also the general cloud services. In the case of AWS, you can reach the object storage system Amazon Simple Storage Service (S3) and many more.

However, these connectivity mechanisms are not capable of directly interconnecting cloud providers. To interconnect cloud providers, you need to use other solutions such as routing them via an on-premises network as described in Figure 4-2 or creating your own VPN connections among the cloud providers to create an overlay network. If managing this interconnection becomes cumbersome, you can leverage third-party vendors that orchestrate these connections for you. Two examples of these vendors are Aviatrix (*https://aviatrix.com*) and Alkira (*https://www.alkira.com*).

Either way, you still need to design a network topology that allows connecting all these environments, with a consistent network addressing and routing plan between network segments. This requires the network skills you have developed in your network engineering career.

Moreover, as the level of complexity grows, the need for automation increases exponentially. There are more "things" to manage and configure—things like transit gateway attachments, VPN connections, or separate subnets for certain types of connections. Managing them effectively will *require* some form of automation.

Network Automation in the Cloud

Networking in the cloud, unlike a lot of on-premises networking, is inherently built for automation. It's a by-product of the qualities of cloud computing per the NIST definition provided in "Brief Definition of Cloud Computing" on page 97. We can approach network automation in the cloud in three ways:

- Using the cloud provider's APIs directly
- Using the cloud provider's CLI tool
- Using a tool purpose-built for automating the cloud

Using the cloud provider's APIs

Cloud providers offer API-first platforms. They have a rich set of APIs that can be used to automate the provisioning of cloud resources. Every other method (i.e., CLI tools or purpose-built tools) is just a wrapper around these APIs.

However, you won't usually use the APIs directly. Even when you want to hit the APIs directly, you will likely use a programming language implementing a wrapper around the API (i.e., software development kit, or SDK). For instance, AWS maintains many SDKs for various programming languages, such as Boto3 (*https://oreil.ly/8MUOf*) for Python and AWS SDK for Go (*https://oreil.ly/CDIrY*). Using an SDK makes API interaction easier because you don't have to worry about the HTTP requests and responses.

The APIs support different versions to maintain backward compatibility in your code. The same applies to the SDKs.

In the following chapters, you will learn about programming languages (Chapters 6 and 7) as well as about HTTP APIs (Chapter 10). Therefore, we won't cover examples of using the APIs here. You will find examples of using REST APIs, such as the ones exposed by AWS, in Chapter 10. There, you will learn about interacting with the APIs with various methods such as cURL, Postman, Python, and Go. Even though those examples are not specific to cloud service provisioning, all the APIs share the same principles so you can apply the knowledge to the cloud service provisioning use case.

Using the cloud provider's CLI tool

The command-line interface is another UI to interact with the cloud provider's APIs. The CLI tool offered by many of these cloud providers is often just a wrapper around that provider's standard APIs, making it easier to interact with them. For instance, the AWS CLI (*https://aws.amazon.com/cli*) tool leverages a Python SDK to expose this UI.

The CLI tool can be used manually by an operator to manage the cloud services, or it can be used in an automated fashion. For instance, you can use the CLI tool in a shell script. In Chapter 12, you will find examples (with the necessary configuration) of using the AWS CLI tool to interact with the AWS cloud. In the meantime, we give

you an example from the AWS CLI repository (*https://oreil.ly/JzEnY*) of how to use
the AWS CLI tool to create a VPC:

```
$ aws ec2 create-vpc \                                                        ❶
    --cidr-block 10.0.0.0/16 \                                                ❷
    --tag-specification ResourceType=vpc,Tags=[{Key=Name,Value=MyVpc}]`       ❸

{                                                                             ❹
    "Vpc": {
        "CidrBlock": "10.0.0.0/16",
        "DhcpOptionsId": "dopt-5EXAMPLE",
        "State": "pending",
        "VpcId": "vpc-0a60eb65b4EXAMPLE",
        "OwnerId": "123456789012",
        "InstanceTenancy": "default",
        "Ipv6CidrBlockAssociationSet": [],
        "CidrBlockAssociationSet": [
            {
                "AssociationId": "vpc-cidr-assoc-07501b79ecEXAMPLE",
                "CidrBlock": "10.0.0.0/16",
                "CidrBlockState": {
                    "State": "associated"
                }
            }
        ],
        "IsDefault": false,
        "Tags": [
            {
                "Key": "Name",
                "Value": MyVpc"
            }
        ]
    }
}
```

❶ `aws ec2 create-vpc` is the command to create a VPC; `ec2` is the AWS service
type (*https://oreil.ly/eJA8b*), and `create-vpc` is the specific action.

❷ Every AWS resource has mandatory and optional arguments. For the VPC, only
the CIDR block is mandatory.

❸ `Tags`, or metadata, is a common parameter for all cloud resources to add more
dimensions to improve the resource classification.

❹ The output of the command is a JSON object with the details of the created VPC,
directly taken from the AWS API response.

You can find the complete AWS CLI tool documentation online (*https://oreil.ly/
BI7Ql*).

Using a tool purpose-built for automating the cloud

On top of the cloud provider's APIs, purpose-built tools have been built to automate the cloud. These tools are usually called *infrastructure as code* tools because they allow you to define your infrastructure as code (in a declarative approach) and then manage it accordingly.

You could also automate the cloud by using an imperative approach (e.g., using Ansible), but we consider that an antipattern for service provisioning, so we recommend it for configuration management. Both approaches can coexist, as you may need to configure some services after provisioning them. We take a deep dive into this topic in Chapter 12.

To classify the tools implementing a declarative approach, we have to consider two dimensions: whether they are cloud-specific or multicloud, and whether they use a programming language or a domain-specific language (DSL) to define the infrastructure.

 A DSL is designed to solve a specific problem; in contrast, a programming language is a general-purpose language that can be used to solve any problem. DSLs are intended to be used by non-programmers, so they are usually easier to learn and use than programming languages, but they are less flexible. Examples of DSLs are Structured Query Language (SQL), HTML, the YAML-based syntax used in Ansible playbooks, and HashiCorp Configuration Language (HCL) used in Terraform (more about YAML in Chapter 8 and about Ansible and HCL/Terraform in Chapter 12).

In Table 4-1, we use these two dimensions to classify a few of the most popular tools.

Table 4-1. Purpose-built tools for automating the cloud

	Programming language	Domain-specific language
Single cloud	AWS Cloud Development Kit (CDK)	AWS CloudFormation, Azure Resource Manager
Multicloud	Pulumi, CDK for Terraform	Terraform

You should choose the most appropriate tool for your context. In Chapter 12, we explain how to use Terraform and its DSL, because it's the most popular tool for multicloud environments.

After this brief introduction to cloud networking, we will now move on to discuss the relationship between containers and cloud services.

Containers

Unless you haven't been paying attention to what's happening in the technology world, you almost surely have heard of containers. *Containers* are, in the end, just processes running on an OS instance. In fact, a key facet to understanding containers is that there is no such thing as a container. What we refer to as a container is a process running on an OS instance that may or may not take advantage of certain OS features. So why are containers getting so much attention? There are some very good reasons:

Isolation

A process running in a container—or you could say a containerized process—is isolated from other processes by a series of OS-level features called *namespaces.* These namespaces can isolate the process in a variety of ways; for example, the process can be made to think it's the only process running on the OS (via the "process identifier," or PID namespace), that it has its own network interfaces (via the network namespace), or that it has its own set of users and groups (via the user namespace). The exact set of namespaces employed will vary based on the *container runtime* (the engine responsible for setting up processes to run in a container), the presence or absence of a *container orchestrator* (a tool responsible for managing the lifecycle of containers), and other factors. You'll see this in action in the section on Kubernetes, a popular container orchestration platform.

Distribution

Another aspect of containers is that they are built from a container image. A *container image* bundles together all the dependencies needed by the process that will run in a container; this includes any executables, system libraries, tools, or even environment variables and other required configuration settings. Because a container image doesn't include the full kernel and OS—it contains what is needed to run only one specific process—images are typically *much* smaller than a VM image. When coupled with the ability for image creators to easily publish (*push*) container images to a registry, and for other users to easily retrieve (*pull*) images from a registry, it becomes easy to widely distribute container images.

Consider an open source project like the Caddy web server (*https://oreil.ly/ j311S*). The maintainers of a project like Caddy can bundle their project and all its dependencies and provide that in a container image for users. Users can pull the Caddy container image and deploy it in a few minutes with a couple of commands.

Reuse

Not only are container images easy to build, easy to distribute, and easy to consume, but they are also easy for others to *reuse*. Consider again the Caddy web server. If a user wants to deploy Caddy along with custom web content, it's trivial to build a new container image based on the Caddy container image. Someone else could, in turn, reuse your custom image to build their own custom image. Arguably, this ease of reuse could be one of the most important and influential aspects of containers and container images.

Speed

A container doesn't run any faster than a "normal" process on a host, but containers themselves are *far* faster to start than other isolation mechanisms, like VMs. The size of a container image—sometimes as low as tens of megabytes in size, compared to hundreds or thousands of megabytes for a VM disk image—makes containers faster to distribute. Finally, new container images can often be built in minutes, making the time investment for creating a new container image significantly lower than the time investment required to build a VM image, even when using VM image creation automation tools like Packer (*https://packer.io*).

Containers became popular in 2013 with the introduction of Docker, but containers have been around for far longer than that. Before Docker's arrival, containers existed in the form of LXC (*https://linuxcontainers.org*), Linux-VServer, OpenVZ, FreeBSD jails, Oracle Solaris Containers (and Solaris Zones), and even going all the way back to the original introduction of chroot. All of these were OS-level mechanisms for isolating processes running on a host. LXC is considered the first complete implementation of containers that leveraged both control groups (cgroups) for limiting resource utilization and namespaces for isolating processes *without* the need for a custom Linux kernel.

If you're interested in more details on Docker, we recommend *Using Docker* by Adrian Mouat (O'Reilly).

Following the rise of Docker, standards around containers began to emerge. One key standardization effort is the Open Container Initiative, or OCI (*https://opencontainers.org*), which was formed in 2015 by Docker, CoreOS (now part of Red Hat, which in turn is part of IBM), and others. OCI helped establish standards around the image specification (how container images are built), the runtime specification (how a container is instantiated from a container image), and the distribution specification (how containers are distributed and shared via a *registry*). Driven in part by this standardization (and to some extent helping to drive this standardization), standard implementations also began to emerge: runc (*https://oreil.ly/Pkg-7*) as a standard implementation of running a container according to the OCI specification, and containerd (*https://oreil.ly/2BfSC*) as a standard implementation of a full-lifecycle container runtime that builds on top of runc.

Although great strides have been made in recent years in adding containerization functionality to Windows, containers remain—even today—largely a Linux-only thing. Throughout the discussion of containers in this chapter, the focus is only on Linux containers.

Now that you have a better understanding of what containers are and what benefits they offer, let's answer the question of why we are discussing containers in a cloud-focused chapter, especially when you've already seen that containers are predominantly a Linux-focused entity. Why not put them in the Linux chapter, instead of the cloud chapter?

What Do Containers Have to Do with the Cloud?

In and of themselves, containers have nothing to do with cloud computing. They are an OS-level construct and are equally at home on your local laptop, on a VM running on a hypervisor in a data center, or on a cloud instance. Since their introduction, however, containers have grown to be a key part of *cloud native computing*. As defined by the Cloud Native Computing Foundation (CNCF) (*https://oreil.ly/GESqd*), cloud-native computing enables "organizations to build and run scalable applications in modern and dynamic environments such as public, private, and hybrid clouds, while leveraging cloud computing benefits to their fullest."

Given the importance of containers to cloud native computing, and given the prevalence of container-based services offered by public cloud providers today—like AWS ECS, Google Cloud Run, and Azure Container Instances (ACI)—we feel the placement of containers in this cloud chapter is appropriate.

What Do Containers Have to Do with Networking?

The placement of containers within a cloud-focused chapter hopefully makes sense, but a larger question still needs answering: what do containers have to do with networking? We feel it's important to include content on containers in a networking programmability and automation book for a few reasons:

- The way in which container networking is handled—especially when containers are used in conjunction with the Kubernetes container orchestration platform—is sufficiently different from what most network engineers already know and understand that it's worth highlighting these differences and building a bridge between Kubernetes concepts and more "typical" networking constructs.

- Network engineers may wish to use containers in conjunction with other tools. A network engineer might, for example, want to create a "network tools" container image that has all of the most important networking and network automation tools (including all necessary dependencies) bundled into a single image that is easily distributed and executed on any compatible platform. Containers also simplify spinning up network development environments, as you will learn in Chapter 5 when we cover Containerlab (*https://oreil.ly/KtnDl*).

- Network vendors may leverage containers in their platforms, especially on Linux-based platforms. The isolation mechanisms of containers combined with the ease of distribution make containers an ideal method for delivering new functionality to networking platforms.

So, we'll review the basics of container networking, including how containers are isolated from one another, and how they can communicate with one another and with the outside world.

Extending Linux Networking for Containers

One reason the Linux chapter (Chapter 3) spends so much time on the basic building blocks of networking is that containers (and container orchestration systems like Kubernetes, as you'll see in "Kubernetes" on page 126) extend these basic building blocks to accommodate container networking. A good understanding of the basic building blocks provides the necessary structure that makes it easier to add container-specific concepts to your skill set.

For networking containers, five Linux technologies are leveraged:

- Network namespaces
- Virtual Ethernet (veth) interfaces
- Bridges
- IP routing
- IP masquerading

Of these, bridges and IP routing—a term used to describe the ability of a Linux-based system to act as a Layer 3 (IP-based) router—were discussed in Chapter 3. The remaining three technologies are discussed in the following sections. We start with Linux network namespaces.

Linux network namespaces

Namespaces are an isolation mechanism; they limit what processes can "see" in the namespace. The Linux kernel provides multiple namespaces; for networking, *network namespaces* are the primary namespaces involved. Network namespaces can be used to support multiple separate routing tables or multiple separate iptables configurations, or to *scope*, or limit, the visibility of network interfaces. In some respects, they are probably most closely related to VRF instances in the networking world.

While network namespaces can be used to create VRF instances, separate work is going on in the Linux kernel community right now to build "proper" VRF functionality into Linux. This proposed VRF functionality would provide additional logical Layer 3 separation within a namespace. It's still too early to see where this will lead, but we want you to know about it nevertheless.

Some use cases for Linux network namespaces include the following:

Per-process routing

Running a process in its own network namespace allows you to configure routing per process.

Enabling VRF configurations

We mentioned at the start of this section that network namespaces are probably most closely related to VRF instances in the networking world, so it's only natural that enabling VRF-like configurations would be a prime use case for network namespaces.

Support for overlapping IP address spaces

You might also use network namespaces to provide support for overlapping IP address spaces, where the same address (or address range) might be used for different purposes and have different meanings. In the bigger picture, you'd probably need to combine this with overlay networking and/or NAT in order to fully support such a use case.

Container networking

Network namespaces are also a key part of the way containers are connected to a network. Container runtimes use network namespaces to limit the network interfaces and routing tables that the containerized process is allowed to see or use.

In this discussion of network namespaces, the focus is on that last use case—container networking—and how network namespaces are used. The focus is further constrained to discuss only how the Docker container runtime uses network namespaces. Finally, as mentioned earlier, we will discuss only Linux containers, not containers on other OSs.

In general, when you run a container, Docker will create a network namespace for that container. You can observe this behavior by using the lsns command. For example, if you run lsns -t net to show the network namespaces on an Ubuntu Linux system that doesn't have any containers running, you would see only a single network namespace listed.

However, if you launch a Docker container on that same system with docker run --name nginxtest -p 8080:80 -d nginx, then lsns -t net will show something different. Here's the output of lsns -t net -J, which lists the network namespaces serialized as JSON:

```
{
  "namespaces": [
    {
      "ns": 4026531840,                                        ❶
      "type": "net",
      "nprocs": 132,
      "pid": 1,
      "user": "root",
      "netnsid": "unassigned",
      "nsfs": null,
      "command": "/sbin/init"
    },
    {
      "ns": 4026532233,                                        ❷
      "type": "net",
      "nprocs": 5,
      "pid": 15422,
      "user": "root",
      "netnsid": "0",
      "nsfs": "/run/docker/netns/b87b15b217e8",
      "command": "nginx: master process nginx -g daemon off;"  ❷
    }
  ]
}
```

❶ The *host* (or *root*, or *default*) namespace that is present on every Linux system. When we interact with network interfaces, routing tables, or other network configurations, we are generally interacting with the default namespace.

❷ The namespace created by Docker when we ran (created) the container. There are multiple ways to determine that this is the namespace Docker created, but in this case looking at the command field gives it away.

In some cases—like the preceding example—it's easy to tell which network namespace is which. For a more concrete determination, you can use the following steps:

1. Use the docker container ls command to get the container ID for the container in question.

2. Use the docker container inspect *container-id* command to have the Docker runtime provide detailed information about the specified container. This will produce a lot of output in JSON; you may find it easier to deal with this information if you pipe it through a utility like jq.

3. Look for the `SandboxKey` property. It will specify a path, like /var/run/docker/ netns/b87b15b217e8. Compare that with the output of `lsns` and its `nsfs` property. With the exception of the /var prefix, the values will match when you are looking at the same container.

 If you don't want to run a container in a network namespace, Docker supports a `--network=host` flag that will launch the container in the host (also known as the root, or default) namespace.

The `ip` command (from the `iproute2` package), which Chapter 3 covers in great detail, also has an `ip netns` subcommand that allows the user to create, manipulate, and delete network namespaces. However, the network namespaces created by Docker and other container runtimes generally aren't visible to the user, even if used with `sudo` to gain elevated permissions. The `lsns` command used in this section, however, *will* show network namespaces created by Docker or another container runtime. (Although we are discussing only network namespaces here, `lsns` can show any type of namespace, not just network namespaces.)

Network namespaces have more use cases than just containers; for a more detailed look at working with network namespaces in a noncontainer use case, refer to the additional online content for this book (*https://oreilly-npa-book.github.io*). There you'll find examples of how to use the `ip netns` command to manipulate the networking configuration of a Linux host, including adding interfaces to and removing interfaces from a network namespace.

Linux network namespaces are a critical component for container networking, but without a mechanism for simulating the behavior of a real network interface, our systems' ability to connect containers to the network would be greatly constrained. In fact, we'd be able to run only as many containers as we could fit physical network interfaces in the host. Virtual Ethernet interfaces are the solution to that constraint.

Virtual Ethernet interfaces

Just as network namespaces enable the Linux kernel to provide network isolation, *Virtual Ethernet* (also called *veth*) interfaces enable you to intentionally break that isolation. Veth interfaces are logical interfaces; they don't correspond to a physical NIC or other piece of hardware. As such, you can have many more veth interfaces than you have physical interfaces.

Further, veth interfaces always come in pairs: traffic entering one interface in the pair comes out the other interface in the pair. For this reason, you may see them referenced as *veth pairs*. Like other types of network interfaces, a veth interface can be assigned to a network namespace. When a veth interface—one member of a veth pair —is assigned to a network interface, you've just connected two network namespaces to each other (because traffic entering a veth interface in one namespace will exit the other veth interface in the other namespace).

This underlying behavior—placing one member of a veth pair in a network namespace and leaving the peer interface in the host (or default) namespace—is the key to container networking. This is how all basic container networking works.

Using the same Docker container spun up in the previous section (which was a simple nginx container launched with the command docker run --name nginxtest -p 8080:80 -d nginx), let's look at how this container's networking is handled.

First, you already know the network namespace the nginx container is using; you determined that using lsns -t net along with docker container inspect and matching up the nsfs and SandboxKey properties from each command, respectively.

Using this information, you can now use the nsenter command to run other commands within the namespace of the nginx Docker container. (For full details on the nsenter command, use man nsenter.) The nsenter flag to run a command in the network namespace of another process is -n, or --net, and it's with that flag you'll provide the network namespace for the nginx container as shown in Example 4-1.

Example 4-1. Running ip link *within a namespace with* nsenter

```
ubuntu2004:~$ sudo nsenter --net=/run/docker/netns/b87b15b217e8 ip link list
1: lo: LOOPBACK,UP,LOWER_UP mtu 65536 qdisc noqueue state UNKNOWN mode DEFAULT
 group default qlen 1000
    link/loopback 00:00:00:00:00:00 brd 00:00:00:00:00:00
4: eth0@if5: BROADCAST,MULTICAST,UP,LOWER_UP mtu 1500 qdisc noqueue state UP  ❶
mode DEFAULT group default
    link/ether 02:42:ac:11:00:02 brd ff:ff:ff:ff:ff:ff link-netnsid 0
```

❶ The interface name is eth0@if5. The interface index—the number at the beginning of the line before the interface name—is 4.

Compare that with the output of ip link list in the host (default) network namespace from Example 4-2.

Example 4-2. Running ip link *in the host network namespace*

```
ubuntu2004:~$ ip link list
1: lo: LOOPBACK,UP,LOWER_UP mtu 65536 qdisc noqueue state UNKNOWN mode DEFAULT
 group default qlen 1000
    link/loopback 00:00:00:00:00:00 brd 00:00:00:00:00:00
2: ens5: BROADCAST,MULTICAST,UP,LOWER_UP mtu 9001 qdisc mq state UP mode DEFAULT
 group default qlen 1000
```

```
    link/ether 02:95:46:0b:0f:ff brd ff:ff:ff:ff:ff:ff
    altname enp0s5
3: docker0: BROADCAST,MULTICAST,UP,LOWER_UP mtu 1500 qdisc noqueue state UP mode
 DEFAULT group default
    link/ether 02:42:70:88:b6:77 brd ff:ff:ff:ff:ff:ff
5: veth68bba38@if4: BROADCAST,MULTICAST,UP,LOWER_UP mtu 1500 qdisc noqueue master ❶
 docker0 state UP mode DEFAULT group default
    link/ether a6:e9:87:46:e7:45 brd ff:ff:ff:ff:ff:ff link-netnsid 0
```

❶ The interface with `veth` in the name is one indicator that this *might* be a veth interface. Names can be changed, though, so this is not a foolproof indicator. However, the name shows `veth68bba38@if4`, and the interface index is 5.

The connection between both outputs is the `@ifX` suffix. On the interface with the index of 5 (that's the `veth68bba38` interface in the host namespace), the suffix points to the interface whose index is 4. The interface with the index of 4 is `eth0` in the nginx container's network namespace (see Example 4-1), and its suffix points to interface index 5 (see Example 4-2).

This is how you can determine veth pairs, and in this case, you see that Docker has created a veth pair for this container. One member of the veth pair is placed in the nginx container's network namespace, and the other member of the veth pair remains in the host namespace. In this configuration, traffic that enters `eth0@if5` in the nginx container's network namespace will exit `veth68bba38@if4` in the host namespace, thus traversing from one namespace to another namespace.

 You can also use `ip -d link list` to show more details in the output. The additional output will include a line with the word `veth` to denote a member of a veth pair. This command will also clearly indicate when an interface is a bridge interface (the additional output will show `bridge`) as well as when an interface is part of a bridge (denoted by `bridge_slave`). Also, in the event the `@ifX` suffix isn't present, you can use `ethtool -S veth-interface`, which will include the line `peer_ifindex:` in the output. The number there refers to the interface index of the other member of the veth pair.

Veth interfaces enable container traffic to move from its own network namespace to the host network namespace (assuming that the container was not started with the `--network=host` flag), but how does traffic get from the veth interface in the host namespace onto the physical network? If you guess a bridge, you guessed correctly! (To be fair, bridges were listed at the beginning of this section as a component of container networking.)

The key in Example 4-2, as discussed in "Bridging (Switching)" on page 86, is the appearance of `master docker0` related to `veth68bba38@if4`. The presence of this text indicates that the specified interface is a member of the `docker0` Linux bridge. If you examine the rest of the interfaces, however, you'll note that none of them is a member of the `docker0` bridge. How, then, does the traffic actually get onto the physical network? This is where IP masquerading comes in, which is the final piece in the puzzle of how Docker containers on a Linux host connect to a network.

Veth interfaces have more uses, although most involve connecting network namespaces together. Refer to the extra online content for this book (*https://oreilly-npa-book.github.io*) for additional examples of using veth interfaces, as well as a look at the commands for creating, modifying, and removing veth interfaces.

IP masquerading

In exploring container networking, so far you've seen how container runtimes like Docker use network namespaces to provide isolation—preventing a process in one container from having any access to the network information of another container or of the host. You've also seen how veth interfaces (also referred to as *veth pairs*) are used to connect the network namespace of a container to the host network namespace. Building upon the extensive coverage of interfaces, bridging, and routing from Chapter 3, you've also seen how a Linux bridge is used in conjunction with the veth interfaces in the host namespace. Only one piece remains: getting the container traffic out of the host and onto the network. This is where IP masquerading gets involved.

IP masquerading enables Linux to be configured to perform NAT. NAT, as you're probably aware, allows one or more computers to connect to a network by using a different address. In the case of IP masquerading, one or more computers connect to a network by using the Linux server's own IP address. RFC 2663 (*https://oreil.ly/ 4qIP0*) refers to this form of NAT as *network address port translation* (*NAPT*); it's also referred to as *one-to-many NAT*, *many-to-one NAT*, *port address translation* (*PAT*), and *NAT overload*.

Before going much further, it's worth noting here that Docker supports several types of networking:

Bridge
This is the default type of networking. It uses veth interfaces, a Linux bridge, and IP masquerading to connect containers to physical networks.

Host

When using host mode networking, the Docker container is not isolated in its own network namespace; instead, it uses the host (default) network namespace. Exposed ports from the container are available on the host's IP address.

Overlay

Overlay networking creates a distributed network spanning multiple Docker hosts. The overlay networks are built using VXLAN, defined in RFC 7348 (*https://oreil.ly/cGWsK*). This mode of networking is directly tied to Docker's container orchestration mechanism, called Swarm.

IPvlan and macvlan

IPvlan networking allows multiple IP addresses to share the same MAC address of an interface, whereas macvlan networking assigns multiple MAC addresses to an interface. The latter, in particular, does not generally work on cloud provider networks. Both IPvlan and macvlan networking are less common than other network types.

 Macvlan networking using macvlan interfaces can be used for other purposes besides container networking. More information on macvlan interfaces and macvlan networking is found at the extra online content for this book (*https://oreilly-npa-book.github.io*).

Throughout this section on container networking, the discussion has centered on bridge mode networking with Docker.

When using bridge mode networking with Docker, the container runtime uses a network namespace to isolate the container and a veth pair to connect the container's network namespace to the host namespace. In the host namespace, one of the veth interfaces is attached to a Linux bridge. If you launch more containers on the same Docker network, they'll be attached to the same Linux bridge, and you'll have immediate container-to-container connectivity on the same Docker host. So far, so good.

When a container attempts to connect to something that's *not* on the same Docker network, Docker has already configured an IP masquerading rule that will instruct the Linux kernel to perform many-to-one NAT for all the containers on that Docker network. This rule is created when the Docker network is created. Docker creates a default network when it is installed, and you can create additional networks by using the `docker network create` command.

First, let's take a look at the default Docker network. Running `docker network ls` shows a list of the created Docker networks. On a freshly installed system, only three networks will be listed (the network IDs listed will vary):

```
ubuntu2004:~$ docker network ls
NETWORK ID      NAME      DRIVER    SCOPE
b4e8ea1af51b    bridge    bridge    local
add089049cda    host      host      local
fbe6029ce9f7    none      null      local
```

Using the `docker network inspect` command displays full details about the specified network. Here's the output of `docker network inspect b4e8ea1af51b` showing more information about the default bridge network (some fields were omitted or removed for brevity):

```
[
    {
        "Name": "bridge",
        "Id": "b4e8ea1af51ba023a8be9a09f633b316f901f1865d37f69855be847124cb3f7c",
        "Created": "2023-04-16T18:27:14.865595005Z",
        "Scope": "local",
        "Driver": "bridge",
        "EnableIPv6": false,
        "IPAM": {
            "Driver": "default",
            "Options": null,
            "Config": [
                {
                    "Subnet": "172.17.0.0/16"                    ❶
                }
            ]
        },
        "Options": {
            "com.docker.network.bridge.default_bridge": "true",
            "com.docker.network.bridge.enable_icc": "true",
            "com.docker.network.bridge.enable_ip_masquerade": "true",  ❷
            "com.docker.network.bridge.host_binding_ipv4": "0.0.0.0",
            "com.docker.network.bridge.name": "docker0",               ❸
            "com.docker.network.driver.mtu": "1500"
        },
        "Labels": {}
        # output omitted for brevity
    }
]
```

❶ The subnet used by containers is `172.17.0.0/16`.

❷ Docker will automatically create the necessary IP masquerading rules for this network.

❸ The name of the bridge for this network is `docker0` (shown in the `Options` section).

You can verify this information by using Linux networking commands covered in Chapter 3 and in this section. For example, to see the IP address assigned to the nginx

Docker container launched earlier, you use a combination of `nsenter` and `ip addr list`, like this:

```
ubuntu2004:~$ sudo nsenter --net=/run/docker/netns/b87b15b217e8 ip addr list eth0
4: eth0@if5: BROADCAST,MULTICAST,UP,LOWER_UP mtu 1500 qdisc noqueue state UP
 group default
    link/ether 02:42:ac:11:00:02 brd ff:ff:ff:ff:ff:ff link-netnsid 0
    inet 172.17.0.2/16 brd 172.17.255.255 scope global eth0 ❶
        valid_lft forever preferred_lft forever
```

❶   Verifies that the container is using an address from the 172.17.0.0/16 network

Similarly, running `ip -br link list` (the `-br` flag stands for *brief* and displays abbreviated output) shows that the bridge created by Docker is indeed named docker0:

```
ubuntu2004:~$ ip -br link list
lo               UNKNOWN   00:00:00:00:00:00 LOOPBACK,UP,LOWER_UP
ens5             UP        02:95:46:0b:0f:ff BROADCAST,MULTICAST,UP,LOWER_UP
docker0          UP        02:42:70:88:b6:77 BROADCAST,MULTICAST,UP,LOWER_UP
veth68bba38@if4  UP        a6:e9:87:46:e7:45 BROADCAST,MULTICAST,UP,LOWER_UP
```

The last piece is the IP masquerading rule, which you can verify by using the `iptables` command. Using iptables is a topic that could have its own book, and does, in fact—see *Linux iptables Pocket Reference* by Gregor N. Purdy (O'Reilly). We can't cover it in great detail but can provide a high-level overview and then explain where the Docker IP masquerading rule fits in.

 Technically, iptables has been replaced by nftables. However, the Linux community still largely references iptables, even when referring to nftables. Additionally, the `iptables` command (and its syntax) continues to work even though the underlying mechanism is now nftables.

Iptables provides several tables, like the filter table, the NAT table, and the mangle table. Additionally, there are multiple chains, like PREROUTING, INPUT, OUTPUT, FORWARD, and POSTROUTING. Each chain is a list of rules, and not every table will have every chain. The rules in a chain match traffic based on properties like source address, destination address, protocol, source port, or destination port. Each rule specifies a target, like ACCEPT, DROP, or REJECT.

With this additional information in hand, let's look at the `iptables` command. In Example 4-3, we use this command to show you all the chains and rules in the NAT table.

Example 4-3. Listing all chains and rules in the NAT table with `iptables`

```
ubuntu2004:~$ iptables -t nat -L -n                    ❶
...output omitted...
Chain POSTROUTING (policy ACCEPT)
target      prot opt source              destination
MASQUERADE  all  --  172.17.0.0/16       0.0.0.0/0  ❷ ❸ ❹
...output omitted...
```

❶ The `-t nat` parameter tells `iptables` to display the NAT table. The `-L` lists the rules, and `-n` simply instructs `iptables` to show numbers instead of attempting to resolve them into names.

❷ The rule specifies the source as `172.17.0.0/16`. We know that to be the subnet assigned to the default Docker bridge network.

❸ The rule specifies a destination of `0.0.0.0/0` (anywhere).

❹ The target for traffic that matches the rule is `MASQUERADE`. This target is available only in the NAT table and in the `POSTROUTING` chain.

By the time traffic hits the `POSTROUTING` chain in the NAT table, routing has already been determined (for more details on how Linux routing works, see "Routing as an End Host" on page 80 and "Routing as a Router" on page 85), and the outbound interface has already been selected based on the host's routing configuration. The `MASQUERADE` target instructs iptables to use the IP address of the outbound interface as the address for the traffic that matches the rule—in this case, traffic from the Docker network's subnet bound for anywhere. This is how, when using a Docker bridge network, traffic actually makes it onto the network: the Linux host determines a route and outbound interface based on its routing table and sends the Docker container traffic to that interface. The rule in the `POSTROUTING` chain of the NAT table grabs that traffic and performs many-to-one NAT using the selected interface's IP address.

Many Linux distributions also provide an `iptables-save` command, which shows the iptables rules in a slightly different format. This is how `iptables-save` shows the rule created by Docker for masquerading a bridge network:

```
ubuntu2004:~$ sudo iptables-save -t nat
...output omitted...
-A POSTROUTING -s 172.17.0.0/16 ! -o docker0 -j MASQUERADE
...output omitted...
```

In this format, you can clearly see the specified source (`-s 172.17.0.0/16`), and the `!` `-o docker0` is shorthand indicating that the outbound interface is *not* the docker0 bridge. In other words, traffic coming from `172.17.0.0/16` is not bound for any destination on the docker0 bridge. The target is specified by `-j MASQUERADE`.

Before moving on to the next section, we present a visual summary of the previous examples in Figure 4-3. You can observe the container running on a network namespace (other namespaces may exist in the same host) that is connected to the default (host) namespace via a veth interface. The veth interface is connected to the docker0 bridge, which is connected to the host's physical interface, and finally, via IP masquerading, to the rest of the network.

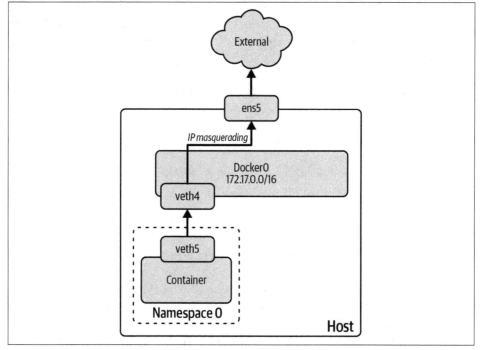

Figure 4-3. Container networking summary

It's now time to transition to Kubernetes, a popular container orchestration tool. Although many of the concepts introduced in this section still apply—Kubernetes is working with containers, after all—a few notable differences exist. The next section touches on those differences and builds on what you already know about container networking.

Kubernetes

Although not necessarily strictly tied to cloud computing—one could make the argument that Kubernetes (*https://oreil.ly/rc7R6*) is a form of PaaS—the use of *cloud native* to describe Kubernetes has inevitably and deeply linked this successful open source project with cloud computing. You've already seen how containers themselves are associated with cloud computing; it's only natural that the position of Kubernetes in the realm of cloud computing is further solidified by the fact that it is a *container orchestrator* and is responsible for orchestrating the lifecycle of containers across a fleet of compute instances.

Finally, the predecessors to Kubernetes were systems internal to Google—Borg and later Omega—that were responsible for managing the compute capacity across thousands of nodes. Kubernetes was, truly, "born from the cloud."

 Kubernetes is not the only container orchestrator but is the most popular. Other container orchestrators include Nomad (*https:// oreil.ly/bQrbG*) and Docker Swarm (*https://oreil.ly/Yk1RY*). Many other container orchestration platforms are built on top of Kubernetes, such as OpenShift (*https://oreil.ly/ez3oX*) and Rancher by SUSE (*https://oreil.ly/d-T69*).

Before discussing networking in Kubernetes, it's important to explain some of the key concepts found in Kubernetes, along with important terminology.

Key Kubernetes Concepts

Kubernetes is, at the core, a distributed system responsible for managing compute workloads across units of compute capacity. The "compute workloads" are *containers*, which is why Kubernetes is often referred to as a container orchestration platform. The "units of compute capacity" are referred to as *nodes*, and they can be bare-metal instances, cloud instances, or VMs running on an on-premises hypervisor like VMware vSphere.

Kubernetes nodes are organized into *clusters*. Each cluster has a control plane, running on one or more nodes, that provides the management functions for the cluster. Nodes that run the control plane components for the cluster are *control plane nodes*. Nodes that aren't part of the control plane are *worker nodes*.

The control plane has three pieces: the API server, the controller manager, and the scheduler. Each performs a different but critical function in the overall operation of the Kubernetes cluster. The scheduler is responsible for placing workloads on worker nodes, while the API server exposes the control plane to users (and other systems). We'll discuss the controller manager shortly.

Backing the control plane is a distributed key-value store named etcd (*https://oreil.ly/ 3cAUb*); this typically runs on the control plane nodes but can run external to the cluster if desired. Etcd—which also forms clusters—needs to have an odd number of instances in order to establish and maintain quorum. Typically, you'll see three etcd instances, along with three control plane instances, in a highly available Kubernetes cluster. It is possible, however, to run a Kubernetes cluster with a single etcd instance and a single control plane node.

Although etcd has requirements about the number of instances to establish and maintain quorum, the Kubernetes control plane components themselves have no such requirements. You can run two control plane nodes for availability, if desired. However, etcd often runs on the control plane nodes themselves, and in that case, you'll find three instances of the Kubernetes control plane components.

The Kubernetes API server implements a RESTful *declarative API*: users (and other systems) don't use the Kubernetes API to tell the cluster what to do (an imperative approach), but rather to tell the cluster *what the desired outcome is* (a declarative approach). For example, using the API, you wouldn't instruct a Kubernetes cluster to create three workloads. Instead, you would tell the Kubernetes cluster you want three workloads running, and you leave the "how" to the cluster itself.

This behavior is known as *reconciliation* of the desired state (the desired outcome you've given the cluster) against the actual state (what is actually running or not running on the cluster). This happens constantly within Kubernetes and is often referred to as the *reconciliation loop*. Reconciling the desired state against the actual state sits at the heart of everything Kubernetes does and the way Kubernetes operates.

Every action that's taken in a Kubernetes cluster happens via the reconciliation loop. For every kind of API object that Kubernetes knows about, something has to implement the reconciliation loop. That "something" is known as a *controller*, and the controller manager—the third part of the Kubernetes control plane, along with the scheduler and the API server—is responsible for managing the controllers for the built-in objects that Kubernetes understands. New types of objects can be created, via a *custom resource definition* (CRD), but the new types of objects will also require a controller that understands the lifecycle of those objects: how they are created, how they are updated, and how they are deleted.

 O'Reilly has published several books focused exclusively on Kubernetes that may be helpful. Titles to consider include *Kubernetes: Up and Running, 3rd Edition*, by Brendan Burns et al.; *Kubernetes Cookbook* by Sébastien Goasguen and Michael Hausenblas; *Production Kubernetes* by Josh Rosso et al.; and *Kubernetes Patterns* by Bilgin Ibryam and Roland Huß.

A lot more could be said about Kubernetes, but this basic introduction gives you enough information to understand the rest of this section. Next we discuss some of the basic building blocks involved in Kubernetes networking.

Building Blocks of Networking in Kubernetes

Kubernetes introduces a few new constructs, but it's important to remember that Kubernetes is built on top of existing technologies. In the following sections, we discuss the basic building blocks of Kubernetes networking, and how they relate to the networking technologies you already know, such as container networking, IP routing, and load balancing, among others.

Pods

A *Pod* is a collection of containers that share network access and storage volumes. A Pod may have one container or multiple containers. Regardless of the number of containers within a Pod, however, certain things remain constant:

- All the containers within a Pod are scheduled together, created together, and destroyed together. Pods are the *atomic* unit of scheduling.

- All the containers within a Pod share the same network identity (IP address and hostname). Kubernetes accomplishes this by having multiple containers share the same network namespace—which means they share the same network configuration and the same network identity. This does introduce some limitations; for example, two containers in a Pod can't expose the same port. The basics of how these containers connect to the outside world remain as described in "Containers" on page 112, with a few minor changes.

- A Pod's network identity (IP address and hostname) is *ephemeral*; it is allocated dynamically when the Pod is created and released when the Pod is destroyed or dies. As a result, you should never construct systems or architectures that rely on directly addressing Pods; after all, what will happen when you need to run multiple Pods? Or what happens when a Pod dies and gets re-created with a different network identity?

- All the containers within a Pod share the same storage volumes and mounts. This is accomplished by having containers share the namespace responsible for managing volumes and mounts.

- Kubernetes provides higher-level mechanisms for managing the lifecycle of Pods. For example, *Deployments* are used by Kubernetes to manage *ReplicaSets*, which in turn manage groups of Pods to ensure that the specified number of Pods is always running in the cluster.

To create a Pod, a cluster user or operator would typically use a YAML file that describes the Pod to the Kubernetes API server. The term given to these YAML files is *manifests*, and they are submitted to the API server (typically via the Kubernetes command-line tool, kubectl, or its equivalent). Example 4-4 shows a manifest for a simple Pod.

Example 4-4. Kubernetes Pod manifest

```
apiVersion: v1     ❶
kind: Pod          ❷
metadata:          ❸
  name: assets
  labels:
    app.kubernetes.io/name: zephyr
spec:
  containers:      ❹
    - name: assets
      image: nginx ❺
      ports:       ❻
        - name: http-alt
          containerPort: 8080
          protocol: TCP
```

❶ The Kubernetes API supports versioning. When the API version is just v1, as here, it means this object is part of the Kubernetes core API.

❷ kind refers to Kubernetes construct types, like Pod, Deployment, Service, Ingress, NetworkPolicy, etc.

❸ Every API object also has metadata associated with it. Sometimes the metadata is just a name, but many times—as in this example—it also includes labels. Labels are heavily used throughout Kubernetes.

❹ A Pod can have one or more containers. In this example, only a single container is in the Pod, but more items could be in the list.

❺ The image specified here is a container image. This container image will be used to create a new container in the Pod. In this example, only a single container is in the Pod.

❻ Pods can expose one or more ports to the rest of the cluster.

When creating Pods, Kubernetes itself doesn't create the containers; that task is left to the container runtime. Kubernetes interacts with the container runtime via a standard interface known as the Container Runtime Interface (CRI). Similar standard interfaces exist for storage (Container Storage Interface, or CSI) and networking (Container Network Interface, or CNI). CNI is an important part of Kubernetes networking, but before discussing CNI, let's take a look at Kubernetes Services.

Services

If you can't connect directly to a Pod, how can applications running in Pods possibly communicate across the network? This is one of the most significant departures of

Kubernetes from previous networking models. When working with VMs, the VM's network identity (IP address and/or hostname) is typically long-lived, and you can plan on being able to connect to the VM in order to access whatever applications might be running on that VM. As you shift into containers and Kubernetes, that's no longer true. A Pod's network identity is ephemeral. Further, what if there are multiple replicas of a Pod? To which Pod should another application or system connect?

Instead of connecting to a Pod (or to a group of Pods), Kubernetes uses a *Service* (Example 4-5 shows a manifest for a simple one). A Service fulfills two important roles:

- Assigning a stable network identity to a defined subset of Pods. When a Service is created, it is assigned a network identity (IP address and hostname). This network identity will remain stable for the life of the Service.

- Serving as a load balancer for a defined subset of Pods. Traffic sent to the Service is distributed to the subset of Pods included in the Service.

Example 4-5. Kubernetes Service manifest

```
apiVersion: v1
kind: Service
metadata:
  name: zephyr-assets
spec:
  selector:              ❶
    app.kubernetes.io/name: zephyr
  ports:
    - protocol: TCP
      port: 80           ❷
      targetPort: 8080   ❸
```

❶ The selector indicates a label, and the effective result of including this label in the selector is that Pods with that label will be "part" of the Service; that is, Pods with this label will receive traffic sent to the Service.

❷ The port by which the Service is accessible to the rest of the cluster.

❸ The port, exposed by the Pods in the Service, to which traffic will be sent.

This example illustrates how the relationship between a Pod and a Service is managed. Using label selectors, the Service will dynamically select matching Pods. If a Pod matches the labels, it will be "part" of the Service and will receive traffic sent to the Service. Pods that don't match the Service's definition won't be included in the Service.

Labels, like the one shown in the preceding example, are simply key-value pairs, like `app.kubernetes.io/name: zephyr`. Labels can be arbitrary, but emerging standards around the labels should be used, and Kubernetes has rules regarding the length of the keys and values in a label.

Various kinds of Services are supported by Kubernetes:

ClusterIP Service
> This default type of Service has a virtual IP address—which is valid *only* within the cluster itself—assigned to the Service. A corresponding DNS name is also created, and both the IP address and the DNS name will remain constant until the Service is deleted. ClusterIP Services are not reachable from outside the cluster.

NodePort Service
> It exposes the Service at a defined port. Traffic sent to a node's IP address on that port is then forwarded to the Service's ClusterIP, which in turn distributes traffic to the Pods that are part of the Service. NodePort Services allow you to expose the Service via an external or manual process, like pointing an external HAProxy instance to the Service's defined NodePort.

LoadBalancer Service
> It requires some type of controller that knows how to provision an external load balancer. This controller might be part of the Kubernetes cloud provider, which supports integration with underlying cloud platforms, or it might be a separate piece of software you install onto the cluster. Either way, Kubernetes sets up a NodePort Service and then configures the external load balancer to forward traffic to the assigned node port. LoadBalancer Services are the primary way to expose Services outside a Kubernetes cluster.

Services operate at Layer 4 of the OSI model (at the TCP/UDP layer). As such, a Service cannot make a distinction between the hostnames used in an HTTP request, for example. Because so many companies were using Kubernetes to run web-based apps over HTTP/HTTPS, this became a limitation of Services. In response, the Kubernetes community created Ingresses.

Ingresses

An *Ingress* is used to perform Layer 7 (HTTP) routing, based on various properties of an HTTP request. An Ingress is managed by an *ingress controller*, which is a specific piece of software deployed onto your Kubernetes cluster to perform the necessary functions. Numerous ingress controllers are available, including (but not limited to) the ginx ingress controller, the HAProxy ingress controller, the Traefik ingress controller, and various Envoy Proxy–based ingress controllers (such as Ambassador, Contour, and Gloo). The exact feature set of these various ingress controllers varies, but all perform the same basic function: receive Ingress definitions from the Kubernetes API and perform HTTP routing based on those definitions.

 The Kubernetes community is in the midst of defining a replacement for Ingress. This project is known as the Gateway API project, and more information is available at the Kubernetes Gateway API website (*https://oreil.ly/4X_g1*). This effort also involves many products and projects that are classified as *API gateways*, since their core functionality is similar to that provided by the Gateway API.

An Ingress definition (or an Ingress object) provides a set of rules that define how HTTP routing should be performed by the ingress controller. Say, for example, that Service A services API requests to the /users API, while Service B services API requests for the /devices API. You might have an Ingress object with multiple rules that directs traffic sent to /users to Service A (referring here to a Kubernetes Service) and directs traffic sent to /devices to Service B. Both routes could be exposed behind a single FQDN, like api.company.com or similar.

Alternatively, you could have an Ingress object that defines rules based on the FQDN in the request and directs traffic to various Services based on that FQDN. Example 4-6 shows an Ingress manifest.

Example 4-6. Kubernetes Ingress manifest

```
apiVersion: networking.k8s.io/v1 ❶
kind: Ingress
metadata:
  name: minimal-ingress
  annotations:
    nginx.ingress.kubernetes.io/rewrite-target: /
spec:
  ingressClassName: nginx-example
  rules:                           ❷
  - http:
      paths:
      - path: /testpath            ❸
        pathType: Prefix
        backend:
          service:                 ❹
            name: test
            port:
              number: 80
```

❶ The API version for an Ingress object also specifies an API group (network ing.k8s.io). As Kubernetes has grown and matured, API groups have been used to help organize the growing API surface area.

❷ These rules define how the ingress controller should direct traffic based on various conditions.

❸ In this case, there's only a single condition (the `path` needs to start with `/test path`). However, adding new items to the `paths` list would allow us to define additional rules to direct traffic to different Services.

❹ In all cases, the destination for traffic being directed by an ingress controller is a Kubernetes Service.

 An ingress controller directs traffic to Kubernetes Services, which are typically defined as ClusterIP Services. However, the ingress controller must be also exposed using a Service, typically a LoadBalancer Service. This allows traffic to enter the Kubernetes cluster via the ingress controller's Service, then be directed by the ingress controller to the appropriate Service. In this fashion, only the ingress controller is reachable from outside the cluster, and all other Services are "gated" behind the ingress controller.

Other networking constructs

Pods, Services, and Ingresses form the bulk of what's used regularly to define how Kubernetes should expose and connect workloads. However, a couple of other constructs are worth briefly mentioning:

NetworkPolicies
 NetworkPolicies provide a means for users to control what traffic is or is not permitted into or out of Pods. They are, essentially, Pod firewalls. Be wary of the firewall comparison, however; while it is convenient, NetworkPolicies do behave differently than most firewalls: there's no deny action, for example, and no sense of rule priority or order.

Namespaces
 Not to be confused with namespaces at the Linux kernel level, Kubernetes namespaces provide logical separation of API objects, like Pods and Services. Namespaces also affect the automatic DNS-based service discovery that Kubernetes performs for all Services.

Thus far, you've seen some of the high-level Kubernetes API objects that form the building blocks of Kubernetes networking. However, a key component sits one level lower and is responsible for handling all the plumbing that makes the higher-level constructs function. It's the CNI introduced earlier in this chapter, and it provides a standard mechanism for plugging various networking models into Kubernetes.

Container Network Interface

The CNI is a generic specification (*https://oreil.ly/-SN0R*) that defines how a container network plug-in should be implemented. It defines a set of APIs and the format of the configuration expected. Kubernetes, as a container orchestrator solution, implements the CNI specification, so any CNI-compliant plug-in can be used with any Kubernetes cluster.

A CNI plug-in can implement one or many networking features, such as assigning IP addresses to Pods, pod-to-pod encapsulation, external connectivity, network policies, and more. Some basic plug-ins are maintained by the CNI community (*https://oreil.ly/CcdGN*), but many third-party plug-ins implement advanced features. Some of them include Calico (*https://oreil.ly/YE5MV*), Cilium (*https://oreil.ly/srk0g*), and Amazon ECS CNI plug-ins (*https://oreil.ly/-Ov1f*).

The CNI specification doesn't dictate how the plug-in should work; it dictates only how to interact with this plug-in using a specific interface. The CNI plug-in can be written in any language, but is expected to be provided and executed as a binary.

> You can find more information about CNI, the CNI specification, and available CNI plug-ins at the CNI GitHub repository (*https://oreil.ly/_QPDf*).

Using the CNI specification, Kubernetes can implement a wide variety of networking models. In Figure 4-4, we depict one of the many Kubernetes network solutions using the kube-router (*https://oreil.ly/s_ir1*) approach to illustrate how both worlds can work together. In this case, each Kubernetes host uses a BGP daemon (running in the default Kubernetes namespace) to advertise the host's CIDRs using the BGP protocol. The external BGP route reflector simplifies the BGP architecture, avoiding the need for a full mesh of BGP peers. All the Kubernetes hosts learn about the others' prefixes as well as external prefixes (e.g., the internet).

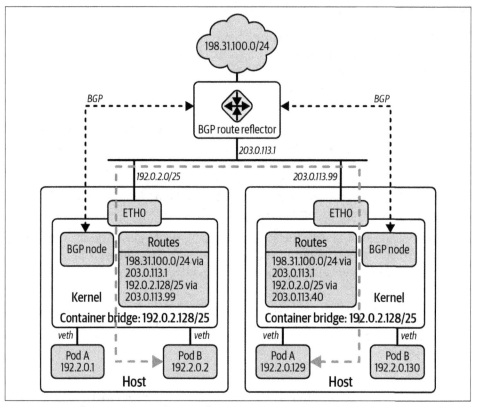

Figure 4-4. Kubernetes networking with BGP

Finally, to complete this high-level Kubernetes exploration, let's take a look at a new networking pattern that's gaining a lot of popularity: the service mesh.

Service Mesh

Modern software applications have led to the recent adoption of microservices architecture (*https://oreil.ly/Vw8wI*). This architecture is characterized by using many small and independent services that work together to provide the functionality of the application, allowing for a more flexible, reusable, and scalable architecture. However, this architecture also introduces challenges, and some are related to networking: how do we ensure that all the services can communicate with one another? And how do we ensure that the communication is secure, reliable, and observable?

An answer to these questions is the service mesh pattern. A *service mesh* is a dedicated infrastructure layer that handles service-to-service communication. It's typically implemented as a set of lightweight proxies that are deployed alongside the application services. These proxies intercept all the traffic to and from the applications to provide the following:

Traffic management
Service discovery, load balancing, and fault tolerance

Security
Encryption, authentication and authorization, and access control

Observability
Application metrics, distributed tracing, and logs

The goal is clear: to offload the common networking tasks from the application to the service mesh. This allows the applications to focus on their core business logic without worrying about connectivity-related details.

Service mesh is not limited to Kubernetes. Netflix, in 2017, already had a tech stack to implement service mesh features. However, nowadays Kubernetes is the most popular platform for deploying service mesh, and the two are often used together (most of the examples we mention next run only in Kubernetes).

To achieve this, the service mesh architecture requires two main components:

Data plane
This communication layer handles the actual service-to-service communication. It's implemented as a set of lightweight proxies (sidecar proxies) that are deployed alongside the application services. These proxies intercept all the traffic to and from the services and implement the service mesh features. Examples of data plane proxies are Envoy (*https://www.envoyproxy.io*), Cilium (*https://oreil.ly/ Ql9Rr*), NGINX (*https://www.nginx.com/products/nginx*), and HAProxy (*https:// www.haproxy.com*).

Control plane
This management layer provides the configuration for the data plane. It takes your service mesh configuration and translates it into the configuration for the data plane proxies. It also distributes service discovery updates and collects observability data from the data plane. Some of the most popular control planes are Istio (*https://istio.io*), Consul (*https://www.consul.io*), and Linkerd (*https://link erd.io*) (which also provides a data plane proxy), or cloud-specific solutions like AWS App Mesh (*https://oreil.ly/BBBcR*).

Mastering Service Mesh by Anjali Khatri and Vikram Khatri (Packt) is a good resource to learn more about it.

In Kubernetes, the data plane is implemented as a set of sidecar containers deployed alongside the application containers in the same Pod. Traffic from the application containers is redirected through the sidecar containers, although the specific mechanism used to do this varies among service mesh implementations. The control plane programs these sidecar containers with the necessary configuration to implement the service mesh features, in a centralized way.

You could understand the service mesh as another *overlay* abstraction, but the closest to the application. But, as with any other overlay, the service mesh relies on the underlying network infrastructure to provide connectivity. Your role as a network engineer will be either to implement the service mesh or to provide the underlying network infrastructure to support it and interconnect with the rest of the network. In both cases, understanding how service mesh works is a skill to master.

Summary

Cloud computing doesn't negate the need for networking skills. Indeed, as you've seen in this chapter, networking and network automation are just as important in cloud-based environments as they are in your on-premises environments.

Cloud network services, container and Kubernetes networking, and service mesh are all networking technologies that solve specific problems. They are not mutually exclusive. You can combine them to provide complete networking solutions for your cloud-based applications while extending them to your on-premises networks.

In the next chapter, we change gears to start your journey into the world of network automation, and we show you how containers can help you bootstrap lab environments. Let's begin with your local network development environment.

## CHAPTER 5

Network Developer Environments

As a network engineer, you probably know how important it is to have an optimized working environment. In the physical sense, this might include things like having the right keyboard, sometimes using multiple monitors, and maybe even a standing desk to give you room for stretching out during those long troubleshooting sessions. You may have a bookshelf close at hand so your platform or protocol references are never too far away. This extends to the digital world too: you might have bookmarks to online references, or your network controller's UI. Maybe you have your favorite terminal emulation tool, set up with scripts and shortcuts to get CLI access to all your network devices quickly.

In the same way, software developers often rely on a series of tools to not only stay productive, but also facilitate the development and eventual deployment of the code they write. Many of these tools are just as useful in a network automation context, and we discuss a few of them in this chapter.

Before we get started, it's important to talk about some of the benefits you can expect by investing time in building a proper development environment:

Functional validation

One of the main reasons it's important to build a development environment is so that we know the code we're writing *actually works*. Professional developers don't simply write code in Notepad and hope it works. They build using a variety of tools that not only provide feedback on their code while they're writing it, but also allow them to *run* their code so they can see it working the way they expect.

Consistency

When a developer environment is more formalized and shared among developers on a team, onboarding new team members becomes much easier. While room can be allowed for customization, having all team members use a common set of tools creates a lot less friction when new members are coming up to speed.

Testability

A formalized developer environment also lends itself to being more conducive to automated testing. For example, if your test suite can be executed with a simple `make test` command, each developer can validate that their own code works locally with ease—and more importantly, so can your CI system. We cover more about this in Chapter 13.

This chapter is not meant to specify the "correct" environment, as everyone has their own way of working. Rather, we want to make you aware of some of the key attributes that a productive developer environment might have, as well as dive into a few popular examples that facilitate each of these attributes. From this, you can decide which tools and techniques work best for you or your team.

To that end, we cover a few topics in this chapter:

- Text editors
- Development tools
- Emulation/simulation tools

Text Editors

Whether you're developing automation solutions using a full-blown programming language like Python or Go (which we cover in Chapters 6 and 7), or with more opinionated tools like Ansible or Terraform (which we cover in Chapter 12), at the end of the day, you'll have to do some typing. Even the most opinionated automation tools typically require complex workflows to be defined in some kind of text format like YAML (which we discuss in Chapter 8), which has its own rules to follow.

The notepad-type of application that may come with your operating system is *technically* capable of allowing you to read and write basic code in a text file, but you'll quickly find it is woefully inadequate for any practical network automation purposes. To understand this, it's first necessary to cover some basic requirements you're certain to have when using a text editor for building out a network automation solution.

No text editor is perfect, and everyone has their own peculiar workflows and preferences. However, any worthwhile text editor should support a core set of requirements, and we discuss these and more in the sections to follow.

Some popular text editors include the following:

Visual Studio Code (https://code.visualstudio.com)
Colloquially referred to as *VS Code*, this is a free, lightweight graphical editor that is well supported and actively developed by Microsoft. It boasts a large eco-system of plug-ins. Because of its accessibility and the support available through plug-ins, VS Code has become a popular first choice.

Vim (https://www.vim.org)
This lightweight and totally customizable text editor has an extremely large ecosystem (it's been around for a while). Really, it's the gold standard for text editors (you might notice that other text editors sometimes advertise support for "Vim key bindings/shortcuts"). Using Vim can be intimidating for those not used to relying so heavily on the keyboard to get around, but you'd be hard-pressed to find a more customizable editor.

Sublime Text (https://www.sublimetext.com)
This minimalist graphical editor is similar to Visual Studio Code but has been around longer. It includes a free evaluation version, but individual licenses are available for purchase. It also has a healthy plug-in ecosystem.

This is just an abbreviated list. Many other text editors are available to choose from, each with its own pros and cons. There's really no "best" editor. Each editor comes with its own workflow, features, and ecosystem, which fit everyone differently. Play around with a few options and get started with the one that seems best for you. For the purposes of illustration, many screenshots used in this chapter use Visual Studio Code.

Next, we highlight some specific features that you should consider when evaluating which text editor is right for you.

Syntax Highlighting

Syntax highlighting allows your editor to highlight certain keywords in a given file to make it easier to read, instead of having a bunch of monochrome text on a monochrome background. Figure 5-1 shows how syntax highlighting can color-code certain keywords and symbols to facilitate reading and writing code.

 If you're reading the print edition of this book, the screenshot in Figure 5-1 is in black-and-white, and therefore the colors used for syntax highlighting aren't apparent. You're encouraged to explore this feature for yourself by using one of the editors mentioned.

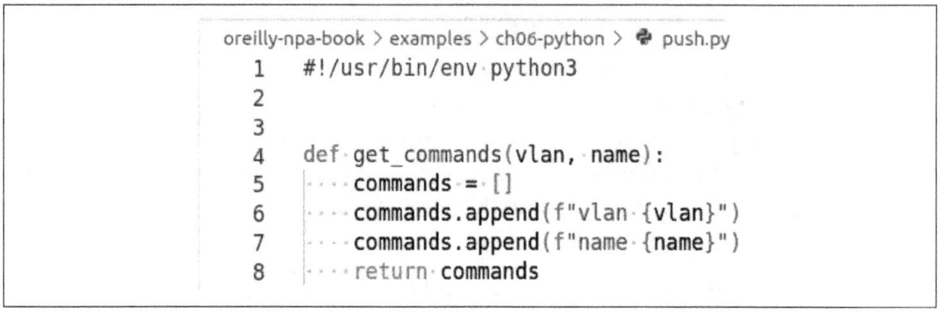

```
oreilly-npa-book > examples > ch06-python > 🐍 push.py
1    #!/usr/bin/env python3
2
3
4    def get_commands(vlan, name):
5        commands = []
6        commands.append(f"vlan {vlan}")
7        commands.append(f"name {name}")
8        return commands
```

Figure 5-1. Syntax highlighting in a text editor

Syntax highlighting can make it easier to read code, as it allows us to make use of our brain's powerful pattern-matching capabilities to quickly recognize well-understood code without having to read every character individually and carefully.

Syntax highlighting is obviously context dependent—for instance, what's considered a keyword in Python will be different from keywords in Go. A good text editor will either include support for syntax highlighting out of the box or, at a minimum, support an ecosystem of plug-ins that can add this kind of functionality.

Customization

Text editors, by design, are minimalistic. You likely can't just download one and have it do everything you need out of the box. However, most text editors allow you to find ways to add or change the functionality you need. This can be done via a combination of settings/preferences or third-party plug-ins that add features and integrations that don't come natively with the editor, as shown in Figure 5-2.

For instance, you might want to be able to interact with Git, for tasks like viewing your local repository's status and making commits, all from within the editor itself. One of the most useful aspects of such an integration is seeing which changes you have made to your local repository at a glance, as shown in Figure 5-3.

Figure 5-2. Customizing text-editor options via plug-ins

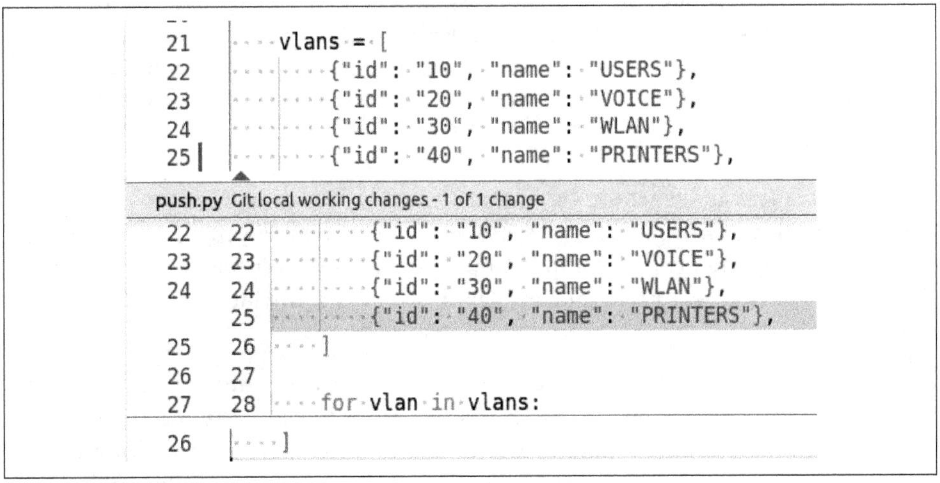

```
21    ····vlans·=·[
22    ·····|·····{"id":·"10",·"name":·"USERS"},
23    ·····|·····{"id":·"20",·"name":·"VOICE"},
24    ·····|·····{"id":·"30",·"name":·"WLAN"},
25 |  ·····|·····{"id":·"40",·"name":·"PRINTERS"},
```

push.py Git local working changes - 1 of 1 change

```
22    22   ·······{"id":·"10",·"name":·"USERS"},
23    23   ·······{"id":·"20",·"name":·"VOICE"},
24    24   ·······{"id":·"30",·"name":·"WLAN"},
      25   ·······{"id":·"40",·"name":·"PRINTERS"},
25    26   ·····]
26    27
27    28   ····for·vlan·in·vlans:
```

```
26    ·····]
```

Figure 5-3. Integrating Git

We dive much deeper into the CLI for Git in Chapter 11; for now, know that little visual hints like this can help reduce friction when working on a complex project. Some editors like Visual Studio Code have this functionality built in; others may support this only via a third-party plug-in.

Plug-ins can also extend an editor's functionality by adding support for intelligent code analysis, which can detect errors, add auto-completion drop-down menus, and provide advanced code navigation. We explore features like these in the following section.

Intelligent Code Analysis

Several features that go well beyond simple syntax highlighting are required and expected for nearly all modern development workflows. They aren't typically referred to by a single cohesive umbrella term, but for the sake of this section, we refer to them as *intelligent code analysis*—as they all enable you, as the developer, to work more productively in a particular language.

Developers of text editors have historically had to add the necessary functionality to provide intelligent code analysis features for a particular language. This nontrivial task may require a lot of time and effort, made worse by the fact that the developers behind each editor had to spend this time and effort independently. This means that support for the language you wanted to work with might not be complete, or available at all, depending on your editor.

To make it much easier for editors to integrate with new languages, the Language Server Protocol, or LSP (*https://oreil.ly/Xh3LP*) allows this integration to be centralized in a *language server*. Editors that support LSP can much more easily integrate with any language server, which is typically developed and maintained by that language's community. Languages including Python, Go, and Rust all have their own language servers.

The first of these intelligent code analysis features is *integrated error checking*. If there's a problem with our code, it's useful to know right away, instead of having to find out only after we've compiled or run the code—especially in production. Figure 5-4 shows how a properly configured editor can provide this feedback as we write our code.

In addition to "hard errors," we also want to know about less critical "stylistic" problems as early as possible. These kinds of problems can be found in code that, for instance, might be functional (it runs or compiles properly) but otherwise violates established idioms of the language you're working in. For instance, Python has PEP 8 (*https://oreil.ly/2409f*), a guide detailing conventions to follow to help make your Python code more readable. Violations of these guidelines can be brought to your attention, as shown in Figure 5-5, and in some cases, even automatically corrected.

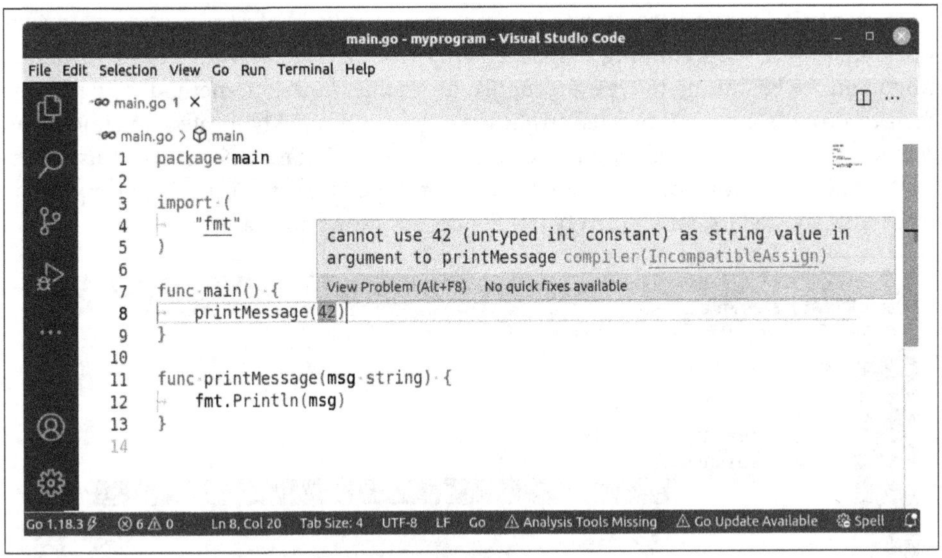

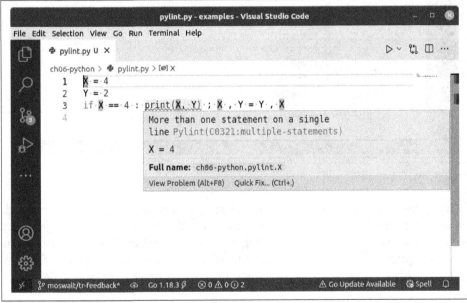

Figure 5-4. Error detection in a text editor

Figure 5-5. Using a text editor for linting

Autocompletion is another extremely common and valuable feature, especially when working with a programming language. This feature enables your editor to detect when you are beginning to type a recognized variable, function, method, or type, and then to provide a drop-down list from which you can quickly locate and choose the correct option, instead of typing the rest. Autocompletion is particularly useful in enumerating the available methods for a given type when relevant, including those methods, parameters, and return types. Figure 5-6 shows an example.

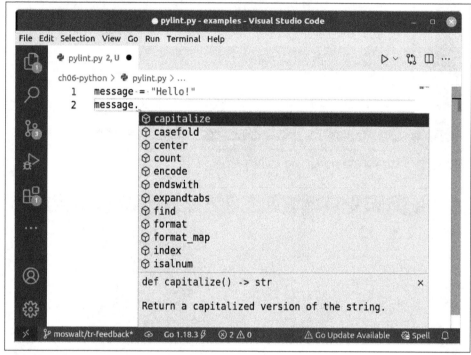

Figure 5-6. A text editor with autocompletion

In many text editors, you can also view the documentation for a given type, method, or function, simply by hovering over it in code. It's easy to forget the right order or type for the function you're trying to use, and being able to refresh your memory quickly is incredibly useful. In Figure 5-7, the documentation for Go's `strings.Split()` function is shown when hovering over a reference to it in source code.

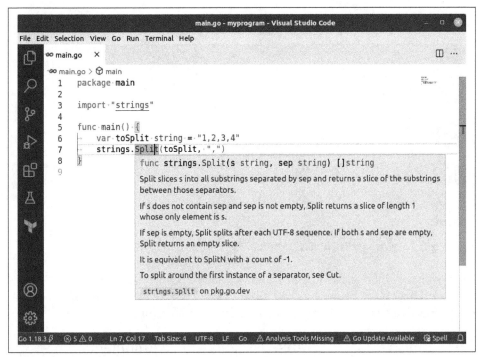

Figure 5-7. Viewing code documentation in a text editor

Options like Go to Definition, Find References, and Refactor within a text editor that includes this kind of integration can be much better than using simple text-searching tools like `grep` or `sed` because they use the deeper understanding of language semantics to avoid finding or updating the wrong thing (for example, partial matches). Code is often not read top to bottom, but rather as a hierarchy of types and function calls, and navigating through a codebase by following references in this way can be useful. While such functionality can vary by editor, Visual Studio Code features these options prominently when right-clicking a variable, function, or method, as shown in Figure 5-8.

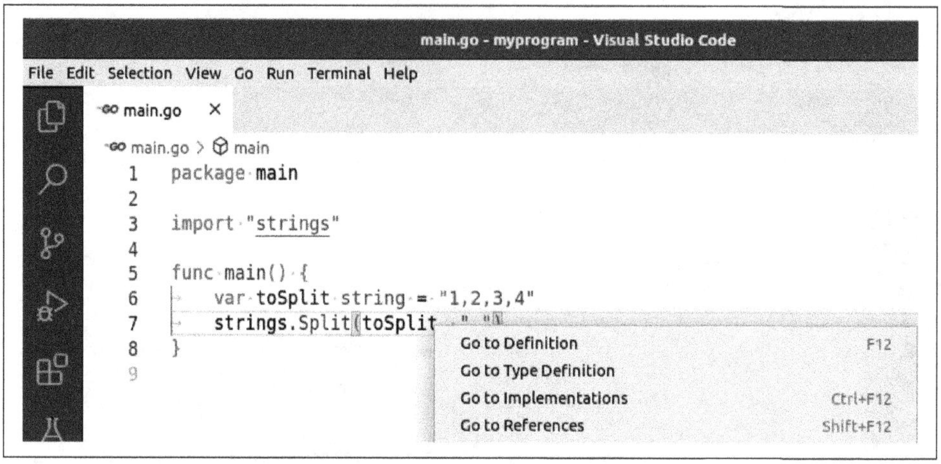

Figure 5-8. Displaying the Go to Definition/References options

Editors that are built and configured to have a deeper understanding of the languages we're working on can provide us with features like these and more, greatly enhancing our productivity when building network automation solutions.

Text Editors Versus Integrated Development Environments

You may have heard the term *integrated development environment*, or *IDE*. Within the world of software development, this term is at times used somewhat loosely to refer to any general text editor. However, it actually means something much more specific. IDEs are similar to text editors in that they are tools for writing code, but they tend to have a lot of features aimed at helping developers work within a particular framework or language. They aim to be a holistic, "one-stop shop" for subspecialties of software development.

For instance, when writing Python code, you might choose something like PyCharm (*https://oreil.ly/R2t8q*), made by JetBrains (shown in Figure 5-9). However, you likely wouldn't want to use this for Go development.

Figure 5-9. PyCharm

An IDE is a popular choice for some, especially for those who want a fully and vertically integrated solution for their development environment. Others may prefer a simpler editor, opting instead for generalized features that work for any programming environment. A popular reason developers might choose a simpler text editor over an IDE is that they tend to be much more lightweight and more broadly customizable. The downside, historically, has been that this lightweight nature came at the cost of maybe not having as many features as a full-blown IDE.

However, as mentioned in the previous section, the advent of language servers has democratized the in-depth language tooling that used to be reserved for these more focused IDEs. Previously, text editor developers had difficulty justifying the time and effort cost associated with adding these smarts natively. Now that these features are standardized and centralized, simple text editors can compete much more easily with IDEs on these features.

There's no wrong answer here. Most modern text editors now have support for all kinds of languages, so their advantage is that you can work in a variety of languages while using the same general UI. Then again, companies like JetBrains are developing IDEs for a wide variety of languages and are making an effort to streamline the experience across the various IDEs they offer. So your choice really does come down to personal preference.

In the next section, we dive into more development tools that you can use directly in your editor or at the command line, and are invaluable for working on network automation solutions.

Development Tools

Aside from the tools you may find integrated with your text editor (natively or through plug-ins) or IDE, a nearly endless list of other tools and frameworks are available to develop, deploy, or debug network automation solutions. Covering them all is impossible, but we can touch on a few you're most likely to run into during your network automation journey.

Even the term *development tools* is quite broad, so it can be useful to break this discussion into a few use cases you're bound to encounter:

Dependency management
> As covered in future chapters, the network automation solutions we'll build are unlikely to be constructed from scratch; typically, they'll be built on top of existing tools and libraries. Tools that help us manage these dependencies will pay dividends from development to deployment.

Packaging and deployment automation
> At some point, you'll want to take that script or workflow you've been developing on your laptop and deploy it to production. Tools that can help you automate the various tasks related to deployment will help you do so safely and predictably.

Working with text-based formats
> Much of the work involved with not only building automation solutions, but also updating and deploying them, often requires working with text-based data formats like YAML. We cover these formats in more detail in Chapter 8, but in this chapter we'll first arm you with some tools you'll want in your repertoire for helping you mutate, search, and manage changes to configurations found in these formats.

While these use cases are quite distinct from one another, you should keep in mind these important traits when looking for tooling in each area:

- Where relevant, inputs and configurations for these tools should be stored and managed as code: meaning that you should manage this data alongside the rest of your automation solution in a version-controlled repository like Git. We cover concepts like these a bit more in Chapters 11 and 13.

- Look for tools that align well with the Unix philosophy. Tools like these are often used as part of a shell script, so they should be simple and designed in such a way that they can be stitched together as part of a cohesive solution.

The following sections include specific examples of tools, but many more are out there, each with its own specialized focus.

Virtualenv

In this book, we discuss a few options for creating automation solutions. Sometimes a full-blown programming language is required. In Chapter 6, we explore the use of Python as part of our automation solutions. Most of the time, the solutions you build in Python should use its huge ecosystem of existing third-party libraries instead of trying to reinvent the wheel.

However, managing these software dependencies can be challenging. For instance, you might be working on two different solutions requiring different versions of a particular Python package to be installed. You might be working on a machine where you don't even have the necessary permissions to install packages in Python's system-wide packages directory. You might want to run your solution with a different version of Python than your system's default.

For these and other reasons, *Virtualenv* (*https://oreil.ly/XuLvC*) exists to make managing Python-based dependencies much easier. It works by creating a virtual environment in a directory of your choice, including a full-blown Python environment plus any dependencies you wish to install. This allows you to not only install these dependencies without elevated permissions, but also manage all of this alongside the program or script you're writing. You'll see more of Virtualenv in action in Chapter 6.

Make

Arguably the original build automation tool is GNU Make (*https://oreil.ly/ahm18*). Historically, this has been extremely popular for compiling and installing software from source code. If you've ever tried to compile a software package from source on Linux, you've almost certainly used this tool.

With Make, you define a set of *targets* in a text file called a *Makefile*. You can run one of these targets on the command line, and the instructions in that target will be executed. However, you're not limited to tasks like compiling source code; you can do just about anything you would normally do using a bash shell script. Example 5-1 shows a Makefile that includes some common tasks you might see in a Go project.

Full versions of the code examples in this chapter can be found in the book's GitHub repo at *https://github.com/oreilly-npa-book/examples/tree/v2/ch05-netdevenv*.

Example 5-1. Makefile

```
SHELL=/bin/bash

all: build                  ❶

build:
        go install ./cmd/... ❷

fmt:
        go fmt ./...         ❸

test:
        go test ./... -cover ❹
```

❶ The `all` target is a special one that allows us to control what happens if the `make` command is run against this file without specifying a target. In this case, we just run the `build` target.

❷ `make build` installs the binaries in the *./cmd* directory.

❸ `make fmt` runs a formatting check against our code.

❹ `make test` executes all testing code found in our project and produces a coverage report.

Makefiles can be especially useful for creating a central place to execute the most common tasks in your project, whatever they are, including building, running, testing, and linting. Instead of having to remember which script to run, with which parameters, in which order, you can just run `make test`, `make lint`, etc.

You can also add dependencies between targets, which allows you to automatically execute other targets first. This allows you to define somewhat complex workflows in the Makefile while keeping the actual user interaction quite simple.

Docker

As we've mentioned, managing software dependencies can be challenging, even for the simplest programs or scripts. This is true during development but also in production. For instance, if your script requires the Requests library, you need to make sure this is installed on every server your script might run on. What if we're writing an Ansible playbook and requiring a particular module to be available? What about other programming languages, where we might compile a program that requires certain libraries to be available on the system?

Historically, the most comprehensive way to solve dependency issues was with VMs. With the advent of virtualization technology, it became possible to build a VM image that had all of these dependencies set up, without having to dedicate an entire hardware platform to running it. However, this approach isn't without its problems. For one thing, building an image to house an entire operating system and then installing your application and dependencies on top can be time- and resource-consuming. Additionally, a VM image with a full operating system requires a lot of overhead to run just a single application—but if we try to run multiple applications within the same operating system, how do we manage conflicting dependencies?

In recent years, another option has emerged to solve this problem: application containers. This approach uses isolation techniques offered by the operating system (e.g., Linux) to allow applications to run—with all their dependencies—in an isolated environment on the same operating system. There are a few ways to build and run container images, but overwhelmingly the most popular choice these days is Docker (*https://www.docker.com*). With Docker, you can create a manifest known as a (*Dockerfile*) that specifies the steps required to build a complete container image optimized to run a particular application, such as installing dependencies, adding configuration files, and setting environment variables. Example 5-2 shows a Dockerfile.

Example 5-2. Dockerfile

```
FROM python:3.8-slim-buster          ❶

COPY requirements.txt requirements.txt  ❷

RUN pip3 install -r requirements.txt    ❸

COPY ./getip.py /getip.py             ❹

CMD [ "python3", "/getip.py"]         ❺
```

❶ Specifies the base image we want to build from. This particular image comes with Python 3.8 already installed for us.

❷ Copies our *requirements.txt* file from our outside filesystem, into the image itself.

❸ The RUN instruction executes a shell command to run inside the container image; in this case, we're installing the Python requirements listed in the file we copied in the prior step.

❹ Copies our Python program into the container image as well.

❺ CMD specifies the command that should be run when the container starts; in this case, we're calling Python to execute our program.

Building and running an instance of a container image from this specification is only a few commands away, as shown in Example 5-3.

Example 5-3. Building an image from a Dockerfile

```
~$ docker build . -t getip:v1.0 ❶
<...build output omitted for brevity...>

~$ docker run --rm getip:v1.0 ❷
Hello from Docker! Your IP address is 104.28.253.219
```

❶ Instructs Docker to build a container image using a Dockerfile found in the current directory, and name it `getip`. It also specifies a tag `v1.0`, so that it can be uniquely identified, should we choose to build multiple versions of the same Docker image.

❷ Instructs Docker to run an instance of the image we just built (and clean it up once it exits).

One of the great advantages of a simple container build system like Docker is that these container images can be run on a production server just as we ran them in the preceding example, without having to worry about installing application dependencies there—they're all bundled in the container image! This makes it much easier to deploy our code to production.

This also makes it easier for other developers to use these images. For instance, you may publish your image to a registry, which is a centralized repository for images that others can download from using the `docker pull` command, shown in Example 5-4.

Example 5-4. Pulling a Docker image from a registry

```
~$ docker pull ghcr.io/nokia/srlinux
Using default tag: latest
latest: Pulling from nokia/srlinux
5021ece2e12c: Pull complete
Digest: sha256:39671cbffaa2e42d584ecacac2070c9fbef0cf5f0295abe13135506375d0e51e
Status: Downloaded newer image for ghcr.io/nokia/srlinux:latest
ghcr.io/nokia/srlinux:latest
```

When an image is published to a registry in this way, other people can simply download it instead of having to build it themselves.

The image used in Example 5-4 is just an example, and you'll see this image in action in an upcoming section. The path to your image depends on the type of registry being used.

Publishing images is a bit more complex than we have time to cover in this chapter, but the `docker push` command can be helpful here. You'll also likely need to set up authentication to your image registry in order to push images. Consult your registry documentation—e.g., Docker Hub (*https://hub.docker.com*)—for more information on how to publish container images.

Sometimes a single container image isn't enough; even the simplest applications can comprise multiple components, each with unique configurations, dependencies, and scalability requirements. Running a single application might require that we instantiate multiple containers and allow them to communicate with one another, but still treat them as a single stack. You can do this by using a Docker Compose file (*https://oreil.ly/L_hiT*). With this, Docker allows you to define a set of services that run together, with particular instructions such as what ports should be opened, and in what order they should be run. This can include a combination of images built using a local Dockerfile you've also defined or a prebuilt container image like `redis`. Example 5-5 shows a Compose file.

Example 5-5. Docker Compose file

```
version: "3.9"
services:
  web:
    build: .
    ports:
      - "8000:5000"
  redis:
    image: "redis:alpine"
```

This is a *very* light introduction to the world of containers and Docker. We explored a bit more of the networking-specific details for container systems like Docker back in Chapter 4, but for a more holistic exploration into Docker, we recommend *Docker: Up & Running*, 3rd Edition, by Sean P. Kane with Karl Matthias (O'Reilly).

dyff

Throughout this book (and indeed, later in this chapter), we use a data format called YAML that allows us to work with structured data in a human-readable way. Although YAML was designed to be human readable, technologies like Kubernetes and Ansible that make heavy use of YAML can result in some pretty unwieldy YAML files.

One common problem when working with large amounts of YAML is understanding changes. Generally, when looking at the difference between two versions of a file, we have to use something like diff. Let's say we have a YAML file that defines a series of switches, each of which has a series of interfaces, each of which includes some configured VLANs. If we add a VLAN to one of these interfaces and view the change in a tool like diff, the output doesn't tell us much about where this change took place (Example 5-6).

Example 5-6. diff output

```
~$ diff before.yaml after.yaml
30c30
<         vlans: [1, 100]
---
>         vlans: [1, 50, 100]
```

This might be OK for some formats, but with YAML, context is important. Knowing where that change is located within the greater YAML data structure is crucial for understanding the impact of the change. Because of YAML's popularity within infrastructure automation circles, tools like dyff (*https://oreil.ly/5Qskd*) have emerged to show changes to a file in a way that preserves the understanding of how YAML works. Example 5-7 illustrates how this tool can show us not only the change in data, but also a path describing where in the data structure that change took place.

Example 5-7. dyff output

```
~$ dyff between -b before.yaml after.yaml

switches.sw02.interfaces.eth3.vlans
  + one list entry added:
    - 50
```

This was only a brief exploration of some of the more relevant development tools you might encounter for network automation. You're likely to encounter far more than we can cover in this section, and new use cases (and tools to solve them) are being discovered all the time. Remain open to incorporating new tools into your repertoire and retiring those that have outlived their usefulness.

In the next section, we explore another important part of building your development environment: tools for simulating network devices and topologies.

Emulation/Simulation Tools

For a long time, if you wanted to build a network lab, you had to buy hardware. Even after the advent of x86 virtualization in the early 2000s, it wasn't until around 2015 that network vendors published VM images for even a portion of their portfolios.

These days, many form factors are available as VMs. While running an NOS as a VM usually involves a few caveats (for instance, certain hardware features are difficult to emulate in software), the majority of use cases related to network automation are a perfect fit for this model. Most of the time when we're looking to develop or test our network automation solutions, we need only a virtual network topology that has the same management interfaces we can expect from "real" equipment. Management APIs and telemetry interfaces like those we discuss in Chapter 10 are typically present in the virtual editions of our favorite NOS, and that's usually all we need.

Now that most vendors have at least one VM image, the need has arisen for tools to help build topologies using these images so that we can (as much as possible) faithfully replicate our "real" production networks in a virtual form-factor by interconnecting multiple devices, establishing routing adjacencies, etc. Doing so makes it easier for us to ensure that the solutions we're building are suitable for production.

For the purposes of integrating tools like these into your development environment, you should look out for the following features:

Configuration as code
> As with other tools in this chapter, it's highly beneficial to use tools that allow their configuration to be represented simply using text files that are easy to read and edit. This allows you to manage these configurations in a version-controlled repository, alongside the rest of your code, scripts, and workflows. Putting a set of config files in a shared repo somewhere is a lot easier than passing around multigigabyte virtual image files. It also allows you to reuse many of the tools covered in this chapter in a continuous integration/continuous delivery (CI/CD) pipeline to automatically validate existing and proposed network changes, which we cover in Chapter 13.

Supports connected topologies
> Being able to run a single instance of an NOS as a VM has some utiliity, but the real power comes from the ability to connect VMs using some of the virtual networking technologies we discussed in Chapter 3, such as bridging. Doing so allows you to not only validate that your solution performs the necessary configuration changes you intend, but also validate the desired operational state and overall connectivity of the topology as a whole.

Supported and accessible

This part of your development environment can be complex, and you don't want to waste time thinking too much about your tools. You want something that works well and is accessible to everyone. It doesn't have to be open source, but you don't want to be spending too many cycles fussing around with flaky tools. You need to use tools that are rock-solid and allow you to get a topology up simply and get on with your work.

Next, we explore some examples of emulation and simulation tools that you're likely to want to add to your repertoire for your network automation journey.

VirtualBox

If you're looking to run VMs of any kind on your laptop, one of your best choices is VirtualBox (*https://www.virtualbox.org*). This open source virtualization platform has been around for a long time. It can run on a variety of operating systems (including Windows, Linux, and macOS) and is free to download. You are, of course, free to use VirtualBox on its own by using the GUI shown in Figure 5-10.

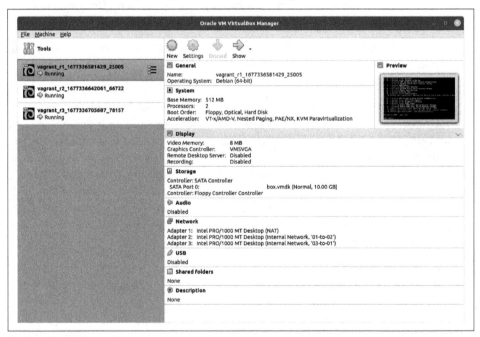

Figure 5-10. VirtualBox

You can download virtual images from just about any network vendor's website and import them into VirtualBox, often with just a few clicks. However, as you'll see in the following section, you can use tools like Vagrant to automate the instantiation and configuration of these VMs.

Vagrant

As we've mentioned, using a platform like VirtualBox directly is certainly possible if you want to emulate your favorite NOS, but this particular workflow has a couple of shortcomings within the context of a proper network development environment:

- Collaborating over changes you might make to your VMs can be difficult. Even "small" VM images can be multiple gigabytes, making them somewhat impractical to share with other developers.

- Even simple configuration changes through the VirtualBox GUI can be tedious. Using this approach to create complex topologies of VMs is quite time-consuming and error prone.

Instead of doing this, you can use a tool like Vagrant (*https://www.vagrantup.com*) to define a full topology in a text file, complete with not only the individual configuration of each VM, but also how they should be connected together. Vagrant integrates with *providers* like VirtualBox to orchestrate the creation and configuration of VMs, following the instructions defined in the configuration file. This *Vagrantfile* uses a Ruby-like syntax for defining VM configurations. Example 5-8 shows a topology containing three interconnected virtual VyOS routers (*https://vyos.io*).

Example 5-8. Vagrantfile describing three-node virtual router topology

```
Vagrant.configure(2) do |config|
    config.vm.box = "vyos/current"        ❶

    config.vm.define "r1" do |r1|         ❷
        r1.vm.host_name = "r1"
        r1.vm.network "private_network",  ❸
                    ip: "192.168.12.11",
                    virtualbox__intnet: "01-to-02"
        r1.vm.network "private_network",
                    ip: "192.168.31.11",
                    virtualbox__intnet: "03-to-01"
    end

    config.vm.define "r2" do |r2|
        r2.vm.host_name = "r2"
        r2.vm.network "private_network",
                    ip: "192.168.23.12",
                    virtualbox__intnet: "02-to-03"
        r2.vm.network "private_network",
                    ip: "192.168.12.12",
                    virtualbox__intnet: "01-to-02"
    end
```

```
config.vm.define "r3" do |r3|
    r3.vm.host_name = "r3"
    r3.vm.network "private_network",
                    ip: "192.168.31.13",
                    virtualbox__intnet: "03-to-01"
    r3.vm.network "private_network",
                    ip: "192.168.23.13",
                    virtualbox__intnet: "02-to-03"
  end
end
```

❶ Specifies the image that should be used for all three of the VMs defined in this Vagrantfile.

❷ Defines the VMs. This `config.vm.define` statement and the block contained within are repeated for each VM in our topology.

❸ Optionally, we can attach networks to each VM. In this case, the network names are chosen in such a way that the three virtual machines are connected in a "triangle" topology.

Vagrant images are distributed in a special format called boxes (*https://oreil.ly/JqfYP*). This is similar to the virtual images you might download to run in VirtualBox natively, but also includes the necessary modifications to use that virtual image in Vagrant. The image in Example 5-8 (`vyos/current`) is already packaged in this format and is also hosted on Vagrant Cloud—Vagrant's official image repository. Vagrant can automatically download and use this image without any modifications, and it should just work.

Unfortunately, most network vendors don't upload their Vagrant boxes to Vagrant Cloud, so you may need to download the Vagrant *.box* file yourself. Worse still, many vendors provide simple VirtualBox-compatible images, which means you may have to do a bit of packaging yourself to get them to work with Vagrant. Fortunately, plenty of guides and tools out there can help in this regard; for instance, the netlab project (*https://oreil.ly/JilA8*) has guides for creating Vagrant boxes from these more general-purpose VM images.

 Some Vagrant boxes also require a Vagrant plug-in to be installed on the VM host, to allow Vagrant to detect and interact properly with the guest operating system. For example, you may need to install the VyOS plug-in via `vagrant plugin install vagrant-vyos` in Example 5-8 to work.

In the directory where this Vagrantfile is located, you need only run `vagrant up`. Once you do this, the relevant image(s) will be downloaded, and three virtual routers will be started and connected to each other as described in the Vagrantfile. Example 5-9 shows the output provided by Vagrant during the instantiation of this virtual topology.

Example 5-9. Starting a virtual topology

```
~$ vagrant up
Bringing machine 'r1' up with 'virtualbox' provider...
Bringing machine 'r2' up with 'virtualbox' provider...
Bringing machine 'r3' up with 'virtualbox' provider...
==> r1: Importing base box 'vyos/current'...
==> r1: Matching MAC address for NAT networking...
==> r1: Checking if box 'vyos/current' version '20230215.03.17' is up to date...
==> r1: Setting the name of the VM: vagrant_r1_1677336581429_25005
==> r1: Clearing any previously set network interfaces...
==> r1: Preparing network interfaces based on configuration...
    r1: Adapter 1: nat
    r1: Adapter 2: intnet
    r1: Adapter 3: intnet
==> r1: Forwarding ports...
    r1: 22 (guest) => 2222 (host) (adapter 1)
==> r1: Booting VM...
==> r1: Waiting for machine to boot. This may take a few minutes...
    r1: SSH address: 127.0.0.1:2222
    r1: SSH username: vyos
    r1: SSH auth method: private key
    r1:
    r1: Vagrant insecure key detected. Vagrant will automatically replace
    r1: this with a newly generated keypair for better security.
    r1:
    r1: Inserting generated public key within guest...
    r1: Removing insecure key from the guest if it's present...
    r1: Key inserted! Disconnecting and reconnecting using new SSH key...
==> r1: Machine booted and ready!
==> r1: Checking for guest additions in VM...
    r1: No guest additions were detected on the base box for this VM! Guest
    r1: additions are required for forwarded ports, shared folders, host only
    r1: networking, and more. If SSH fails on this machine, please install
    r1: the guest additions and repackage the box to continue.
    r1:
    r1: This is not an error message; everything may continue to work properly,
    r1: in which case you may ignore this message.
==> r1: Setting hostname...
==> r1: Configuring and enabling network interfaces...
==> r1: Rsyncing folder: ~/examples/ch05-netdevenv/vagrant/ => /vagrant

[output omitted for similar output from r2 and r3...]
```

You can connect via SSH to any of the VMs in this topology, and even ping between them (thanks to the networking configuration in our Vagrantfile), as shown in Example 5-10.

Example 5-10. Connecting to a virtual topology

```
~$ vagrant ssh r1
Welcome to VyOS!

vyos@r1:~$ ping 192.168.12.12 count 1
PING 192.168.12.12 (192.168.12.12) 56(84) bytes of data.
64 bytes from 192.168.12.12: icmp_seq=1 ttl=64 time=0.431 ms

--- 192.168.12.12 ping statistics ---
1 packets transmitted, 1 received, 0% packet loss, time 0ms
rtt min/avg/max/mdev = 0.431/0.431/0.431/0.000 ms
```

Vagrant also includes a feature called *provisioners* that allows you to perform additional configuration steps after the VMs have been provisioned and booted up. One relevant provisioner for our purposes is `ansible`, which allows you to run an Ansible playbook on your VMs. This can be used to bootstrap your topology with a more real-world configuration, including routing adjacencies and ACLs. You can do this by adding a stanza to the VM configuration in the Vagrantfile, like the one shown in Example 5-11.

Example 5-11. Adding a provisioner to a Vagrant topology

```
config.vm.provision "ansible" do |ansible|
    ansible.playbook = "playbook.yml"
end
```

The benefit, of course, is that you can store both the Ansible playbook and the Vagrantfile in the same version-controlled repository, making it easier for anyone to stand up the same topology, with all of the relevant configurations in place. We explore Ansible in greater detail in Chapter 12. Once you've learned more about Ansible, consider circling back here and adding a playbook to your Vagrant topology!

When you're all done with your Vagrant topology, you can clean it up as simply as you created it, using the single command `vagrant destroy`, as shown in Example 5-12.

Example 5-12. Destroying the vagrant topology

```
~$ vagrant destroy -f
==> r3: Forcing shutdown of VM...
==> r3: Destroying VM and associated drives...
==> r2: Forcing shutdown of VM...
==> r2: Destroying VM and associated drives...
==> r1: Forcing shutdown of VM...
==> r1: Destroying VM and associated drives...
```

Vagrant and VirtualBox represent a powerful combination for creating simulated network topologies from the comfort of your laptop, but sometimes you need something a bit more modern and lightweight. In the next section, we explore a fairly new tool for creating simulated network topologies, using containers instead of VMs.

Containerlab

A great advantage of Vagrant is that it allows VM topologies to be easily orchestrated via text files that can be shared. However, VMs can often consume a lot of system resources. It would be great if you could use container images instead, while retaining many of these benefits.

Fortunately, a relatively new tool called *Containerlab* (*https://oreil.ly/kcahb*) allows you to do this. With Containerlab, you can create lab topologies using a simple text-based format, and then instantiate these topologies using container images. Whereas Vagrant used a Ruby-like syntax for defining the topology configuration, Containerlab uses a simpler YAML-based language in *clab* files, as shown in Example 5-13.

Example 5-13. Containerlab topology clab file

```
name: example-lab            ❶
topology:
  nodes:                     ❷
    srl01:
      kind: srl
      image: ghcr.io/nokia/srlinux
      startup-config: srl1.cfg  ❸

    srl02:
      kind: srl
      image: ghcr.io/nokia/srlinux
      startup-config: srl2.cfg

links:                       ❹
  - endpoints: ["srl01:e1-1", "srl02:e1-1"]
```

❶ The name of the topology as a whole. This allows Containerlab to understand which nodes are in which topology—especially useful for running multiple topologies at once.

❷ The nodes in the topology. We can specify which image the nodes use as well as what they should be named.

❸ An optional parameter specifying a configuration that should be applied to the node once instantiated.

❹ Creates connectivity between the nodes in our topology.

We explore YAML in much greater detail in Chapter 8, so don't worry about the details of this syntax for now. This is just an example to get you started.

You can deploy this topology by using the single command `containerlab deploy`, shown in Example 5-14.

Example 5-14. Containerlab deployment

```
~$ containerlab deploy
INFO[0000] Containerlab v0.36.1 started
INFO[0000] Parsing & checking topology file: topology1.clab.yaml
INFO[0000] Creating lab directory: /examples/ch05-netdevenv/containerlab/clab-srl02
INFO[0000] Creating docker network: Name="clab", IPv4Subnet="172.20.20.0/24", IPv6Subnet="2001:172:20:20::/64"
INFO[0000] Creating container: "srl1"
INFO[0000] Creating container: "srl2"
INFO[0001] Creating virtual wire: srl1:e1-1 <--> srl2:e1-1
INFO[0001] Running postdeploy actions for Nokia SR Linux 'srl2' node
INFO[0001] Running postdeploy actions for Nokia SR Linux 'srl1' node
INFO[0010] Adding containerlab host entries to /etc/hosts file
+---+--------------+--------------+------------------------+------+---------+------------------+--------------------------+
| # |     Name     | Container ID |         Image          | Kind |  State  |   IPv4 Address   |       IPv6 Address       |
+---+--------------+--------------+------------------------+------+---------+------------------+--------------------------+
| 1 | clab-srl02-srl1 | ea5012df1061 | ghcr.io/nokia/srlinux | srl  | running | 172.20.20.2/24 | 2001:172:20:20::2/64 |
| 2 | clab-srl02-srl2 | 08b9f9ec660a | ghcr.io/nokia/srlinux | srl  | running | 172.20.20.3/24 | 2001:172:20:20::3/64 |
+---+--------------+--------------+------------------------+------+---------+------------------+--------------------------+
```

You can connect via SSH (or other available methods) by using the management address in the preceding table, as shown in Example 5-15.

Example 5-15. Connecting to Containerlab topology via SSH

```
~$ ssh admin@172.20.20.2

A:srl1# ping network-instance default 192.168.0.1 -c 1
Using network instance default
PING 192.168.0.1 (192.168.0.1) 56(84) bytes of data.
64 bytes from 192.168.0.1: icmp_seq=1 ttl=64 time=10.5 ms

--- 192.168.0.1 ping statistics ---
1 packets transmitted, 1 received, 0% packet loss, time 0ms
rtt min/avg/max/mdev = 10.518/10.518/10.518/0.000 ms
```

However, Containerlab is just orchestrating Docker containers behind the scenes, so you can use `docker exec` to access the CLI of these nodes as well, as shown in Example 5-16.

Example 5-16. Connecting to Containerlab topology via docker exec

```
~$ docker ps
CONTAINER ID   IMAGE                  COMMAND               CREATED        STATUS ...
08b9f9ec660a   ghcr.io/nokia/srlinux  "/tini -- fixuid -q …" 7 minutes ago  Up 7   ...
ea5012df1061   ghcr.io/nokia/srlinux  "/tini -- fixuid -q …" 7 minutes ago  Up 7   ...

~$ docker exec -it clab-srl02-srl1 sr_cli
Using configuration file(s): []
Welcome to the srlinux CLI.
A:srl1#
```

You can also use the `containerlab graph` subcommand to start a local web server that allows you to inspect your running topology in the browser (Figure 5-11).

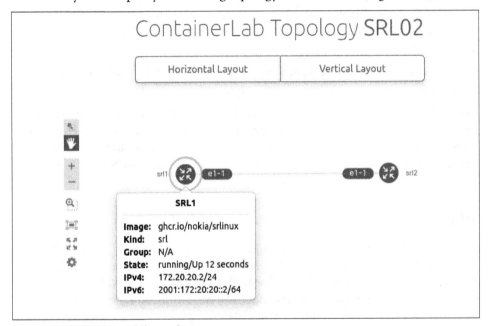

Figure 5-11. Containerlab graph

While the idea of running a network topology by using containers is still fairly new, many vendors provide container images for learning purposes. Such a form factor for learning, or validating that automation solutions work as we expect, is proving to be an invaluable recent addition to our repertoire.

Other Tools

This section lists a few other popular tools for simulating network topologies that we can't cover in detail here. They all have varying capabilities and design goals but may be worth knowing about:

GNS3 (https://www.gns3.com)
A popular network emulation platform that includes a great interface for drag-and-drop building of virtual topologies. Historically, it relied on emulation software called *dynamips*, which was specifically created to emulate Cisco hardware. However, it has since expanded greatly with many new features, including the ability to run non-Cisco images.

EVE-NG (https://www.eve-ng.net)
Another great network emulation platform with a web-based UI. Includes free and paid versions.

Terraform (https://www.terraform.io)
A popular tool for IaC automation. Particularly useful for building cloud-based labs. We explore Terraform in much greater detail in Chapter 12.

Hopefully, this chapter has provided insight into the kinds of tools and techniques you can use in your own network automation development environment. Again, this is an ever-changing space, so take this chapter not as an exhaustive checklist, but as a source of inspiration for building out an environment that works for you and your team.

Summary

The best network development environment is the one that works for you. The tools and techniques discussed here are just some popular examples, and the environment you construct for yourself will be influenced heavily by your own background, the programming and automation technologies you work with, and the organization and team you're a part of. Play around with different options, and be open to adapting when new tools become available.

In the chapters to follow, we're going to make heavy use of this environment, diving into concepts like Python, Go, data formats, and templates.

CHAPTER 6
Python

As a network engineer, there has never been a better time for you to learn to automate and write code. As we noted in Chapter 1, the network industry is fundamentally changing. It is a fact that networking had not changed much from the late 1990s to about 2010, both architecturally and operationally. In that span of time, network engineers undoubtedly typed in the same CLI commands hundreds, if not thousands, of times to configure and troubleshoot network devices. Why the madness?

It is specifically around the operations of a network that learning to read and write some code starts to make sense. In fact, scripting or writing a few lines of code to gather information on the network, or to make changes, isn't new at all. It's been done for years. Some engineers took on this feat—programming in their language of choice, learning to work with raw text using complex parsing and regular expressions, and querying SNMP MIBs in a script. If you've ever attempted this yourself, you know firsthand that it's possible, but working with regular expressions and parsing text is time-consuming and tedious.

Luckily, things are starting to move in the right direction, and the barrier to entry for network automation is more accessible than ever. We are seeing advances from network vendors, but also in the open source tooling available for automating the network, both of which we cover in this book. For example, there are now network device APIs, vendor- and community-supported Python libraries, and freely available open source tools that give you and every other network engineer access to a growing ecosystem to jump-start your network automation journey. This ultimately means that you have to write less code than you would have in the past, and less code means faster development and fewer bugs.

Before we dive into the basics of Python, we'll consider one more important question because it always comes up in conversations among network engineers: *should network engineers learn to code?*

Should Network Engineers Learn to Code?

Unfortunately, you aren't getting a definitive *yes* or *no* from us. Clearly, we have a full chapter on Python and another on Go, and plenty of examples throughout the book on how to use Python or Go to communicate to network devices via network APIs and extend DevOps tools like Ansible and Terraform, so we definitely think learning the basics of any programming language is valuable. We also think it'll become an even more valuable skill as the network and IT industries continue to transform at such a rapid pace, and we happen to think Python is a pretty great first choice.

 We consider Python a great first choice when it comes to network automation for several reasons. First, Python is a dynamically typed language that allows you to create and use Python objects (such as variables and functions) where and when needed, meaning they don't need to be defined before you start using them. This simplifies getting started. Second, Python is also super readable. It's common to see conditional statements like `if device in device_list:`, and in that statement, you can easily decipher that we are simply checking to see if a device is *in* a particular list of devices. Another reason is that network vendors and open source projects are building a great set of libraries and tools using Python. This just adds to the benefit of learning to program with Python.

The real question, though, is *should every network engineer know how to read and write a basic script*? The answer is a definite *yes*. Now *should every network engineer become a software developer*? Absolutely not. Many engineers will gravitate more toward one discipline than the next, and maybe some network engineers do transition to become developers, but all types of engineers, not just network engineers, *should not* fear trying to read through some Python or Ruby, or even more advanced languages like C, Go, or Rust. System administrators have done fairly well already with using scripting as a tool to allow them to do their jobs more efficiently by using bash scripts, Python, Ruby, and PowerShell.

On the other hand, this hasn't been the case for network administrators (which is a major reason for this book!). As the industry progresses and engineers evolve, it's realistic for you, as a network engineer, to be more *DevOps oriented*, in that you end up somewhere in the middle—not as a developer, but also not as a traditional CLI-only network engineer. You could end up using open source configuration management and automation tools and then add a little code as necessary (and if needed) to accomplish and automate the workflows and tasks in your specific environment.

Unless your organization warrants it based on size, scale, compliance, or control, it's not common or recommended to write custom software *for everything* and build a home-grown automation platform. It's not an efficient use of time. We do recommend that you understand the components involved in programming, software development, and especially fundamentals such as core data types that are common to all tools and languages, as we cover in this chapter focused on Python.

So we know the industry is changing, devices have APIs, and it makes sense to start the journey to learn to write some code. This chapter provides you with the building blocks to go from 0 to 70 as you start your Python journey. Throughout the rest of this chapter, we start with the basics of Python (e.g., data types and flow logic), and then explore more advanced topics such as functions, classes, modules, and other patterns.

Get ready—you are about to jump in and learn some Python!

This chapter's sole focus is to introduce foundational Python concepts to network engineers looking to learn Python to augment their existing skill sets. It is not intended to provide an exhaustive education for full-time developers to write production-quality Python software. A useful book to go deeper on Python is *Fluent Python* by Luciano Ramalho (O'Reilly).

Additionally, the concepts covered in this chapter are heavily relevant outside the scope of Python. For example, you *must* understand concepts like loops and data types—which we explore here—to work with tools like Ansible, Nornir, and Terraform.

Finally, once you finish this chapter, you might realize that we didn't explore many real-world network automation use cases. This is intentional; as with any programming language, sometimes entire books are often not enough to cover even the basics, and we aim to give a sufficient foundation for our purposes in a single chapter. So, in this chapter we focus solely on this foundation. Chapter 10 then revisits many of these concepts to tackle some real-world network automation tasks.

Using the Python Interactive Interpreter

The *Python interactive interpreter* isn't always known by those just starting out to learn to program or even those who have been developing in other languages, but it is a tool that everyone should know and learn before trying to create standalone executable scripts.

The interpreter is instrumental to developers of all experience levels. This tool, also commonly known as the Python *shell*, is used as a learning platform for beginners, but it's also used by the most experienced developers to test and get real-time feedback without having to write a full program or script.

The Python shell, or interpreter, is found on nearly all native Linux distributions as well as many of the more modern network OSs from vendors including, but not limited to, Cisco, HPE, Juniper, Cumulus, and Arista. To access the Python interactive interpreter, you simply open a Linux terminal window, or SSH to a modern network device, type in the command python3, and hit Enter.

 All examples throughout this chapter that denote a Linux terminal command start with $. While you're at the Python shell, all lines and commands start with >>>. Additionally, all the examples are from a system running Ubuntu 20.04 LTS and Python 3.8.12.

Since the first version of this book was published, Python 2.7 has reached End of Life. As a result, this chapter now exclusively uses Python 3 syntax and libraries.

For an explicit usage of Python 3 across the book, we use python3 to run Python scripts and launch the interactive interpreter, disambiguating with the python alias, which could still be pointing to Python 2.

After entering the python3 command and hitting Enter, you are taken directly into the shell. While in the shell, you start writing Python code immediately! There is no text editor, no IDE, and no prerequisites to getting started:

```
$ python3
Python 3.8.12 (default, Feb 26 2022, 00:05:23)
[GCC 10.2.1 20210110] on linux
Type "help", "copyright", "credits" or "license" for more information.
```

Although we jump into much more detail on Python throughout this chapter, we'll take a quick look at a few examples right now to see the power of the Python interpreter. Let's start by simply creating a variable called hostname and assigning it the value of ROUTER_1:

```
>>> hostname = 'ROUTER_1'
```

Notice that you do not need to declare the variable first or define that hostname is going to be of type string. This is a departure from some programming languages such as C and Java, and a reason Python is called a dynamic language.

Now, you can print the variable `hostname`:

```
>>> print(hostname)
ROUTER_1
>>>
>>> hostname
'ROUTER_1'
```

Once you've created the variable, you can easily print it using the `print` command, but while in the shell, you can also display the value of `hostname` or any variable by just typing in the name of the variable and pressing Enter. One difference between these two methods is that when you use the `print` statement, characters such as the end of line, or EOL (\n), are interpreted, but are not when you're not using the `print` statement.

For example, using `print` interprets the \n and a new line is printed, but when you're just typing the variable name into the shell and hitting Enter, the \n is not interpreted and is just displayed to the terminal:

```
>>> banner = "\n  WELCOME TO ROUTER_1  \n"
>>>
>>> print(banner)

  WELCOME TO ROUTER_1

>>>
>>> banner
'\n  WELCOME TO ROUTER_1  \n'
```

Can you see the difference?

When you are validating or testing, the Python shell is a great tool to use. In the preceding examples, you may have noticed that single quotes and double quotes are both used. Now you may be thinking, could they be used together on the same line? Let's not speculate about it; let's use the Python shell to test it out:

```
>>> hostname = 'ROUTER_1"
  File "<stdin>", line 1
    hostname = 'ROUTER_1"
                        ^
SyntaxError: EOL while scanning string literal
```

And just like that, you verify that Python supports both single and double quotes, and learn that they cannot be used together.

Most examples throughout this chapter continue to use the Python interpreter—feel free to follow along and test them out as they're covered. We'll continue to use the Python interpreter as we review Python data types, with a specific focus on networking.

Understanding Python Data Types

This section provides an overview of various Python data types, including strings, numbers (integers and floats), booleans, lists, and dictionaries. This section also touches upon tuples and sets.

The content on strings, lists, and dictionaries is broken into two parts. The first is an introduction to the data type and the second covers some of its built-in methods. As you'll see, *methods* are natively part of Python, making it extremely easy for developers to manipulate and work with each respective data type.

For example, a method called `upper` that takes a string and converts it to all uppercase letters can be executed with the statement, `"router1".upper()`, which returns ROUTER1. We show many more examples of using methods throughout this chapter.

The sections on integers and booleans provide an overview to show you how to use mathematical operators and boolean expressions while writing code in Python.

Finally, we close the section on data types by providing a brief introduction to tuples and sets. They are more advanced data types, but we feel they were still worth covering in an introduction to Python.

Table 6-1 describes and highlights each data type covered in this chapter. You can use this as a reference throughout the chapter.

Table 6-1. Python data types

Data type	Description	Short name (type)	Characters	Example
String	Series of any characters surrounded by quotes.	`str`	`""`	`hostname="nycr01"`
Integer	Whole numbers represented without quotes.	`int`	n/a	`eos_qty=5`
Float	Floating-point number (decimals).	`float`	n/a	`cpu_util=52.33`
Boolean	Either `True` or `False` (no quotes).	`bool`	n/a	`is_switchport=True`
List	Ordered sequence of values. Values can be any data type.	`list`	`[]`	`vendors=['cisco', 'juni per', 'arista', 'cisco']`
Dictionary	Ordered collection of key-value pairs.	`dict`	`{}`	`facts={"vendor":"cisco", "platform":"catalyst", "os":"ios"}`
Set	Unordered collection of unique elements.	`set`	`set()`	`set(vendors) returns {'aris ta', 'cisco', 'juniper'}`
Tuple	Ordered and unchangeable sequence of values.	`tuple`	`()`	`ipaddr=('10.1.1.1', 24)`

Let's get started and take a look at Python strings.

Strings

Strings—a sequence of characters enclosed by quotes—are arguably the most well-known data type in all programming languages.

Although strings look like a simple data type, they are slightly more complex. A string can represent two kinds of data: *text* and *bytes*. In Python 2, both types were represented as a `str`, but in Python 3, each is a separate and incompatible type.

You can go deeper on the differences (*https://oreil.ly/RuNfW*), but in short, in Python 2 strings are ASCII characters and in Python 3 strings are Unicode characters (by default UTF-8), so if you receive *bytes* you will need to *encode* them to use string methods, using one of the available encode types, such as UTF-8, UTF-16, ASCII, or others.

Earlier in the chapter, we presented a few basic examples for creating variables that were of type `str`. Let's examine what else you need to know when starting to use strings.

First, you'll define two new variables that are both strings, `final` and `ipaddr`:

```
>>> final = 'The IP address of router1 is: '
>>>
>>> ipaddr = '192.0.2.1'
```

You can use the built-in function called `type` to verify the data type of any given object in Python:

```
>>> type(final)
<class 'str'>
```

This is how you can easily check the type of one object, which is often helpful in troubleshooting code, especially if it's code you didn't write.

Next, let's look at how to combine, add, or *concatenate* strings:

```
>>> final + ipaddr
'The IP address of router1 is: 192.0.2.1'
```

So far, you've created two new variables: `final` and `ipaddr`. Each is a string. After both are created, you *concatenate* them using the + operator, and finally print them out. Fairly easy, right?

The same could be done even if `final` is not a predefined object:

```
>>> print('The IP address of router1 is: ' + ipaddr)
The IP address of router1 is: 192.0.2.1
```

Using built-in methods of strings

To view the available built-in methods for strings, you use the built-in `dir()` function while in the Python shell. You first create any variable that is a string or use the formal data type name of `str` and pass it as an argument to `dir()` to view the available methods. You can always find more detailed information in the Python official docs (*https://oreil.ly/ICC4d*).

`dir()` can be used on any Python object, not just strings, as we show throughout this chapter.

```
>>> dir(str)
# output has been omitted
['__add__', '__class__', '__contains__', '__delattr__', '__doc__',
'endswith', 'expandtabs', 'find', 'format', 'index', 'isalnum', 'isalpha',
'isdigit', 'islower', 'isspace', 'istitle', 'isupper', 'join', 'lower',
'lstrip', 'replace', 'rstrip', 'split', 'splitlines', 'startswith',
'strip', 'upper']
```

To keep the output clean and simplify examples throughout the chapter, we add an *omitted* comment in some outputs. In this example, we've removed some objects that start and end with double underscores (_), also known as *dunders*. These internal methods are used to implement some *magic* operations without explicitly calling them.

For instance, as you will see in "Understanding Python Classes" on page 230, when an object is created from a class, there is an implicit call to the `__init__()` method (the *constructor*) and it returns an object. By overwriting this dunder, you can customize how your objects will be created.

To reiterate what we said earlier, it's possible to also pass any string to the `dir()` function to produce the same output as previously. For example, if you define a variable such as `hostname = 'ROUTER'`, `hostname` can be passed to `dir()`—that is, `dir(hostname)`—producing the same output as `dir(str)` to determine what methods are available for strings.

Let's take a look at several of the string methods, including count(), endswith(), startswith(), format(), isdigit(), join(), lower(), upper(), and strip().

As we review each method, you should be asking yourself two key questions. What value is returned from the method? And what action is the method performing on the original object?

Using the upper() and lower() methods. Using the upper() and lower() methods is helpful when you need to compare strings that do not need to be case-sensitive. For example, maybe you need to accept a variable that is the name of an interface such as Ethernet1/1, but want to also allow the user to enter ethernet1/1. The best way to compare these is to use upper() or lower():

```
>>> interface = 'Ethernet1/1'
>>>
>>> interface.lower()
'ethernet1/1'
>>>
>>> interface.upper()
'ETHERNET1/1'
```

You can see that when you're using a method, the format is to enter the object name, or string in this case, and then append *.methodname()*:

- The period (.) indicates accessing a method (or an attribute) of an object.
- methodname is the name of the method.
- The parentheses, (), indicate calling the method. As you will see soon, it could take arguments.

Next, after executing interface.lower(), notice that ethernet1/1 is printed to the terminal. This is telling you that ethernet1/1 was *returned* when lower() was executed. The same holds true for upper(). When something is returned, you also have the ability to assign it as the value to a new or existing variable:

```
>>> intf_lower = interface.lower()
>>>
>>> print(intf_lower)
ethernet1/1
```

In this example, you can see how to use the method, but also assign the data being returned to a variable.

What about the original variable called interface? Let's see what, if anything, changed with interface:

```
>>> print(interface)
Ethernet1/1
```

Since you are exploring the first examples, it still may not be clear what you're looking for to see if something changed in the original variable interface, but you do know that it still holds the value of Ethernet1/1, which hasn't changed. Don't worry, you'll see plenty of examples of when the original object is modified throughout this chapter.

Using the startswith() and endswith() methods. As you can probably guess, starts with() is used to verify whether a string starts with a certain sequence of characters, and endswith() is used to verify whether a string ends with a certain sequence of characters:

```
>>> ipaddr = '10.100.20.5'
>>>
>>> ipaddr.startswith('10')
True
>>>
>>> ipaddr.startswith('100')
False
>>>
>>> ipaddr.endswith('.5')
True
```

The lower() and upper() methods return a string, which is a modified string with all lowercase or uppercase letters. However, startswith() and endswith() do not return a string, but rather a boolean (bool) object. As you'll learn later in this chapter, boolean values are True and False. The startswith() method returns True if the sequence of characters being passed in matches the respective starting or ending sequence of the object. Otherwise, it returns False.

 For the boolean values True and False, no quotes are used, and the first letter must be capitalized. Booleans are covered in more detail later in the chapter.

Using these methods proves to be valuable when you're looking to verify the start or end of a string. Maybe you want to verify the first or fourth octet of an IPv4 address or verify an interface name, as you did in the previous example using lower(). Rather than assume that a user of a script is going to enter the full name, it's advantageous to do a check on the first two characters to allow the user to input ethernet1/1, eth1/1, or et1/1.

For this check you'll combine methods, or use the return value of one method as the base string object for the second method:

```
>>> interface = 'Eth1/1'
>>>
>>> interface.lower().startswith('et')
True
```

You verify that it is an Ethernet interface by first executing lower(), which returns eth1/1, and then the boolean check is performed to see whether eth1/1 starts with et. And, clearly, it does.

Of course, other parts could be invalid beyond the eth in an interface string object, but the point is that methods can be easily used together.

Using the strip() method. Some legacy network devices still don't have APIs. If you want to write a script, it's plausible that at some point you'll try it out on an older CLI-based device. If you do this, you'll be sure to encounter globs of raw text coming back from the device—this could be the result of any show command from the output of show interfaces to a full show running-config.

When you need to store or simply print something, you may not want any whitespace wrapping the object you want to use or see. To be consistent with previous examples, let's say this is an IP address.

What if the object you're working with has the value of " 10.1.50.1 " including the whitespace. The methods startswith() or endswith() don't work because of the spaces. For these situations, you use strip() to remove the whitespace:

```
>>> ipaddr = '    10.1.50.1    '
>>>
>>> ipaddr.strip()
'10.1.50.1'
```

Using strip() returns the object without any spaces on both sides. Examples aren't shown for lstrip() or rstrip(), but they are two other built-in methods for strings that remove whitespace specifically on the left or right side of a string object, respectively.

Using the isdigit() method. While working with strings, you'll need to verify that the string object is a number at times. Technically, integers are a different data type (covered in the next section), but numbers can still be values in strings.

Using isdigit() makes it extremely straightforward to see whether the character or string is actually a *digit*:

```
>>> ten = '10'
>>>
>>> ten.isdigit()
True
>>>
>>> bogus = '10a'
>>>
>>> bogus.isdigit()
False
```

Just as with startswith(), isdigit() also returns a boolean. It returns True if the value is an integer; otherwise, it returns False.

Using the count() method. Imagine working with a binary number—maybe it's to calculate an IP address or subnet mask. Although some built-in libraries can do binary-to-decimal conversion, what if you just want to *count* how many 1s or 0s are in a given string? You can use count() to do this for you:

```
>>> octet = '11111000'
>>>
>>> octet.count('1')
5
```

This example shows how easy it is to use count(). This method, however, returns an int (integer), unlike any of the previous examples.

When using count(), you are not limited to sending a single character as a parameter either:

```
>>> octet.count('111')
1
>>>
>>> test_string = "Don't you wish you started programming a little earlier?"
>>>
```

```
>>> test_string.count('you')
2
```

Using the format() method. You saw earlier how to concatenate strings. Imagine needing to create a sentence, or better yet, a command to send to a network device that is built from several strings or variables. How would you *format* the string, or CLI command?

Let's use `ping` as an example and assume that the command you need to create is the following:

```
ping 8.8.8.8 vrf management
```

 The examples in this chapter use generic network CLI commands, as no actual device connections are being made. Thus, they map to no specific vendor and are the de facto "industry standard" examples that work on various systems including Cisco IOS, Cisco NXOS, Arista EOS, and many others.

If you were writing a script from the preceding command, you could identify two variables: `'8.8.8.8'` (the IP address) and `management` (the VRF name). These variables can become user-input parameters that change at every execution.

One way to build the string is to start with the following:

```
>>> ipaddr = '8.8.8.8'
>>> vrf = 'management'
>>>
>>> ping = 'ping' + ipaddr + 'vrf' + vrf
>>>
>>> print(ping)
ping8.8.8.8vrfmanagement
```

You see the spacing is incorrect, so you have two options: add spaces to your input objects or within the `ping` object. Let's try adding them within `ping`:

```
>>> ping = 'ping' + ' ' + ipaddr + ' ' + 'vrf ' + vrf
>>>
>>> print(ping)
ping 8.8.8.8 vrf management
```

As you can see, this works quite well and is not too complicated, but as the strings or commands get longer, dealing with all the quotes and spaces can get messy. Using the `format()` method can simplify this:

```
>>> ping = 'ping {} vrf {}'.format(ipaddr, vrf)
>>>
>>> print(ping)
ping 8.8.8.8 vrf management
```

The format() method takes multiple arguments, which are inserted between the curly braces ({}) found within the string. Notice that format() is being used on a raw string, unlike in the previous examples.

It's possible to use any of the string methods on both variables or raw strings. This is true for any other data type and its built-in methods as well.

The next example shows using the format() method with a pre-created string object (variable), in contrast to the previous example:

```
>>> ping = 'ping {} vrf {}'
>>>
>>> command = ping.format(ipaddr, vrf)
>>>
>>> print(command)
ping 8.8.8.8 vrf management
```

This scenario is more likely, in that you would have a predefined command in a Python script with users inputting two arguments, and the output is the final command string that gets pushed to a network device.

Another option to concatenate strings is to use the % operator. One example for inserting strings (s) is provided here:

```
>>> hostname = 'r5'
>>> interface = 'Eth1/1'
>>>
>>> test = 'Device %s has one interface: %s' % (hostname,
    interface)
>>> print(test)
Device r5 has one interface: Eth1/1
```

Since Python 3.6, a new formatting option for strings is available: *f-strings*, which has an f at the beginning of the string and uses {} to contain the expressions that will be *rendered* to strings. This formatting option has gained a lot of popularity within the Python community because it helps visualize where the variables are used:

```
>>> f'ping {ipaddr} vrf {vrf}'
'ping 8.8.8.8 vrf management'
```

When using *f-strings* for debugging, you can use = after the object name to populate the name of the object rendered:

```
>>> f'Rendering command with: {ipaddr=} {vrf=}'
"Rendering command with: ipaddr='8.8.8.8' vrf='management'"
```

Using the join() and split() methods. We saved `join()` and `split()` for last since they include working with another data type called `list`.

 Although lists are formally covered later in this chapter, we include a brief introduction here to show the `join()` and `split()` methods for string objects.

Lists are exactly what they sound like. They are a *list* of objects, and each object is called an *element*. The elements in a list don't have to be of the same data type.

In an environment with five routers, you might have a list of hostnames:

```
>>> hostnames = ['r1', 'r2', 'r3', 'r4', 'r5']
```

You can also build a list of commands to send to a network device to make a configuration change. The next example is a list of commands to shut down an Ethernet interface on a switch:

```
>>> commands = ['config t', 'interface Ethernet1/1', 'shutdown']
```

Building a list like this is common, but if you're using a traditional CLI-based network device, you might not be able to send a `list` object directly to the device. The device may require strings to be sent (or individual commands).

`join()` is one such method that can take a list and create a string, but insert required characters, if needed, between them.

Remember that \n is the EOL character. When sending commands to a device, you may need to insert \n between commands to allow the device to render a new line for the next command.

If you take `commands` from the previous example, you can see how to leverage `join()` to create a single string with a \n inserted between each command:

```
>>> '\n'.join(commands)
'config t\ninterface Ethernet1/1\nshutdown'
```

Another practical example is when using an API such as NX-API that exists on Cisco Nexus switches. Cisco gives the option to send a string of commands, but they need to be separated by a semicolon (;). To do this, you use the same approach:

```
>>> ' ; '.join(commands)
'config t ; interface Ethernet1/1 ; shutdown'
```

In this example, you add a space before and after the semicolon, but it's the same overall approach.

In these examples, a semicolon and an EOL character are used as the separator, but you don't need to use any characters at all. It's possible to concatenate the elements in the list without inserting any characters, like this: `''.join(list_name)`.

You've learned how to use `join()` to create a string out of a list, but what if you need to do the exact opposite and create a list from a string? One option is to use the `split()` method.

Let's start with the previously generated string and convert it back to a list:

```
>>> commands = 'config t ; interface Ethernet1/1 ; shutdown'
>>>
>>> cmds_list = commands.split(' ; ')
>>>
>>> print(cmds_list)
['config t', 'interface Ethernet1/1', 'shutdown']
```

This shows how simple it is to take a string object and create a list from it. Another common example for networking is to take an IP address (string) and convert it to a list by using `split()`, creating a list of four elements—one element per octet:

```
>>> ipaddr = '10.1.20.30'
>>>
>>> ipaddr.split('.')
['10', '1', '20', '30']
```

That covers the basics of working with Python strings. Let's move on to the next data type, which is numbers.

Numbers

In this section, we don't spend much time on different types of numbers such as floats (decimal numbers) or imaginary numbers (complex numbers with a zero real part), but we do briefly look at the data type denoted as `int`, better known as an *integer*. Frankly, this is because most people understand numbers, and there aren't built-in methods that make sense to cover at this point. Rather than cover built-in methods for integers, we take a look at using mathematical operators while in the Python shell.

Decimal numbers in Python are referred to as *floats*. Remember, you can always verify the data type by using the built-in function `type()`:

```
>>> cpu = 41.3
>>>
>>> type(cpu)
<class 'float'>
```

To add numbers, nothing fancy is needed; just add them:

```
>>> 5 + 3
8
>>> a = 1
>>> b = 2
>>> a + b
3
```

A counter might be needed as you are looping through a sequence of objects. You may want to say counter = 1, perform some type of operation, and then do counter = counter + 1. While this is perfectly functional and works, it is more idiomatic in Python to perform the operation as counter += 1, as shown here:

```
>>> counter = 1
>>> counter = counter + 1
>>> counter
2
>>>
>>> counter = 5
>>> counter += 5
>>> counter
10
```

Like addition, subtraction requires nothing special. Let's dive right into an example:

```
>>> 100 - 90
10
>>> count = 50
>>> count - 20
30
```

When multiplying, yet again, there is no difference:

```
>>> 100 * 50
5000
>>>
>>> print(2 * 25)
50
```

The nice thing about the multiplication operator (*) is that you can also use it on strings. You may want to format something and make it nice and pretty:

```
>>> print('=' * 50)
==================================================
```

The preceding example is basic but powerful. Not knowing this is possible, you may be tempted to print one line a time and print a string with the command print(==================), but in reality after learning this and a few other tips covered later in the chapter, pretty-printing text data becomes much simpler.

If you haven't performed any math by hand in recent years, division may seem like a nightmare. As expected, though, it is no different from the previous three mathematical operations reviewed—well, sort of.

To perform a division operation, you still begin by entering 10 / 2, or 100 / 50, and so on, like so:

```
>>> 100 / 50
2
```

These examples are probably what you expected to see.

However, you might see a difference in the result, as compared to manual division:

```
>>> 12 / 10
1
```

As you know, the number 10 goes into 12 *one* time. This is called the *quotient*, so here the quotient is equal to 1. What is not displayed or returned is the *remainder*. To see the remainder in Python, you must use the %, or modulus, operation.

```
>>> 12 % 10
2
```

This means to fully calculate the result of a division problem, you use both the / and % operators.

You can convert (or cast) an integer to a string by using str(10), and also do the opposite, converting a string to an integer by using int('10'):

```
>>> str(10)
'10'
>>> int('10')
10
```

That was a brief look at how to work with numbers in Python. We'll now move on to booleans.

Booleans

Boolean objects, otherwise known as objects that are of type bool in Python, are fairly straightforward. Let's first review the basics of general boolean logic by looking at a *truth table* (Table 6-2).

Table 6-2. Boolean truth table

A	B	A and B	A or B	Not A
False	**False**	False	False	True
False	**True**	False	True	True
True	**False**	False	True	False
True	**True**	True	True	False

Notice that all values in the table are either True or False. This is because with boolean logic, all values are reduced to either True or False. This makes booleans easy to understand.

Since boolean values can be only True or False, all expressions also evaluate to either True or False. You can see in the table that *both* values, for A and B, need to be True, for "A and B" to evaluate to True. And "A or B" evaluates to True when *any* value (A or B) is True. You can also see that when you take the *NOT* of a boolean value, it calculates the inverse of that value. This is seen clearly as NOT False yields True and NOT True yields False.

From a Python perspective, nothing is different. We still have only two boolean values: True and False. To assign one of these values to a variable within Python, you must enter it just as you see it (with a capitalized first letter, and without quotes):

```
>>> exists = True
>>>
>>> exists
True
>>>
>>> exists = true
Traceback (most recent call last):
  File "<stdin>", line 1, in <module>
NameError: name 'true' is not defined
```

As you can see, using booleans is quite simple. Based on the real-time feedback of the Python interpreter, you can see that using a lowercase *t* doesn't work when you're trying to assign the value of True to a variable.

Here are a few more examples of using boolean expressions while in the Python interpreter:

```
>>> True and True
True
>>>
>>> True or False
True
>>>
>>> False or False
False
```

In the next example, these same conditions are evaluated, assigning boolean values to variables:

```
>>> value1 = True
>>> value2 = False
>>>
>>> value1 and value2
False
>>>
>>> value1 or value2
True
```

Notice that boolean expressions are also not limited to two objects:

```
>>> value3 = True
>>> value4 = True
>>>
>>> value1 and value2 and value3 and value4
False
>>>
>>> value1 and value3 and value4
True
```

When extracting information from a network device, using booleans for a quick check is common. Is the interface a routed port? Is the management interface configured? Is the device reachable? While a complex operation may be required to answer each of those questions, the result is stored as True or False.

The opposite of those questions would be, is the interface a switched port or is the device not reachable? Having variables or objects for each question wouldn't make sense, but we could use the not operator, since we know the not operation returns the inverse of a boolean value.

Let's take a look at using not in an example:

```
>>> not False
>>> True
>>>
>>> is_layer3 = True
>>> not is_layer3
False
```

This example uses a variable called is_layer3. It is set to True, indicating that an interface is a Layer 3 port. If you take the not of is_layer3, you would then know if it is a Layer 2 port.

We introduce conditionals (if-else statements) later in the chapter, but based on the logic needed, you may need to know whether an interface is in fact Layer 3. If so, you would have something like if is_layer3:, but if you needed to perform an action if the interface was Layer 2, then you would use if not is_layer3:.

In addition to using the and and or operands, the *equal to* (==) and *does not equal to* (!=) expressions are used to generate a boolean object. With these expressions, you can do a comparison, or check, to see whether two or more objects are (or not) equal to one another:

```
>>> True == True
True
>>> True != False
True
>>> 'network' == 'network'
True
>>> 'network' == 'no_network'
False
```

Empty Objects

Python offers a simple and readable way to *evaluate* whether an object is empty. If the object is not empty, the evaluation will return `True`, and if empty, will return `False`. In the following example, you can notice how easy it is to read the code `if not devices:`. It's almost literal: if there are no `devices`, the assessment will match the `if` statement:

```
>>> devices = []
>>> if not devices:
...     print('devices is empty')
...
devices is empty
>>>
>>> hostname = 'something'
>>>
>>> if hostname:
...     print('hostname is not empty')
...
hostname is not empty
```

However, even though this *evaluation* usually matches what we understand as *emptiness*, the actual logic applied is the boolean evaluation of the object, implemented via the `__bool__` dunder method, and could be customized for our own class, as we will explore in "Understanding Python Classes" on page 230.

After a quick look at working with boolean objects, operands, and expressions, we are ready to cover working with Python lists.

Lists

You had a brief introduction to lists when we covered the string built-in methods called `join()` and `split()`. This section covers lists in a bit more detail.

Lists are the object type called `list`, and at their most basic level are an ordered sequence of objects. The examples from earlier in the chapter when we looked at the `join()` method with strings are provided again next to provide a quick refresher on how to create a list. Those examples were lists of strings, but it's also possible to have lists of any other data type as well, which you'll see shortly.

```
>>> hostnames = ['r1', 'r2', 'r3', 'r4', 'r5']
>>> commands = ['config t', 'interface Ethernet1/1', 'shutdown']
```

Here is a list of objects in which each object is a different data type:

```
>>> new_list = ['router1', False, 5]
>>>
>>> print(new_list)
['router1', False, 5]
```

Now you understand that lists are an ordered sequence of objects and are enclosed by brackets. One of the most common tasks when you're working with lists is to access an individual element of the list.

Let's create a new list of interfaces and show how to print a single element of a list:

```
>>> interfaces = ['Eth1/1', 'Eth1/2', 'Eth1/3', 'Eth1/4']
```

The list is created, and now three elements of the list are printed one at a time:

```
>>> print(interfaces[0])
Eth1/1
>>>
>>> print(interfaces[1])
Eth1/2
>>>
>>> print(interfaces[3])
Eth1/4
```

To access the individual elements within a list, you use the element's *index* value enclosed within brackets. It's important to see that the index begins at 0 and ends at the "length of the list minus 1." This means in our example, to access the first element, you use interfaces[0] and to access the last element, you use interfaces[3].

You can easily see that the length of the preceding list is 4, but what if you didn't know the length of the list?

Luckily, Python provides a built-in function called len() to help with this:

```
>>> len(interfaces)
4
```

So, you can access the last element of the list by subtracting 1 from its length: list_name[len(list_name) - 1]:

```
>>> interfaces[len(interfaces) - 1]
'Eth1/4'
```

Another way, more Pythonic, to access the last element in any list is: list_name[-1]. So, with the minus we are indexing the list from the end, instead of the beginning:

```
>>> interfaces[-1]
'Eth1/4'
```

Often, the terms *function* and *method* are used interchangeably, but until now we've mainly shown methods, not functions. The slight difference is that a function is called without referencing a parent object. As you saw, when you use a built-in method of an object, it is called using the syntax *object.method()*, and when you use a function like len(), you call it directly. That said, it is common to call a method a function.

The same *indexing* access used for *lists* also works for *strings*. If a variable called router is assigned the value of "DEVICE", then router[0] returns "D".

However, a string is not a list, so you can't assign a new value to the indexed position. String is an *immutable* type; it cannot be modified. Notice that if you assign a different value, hostname = 'something else', you are not modifying the string; you are creating a new one. If you try to modify an element of a string, you will observe an error raised:

```
>>> hostname[1] = 'A'
Traceback (most recent call last):
  File "<stdin>", line 1, in <module>
TypeError: 'str' object does not support item assignment
```

A useful technique, to produce a subset of a sequence (such as lists or strings), is *slicing*. Using a colon (:) before or after the index, you can indicate that you want to retrieve all the elements before or after the index, respectively. This can become pretty powerful when you need to parse through different types of objects:

```
>>> hostname = 'DEVICE_12345'
>>>
>>> hostname[4:]
'CE_12345'
>>>
>>> hostname[:-2]
'DEVICE_123'
```

Using built-in methods of Python lists

To view the available built-in methods for lists, the dir() function is used just as we showed previously when working with string objects. You can create any variable that is a list or use the formal data type name of list and pass it as an argument to dir(). You'll use the interfaces list for this:

```
>>> dir(interfaces)
[... omitted dunders ..., 'append', 'clear', 'copy', 'count', 'extend', 'index',
'insert', 'pop', 'remove', 'reverse', 'sort']
```

Let's take a look at a few of these built-in methods.

Using the append() method. The great thing about these method names, as you'll continue to see, is that they are human-readable, and for the most part, intuitive. The append() method is used to *append*, or add, an element to an existing list.

This is shown in the next example, but let's start with creating an empty list. You do so by assigning empty brackets to an object:

```
>>> vendors = []
```

Let's append vendors to this list:

```
>>> vendors.append('arista')
>>>
>>> print(vendors)
['arista']
>>>
>>> vendors.append('cisco')
>>>
>>> print(vendors)
['arista', 'cisco']
```

You can see that using append() adds the element to the *last* position in the list. In contrast to many of the methods reviewed for strings, this method is *not* returning anything, but modifying the original variable, or object.

Using the insert() method. Rather than just append an element to a list, you may need to *insert* an element at a specific location. This is done with the insert() method.

To use insert(), you need to pass it two arguments. The first argument is the position, or index, where the new element gets stored, and the second argument is the object getting inserted into the list:

```
>>> commands = ['interface Eth1/1', 'ip address 192.0.2.1/32']
```

 As a reminder, the commands in these examples are generic and do not map back to a specific vendor or platform.

Let's now assume you need to add two more commands to the previous commands list. The command that needs to be added as the first element is config t, and the one that needs to be added just before the IP address is no switchport:

```
>>> commands = ['interface Eth1/1', 'ip address 192.0.2.1/32']
>>>
>>> commands.insert(0, 'config t')
>>>
>>> print(commands)
['config t', 'interface Eth1/1', 'ip address 192.0.2.1/32']
>>>
>>> commands.insert(2, 'no switchport')
>>>
>>> print(commands)
['config t', 'interface Eth1/1', 'no switchport', 'ip address 192.0.2.1/32']
```

Using indexes bigger than the actual length of the list will not raise an error. It will simply insert the objects at the end of the list:

```
>>> commands.insert(9999, "shutdown")
>>> commands
['config t', 'interface Eth1/1', 'no switchport',
'ip address 192.0.2.1/32', 'shutdown']
```

Using the count() method. If you are doing an inventory of types of devices throughout the network, you may build a list that has more than one of the same object within a list. To expand on the earlier example, you may have a list that looks like this:

```
>>> vendors = ['cisco', 'cisco', 'juniper', 'arista', 'cisco', 'hp', 'cumulus',
'arista', 'cisco']
```

You can *count* how many instances of a given object are found by using the count() method. In our example, this can help determine how many Cisco or Arista devices are in the environment:

```
>>> vendors.count('cisco')
4
>>>
>>> vendors.count('arista')
2
```

Note that count() returns an int, or integer, and does not modify the existing object—unlike insert(), append(), and a few others reviewed in the upcoming examples.

Using the pop() and index() methods. Most of the methods thus far have either modified the original object or returned something. The pop() method does both:

```
>>> hostnames = ['r1', 'r2', 'r3', 'r4', 'r5']
```

The preceding example has a list of hostnames. Let's pop (remove) r5 because that device was just decommissioned from the network:

```
>>> hostnames.pop()
'r5'
>>>
>>> print(hostnames)
['r1', 'r2', 'r3', 'r4']
```

As you can see, the element being popped is returned, *and* the original list is modified as well. You should also notice that no element or index value was passed in, so you can see by default, pop() pops the last element in the list.

What if you need to pop r2? It turns out that to *pop* an element that is not the last one, you need to pass in an index value of the element that you wish to pop. But how do you find the index value of a given element? This is where the index() method comes into play.

To find the index value of a certain element, use `index()`:

```
>>> hostnames.index('r2')
1
```

Here you see that the index of the value r2 is 1.

So, to pop r2, you would perform the following:

```
>>> hostnames.pop(1)
'r2'
>>>
>>> print(hostnames)
['r1', 'r3', 'r4']
```

You could also do this in a single step:

```
>>> hostnames.pop(hostnames.index('r2'))
```

Using the sort() method.   The last built-in method to take a look at for lists is `sort()`. As you may have guessed, `sort()` is used to *sort* a list.

In the next example, you have a list of IP addresses in nonsequential order, and you use `sort()` to update the original object. Notice that nothing is returned:

```
>>> available_ips = ['10.1.1.1', '10.1.1.9', '10.1.1.8', '10.1.1.7', '10.1.1.4']
>>>
>>> available_ips.sort()
>>>
>>> available_ips
['10.1.1.1', '10.1.1.4', '10.1.1.7', '10.1.1.8', '10.1.1.9']
```

The sort from the previous example sorts IP addresses as strings instead of as IP addresses. So, if in `available_ips` you had 2.2.2.2, this "smaller" IP address will be sorted to be the last, because, as characters, 10 < 2.

A useful practice when working with methods is to check the available *customization* options. Usually, a method behavior has already implemented some tuning options to cover the common use cases. The `help()` method will show you all the detail:

```
>>> help(list.sort)
Help on method_descriptor:

sort(self, /, *, key=None, reverse=False)
    Sort the list in ascending order and return None.
    ...

    The reverse flag can be set to sort in descending order.
(END)
```

The `sort()` method supports a named boolean argument, `reverse`, that can sort the list in *descending* order:

```
>>> available_ips.sort(reverse=True)
>>>
>>> available_ips
['10.1.1.9', '10.1.1.8', '10.1.1.7', '10.1.1.4', '10.1.1.1']
```

In nearly all our list examples, the elements of the list are the same type of object; that is, they are all strings: commands, IP addresses, vendors, or hostnames. However, Python allows you to create lists that store different types of objects.

A prime example of storing different objects arises when storing information about a particular device. Maybe you want to store the hostname, vendor, and OS. A list to store these device attributes would look something like this:

```
>>> device = ['router1', 'juniper', '12.2']
```

Since elements of a list are indexed by an integer, you need to keep track of which index is mapped to which particular attribute. While it may not seem hard for this example, what if 10, 20, or 100 attributes need to be accessed? Even if mappings were available, it could get extremely difficult since lists are *ordered*. Replacing or updating any element in a list would need to be done carefully.

Wouldn't it be nice if you could reference the individual elements of a list by *name* and not worry so much about the *order* of elements? So, rather than access the hostname by using `device[0]`, you could access it like `device['hostname']`. As luck would have it, this is exactly where Python dictionaries come into action, and they are the next data type we cover in this chapter.

Python Dictionaries

We've now reviewed some of the most common data types, including strings, integers, booleans, and lists, which exist across all programming languages. In this section, we introduce the *dictionary*, which is a Python-specific data type. In other languages, they are known as *associative arrays*, *maps*, or *hash maps*.

Dictionaries are ordered lists by *insertion*, and their *values* are accessed by names, otherwise known as *keys*, instead of by index (integer). Dictionaries are simply a collection of *key-value* pairs called *items*.

In earlier versions of Python, dictionaries were an *unordered* data structure. You were not able to warrant the order of the items. However, as of Python 3.7, dictionaries are guaranteed to preserve the order in which key-value pairs are inserted.

We finished the previous section on lists with this example:

```
>>> device = ['router1', 'juniper', '12.2']
```

If you build on this example and convert the list device to a dictionary, it would look like this:

```
>>> device = {'hostname': 'router1', 'vendor': 'juniper', 'os': '12.1'}
```

The notation for a dictionary is a curly brace ({), then key, colon, and value, for each key-value pair, separated by a comma (,), and then it closes with another curly brace (}).

Once the dict object is created, you access the desired value by using *dict[key]*:

```
>>> print(device['hostname'])
router1
>>>
>>> print(device['os'])
12.1
>>>
>>> print(device['vendor'])
juniper
```

You can create the same dictionary from the previous example in a few ways. Two are shown here:

```
>>> device = {}
>>> device['hostname'] = 'router1'
>>> device['vendor'] = 'juniper'
>>> device['os'] = '12.1'
>>>
>>> print(device)
{'hostname': 'router1', 'vendor': 'juniper', 'os': '12.1'}

>>> device = dict(hostname='router1', vendor='juniper', os='12.1')
>>>
>>> print(device)
{'hostname': 'router1', 'vendor': 'juniper', 'os': '12.1'}
```

Using built-in methods of Python dictionaries

Python dictionaries have a few built-in methods worth covering, so as usual, we'll dive right into them. Just as with the other data types, we first present all available methods minus those that start and end with underscores:

```
>>> dir(dict)
['clear', 'copy', 'fromkeys', 'get', 'items', 'keys', 'pop', 'popitem',
'setdefault', 'update', 'values']
```

Using the get() method. You saw earlier how to access a key-value pair of a dictionary by using the notation of *dict[key]*. That is a popular approach, but with one caveat. If the key does not exist, Python raises a KeyError (similarly, a list would raise an IndexError when accessing a nonexistent position):

```
>>> device
{'hostname': 'router1', 'vendor': 'juniper', 'os': '12.1'}
>>>
>>> print(device['model'])
Traceback (most recent call last):
  File "<stdin>", line 1, in <module>
KeyError: 'model'
```

Using the `get()` method provides another approach that is arguably safer, unless you *want* to raise an exception. We explore more about exceptions in "Embracing Failure with try/except" on page 234.

Let's first look at an example using `get()` when the key exists:

```
>>> device.get('hostname')
'router1'
```

And now an example of when a key doesn't exist:

```
>>> device.get('model')
>>>
```

As you can see, absolutely nothing is returned when the key isn't in the dictionary, but it gets better than that. The `get()` method also allows the user to define a value to return when the key does not exist! Let's take a look:

```
>>> device.get('model', False)
False
>>>
>>> device.get('model', 'DOES NOT EXIST')
'DOES NOT EXIST'
>>>
>>> device.get('hostname', 'DOES NOT EXIST')
'router1'
```

Pretty simple, right? You can see that the value to the right of the key is returned only if the key does not exist within the dictionary.

Using the keys() and values() methods.   Dictionaries are a list of key-value pairs. Using the built-in methods `keys()` and `values()`, you can access each object individually.

In Python 3, these methods do not return a simple list but dictionary *view objects* that can be iterated to yield the data, as you will see in "Using Loops in Python" on page 203. Notice that the order of the items is preserved:

```
>>> device.keys()
dict_keys(['hostname', 'vendor', 'os'])
>>>
>>> device.values()
dict_values(['router1', 'juniper', '12.1'])
```

However, these view objects can't be accessed directly:

```
>>> device.keys()[0]
Traceback (most recent call last):
  File "<stdin>", line 1, in <module>
TypeError: 'dict_keys' object is not subscriptable
```

To access a specific object, you need to first convert the data to a list with list():

```
>>> list(device.keys())[0]
'hostname'
```

Using the pop() method. We introduced the built-in method pop() earlier in the chapter when we were reviewing lists. It just so happens dictionaries also have a pop() method, and it's used similarly. Instead of passing the method an index value as you did with lists, you pass it a key:

```
>>> device
{'hostname': 'router1', 'vendor': 'juniper', 'os': '12.1'}
>>>
>>> device.pop('vendor')
'juniper'
>>>
>>> device
{'hostname': 'router1', 'os': '12.1'}
```

You can see that pop() modifies the original object *and* returns the value being popped.

Using the update() method. There may come a time when you are extracting device information such as hostname, vendor, and OS from a network device and storing it in a Python dictionary. And down the road you need to add to or *update* it with another dictionary that has other attributes about a device.

The following shows two dictionaries:

```
>>> device = {'hostname': 'router1', 'vendor': 'juniper', 'os': '12.1'}
>>>
>>> oper = dict(cpu='5%', memory='10%')
>>>
>>> oper
{'cpu': '5%', 'memory': '10%'}
```

You can use the update() method to update one of the dictionaries, basically adding one dictionary to the other. Let's add oper to device:

```
>>> device.update(oper)
>>>
>>> print(device)
{'hostname': 'router1', 'vendor': 'juniper', 'os': '12.1', 'cpu': '5%',
'memory': '10%'}
```

If a *match* occurs with a dictionary key, the update() method will *update* the old value with the new value from the new dictionary. In the next example, the vendor key from device is changed from the original juniper to arista because the data from new_vendor is updated on the reference dictionary:

```
>>> new_vendor = {'vendor': 'arista'}
>>>
>>> device.update(new_vendor)
>>>
>>> print(device)
{'hostname': 'router1', 'vendor': 'arista', 'os': '12.1', 'cpu': '5%',
'memory': '10%'}
```

Notice that nothing is returned with update(). Only the object being updated, or device in this case, is modified.

Using the items() method. When working with dictionaries, you'll see items() used *a lot*, so it is extremely important to understand—not to discount the other methods, of course!

You saw how to access individual values via get() and how to get a list of all the keys and values via the keys() and values() methods, respectively. What about accessing a particular key-value pair of a given item at the same time, or iterating over all items? If you need to iterate (or loop) through a dictionary and simultaneously access keys and values, items() is a great tool for your tool belt.

 We formally introduce loops later in this chapter, but because items() is commonly used with a for loop, we are showing an example with a for loop here. The important takeaway is that when using the for loop with items(), you can access a key and value of a given item at the same time.

The most basic example is looping through a dictionary with a for loop and printing the key *and* value for each item. Again, loops are covered later in the chapter, but this is meant just to give a basic introduction to items():

```
>>> for key, value in device.items():
...     print(f'{key}: {value}')
...
hostname: router1
vendor: arista
os: 12.1
cpu: 5%
memory: 10%
```

In the for loop, key and value are user-defined and could have been anything, as you can see in this example:

```
>>> for my_attribute, my_value, in device.items():
...     print(f'{my_attribute}: {my_value}')
...
hostname: router1
vendor: arista
os: 12.1
cpu: 5%
memory: 10%
```

Now that we've covered the major data types in Python, you should have a good understanding of how to work with strings, numbers, booleans, lists, and dictionaries. Next we introduce two more data types—sets and tuples—that are a bit more advanced than the previous data types covered.

Sets and Tuples

The next two data types don't necessarily need to be covered in an introduction to Python, but as we said at the beginning of the chapter, we want to include a quick summary of them for completeness. These data types are `set` and `tuple`.

If you understand lists, you'll understand sets. *Sets* are a list of elements, but there can be only one of a given element in a set, and additionally, elements cannot be indexed (or accessed by an index value, like a list).

You can see that a set looks like a list, but is surrounded by `set()`:

```
>>> vendors = set(['arista', 'cisco', 'arista', 'cisco', 'juniper', 'cisco'])
```

This set is being created with multiple elements that are the same. We used a similar example when using the `count()` method with lists to count the number of devices from a given vendor. But what if you want to know only how many, and which, vendors exist in an environment? You can use a set:

```
>>> vendors = set(['arista', 'cisco', 'arista', 'cisco', 'juniper', 'cisco'])
>>>
>>> vendors
set(['cisco', 'juniper', 'arista'])
>>>
>>> len(vendors)
3
```

Notice that `vendors` contains only three elements.

The next example shows what happens when you try to access an element within a set. You must iterate through the elements, using a `for` loop as an example:

```
>>> vendors[0]
Traceback (most recent call last):
  File "<stdin>", line 1, in <module>
TypeError: 'set' object is not subscriptable
```

We leave as an exercise for you to explore the built-in methods for `sets`.

The tuple is an interesting data type and also best understood when compared to a list. It is like a list but cannot be modified. You saw that lists are *mutable*, meaning that you can update, extend, and modify them. Tuples, on the other hand, are *immutable*, and you can't modify them after they're created. Also, as with lists, it's possible to access individual elements of tuples:

```
>>> description = ('ROUTER1', 'PORTLAND')
>>>
>>> description
('ROUTER1', 'PORTLAND')
>>>
>>> print(description[0])
ROUTER1
```

After the variable object `description` is created, there is no way to modify it. You cannot modify any of the elements or add new elements. This could help if you need to create an object and want to ensure that no other function or user can modify it. The next example shows that you cannot modify a tuple and that a tuple has no methods such as `update()` or `append()`:

```
>>> description[1] = 'trying to modify one'
Traceback (most recent call last):
  File "<stdin>", line 1, in <module>
TypeError: 'tuple' object does not support item assignment
>>>
>>> dir(tuple)
[... omitted dunders ..., 'count', 'index']
```

To help compare and contrast lists, tuples, and sets, we have put this high-level summary together:

Lists
> Are mutable, can be modified, contain individual elements they can be accessed directly, and can have duplicate values

Sets
> Are mutable, can be modified, contain individual elements that cannot be accessed directly, and cannot have duplicate values

Tuples
> Are immutable, cannot be updated or modified after they're created, contain individual elements that can be accessed directly, and can have duplicate values

You have learned about various Python types, each with its own behavior and methods. So, in your programs you might like to validate the variable's type before using it. The `isinstance()` built-in function can identify a type, not only for built-in types but also custom-class types:

```
>>> hostname = ''
>>> devices = []
```

```
>>> if isinstance(devices, list):
...     print('devices is a list')
...
devices is a list
>>>
>>> if isinstance(hostname, str):
...     print('hostname is a string')
...
hostname is a string
```

This concludes the section on data types. We'll now shift gears a bit and jump into using conditionals (*if then* logic) in Python.

Adding Conditional Logic to Your Code

By now you should have a solid understanding of working with various types of objects. The beauty of programming comes into play when you start to use those objects by applying logic within your code, such as executing a task or creating an object when a particular condition is true (or not true!).

Conditionals are a key part of applying logic within your code, and understanding conditionals starts with understanding the if statement. Let's start with a basic example that checks the value of a string:

```
>>> hostname = 'NYC'
>>>
>>> if hostname == 'NYC':
...     print('The hostname is NYC')
...
The hostname is NYC
```

Even if you did not understand Python before starting this chapter, odds are you know what is being done in this example. This is part of the value of working in Python—it tries to be as human-readable as possible.

When you're working with an if statement, note two parts of the syntax. First, *all* if statements end with a colon (:). Second, the code that gets executed *if* your condition is true is part of an indented block—this indentation *should be* four spaces, but the number of spaces technically does not matter. All that *technically* matters is that you are consistent.

 Generally speaking, it is good practice to use a four-space indent when writing Python code. This is widely accepted by the Python community as the norm for writing idiomatic Python code. This makes code sharing and collaboration much easier.

The following shows a full indented code block:

```
>>> if hostname == 'NYC':
...     print('This hostname is NYC')
...     print(len(hostname))
...     print('The End.')
...
This hostname is NYC
3
The End.
```

Now that you understand how to construct a basic `if` statement, let's add to it.

What if you need to do a check to see if the hostname is NJ in addition to NYC? To accomplish this, you use the *else if* statement, or `elif`:

```
>>> hostname = 'NJ'
>>>
>>> if hostname == 'NYC':
...     print('This hostname is NYC')
... elif hostname == 'NJ':
...     print('This hostname is NJ')
...
This hostname is NJ
```

Similar to the `if` statement, the `elif` statement needs to end with a colon, and the associated code block to be executed must be indented. The `elif` statement also must be aligned to the `if` statement.

What if NYC and NJ are the only valid hostnames, but now you need to execute a block of code if another hostname is being used? This is where you use the `else` statement:

```
>>> hostname = 'DEN_CO'
>>>
>>> if hostname == 'NYC':
...     print('This hostname is NYC')
... elif hostname == 'NJ':
...     print('This hostname is NJ')
... else:
...     print('UNKNOWN HOSTNAME')
...
UNKNOWN HOSTNAME
```

Using `else` isn't any different from using `if` and `elif`. It needs a colon (:) and an indented code block underneath it to execute.

When Python executes conditional statements, the conditional block is exited as soon as a match occurs. For example, if `hostname` is equal to NYC, there would be a match on the first line of the conditional block, the print statement `print('This hostname is NYC')` would be executed, and then the block would be exited (no other `elif` or `else` would be executed).

The following is an example of an error produced because of incorrect indentation. The example has extra spaces in front of `elif` that should not be there:

```
>>> if hostname == 'NYC':
...     print('This hostname is NYC')
...   elif hostname == 'NJ':
  File "<stdin>", line 3
    elif hostname == 'NJ':
                        ^
IndentationError: unindent does not match any outer indentation level
```

And the following shows an error produced by a missing colon:

```
>>> if hostname == 'NYC'
  File "<stdin>", line 1
    if hostname == 'NYC'
                       ^
SyntaxError: invalid syntax
```

The point is, even if you have a typo in your code when you're just getting started, don't worry; you'll see pretty intuitive error messages.

You will continue to see conditionals in upcoming examples, including the next one, which introduces the concept of containment.

Understanding Containment

When we say *containment*, we are referring to the ability to check whether an object *contains* a specific element or object. Specifically, let's look at the usage of in, building on what you just learned with conditionals. Although this section covers only in, don't underestimate this powerful containment feature of Python.

If you use the vendors variable that has been used in previous examples, how would you check to see if a particular vendor exists? One option is to loop through the entire list and compare the vendor you're looking for with each object. That's definitely possible, but why not just use in?

Using containment is not only readable, but also simplifies the process for checking whether an object has what you are looking for:

```
>>> vendors = ['arista', 'juniper', 'cumulus', 'cisco']
>>>
>>> 'arista' in vendors
True
```

This syntax is straightforward, and a bool is returned. It's worth mentioning that this syntax is another one of those expressions that is considered writing idiomatic Python code.

This can now be taken a step further and added into a conditional statement:

```
>>> if 'arista' in vendors:
...     print('Arista is deployed.')
...
'Arista is deployed.'
```

Just as in previous examples, where you checked whether an element was in a list, in this next example, check to see if part of a string is *in* another string. You use a basic boolean expression and then use the expression in a conditional statement:

```
>>> version = "CSR1000V (X86_64_LINUX_IOSD-UNIVERSALK9-M), Version 16.3.1"
>>>
>>> "16.3.1" in version
True
>>>
>>> if "16.3.1" in version:
...     print("Version is 16.3.1!!")
...
Version is 16.3.1!!
```

 The in operator is implemented by the __contains__ dunder method. So, any object that implements this method can be used with the in operator.

As we previously stated, containment when combined with conditionals is a simple yet powerful way to check whether an object or value exists within another object. In fact, when you're just starting out, it is quite common to build really long and complex conditional statements, but what you really need is a more efficient way to evaluate the elements of a given object.

One such way is to use loops while working with objects such as lists and dictionaries. Using loops simplifies the process of working with these types of objects. This will become much clearer soon, as our next section formally introduces loops.

Using Loops in Python

We've finally made it to loops. As objects continue to grow, especially those that are much larger than our examples thus far, loops are absolutely required. Start to think about lists of devices, IP addresses, VLANs, and interfaces. We'll need efficient ways to search data or perform the same operation on each element in a set of data (as examples). This is where loops begin to show their value.

In this section, we cover two main types of loops: the for loop and while loop. From the perspective of a network engineer who is looking at automating network devices and general infrastructure, you can get away with almost always using a for loop. Of course, it depends on exactly what you are doing, but generally speaking, for loops in Python are pretty awesome, so we'll save them for last.

The while Loop

The general premise behind a while loop is that a set of code is executed *while* a certain condition is true. In the example that follows, the variable counter is set to 1 and then for as long as, or *while*, it is less than 5, the variable is printed, and then increased by 1.

The syntax required is similar to what we used when creating if-elif-else statements. The while statement is completed with a colon (:), and the code to be executed is indented four spaces:

```
>>> counter = 1
>>>
>>> while counter < 5:
...     print(counter)
...     counter += 1
...
1
2
3
4
```

This introduction is all we are going to cover on the while loop, as we'll be using the for loop in the majority of examples going forward.

The for Loop

The for loop in Python is awesome because when you use it, you are usually looping, or *iterating*, over a set of objects, like those found in a list, string, or dictionary. In other programming languages, for loops require an index and increment value to always be specified, which is not the case in Python.

Let's start by reviewing a *for-in*, or *for-each* loop, which is the most common type of for loop in Python. As in the previous sections, we start by reviewing a few basic examples.

The first prints each object within a list. You can see in the following example that the syntax is simple, and again, much like what you learned when using conditionals and the while loop. The first statement, or the beginning of the for loop, needs to end with a colon (:), and the code to be executed must be indented:

```
>>> vendors = ['arista', 'juniper', 'cisco']
>>>
>>> for vendor in vendors:
...     print(f'VENDOR: {vendor}')
...
VENDOR:  arista
VENDOR:  juniper
VENDOR:  cisco
```

As mentioned earlier, this type of for loop is often called a *for-in* or *for-each* loop because you are iterating over *each* element *in* a given object.

In the example, the name of the object vendor is totally arbitrary and up to the user to define, and for each iteration, vendor is equal to that specific element. For example, in this example vendor equals arista during the first iteration, juniper in the second iteration, and so on.

To show that vendor can be named anything, let's rename it network_vendor:

```
>>> for network_vendor in vendors:
...     print(f'VENDOR: {network_vendor}')
...
VENDOR:  arista
VENDOR:  juniper
VENDOR:  cisco
```

Let's now combine a few of the things you've learned so far with containment, conditionals, and loops.

In the next example, you have a new list of vendors. One of them is a *great* company, but just not cut out to be a network vendor! Then, you define approved_vendors, which is basically the approved vendors for a given customer. This example loops through the vendors to ensure that they are all approved, and if not, prints a statement saying so to the terminal:

```
>>> vendors = ['arista', 'juniper', 'cisco', 'oreilly']
>>>
>>> approved_vendors = ['arista', 'juniper', 'cisco']
>>>
>>> for vendor in vendors:
...     if vendor not in approved_vendors:
...         print(f'NETWORK VENDOR NOT APPROVED: {vendor}')
...
NETWORK VENDOR NOT APPROVED:  oreilly
```

You can see that not can be used in conjunction with in, making the code powerful and easy to read.

Example 6-1 is a more challenging example: you loop through a dictionary, while extracting data from another dictionary, and even get to use some built-in methods you learned earlier in this chapter.

Full versions of the code examples in this chapter can be found in the book's GitHub repo at *https://github.com/oreilly-npa-book/exam ples/tree/v2/ch06-python*.

Example 6-1. Using a for loop with items()

```
>>> COMMANDS = {
...     'description': 'description {}',
...     'speed': 'speed {}',
...     'duplex': 'duplex {}',
... }
>>> CONFIG_PARAMS = {
...     'description': 'auto description by Python',
...     'speed': '10000',
...     'duplex': 'auto'
... }
>>> commands_list = []
>>>
>>> for feature, value in CONFIG_PARAMS.items():
...     command = COMMANDS.get(feature).format(value)
...     commands_list.append(command)
...
>>> commands_list.insert(0, 'interface Eth1/1')
>>>
>>> print(commands_list)
['interface Eth1/1', 'description auto description by Python',
'speed 10000', 'duplex auto']
```

Using uppercase variables (e.g., COMMANDS or CONFIG_PARAMS) is a Python convention to refer to variables containing constant values, which do not change during execution.

In this example, you start building a dictionary that stores CLI commands to configure certain features on a network device into the COMMANDS variable.

You have a dictionary of three items (key-value pairs). Each item's key is a network feature to configure, and each item's value is the start of a command string that'll configure that respective feature. These features include speed, duplex, and description. Each value of the dictionary is followed by curly braces ({}) because you'll be using the format() method of strings to insert variables.

After the COMMANDS dictionary is created, you create a second dictionary called CON FIG_PARAMS that will be used to dictate which commands will be executed and which value will be used for each command string defined in COMMANDS.

Then you use a for loop to iterate through CONFIG_PARAMS() using the items built-in method for dictionaries. As you iterate through, you'll use the key from CONFIG_PARAMS to get the proper value, or command string, from COMMANDS. This is possible because they were prebuilt using the same key structure. The command string is returned with curly braces, but as soon as it's returned, you use the format() method to insert the proper value, which happens to be the value in CONFIG_PARAMS.

Now we'll walk through this in even more detail. Please take your time and even test this out yourself while on the Python interactive interpreter.

In the first line, `commands_list` is creating an empty list `[]`. This is required in order to `append()` to this list later.

You then use the `items()` built-in method as you loop through `CONFIG_PARAMS`. This was covered briefly earlier in the chapter, but `items()` is giving you, the network developer, access to both the key *and* value of a given key-value pair at the same time. This example iterates more than three key-value pairs: `description`/`auto descrip tion` by Python, `speed`/`10000`, and `duplex`/`auto`.

During each iteration—that is, for each key-value pair that is being referred to as the variables `feature` and `value`—a command is being pulled from the `COMMANDS` dictionary. As you may recall, the `get()` method is used to get the value of a key-value pair when you specify the key. In the example, this key is the `feature` object. The value being returned is `description {}` for `description`, `speed {}` for `speed`, and `duplex {}` for `duplex`. As you can see, all of these objects being returned are strings, so then you are able to use the `format()` method to insert the `value` from `CONFIG_PARAMS` because you also saw earlier that multiple methods can be used together on the same line. Once the value is inserted, the command is appended to `commands_list`.

Finally, after the commands are built, you insert interface `Eth1/1` as the first item of the list. This could have also been done first, with `commands_list = ['interface Eth1/1']`. If you understand this example, you're at a really good point already with getting a grasp on Python!

You've now seen some of the most common types of `for` loops that allow you to iterate over lists and dictionaries. We'll now take a look at another way to construct and use a `for` loop.

Using the enumerate() function

Occasionally, you may need to keep track of an index value as you loop through an object. We show this fairly briefly, since most of these examples are like the previous examples already covered.

The `enumerate()` function is used to enumerate the list and give an index value, and is often handy to determine the exact position of a given element.

The next example shows how to use `enumerate()` within a `for` loop. You'll notice that the beginning part of the `for` loop looks like the dictionary examples, only unlike `items()`, which returns a key and value, `enumerate()` returns an index, starting at 0, and the object from the list that you are enumerating.

The example prints both the index and value to help you understand what it is doing:

```
>>> vendors = ['arista', 'juniper', 'cisco']
>>>
>>> for index, each in enumerate(vendors):
...     print(f'{index} {each}')
...
0 arista
1 juniper
2 cisco
```

Maybe you don't need to print all indices and values. Maybe you need only the index for a given vendor. This is shown in this example:

```
>>> for index, each in enumerate(vendors):
...     if each == 'arista':
...         print(f'arista index is: {index}')
...
arista index is:  0
```

Flow control within loops

Loops can become a trap. In the *enumerate* example, you started and completed a full iteration over the objects in vendors, even though you were interested in only the ones matching arista. In that case, this was not a big issue because the list had three items. But, what if vendors had thousands of elements? Should you continue iterating over the list when you have already found the item you were looking for?

Luckily, Python has a break statement to stop a loop iteration at any point—for example, when the purpose of the loop is fulfilled. In the following variation, you add a print() for each iteration and a break to stop the loop once you find arista, so you can see how the loop is stopped when a condition is met:

```
>>> vendors = ['arista', 'juniper', 'cisco']
>>>
>>> for index, each in enumerate(vendors):
...     print(index)
...     if each == 'arista':
...         print(f'arista index is: {index}')
...         break
...
0
arista index is: 0
```

Another useful statement is continue, to jump to the next iteration of the loop and skip any pending logic for the present iteration. In the next example, you use continue to achieve the same goal, printing the arista index:

```
>>> for index, each in enumerate(vendors):
...     print(index)
...     if each != 'arista':
...         continue
...     print(f'arista index is: {index}')
...
0
```

```
arista index is: 0
1
2
```

Obviously, in this case you are not *breaking* the loop (you are not using break), and you print all the *indexes* but not the strings. Using continue makes the code easy to read: adding a condition at the beginning of the iteration helps you understand whether it makes sense to continue with the iteration or to move to the next one.

We've covered quite a bit of Python so far, from data types to conditionals to loops. However, we still haven't discussed how to efficiently reuse code via functions. This is what we cover next.

Using Python Functions

Because you are reading this book, you probably at some point have heard of functions, but if not, don't worry—we have you covered! Functions are all about eliminating redundant and duplicate code and easily allowing for the reuse of code.

On a daily basis, network engineers are configuring VLANs over and over again. And they are likely proud of how fast they can enter the same CLI commands into a network device or switch over and over. Writing a script with functions eliminates writing the same code *over and over*.

Let's assume you need to create a few VLANs across a set of switches. Based on a device from Cisco or Arista, the commands required may look something this:

```
vlan 10
  name USERS
vlan 20
  name VOICE
vlan 30
  name WLAN
```

Imagine you need to configure 10, 20, or 50 devices with the same VLANs! You likely would type in those six commands for as many devices as you have in your environment.

This is actually a perfect opportunity to create a function and write a small script. Since we haven't covered scripts yet, we'll still be working in the Python shell.

For our first example, you'll start with a basic print() function and then come right back to the VLAN example:

```
>>> def print_vendor(net_vendor):
...     print(net_vendor)
...
>>>
>>> vendors = ['arista', 'juniper', 'cisco']
>>>
>>> for vendor in vendors:
```

```
...      print_vendor(vendor)
...
arista
juniper
cisco
```

Here, print_vendor() is a function that is created and *defined* using def. If you want to pass variables (parameters) into your function, you enclose them within parentheses next to the function name. This example is receiving one parameter and is referenced as net_vendor while in the function called print_vendor(). Like conditionals and loops, function declarations also end with a colon (:). Within the function, an indented code block has a single statement—it simply prints the parameter being received.

Once the function is created, it is ready to be immediately used, even while in the Python interpreter.

For this first example, we looped through vendors. During each iteration of the loop, we passed the object, which is a string of the vendor's name, to print_vendor().

Notice that the variables have different names based on where they are being used, meaning that you are passing vendor, but it's received and referenced as net_vendor from within the function. There is no requirement to have the variables use the same name within the function, although it'll work just fine if you choose to do it that way.

Since you now understand how to create a basic function, let's return to the VLAN example and create two functions to help automate VLAN provisioning; see Examples 6-2 and 6-3.

Example 6-2. get_commands() function

```
>>> def get_commands(vlan, name):  ❶
...      commands = []
...      commands.append(f'vlan {vlan}')
...      commands.append(f'name {name}')
...      return commands              ❷
...
```

❶ The get_commands() function accepts two parameters: vlan indicates the VLAN ID, and name indicates the name.

❷ Returns a list of commands crafted from the input arguments.

Example 6-3. push_commands() function

```
>>> def push_commands(device, commands):      ❶
...     print(f'Connecting to device: {device}')
...     for cmd in commands:
...         print(f'Sending command: {cmd}')  ❷
...
```

❶ This function also accepts two parameters: device, which is the device to send the commands to, and commands, which is the list of commands to send.

❷ In reality, the actual configuration push isn't happening in this function, but rather it is printing commands to the terminal to simulate the command execution.

To use these functions, you need two things: a list of devices to configure and the list of VLANs to send. The list of devices to be configured is as follows:

```
>>> devices = ['switch1', 'switch2', 'switch3']
```

To create a single object to represent the VLANs, we have created a list of dictionaries. Each dictionary has two key-value pairs, one pair for the VLAN ID and one for the VLAN name:

```
>>> vlans = [{'id': '10', 'name': 'USERS'}, {'id': '20', 'name': 'VOICE'},
{'id': '30', 'name': 'WLAN'}]
```

As you may recall, Python provides more than one way to create a dictionary. Any of those options could have been used here.

In Example 6-4, we use these functions. The following code loops through the vlans list. Remember that each element in vlans is a dictionary. For each element, or dictionary, the id and name are obtained by way of the get() method. There are two print statements, and then the first function, get_commands(), is called—id and name are parameters that get sent to the function, and then a list of commands is returned and assigned to commands.

Example 6-4. Using defined functions

```
>>> for vlan in vlans:                        ❶
...     vid = vlan.get('id')
...     name = vlan.get('name')
...     print(f'CONFIGURING VLAN: {vid}')
...     commands = get_commands(vid, name)    ❷
...     for device in devices:                ❶
...         push_commands(device, commands)   ❸
...         print()
...
```

❶ Combining two `for` loops, for `vlans` and `devices`, will provide full coverage of VLAN configuration per device.

❷ Using the `get_commands()` function from before, we can obtain all the necessary commands per VLAN.

❸ Once we have the commands for a given VLAN, they are executed on each device by looping through `devices`.

And this is the output generated:

```
CONFIGURING VLAN: 10
Connecting to device: switch1
Sending command: vlan 10
Sending command: name USERS

Connecting to device: switch2
Sending command: vlan 10
Sending command: name USERS

Connecting to device: switch3
Sending command: vlan 10
Sending command: name USERS

CONFIGURING VLAN: 20
Connecting to device: switch1
Sending command: vlan 20
Sending command: name VOICE

Connecting to device: switch2
Sending command: vlan 20
Sending command: name VOICE

Connecting to device: switch3
Sending command: vlan 20
Sending command: name VOICE

CONFIGURING VLAN: 30
Connecting to device: switch1
Sending command: vlan 30
Sending command: name WLAN

Connecting to device: switch2
Sending command: vlan 30
Sending command: name WLAN

Connecting to device: switch3
Sending command: vlan 30
Sending command: name WLAN
```

Remember, not all functions require parameters, and not all functions return a value.

In this output, you may notice that we pivoted on the VLANs instead of the devices, which resulted in tearing up and down several connections to the devices (one per VLAN). Swapping the for loops and pivoting on the devices could have reduced the number of necessary device connections by consolidating all the VLAN changes.

You should now have a basic understanding of creating and using functions, understanding how they are called and defined with and without parameters, and how it's possible to call functions from within loops. Next, we cover how to read and write data from files in Python.

Working with Files

This section shows you how to read and write data from files. Our focus is on presenting the basics so you'll then be able to easily pick up other sources to continue learning about working with files.

Reading from a File

For our example, a configuration snippet is located in the same directory from where you entered the Python interpreter. The file, named *vlans.cfg*, looks like this:

```
vlan 10
  name USERS
vlan 20
  name VOICE
vlan 30
  name WLAN
vlan 40
  name APP
vlan 50
  name WEB
vlan 60
  name DB
```

With just two lines in Python, you can *open* and *read* the file:

```
>>> vlans_file = open('vlans.cfg', 'r')
>>>
>>> vlans_file.read()
'vlan 10\n  name USERS\nvlan 20\n  name VOICE\nvlan 30\n
name WLAN\nvlan 40\n  name APP\nvlan 50\n  name WEB\nvlan 60\n
  name DB'
>>>
>>> vlans_file.close()
```

You read the full file as a complete str object by using the read() method for file objects.

The next example reads the file and stores each line as an element in a list by using the readlines() method for file objects:

```
>>> vlans_file = open('vlans.cfg', 'r')
>>>
>>> vlans_file.readlines()
['vlan 10\n', '  name USERS\n', 'vlan 20\n', '  name VOICE\n', 'vlan 30\n',
'  name WLAN\n', 'vlan 40\n', '  name APP\n', 'vlan 50\n', '  name WEB\n',
'vlan 60\n', '  name DB']
>>>
>>> vlans_file.close()
```

Let's reopen the file, save the contents as a string, but then manipulate it in order to store the VLANs as a dictionary (similar to the way you used the vlans object in Example 6-4):

```
>>> vlans_file = open('vlans.cfg', 'r')
>>>
>>> vlans_text = vlans_file.read()
>>>
>>> vlans_list = vlans_text.splitlines()
>>>
>>> vlans_list
['vlan 10', '  name USERS', 'vlan 20', '  name VOICE', 'vlan 30',
'  name WLAN', 'vlan 40', '  name APP', 'vlan 50', '  name WEB',
'vlan 60', '  name DB']
```

The file is read, and the contents are stored as a string in vlans_text. A built-in method for strings called splitlines() is used to create a list; each element in the list is each line within the file. This new list is called vlans_list and has a length equal to the number of commands that were in the file.

Next, in Example 6-5, we normalize the raw text content into a list of dictionaries.

Example 6-5. Normalizing raw text into a list of dictionaries

```
>>> vlans = []
>>> for item in vlans_list:                              ❶
...     if 'vlan' in item:
...         temp = {}                                    ❷
...         id = item.strip().strip('vlan').strip()      ❸
...         temp['id'] = id
...     elif 'name' in item:
...         name = item.strip().strip('name').strip()
...         temp['name'] = name
...         vlans.append(temp)
...
>>>
>>> vlans
[{'id': '10', 'name': 'USERS'}, {'id': '20', 'name': 'VOICE'},
```

```
{'id': '30', 'name': 'WLAN'}, {'id': '40', 'name': 'APP'},
{'id': '50', 'name': 'WEB'}, {'id': '60', 'name': 'DB'}]
>>>
```

❶ Once the list is created, it is iterated over within a `for` loop. The variable `item` is used to represent each element in the list as it's being iterated over. In the first iteration, `item` is `'vlan 10'`; in the second iteration, `item` is `' name USERS'`; and so on.

❷ Within the `for` loop, a list of dictionaries is ultimately created; each element in the list is a dictionary with two key-value pairs: `id` and `name`. We accomplish this by using a temporary dictionary called `temp`, adding both key-value pairs to it, and then appending it to the final list only after appending the VLAN name. Per the following note, `temp` is reinitialized *only* when it finds the next VLAN, so it's assuming a certain order of the input data.

❸ Notice how `strip()` is being used. We can use `strip()` to strip not only white-space but also particular substrings within a string object. Additionally, we *chain* multiple methods together in a single Python statement. For example, with the value `' name WEB'`, when `strip()` is first used, it returns `'name WEB'`. Then, we use `strip('name')`, which returns `' WEB'`, and then finally `strip()` to remove any whitespace that still remains to produce the final name of `'WEB'`.

 The previous example is not the only way to perform an operation for reading in VLANs. That example *assumes* a VLAN ID and name for every VLAN, which is usually not the case, but is done this way for conveying certain concepts. It initializes `temp` only when VLAN is found, and appends `temp` only after the "name" is added (this would not work if a name did not exist for every VLAN and is a good use case for using Python error handling using `try`/`except` statements, as we cover in "Embracing Failure with try/except" on page 234).

Writing to a File

The next example shows how to write data to a file. The `vlans` object created in the previous example is used here too:

```
>>> vlans
[{'id': '10', 'name': 'USERS'}, {'id': '20', 'name': 'VOICE'},
{'id': '30', 'name': 'WLAN'}, {'id': '40', 'name': 'APP'},
{'id': '50', 'name': 'WEB'}, {'id': '60', 'name': 'DB'}]
```

A few more VLANs are created before you try to write the VLANs to a new file:

```
>>> add_vlan = {'id': '70', 'name': 'MISC'}
>>> vlans.append(add_vlan)
>>>
>>> add_vlan = {'id': '80', 'name': 'HQ'}
>>> vlans.append(add_vlan)
>>>
>>> print(vlans)
[{'id': '10', 'name': 'USERS'}, {'id': '20', 'name': 'VOICE'},
{'id': '30', 'name': 'WLAN'}, {'id': '40', 'name': 'APP'},
{'id': '50', 'name': 'WEB'}, {'id': '60', 'name': 'DB'},
{'id': '70', 'name': 'MISC'}, {'id': '80', 'name': 'HQ'}]
```

Eight VLANS are now in the vlans list. Let's write them to a new file but keep the formatting the way it should be with proper spacing.

The first step is to open the new file. If the file doesn't exist, which it doesn't in our case, it'll be created:

```
>>> write_file = open('vlans_new.cfg', 'w')
```

Once the file is open, you use the get() method again to extract the required VLAN values from each dictionary and then use the file method called write() to write the data to the file. Finally, you close the file:

```
>>> for vlan in vlans:
...     id = vlan.get('id')
...     name = vlan.get('name')
...     write_file.write(f'vlan {id}\n')
...     write_file.write(f'  name {name}\n')
...
>>>
>>> write_file.close()
```

You've created the *vlans_new.cfg* file and generated the following contents in the file:

```
$ cat vlans_new.cfg
vlan 10
  name USERS
vlan 20
  name VOICE
vlan 30
  name WLAN
vlan 40
  name APP
vlan 50
  name WEB
vlan 60
  name DB
vlan 70
  name MISC
vlan 80
  name HQ
```

As you start to use file objects more, you may see some interesting things happen. For example, you may forget to close a file, and wonder why there is no data in the file that you know should have data!

By default, what you are writing with the write() method is held in a buffer and is written to the file only when the file is closed. This setting is configurable.

You can also use the with statement, a context manager, to help manage this process. A context manager is a Python object that defines a runtime context: what to do when entering it and what to do when exiting it. In this example, you see how the return object of the open() method is used as a context manager, so it closes the file when exiting the context *automatically*:

```
>>> with open('vlans_new.cfg', 'w') as write_file:
...     write_file.write('vlan 10\n')
...     write_file.write('  name TEST_VLAN\n')
...
```

When you open a file with open('vlans.cfg', 'r'), two parameters are passed. The first is the name of the file, including the relative or absolute path of the file. The second is the *mode*, which is an optional argument, but if not included, defaults to read-only, which is the r mode. Other modes include w, which opens a file only for writing (if you're using the name of a file that already exists, the contents are erased), a opens a file for appending, and r+ opens a file for reading and writing. You can find more details in the official Python docs (*https://oreil.ly/_Zx55*).

Since Python 3, the file's content is handled as bytes and *encoded* to text with an implicit UTF-8 encoding. If you want to change the encoding type, you can use the named argument encoding:

```
>>> vlans_file = open('vlans.cfg', 'r', encoding='ascii')
```

Everything in this chapter thus far has been using the dynamic Python interpreter. This showed how powerful the interpreter is for writing and testing new methods, functions, or particular sections of your code. No matter how great the interpreter is, you still need to be able to write programs and scripts that can run as a standalone entity. This is exactly what we cover next.

Creating Python Programs

Let's take a look at how to build on what you've been doing in the Python shell and learn how to create and run a standalone Python script, or program. This section shows how to easily take what you've learned so far and create a script within just a few minutes.

 If you're following along, feel free to use any text editor you are comfortable with, including, but not limited to vi, Vim, Sublime Text, Notepad++, or even a full-blown IDE, such as PyCharm or VS Code, as introduced in Chapter 5.

Let's look at a few examples.

Creating a Basic Python Script

The first step is to create a new Python file that ends with the *.py* extension. From the Linux terminal, you can create a new file by typing **touch net_script.py** and opening it in your text editor. As expected, the file is completely empty.

The first script you'll write simply prints text to the terminal. Add the following five lines of text to *net_script.py* to create a basic Python script:

```
#!/usr/bin/env python3

if __name__ == "__main__":
    print('^' * 30)
    print('HELLO NETWORK AUTOMATION!!!!!')
    print('^' * 30)
```

Now that the script is created, let's execute it. To execute a Python script from the Linux terminal, you use the `python3` command. All you need to do is append the script name to the command as shown here:

```
$ python3 net_script.py
^^^^^^^^^^^^^^^^^^^^^^^^^^^^^^
HELLO NETWORK AUTOMATION!!!!!
^^^^^^^^^^^^^^^^^^^^^^^^^^^^^^
```

And that's it! If you were following along, you just created a Python script. You might have noticed that everything under the `if __name__ == "__main__":` statement is the same as if you were on the Python interpreter.

Now we'll take a look at the two unique statements that are optional, but recommended, when you are writing Python scripts.

Using Comments in Python

Python code is usually easy to read, even without adding extra *comments*. However, adding comments in your programs can sometimes help new developers jumping into the code (reviewing, fixing or extending it), or even you, when you're coming back to your code after a while and don't fully remember the original context.

This book isn't about *clean code* best practices, but an accepted rule of thumb is that comments should be used to explain or clarify your intent when it is not obvious enough.

In Python you can use the # (known as a hashtag, number sign, or pound sign) for inline comments:

```
commands = []
# The order of the commands is relevant, do not change it
commands.append(f'vlan {vlan}')
# Due to the naming convention, the name of a vlan includes the vlan ID
commands.append(f'name {name}_{vlan}')
```

Python linters used to perform checks on the code can also act upon the text that comes after comments starting with #.

Now we'll take a look at a special comment type, optional but recommended, when you are writing Python scripts, the shebang. We introduced the shebang in Chapter 3.

Understanding the shebang

The *shebang* is the first line in the script: `#!/usr/bin/env python3`. This is a special and unique line for Python programs.

It is the only line of code, other than comments, that uses the # as the first character. The shebang needs to be the first line in a Python program when used.

The shebang instructs the system which Python interpreter to use to execute the program. Of course, this also assumes file permissions are correct for your program file (i.e., that the file is executable). If the shebang is not included, you must use the `python` keyword to execute the script, which you have in all our examples anyway.

For example, say you have the following script in *hello.py*:

```
if __name__ == "__main__":
    print('Hello Network Automation!')
```

You could execute the code by using the statement `$ python3 hello.py`, assuming the file was saved as *hello.py*. But you could not execute it using the statement `$ ./hello.py`. In order for the statement `$ ./hello.py` to be executed, you need to add the shebang to the program file because that's how the system knows how to execute the script. Also, remember to add execute permissions to the file with `chmod +x hello.py`!

```
#!python3

if __name__ == "__main__":
    print('Hello Network Automation!')
```

The shebang as we have it, python3, defaults to using Python 3.8.12 on the system we're using to write this book. We can check the exact Python version with which python3:

```
$ which python3
/usr/bin/python3
```

If your machine has different installations of Python, you can refer directly to the desired one in your shebang. For instance, using #!/usr/bin/python3.9 will use the Python 3.9 executable. However, this approach has the drawback of being inflexible (for instance, this will cause problems in Virtualenv, covered in "Isolating Your Dependencies with Virtualenv" on page 229).

A better approach is to use /usr/bin/env python3, which allows the external environment to influence the specific installation your script uses.

Now that you understand the shebang, we can continue to present another optional statement that will open the door to start creating your first Python scripts.

Migrating Code from the Python Interpreter to a Python Script

A common component of a Python script is the if __name__ == "__main__": statement. Based on the quotes, or lack thereof, you can see that __name__ is a variable, and "__main__" is a string. When a Python file is executed as a standalone script, the variable name __name__ is automatically set to "__main__". Thus, whenever you use python3 *script*.py, everything underneath the if __name__ == "__main__": statement is executed.

At this point, you are probably thinking, when wouldn't __name__ be equal to "__main__"? That is discussed in "Working with Python Modules" on page 222, but here's the short answer: when you are importing particular objects from Python files, but not necessarily using those files as a standalone program.

In Example 6-6, we use the same Python script as in "Using Python Functions" on page 209. The reason is to show you firsthand how easy it is to migrate from using the Python interpreter to writing a standalone Python script.

Example 6-6. Script to render push commands

```python
#!/usr/bin/env python3              ❶

def get_commands(vlan, name):      ❷
    commands = []
    commands.append(f'vlan {vlan}')
    commands.append(f'name {name}')
    return commands

def push_commands(device, commands):  ❷
    print(f'Connecting to device: {device}')
    for cmd in commands:
        print(f'Sending command: {cmd}')

if __name__ == "__main__":         ❸

    devices = ['switch1', 'switch2', 'switch3']

    vlans = [
        {'id': '10', 'name': 'USERS'},
        {'id': '20', 'name': 'VOICE'},
        {'id': '30', 'name': 'WLAN'}
    ]

    for vlan in vlans:             ❹
        vid = vlan.get('id')
        name = vlan.get('name')
        print(f'CONFIGURING VLAN: {vid}')
        commands = get_commands(vid, name)
        for device in devices:
            push_commands(device, commands)
            print()
```

❶   The shebang instructs the system about the Python interpreter to use.

❷   The functions are defined before using them.

❸   The if statement indicates to run this code when it's executed as a script instead of being imported.

❹   The same nested for loop defined in Example 6-4 is executed.

You can execute this script with the commands python3 push.py or ./push.py. The output you see is exactly the same output you saw when it was executed on the Python interpreter in Example 6-4.

Python offers the -i flag to be used when executing a script, but instead of exiting the script, it enters the interpreter, giving you access to all the objects built in the script. This is *great* for testing.

Let's see what happens when you run the script with the -i flag set:

```
$ python3 -i push.py
>>>
>>> print(devices)
['switch1', 'switch2', 'switch3']
>>>
>>> print(commands)
['vlan 30', 'name WLAN']
```

Notice that it executes, but then drops you right into the Python shells and you have access to those objects at the end of the execution. Pretty cool, right?

If you are creating several scripts that perform various configuration changes on the network, you can intelligently assume that the push_commands() function will be needed in almost all scripts. One option is to copy and paste the function into all the scripts. Clearly, that would not be optimal because if you need to fix a bug in that function, you would need to make that change in *all* the scripts.

Just as functions allow you to reuse code within a single script, Python provides a way to reuse and share code among scripts/programs. You do so by creating a Python module, which is what we cover next as we continue to build on the previous example.

Working with Python Modules

We are going to continue to leverage the *push.py* file we just created in the previous section to better articulate how to work with a Python module. You can think of a *module* as a type of Python file that holds information, (e.g., Python objects), that can be used by other Python programs but is not a standalone script or program itself.

For this example, you are going to enter back into the Python interpreter while in the same directory where the *push.py* file exists.

Let's assume you need to generate a new list of commands to send to a new list of devices. Remember that you have this function called push_commands() in another file that already has the logic to push a list of commands to a given device. Rather than re-create the same function in your new program (or in the interpreter), you can reuse push_commands() from within *push.py*. Let's see how to do it.

While at the Python shell, you type in `import push` and hit Enter. This imports all the objects within the *push.py* file:

```
>>> import push
```

Take a look at the imported objects by using `dir(push)`:

```
>>> dir(push)
['__builtins__', '__cached__', '__doc__', '__file__', '__loader__', '__name__',
'__package__', '__spec__', 'get_commands', 'push_commands']
```

Just as with the standard Python data types, `push` has methods that start and end with underscores (dunders), but you should also notice the two objects called `get_commands` and `push_commands`, which are the functions from the *push.py* file!

As you may recall, `push_commands()` requires two parameters. The first is a device, and the second is a list of commands. Let's now use `push_commands()` from the interpreter:

```
>>> device = 'router1'
>>> commands = ['interface Eth1/1', 'shutdown']
>>>
>>> push.push_commands(device, commands)
Connecting to device: router1
Sending command: interface Eth1/1
Sending command: shutdown
```

If you import multiple modules, there could be objects with duplicated names. Using `import push` is definitely a good option because it enables you to specify the module where the object exists (i.e., `push.push_commands`). On the other hand, there are other options for importing objects.

One other option is to use `from import`. In our example, it would look like this: `from push import push_commands`. Notice in the following code, you can directly use `push_commands()` without referencing push:

```
>>> from push import push_commands
>>>
>>> push_commands(device, commands)
Connecting to device: router1
Sending command: interface Eth1/1
Sending command: shutdown
```

We recommend making `import` statements as specific as possible and to import only what's used in your code. You should *not* use wildcard imports, such as `from push import *`. Statements like this load all objects from the module, potentially overloading and causing namespace conflicts with objects you've defined. And it also complicates troubleshooting, as it makes it difficult to decipher where an object was defined or came from.

Another option is to rename the object as you are importing it, using from import as. If you happen to not like the name of the object or think it is too long, you can rename it on import. The code looks like this for our example:

```
>>> from push import push_commands as pc
>>>
>>> pc(device, commands)
Connecting to device: router1
Sending command: interface Eth1/1
Sending command: shutdown
```

Notice how easy it is to rename the object and make it something shorter and/or more intuitive.

Reusing functions is great, but it implies that the consumer of the code may not know the concrete purpose, or usage, of the imported function. To make reusability easier, the next step is to learn how to document your functions.

Documenting Functions

When you create functions that will be used by others, it's helpful to document how your function should be used. In Python, you can add *docstrings* to describe functions, methods, and classes; you use triple quotes (""") to define a docstring, and you can document the expected arguments and what the function returns:

```
def get_commands(vlan, name):
    """Get commands to configure a VLAN.

    Args:
        vlan (int): vlan id
        name (str): name of the vlan

    Returns:
        List of commands is returned.
    """

    commands = []
    commands.append(f'vlan {vlan}')
    commands.append(f'name {name}')
    return commands
```

You learned how to import a module—namely, *push.py*. Let's import it again now to see what happens when you use help on get_commands() since you now have a docstring configured. You see the whole function's *docstring* when you use help(). Additionally, you see information about the parameters and what data is returned, if properly documented:

```
>>> import push
>>>
>>> help(push.get_commands)

Help on function get_commands in module push:
```

```
get_commands(vlan, name)
    Get commands to configure a VLAN.

    Args:
        vlan (int): vlan id
        name (str): name of the vlan

    Returns:
        List of commands is returned.
(END)
```

 Some code editors provide contextual help to automatically render the docstring information when you are typing a function name.

By now you should understand how to create not only a script, but also a Python module with functions (and other objects), and how to use those reusable objects in other scripts and programs.

Passing Arguments into a Python Script

The preceding two sections covered writing Python scripts and using Python modules. The `sys` module is part of the Python standard library (i.e., comes with Python by default), and now you will see how it allows you to easily pass in arguments from the command line into a Python script. Specifically, you're going to use an attribute (or variable) within the module called `argv`.

Let's take a look at a basic script called *send_command.py* that has only a single `print` statement:

```
#!/usr/bin/env python3

import sys

if __name__ == "__main__":
    print(sys.argv)
```

 `sys.args` is available only when running a Python script. It doesn't exist in the Python interpreter.

Now you'll execute the script, passing in a few arguments simulating data required to log in to a device and issue a `show` command:

```
ubuntu2004:~$ python3 send_command.py username password 10.1.10.10 "show version"
['send_command.py', 'username', 'password', '10.1.10.10', 'show version']
```

You can see that sys.argv is a list. In fact, it's simply a list of the strings that you passed in from the Linux command line. You can also infer what really happened: Python did a split (str.split(" ")) on send-command.py username password 10.1.10.10 "show version", which created the list of five elements!

Finally, note that when you're using sys.argv, the first element is always the script name.

If you'd like, you can assign the value of sys.argv to an arbitrary variable to simplify working with the parameters passed in. In either case, you can extract values by using the appropriate index values as shown:

```
#!/usr/bin/env python3

import sys

if __name__ == "__main__":
    args = sys.argv
    print(f"Username:  {args[1]}")
    print(f"Password:  {args[2]}")
    print(f"Device IP: {args[3]}")
    print(f"Command:   {args[4]}")
```

If you execute this script, you get the following output:

```
$ python3 send_command.py username password 10.1.10.10 "show version"
Username:  username
Password:  password
Device IP: 10.1.10.10
Command:   show version
```

 When using sys.argv, you still need to account for input error handling (at a minimum, check the length of the list). Additionally, the user of the script must know the precise order of the elements that need to be passed in.

In our example, if you call the script with fewer than the four expected arguments, you will hit an IndexError because you are accessing an index in a list that doesn't exist:

```
$ python3 send_command.py
Traceback (most recent call last):
  File "/your/path/examples/ch06-python/send_command.py",
    line 8, in <module> print(f"Username:  {args[1]}")
IndexError: list index out of range
```

For more advanced argument handling, you should look at the Python module argparse, which offers a user-intuitive way of passing in arguments with flags and a built-in help menu. This is beyond the scope of this book.

You can build on this to perform more meaningful network tasks as you continue reading this book. For example, after reading Chapter 10, you'll be able to pass parameters like this into a script that actually connects to a device and issues a show command (or equivalent).

Using pip and Installing Python Packages

As you get started with Python, you'll likely need to install third-party software. For example, you may want to automate network devices with Netmiko, a popular SSH client for Python that we cover in Chapter 10. The most common way to distribute Python software, including Netmiko, is the Python Package Index (PyPI), pronounced "pie-pie." You can also browse and search the PyPI repository directly at *https://pypi.python.org/pypi*.

> pip, by default, installs the packages in the system. We strongly recommend using virtual environments to isolate your Python package installations. This topic is introduced next in "Isolating Your Dependencies with Virtualenv" on page 229.

You can use the pip program to install any software that's hosted on PyPI (such as Netmiko) to your machine directly from PyPI. The pip installer by default goes to PyPI, downloads the software, and installs it on your machine.

> pip3, an updated version of the original pip from Python 2, installs packages for Python 3+. Even though pip as a soft link could be also pointing to pip3, to avoid ambiguity, we use pip3 consistently in this book.

Using pip3 to install Netmiko can be done with a single line on your Linux machine:

```
ubuntu2004:~$ pip3 install netmiko
# output has been omitted
```

By default, this command will install the latest (stable release) of a given Python package in a system path (the path will vary based on the OS). However, you may want to ensure that you install a specific version—this is helpful so you don't automatically install the next release without testing. This is referred to as *pinning*: you can *pin* your install to a specific release. In the next example, we show how you can pin the installation of Netmiko to version 3.4.0:

```
ubuntu2004:~$ pip3 install netmiko==3.4.0
# output has been omitted
```

You can use `pip3` to upgrade versions of the software too. For example, you may have installed version 3.4.0 of Netmiko and when a new release is available, you can upgrade to the latest release by using the `--upgrade` or `-U` flag on the command line:

```
ubuntu2004:~$ pip3 install netmiko --upgrade
# output has been omitted
```

It's also common to install Python packages from *source*. That means getting a specific version from the source code (not released to PyPI)—for example, from GitHub, a version control system that we cover in Chapter 11. Perhaps the code under development in GitHub has a bug fix you need, but it hasn't been published.

When you get the source code of a Python project, there is a good chance you'll see two files in the root of the project: *requirements.txt* and *setup.py*. You can use these to install the Python package from source. The requirements file lists the requirements needed for the application to run. For example, here is the current *requirements.txt* for Netmiko:

```
paramiko>=2.0.0
scp>=0.10.0
pyyaml
pyserial
textfsm
```

You can see that Netmiko has five dependencies, commonly referred to as *deps*. You can also install these deps directly from PyPI by using a single statement:

```
ubuntu2004:~$ pip3 install -r requirements.txt
# output has been omitted
```

To completely install Netmiko (from source) including the requirements, you can also execute the *setup.py* file that you'd see in the same source code directory:

```
ubuntu2004:~$ python3 setup.py install
# output has been omitted
```

By default, installing the software with *setup.py* will also install directly into a system path. If you want to contribute back to a given project and actively develop the project, you can also install the application directly from where the files exist and are being developed:

```
ubuntu2004:~$ python3 setup.py develop
# output has been omitted
```

This makes it such that the files in your local directory are the ones running Netmiko. Otherwise, with the `install` option, you'll need to modify the files in your system path to affect the Netmiko install (for example, when troubleshooting an external library).

There is an even easier way to install a Python project from the source code without cloning the repository locally. This approach is especially useful when you don't need to develop code but just use a specific version, from a branch or a commit (see Chapter 11 for details). To target a specific branch, you can append @develop after the repository URL. The name of the branch is develop, but you could point to a specific commit or tag. This is particularly useful when the library is still not released to PyPI or when you want to use a feature that hasn't been released yet:

```
ubuntu2004:~$ pip3 install \
    git+https://github.com/ktbyers/netmiko.git@develop
# output has been omitted
```

Isolating Your Dependencies with Virtualenv

By default, pip3 installs the packages into your global Python environment. This works well for single-purpose applications (such as a container running one process), but your local development environment is going to become a nightmare sooner rather than later.

For example, when you work on your first Python project, say you install a specific version of an external library. Then a new project comes up, and one of its dependencies depends on exactly the same library you already have, but on a different version. Because pip3 installs the libraries globally, you have a problem.

But don't worry; Python offers you a solution by creating *virtual environments*, or *virtualenvs*. These isolated Python environments live inside a folder, with all the dependencies of a specific project. This *folder* could be placed wherever you prefer, and one common option is to put it directly in each project folder with the name *.venv*.

To create a new Python virtualenv, you use python3 -m venv, followed by the folder name. This command creates a brand-new Python environment in this folder, where the packages will be installed:

```
ubuntu2004:~$ python3 -m venv .venv
ubuntu2004:~$ ls .venv
bin  include  lib  lib64  pyvenv.cfg
```

But so far, you have created only the virtualenv, and you are still not using it because it's not *active*. The next step is to activate it. Run source on bin/activate within the virtualenv, and you will see how the *path* changes to (.venv), the name of your virtualenv, indicating that now the Python environment is not the global one but the one that has been activated. Now, if you check your Python binary path, it points to the one within the *.venv* folder:

```
ubuntu2004:~$ source .venv/bin/activate
(.venv) ubuntu2004:~$
(.venv) ubuntu2004:~$ which python
/home/ntc/.venv/bin/python
```

Do you remember installing Netmiko before? If you check the installed packages within the virtualenv, you won't find it! Similarly, anything you install while the virtualenv is activated is kept only on this virtualenv and won't affect the global environment or other virtualenvs:

```
(.venv) ubuntu2004:~$ pip3 list
Package    Version
---------- -------
pip        21.2.4
setuptools 57.5.0
wheel      0.37.1
```

Finally, you can go back to the global mode simply by *deactivating* the virtualenv:

```
(.venv) ubuntu2004:~$ deactivate
ubuntu2004:~$ which python
/usr/bin/python
```

Python has several packages (Pipenv, Poetry, and others) that can help you with dependency management, installation, and packaging. We strongly recommend you give them a try; they are really helpful!

As a best practice, keep every Python project in a different virtual environment. This approach will make your life much easier because you will avoid the pain of inconsistent package versions, inherited from each project's direct package dependencies.

Now that you have learned about installing and importing others' code, and have explored the Python built-in data types in "Understanding Python Data Types" on page 172, the next stop is to understand how to define your own data types: *classes*.

Understanding Python Classes

A *class*, in a programming language, contains *data* (attributes) and *procedures* (methods) that are related to its data. A class is one of the key abstractions that enable object-oriented programming (OOP) in Python (and similarly in other programming languages). OOP is about modeling real-world entities and how they interact; used correctly, OOP can make your code more readable, maintainable, and even more testable.

But, before going into defining your classes, you need to understand how to use others' defined classes.

Using Classes

To get access to classes from other modules, you use the same import statement you used to import functions in "Working with Python Modules" on page 222. Here, you import the class Device from your package vendors.cisco.device (from within the *ch6-python* directory):

```
>>> from vendors.cisco.device import Device
```

Classes are just abstract representations of an object. However, to create a specific instance of an object, you must *instantiate* the class. This looks similar to the way you call functions, and you can think of this syntax as calling a function that returns an instance of the class.

Then you can instantiate an instance of the Device class and get a Device object. As with functions, you pass some arguments, which are used to *construct* the instance. When you instantiate a class, you are actually calling the __init__() method, known as the *constructor*. The following snippet describes how to create three objects from the Device class and save them in different variables:

```
>>> switch1 = Device(ip='10.1.1.1', username='cisco', password='cisco')
>>> switch2 = Device(ip='10.1.1.2', username='cisco', password='cisco')
>>> switch3 = Device(ip='10.1.1.3', username='cisco', password='cisco')
```

Notice that each variable is a separate instance of Device:

```
>>> type(switch1)
<class 'vendors.cisco.device.Device'>
```

Once the class object is initialized, you can start using its *methods*. This is just like using the built-in methods for the data types you learned about earlier in the chapter. The syntax is *class_object.method*:

```
>>> switch1.show('show version')
```

> As a reminder, using method objects of a class is just like using the methods of the data types such as strings, lists, and dictionaries.

If you execute show for switch2 and switch3, you would get the proper return data back from each device as expected, since each object is a different instance of Device, and the show() method will use the connection data from each instance.

Now that you understand how to use classes, let's create your first class!

Building Your Own Classes

In the previous section, we introduced two main elements you need to define when building your own class:

- The *constructor* method (__init__()) to initialize the instance data (attributes)
- The methods that the objects of this class will expose

Taking as a reference the example from "Using Classes" on page 231, Example 6-7 implements the Device class, starting with the __init__() method.

Example 6-7. Building a class

```
>>> class Device:
...     def __init__(self, ip, username, password):
...         self.host_ip = ip
...         self.user = username
...         self.pswd = password
...
>>> router = Device(ip='192.0.2.1', username='abc', password='123')
>>>
>>> router.host_ip
'192.0.2.1'
>>>
>>> router.__dict__
{'host_ip': '192.0.2.1', 'user': 'abc', 'pswd': '123'}
```

With the class statement, you start the class definition (by convention, starting with a capital letter, but that's not mandatory).

And right after it, you define the __init__() constructor method (with def). Remember that this method is a dunder that will be called, magically, when the class is instantiated via Device(), returning an actual instance object. This newly created object is referenced, within the method definition, by self. As you build more class methods, you will use self to represent the instance of the class. However, self is a convention, not an actual Python keyword. It is simply the first argument a class method takes. In Example 6-7, the __init__() method stores only input arguments into object attributes, but this method could contain a more complex logic.

After the class definition, you instantiate it and assign it to the router variable, and then you access the data from one of its attributes with router.host_ip, similar to the way you would call the methods that will expose later, but without the parentheses.

Last, you access a hidden attribute, __dict__, that returns a default conversion of all attributes as a dictionary. This could look like magic now because you have not explicitly defined it, but you will understand when we explain *inheritance* in Example 6-9.

Defining class methods is pretty similar to defining functions, but with the context reference to `self` that points to the instance object created when the class is instantiated. See Example 6-8.

Example 6-8. Adding a method to a class

```
>>> class Device:
...     def __init__(self, ip, username, password):
...         # omitted for brevity
...
...     def show(self, command):                        ❶
...         return f'{command} output from {self.host_ip}'  ❷
...
>>> router = Device(ip='192.0.2.1', username='abc', password='123')
>>>
>>> router.show('show version')
'show version output from 192.0.2.1'
```

❶ The show() method, in the Device class, returns a string, combining an internal class attribute, `self.host_ip`, and a method argument, `command`.

❷ Class methods have access to the class instance object, via the first argument (usually named `self`).

Sometimes you don't need to completely create a brand-new class only to add a new attribute or a new method. In these cases, it's wiser to *extend* a class via *inheritance*. We will not go deep on this topic, but Example 6-9 shows how simple is to extend a class for your convenience while keeping the definition (attributes and methods) from the *parent* class.

Example 6-9. Extending a class

```
>>> class Router(Device):                               ❶
...     def disable_routing(self):                      ❷
...         return f'Routing is disabled for {self.host_ip}'
...
>>>
>>> router = Router(ip='192.0.2.1', username='abc', password='123')  ❸
>>>
>>> router.show('show version')                         ❹
'show version output from 192.0.2.1'
>>>
>>> router.disable_routing()
'Routing is disabled for 192.0.2.1'
```

❶ We define the new class `Router` as in Example 6-7, but taking the argument `Device`. At this point, `Router` is a copy of the original `Device` class, with a different name.

❷ After inheriting from a parent class, we can add new methods, as we do with `def disable_routing(self)`, or we can add other class attributes. Similarly as we add a new method, we can overwrite a previously existing one by redefining it in the child class.

❸ The initialization of the `router` object (`router = Router(...)`) is exactly the same as in Example 6-8, even though we have not defined a new `__init__()` method.

❹ The methods from the parent class are still available for the child objects.

Moreover, when an object is created from a class that inherits from another class, the object *belongs* to all the classes. In our example, `router` is, at the same time, a `Device` and a `Router`, as you can check with the `isinstance()` function:

```
>>> isinstance(router, Router)
True
>>> isinstance(router, Device)
True
```

We have barely touched the surface of Python classes, giving you the basics to start using OOP in your programs. Next, you will learn how to make your code execution more robust.

Embracing Failure with try/except

When you write code, you try to build it to provide a seamless execution, without flow execution crashes. However, as the code grows in complexity, guaranteeing an execution without errors becomes a big challenge because of the multiple cases to cover.

Every programming language provides a pattern or mechanism to facilitate error handling. In Python, error handling is built around exceptions (you've already seen some of them, such as `KeyError`, in previous code examples) and the try/except block.

Functions and methods communicate that something special has happened via *raising* an *exception*. Python has a `raise` statement to enable your code to signal to the caller of the function that a specific event has happened. Usually, this event is something wrong and must be handled by the caller, but its meaning is not necessarily negative.

From the caller's perspective, you can use the try/except block to handle exceptions. The *try* block is where the code is executed and exceptions may be raised, and the *except* captures specific exceptions, in order to handle them appropriately.

When exploring the dictionaries access, you saw that a `KeyError` exception is raised when you access a *key* that doesn't exist. Now let's try to not break the execution using the try/except block:

```
>>> device = {'hostname': 'router1', 'vendor': 'juniper', 'os': '12.1'}
>>>
>>> device["random_key"]
Traceback (most recent call last):
  File "<stdin>", line 1, in <module>
KeyError: 'random_key'
```

Here, when you access `random_key` without the try/except block, a `Traceback` is printed. This report contains *where* and *how* your code failed and broke the execution, and is useful to diagnose the issue and debug your code. To better understand the `Traceback` content, we should read it from the bottom up:

`KeyError`
  Exception name raised.

`'random_key'`
  The error message—in this case, the key that you are accessing.

`File "<stdin>", line 1, in <module>`
  Calls involved, pointing out to the file and the line of code. In this case, because we are using interactive mode, `stdin` is shown.

Now, using the try/except block, you make your code ready to handle the `KeyError` exception gracefully, simply printing a message and resuming the code execution:

```
>>> try:
...     device["random_key"]
... except KeyError:
...     print('The key is not present')
...
The key is not present
```

Python has a built-in class `Exception` that is the parent of all the other exceptions. Indeed, the `KeyError` exception inherits from `Exception`. Thus, you can use `Exception` as a wildcard to catch *all* Python exceptions and protect your code execution against any unexpected failure. However, use this with caution because it could mask real programming errors.

`Exception` is yet another class, with certain dunders that make it *special*. All you learned about classes still applies here, so you can create your own *exceptions* from the base `Exception` class, overwriting methods or adding extra attributes, and catch them in *try/except* blocks. When you build a Python library, the exception classes have a relevant role too, besides the other functions and classes you expose.

Before closing this chapter, we want to explain a slightly more advanced concept to introduce you to a new programming paradigm: parallel code execution.

Parallelizing Your Python Programs

By default, Python programs follow a *serial* execution pattern. Starting from an entry point, your code is executed one task after another, so the second task doesn't start until the previous task is completed. This is not a problem when you have a small program or when the time spent on each task is not significant. But what if one task takes too long, simply waiting for an external process to complete? Should your precious CPU stay empty until you get the response? Or, having multiple CPU cores, why not distribute processing load across them, instead of leaving them on the bench?

The solution to this challenge is performing multiple operations at the same time. Figure 6-1 illustrates the difference between running your code tasks in serial or running them in parallel.

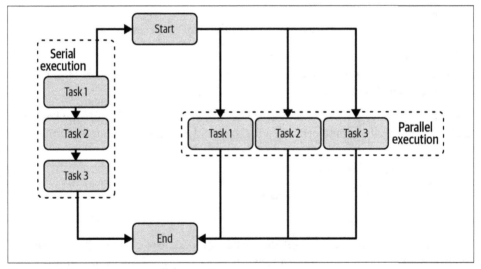

Figure 6-1. Serial versus parallel execution

The most common network automation use cases, interacting with APIs or remote network devices, are *I/O-bound* operations (entering a *blocking* state when waiting for the input/output data). To parallelize these operations, you can use threads. A *thread* is a separate flow of execution that runs at *the same time*.

Python supports multiple implementation options for parallelization. We don't cover all of them, but use the ThreadPoolExecutor utility to exemplify the idea.

 For *CPU-bound* operations, where it's necessary to spread the load over multiple processes (instead of multiple threads on the same process), you can use ProcessPoolExecutor, similarly to using ThreadPoolExecutor here.

First, you *simulate* a long-standing I/O task adding a *blocking* call, time.sleep(5), in the get_commands() function, the same function defined in Example 6-2:

```
>>> import time
>>>
>>> def get_commands(vlan, name):
...     time.sleep(5)
...     commands = []
...     commands.append(f'vlan {vlan}')
...     commands.append(f'name {name}')
...     return commands
...
```

As expected, in Example 6-10, if we execute the get_commands() function in a three-iteration loop, the total execution time is 15 seconds, because each function is called when the previous ends in a serial way.

Example 6-10. Serial execution

```
>>> def run_task(vlans):                              ❶
...     start_time = time.time()
...     for vlan in vlans:
...         result = get_commands(vlan=vlan['id'], name=vlan['name'])
...         print(result)
...     print(f'Time spent: {time.time() - start_time} seconds')  ❷
...
>>> vlans = [{'id': '10', 'name': 'USERS'}, {'id': '20', 'name': 'VOICE'},
{'id': '30', 'name': 'WLAN'}]
>>>
>>> run_task(vlans)
['vlan 10', 'name USERS']
['vlan 20', 'name VOICE']
['vlan 30', 'name WLAN']
Time spent: 15.008316278457642 seconds
```

❶ Wraps the loop into a run_task() function.

❷ Prints the time spent subtracting the initial and final time, using the time.time() function, which returns the time in seconds since the epoch.

Now, in Example 6-11, using ThreadPoolExecutor, the overall time spent is only 5 seconds instead of 15 seconds because the three tasks are executed concurrently. Imagine what this means when you have to execute a 30-second operation for hundreds of devices. Even though the code may look a bit overwhelming in the beginning, we hope this sounds appealing to you.

Example 6-11. Parallel execution

```
>>> import concurrent.futures
>>>
>>> with concurrent.futures.ThreadPoolExecutor() as executor:    ❶
...     start_time = time.time()
...     tasks = []
...     for vlan in vlans:                                        ❷
...         tasks.append(
...             executor.submit(
...                 get_commands, vlan=vlan['id'], name=vlan['name']
...             )
...         )
...     for task in concurrent.futures.as_completed(tasks):       ❸
...         print(task.result())
...     print(f'Time spent: {time.time() - start_time} seconds')
...
['vlan 10', 'name USERS']
['vlan 20', 'name VOICE']
['vlan 30', 'name WLAN']
Time spent: 5.001068830490112 seconds
```

❶ We introduce the ThreadPoolExecutor class, imported from concurrent .futures, to implement concurrency running the same get_commands() function. We use it as a context manager with the executor variable, automatically cleaning up threads upon completion.

❷ The first loop appends *future* tasks (using the executor).

❸ The second iterates over these tasks, getting the results when completed.

This example helps illustrate the potential of using parallelization in Python. Getting into the details of this code, or exploring other options, such as asyncio, are beyond the scope of this book.

However, this paradigm introduces some collateral effects that must be taken into account when building your code:

- When running code in parallel, by default, you don't control the ending order of the tasks. If your task's execution has dependencies, some kind of coordination will be needed (for instance, using *semaphores*).

- Depending on the parallelization approach, your functions may need to be rewritten, slightly. For instance, you might need to adopt asynchronous behavior when using the `async`/`await` pattern.
- Multiple tasks accessing the same memory object could cause data inconsistency. For instance, two tasks could update the value of the same variable at the exact same time. This can be solved using a *locking* mechanism, preventing concurrent access.
- Increasing the number of parallel tasks, and running concurrent connections, could overload the target endpoint if it's not ready to handle so many sessions. A good approach is to check the concurrency impact in the target endpoint, progressively, so as to not completely knock it down.

Despite the previous considerations, running code in parallel, with the appropriate design, can save a lot of time. With this last superpower, we end the Python chapter, where you have hopefully gained the basic knowledge to start building your Python applications.

Now, you are ready to start programming your first Python program, and as a bonus point, we give you a simple trick to learn more about Python's design philosophy. Try `import this` and see what happens!

Summary

This chapter provided a grassroots introduction to Python for network engineers. We covered foundational concepts such as working with data types, conditionals, loops, functions, and files, and even how to create a Python module that allows you to reuse the same code in different Python programs/scripts. We also got into more advanced topics such as classes and error handling, ending with a quick glance at parallel execution. All these topics should help you as a reference as you continue on with your Python and network automation journey.

In Chapter 8, we introduce you to data formats such as YAML, JSON, and XML, and in that process, we also build on the content in this chapter. For example, you'll take what you learned and start to use Python modules to simplify the process of working with these data types, and also see the direct correlation among YAML, JSON, and Python dictionaries.

But Python is not the only programming language used in network automation. Next, in Chapter 7, you will learn about another popular programming language for automation (Go), and you will start noticing commonalities and differences.

CHAPTER 7
Go

Earlier editions of this book covered a wide variety of tools and techniques within the world of network automation. Even at that time (when automation was still largely considered to be a nascent discipline), a multitude of tools existed to address the most common use cases. However, an alternative approach has always existed for use cases where those tools aren't sufficient on their own. Given Python's popularity and approachability, including a chapter focusing on that language makes sense. With this knowledge, network automation professionals always have the option of writing custom Python scripts to fill in any gaps in the existing ecosystem, should the existing tools prove insufficient on their own.

However, Python is no longer the only kid on the block. These days, another programming language can often be found in network automation initiatives of any scale: Go. Initially designed by Google in 2007, Go is used today by thousands of companies around the world. According to the 2021 Go Developer Survey (*https:// oreil.ly/-Y_PE*), 76% of respondents use Go at work. As might be expected, this includes a healthy percentage of technology-focused companies, but also includes industries like healthcare, retail, and manufacturing. Among many others, nearly 40% of respondents said they use Go for automation or scripting use cases. Clearly, something powerful in this relatively young language warrants a closer look for our purposes in the world of network automation.

Before we dig into Go, you should be aware of three significant industry trends, which will help place this chapter in the appropriate context:

Maturity of discipline and demand for specialized skills
> Despite the explosion of additional tools, demand for programming skills in network automation has *increased*, not decreased. This is not entirely unexpected: as the discipline matures, and the common, shared problems are solved by canned tooling, we move up the stack and require more specialized tools that are unique to our individual organizations/environments. Because of this, we also have a much more well-understood set of requirements for what we need our languages and tools to be able to provide.

Cloud native
> Go has an incredibly strong foothold in the area of cloud native technologies. Just as the server virtualization movement in the early 2010s had an immense influence and demand on increasing network agility (which eventually led to SDN), so too is the cloud native movement now having a profound impact on the techniques and technologies that network engineers must use to keep up. More than any other language, Go is the number one choice for integrating modern application infrastructure with the network automation discipline.

Growing community
> Just as the proliferation of libraries and general support for Go has exploded because of the cloud native movement, the last few years in particular have seen a surge of tools, libraries, and training materials focused on using Go for network automation. While Python is still the undisputed leader here because of its extensive, mature network automation ecosystem, the network automation community around Go has grown substantially and has made significant strides toward closing that gap.

These factors have led us to add this chapter to the book. We'll introduce you to Go and its application to network automation. We will, of course, explore each of these factors in the sections to follow. This will provide you with a potentially complementary alternative to Python, for those times when a custom solution is required.

As with the Python chapter, it's impossible to cover everything you need to know about Go in a single chapter. There's a reason programming languages dedicate entire books to even the most introductory concepts. We cover the basics using a few relevant examples so that by the end of this chapter you'll have a solid foundation, but consider this a starting point of your journey; in fact, we cover a few great next-steps at the end of this chapter. Along the way, we highlight some of Go's unique strengths so that you'll have a better understanding of when it might suit your purposes.

Why Go?

With Python dominating the network automation space, you might be wondering, why learn another programming language? Why specifically Go? To answer either question, we should first answer a more fundamental one: what requirements does the typical network automation professional have for any programming language? This is a question we as an industry haven't had to contend with often, given that for many years, Python was our only practical choice. However, it's an important one to consider these days; understanding these requirements will help us understand why the industry gravitated toward Python so strongly, and will enable us to identify other languages that may do the job as well, taking into account the unique strengths they may bring to the table.

We propose the following requirements:

Speed of development

Most network engineers are not seasoned developers and don't necessarily want to be (nor do their employers). The language must be simple enough that it's easy to get to value and iterate quickly. This requirement has two subrequirements. First, the language should be easy to adopt; a newcomer must be able to adopt this new language and its patterns and become moderately productive with it within a week or two. Second, the language should have low maintenance overhead: the language has to be easy enough to work with and maintain so that when problems arise, we can solve them quickly and simply.

Ecosystem

Again, we as network automators don't have the time to write everything from scratch. We must rely on an established ecosystem of libraries and tools to build upon. The language we choose must have at least a growing community of others working with this language, publishing these kind of integrations and collaborating to improve the developer experience for everyone.

Operational stability

The code we write controls the network, which powers everything else in our organization—so our code has to be rock-solid. For example, some modern languages do quite a bit of heavy lifting here, through static type checking, race condition detection, and memory safety guarantees. The language we choose must have the necessary tools to create a stable service, while not violating the other requirements.

No language is perfectly suited nor perfectly flawed when it comes to any of these requirements for network automation. Too much nuance exists to have an absolutist's view. For instance, Python has multiple implementations, each with its own trade-offs. In addition, Python and Go have many design patterns with their own strengths and weaknesses. In light of this, we will view the satisfaction of these requirements through a more subjective lens, from the perspective of the typical network automation professional. Our aim is to help guide you to making your own decision about which of these languages to pursue.

How do Python and Go compare when it comes to satisfying these requirements? Arguably, both do pretty well—each covering all three, with perhaps one slight weakness versus the other. For instance:

- Both Python and Go satisfy our speed-of-development requirement quite well. Both are extremely easy to adopt and require little maintenance overhead over the long-term. One of Go's strengths is that it was built for simplicity from the beginning; it typically provides only one or two ways to do something. This means that once you can understand Go code generally, reading others' code is not too difficult.

- When it comes to the network automation ecosystem, Python has the lead, without question. While Go's community is still growing rapidly, the early lead established by Python in the network automation community will be hard to beat. However, other, somewhat related communities may prefer Go in certain circumstances. For instance, the cloud native community rallied early around Go, and technologies from that ecosystem (e.g., gRPC and gNMI, both discussed in Chapter 10) are often biased toward Go support, or at least have supported Go for a longer period of time.

- For stability and reliability, Go is a much more modern systems-focused language, with a lot of safety-related features built right into the compiler. While creating a stable, reliable service in Python is certainly possible, it can take a considerable amount of extra work because of Python's runtime-focused nature. Additionally, Go programs can be compiled to a single, statically linked binary. Once a Go program is compiled, you don't need to install Go on every machine that will run the program or any third-party libraries you want to include in your program. This tends to result in a lower operational burden.

As you can see, both languages cover these requirements handily. Python isn't going anywhere anytime soon, but Go provides an attractive alternative that may be more suitable in certain cases.

You may also be asking, as many do when they first encounter these subjects, "Which do I learn first?" Take comfort in knowing that there's probably no wrong answer to this question, especially very early in your learning journey. There are definitely reasons to pick one language over the other, but these reasons are typically self-evident: for instance, if your organization is primarily a Python shop, it might be best to stick with that for now. On the other hand, if no precedent has been established, picking a more modern language like Go has advantages. In the absence of these kinds of external factors, the choice is mostly up to you. Explore both languages at a high level, and maybe write a little in each, before making your own decision.

This chapter is not promoting Go over Python, and this book as a whole does not suggest that you *have* to learn both, or even either. We do our best to highlight the strengths and weaknesses of all approaches, so that you can decide what works best in your particular case.

Is Go Faster Than Python?

Inevitably, when comparing these two languages, the question of speed comes up. Python does have a reputation for being slower than other languages, and while you can certainly apply optimizations to improve this, such as choosing different runtimes, this is a generally accepted fact of life for most Python developers. In any objective test, Go will be many times faster than Python, without a doubt.

How important, though, is the speed of our language in the world of network automation? You'll notice we didn't add this to our list of requirements. For most network automation use cases, seeking out Go solely for the purpose of addressing performance-related concerns is likely to be a red herring. *Most* use cases in network automation involve a lot of waiting for I/O, so any performance gains simply by language choice are usually moot. That said, speed is not something to disregard entirely, and performance is definitely a more significant factor in some use cases. Until those use cases present themselves, however, prioritize the other requirements listed in the preceding section.

Is Go Harder than Python?

It's not uncommon for those learning Go for the first time (especially those with primary experience in a language like Python) to develop the perception that Go is relatively difficult to adopt. This perception takes a few forms:

- Go is a statically typed language, whereas Python is dynamically typed (we cover this in more detail in an upcoming section). Python tends to be much more forgiving about which types are used in function parameters, for example.

- Go is a compiled language, which means a seemingly obstructive "extra step" must be performed before a working program is produced.

- Go often complains about things like invalid types and unused variables, preventing a program from even compiling until they're resolved.

Because of perceptions like these, it's not hard to understand why, to an outside observer, languages like Go can be viewed as more difficult compared to Python. Python is far more permissive in comparison.

Modern systems languages like Go have been moving in the direction of having the compiler do more work, and for good reason: the more errors we catch at compile time, the fewer we have to deal with at runtime. A junior engineer may view this extra compilation step (and any errors that surface here) as a hurdle or an impediment; a senior engineer will be thankful for the compiler's brief pause and will try to solve as many problems as possible *before* runtime, when it costs us and our organization much more severely.

Go—like Python—is also known as a *garbage-collected language*. This means it comes with a runtime that takes care of cleaning up unused memory references in the background, allowing you to focus just on the code you want to write. In contrast, languages like C and C++ require you to allocate and free memory yourself, which can not only be arduous but also vulnerable to memory management bugs. So, while it might be easy to write Go off as difficult because of the previous points we've discussed, it should be remembered that Go is much more like Python in this respect, and as a result, has a far lower barrier to entry than its compiled counterparts.

It's important to not overfocus solely on this requirement (speed of adoption is, after all, only one of our requirements). We want a language that's easy to adopt, stable, *and* resilient to operate in production. Fortunately, Go hits a bit of a sweet spot here: the learning curve is not that much steeper than for Python, but we get a tremendous amount of built-in value in the form of compile-time checks that provide a lot of stability and maintainability advantages for free.

Now that we've spent time setting the context for learning Go, let's dive into the fundamental concepts you'll need to know to understand this powerful language.

 Just as we mentioned in Chapter 6, we need to cover a lot of fundamental Go concepts before we can use these concepts to tackle real-world, complex network automation workflows. While the concepts discussed here are certainly relevant to network automation, this chapter is focused purely on these fundamentals, so that you have a solid foundation. Chapter 10 builds on this foundation by using some popular Go libraries and other APIs for performing common network automation tasks.

Fundamental Go Concepts

When first learning any programming language, it's helpful to start with a "Hello, world" example—that is, a minimal example of a working program that prints a short message to the terminal. You can run this program, see its output, and know that you're starting with a working example you can build on. Let's start with Example 7-1.

Full versions of the code examples in this chapter can be found in the book's GitHub repo at *https://github.com/oreilly-npa-book/examples/tree/v2/ch07-go*.

Example 7-1. Your first Go program

```
package main                                        ❶

import "fmt"                                         ❷

func main() {                                       ❸
    fmt.Println("Hello, network automators!")       ❹
}
```

❶ Packages allow us to organize the code into a logical hierarchy. We are specifying the `main` package here because we want to create an executable program. We'll explore packages in greater detail in later examples.

❷ The `import` keyword allows us to use other packages in the code. In this case, the `fmt` package is part of the standard library and is used for formatted I/O.

❸ The `main()` function is the primary entry point when creating an executable program. When we run a compiled Go program, this code represents the beginning of that program's logical flow. While indentation isn't as crucial in Go as it is in Python (in Go, scope is formally indicated using curly braces), automated formatting tools like `gofmt` will automatically indent scopes, such as this function.

❹ The `Println()` function is part of the `fmt` package we imported previously and allows us to print a simple string to the terminal as a line of output. You'll see this quite a few times in the examples to follow—if you're trying to follow along, don't forget to import `fmt`!

Future examples in this chapter are shortened for brevity. Unless otherwise noted, you can assume they can be found within a similar structure: a main package and a main() function. You can view the full, working version of any example at *https://git hub.com/oreilly-npa-book/examples/tree/v2/ch07-go*.

You can use `go run` to quickly compile and execute this program with a single command in your bash terminal, as shown in Example 7-2. This is extremely useful and gives you the same "scripting" experience you've come to love from Python, but with all of Go's unique benefits.

Example 7-2. Running your first Go program

```
~$ go run 1-first-program.go
Hello, network automators!
```

The `go run` command is a great way to quickly get started running Go code, but it has its limitations. You should also be aware of the `go build` and `go install` commands, especially if you want to build a reusable binary that you can distribute to other machines that don't have Go installed.

Now that we have a solid foundation to build on, let's get into some concepts. Next, we explore variables, common types, and how they compare with those found in Python.

Types and Variables

As with nearly any programming language, Go comes with a set of basic types. For the most part, they are comparable to the equivalent types in Python, so if you're familiar with those, these work much the same way. Table 7-1 shows the most commonly used types in Go.

Table 7-1. Common Go built-in types

Type	Example	Description
bool	false	Boolean value; true or false
int	3	Commonly used numeric type; used for integers
float	3.0	Numeric value for nonwhole numbers
string	"hello"	A series of textual characters

However, Go has some additional variations that you'll want to be aware of. For instance, int is short for a *signed integer*, which can be used to represent either negative or positive values. On the other hand, uint, which represents unsigned integers, can represent only positive integers.

Additionally, both uint and int, as well as float, may optionally include a number at the end, such as uint8 or float64. This is a way of statically specifying the size for that type: a uint8 is an 8-bit unsigned integer (also called a byte), and a float64 is a 64-bit floating-point number.

For types like uint and int that omit this size, the target system determines the size; for example, int is 32 bits long on 32-bit systems, and 64 bits long on 64-bit systems. It is overwhelmingly common (and indeed a Go best practice) to use these more flexible types when possible.

We later get into a few other built-in types, not to mention the multitude of externally defined types (or structs), but this simple set of types suffices for now. Next, we explore the use of variables in Go and make use of these types.

Variables in Go

In Go, variables are one of the fundamental building blocks of the language, as they are in many other programming languages. Variables allow you to create unique, ideally self-describing references to a value of a given type. Instead of passing around the string "Hello, network gophers!", you can assign this value to a variable—say, myString1—and then use the variable to reference that value. Variables, as the name implies, also allow you to reassign new values to that same reference, so you have to change this value in only one place.

You can create a variable in Go in a few ways. In general, the approach you choose depends on whether you want to initialize the variable with a value or leave to a default, or zero value. You may also want to explicitly specify the type, or let the compiler infer the type based on the value you initialize the variable with.

Example 7-3 explains these options:

Example 7-3. Initializing variables in Go

```
var myString1 string = "Hello, network gophers!"  ❶

var myString2 string                              ❷

var myString3 = "Hello, network gophers!"         ❸

myString4 := "Hello!"                             ❹

var (                                             ❺
    myString5 string
    myString6 = "Hello, network gophers!"
)
```

```
// This is invalid, as there is no explicit type declaration
// or a value from which the type can be inferred.
// So, this will fail to compile.
var whatIsThis
```

❶ This is the most explicit form; it initializes the variable with a value, while also explicitly stating its type.

❷ Omitting the value defaults to the *zero value* for that type—in this case, a zero-length string (`""`). Other types have different zero values; for instance, a `bool` will default to `false`, and an `int` type will default to `0`.

❸ The Go compiler can also infer the type based on the value passed in.

❹ The `:=` operator is shorthand for the previous example, which infers the type based on the provided value.

❺ The `var` keyword allows you to group variable declarations together, to improve readability.

If you were to copy this code into your own project as is, it would fail to compile, with the message *variable name* `declared but not used`. This is one major difference between Python and Go: Python has no problem running a program with unused variables (though it's common to use external linting tools to help catch such occurrences), whereas Go won't even compile a program successfully if unused variables are present. To fix this, we must *use* the variable—for instance as a parameter to a function call.

 This is another instance where "stricter" languages like Go seem to be looked at unfavorably in the network industry. After all, Python doesn't care if variables are unused or not, so why can't Go just let us do what we want so we can get this script written? Think of it this way: within a network device's configuration, ACLs often get unwieldy and hard to manage because we fear that removing an entry might break something, so they inevitably grow over time. To prevent this kind of thing from happening in our Go programs, the compiler is doing us a favor by letting us know upfront if a variable is unused. This helps improve readability and maintainability.

You can represent values in Go by using another approach that's particularly well suited for values that do not change. These are known as *constants*. Whereas variables allow you to reassign new values to them, constants do not; instead, they always retain the value they were initialized with.

Using constants has advantages: since they are unchanging by design, the compiler can safely make optimizations that aren't always possible with variables. Constants can also be used for potentially larger values—for instance, a floating-point number defined as a constant can have much higher precision than even the float64 type.

Their usage is similar to variables, but with a few nuances—particularly, the use of the const keyword. Also, unlike variables, unused constants are permitted at compile time. Example 7-4 shows a few ways to declare constants in your code.

Example 7-4. Initializing constants in Go

```
const myString string = "Hello, network gophers!"                                  ❶

// myString = "new value"                                                          ❷

const Pi = 3.14159265358979323846264338327950288419716939937510582097494459       ❸

const (                                                                            ❹
    myString2 = "Hello, network gophers!"
    retries   = 3
)
```

❶ This is the most explicit form of constant declaration.

❷ This will fail to compile; myString is declared above as a const, so a re-assignment like this is not permitted (thus this line is commented out).

❸ As with variables, the compiler will infer the type from the assigned value if not explicitly stated.

❹ Multiple assignment blocks work the same as variables as well.

Practically speaking, constants should be used when a particular value is known ahead of time and is guaranteed to not change. The maximum value for a VLAN or VXLAN identifier, or the speed for a Gigabit Ethernet interface, are good examples.

Static versus dynamic type systems

Especially if you have experience with Python, much of what's been discussed thus far may not be that new to you. Other than the obvious syntax differences, these concepts translate across language boundaries fairly well. Python also has variables and simple types like strings and integers. However, the two languages differ greatly in the way these types are verified and enforced.

Python uses a *dynamic type system*: the types used within a Python program are not checked for validity until runtime. If you write a program that uses an inappropriate type (say, as a parameter for a function), the program will run just fine until it encounters the line of code that makes this mistake. Trying to do math using strings and integers is a classic example, as shown in Example 7-5.

Example 7-5. TypeError in Python

```
>>> x = 1
>>> y = "2"
>>> x + y
Traceback (most recent call last):
  File "<stdin>", line 1, in <module>
TypeError: unsupported operand type(s) for +: 'int' and 'str'
```

If you had a program with this code, the error wouldn't occur until those lines executed. Imagine if your network automation system failed to handle this kind of error at 2:00 a.m. while you were fast asleep!

In contrast, Go uses a *static type system*: types are checked at compile time. You are unable to compile/build your program until these errors are addressed. Example 7-6, which is similar to the Python program shown in Example 7-5, will fail to compile, with the message `invalid operation: x + y (mismatched types int and string)`.

Example 7-6. Type mismatch in Go

```
x := 1
y := "2"
z := x + y
```

You are also not permitted to change the type of a variable once initialized. Example 7-7 will fail to compile because you've tried to assign a string value to x, which was first initialized as an `int`.

Example 7-7. Trying to change type in Go

```
var x = 1
x = "foo"
```

Another important point to understand is that even though in this example, x is initialized as an `int` implicitly because of the value it is initialized with, this still follows the rules of a static type system. The x variable is still just as much an `int` as if we'd explicitly stated so; this kind of type inference is purely for convenience.

This strict enforcement of types extends well beyond these simple examples, and you'll see their influence in many of the sections to follow.

Again, on the surface this all seems rather obstructive, doesn't it? After all, we're busy network engineers who just want to get on with our day job, much of which doesn't involve writing code.

However, most programmers (especially those also operating the software they write, as most network engineers do) would choose to encounter these kinds of errors on our terms, rather than encountering them later on, in the middle of the night.

While no compiler will ever completely prevent all runtime errors, modern systems languages like Go have made great strides to make the compiler as smart as possible—resulting in a program that's simpler and stabler—while still trying to make the development process as smooth as possible.

You may have also heard languages described as either *strongly* or *weakly* typed. This concept is tangentially related to the dynamic versus static spectrum we've discussed in this section, but ultimately describes a different way of looking at type systems. Recall that a static or dynamic type system is defined by *when* types are checked for validity (compile time versus run time). While there is no official definition, *strict versus weak* is generally used to describe how *lenient* the language is when a type mismatch occurs.

Recall Examples 7-5 and 7-6, from earlier in this section where we tried to perform a mathematical addition of the integer 1 and the string "2". Even though Python and Go differ in *when* they produce an error (Python does this at runtime, whereas Go won't even compile the program), neither will allow such an operation without an explicit conversion of some kind. These are both strongly typed systems.

In contrast, a language like JavaScript—which is considered weakly typed—will make an attempt to implicitly convert types whenever possible. Attempting to perform the operation 1 + "2" will automatically convert 1 to a string and *concatenate* the two operands, resulting in the string "12". While this does avoid a runtime error, this behavior could be entirely against the programmer's actual intent and could result in serious problems.

Now that you understand the basics of types and variables in Go, it's time to move on to the backbone of any real-world application of programming: flow control.

Flow Control

Flow control is a language-agnostic term used to describe logical constructs that allow you to specify the decisions your program should make, and the order in which certain tasks are carried out. If you've already read Chapter 6, this should sound familiar.

In Python, flow control is accomplished with loops, conditionals, and match statements. In fact, primitives like these are common across a wide variety of programming languages, which is why learning a second or third programming language is usually easier than learning programming for the first time in any language.

Let's start with conditionals. Like many programming languages (including Python), this is accomplished with an if statement. In Go, these work by testing whether an expression evaluates to a boolean true or false. This can be a simple expression (even a single boolean variable), or a more complex one, with chained logical or arithmetic operators, but ultimately it must evaluate to either true or false. Example 7-8 shows a simple Go conditional statement.

Example 7-8. Conditionals in Go

```
var snmpConfigured bool = true       ❶
if snmpConfigured {                  ❷
    fmt.Println("SNMP is configured!") ❸
}
```

❶ This is a boolean variable that we're setting explicitly here, but this could be set any number of ways, such as in response to parsing a config file.

❷ Because snmpConfigured is itself a boolean type, it can be used as an expression.

❸ Code within the braces will execute if the preceding expression is true.

The ! operator is used for negation. It can negate all or part of an expression, as in Example 7-9.

Example 7-9. Negating conditional expressions in Go

```
// In this case, the "!" negates the value of snmpConfigured,
// so the inner statement will execute only if snmpConfigured
// is false.
if !snmpConfigured {
    fmt.Println("SNMP is not configured.")
}
```

Sometimes you want to handle multiple outcomes within the same statement. The else keyword serves this purpose in Example 7-10.

Example 7-10. Else statement in Go

```
// Both conditions can be handled by using the else
// keyword.
if snmpConfigured {
    fmt.Println("SNMP is configured!")
```

```
} else {
    fmt.Println("SNMP is not configured.")
}
```

Boolean values can be only true or false. Other types, like integers, can have a wider variety of possibilities. For these, we must employ a few additional tricks:

- Relational operators such as greater-than (>) and less-than (<) can capture a range of numeric values.

- The else if phrase is used to capture another expression, should an earlier one fail to evaluate to true.

- Logical operators such && (AND) and || (OR) can be used to create more complex expressions.

Example 7-11 illustrates a few of these more complex expressions.

Example 7-11. More complex conditionals in Go

```
var vlanID int = 1024
if vlanID < 100 {
    fmt.Println("VLAN ID is less than 100")
} else if vlanID > 100 && vlanID < 1000 {
    fmt.Println("VLAN ID is between 100 and 1000")
} else {
    fmt.Println("VLAN ID is greater than 1000")
}
```

Sometimes you want to run a bit of code multiple times. In these cases, loops are a common choice.

Go has only a single type of loop, the for loop. As in Python, this can be used to loop, or iterate, over a set of values. However, it also can be used to simply execute a set of instructions until a specified condition is met.

The number of times a loop repeats is determined by the same logic that governs conditionals. In general, while a given statement evaluates to true, the loop continues to repeat itself. Once that expression evaluates to false, the loop exits. In many programming languages, this expression is often referred to as the *exit condition*.

Example 7-12 is a simple loop that initializes a counter variable i, and repeatedly prints its value and increments it by 1 while its value is less than or equal to 5.

Example 7-12. Simple loop with counter

```
// Simple loop that prints VLAN IDs in order from 1-5. It
// accomplishes this by incrementing a counter
// and exits once it's greater than 5
i := 1
```

```
for i <= 5 {
    fmt.Printf("VLAN %d\n", i)
    i = i + 1
}
```

 Printf(), another function from the fmt package that is similar to Println(), also allows you to create formatted strings where you can dynamically inject the VLAN ID into the output. You can read more about the formatting syntax in the the fmt package documentation (*https://pkg.go.dev/fmt*).

When the value of i is greater than 5, the loop's condition no longer evaluates to true, and the loop exits. The output produced by this code confirms this:

```
VLAN 1
VLAN 2
VLAN 3
VLAN 4
VLAN 5
```

Example 7-13 shows a more common way to write a simple loop like this. You place the initialization of i, the loop's exit condition, and the increment of i all on one line. While the syntax is different, the behavior of this loop is identical to the one in Example 7-12.

Example 7-13. Simple loop (classic notation)

```
for i := 1; i <= 5; i++ {
    fmt.Printf("VLAN %d\n", i)
}
```

Sometimes you need more fine-grained control over the behavior of these loops. For instance, in these examples, any instructions you place within the loop will be executed every time the loop repeats. What if you want the loop to repeat—or even exit—before the end of these instructions is reached?

For cases such as these, the continue and break keywords are essential. In Go, these keywords work almost exactly as they do in Python.

The continue keyword allows you to effectively skip over any remaining instructions. In Example 7-14, continue is used with a conditional that causes the loop to repeat before printing the value of i, only when that value is equal to 3.

Example 7-14. Using continue in Loops

```go
// We can use the continue keyword to cause the loop to repeat
// earlier than it normally would
for i := 1; i <= 5; i++ {
    if i == 3 {
        continue
    }

    // Because of the continue statement above,
    // this line will not run when i == 3
    fmt.Printf("VLAN %d\n", i)
}
```

The break keyword is used to exit from a loop entirely, even if the exit condition hasn't yet been reached. Example 7-15 uses the break keyword in a loop that doesn't even have an exit condition. This allows you to control exactly when and how this loop ends.

Example 7-15. Using break in loops

```go
vlanID = 1

for {                                              ❶
    fmt.Printf("Looking at VLAN %d\n", vlanID)     ❷

    if vlanID > 5 {
        break                                      ❸
    }

    vlanID++
}
```

❶ Loops with no exit condition (like this one) will loop indefinitely unless a break or return statement is used.

❷ This line will always execute as long as the loop is running.

❸ Because the loop doesn't have an exit condition, this break statement is the only way this loop will end.

In this example, the break statement is called when the value of vlanID is greater than 5. Since this takes place near the end of the loop, any preceding instructions will still be executed, even if vlanID is greater than 5 (a traditional loop with an exit condition would not have this behavior). Therefore, you see six lines of output:

```
Looking at VLAN 1
Looking at VLAN 2
```

```
Looking at VLAN 3
Looking at VLAN 4
Looking at VLAN 5
Looking at VLAN 6
```

One important point to keep in mind is that the `continue` and `break` statements by default apply only to the loop in which they appear. In the preceding examples, this is simple because you have only one loop—but if they appeared within nested loops, for example, it would be hard for the compiler to know which loop we are referring to when using these keywords.

The next section illustrates a method for solving this problem and presents other use cases for loops as we explore collection types in Go.

Collection Types

We've covered the basic types in Go, including `string`, `int`, and `bool`. However, sometimes a single instance of one of these types is not enough, and you may want to be able to work with a series of them.

This is a common use case for just about any practical programming task, and while the terminology may differ, you'll find tools to support this in any modern programming language.

Different languages have their own specific ways of storing series of values, which may have some language-specific behavior. For instance, in dynamic languages like Python we have the *list*, which is similar to an array but offers more flexibility, like being able to grow or shrink the series at will, as well as store a variety of types.

The generalized version you might learn about in a computer science course is the *array*, which is simply a fixed-length series of values of a given type. Go has the concept of an array, as shown in Example 7-16.

Example 7-16. Arrays in Go

```
// This declares "vlans" as an array of type "int"
// and a size of 3.
var vlans [3]int

// Once initialized, we can set values in the array
// by their index. Since arrays have a fixed size,
// the compiler can warn us if we use an invalid index
//
// Don't forget, slices and arrays start with index 0!
vlans[0] = 1

// You can also initialize arrays with values at
// the same time
vlans2 := [3]int{1, 2, 3}
```

Arrays are a commonly supported collection type, especially in compiled, statically typed languages like Go, because the compiler can easily calculate how much memory is required to store an array. On a 64-bit machine, int is 64 bits, and the arrays in Example 7-16 have a fixed size of 3, so a minimum of 192 bits of memory is needed to store each of them (though in practice this ends up being slightly higher because of padding).

From a practical standpoint, however, you'll almost never see arrays used in Go code. This is because arrays are inflexible—for instance, arrays have a fixed size. If you want to add an element to an array, you have to create a new one with the size you want and then copy the values from the smaller one yourself.

Fortunately, Go offers another option: the slice. *Slices* are similar to arrays in that they store a sequence of values, but they're more flexible. For instance, slices don't have a fixed size; you can grow them as needed. For this reason, slices are an overwhelmingly more popular choice than arrays in Go.

However, slices and arrays in Go aren't totally unrelated concepts. In fact, slices are really just a thin abstraction on top of arrays, and it is in this abstraction where slices gain their flexibility advantage. You can think of slices as simply a *view* into an array—or as the Go blog puts it (*https://oreil.ly/mTBVn*), a "descriptor of an array segment." The advantage of using slices, and the built-in functions for working with them (as we'll explore in the following examples), is that the management of this *backing* array (the array to which the slice is providing a view) is done for you.

The syntax for initializing a slice is similar to that in Example 7-16, but with slices, we can omit the size parameter. Example 7-17 shows a few ways you can initialize slices in Go.

Example 7-17. Initializing a slice

```
var intSlice []int                          ❶

var stringSlice []string                    ❷

var vlanSlice = []int{11, 22, 33, 44, 55}   ❸

vlanSlice2 := []int{11, 22, 33, 44, 55}     ❹
```

❶ Initializing a slice is similar to initializing an array—just leave out the size! Note, though, that this slice is empty; we need to append values to it before we can do much with it.

❷ We can create slices of just about any type; here's a slice of strings!

❸   The literal method using curly braces also allows us to initialize the slice with values at the same time.

❹   This is identical to ❸.

As mentioned previously, slices are more flexible than arrays, and one of the most obvious benefits of this flexibility is that they don't have a fixed size; you can add elements as needed. This is done with the `append()` built-in function, as illustrated in Example 7-18.

Example 7-18. Appending elements to a slice

```
// append() takes the original slice from the previous example, adds
// a new element, and returns the resulting new slice.
// That's why we're passing "vlanSlice" as the first parameter but then
// overwriting it with the result.
vlanSlice = append(vlanSlice, 66)

fmt.Println(vlanSlice) // output: [11 22 33 44 55 66]
```

As mentioned previously, slices are really just a view into a backing array that is managed for you. This view is defined by two properties:

Length
   The current size of the segment of the backing array that the slice represents.

Capacity
   The maximum size of the slice, which is another way of saying "the size of the backing array."

You can use the `cap()` and `len()` functions to find out the capacity and length of a given slice, as shown in Example 7-19.

Example 7-19. Slice capacity and length

```
// Let's redefine vlanSlice back to a length of 5 elements
vlanSlice = []int{11, 22, 33, 44, 55}

// output: vlanSlice cap is 5, len is 5
//
// The "cap()" function returns an integer containing the slice's capacity,
// len() returns the slice's length. We can see that after initialization,
// both are set to 5, meaning that the backing array has a capacity of 5,
// and the "segment" of that backing array that the slice provides a view
// to is also 5.
fmt.Printf("vlanSlice cap is %d, len is %d\n", cap(vlanSlice), len(vlanSlice))
```

The difference between these two properties can be seen by repeating this print statement after appending some additional values to the slice that we defined in Example 7-19. See Example 7-20.

Example 7-20. Slice capacity and length after appending

```
vlanSlice = append(vlanSlice, 66)

// output: vlanSlice cap is 10, len is 6
//
// After appending a value, the slice length increased to 6
// as expected, but the capacity is now 10! This is because we reached
// the maximum capacity of the backing array, so append() had to allocate
// a new one.
fmt.Printf("vlanSlice cap is %d, len is %d\n", cap(vlanSlice), len(vlanSlice))

// Append one more time
vlanSlice = append(vlanSlice, 77)

// output: vlanSlice cap is 10, len is 7
//
// After another append, the length has yet again increased to 7, but the
// capacity remains unchanged, because it is greater than the length.
// This means that append() did not have to allocate a new backing array;
// it had enough room to spare to accommodate the additional element.
fmt.Printf("vlanSlice cap is %d, len is %d\n", cap(vlanSlice), len(vlanSlice))
```

 You may see different allocations after calling append() as the behavior of this reallocation may vary based on the types used and the platform your code is running on, etc. The important point to remember is that this reallocation is done for you, so you don't need to do it yourself.

The lesson to learn here is that being able to dynamically append elements to a slice does come with potential drawbacks to consider. Repeatedly appending elements to a slice may cause its length to outgrow its capacity. When this happens, a new backing array will have to be allocated, and then on top of that, the elements from the old backing array will have to be copied over to the new.

The good news is that append() does all that for you, so you don't have to do it yourself. However, these operations can have a significant negative impact on performance, especially for large slices. Imagine appending elements to a slice with millions of elements!

One way to deal with this is to use make() to initialize a slice. When using this function, you must specify the type and length of the slice you wish to create, but you can also optionally specify the capacity for the slice, as shown in Example 7-21.

Example 7-21. Using make() to set slice capacity

```
preallocatedVlanSlice := make([]int, 2, 50)  ❶

// output: preallocatedVlanSlice cap is 50, len is 2
fmt.Printf("preallocatedVlanSlice cap is %d, len is %d\n",
    cap(preallocatedVlanSlice), len(preallocatedVlanSlice))

preallocatedVlanSlice[0] = 1                  ❷
preallocatedVlanSlice[1] = 2                  ❷

for i := 3; i <= 50; i++ {                    ❸
    preallocatedVlanSlice = append(preallocatedVlanSlice, i)
}

// output: preallocatedVlanSlice cap is 50, len is 50
fmt.Printf("preallocatedVlanSlice cap is %d, len is %d\n",
    cap(preallocatedVlanSlice), len(preallocatedVlanSlice))
```

❶ We can get the flexibility benefits of slices and the predictability/performance of arrays by using make() to declare slices with a length (and capacity) ahead of time.

❷ Because our slice's length is 2, we can set the first two elements to indices 0 and 1.

❸ If we go beyond this length, we must use append()—but since the slice has a capacity of 50, we can add 48 more elements before append() must allocate a new backing array. Until then, this will simply grow the length and set values at the referenced index. Efficient!

If you know in advance how large a slice might become, you can use make() to avoid the costly reallocation that can happen when using append().

You can use what you learned earlier about loops to iterate over a slice. This is useful when you want to perform an operation over the elements of a slice individually. Example 7-22 does this while printing each element of the slice.

Example 7-22. Iterating over slices with for loops

```
var vlanSliceIter = []int{11, 22, 33, 44, 55}

for i := 0; i < len(vlanSliceIter); i++ {  ❶
    fmt.Printf("vlanSliceIter index %d has a value of %d\n", i, vlanSliceIter[i])
}

for i := range vlanSliceIter {              ❷
    fmt.Printf("vlanSliceIter index %d has a value of %d\n", i, vlanSliceIter[i])
}
```

```
for i, val := range vlanSliceIter {          ❸
    fmt.Printf("vlanSliceIter index %d has a value of %d\n", i, val)
}
```

❶ We can use a for loop with a counter variable to iterate over the slice. Starting at 0 and ending before we reach the end of the slice allows us to iterate over each element one at a time.

❷ Alternatively, we can use the range keyword to do the same thing. At each iteration, the variable i will be set to the next index of the slice.

❸ The range keyword can also provide the value at each index.

Combining range with some of the other keywords you learned like break or con tinue can be useful for controlling when to act on a particular element in a slice, or when to stop iterating entirely, as shown in Example 7-23.

Example 7-23. Breaking out of slice iteration

```
// When searching an array or slice for a particular value, you can use
// the break statement to stop iterating once you've found it.
toFind := 33
for i, val := range vlanSliceIter {
    if val == toFind {
        fmt.Printf("Found! Index is %d\n", i)

        // Since we've found our value, there's no point in looping any further.
        // We can use break to stop iterating over the slice.
        break
    }
}
```

As we stated previously, continue and break statements by default apply only to the loop in which they appear. As in Example 7-23, this can be quite simple when you have only one loop. However, for multiple loops nested within one another, these keywords may not be sufficient on their own, as the compiler will assume you're referring to the innermost loop. To solve this problem, you can use *labels*, which allow you to refer to a loop scope other than the immediately local scope. If you have a set of deeply nested loops, this allows you to break out of a loop scope of your choosing.

Let's say you have a data structure made of nested slices of varying types, which represents a series of network devices. Each device has a series of interfaces, and each interface has a series of VLANs configured on them. If you want to find the first device and interface that was configured with VLAN 400, you'd need to use a series of nested loops to search for this. Once found, it's not very useful to continue iterating, so you want a way to stop all loops from iterating.

Example 7-24 uses a label on the outermost scope of a nested loop so that you can break out of it even if you use the break keyword on the innermost loop.

Example 7-24 uses structs so you can more easily refer to the slices you're iterating over by name (e.g., .interfaces, .vlans, etc.), which are defined outside this particular example. We cover this concept in "Structs" on page 275, and you can always see the full example in the repository at *https://github.com/oreilly-npa-book/examples/tree/v2/ch07-go*.

Example 7-24. Using labels on loops

```
deviceloop:                                              ❶
    for _, device := range devices {                     ❷
        for i, iface := range device.interfaces {        ❸
            for _, vlanID := range iface.vlans {          ❹

                if vlanID == 400 {
                    fmt.Printf("Device %s has vlan 400 configured on interface %d\n",
                        device.hostname, i)
                    break deviceloop                       ❺
                }
            }
        }
    }
```

❶ This label deviceloop applies to the outer loop, which is declared immediately in line ❷. We can use continue or break statements at any level of nested loop to refer explicitly to this outer loop scope by name.

❷ This outer loop iterates through a slice of devices.

❸ This middle loop iterates through a slice of that device's interfaces.

❹ This inner loop iterates through a slice of that interface's VLAN IDs.

❺ A typical break statement would break out of only the inner loop. By referring to the deviceloop label we declared earlier, we can specify that we want to break out of the outermost loop. This means that all three loops stop iterating.

Note that continue statements work the same way; if you want to skip other interfaces on a particular device but still look at the interfaces of the next device in the slice, you could use continue in this example to print all devices that have an interface configured with VLAN 400, while skipping any unnecessary iterations in the process.

While labels have their place, using them to solve challenges with nested loops can have a negative impact on the maintainability of your code. Even the simple code in Example 7-24 can be difficult to follow, and this will only increase as the complexity of your program grows. In many cases, the use of labels can be taken as a hint that it may be time to break up your code a little more. In an upcoming section, you'll learn about using functions to build reusable blocks of code, and how you can use them to solve this problem in a more maintainable way.

As you can see, slices are a powerful tool for storing a sequence of values. However, they're not the only collection type in Go. In some use cases, a slice might not be the best choice; for instance, as you saw in the previous example, in order to find a value in a slice, you don't implicitly know its index up front. Rather, to find it, you must iterate over the slice until the element is found. For large slices, this can take a long time.

Sometimes, a key-value data structure could be a more appropriate choice. These work by storing a particular value using a corresponding *key*, forming a key-value pair. Once stored, the value can be looked up simply using this key, regardless of where that value is stored in memory. Unlike with slices or arrays, this operation is extremely fast, as it doesn't require iteration.

This kind of data structure is also common in many programming languages, but may be known by different names. You saw this in Chapter 6 in the form of dictionaries. Go's key-value data structure is called the *map*. The methods for initializing maps are somewhat similar to slices, but have a few minor differences and some important considerations. Example 7-25 shows a few of these.

Example 7-25. Initializing maps

```
// CAREFUL - this syntax will only declare the map but will not
// initialize it.
var nilMap map[string]int
// Trying to write to this map will cause a runtime panic!
nilMap["foo"] = 80

// It's much safer to declare and initialize the map at the same time.
// Each of these examples is equivalent - they each declare and initialize
// a map with a "string" type for the keys, and an "int" type for the values.
var myMap = make(map[string]int)
var myMap2 = map[string]int{}
myMap3 := map[string]int{}

// The "literal" method using curly braces also allows us to initialize
// the map with some values at the same time.
vlanMap := map[string]int{
    "VLAN_100": 100,
```

```
        "VLAN_200": 200,
        "VLAN_300": 300,
}
```

If you've already gone through Chapter 6, some of the syntax for reading from or writing to this map should be somewhat familiar, perhaps with some minor differences. Example 7-26 illustrates reading a value from a map, writing new keys (or overwriting existing ones) to the map, and deleting existing keys.

Example 7-26. Reading, writing, and deleting keys from maps

```
vlan := vlanMap["VLAN_300"]        ❶
fmt.Printf("vlan is %d\n", vlan)

vlanMap["VLAN_400"] = 401          ❷
vlanMap["VLAN_400"] = 400          ❸

delete(vlanMap, "VLAN_300")        ❹
fmt.Println(vlanMap)

fmt.Println(vlanMap["VLAN_999"])   ❺
// output: 0
```

❶ This reads a value from the map using the expected key and creates a new variable `vlan` with this value.

❷ This syntax adds a single key-value pair to the map. Note that the key is a string, and the value is an int, which matches the types declared when the map was created.

❸ We can overwrite an existing key.

❹ We can delete a key-value pair from a map by using the `delete()` function. This requires two parameters: first the map itself, and then the key to delete.

❺ Reading a key that doesn't exist will return the zero value for the value's type—in this case, 0.

One important point to take away from Example 7-26 is that looking up a key that doesn't exist in a map will not produce an error, as it does in other languages like Python. Rather, if you attempt to read a key from a map that doesn't exist, you'll get back the zero value for the type used as that map's value.

The *zero value* for a type is another way of saying the *default* value for a type. If you create a string variable but don't initialize it with a value, the value will be an empty string (""). Boolean variables default to false, and int variables default to 0. Since your map uses int for its value type, this is what you'll get back if you try to read a key that doesn't exist.

Because you'll get a zero value instead of an error, knowing whether a given key exists in the map can be important. Imagine reading a key that *does* exist in the map, but the value for that key just happens to be that type's zero value. It's a totally reasonable scenario—and in this case, it would be impossible to rely solely on the value retrieved to determine whether the key actually exists in the map, since you'd get the zero-value back either way.

Another problem is the behavior around writing keys to the map. If the key doesn't already exist, writing a new key is no problem. However, if the key does already exist, writing to this key will silently replace its old value, which may not be desired. In some cases, knowing first whether the key already exists can be useful, so you can then decide whether to replace the existing value.

Fortunately, Go offers precisely what you need for both of these use cases: a way to test whether a key exists in a map. You can use this within a conditional (if) statement to perform instructions depending on whether the key is found in the map. Example 7-27 shows this idea in action.

Example 7-27. Testing whether a key exists in a map

```
if val, found := vlanMap["VLAN_999"]; found {        ❶
    fmt.Printf("Found vlan %d\n", val)               ❷
}

if _, found := vlanMap["VLAN_999"]; !found {         ❸
    fmt.Println("Did not find VLAN_999 in the map")  ❹
}

if val, found := vlanMap["VLAN_400"]; found {
    fmt.Printf("Found vlan %d\n", val)               ❺
}
```

❶ The same syntax used for reading a key from a map can optionally return a second boolean value, which is set to found. We can then test whether found is true (which indicates the key already exists) on the same line by adding a semicolon and then the variable found on its own (remember, booleans can be used as entire expressions in conditionals).

❷ The key doesn't exist, but the conditional in ❶ evaluates to true only if it is found—so this line will *not* execute.

❸ We can test the reverse by simply negating found; this is an easy way to test that a key is *not* found in a map. In this case, we don't expect the retrieved value to be useful, so we can ignore it by replacing val with an underscore. This tells the compiler to discard the retrieved value.

❹ This key still doesn't exist, but unlike the preceding conditional, this one evaluates to true if the key is *not* found, so this line *will* execute.

❺ This conditional specifies a key that *does* exist, and evaluates to true if it's found in the map—so this print statement *will* execute.

You can, of course, include much more than print statements within these conditionals. You may choose to delete a key if it exists, or perhaps write a key to a map *only* if it doesn't already exist, for example. Having the ability to first understand whether a key exists in a map enables you to decide about the behavior of your program based on a map's state.

As with slices, you may want to be able to iterate over the key-value pairs in a map, as shown in Example 7-28. You might notice the syntax is similar to iterating over a slice (using the range keyword).

Example 7-28. Iterating over key-value pairs in a map

```
// As with slices, the range keyword allows us to easily
// iterate over the key-value pairs in the map.
// Note that unlike slices, maps are not ordered.
for key, value := range vlanMap {
    fmt.Printf("%s has a value of %d\n", key, value)
}

// If we don't need the values, we can omit the second variable to retrieve only the
// keys out of the map.
for key := range vlanMap {
    fmt.Printf("Found key %s\n", key)
}
```

Thus far in this chapter, we've explored quite a few of Go's built-in types: singular types like int, string, and bool, as well as collection types like maps and slices. We've also explored flow-control tools like conditionals and loops. Even the simplest program or script will use most or all of these concepts. However, inevitably, those small scripts grow to a point where it may be necessary to break up the code and create reusable chunks. The next section explores how to do this in Go with functions.

Functions

The vast majority of programming languages you might run into offer the ability to create blocks of code that are somewhat self-contained and can be used to accomplish a specific task. These are often called *functions*. They have a few benefits that apply in just about any programming language:

Reusable code
> Functions can make it possible for you to create chunks of code that can be reused by you or even other programmers. For instance, the `fmt` package in the standard library has the `Println()` function, which we've made liberal use of in this chapter thus far. You didn't have to worry about the details of how to actually write text to standard output; you just called the function, and it did the rest. Creating functions that perform even moderately complex tasks on their own can make future programming more productive.

Improved readability and maintainability
> Focusing on accomplishing a specific task in a function makes that task much easier to reason about. Code within the function is there only to facilitate that single task, and the rest of your program can simply call this function without worrying about what's happening inside.

You've already seen functions in use in this chapter; recall that all the examples thus far are designed to be executed within a `main()` function. This function, defined within a package named `main`, will be automatically called when the resulting binary is executed. Example 7-29 shows a simple program that illustrates this.

Example 7-29. The main function

```
// This is a function like any other - but because it
// has the special name main and is located within a
// package also called main, it will be automatically
// called when this program is executed.
func main() {
    fmt.Println("Hello, network automators!")
}
```

However, you can also define your own functions. For instance, Example 7-30 shows that the call to `fmt.Println()` can be wrapped in a custom function `doPrint()`, which can then be called from `main()`.

Example 7-30. A minimal function

```
func main() {
    doPrint()
}
```

```
func doPrint() {
    fmt.Println("Hello network automators!")
    fmt.Println("Welcome to Network Programmability and Automation!")
    fmt.Println("Enjoy this chapter on the Go programming language.")
}
```

This can be useful if you simply want to make a set of tasks more repeatable. Calling a single function to perform many tasks can keep the code in `main()` much simpler and easier to understand.

However, while certainly permissible, it's not always practical for functions like this to be truly self-contained. Functions often require *input* to be able to do their tasks; the tasks themselves may be defined in the function, but they often need some kind of data from elsewhere in the program to do their work. For instance, the call to `fmt.Println()` isn't that useful unless you provide it with the string you want to print to standard output.

For this reason, many functions have one or more *parameters*. These work like variables that are initialized and usable within the scope of the function, but are populated with values passed when the function is called. These follow the same strict typing rules as normal variables, and their type has to be explicitly declared within the function definition. Example 7-31 shows a function `printMessage()` with a parameter `msg`, which is a `string` type. You can then refer to `msg` as if it were any other string variable.

Example 7-31. Function with a parameter

```
func printMessage(msg string) {
    fmt.Printf("Hello network automators, today we're learning %s!\n", msg)
}
```

To reiterate a point made earlier, this strict type system behavior is often one of the arguments made in favor of languages like Python. Because these languages don't require function parameters to have an explicit type like this, they are perceived as easier to learn. However, this kind of flexibility adds a nontrivial amount of complexity for the programmer, who will inevitably have to add type checks to ensure that the function won't fail at runtime if the wrong type is used.

Strict type systems like this may seem overly cumbersome on the surface, but don't take for granted the time and mental energy saved in avoiding the kind of runtime checks necessary in dynamic languages. These systems also make your code easier to understand. Remember, the smarter your compiler is, the more maintainable and stable your program will be!

Functions not only accept input in the form of parameters, but can also return values to be consumed by the caller (perhaps to initialize a new variable). Like parameters, the return type must be explicitly declared. Example 7-32 shows a function that calculates the total number of addresses in an IPv4 prefix. The caller must only provide the length of the prefix as an `int` parameter, and the function will return an `int` value representing the number of addresses.

Example 7-32. Function with parameter and return type

```
func totalIPv4Addresses(prefixLen int) int {   ❶
    x := 32 - prefixLen                         ❷

    addrCount := math.Pow(2.0, float64(x))      ❸

    return int(addrCount)                        ❹
}
```

❶ `totalIPv4Addresses()` is a function for calculating the number of addresses in an IPv4 prefix of a provided length. `prefixLen` is a parameter of type `int`. The return type for this function is also `int`, which is declared after the set of parentheses containing the function parameter(s).

❷ To calculate the number of addresses in an IPv4 address, we must calculate 2^x, where x is `prefixLen` subtracted from 32. So let's first get x.

❸ Go doesn't have an exponent operator, but we can use the `Pow()` function in the `math` package. This function has two parameters, and each has a type of `float64`, which is why we're converting the latter using the `float64` built-in function (`2.0` is already a `float64`).

❹ `math.Pow()` also has a return type of `float64`, so we must convert it to an `int` before returning it, to satisfy the function's return type. The `return` keyword allows us to exit a function immediately and return the value provided.

Because this function returns a value, you can capture it in a new variable to be used later, as illustrated in Example 7-33.

Example 7-33. Calling a function with a parameter and return type

```
func main() {
    // Create a variable to hold the prefix length we'll pass in to
    // totalIPv4Addresses()
    prefixLen := 22

    // Call totalIPv4Addresses and provide the variable prefixLen as the
    // required parameter. (We could provide a value of 22 directly as well,
```

```
    // but this way we can reuse this variable in the log message below.)
    //
    // Note also that we're assigning the return value to a new variable
    // called "addrs"
    addrs := totalIPv4Addresses(prefixLen)

    fmt.Printf("There are %d addresses in a /%d prefix\n", addrs, prefixLen)
    // output: There are 1024 addresses in a /22 prefix
}
```

Example 7-34 shows that functions can have multiple parameters or multiple return types.

Example 7-34. Function with multiple parameters and return values

```
func main() {
    // both input parameters and return values are separated by commas
    sum, product := sumAndProduct(2, 6)
    fmt.Printf("Sum is %d, product is %d\n", sum, product)
}

// sumAndProduct takes in two integers x and y, and returns their sum and product,
// respectively.
//
// Note that the input parameters x and y are separated only by a comma - since
// they're both integers, we can just specify int once after them.
//
// Also, note that the return types are also separated by a comma and also wrapped
// in parentheses.
func sumAndProduct(x, y int) (int, int) {
    sum := x + y
    product := x * y
    return sum, product
}
```

The examples thus far are fairly simple functions performing basic mathematic tasks that have a predictable outcome. However, some functions include operations that can fail, such as those that rely on I/O from the network or filesystem. It's important to know when a particular operation has succeeded or failed, so we can decide what to do next; we could perhaps log a message to our user and/or try the operation again.

Go handles errors like these with a special error type. You can see this type in the declaration of the function createVLAN() in Example 7-35.

Example 7-35. Function that returns an error value

```
func createVLAN(id uint) error {                         ❶

    if id > 4096 {                                       ❷
        return errors.New("VLAN ID must be <= 4096")     ❸
```

```
    }
    fmt.Printf("Creating VLAN with ID of %d\n", id)  ❹
    return nil
}
```

❶ createVLAN() takes in an unsigned integer parameter for the VLAN ID and returns an error type if a problem is encountered.

❷ Even though the uint type (used for the id parameter) can support billions of values, you know that 4096 is the maximum VLAN ID. So we can add a conditional that checks for this and returns a new error if the ID is over this value.

❸ New() is a function in the errors package that allows us to initialize a new error value from a string containing your custom error message.

❹ This will execute only if id is a valid VLAN ID, so to simulate the creation of a VLAN, we'll print a log message and return nil as the error value, which indicates that no error occurred.

In Go, after calling a function that returns an error, it's necessary to explicitly check this error value. In the vast majority of cases, you'll want to do this immediately after the function returns. Unlike languages like Python, which work by throwing exceptions that could stop your program if you don't handle them properly, Go requires that you explicitly check the returned error for a non-nil value to determine whether an error took place. Example 7-36 illustrates a common pattern that occurs after most function calls.

Example 7-36. Handling errors

```
// It is conventional to assign error return types to a variable err.
err := createVLAN(50)

// If err is not a nil value, it means an error occurred, so we should
// check for that immediately after calling the function above.
if err != nil {
    // This is where you could take steps to recover from the error
    // if possible.
    fmt.Println(err)
}
```

Not every function returns an error type. Some functions return only concrete types like int or bool, and others return nothing at all. When calling a function, especially one that you didn't write, take the time to understand the function's documentation if it's available so you can properly interpret any values it returns.

Previously, you used the continue and break keywords to more carefully control the operation of loops in Go. In Example 7-24, you also used labels to disambiguate which loop scope is being targeted by these keywords, in the event of nested loops. However, you can use what you just learned about functions as a potentially more maintainable alternative to using labels.

Anywhere within the scope of a function, you can use the return keyword to exit from that function, regardless of any additional level of scope (i.e., from conditionals, loops, etc.) in which it is called. Example 7-37 makes a nested loop more readable by putting it in its own function and relying on the return keyword to break execution when desired.

Example 7-37. Returning from a function to break out of nested loops

```go
func returnFromNestedLoops() {
    for _, device := range devices {         ❶
        for i, iface := range device.interfaces {
            for _, vlanID := range iface.vlans {
                if vlanID == 400 {
                    fmt.Printf("Device %s has vlan 400 configured on interface %d\n",
                        device.hostname, i)
                    return              ❷
                }
            }
        }
    }
}
```

❶ No label is needed here!

❷ The return keyword immediately exits from the entire function, so this effectively breaks out of all three loops.

In some cases, using return can provide a more readable alternative than the label-based approach. In this example, you are not only avoiding the use of labels (which can be difficult to keep track of), but also enclosing the entire nested loop structure within the function, making it easier to reason about.

Next, we move beyond the built-in types like int and string we've been using thus far to work with custom-defined types and the variety of tools Go offers to work with them.

Structs

Sometimes the built-in types like integer, boolean, and string are not sufficient to create representations of complex logical or even physical constructs that you want to be able to represent in your programs. For instance, using one of these built-in types, how might you represent a network device such as a switch or a router? Would you use a string to represent this? A string type might capture the hostname of this device, but that's it—what about that device's port layout, its configuration, or its operational status? Even a far simpler example—the humble VLAN—still has two properties that are typically described together: an ID and a name.

It's important to be able to model constructs like this in your code; doing so makes your code far easier to understand and maintain. In Go, the *struct* allows you to create your own type definitions, which are composed of properties, or fields, which have their own types (which can themselves be built-in types or other struct types). In Example 7-38, you define a struct type vlan with two fields, id and name.

Example 7-38. Struct definition

```
// This is where we define our custom struct vlan
// Note that this is just a definition - we'll actually create
// an instance of this later.
type vlan struct {

    // id and name are fields of our vlan struct.
    // They each have their own type definition (in this
    // case, uint and string)
    id    uint
    name string
}
```

 Go is far less of an object-oriented language when compared to Python (Go doesn't include traditional object-oriented features you might know from Python, such as inheritance). But thinking of structs as Go's analog to Python's classes (covered in Chapter 6) is a reasonably close approximation for learning purposes. Like Python's classes, structs are a way to model real-world objects with properties (fields) and behaviors (methods).

As shown in Example 7-39, you can then create an instance of this struct and store this value as a single variable—the type of which is vlan. That variable will hold both the ID and name of this VLAN together as fields of the same object.

Example 7-39. Instantiating a struct

```
// instantiate a vlan type using the literal syntax.
//
// You can populate every field with a value, or you can leave it out, and the
// field will be set to the zero value for that field's type.
myVlan := vlan{
    id:   5,
    name: "VLAN_5",
}

// We can also set these fields after instantiation
myVlan.id = 6
myVlan.name = "VLAN_6"
```

As we mentioned previously, a valid VLAN ID must be less than or equal to 4096. However, when instantiating structs directly in this fashion, you could set the id field to any valid uint value, which can contain many more values than this.

To provide a more opinionated way of instantiating structs so that you can check for constraints like this, it's not uncommon to create a constructor function, as shown in Example 7-40. This function takes in a set of parameters needed to instantiate the struct type but is also able to perform checks that ensure that the values are valid.

Example 7-40. Instantiating a struct within a constructor function

```
func NewVLAN(id uint, name string) (vlan, error) {        ❶ ❷
    if id > 4096 {
        return vlan{}, errors.New("VLAN ID must be <= 4096")  ❸
    }

    return vlan{                                          ❹
        id,
        name,
    }, nil
}
```

❶ NewVLAN() is a constructor function, which returns an instantiated vlan instance but also ensures that the id field is populated with a valid VLAN ID. The first letter in this function is capitalized, indicating it is *exported* (accessible from outside the current package).

❷ This function has two return types: the first is vlan, and the second is error.

❸ When returning a non-nil error alongside a struct type, it's conventional to return the zero value for those struct types. We did this with the empty braces as in ❹.

❹ We already determined that the `id` parameter satisfies your requirements, so we can instantiate and return a `vlan` right here in the `return` statement, passing in the `id` and `name` variables as fields.

In a practical setting, instantiating a struct often requires more than simply populating its fields with static values. It's not out of the ordinary for more complex setup tasks to be required in order to populate the struct with the information needed. Constructor functions like these allow all this logic to be contained in a single function, which enables consumers to easily create a working instance of the struct.

 Example 7-40 mentions that the constructor function is exported, which means it is accessible outside the current package. This is common for constructor functions such as this. Constructor functions provide a more stable API for instantiating structs, while also performing checks like the ID range check you saw in the example. We cover the differences between exported and unexported in "Packages and Modules" on page 297; for the time being, we'll continue to operate in the `main` package as we have thus far.

Structs can use other structs in their field definitions. Given the definition `vlan` in Example 7-38, you can include this type in the fields of a new struct, such as `device`, as defined in Example 7-41.

Example 7-41. Using struct types in other struct definitions

```
type device struct {
    hostname string

    // Here, vlans is a field on the device struct. Its type
    // is a slice of vlan instances.
    vlans []vlan
}
```

However, the physical or logical constructs we're trying to model with structs are usually more than just a set of properties we want to store in memory. If structs represent what something *is*, we need something to also describe what something *does*. We need a way to represent *behavior*. For this, structs can have methods.

Methods

Methods are similar to functions in that they can have parameters, return types, and keywords that are specific to functions, like `return`. However, one significant difference is that methods include a receiver. A *receiver* is like a function parameter: it is made available to the function body in the same way, but always represents the instance of the struct it's defined on. You'll also see receivers declared prior to the method name, rather than in the usual place function parameters are declared.

For a practical demonstration, Example 7-42 builds on Example 7-41 by defining a new method on the device type that prints the hostname of the device to the terminal.

Example 7-42. Defining a method on a struct

```
type device struct {
    hostname string
    vlans []vlan
}

// printHostname has no explicit parameters, but does have a receiver of type
// device named d.
func (d device) printHostname() {
    // We can refer to d in the body of the method
    // to access the fields of the instantiated struct object.
    fmt.Println(d.hostname)
}
```

Since methods are, by definition, functions declared on an *instance* of a struct, in Example 7-43, you must first instantiate your device struct in order to be able to call the printHostname() method on it.

Example 7-43. Invoking a method

```
// Methods are defined on a struct instance, so we must first instantiate device
// as a new variable myDevice.
myDevice := device{hostname: "r1"}

// While functions are called from a package (i.e., fmt), methods are called
// from an instance of a struct, which we created above.
//
// Note that there's no need for this method to have a hostname parameter;
// since the receiver is passed implicitly, the method already has access to
// this receiver's hostname field.
myDevice.printHostname() // output: "r1"
```

What if you want to create a method that *sets* the hostname? This could be useful; perhaps you could enforce some kind of length limit here. Example 7-44 shows that you can assign a new value to the fields of the receiver the same way you might do this for a struct instance outside a method.

Example 7-44. Defining the setHostname() method

```go
func (d device) setHostname(hostname string) {
    // If the length of the hostname parameter is greater than 10,
    // use slicing syntax to shorten to 10 characters.
    if len(hostname) > 10 {
        hostname = hostname[:10]
    }

    // Assign the result to the hostname field of receiver d
    d.hostname = hostname
}
```

However, when you execute this method and call printHostname() once more, you see some strange behavior, shown in Example 7-45.

Example 7-45. setHostname() not updating the hostname as expected

```go
myDevice.printHostname() // output: "r1"
myDevice.setHostname("r2")
myDevice.printHostname() // output: "r1" ??
```

Interestingly, even though you call setHostname() with a parameter of r2, if you call printHostname() once more afterward, it still produces an output of r1, which is the original hostname you used to initialize the struct in previous examples.

To explain this, you need to dive into a concept that you may not have had much exposure to if you're new to programming or if your primary experience comes from Python: the concept of pointers. For those who don't write low-level code every day, this may come off as a bit of an advanced topic, but have no fear. Go makes this much easier to deal with than most languages that include this concept.

When you call a function (or method) in most programming languages, your program (under the hood) will allocate additional memory for that function on a region of memory known as the *stack*. The portion of the stack allocated for a particular function, known as a *stack frame*, is used to store values that are needed by that function while it's running. It's also generally pretty fast.

Go is typically referred to as a *pass-by-value* language. One way this behavior is observed is that whenever you invoke a function or method, stack memory is allocated, and any parameters for that function are *copied* into that memory space. For methods, this includes the receiver; the values that make up that receiver's fields are also copied into this region of memory, as illustrated in Figure 7-1.

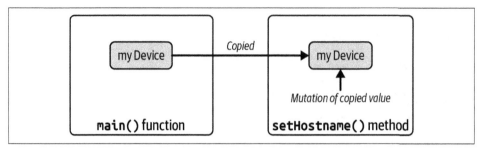

Figure 7-1. Mutating a value receiver

When you changed the `hostname` field on your receiver d in Example 7-44, you did this on the *copied value* of this receiver within the method. Outside the method, in your `main()` function, `myDevice`—which is what your method copied *from*—still has the hostname `r1` because you modified only its copy, which was then discarded when the function exited. The original `myDevice` remains unaffected.

So, you need a way to mutate the original value. But how can you do this if everything in Go is passed by value and is therefore copied into contexts like functions or methods? In Go, you can use *pointers*—and in this particular case, *pointer receivers*. A pointer is exactly what it sounds like: it "points" to a specific memory address where a value is stored. In this case, rather than copying a struct's value (all of its constituent fields) into the stack, only the value of the pointer—the address in memory it refers to—is copied. This allows the code in `setHostname()` to mutate the original value, as illustrated in Figure 7-2.

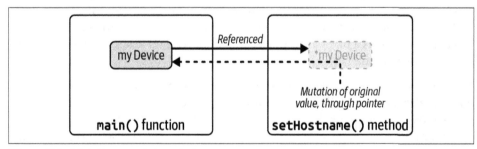

Figure 7-2. Mutating a pointer receiver

When we manipulate the fields of a pointer to our struct within the method, those changes will outlast the stack frame and be made on the original copy of that struct instance. In some cases, this is made possible because the language's runtime will store the original value not on the stack, but on a different region of memory known as the *heap*. Allocating memory on the heap is more computationally expensive than using stack memory, but when you need to mutate the original value, the trade-off can be worthwhile.

In our example, you need to convert the setHostname() method to use a pointer receiver rather than a value receiver. Thankfully, this change is remarkably simple: you add an asterisk (*) just before the receiver's type. This indicates the receiver is a *pointer* to a device value rather than a copy of that value. Any changes you make to the fields of your receiver d will be applied to the original myDevice instance you created in the main() function. Example 7-46 shows the use of a pointer receiver to update the hostname field of the device struct.

Example 7-46. Defining the setHostname() method with a pointer receiver

```
// This has a pointer receiver, denoted by the asterisk before the device
// receiver type. This means that setting the hostname field here will apply
// to the original copy of this struct instance.
func (d *device) setHostname(hostname string) {
    // If the length of the hostname parameter is greater than 10,
    // use slicing syntax to shorten to 10 characters.
    if len(hostname) > 10 {
        hostname = hostname[:10]
    }

    // Assign the result to the hostname field of receiver d
    d.hostname = hostname
}

func main() {

    myDevice := device{hostname: "r1"}

    // Since the setHostname() method is declared with a pointer receiver,
    // it will mutate the hostname field in the original instance,
    // represented here by the variable myDevice.
    myDevice.setHostname("r2")
    myDevice.printHostname() // output: r2
}
```

Most of the time, if you're simply using an existing struct or its methods, you don't have to care about whether they're using a value or pointer receiver, because Go handles this for you (you'll notice that no change to how you *called* this function was needed). This isn't always true, though, as you'll see in the next section.

You might be asking yourself, "Why not just use pointer receivers everywhere?" Often it does seem more convenient to always use pointer receivers so you never have to run into this problem. For programs that aren't particularly performance-sensitive, this may be a sensible approach. For others, more consideration may be necessary.

For example, copying values onto the stack sounds bad, but it's usually quite fast, since stack memory is calculated at compile time and allocated for your program when it starts. In contrast, the use of a pointer receiver often implies an allocation on the heap, which can be computationally expensive since this must be requested via the operating system at runtime. So, for small receiver values, it may be best to avoid pointer receivers if you don't need to mutate the receiver. However, for large receiver values, and especially if you're repeatedly calling a method, the opposite may be true: copying onto the stack may be tremendously costly, whereas passing a pointer around is pretty cheap after the memory it points to has been allocated. So in some cases, using a pointer receiver, even if you're not mutating it, can be a better choice.

 In many programming languages (including Go), it's not always possible to determine whether something is allocated on the stack or heap just by reading the code. A lot of other factors and optimizations (many of which are implementation-specific) influence this decision but are well beyond the scope of this chapter.

Unfortunately, it's not possible to give a one-size-fits-all answer when it comes to performance analysis. If performance is important to you, explore the use of profilers to identify areas in your program that can be optimized. For most use cases, especially those that pertain to emerging network automation programmers, this is not something you need to worry about too much. Instead, use this general guideline when you define your own methods: use pointer receivers if you need to mutate the original value, and use value receivers if you don't.

Next, we'll explore a powerful feature of Go that allows us to create far more flexible APIs while retaining the benefits of a strict type system: interfaces.

Interfaces

As you saw in previous examples, functions can use structs as parameter types, allowing callers to pass more complex types into functions instead of the simpler built-in types like int or string. However, using strictly defined types like this (also known as *concrete types*) can be inflexible.

Imagine you're designing a function to print the hostname of a network device. You may already have a custom type defined (say, Router), which includes the hostname field, as well as some fields that might be relevant to routers in particular (say, a list of VRFs). Example 7-47 shows this idea in action.

Example 7-47. Using a concrete type as a function parameter

```
type Router struct {
    hostname string
    vrfs     []string
}
```

```
// This function takes a concrete type (the "Router" struct)
// and therefore, no other type can be used when calling this
// function.
func printHostname(device Router) {
    fmt.Printf("The hostname is %s\n", device.hostname)
}
```

This approach has one major drawback: you can use the Router type only when passing in the device parameter. If you had other types (say, Firewall or Switch), even if they had a hostname field, you could not use them in this case. You'd end up having to create different functions for each parameter type you wanted to be able to use, which can get messy. Is there a better way?

There is! In cases like these, you often don't actually require a specific type, but only a particular behavior that you expect that type to have. In this example, you don't care about the parameter's type, but only that it has a hostname. While today there's no way in Go to allow any type with a particular field (this is somewhat nuanced situation we explore in "Generics" on page 295), there *is* a way to allow any type that implements a particular set of *methods*. This is where interfaces come in.

Interfaces allow you to describe the behavior you want a particular type to have. They mandate a set of one or more methods (with their parameter and return types as applicable), and instead of using this concrete type when declaring your function parameter, you can use this interface type. Any concrete type can be used as long as it implements the method requirements described by that interface. A concrete type that implements all the methods required by an interface is said to have "satisfied" or "implemented" that interface. Example 7-48 shows the use of interfaces to capture any concrete type that implements the GetHostname() method.

Example 7-48. Interface type as a function parameter

```
type Hostnamer interface {          ❶
    GetHostname() string
}

type Router struct {
    hostname string
    vrfs     []string
}

func (r Router) GetHostname() string {  ❷
    return r.hostname
}

func printHostname(device Hostnamer) {  ❸
    fmt.Printf("The hostname is %s\n", device.GetHostname())
}
```

❶ This interface type describes any concrete type that implements a `GetHostname()` method that has no parameters, and a single `string` return type.

❷ This method allows the `Router` type to satisfy the `Hostnamer` interface.

❸ This function uses the `Hostnamer` interface for the `device` parameter, so any type that implements that interface can be used.

The reason this is useful is that you are now no longer required to use only the concrete type `Router`. You can use any type that satisfies the `Hostnamer` interface. For instance, the `Firewall` and `Switch` types in Example 7-49 also implement the `Hostnamer` interface.

Example 7-49. Additional concrete types for the `Hostnamer` interface

```go
type Switch struct {
    hostname string
    vlans    []int
}

func (s Switch) GetHostname() string {

    // There's no rule that says we **have** to return r.hostname directly.
    // What we do inside the method doesn't affect whether it implements
    // the Hostnamer interface. We can give the hostname a prefix of "switch-"!
    return fmt.Sprintf("switch-%s", s.hostname)
}

type Firewall struct {
    hostname string
    zones    []string
}

func (f Firewall) GetHostname() string {
    return fmt.Sprintf("firewall-%s", f.hostname)
}
```

Each of these concrete types satisfies the `Hostnamer` interface so they can all be used as a parameter for `printHostname()`.

The *contents* of the methods required by this interface don't matter; what matters is the method signature. This is why each of the `GetHostname()` methods shown in Example 7-49 can do things like prepend a prefix of `switch-` or `firewall-` if desired before returning a value. This means you have great flexibility in the kind of behavior that each of these types exhibits.

In Go, satisfaction of an interface is checked at compile time. Therefore, if you try to use a concrete type for an interface parameter, but that type doesn't satisfy that interface, your program will fail to compile. However, this check is done implicitly. The only way the Go compiler will know to even bother checking for whether a type satisfies a given interface is if your program tries to actually use that type to satisfy an interface parameter, as you saw in printHostname(). This is in contrast to other languages like Rust or Java, which require you to explicitly declare that a given type satisfies an interface or trait, even if it's never used in such a context.

Now, let's backtrack a little bit to our discussion on method receivers. Recall that these are implicitly passed parameters that provide a handle to the instance of an object on which that method is defined. You should also remember that you can have value and pointer receivers, and that each has pros and cons.

Generally speaking, when you're *calling* a method, you don't have to care about whether it's defined using a value or pointer receiver. This is an implementation detail that doesn't change the way methods are called. However, in one important exception, you still might need to do something a bit different, and it comes into play when you're using interfaces, which we'll explore next.

Let's build on the previous examples and define a new interface Trimmable, which includes the same method from your Hostnamer interface but adds a second method TrimHostname(). You'll then implement the TrimHostname() method on your Router type so that it is able to satisfy the Trimmable interface. Finally, you'll create a new printHostnameTrimmed() function that accepts a parameter of this interface type Trimmable, as well as an integer to specify the maximum length for your hostname—anything over this will be trimmed. This is shown in Example 7-50.

Example 7-50. Implementing the Trimmable interface with a pointer receiver method

```
type Trimmable interface {                                        ❶
    TrimHostname(int)
    GetHostname() string
}

func (r *Router) TrimHostname(length int) {                       ❷
    if len(r.hostname) > length {                                 ❸
        r.hostname = r.hostname[:length]
    }
}

func printHostnameTrimmed(device Trimmable, trimLength int) {
    device.TrimHostname(trimLength)                               ❹
```

```
fmt.Printf("The device hostname trimmed to %d characters is %s\n", ❺
    trimLength, device.GetHostname())
}
```

❶ As we can see, interfaces can specify more than one method.

❷ Remember, when mutating the fields of the receiver, we usually want to use a
    pointer receiver. Otherwise, we'll just mutate a copy of the receiver value.

❸ This syntax trims the string so that it's no longer than the length parameter. Of
    course, if it's already shorter, we don't need to do anything.

❹ Trimmable requires the TrimHostname() method to be defined, so we know we
    can use it here.

❺ Trimmable also uses the GetHostname() method so we can use this to retrieve the
    result after we've trimmed it.

What happens if we create an instance of Router and try to pass it to printHostname
Trimmed()? This is exactly what we do in Example 7-51.

Example 7-51. Compilation error—Router does not implement Trimmable

```
rtr := Router{hostname: "rtr1-dc1"}

// Fails to compile!
//
// ./10-interfaces.go:23:23: cannot use rtr (variable of type Router) as
//      type Trimmable in argument to printHostnameTrimmed:
// Router does not implement Trimmable (TrimHostname method has pointer receiver)
printHostnameTrimmed(rtr, 4)
```

This code fails to compile! The error message you get from the compiler is also somewhat cryptic, indicating that Router does not implement the Trimmable interface.

This is a bit misleading because there's nothing actually wrong with the way you
defined the TrimHostname() method on Router. On paper, this method should allow
the Router type to satisfy the Trimmable interface. Rather, the problem is with what
you passed in to printHostnameTrimmed().

In Go, the *method set* of a type determines which methods can be called on that
type. A we've discussed in earlier examples, types can be represented in more than
one form—values, pointers, and now interfaces. The method set available depends
on which of these you're dealing with. In Example 7-51, you're passing a *value* to
printHostnameTrimmed(). However, the method set for such a value does not include
methods defined with a pointer receiver; it's as if your TrimHostname() method

doesn't exist! This is why the compiler believes you haven't satisfied the `Trimmable` interface.

In constrast, the method set of a *pointer* to a type includes not only all the methods with a value receiver type, but also the methods with a *pointer* receiver type, such as `TrimHostname()`. To use `Router` to satisfy `Trimmable`, you must pass a pointer, rather than a value, to `printHostnameTrimmed()`. Fortunately, this is easy to do, as shown in Example 7-52.

Example 7-52. Passing a pointer to `Router` as `Trimmable`

```
// We can create a pointer to a value by using the ampersand symbol. Whereas rtr was
// type Router, rtrPointer is type *Router (pointer of type Router)
rtrPointer := &rtr

// This works, because we're passing a pointer (*Router) to printHostnameTrimmed()
// rather than a value. This means the method set now includes the method required
// to satisfy Trimmable
printHostnameTrimmed(rtrPointer, 4)

// We could also skip defining a separate variable and do this all in one step
printHostnameTrimmed(&rtr, 4)
```

You've learned that, with interfaces, you can still benefit from the compile-time safety of a static type system while also creating the flexibility needed to create reusable and ergonomic APIs. Interfaces are in use in all kinds of Go programs and libraries. Many of the functions you use from Go's standard library accept interface parameters.

This wraps up the more fundamental concepts in Go. With the concepts we've covered thus far, you'll be well equipped to start your Go journey. The next section covers a few concepts that are a little more advanced but crucial for understanding how to use Go most effectively.

Advanced Concepts

The previous sections have mostly focused on fairly basic Go concepts; these are things you need to know if you're going to be productive with Go. Some of these concepts are easier to understand than others, to be sure; while loops and conditionals are second nature if you come from Python, for example, interfaces and strict type systems can be difficult if you've never been exposed to them before. In either case, you'll likely need to build a solid understanding of all these concepts to be productive with Go in just about any capacity.

This section dives into some slightly more advanced topics. This isn't to say you don't need to know these topics, or that you'll never run into them, but they do require a bit more effort to truly master than can be covered in a single subsection in this book. As a result, the coverage of these topics and the examples provided are not comprehensive, but rather a brief introduction.

The goal of this section is to introduce these concepts and explain as simply as possible why they're important—especially within the context of network automation. With this foundation, you can build a more detailed understanding by using the numerous fantastic resources out there. We cover a few of these resources at the end of this chapter.

Concurrency

If you've heard about Go, you've probably also heard that one of its strengths is concurrency. But what does this mean?

When you write scripts or programs to perform some kind of automation workflow, you typically start out writing a series of tasks to be executed serially; in other words, do task A, then task B, then task C, as shown in Figure 7-3.

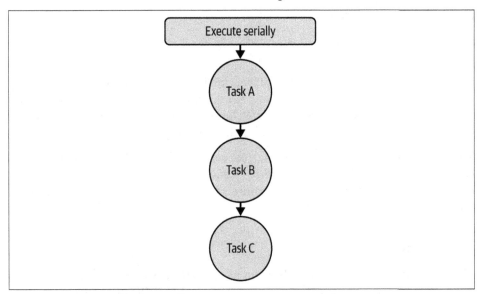

Figure 7-3. Executing tasks serially

Concurrency is a program's capability to handle multiple tasks at the same time. This allows us to do things like execute tasks A and B simultaneously, wait for them to finish, and only then execute task C, as illustrated in Figure 7-4.

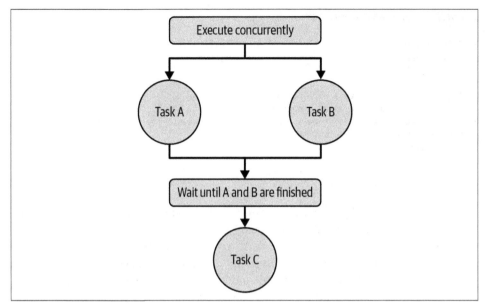

Figure 7-4. Executing tasks concurrently

Concurrency is frequently brought up when discussing Go's strengths for two reasons. First, Go includes native support for concurrency (it's built into the language itself, as opposed to being available only via third-party libraries). Second, the way Go exposes concurrency primitives is remarkably simple, compared to how it's done in other languages.

Given that concurrency is one of Go's most popular features, do you *have* to learn concurrency to learn Go? Certainly not, in the same way that it's possible to become quite proficient in Python without learning one of the concurrency frameworks in that language (though Chapter 6 covers these topics, if you're interested). Perfectly stable and efficient programs are deployed to production all the time that do not make use of concurrency.

Like most concepts we discuss in this book, concurrency is simply a tool to solve a particular set of problems. While Go aims to make concurrency as simple as possible, there's still something to be said for avoiding the added complexity that it will inevitably bring. However, as with any tool, sometimes it's the right one for the job, and it's important to be aware of it as well as the context in which it shines.

The primary building block of concurrency in Go is the goroutine. A play on the established term coroutine, goroutines are lightweight threads that allow you to execute a function or method in parallel to the rest of your code. Creating a goroutine is incredibly easy, as you're able to start one by simply prepending the word go before invoking a function or method; see Example 7-53.

Example 7-53. A simple goroutine

```
// This call to time.Sleep() will "block", meaning it will halt execution
// of the rest of this program until the timer expires.
time.Sleep(1 * time.Second)

// This call to time.Sleep() will not block execution of this program,
// because it is launched as a goroutine. The timer will still count down,
// but this will happen in a separate lightweight thread, so the following
// instruction(s) will execute immediately.
go time.Sleep(10 * time.Second)

// We will see this immediately - not after 10 seconds.
fmt.Println("Program finished!")
```

However, this code isn't very useful because the program will end before the goroutine is able to finish. Typically, after launching a concurrent task using a goroutine, you should wait for that goroutine to complete before moving forward. This approach is common when launching many goroutines at once, which you might do when you want to perform a certain number of similar tasks, all in parallel. A common tool for this situation is the WaitGroup, found in the sync package. This is essentially a counter that keeps track of the number of goroutines and then blocks execution until they all finish, as shown in Example 7-54.

Example 7-54. Waiting for goroutines to finish

```
var wg sync.WaitGroup
var numGoroutines = 5

wg.Add(numGoroutines)                              ❶

for i := 1; i <= numGoroutines; i++ {  ❷
    go func(i int) {
        defer wg.Done()                            ❸

        fmt.Printf("Goroutine started with duration of %d seconds\n", i)
        time.Sleep(time.Duration(i) * time.Second)
        fmt.Printf("%d second goroutine finished!\n", i)
    }(i)
}

wg.Wait()                                          ❹

fmt.Println("Program finished!")
```

❶ The Add() method allows us to configure the wait group with the number of goroutines to wait for.

❷ This loop allows us to launch all the goroutines in quick succession.

❸ This will decrement (subtract) the wait group by a value of 1. Remember, defer statements run at the *end* of a function.

❹ The Wait() method will block execution until all of the goroutines complete. Remember, we set the number of goroutines to wait for via the Add() method.

Example 7-55 shows the output from this program. Although the goroutines are started in no particular order (the wait duration printed for each appears random), they finish in chronological order because each has a different sleep value. What's more is that because of your wait group, your program doesn't exit until all the goroutines have finished.

Example 7-55. The output after waiting for goroutines to finish

```
~$ ~go run 11-concurrency.go
Goroutine started with duration of 5 seconds
Goroutine started with duration of 3 seconds
Goroutine started with duration of 4 seconds
Goroutine started with duration of 1 seconds
Goroutine started with duration of 2 seconds
1 second goroutine finished!
2 second goroutine finished!
3 second goroutine finished!
4 second goroutine finished!
5 second goroutine finished!
Program finished!
```

Another common method of synchronizing goroutines is accomplished through the use of *channels*. Channels are commonly used to communicate values between goroutines. In addition, channels block execution until the value you're sending is received by the other goroutine. This gives you the same synchronization power as with wait groups, but in more than one place, while also communicating an actual value across the goroutine boundary. Quite powerful! Example 7-56 shows channels in action.

Example 7-56. Synchronizing goroutines with channels

```
fChan := make(chan float32)        ❶

getDeviceCPU := func() float32 { ❷
    time.Sleep(250 * time.Millisecond)
    return rand.Float32()
}

go func(iChan chan float32) {        ❸
    for {
        cpu := getDeviceCPU()
```

```
        if cpu >= 0.8 {              ❹
            iChan <- cpu             ❺
        }
    }
}(fChan)

for {                                ❻
    fmt.Println(<-fChan)             ❼ ❽
}
// Output:
// 0.9405091
// 0.81363994
// 0.8624914
// 0.865335
// 0.975241
```

❶ Channels have a type (in this case, float32) as well as a length. By omitting the length parameter to make(), we're creating an unbuffered channel, which has a length of 0.

❷ getDeviceCPU() simulates an API call to a network device to get the current CPU utilization.

❸ Here, we're doing a fairly common task of retrieving a device's CPU via an API call. We want to do ongoing monitoring (and keep sending values into the channel), so we'll do this in an infinite loop.

❹ We don't really care about values less than 0.8. But for any higher values, let's notify the main goroutine by sending those values on the channel.

❺ The send syntax places the channel on the *left* side of the <- operator. Remember, this will block execution of the goroutine until you receive a value from this channel in the main goroutine.

❻ This is an infinite loop so that the program continually receives values from the channel.

❼ Remember, channels allow for synchronization of goroutines, as well as conveying values. When receiving a value here, we know that the goroutine is sending a value at the same time. This will block execution of this main goroutine until the goroutine we launched earlier sends a value into the channel.

❽ The receive syntax places the channel on the *right* side of the <- operator.

Channels can be created with a length greater than 0. These are known as *buffered channels*, and unlike unbuffered channels, they block execution on send operations only if their buffer is full. Unbuffered channels, effectively having no buffer, always block on a send operation until that value is received from the channel. While buffered channels have their use cases, they do dull the synchronization benefits of channels a bit, and as a result, they are not as popular of a choice in the broader Go community. A common convention is to default to using unbuffered channels and to use buffered channels only if you know you require them.

In Chapter 10, you will see additional, practical examples of goroutines and channels in action, as these are helpful when working with modern network automation RPC frameworks like gNMI.

Goroutines may require access to shared resources. Often the most practical solution is to allow goroutines direct access to resources managed in other goroutines, rather than through channels or a similar mechanism. This is often done by passing a pointer (rather than a value) into a goroutine or into popular reference types like maps or slices. As you saw with methods during our exploration of pointer and value receivers, pointers allow you to pass around a handle to the same region in memory.

However, when writing concurrent code as you have been with goroutines, you must be careful. Concurrent access to shared resources should be done with care. For instance, if Go detects that multiple goroutines are trying to write to a map at the same time, it will trigger a panic, and your program will crash.

To avoid this, you must ensure that only one goroutine is actually accessing a shared resource at a time. A popular choice for accomplishing this is the *mutex*, which works in the same way you might check out a book from the library. When you want to read a book, you check it out. Then, you read it; and while you're reading it, others are waiting for it to become available. When you check the book back in, other people are able to repeat the same process in order to read it for themselves.

A mutex works much the same way: when you want to access a shared resource, you Lock the corresponding mutex (check out the book). When you're finished, you Unlock the mutex (check the book back in). In Example 7-57, we are monitoring the CPU utilization of several network devices concurrently, and updating a shared map where these values are stored and in turn printed to the console.

Example 7-57. Protecting shared resources with a mutex

```
var cpuMap = make(map[string]float32)     ❶
var cpuMapMut = sync.Mutex{}

getDeviceCPU := func() float32 {          ❷
```

```
        return rand.Float32()
}

monitorFunc := func(hostname string) {  ❸
    for {
        cpu := getDeviceCPU()
        cpuMapMut.Lock()                 ❹
        cpuMap[hostname] = cpu           ❺
        cpuMapMut.Unlock()               ❻
    }
}

go monitorFunc("sw01")                   ❼
go monitorFunc("sw02")
go monitorFunc("sw03")

for {                                    ❽
    time.Sleep(1 * time.Second)
    fmt.Printf("cpuMap: %v\n", cpuMap)
}
```

❶ We're declaring the map and the mutex. Because they are contained in the outer scope, they can be referenced directly by the goroutines we'll launch later.

❷ getDeviceCPU simulates an API call to a network device to get the current CPU utilization.

❸ monitorFunc is the function that we'll eventually launch as a goroutine, and it contains the infinite for loop as well as the updates to cpuMap, including the mutex Lock and Unlock operations.

❹ This call will block execution if another goroutine already has a lock. Only when we're able to successfully acquire a lock in *this* goroutine will execution continue. This is how we can safely write to a map from multiple concurrent goroutines.

❺ Now that we have a lock on the mutex, we can write to the map safely. Without the mutex (or another similar tool offering the same kind of synchronization), the program might crash when multiple goroutines try to access the map at the same time.

❻ Don't forget to unlock the mutex when you're done so that other goroutines can use it! Sometimes you'll see defer used to call Unlock() automatically at the end of the function.

❼ Launch three goroutines—one for each device.

❽ Repeatedly print the contents of the map to the terminal.

In Go, mutexes are not tied directly to the shared resource itself; it's up to you to ensure that you're accessing the resource only after you've acquired a lock (other languages might force you to take a lock before you can even access the resource). It's common for library authors to wrap all of this lock/unlock logic in functions so that you don't have to worry about it, but in the event you're working with your own goroutines and shared resources, the mutex is an important concept to understand.

Goroutines (and concurrency in general) are a powerful, and sometimes necessary, tool when performing the same task on multiple network devices. However, as you can see even in the few preceding examples, using goroutines can get complex, fast. Writing concurrent code—even in a language like Go, which makes it as easy as possible—is about much more than simply prepending a function call with go. Creating concurrent code opens you up to a new class of problems that require their own solutions.

In other words, be careful not to introduce concurrency into your program for the wrong reasons. It is not a panacea that will automatically make your program faster. Modern languages like Go are quite fast without concurrency, and you may find that the perceived inefficiency of performing tasks serially (without concurrency) isn't as problematic for your particular use case as it seemed on paper. That said, sometimes it's the right tool for the job, and in those cases, you'll be glad you're armed with a language like Go, which makes it as approachable as possible, and comes with the tools we've discussed in this section.

Generics

In an earlier section, we talked about interfaces. These enable you to inject a little flexibility into your APIs by requiring a given type to exhibit a certain kind of *behavior*, rather than working only with concrete types like integers, strings, or specific structs. However, this comes with important caveats. For example, interfaces work by requiring a method set—which means that any type used as an interface parameter *must* implement that interface's methods. If you want your function parameters to flexibly handle a variety of types, but those types don't implement any methods, interfaces won't be a good solution.

For quite a long time, this situation was the status quo in Go. However, Go 1.18 introduced *generics*, which is a well-established concept in other programming languages. Just as interfaces did before Go 1.18, generics allow you to have much more flexibility over concrete types—but rather than requiring that a type adhere to a particular method set, they work by specifying a *type set*. This is a broader categorization than method sets, in that they can capture a set of just about any type, not just types that implement a particular method. Example 7-58 shows generics in actions.

Example 7-58. Type flexibility with generics

```go
func main() {
    fmt.Println(Min(3, 5))              ❶
    fmt.Println(Min(2.5, 6.3))
    fmt.Println(Min("foo", "fooooo"))
}

type comparable interface {            ❷
    int | float64 | string
}

func Min[T comparable](x, y T) T {     ❸
    if x < y {
        return x
    }
    return y
}
```

❶ Because Min uses generic parameters, you can pass a variety of types as parameters to x and y; in these examples, you're passing integers, then floats, then strings. Because all of these are listed in the type set declared in the comparable interface, this approach works.

❷ Rather than declaring methods in your comparable interface, you can specify types that you know can be compared using the < operator. This allows you to pass any of these types into Min(). This is the upgrade that interfaces received in Go 1.18: they can be used to define method sets and/or type sets.

❸ This declares a generic type T that must implement the comparable interface. Then, when declaring parameters x and y, you can reference this type T. This means that both x and y must in turn implement comparable. Also, because they're both generic type T, they cannot be different types from each other when the function is invoked. Without generics, you'd either have to use interfaces (and therefore each of these types would have to have methods the interface would match on) or you'd have to create a copy of this Min() function for each type we want to be able to pass in (MinInt, MinFloat64, etc.).

In addition to working on type sets and not just on method sets, generics differ from the traditional use of interfaces in Go in their implementation. Before the introduction of generics in Go, each type in Example 7-58 would need its own Min() function that used concrete types for this comparison (i.e., MinInt, MinFloat64, etc.). This is actually what the compiler does on your behalf when you compile a program using generics: the compiler creates a copy of that generic function for every concrete type passed in to it. You never see these copies; they're present only in the resulting binary.

As programmers, we can keep our code simple by dealing only with generic types; this is known as *monomorphization*. This technique retains the benefits of a static type system, but with the flexibility that previously required the use of interfaces with method sets.

 In some cases, using generics can be more efficient than the equivalent traditional approach with interfaces and method sets. For instance, when using a traditional interface, your program will have to do a runtime lookup to find the actual concrete type being referenced. With generics, this is unnecessary because the mapping of type to function is done at compile time. Naturally, the size of your program's resulting binary after compilation will be larger.

However, whether generics *actually* speed up your program in a meaningful way is extremely use-case dependent. The decision of whether to use generics should be first and foremost driven by readability and maintainability concerns, and any perceived performance gains should be backed up with data from profiling your program.

While generics are a useful tool for a certain class of problems, you will almost certainly be able to address any automation use case in Go without them. At the time of this writing, generics are still an incredibly new concept in the Go programming language, and it will take years for the ecosystem and best practices around them to be established. As with any other advanced topic in this section, reach for generics only when you've gone through the work of proving you really need them.

Next, we explore how Go code is organized and shared via packages and modules.

Packages and Modules

As with any programming language, the more code you write in Go, the more you'll want to organize your code into logical groups. For instance, you may have a set of *.go* files that pertain to interacting with network devices. Then, you may have another set of files for generating config files, and another still for retrieving intended state from your single-source-of-truth platform, and on and on. Eventually, it will become difficult to manage a growing codebase that blurs the lines between these logical groupings.

Packages are one way to solve this problem in Go. Using *packages*, you can create logical groupings to organize your code better. For instance, you might have three packages, given the previous examples: devices, generator, and ssot. Example 7-59 shows what the filesystem structure of such a package might look like.

Example 7-59. Go packages

```
myprogram
├── devices
│   ├── arista.go
│   ├── cisco.go
│   ├── devices.go
│   └── juniper.go
├── generator
│   └── generator.go
├── main
│   └── main.go
└── ssot
    ├── ssot.go
    └── state.go
```

Remember that when you execute a Go program, the main() function is invoked automatically. This function must exist within a package called main (recall, all the way back to Example 7-1, that you declared this by using the package keyword). In Example 7-59, you have a package main in addition to the other three. From our code in this package, you can refer to the other three packages when calling their functions or using their types.

You've already done this several times throughout this chapter. As mentioned before, functions like Println() and Printf() are from the fmt package, which is part of Go's standard library (we'll explain what that means in the next section). Similarly, if the generator package included a function Generate(), and you wanted to call it from your main package, you'd probably call it with generator.Generate().

You may have also noticed that anytime you call a function or use a type from a different package, that function or type always starts with a capital letter. This is because Go uses the capitalization (or lack thereof) to indicate whether the thing being identified should be available outside its package. This applies to a lot of constructs in Go, including functions, methods, structs, interfaces, and even field names. If a given identifier starts with a capital letter, it is known to be *exported* and is usable by code both inside and outside the package in which it's declared. A lowercase letter means that identifier can be used only from within that package (*unexported*). This is comparable to concepts like *public* and *private* (respectively) in other languages. This syntax allows you to be more precise when defining your package's API surface—the more stable points of interaction between your package and other programmers who wish to use it.

Packages, however, are just part of the picture. In Go, *modules* describe a collection of packages and are useful for a few things. First, they provide a way to unify a set of related packages into one easily distributable repository. In fact, it's common to see a Go module located at the root of a corresponding Git repository. This can be particularly useful if you're developing a Go library for other developers to consume.

Modules play another role, though: they are the mechanism by which Go *manages dependencies*, such as third-party libraries you want to use in your own code. We haven't talked too much about this yet because all of the prior examples exclusively use the standard library. However, if you want to go beyond the standard library (which you almost certainly will at some point), you'll need to configure your own module to properly handle the dependencies your code has on other modules. In "Third-Party Modules and Packages" on page 310, you'll learn more about how to work with modules in order to bring third-party code into your project.

At the beginning of this chapter, we make the assertion that Go is an important language to know in the world of network automation, and that a big reason for that is the growing ecosystem of tools and packages that are particularly useful for network automation use cases. Now that you understand the basics of packages and modules, it's time to explore this a bit further. Let's look a bit more deeply at some popular packages—those in Go's standard library as well as those maintained by third parties—that you'll want to be aware of as you move forward in your journey.

 Though we do our best in these sections to explore some of the more popular packages you might run into, it's impossible to cover them all and equally difficult to cover any one of them exhaustively. In addition, the network automation ecosystem in Go is constantly growing and changing, so a large portion of these specific examples will almost certainly change dramatically within the next few years. The goal of this section is to provide you with a repertoire for common network automation use cases. At the end of this section, you will have a solid base upon which you can continue to build as you progress in your journey.

Standard Library Packages

Programming languages are rarely just a spec and a compiler that converts that spec into machine code. They often come with a set of types and functions used for common tasks. Some of these are provided as *built-ins*, meaning they are baked into the language specification so you don't need to do anything special to use them.

Go built-ins include types like int and string but also functions like make() and new(). Other Go built-ins do require you to import a package in your code, but otherwise don't require any special installation to be usable. The fmt package is a good example; we've made liberal use of functions like Println() and Printf() throughout this chapter, both of which are from the fmt package.

This paradigm of built-ins versus standard library is true of many programming languages. As you saw in Chapter 6, for instance, Python has built-ins like str and print() but also a diverse standard library including packages like time and sys.

The fmt package is one of many considered part of Go's *standard library* (sometimes abbreviated stdlib or std). This is a collection of packages that are useful for common tasks you'd need in just about any program you're writing in Go. These packages also have an extremely stable API, which is required as part of the Go version 1 compatibility guarantee. You don't have to worry about Go version upgrades breaking code that uses standard library types or functions.

Go has a robust standard library, including several packages that are particularly useful for network automation use cases. We've covered a few of these already in this chapter. Again, fmt (*https://pkg.go.dev/fmt*) is where we find functions like Println() and Printf(), but is broadly useful for formatted I/O in general. We also used sync (*https://pkg.go.dev/sync*), which is definitely a package you'll want to be familiar with if you use concurrency in your programs.

strings

To start, we'll explore a few packages that specifically relate to working with string data. If you want to perform tasks like find a substring (such as a prefix or suffix), trim off parts of a string, or otherwise parse string data, your first stop should absolutely be the strings package. This package includes many functions that are useful for doing all kinds of common things to parse, edit, and search within strings, and you will almost certainly run into a handful of them in your network automation. Example 7-60 shows some of the more commonly used functions in this package.

Example 7-60. Using strings to work with...strings!

```
exampleString := `
Hello network automators! Welcome to Network Programmability and Automation.
`

doesContain := strings.Contains(exampleString, "Automation")        ❶
fmt.Println(doesContain) // output: true


substringIndex := strings.Index(exampleString, "Welcome")           ❷
fmt.Println(substringIndex) // output: 27

strSplit := strings.Split(exampleString, " ")                       ❸
fmt.Println(strSplit[4]) // output: "Welcome"

strTrimmed := strings.TrimSpace("   Automation!   ")                ❹
fmt.Println(strTrimmed)       // output: "Automation!"
```

```
fmt.Println(len(strTrimmed)) // output: "11"

strReplaced := strings.ReplaceAll(exampleString, "network", "gopher") ❺
fmt.Println(strReplaced)
// output:
// "Hello gopher automators! Welcome to Network Programmability and Automation."
```

❶ Contains() returns true or false, depending on whether the string (first parameter) contains the indicated substring (second parameter).

❷ strings.Index() returns the index (location within the string) of the first instance of the substring.

❸ strings.Split() creates a slice of strings ([]string) from the input string based on a provided delimiter. The following example uses a space as a delimiter, which will result in each word of the input string being placed in its own slice element. We can perform the reverse of this operation by using strings.Join(), which creates a single string from a []string, joined with a delimiter of your choice.

❹ strings.TrimSpace() is a super handy function for easily removing extra spaces at the beginning or end of a string. Plenty of other trim functions are in strings, each with its own specialized use cases, including Trim(), TrimPrefix()/Trim Suffix(), and TrimLeft()/TrimRight().

❺ strings.ReplaceAll() can replace all instances of a given substring with another string of our choice. If we want to replace only a limited number of instances, we can use strings.Replace().

strconv

Example 7-61 shows another strings-related (but much more narrowly focused) package: strconv. This contains functions for parsing and converting between strings and other built-in types like integers.

Example 7-61. Converting to and from strings by using strconv

```
// strconv.Atoi converts a string to an integer. It returns the integer
// value but also an err, as the parse might fail because of integer overflow,
// non-integers, etc.
i, err := strconv.Atoi("-42")
if err != nil {
    fmt.Printf("Unable to convert string to integer: %s\n", err)
} else {
    fmt.Printf("Parsed integer is %d\n", i)
}

// strconv.ItoA performs the reverse, converting an integer to a string.
```

```
// This cannot fail, so we see only one return type from this function.
i42 := strconv.Itoa(42)
fmt.Printf("i42 as a string is %s\n", i42)
```

strconv has several other functions, including those that work with other types like booleans and floating-point numbers.

regexp

Inevitably, especially in the world of network automation, the somewhat basic string-searching functions in strings just aren't sufficient, and we need something a bit more advanced. In any language or tool, this generally means the introduction of *regular expressions* (*regexes*) for more advanced string-search or even-replacement tasks. Fortunately, Go's standard library has the regexp package, which includes robust regex support. Example 7-62 contains practical examples of using this package to perform common parsing tasks in network automation.

Example 7-62. Using regular expressions in Go with the regexp package

```
outputStr := `
eth0: flags=4099<UP,BROADCAST,MULTICAST>  mtu 1500
    inet 172.17.0.1  netmask 255.255.0.0  broadcast 172.17.255.255
    ether 02:12:2a:24:5b:98  txqueuelen 0  (Ethernet)
`                                                                     ❶

re, err := regexp.Compile(`([0-9a-f]{2}:){5}[0-9a-f]{2}`)           ❷
if err != nil {
    panic(err)
}

fmt.Println(re.MatchString(outputStr))                               ❸
// output: true

fmt.Println(re.FindString(outputStr))                               ❹
// output: 02:12:2a:24:5b:98

fmt.Println(re.ReplaceAllString(outputStr, "00:00:00:00:00:00"))   ❺
// output:
//
// eth0: flags=4099<UP,BROADCAST,MULTICAST>  mtu 1500
//     inet 172.17.0.1  netmask 255.255.0.0  broadcast 172.17.255.255
//     ether 00:00:00:00:00:00  txqueuelen 0  (Ethernet)
```

❶ outputStr is a large multiline string you can parse with the regexp package. A variable containing contents retrieved from a file or from an API call would work just as well.

❷ This regex matches MAC addresses. regexp.Compile() returns a *regexp.Regexp, which we can use for later tasks. All following tasks are done using methods of this returned instance re. This is a common step in many implementations of regexes, including in languages other than Go. This helps ensure that you have a valid expression before continuing.

❸ We can use the MatchString() method of the returned instance re to get a basic boolean true/false to indicate whether any substring in outputStr matches your regular expression.

❹ FindString() goes a step further and returns the first specific substring that matches our expression. Other methods like FindAllString() and FindAll StringIndex() can be used to find all instances that match, returning a slice of strings ([]string) that can be inspected afterward or perhaps even iterated over.

❺ ReplaceAllString() allows us to replace all instances that match the expression with a given string literal. In this case, we're overwriting the MAC address with all 0s, leaving the rest untouched.

encoding

A common task in Go, especially in network automation, is the serialization and deserialization of data structures to and from formats like JSON and XML. This is often necessary to send/receive data between disparate systems—for instance, the HTTP API on your favorite network device. For this, as shown in Example 7-63, the encoding package is invaluable—and in particular, encoding/json and encoding/xml for working with JSON and XML, respectively.

Example 7-63. JSON/XML serialization with the encoding package

```go
type NetworkInterface struct {                    ❶
    Name  string `xml:"name" json:"name"`         ❷
    Speed int
}

type Device struct {
    Hostname   string
    Interfaces []NetworkInterface
}

r1 := Device{
    Hostname: "r1",
    Interfaces: []NetworkInterface{
        {
            Name:  "eth0",
            Speed: 1000,
        },
    },
```

```
}

jsonOut, err := json.Marshal(&r1)
if err != nil {
    panic(err)
}
fmt.Println(string(jsonOut))
// output:  {"Hostname":"r1","Interfaces":[{"name":"eth0","Speed":1000}]}

xmlOut, err := xml.Marshal(&r1)
if err != nil {
    panic(err)
}
fmt.Println(string(xmlOut))
// output:  <Device><Hostname>r1</Hostname><Interfaces>
//                  <name>eth0</name><Speed>1000</Speed></Interfaces></Device>
```

❶ The encoding package (and generally any package that performs serialization/deserialization) will work with only exported types and fields (which start with a capital letter).

❷ You may wonder about this strange string after this field. This is called a *struct tag*, and while not required, it is extremely common to see these for structs that will be used for serialization/deserialization purposes, such as to/from JSON or XML. Generally, struct tags are just metadata; they have no implicit purpose on their own. However, both the xml and json package can use these if present to specify a field name that is different from the actual struct field's name.

Chapter 8 covers JSON and XML in much more detail, but Example 7-63 will help you get started working with these extremely popular data formats.

net

The Go standard library includes a robust networking package known as net. Here, you can find all kinds of useful types and functions for working with the network stack, from setting up an arbitrary TCP connection to full-blown application-level network interactions.

As you'll see in Chapter 10, it's common for a REST API to have a companion client-side library that you can integrate with easily. However, this isn't always the case, and sometimes you have to query an HTTP API directly. A specific subset of Go's net package known as net/http has an easy-to-use HTTP client, which you use in Example 7-64 to query a public HTTP API.

Example 7-64. Querying an HTTP API with the net/http package

```go
resp, err := http.Get("https://api.ipify.org?format=json")          ❶
if err != nil {
    panic(err)
}
defer resp.Body.Close()
body, err := io.ReadAll(resp.Body)
if err != nil {
    panic(err)
}

ipifyResponse := struct {                                           ❷
    IP string `json:"Ip"`
}{}
err = json.Unmarshal(body, &ipifyResponse)
if err != nil {
    panic(err)
}
fmt.Println(ipifyResponse.IP)

client := &http.Client{}                                           ❸
req, err := http.NewRequest("GET", "https://api.ipify.org?format=json", nil) ❹
if err != nil {
    panic(err)
}
req.Header.Add("My-Header", `foo`)                                 ❺
resp, err = client.Do(req)                                          ❻
```

❶ The net/http package includes high-level functions like Get() for performing requests easily with some sensible defaults.

❷ We can use what you learned in Example 7-63 to unmarshal the raw JSON string into a struct type.

❸ Sometimes we need a bit more control than these high-level functions offer. For instance, we may need to send specific HTTP headers with our request. This requires that we create our own Client and Request.

❹ The method (GET) is defined here as a parameter to http.NewRequest, as is the URL.

❺ Headers are defined on the request object after they're created.

❻ Once prepared, the request is passed as a parameter to Do(), which is a method on client that we created earlier.

This is a brief example of one of the more common tasks you'll run into, but the net/http package has far more utility than this demonstration. For instance, we explored the use of this package to query an HTTP API, but you can also use this package to make your own HTTP API server! You'll also use this package in Chapter 10 to query a RESTCONF server on a network device.

Zooming out a bit, the net package itself also has a few useful things to know about. You can spin up your own raw TCP client or server, perform DNS resolution, and query the local system's network interfaces. However, one of the most likely use cases you'll have for this package is the ability to work with IP addresses and networks. Example 7-65 shows a few helpful examples of these types and functions in action.

Example 7-65. Working with IP addresses and networks via the net package

```
var ipFromByteSlice net.IP = []byte{192, 168, 0, 1} ❶
fmt.Println(ipFromByteSlice)

addrOne := net.ParseIP("192.168.0.1")                ❷
addrTwo := net.ParseIP("2001:db8::1")
fmt.Println(addrOne)
fmt.Println(addrTwo)

network := net.IPNet{                                ❸
    IP: net.ParseIP("192.168.0.0"),
    Mask: net.CIDRMask(24, 32),                      ❹
}

fmt.Println(network.Contains(addrOne))               ❺
 // output: true
fmt.Println(network.Contains(addrTwo))
 // output: false
```

❶ The net.IP type is used to represent IP addresses. While it includes many helpful methods, at its core it is really just a slice of bytes, so we can initialize a net.IP instance by constructing this byte slice ourselves.

❷ For convenience, net.ParseIP() allows us to construct IP instances with a string as input. This is a much more common way of constructing net.IP instances. You'll notice that either IPv4 or IPv6 addresses can be passed here. This is because of the flexibility of the byte slice representation, with a length suited to the address being represented.

❸ net.IPNet is used to represent a network/subnet. It is defined by two fields: an IP (net.IP) and a mask (net.CIDRMask). Like net.IP, net.IPNet is v4/v6 agnostic.

❹ We're defining a bitmask that's 24 bits long, with a total size of 32 bits. In other words, this is the v4 subnet mask 255.255.255.0.

❺ We can then use the Contains() method on network to easily determine if a given IP address is a member of this network.

The net/netip package is a relatively recent addition to the standard library. Initially developed as a third-party module by Tailscale (*https://oreil.ly/b7IW9*), this package was moved into the standard library in Go 1.18. The package contains alternatives to the net.IP type and related functions we explored in Example 7-65. Example 7-66 shows the use of this new netip.Addr type and its associated functions.

Example 7-66. The net/netip package

```
// ParseAddr allows us to parse an IP address (v4 or v6) from a string. Once we
// have the resulting netip.Addr type, we can call helpful methods like
// IsGlobalUnicast() or IsLoopback() to quickly identify properties of the
// address we parsed.
ipv6, err := netip.ParseAddr("2001:db8::1")
if err != nil {
    panic(err)
}
fmt.Println(ipv6.IsGlobalUnicast()) // output: true

// ParseAddr does work for IPv4 addresses as well, but an alternative is the
// AddrFrom4() function, which allows us to pass the address as a 4-length byte
// array, removing the need for error handling (no parsing is being done here).
fmt.Println(netip.AddrFrom4([4]byte{127, 0, 0, 1}).IsLoopback()) // output: true

// We can parse entire prefixes from a string using ParsePrefix()
prefixString := "192.168.0.0/24"
prefix, err := netip.ParsePrefix(prefixString)
if err != nil {
    panic(err)
}
```

At the time of this writing, the remainder of the original third-party netaddr module that didn't make it into Go's standard library in 1.18 is available as netipx (*https://oreil.ly/QSzjF*). This includes functions and types for working with ranges of IP addresses, which can be helpful if you want to iterate over all addresses in a given prefix. This might also be made available in Go's standard library in the future.

time

You'd be hard-pressed to find a use case that doesn't require the time package, as working with time is an extremely common element of just about any network automation workflow. Example 7-67 illustrates uses frequently found in network automation projects. For instance, pausing execution for a certain period of time (for instance, to wait for another task to complete) is, of course, something we must rely on frequently. Other tasks like comparing date/times, or triggering events based on a period of elapsed time are also invaluable tools to add to any network automation-related Go program.

Example 7-67. Working with the `time` package

```
now := time.Now()                                                    ❶
fmt.Println(now)

moonLanding := time.Date(1969, time.July, 20, 20, 17, 45, 0, time.UTC) ❷

var oneSecond time.Duration = 1000000000                             ❸

tenSeconds := 10 * time.Second                                      ❹

fmt.Println(time.Since(moonLanding))                                ❺

time.Sleep(tenSeconds)                                             ❻
```

❶ The `time.Time` type is a singular point in time. One of the most common ways of getting this is via the `Now()` function, which returns the current time.

❷ However, we can create an instance of `time.Time` representing any arbitrary date/time.

❸ `time.Duration` is a type alias for `int64`, and it's used to represent a time duration in nanoseconds. The following example is equivalent to 1 second of duration.

❹ However, the `time` package also includes convenient constants such as `time.Second`, which make it easier to represent durations in a more readable way.

❺ `time.Since()` is a common way to derive a `Duration` between an event in the past and the current time.

❻ Finally, the ever-useful `Sleep()` function—you guessed it—sleeps the current goroutine for the specified `Duration`.

In addition to these fairly common tasks, you can expand on what you learned in "Concurrency" on page 288, and use functions like `time.After()` in conjunction perhaps with other channels to build more complex event-handling systems.

os

The `os` package is extremely useful for working with underlying operating system concepts, like working with reading and writing files, as shown in Example 7-68.

Example 7-68. Reading and writing files with the os package

```
// Reading a text file is easy with os.ReadFile
dat, err := os.ReadFile("sampleconfig.yaml")
if err != nil {
    panic(err)
}
fmt.Println(string(dat))

// Next, let's write a file. Here we're first marshaling a struct into JSON
// so we can write the result to the file.
jsonOut, err := json.Marshal(struct {
    Hostname   string
    Interfaces []string
}{
    "sw01",
    []string{"eth0", "eth1", "eth2"},
})
if err != nil {
    panic(err)
}
// Just like ReadFile returns a []byte value, so does WriteFile require
// this type as an argument. Fortunately that's exactly what json.Marshal returns
err = os.WriteFile("sampleconfig.json", jsonOut, 0644)
if err != nil {
    // Here, instead of calling panic(), we can use os.Exit to more gracefully exit
    // our program, while returning an error code to the operating system.
    fmt.Printf("Unable to write file: %s\n", err)
    os.Exit(1)
}
```

It can also be handy for returning exit codes as we exit our program and handling incoming signals, illustrated in Example 7-69.

Example 7-69. Handling signals with the os package

```
sigs := make(chan os.Signal, 1)                           ❶

signal.Notify(sigs, syscall.SIGINT, syscall.SIGTERM)      ❷
go func() {                                               ❸
    for {
        fmt.Println("Doing some work...")
        time.Sleep(1 * time.Second)
    }
}()

<-sigs                                                    ❹

fmt.Println("exiting")                                    ❺
os.Exit(0)
```

❶ We can use a combination of packages like os, os/signal, and syscall to handle incoming signals from the operating system. This allows us to more gracefully handle these signals. Here, we're creating a channel of type os.Signal.

❷ We then pass this channel into signal.Notify(), along with a list of signals we wish to handle.

❸ This line launches a goroutine to simulate doing some actual work.

❹ If the operating system sends any of the prevously listed signals to our application, this channel will receive this, and the following code will execute. However, until then, it will block, as it is an unbuffered channel.

❺ Here, we add a simple print statement, but we could add any logic we want, to make sure we take care of any cleanup tasks before the program shuts down.

A few other packages are worth a brief mention:

io
> This is one of those packages that shows up everywhere. We already used this in our exploration of net/http in Example 7-64, as resp.Body implements the io.Reader interface.

encoding/binary
> Used for encoding to/from binary formats. While we don't cover this package explicitly, we do cover other binary formats in Chapter 8.

text/template
> Used for Go's templating functionality, which is powerful. You'll learn more in Chapter 9.

Despite the varied and robust examples presented thus far, we're still only scratching the surface. There's a lot more to Go's standard library, and you would be well served to peruse the full package list (*https://pkg.go.dev/std*) to see what else comes with Go. For now, let's turn our attention to the ecosystem of third-party libraries that has emerged to support network automation.

Third-Party Modules and Packages

While Go does enjoy a robust standard library, it cannot address every use case. Inevitably, you'll encounter a situation that may be addressed more comprehensively by code that someone else wrote and published to a platform like GitHub. Remember that Go code is distributed via modules, and to use them, you must first explore how to initialize your own code as its own module.

Fortunately, the vast majority of the tooling you'll need for common development tasks in Go are built right into the same tooling we've used this far to run and build our code—and working with modules and third-party dependencies are no exception. Example 7-70 shows how to initialize a new Go module (these commands should be executed within the bash terminal).

Example 7-70. Initializing a Go module

```
mkdir myfirstmodule && cd myfirstmodule          ❶
go mod init github.com/oreilly-npa-book/myfirstmodule ❷
```

❶ This command creates the new directory *myfirstmodule* and then enters into it.

❷ The argument after go mod init is the *module path*. It's really a prefix for the packages that the module contains. You'll notice that a popular convention is to use the location of the Git repository containing this module; while this isn't required, it does make it easier for other commands like go get to find and download the source for this module.

As a result of running the go mod init command, you have a new file *go.mod* in your directory, with some fairly simple contents, showing the module path as well as the version of Go it was initialized with. A newly initialized *go.mod* file will look very similar to Example 7-71.

Example 7-71. Bare-bones go.mod *file*

```
~$ cat go.mod
module github.com/oreilly-npa-book/myfirstmodule

go 1.18
```

Now that you have an initialized module, you can explore the use of third-party libraries in your code. One extremely popular package for structured logging is Logrus. You'll create a new file *main.go* with the contents shown in Example 7-72.

Example 7-72. Source of myfirstmodule *program*

```
package main

import (
    "fmt"

    // It's conventional to place third-party dependencies in a separate section,
    // to help distinguish them from standard-library and intra-module imports.
    //
    // You can also optionally specify an alias prior to the package path,
    // which may or may not be different from the original package name. In this
```

```
    // case, the logrus package is being aliased to log.
    log "github.com/sirupsen/logrus"
)

func main() {
    vlanIDs := []int{
        100, 200, 300,
    }

    log.Infof("Hello from logrus! There are %d VLANs in the vlanIDs slice.",
        len(vlanIDs))

    fmt.Println("End of program.")
}
```

As you can see, you referred to the logrus package within the import block of Example 7-72. However, you need to do one more thing before your program can compile and run: actually download the logrus source code so it can be compiled alongside your program. For this, you can use two particularly helpful go mod subcommands, shown in Example 7-73.

Example 7-73. Downloading module dependencies

```
# This useful command makes sure that the go.mod file matches what your program
# needs. It will download/add any missing modules, but also remove any unused
# modules as well.
~$ go mod tidy

# By default, modules are downloaded to the system's module cache. However,
# if you want the source for the modules you depend on to be stored alongside
# your code, you can "vendor" them - in this case, these modules will literally
# be stored in a vendor/ subdirectory within your module's directory.
~$ go mod vendor
```

At this point, the *go.mod* file is now much more interesting. Of particular note is the addition of the third-party module you're depending on, including the module's version at the time it was added. You can see this updated file in Example 7-74.

Example 7-74. Updated go.mod *contents*

```
module github.com/oreilly-npa-book/myfirstmodule

go 1.18

require github.com/sirupsen/logrus v1.9.0

require golang.org/x/sys v0.0.0-20220715151400-c0bba94af5f8 // indirect
```

You will usually notice other modules listed in *go.mod* that aren't directly referenced in your code—such as those in Example 7-74 that are followed by `// indirect`. These are modules that your *dependencies* rely on. When managing your program's dependencies, the Go tooling navigates the full tree of dependencies and makes sure they're all available on the system so that your program can compile.

While you'll definitely run into other subcommands and tools while working with Go modules, this covers the basics of initializing your own module and importing other third-party modules. However, knowing how to import other modules is just the first step. You now need to learn where to find third-party modules and how to vet them for quality. We'll also briefly explore a handful of existing third-party modules that you may find useful for network automation in particular.

A great starting point for locating a new module is *https://pkg.go.dev*, which offers a search engine for Go packages and modules. Search for anything you want—maybe "network automation"—and you'll immediately get a bunch of results for Go packages. From here, you can view the README file for a given module and follow the provided links to the code repository (e.g., GitHub), so you can vet the module more thoroughly for your use cases.

This leads to an interesting question; how to know if a module is "good"? We are often looking to bring in third-party modules so that we can complete an automation project and put it into production, so we have to be somewhat rigorous about the code we add to our services. What does this entail?

Unfortunately, there's no silver-bullet answer here. You'll find that most programmers have varying standards for vetting third-party libraries in any language, and this is also true for organizations as a whole. If you're a solo developer working on a network team for a traditional enterprise, your company might have no established standards. Others with more well-established software practices may have more explicit requirements for qualifying third-party code. As this can be a bit of a rabbit hole, we'll focus instead on a few common sense guidelines that make sense for most situations:

Code auditability
    When you're bringing a third-party module into your project, it becomes just as much a part of your program as the code you wrote yourself. So, make it a practice to become comfortable with reading others' code, especially for the modules you're evaluating. The code, or at the very least, its intent, must be clear; if after an hour or two of reading you still have no idea how the code does what it's supposed to do, bringing it into your project may not be a good idea.

Suitability

Does the module actually do what you want it to? Even for a single use case, there could be several potential options to choose from, each with their own design constraints and trade-offs. Become familiar with these and choose the module that best aligns with your goals.

Tests

Does the module come with tests, (e.g., unit tests)? Are the tests reasonably comprehensive; do they provide suitable validation that the code does what it claims to do? Is there a CI/CD infrastructure in place that ensures these tests are run against the existing code, as well as any new contributions?

API stability

What guarantees does the module offer (if any) around breaking API changes? Particularly new modules that are under active development may be changing frequently, which could cause you to have to update your code when updating the module to a new version. This is not always a bad thing, but it's something to consider and be aware of before relying on a module.

Active development

You may find problems with a module after bringing it into your project, so knowing whether the developers of that module are still active and working on improvements can be helpful. Red flags include things like a backlog of unanswered pull requests or issues/bug reports, or the most recent commits being months or years old. Keep in mind that active development is not a panacea; many high-quality libraries are *feature complete*, meaning they reached their original design goal, and nothing is left to work on.

Again, remember that when you bring a third-party library into your program, it becomes just as much a part of your program as the code you wrote yourself, so it's important to take this part seriously. Just because a Go module is published on GitHub doesn't mean it is "good" (or that it even works at all), so don't skip the due diligence here. Even though the preceding guidelines work particularly well for evaluating Go libraries, they contain good advice for working in just about any language.

Obviously, the types of libraries you need depends greatly on what you're trying to accomplish. However, to help get you started, the following is a diverse list of popular libraries that can be used to solve some of the more common network automation use cases:

ygot (https://oreil.ly/pKMvl)

Generates Go code from YANG models and validates/generates data against these models.

goSNMP (https://oreil.ly/8s23s)
Works with SNMP in Go.

Protobuf (https://oreil.ly/0k3KF)
Works with protobuf, a binary serialization format. We cover this must-have library in more detail in Chapter 8 and build on this knowledge when exploring gRPC in Chapter 10.

goBGP (https://oreil.ly/5Vb8g)
An open source BGP implementation in Go. Can be used as a standalone routing stack or integrated as a library into your own application.

netlink (https://oreil.ly/xPC6i)
Interacts with the Linux networking stack via netlink.

gotextfsm (https://oreil.ly/rZDQ3)
Works with TextFSM (a text-parsing language).

goeapi (https://oreil.ly/Q2Kl6)
Works with Arista's eAPI, the programmability option offered on most Arista products.

A few other third-party libraries are extremely common when working with APIs in Go (Chapter 10 covers these in more detail):

gRPC (https://oreil.ly/pRbNC)
This library is a must-have for working with gRPC, a lightweight, modern RPC framework.

gNMI (https://oreil.ly/bLAx6)
The official OpenConfig library for working with gNMI, a protocol for config manipulation and state retrieval built on gRPC.

gNMIc (https://oreil.ly/4We1M)
A CLI client and collector application for gNMI.

This is by no means an exhaustive list, but it should be enough to get you started. Be sure to begin any exploration or search for libraries with a solid understanding of your core requirements. This will help you find the library that best matches the trade-offs you're willing to make.

Summary

We wrote this chapter for the same reason that drives all chapters in this book: to provide you with a properly constrained but still diverse set of tools for solving problems in your network automation journey. You'll inevitably run into a use case that's better suited for Python, even after reading this chapter or getting more hands-on experience with Go. This is expected; in practice, there is no room for absolutism in the ever-changing world of network automation or software development as a whole. As they say, "the right tool for the right job."

That said, Go does strike the sweet spot for today's network automator: it combines the ease of adoption of a language like Python, with the safety and performance typically associated with much less accessible languages. Even if you don't consider yourself a programmer, giving Go a chance is worthwhile. You might find it a useful tool to have in your toolchest.

A subject as vast as a programming language is impossible to cover exhaustively in a single chapter. For next steps, we encourage you to get your hands dirty and consider building something in Go as a prototype. For many of us, learning by doing can be a powerful strategy. Additionally, a great new book has been published called *Network Automation with Go* by Nicolas Leiva and Michael Kashin (Packt Publishing). If you want to go deeper with your knowledge of Go, this book would be a great next step. In addition, the Go Tour (*https://oreil.ly/14k2w*) is a fantastic way to get your hands dirty with Go right away, all in the browser (no need to install anything).

In Chapter 8, you'll see a little bit of both Python and Go in action, as we explore the various data formats that you'll run into in your network automation journey.

Data Formats and Models

If you've done any amount of exploration into the world of APIs, you've likely heard about data formats like JSON, XML, or YAML. You may have heard about concepts like data modeling, or model-driven APIs. Terms like *data serialization* and *markup language* may have popped into the foreground. You'd be right to wonder what all of this means and how it all applies to network automation.

It turns out that these concepts are at the heart of any reasonably complex modern software system, including those built and operated for the purpose of network automation. Even if you're writing a simple script to change the hostname on a switch, at some point, your script will need to transmit some kind of information over the network that the switch will successfully receive and correctly interpret. How can you get your script and that switch to speak the same language?

Data formats like the aforementioned are those shared languages. They are broadly supported in all popular programming languages and are under the covers of nearly all the libraries and tools that you'll use in your network automation journey. They are used by your network device's built-in software for the purpose of being able to reliably and programmatically communicate with external entities, whether a full-blown fabric manager or a simple script on your laptop.

Understanding these formats, and how to work with the data they represent, is therefore crucial for you to be able to work effectively as a network automation professional. This chapter covers a variety of technologies and tools used to represent, transmit, store, and model data formats, with a specific focus on those that you're most likely to run into in your network automation work.

Benefits and Fundamentals of Structured Data Formats

A programmer typically uses a wide variety of tools to store and work with data. You could use simple scalar values (single values), collections (arrays, hashmaps), or even custom types built in the syntax of the language you're using. While the specifics often differ, all languages offer primitives like this to give the programmer multiple ways to solve problems. When passing data within the context of a single program, this is often sufficient. A compiler knows exactly how much memory to allocate for a given type, so all you have to do as the programmer is reference that type when you need it, and the compiler will handle everything.

However, sometimes a more abstract, portable format is required. For instance, a non-programmer may need to be able to feed data into, or retrieve data from, a running program. Multiple programs may need to communicate with one another somehow—and the programs may not even be written in the same language; this is often the case with traditional client-server applications using a script you've written to automate a task on a network device, for example.

The data formats discussed in this chapter were designed to enable these kinds of use cases. They are well-established standards for communicating between generic software systems, and as a result, they're well supported in any language or tool you choose to use. They give you the ability to describe data that would otherwise be represented as a series of bytes in memory.

 Without standardization of data formats, our networks wouldn't even function! Protocols like BGP, OSPF, and TCP/IP were standardized out of a necessity for network elements to have a predictable, shared language in order to effectively communicate across a globally distributed system—the internet!

The formats discussed in this chapter have three key traits that make them extremely useful and preferable, especially within the context of network automation:

Structured

> These data formats, based on an agreed-upon set of rules, were designed to be easier for machines to understand. Computers are much more literal than humans and can't intuitively understand data without a strict, predictable structure. For instance, the unstructured data you might see in the output of a show command on your router or switch may be formatted well for human consumption, but is not ideal for a computer to readily parse and understand.

Supported

> Since these formats are standardized and widely adopted, you'll almost never have to write your own code to understand them directly. You can reuse existing

(and often extremely mature) software and tools for this. Many programming languages like Python and Go have built-in mechanisms that make it easy to import and export data to these formats, either on the filesystem or on the network.

Portable

While some languages have their own intermediate representations (i.e., *pickle* in Python or *gobs* in Go), the formats we discuss here are language agnostic, meaning they work with a wide variety of software ecosystems.

These are all important to consider, but let's ponder the first point a little longer through some examples. Why are structured data formats easier for computers to understand, as opposed to the output you might see as a result of a simple show command?

Whenever you run a command like this, the software on your network device first gathers any data it needs from its subsystems or other network devices. At this stage, the information is little more than bytes in memory. To meaningfully display the results, the software then represents that information in a format that a human being can easily and quickly understand:

```
root@vqfx1> show interfaces em0
Physical interface: em0    , Enabled, Physical link is Up
  Interface index: 8, SNMP ifIndex: 17
  Type: Ethernet, Link-level type: Ethernet, MTU: 1514, Speed: 1000mbps
  Device flags   : Present Running
  Interface flags: SNMP-Traps
  Link type      : Full-Duplex
  Current address: 52:54:00:b1:f5:8d, Hardware address: 52:54:00:b1:f5:8d
  Last flapped   : 2019-01-10 17:49:55 UTC (00:17:33 ago)
    Input packets : 1039
    Output packets: 778
```

The nice thing about output like this is that it requires little effort (or even expertise) to see that the name of this interface is em0. Our brains have the tools to flexibly identify data by using helpful phrases like Physical interface. Even if what we have in mind isn't exactly this, we know that it will get us what we need.

However, it's actually not obvious to a computer where the interface name is located in this output. To us, the term Physical interface is a useful indicator to describe the nature of the text that follows. To a computer, it's all just undifferentiated text. If you were to write a program to pull out the bits of valuable data from this output, you'd have to answer some important questions:

- How do you know which portion of the text represents the value you want to access? Is it before or after the colon? What about commas? Why do some values share a line, whereas others get their own dedicated line?

- What happens if the output doesn't follow a consistent set of formatting rules?

- What happens when another command (e.g., show bgp neighbor) formats things differently? Do you have to write a separate program or function for each command?

- Since the primary use case for this output is human readability, what happens when the network vendor hires a UX expert to review and make changes to the format of this output?

When writing your parsing program or function, you'll have to answer these questions, and more often than not, that will require a lot of extra time and energy that you may not be able to afford. In contrast, structured formats like JSON and XML were built to handle these concerns well.

For example, some configuration models are friendly to automated methods, by representing the configuration model in these data formats like XML or JSON. It is easy in Junos OS to see the XML representation of the show command we ran earlier, as shown in Example 8-1.

 Full versions of the code examples in this chapter can be found in the book's GitHub repo at *https://github.com/oreilly-npa-book/exam ples/tree/v2/ch08-dataformats*.

Example 8-1. Displaying the XML-RPC equivalent for Junos commands

```
root@vqfx1> show interfaces em0 | display xml
<rpc-reply xmlns:junos="http://xml.juniper.net/junos/15.1X53/junos">
    <interface-information>
        <physical-interface>
            <name>em0</name>
            <admin-status junos:format="Enabled">up</admin-status>
            <oper-status>up</oper-status>
            <local-index>8</local-index>
            <snmp-index>17</snmp-index>
            <if-type>Ethernet</if-type>
            <link-level-type>Ethernet</link-level-type>
            <mtu>1514</mtu>
            <speed>1000mbps</speed>

 ... output truncated for brevity ...
```

Comparing this output to the preceding example, you might point out that this is quite a bit harder to read, and you'd be right. You'd even be right to argue that the latter is potentially a little less efficient; in some cases, more raw text would be needed to represent the same data.

From a programmatic perspective however, this is ideal. Example 8-1 provides key advantages over the previous, human-readable code when it comes to being able to programmatically parse the data contained within:

- XML follows a stable set of rules, so there's no need to constantly rewrite low-level text-parsing logic. You need to care about only the data being represented.

- There is consistent use of delimiting structures. It's clear that any tag starts with < and ends with >, and an opening tag should eventually be closed with a corresponding closing tag, such as </tag>.

- Each piece of data is given its own easily parsable field. You know that the space inside the tags represents the entirety of the actual value, and everything else is just structure.

- This format is inherently hierarchical. You know based on the order of opening and closing tags which values have parent/child relationships.

- There is an established convention for metadata—that is, data about data (e.g., the xmlns tag).

While some of the particulars here are specific to XML, all structured data formats provide the same advantages in their own way.

So, in short, structured data formats like those discussed here are designed to allow software systems to communicate reliably and predictably with one another, no matter what language they're written in.

When Structured Data Isn't Available: Screen Scraping

When the first version of this book was written, numerous platforms offered only human-readable text as output to be consumed by automation tools and scripts, as opposed to structured formats like JSON or XML. In cases like these, *screen scraping* can be used to retrieve data from a network device. This technique uses a protocol like SSH to emulate user behavior by sending a series of terminal commands, retrieving the raw text output, and attempting to format this output into a more structured representation. Whether done using a language like Python, or other tools that may provide a slightly more abstract framework, this approach requires you to provide your own set of low-level rules for parsing raw text, or depend on those created/maintained by others. However, these days, platforms that require this approach are becoming more and more rare.

Screen scraping not only makes your automation software extremely fragile, but is also enormously wasteful to your time, and by extension, that of the organization you're working in. The lesson to learn here isn't that it is *impossible* to write a program to parse some kind of text blob that follows from a show command. Instead, remember that the unstructured output you see in your terminal—and the subsystems required to produce it—simply weren't designed to be accessed programmatically. Even those who have successfully created screen-scraping scripts will tell you that this approach is fraught with danger. Some network platforms will literally crash if too many commands are sent at once—not exactly a solid foundation for automation.

In contrast, choosing an architecture that aligns best with your own use case means you can achieve a valuable outcome more quickly and avoid having to deal with problems that were solved decades ago. Your job as network automation professionals is to provide value to your organization as quickly and effectively as possible, and if you are able to choose an approach that doesn't require you to constantly reinvent parsing logic, you should.

Platforms that don't offer any form of support for structured data formats are being phased out, and any serious automation initiative should include a requirement for platforms that do support these options. This not only saves you the time from having to do screen scraping yourself, but also frees you from having to use tools built on this fragile foundation.

Types of Data

As discussed in Chapters 6 and 7, you can use a variety of built-in data types in any modern programming language. We refer to these throughout the text, so if you're not familiar with them, we recommend you start there. We might use terms like *string*, *integer*, and *boolean* for representing different types of scalar (singular) values, *list* or *array* to describe a collection of values, or *dictionary* for key-value pairs.

However, all of these may be known by slightly different names in the various data formats and programming languages we reference, and within those contexts we may use different terms. This is OK and expected; it's more important that you understand the basic concepts behind all of these, rather than trying to be unified and precise in the terminology across the board.

Documents Versus Data

You may have heard the term *markup language* within the context of some of these formats. This is an important term to understand because it is a big part of the history of some of the formats we discuss, and we should be clear about the primary reasons we're even talking about these formats in the first place.

Markup languages can also be referred to as *document-oriented languages*. The canonical example for this is HTML, which includes tags for things like headers, images, and links to external dependencies like JavaScript and CSS files:

```
<html>
    <body>
        <div>
            <p>Hello, World!</p>
        </div>
    </body>
</html>
```

Markup languages like HTML are ultimately used to *describe/annotate a document*, which is then rendered together to form a web page that shows up in your browser.

However, this chapter is not focused on this use case. While some formats (in particular XML) can be used for this purpose, the data formats we're looking at are designed for the task of *data serialization*—that is, representing data (not documents) in a structured way. Remember that the primary reason we're looking at these formats is so that you can understand how software systems exchange data with one another.

So in short, you can think of markup languages as describing *documents* and data serialization formats as describing *data*. It is this second use case that we're focusing on in this chapter.

Categories of Data Formats

The data formats we explore in this chapter fall into two broad categories:

Text-based
    Data is first serialized into an intermediate format like UTF-8 and then encoded into bytes for storage or transmission.

Binary
    Data is encoded directly into an efficient, binary format.

We'll start by looking at text-based data formats.

Text-Based Data Formats

We've already teased a few text-based formats so far in this chapter, but now it's time to look at them more closely. Text-based formats have some key advantages:

- You can easily edit them using a standard text editor or view them plainly using inspection tools in your browser.

- They are well-established standards, and it's extremely easy to find support for them in libraries and tools.

- They're abstract enough to map into just about any common data structure in a variety of programming languages.

The main disadvantage to these formats is that they can be inefficient. One reason is because text-based formats include not only the raw data you want to transmit (strings, integers, arrays, key-value pairs) but also the various characters used to represent that data, such as curly braces and square brackets in JSON or <> tags in XML.

Text-based formats generally have to use more raw storage or bandwidth capacity to accommodate this extra information. These formats also require more processing to both send and receive data. This can become a problem when sending large amounts of data, as this inefficiency can compound. Fortunately, for the vast majority of network automation use cases and workflows, this is rarely a problem.

Whether at rest or in transit, any data you bring into an automation tool or script is ultimately represented as 0s and 1s: *bits*. Most of the time, you deal with these in multiples of 8: *bytes*. We loosely refer to this as *raw binary data*. However, before you can do something practical with this data, it needs to be processed and converted into a form you can work with. For example, computers don't implicitly know that a series of bytes you're receiving from an API request is ultimately meant to be interpreted as a Python list.

To get data from this raw binary format to something you can use (or vice versa), two distinct phases must take place:

1. Decoding and deserializing
2. Serializing and encoding

Figure 8-1 shows that to make sense of data using one of these formats—say, as a payload in an API response that you're receiving—your computer must first decode the raw bits that come off the wire and into a text-encoding standard like UTF-8. This is the *decoding* step.

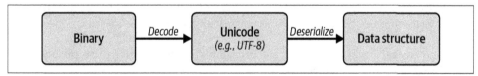

Figure 8-1. Decoding and deserializing text-based data formats

However, at this point you effectively have the equivalent of one big string. A JSON payload, for example, might look something like Example 8-2.

Example 8-2. Decoded JSON string

```
"{\"vendors\":[\"Cisco\",\"Juniper\",\"Arista\"]}"
```

Data that's been transmitted using these formats is most useful when it's been *deserialized* into types and structures within the programming language or tool you're using. For instance, this JSON document would map nicely into a Python dictionary, with a single key, vendors. This key's value would map into a Python list for the three elements in the JSON array. Only after the data is decoded and then deserialized can you do something useful with the data contained within the response payload.

The same process must be followed in reverse to store or transmit data from these types. First, the data must be *serialized* into one of these formats and then *encoded* into bytes, as in Figure 8-2.

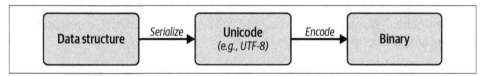

Figure 8-2. Serializing and encoding of text-based data formats

This approach sacrifices a bit of efficiency for enhanced portability, and the potential for humans to more easily understand and even make changes to data found in one of these intermediate formats. Next, we'll explore some of these specific formats in greater detail.

YAML

If you're reading this book because you've seen compelling examples of network automation online or in a presentation and you want to learn more, you may have heard of YAML. This is because YAML is a particularly human-friendly data format, and for this reason, it is used in many network automation tools and initiatives. For instance, YAML is used by Ansible to describe playbooks, variable files, inventory files, and more, as you'll see in Chapter 12.

Previously, we explored the difference between markup and data serialization formats, and you may be wondering which category best describes YAML. Fortunately, the website that hosts the YAML specification (*https://www.yaml.org*) explicitly states that *YAML* stands for *YAML Ain't Markup Language* and that "YAML is a human-friendly data serialization language for all programming languages." So, YAML is primarily intended as a data serialization language, with the added goal of being as human-friendly as possible.

If you compare YAML to the other data formats like XML or JSON, it seems to do much the same thing: it represents constructs like lists, key-value pairs, strings, and integers. However, as you'll soon see, YAML does this is a uniquely human-readable way. YAML is very easy to read and write once you understand how its syntax maps to these basic data structures.

This is a big reason that many automation tools use YAML as a method of defining an automation workflow or providing a data set to work with (like a list of VLANs). YAML also has the added benefit of helping to enable IaC approaches, covered in Chapter 13.

At the time of this writing, the latest YAML specification is YAML 1.2.2, published at *https://www.yaml.org*. Also provided on that site is a list of software projects that implement YAML, typically for the purpose of being read into language-specific data structures and doing something with them. If you have a favorite language, it might be helpful to follow along with the YAML examples in this chapter and try to implement them using one of these libraries.

Let's take a look at some examples. Let's say you want to use YAML to represent a list of network vendors. If you paid attention in the preceding section, you're probably thinking that you want to use a string to represent each vendor name—and you'd be correct! This example is simple:

```
- Cisco
- Juniper
- Brocade
- VMware
```

This YAML document contains four items. You know that each item is a string. One of the nice features of YAML is that you usually don't need quotes or double quotes to indicate a string; a string is usually automatically discovered by the YAML parser (e.g., PyYAML). Each of these items has a hyphen in front of it. Since all four of these strings are shown at the same level (no indentation), you can say that these strings compose a list with a length of 4.

YAML closely mimics the flexibility of Python's type system. A good example of this flexibility is shown by mixing data types in a list:

```
- Core Switch
- 7700
- false
- ['switchport', 'mode', 'access']
```

This is another list, again with a length of 4. However, each item is a totally unique type. The first item, Core Switch, is a string type. The second, 7700, is interpreted as an integer. The third is interpreted as a boolean. This interpretation is performed by a YAML interpreter, such as PyYAML. PyYAML, specifically, does a pretty good job of inferring the kind of data the user is trying to communicate.

The fourth item in this example is itself a list, containing three `string` items. This is an example of a nested data structure in YAML. You've also seen the various ways that some data can be represented. Our "outer" list is shown on separate lines, with each item prepended by a hyphen. The "inner" list is shown on one line, using brackets and commas. These are two ways of writing the same thing: a list.

 Sometimes it's possible to help the parser figure out the type of data you wish to communicate. For instance, if you want the second item to be recognized as a `string` instead of an `integer`, you can enclose it in quotes (`"7700"`). You also enclose data in quotes if a `string` contains a character that is part of the YAML syntax itself, such as a colon (:). Refer to the documentation for the specific YAML parser you're using for more information.

Early on in this chapter, we briefly talked about key-value pairs (or dictionaries, as they're called in Python). YAML supports this structure quite simply. Let's see how you might represent a dictionary with four key-value pairs (Example 8-3).

Example 8-3. YAML dictionary with mixed types

```
Juniper: Also a plant
Cisco: 6500
Brocade: True
VMware:
  - esxi
  - vcenter
  - nsx
```

Here, your keys are shown as `strings` to the left of the colon, and the corresponding values for those keys are shown to the right. If you want to look up one of these values in a Python dictionary, for instance, you reference the corresponding key for the value you are looking for.

Similar to lists, dictionaries are flexible with respect to the data types stored as values. In Example 8-3, you are storing a myriad of data types as the values for each key-value pair.

YAML dictionaries—like lists—can be written in multiple ways. From a data representation standpoint, the previous example is identical to this:

```
{Juniper: Also a plant, Cisco: 6500, Brocade: true,
VMware: ['esxi', 'vcenter', 'nsx']}
```

Most parsers will interpret these two YAML documents precisely the same, but the first is obviously far more readable. The latter is a good illustration of the close relationship between YAML and JSON, but from a practical perspective, you'll rarely need to use the latter format. Again, the primary use case for YAML is to be human readable, so stick with the conventions that most closely align with this.

Finally, you can use a hash sign (#) to indicate a comment. This can be on its own line or after existing data:

```
- Cisco    # ocsiC
- Juniper  # repinuJ
- Brocade  # edacorB
- VMware   # erawMV
```

Anything after the hash sign is ignored by the YAML parser.

As you can see, YAML offers a friendly way for human beings to provide structured data to software systems. However, YAML is fairly new as far as data formats go. When it comes to data formats used for communication directly between software elements (i.e., no human interaction), other formats like XML and JSON are much more popular and have much more mature tooling that is conducive to that use case.

Working with YAML in Python

Let's narrow in on a single example to see exactly how a YAML interpreter will read in the data you've written in a YAML document. Let's reuse one of the previous examples to illustrate the various ways to represent certain data types:

```
Juniper: Also a plant
Cisco: 6500
Brocade: true
VMware:
  - esxi
  - vcenter
  - nsx
```

Let's say this YAML document is saved to your local filesystem as *example.yml*. Your objective is to use Python to read this YAML file, parse it, and represent the contained data as some kind of variable.

Fortunately, the combination of native Python syntax and the aforementioned third-party YAML parser, PyYAML, makes this easy:

```
import yaml
with open("example.yml") as f:
    result = yaml.load(f)
    print(result)
    type(result)

{'Brocade': True, 'Cisco': 6500, 'Juniper': 'Also a plant',
'VMware': ['esxi', 'vcenter', 'nsx']}
<type 'dict'>
```

The Python snippet in the preceding example uses the yaml module that is installed with the PyYAML Python package. This is easily installed using pip as discussed in Chapter 6.

This example shows how easy it is to load a YAML file into a Python dictionary. First, a context manager is used to open the file for reading (a common method for reading any kind of text file in Python), and the load() function in the yaml module allows us to load this directly into a dictionary called result. The lines that follow this code show that this has been done successfully.

XML

As mentioned in the previous section, while YAML is a suitable choice for human-to-machine interaction, other text-based formats like XML and JSON tend to be favored when software elements need to communicate with one another. This section covers Extensible Markup Language (XML), why it is suitable for this use case, and some of the ecosystem tools that exist for working with it.

The XML specification is defined and maintained by the World Wide Web Consortium, or W3C (*https://oreil.ly/47r0N*). XML was derived from a similar but older format called Standard Generalized Markup Language (SGML). XML is considered a subset of SGML, and as a result, any existing SGML parsers should be able to parse XML.

XML was originally created in the late 1990s, when the World Wide Web was moving from static HTML pages to more dynamic content that required lightweight update mechanisms. During this time, the limitations of HTML on its own in this respect were becoming obvious. HTML was designed for the sole purpose of describing the format and structure of a web page, and as a result was quite static and not very extensible. XML was created so that arbitrary data—not just web-focused markup—could easily be transmitted over the network. Some of the earliest use cases for XML were applied toward creating a more dynamic web, but XML itself is a generic format for representing just about anything.

An early popular use case for XML was in the implementation of Asynchronous JavaScript and XML, or Ajax. This was one of the first web development techniques for making web content more dynamic. It accomplished this by having web applications send and receive data in the background, and use this data to dynamically refresh components within the application, without requiring a full page refresh. Another popular use case was SOAP, which was an RPC technique based on XML. At the time of this writing, both use cases have been supplanted by more modern, lightweight alternatives.

In the world of modern network automation, the most popular use case for XML is within the NETCONF protocol. In addition, while JSON is generally a more popular option, XML can be used as the data format for REST APIs as well. We talk about both of these in Chapter 10.

XML shares some similarities with YAML. For instance, it is inherently hierarchical. We can easily embed data within a parent construct, as shown in Example 8-4.

Example 8-4. Basic XML document

```
<device>
  <vendor>Cisco</vendor>
  <model>Nexus 7700</model>
  <osver>NXOS 6.1</osver>
</device>
```

In this example, the <device> element is said to be the *root*. While spacing and indentation don't matter for the validity of XML, you can easily see the root, as it is the first and outermost XML tag in the document. It is also the parent of the elements nested within it: <vendor>, <model>, and <osver>. These are referred to as the *children* of the <device> element, and they are considered siblings of one another. This structure is conducive to storing metadata about network devices, as you can see in this particular example. An XML document may contain multiple instances of the <device> tag (or multiple <device> elements), perhaps nested within a broader <devices> tag.

You'll also notice that each child element contains data within. Whereas the root element contains XML children, these tags contain text data. Thinking back to the section on data types, it is likely these would be represented by string values in a Python program, for instance.

XML elements can also have attributes:

```
<device type="datacenter-switch" />
```

When a piece of information has associated metadata, it may not be appropriate to use a child element to describe that metadata, but rather an attribute. Of course, you can do both if needed. The key is to understand the difference between data and metadata (data about data) and use the appropriate tool to describe it.

An XML document can contain tags with just about any kind of name, depending on the use case. You could, therefore, encounter a naming conflict when creating tags for your own XML data structure. For instance, you might choose to use the tag <device> to describe one of those fancy new "smartphones":

```
<device>Palm Pilot</device>
```

However, what if you also want to use the tag <device> to describe a ToR switch? Fortunately, the XML specification has implemented a namespace system, which helps disambiguate collisions like this. XML allows you to define these namespaces, and refer to them using the xmlns attribute (Example 8-5).

Example 8-5. XML namespaces

```
<root>
  <e:device xmlns:c="https://example.org/enduserdevices">Palm Pilot</e:device>
  <n:device xmlns:m="https://example.org/networkdevices">
    <n:vendor>Cisco</n:vendor>
    <n:model>Nexus 7700</n:model>
    <n:osver>NXOS 6.1</n:osver>XML Schema Definition
  </n:device>
</root>
```

The basic primitives of XML are quite simple. However, to do something meaningful with XML, you should look at the tools available for working with XML in a programming language like Python.

Working with XML in Python

Python includes native support for searching and creating XML documents in its standard library, under the xml module. Popular third-party libraries, such as lxml (*https://lxml.de*), offer a similar API but different underlying implementation. For the sake of simplicity, we stick with what's available natively in Python for these examples.

XML is inherently hierarchical, which makes it a good fit for a tree structure. This is made a bit more apparent in Figure 8-3, which provides a visual representation of the basic XML document in Example 8-4.

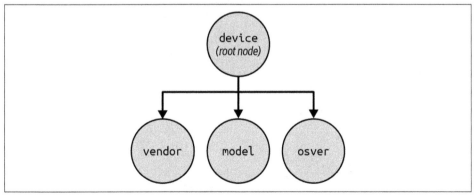

Figure 8-3. Visualization of an XML tree structure

Visualizations like these can be helpful when navigating XML documents by using a programming language like Python.

There are a few ways to search a tree for a particular piece of information, each with its own pros and cons. In this section, we stick with whatever's most pragmatic and straightforward to understand for a given example.

 This section is an extremely condensed explanation of tree structures and how to iterate through them. Courses and other learning resources focused on data structures and algorithms will give you a deeper understanding of the various kinds of tree structures and what they're used for.

The API for working with XML in Python is based on the concept of an element tree: literally, a tree of XML elements. This is in fairly stark contrast to the way you work with data from YAML or JSON, which maps directly into data structures like dictionaries and lists, which can be easier to understand at first glance. However, if you're able to understand the very basics of tree structures, the ElementTree API should be fairly straightforward.

You can import the `ElementTree` class directly from the standard library. You're also creating the simpler alias `ET` so you can easily refer to it in the following examples:

```
>>> import xml.etree.ElementTree as ET
```

There are a few ways to import an XML document, such as with `ET.parse()`, which loads from a file on the filesystem. However, you can also load XML from a string variable, which you might have if you're looking at a response to an API request. In the next example, you're declaring your own variable `data` and then using the `ET.fromstring()` method to read this string and create a new element tree from it:

```
data = """
<devices>
    <device name="sw01">
        <vendor>Cisco</vendor>
        <model>Nexus 7700</model>
        <osver>NXOS 6.1</osver>
    </device>
    <device name="sw02">
        <vendor>Arista</vendor>
        <model>Arista 7800</model>
        <osver>EOS 4.27</osver>
    </device>
    <device name="sw03">
        <vendor>Juniper</vendor>
        <model>QFX 10008</model>
        <osver>Junos 21.3</osver>
    </device>
</devices>
"""

tree = ET.fromstring(data)
```

You can simply print the value of your new `tree` variable to see what has been created for you:

```
>>> print(tree)
<Element 'devices' at 0x7f953cc8e1d0>
```

You'll notice that the type for this variable is `Element`. This doesn't fully represent the whole tree, but only the root element, which is the outermost tag in your XML document: `<devices>`. This element will have references to its children that you can access, and those will have their own children, and so on.

The main way to access the children for a given `Element` is through iteration. You can create a `for` loop to iterate over this element, and the items provided at each iteration will be one of that element's children:

```
>>> for device in tree:
...     print(f"Device {device} found!")
...
Device <Element 'device' at 0x7f953cc3c590> found!
Device <Element 'device' at 0x7f953cbeb6d0> found!
Device <Element 'device' at 0x7f953cbeb860> found!
```

Of course, this doesn't tell you much about each device, only that there are three of them. To access more information, you must go a bit deeper, since the elements like `model` and `vendor` are child elements of the `device` elements. You can use the `find()` method to search within the children of a given node and find the first one that matches a given tag:

```
>>> for device in tree:
...     model = device.find('model').text
...     print(f"Device model is {model}")
...
Device model is Nexus 7700
Device model is Arista 7800
Device model is QFX 10008
```

Since you were already iterating through the children of `tree` to get the `device` elements, the `find()` method can be used directly on a `device` element to search its children.

In some cases, especially when you have a deeply nested structure and are trying to get to a particular element, the `iter()` method can be useful. It allows you to iterate over all tree elements with a certain tag:

```
>>> for vendor in tree.iter('vendor'):
...     print(vendor.text)
...
Cisco
Arista
Juniper
```

This saves you from having to use things like nested `for` loops, or chained `find()` or `findall()` calls. In this case, you can just ask for all `vendor` elements in the entire tree and iterate over them.

As you might imagine, searching large trees can get a little complicated. Fortunately, Python includes limited support for XPath, an expression language that helps simplify searching through an XML document. You can provide a simple XPath expression as a parameter to the `findall()` method, which will then return all elements in the tree that match that expression:

```
>>> for model in tree.findall("./device/model"):
...     print(model.text)
Nexus 7700
Arista 7800
QFX 10008
```

You can also locate nodes based on a combination of their metadata attributes (e.g., the `name` attributes) as well as their element name. This is where things can get *really* powerful. Let's say you want to look up the model for the device named `sw01`:

```
>>> tree.find("./device[@name='sw01']/model").text
'Nexus 7700'
```

You built on the previous expression by specifying the attribute and the desired value alongside `device` in the path. However, you are still able to get a handle on the `model` element, because of the remaining `/model` portion of the expression.

A lot more remains to dig into here, but a detailed explanation of XPath is a bit outside the scope of this section. That said, if you're planning to work with XML frequently, especially large XML documents, XPath is an important tool to have in your toolbox. The official Python documentation on the `xml` module contains a lot of helpful examples.

 Another tool for working with XML data is XQuery (*https://oreil.ly/gJX12*). XQuery is a full-blown query language, similar to what SQL is for relational databases, whereas XPath is a way of providing simple expressions—typically, one-liners for locating data within an XML document. Because of their similarities, you may wonder whether you should learn both. XQuery is rarely needed in the context of network automation. Most of the time, a little bit of Python and XPath can get you just about anything you might need.

While XML is well represented throughout the history of network automation, you should be aware of at least one other text-based format, as we'll explore next.

JSON

JavaScript Object Notation (JSON) is the final text-based data format we'll look at, and arguably the most widely used. XML has seniority, and YAML fills a need for a human-readable format, but when it comes to the format chosen for transporting structured data within networked applications, especially those that use HTTP, JSON is the undisputed champion. Many of the tools and libraries that communicate with network APIs, such as those in Chapters 10 and 12, use JSON to send/receive structured data over the network.

The origin story of JSON is similar to that of XML, albeit slightly more recent. It too was created as a lightweight mechanism for exchanging data over the web, to enable more dynamic content. It was based on a subset of the JavaScript programming language (thus the name), and the types used within the JSON specification closely reflect those within JavaScript. However, JSON is a language-independent format that's well supported by a multitude of programming languages and automation tools. Languages like Go and Python have native JSON support in their standard libraries.

JSON has gone through a few iterations when it comes to standardization but remains largely consistent with the original ECMA-404 standard even to this day. The current version of the Internet Standard for JSON is described in RFC 8259 (*https://oreil.ly/wlcYk*). As you can see from this, JSON is a remarkably simple format; RFC 8259 is only 16 pages long!

JSON can also be used for configuration-related use cases. Node Package Manager (npm) uses JSON to describe the configuration of an npm package. Cloud providers like AWS and GCP use JSON files to configure a variety of their command-line utilities. JSON does have subjective advantages over YAML in this regard. Unlike YAML, JSON does not use indentation to indicate the scope of a given block of data, but rather the more explicit curly brace ({}) and square bracket ([]) syntax. This can make it easier to read and edit JSON documents for those unaccustomed to using indentation for scoping, as is done in programming languages like Python. However, this is almost entirely a matter of preference.

> JSON is widely considered a subset of YAML. In fact, many popular YAML parsers can also parse JSON data as if it were YAML (you may recall some of the "alternative" syntax we used in that section, which is remarkably similar to JSON). However, some of the details of this relationship are a bit more nuanced. See the YAML specification (*https://oreil.ly/RTKLL*) for more information.

When compared directly against XML, it's easy to see that JSON is more lightweight; it is generally able to describe the same underlying data with less overall text structure. Let's say you want to represent a list of book authors in XML. You might do it like this:

```
<authors>
    <author>
        <firstName>Christian</firstName>
        <lastName>Adell</lastName>
    </author>
    <author>
        <firstName>Scott</firstName>
        <lastName>Lowe</lastName>
    </author>
    <author>
        <firstName>Matt</firstName>
        <lastName>Oswalt</lastName>
    </author>
</authors>
```

Example 8-6 shows the equivalent data structure in JSON.

Example 8-6. Equivalent JSON

```
{
    "authors":[
        {
            "firstName": "Christian",
            "lastName": "Adell"
        },
        {
            "firstName": "Scott",
            "lastName": "Lowe"
        },
        {
            "firstName": "Matt",
            "lastName": "Oswalt"
        }
    ]
}
```

You can see that JSON is clearly a more lightweight way of representing data. This results in a more efficient way of transmitting the same underlying data. Especially in the early 2000s, this had a meaningful impact on web performance.

JSON has a fairly straightforward set of built-in types that are similar to those you might find in most programming languages, with some minor terminology differences. You'll find they map to our YAML experience quite nicely:

Number
    A signed decimal number.

String
    A collection of characters, such as a word or a sentence.

Boolean

> True or False.

Array

> An ordered list of values enclosed in square brackets, []; items do not have to be the same type.

Object

> An unordered collection of key-value pairs; keys must be strings (enclosed in curly braces, {}).

Null

> Empty value. Uses the word null.

In Example 8-6, you can see several of these types in use. You'll notice that the whole document is wrapped in curly braces. This means that the outermost (or root) type is an object, which contains key-value pairs.

> A JSON document that uses an object as its root, or outermost, type isn't uncommon, but also isn't the only option. The outermost type could also be an array, containing elements of any type.

In this example, the object being described contains only a single key-value pair (note that the keys within a JSON object are always strings). The key is authors, and the value for that key is an array. This is also equivalent to the list format we discussed in YAML—an ordered list of zero or more values. This is indicated by the square brackets [].

Contained within this list are three objects (separated by commas and a newline), each with two key-value pairs. The first pair describes the author's first name (key of firstName) and the second, the author's last name (key of lastName).

Working with JSON in Python

JSON enjoys wide support across a myriad of languages. A JSON document can often be mapped directly into native data structures in languages like Python (dictionaries, lists) and Go (slices, maps, structs). We'll now look more specifically at how to work with JSON in Python.

Our JSON data is stored in a simple text file:

```
{
  "hostname": "CORESW01",
  "vendor": "Cisco",
  "isAlive": true,
  "uptime": 123456,
```

```
    "users": {
      "admin": 15,
      "storage": 10,
    },
    "vlans": [
      {
        "vlan_name": "VLAN30",
        "vlan_id": 30
      },
      {
        "vlan_name": "VLAN20",
        "vlan_id": 20
      }
    ]
  }
```

Python has tools for working with JSON built right into its standard library, aptly called the `json` package. In Example 8-7, you can read this JSON file, convert it (load) into a Python dictionary, and print out some useful information about it (the inline comments can help explain each step in a bit more detail):

Example 8-7. Importing JSON to a Python dictionary

```
# Python contains very useful tools for working with JSON, and they're
# part of the standard library, meaning they're built into Python itself.
import json

# We can load our JSON file into a variable called "data"
with open("json-example.json") as f:
    data = f.read()

# Since our JSON document is an Object, json.loads() returns a dictionary.
# If our document was an Array, this would result in a list.
json_dict = json.loads(data)

# Printing information about the resulting Python data structure
print("The JSON document is loaded as type {0}\n".format(type(json_dict)))
print("Now printing each item in this document and the type it contains")
for k, v in json_dict.items():
    print(
        "-- The key {0} contains a {1} value.".format(str(k), str(type(v)))
    )
```

Those last few lines show exactly how Python views this data once it's imported. The output that results from running this Python program is shown in Example 8-8.

Example 8-8. Results of importing JSON to a Python dictionary

```
~ $ python json-example.py

The JSON document is loaded as type <type 'dict'>
```

```
Now printing each item in this document and the type it contains
-- The key uptime contains a <type 'int'> value.
-- The key isAlive contains a <type 'bool'> value.
-- The key users contains a <type 'dict'> value.
-- The key hostname contains a <type 'unicode'> value.
-- The key vendor contains a <type 'unicode'> value.
-- The key vlans contains a <type 'list'> value.
```

You might be seeing the unicode data type for the first time. In Python, the str type is just a sequence of bytes, whereas unicode specifies an actual encoding. The reason you're seeing it here is that the JSON specification requires text to be encoded in Unicode. So, if you're new to text encoding, you can conceptually think of unicode as a specific type of string and useful for the same kind of things as the str (string) type, discussed in Chapter 6.

Now that you've imported your JSON document into a native Python data structure, all the tools and techniques you learned in Chapter 6 can be used to find whatever information you're looking for.

You can also perform the reverse action—that is, taking a Python data structure and creating a JSON document from it. Example 8-9 creates a Python list vendors and uses the method json.dumps() to create a JSON document containing an array.

Example 8-9. Dumping a Python list as a JSON array

```
>>> import json
>>> vendors = []
>>> vendors.append("Cisco")
>>> vendors.append("Arista")
>>> vendors.append("Juniper")
>>> print(json.dumps(vendors, indent=2))
[
  "Cisco",
  "Arista",
  "Juniper"
]
```

Binary Data Formats

So far in this chapter, we've been discussing text-based data formats. These data formats leverage an intermediate representation for enhanced portability. The vast majority of languages and tools can easily understand formats like JSON. Therefore, when you're sending data over the network, you can use this format and know that the other end can understand it, even if it's written in another language, by another team, on another continent.

Hopefully, it has also been clear that while this intermediate step sacrifices a bit of efficiency to achieve this portability, the vast majority of use cases in network automation simply do not have the performance requirements for this inefficiency to become a problem. That said, in a few situations, the extra time and storage/band-width required to serialize and deserialize into these formats is considered prohibitively inefficient. For these, a more efficient type of format is called for: a *binary data format*. To understand this format, we first have to explore data types a bit more and how they actually work under the hood.

The type system in any statically typed programming language can usually be thought of as a set of aliases that the compiler uses to represent various lengths of bytes. For example, an int in Go, which defaults to a 32-bit integer, is just a way of allocating 4 bytes of memory. It follows, then, that if we were to define our own type composed of fields like these, that type would occupy as much memory as the sum of its constituent parts; see Example 8-10.

Example 8-10. A simple Go struct

```
type Coords struct {
    X int32
    Y int32
}
```

This type is another way of saying "a 64 bit chunk of memory." The fields used within this type are a way of telling the compiler that the first 32 bits are used for one purpose and the second 32 bits for another.

As you might imagine, this mapping is language-specific. The way Go maps its own type system into memory is very different from the way Python, Rust, or C does it. However, applications written in these languages still need to communicate somehow. We've established that applications can serialize into one of the aforementioned text-based formats to solve this problem, but as we've also shown, this comes at a computational and storage cost that can be unacceptable for some use cases. This is where binary data formats come in.

The primary difference between binary data formats and the text-based formats you've seen thus far is that text-based formats require two separate steps to store or transmit information (encoding/decoding and serialization/deserialization), whereas binary data formats do it all in a single step. This is because applications using binary data formats do not have to first serialize data to an intermediate format like JSON or XML, but rather, they are able to read the raw bytes off of a network request or file on the filesystem, and map those bytes directly into a data structure, as shown in Figure 8-4.

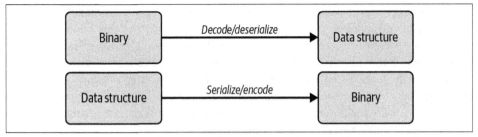

Figure 8-4. Decoding/deserialization and serialization/encoding binary data formats

Of course, even JSON messages must eventually be translated into binary in order to be transmitted or stored; everything your computer does is eventually a bunch of 0s and 1s, after all. However, because binary data formats do not require a text-based serialization step, they require much less work to get to that stage, and ultimately require a smaller number of bits in which to do it. You can think of binary data formats as being "closer" to that low-level representation.

For a more networking-centric example of binary data formats, you need look no further than your earliest Cisco Certified Network Associate (CCNA) or CompTIA Network+ studies. Packet headers are laid out as raw bits and bytes. You are taught to understand that bits 64–72 of an IPv4 packet are for that packet's time to live (TTL), and that the source and destination address are both 32 bits long. You know this because you spend time understanding the concepts that each field represents, and then you understand how many bits are required to represent them. Most importantly, this layout of bits is standardized and must be strictly adhered to; otherwise, two network endpoints wouldn't be able to communicate effectively.

The binary data formats we're talking about here are really no different: they're intended to represent a variety of data structures in such a way that it can be transmitted/stored and encoded/decoded as efficiently as possible. Imagine for a second if this wasn't the case—that the IPv4 packet header was some agreed-upon JSON object that first needed to be deserialized before it could be read by your router. What a preposterously inefficient design that would be! Why, then, is such an idea so patently absurd, yet it's totally acceptable to use formats like JSON for our automation-related APIs? Why wouldn't we just use binary data formats everywhere? Well, the reality is that some APIs have gone in this direction. As we discuss in Chapter 10, binary data formats are quite popular in newer technologies like gRPC. However, JSON-based APIs are hardly going away. And don't forget, text-based data formats still have their unique advantages: they're more readable, easier to debug, and enjoy broader application support.

Application developers have a slew of considerations when deciding between binary data formats and text-based data formats. However, given that this book is focused specifically on network automation, we can boil this down a bit. The first thing you should know is that not many use cases really *require* the efficiencies gained by using binary data formats. Most of the time when you're running network automation workflows, the *vast* majority of your computer's time is spent idle. Typically, your script or tool will send a few API requests and wait for a response. Using text-based data formats for use cases like this is perfectly fine.

Binary data formats are preferred by a network automation professional for two main reasons:

Developer preference

As you've seen, all data formats come with their own set of tools and techniques for working with them. Developers become accustomed to using certain tools, and barring a compelling reason to do otherwise, sticking with what you know is sometimes useful. In some cases, this manifests in the form of a vendor building an API that uses only a certain format; if you're writing a script to work with this API, you too will have to understand how to work with this format.

Performance

This is a nuanced point that shouldn't be taken for granted. Again, most of what is done in network automation is trivial for a computer to handle, However, some use cases, such as streaming network telemetry, do benefit from these kinds of efficiencies. The key questions to ask here are, "How much information is being transmitted, and how often is it being transmitted?" One of the reasons streaming telemetry often uses binary data formats is that it's sending *very* frequent updates, each of which could contain a significant amount of data.

 Binary formats aren't *always* faster or more efficient than text-based formats. A lot of nuance can be found in the implementations behind each technology, and in how well the data itself is laid out in each format. It's totally possible that a text-based format could outperform a binary format. While the scales are definitely tipped in favor of binary formats when it comes to performance, this outcome is not guaranteed by any means.

Because most of the specific benefits and drawbacks of binary data formats tend to vary based on the format in question, it's time to dive into some examples. We have quite a few options when it comes to binary data formats, and we'll start with Protocol Buffers.

Protocol Buffers

By far, the most likely binary data format you'll run into in your network automation journey is that provided by Protocol Buffers (*https://protobuf.dev*), also known as *protobuf*. As described on its website, protobuf was originally developed by Google for internal use, as a smaller and faster alternative to XML.

Since then, the specification and tooling for protobuf have become open source, so that anyone can use them. Previously, if you wanted to store or transmit information between applications, you had to either pick one of the well-known text-based formats like XML (which can be very slow when you're operating at Google scale), or use a binary format specific to a programming language like Python or Go, which solves the performance problem to some extent but then locks you into that format's language and ecosystem.

Protobuf, in contrast, is language agnostic, with nine languages supported by the latest version of the specification, and more being added all the time. This is the result of two important and distinct components:

- A schema definition language that allows you to specify services and messages in a way that's not specific to any one application language (e.g., Python or Go)
- Tools for automatically generating source code in any of the supported languages based on these definitions

We'll explore both of these aspects in the following sections.

Protobuf definitions

Many text-based formats like JSON and XML are self-describing, in that they have formally defined textual conventions for indicating the type of data that they contain. Most binary data formats, on the other hand, are not self-describing. Because they're just an opaque blob of bytes, you need some kind of external type definition so these bytes can be translated into types that both ends of a communication stream can make sense of.

Protobuf is no exception to this. To use protobuf to communicate, developers must first define their message format in the *protobuf interface definition language*, usually stored as *.proto* files. This language allows you to define the complex types that will eventually be serialized into binary data and transmitted to another application. Protobuf is a language-agnostic, human-editable way of representing otherwise opaque, binary data. It's like a Rosetta Stone for binary data—and both sides of a protobuf-based communication channel must have the same copy of it in order to communicate.

A *type* in this language is referred to as a *message*. With this, you can define a custom type that you would like to be serialized via protobuf (Example 8-11).

Example 8-11. A protobuf message

```
message Router {
    int32 id = 1;
    string hostname = 2;
}
```

Before we go much further, a closer examination of the protobuf message in Example 8-11 is warranted:

- `message Router` is a top-level declaration of the message named `Router`. You can use this message definition within other messages or as a parameter or return value for services, which we cover later.

- There are two *singular* fields: `id`, which is of type `int32`, and `hostname`, which is of type `string`.

- Each field has a number to the right that's known as the *field identifier*. Since the order of serialized protobuf data is an implementation detail (and therefore can vary), this helps ensure that the raw binary is deserialized into the right fields.

At no point is the textual data in Example 8-11 transmitted on the wire (this is a key distinction between this and other text-based formats presented thus far, like XML or JSON). It is merely a human-editable specification that the protobuf tooling can read, and "compile" into a more efficient format. For the same reason you would define a class or a struct (as in Example 8-10) so your program knows how to allocate and read a chunk of memory on your computer, you can define a protobuf message in a *.proto* file so that your software knows how make sense of the raw binary data you're retrieving or sending.

Protobuf messages can also reference other messages when the built-in types like `int32` and `string` aren't enough on their own. Let's add a second message type called `Interface`, and then add a field to the `Router` message that uses it:

```
message Router {
    int32 id = 1;
    string hostname = 2;
    repeated Interface interfaces = 3;
}

message Interface {
    int32 id = 1;
    string description = 2;
}
```

The `repeated` keyword is the protobuf equivalent of a list or array. It indicates that the field `interfaces` is not just a single instance of the `Interface` message type, but multiple instances.

Protobuf also allows you to define a `Service`, which describes a set of RPC functions that can use either the built-in types, or the messages you've defined as parameters or return types:

```
service RouterService {
    rpc GetRouter(RouterRequest) returns (Router);
}
```

 Service declarations can be used to define service endpoints for frameworks like gRPC and gNMI. For these, protobuf is one of the most popular data representation technologies, and Chapter 10 covers this in more detail.

This is an *extremely* light introduction to protobuf definitions. There are several more built-in types and important keywords to know if you want to write your own definitions or even read an existing definition. The Protocol Buffers Language Guide (*https://oreil.ly/Wnsdb*) is a great next step if you want to dig in further.

Protobuf tooling and code generation

The second important component that makes protobuf work is the tooling that can automatically generate code in the language of your choice, from these message and service definitions. This automatically generated code makes it much easier to send and receive binary-encoded protobuf data that follows those definitions in your applications.

You looked at individual pieces of our protobuf definition in the preceding section, and a full working example is shown in Example 8-12.

Example 8-12. Full protobuf definition

```
syntax = "proto3";
package networkstuff;

service RouterService {
    rpc GetRouter(RouterRequest) returns (Router);
}

message RouterRequest {
    int32 id = 1;
}

message Router {
    int32 id = 1;
```

```
    string hostname = 2;
    repeated Interface interfaces = 3;
}

message Interface {
    int32 id = 1;
    string description = 2;
}
```

The number one tool you'll want to familiarize yourself with, and make sure you have installed anywhere you want to write code that uses protobuf, is protoc. This is the *protobuf compiler*, and it allows you to go from the generic message definitions you've been working with thus far to "real" code that you can use in languages like Python or Go. Instructions for downloading and installing protoc can be found on the main Protocol Buffers website (*https://oreil.ly/ak-_A*).

Once installed, protoc can be used to generate code for a variety of languages, even simultaneously. This can be executed on the bash command line. The following example instructs protoc to generate Go and Python code in the local directory, from the protobuf definition (as shown in Example 8-12) in the file *networkstuff.proto*:

```
protoc --go_out=. --python_out=. networkstuff.proto
```

This creates two files, one for Python (*networkstuff_pb2.py*), and one for Go (*networkstuff.pb.go*). These contain automatically generated type definitions and constructors for working with the language-specific implementation of the messages and services defined in our protobuf source file. You can then refer to these in your own code in order to use those types.

Let's take a closer look at how to work with the generated Python code. You can open an interactive Python shell in the current directory and import the new module by name:

```
>>> import networkstuff_pb2
```

Within this module, each of your protobuf messages is given its own class, which you can instantiate:

```
>>> router = networkstuff_pb2.Router()
>>> router.id = 1337
>>> router.hostname = "r1"
```

It turns out the Python implementation is pretty smart. Normally, instances of Python classes permit the addition of attributes on the fly, but if you try to do that with your protobuf-generated class, you get an exception:

```
>>> router.foo = "bar"
Traceback (most recent call last):
  File "<stdin>", line 1, in <module>
AttributeError: Assignment not allowed (no field "foobar" in message object).
```

This adds a little bit of safety against things like "fat fingering" attribute names. It's still Python, so this check doesn't happen until runtime (with languages like Go, this would be caught at compile time), but it's better than nothing.

You can also use the `add()` method on the `router.interfaces` attribute to instantiate a new `Interface` object:

```
>>> if1 = router.interfaces.add()
>>> if1.id = 1
>>> if1.description = "outside interface"
>>> if2 = router.interfaces.add()
>>> if2.id = 2
>>> if2.description = "inside interface"
```

Now that you have instantiated your protobuf-defined `Router` object in Python and populated it with sample data, you can use the `SerializeToString()` method to see the byte-level representation of this instance, printed as a Python byte string:

```
>>> router.SerializeToString()
b'\x08\xb9\n\x12\x02r1\x1a\x15\x08\x01\x12\x11outside interface\x1a\x14...'
```

You can write this binary data to the filesystem:

```
>>> f = open('serialized.bin', 'w+b')
>>> f.write(router.SerializeToString())
>>> f.close()
```

Back at the bash shell, you can then use a tool like `hexdump` to inspect the raw bytes in the file:

```
~$ hexdump serialized.bin
0000000 b908 120a 7202 1a31 0815 1201 6f11 7475
0000010 6973 6564 6920 746e 7265 6166 6563 141a
0000020 0208 1012 6e69 6973 6564 6920 746e 7265
0000030 6166 6563
0000034
```

Finally, to go full circle with this example, you can use `protoc` to decode these raw bytes back into a readable format. This decoding requires the original *.proto* file, as well as the name of the message you intend to decode and, of course, the binary file itself (passed via `stdin`):

```
~$ protoc --decode networkstuff.Router networkstuff.proto < serialized.bin

id: 1337
hostname: "r1"
interfaces {
  id: 1
  description: "outside interface"
}
interfaces {
  id: 2
  description: "inside interface"
}
```

The latest protobuf specification supports a canonical encoding in JSON (*https:// oreil.ly/3LmDI*), which can be *really* useful for working with systems that require a more traditional format. This way, you can primarily define your message types in protobuf, and serialize to binary data when you can, but still have the option to generate JSON from a given message when needed.

The method for producing this will vary based on the language, but the protobuf Python library contains a package for working with JSON from protobuf types:

```
>>> from google.protobuf.json_format import MessageToJson
>>> print(MessageToJson(router))
{
  "id": 1337,
  "hostname": "r1",
  "interfaces": [
    {
      "id": 1,
      "description": "outside interface"
    },
    {
      "id": 2,
      "description": "inside interface"
    }
  ]
}
```

Truthfully, as a network automation professional, you're unlikely to use protobuf to write serialized binary data to the filesystem. Things get *really* exciting when you are able to build on what we've only started to explore here and leverage protobuf in modern RPC frameworks like gRPC. Technologies like this will also leverage the code generated by `protoc` not only for the message definitions, but also to generate functions that represent the services we defined. It doesn't matter if you have an API client written in Python and an API server written in Go (or many other combinations); as long as both sides are working from the same protobuf definitions, they can communicate. Chapter 10 covers this in much more detail.

Protobuf is a modern, lightweight binary data format that in the world of network automation has already been widely adopted. However, before we move on, we should touch on a few other binary data formats that you may come across.

Other Binary Data Formats

Within the scope of network automation, protobuf is really the only binary data format you *need* to know about, since it is a key component in many modern network programmability options. However, a few other binary data formats are potentially relevant. It's useful to be aware of some of these alternatives, so we'll spend a few sentences discussing a few of them and their pros and cons:

Pickle

Pickle (*https://oreil.ly/bb0p7*) is a binary format for serializing Python objects. It is specific to Python and therefore will not work in other languages, but offers support for serializing just about any kind of object structure you have in your Python programs. It has advantages like built-in de-duplication (will not serialize the same object twice) and backward compatibility.

Gob

Gob (*https://go.dev/blog/gob*) is a binary format for serializing Go types. It aims to have the same speed advantages as Protocol Buffers, but presented in a way that's much easier to use and doesn't require a separate interface definition language, as you would have in *.proto* files. You need only define your types in code, and the gobs package will be able to determine how best to serialize those types by using reflection techniques.

BSON

BSON (*https://bsonspec.org*) is a "binary-encoded serialization of JSON-like documents." It was originally invented as an internal representation of data for the MongoDB database. It's more efficient than its textual counterpart JSON, but still somewhat less efficient than other binary formats, since it includes things like field names within the serialized data. It does include some additional types that are not supported in the JSON specification.

FlatBuffers

FlatBuffers (*https://flatbuffers.dev*) is similar to protobuf, including the fact that both were originally developed at Google. However, unlike protobuf, FlatBuffers allows you to directly access the serialized data in the form of a flat binary buffer, without having to unpack or deserialize it first. You can also deserialize a portion of the buffer, as opposed to having to deserialize the entire buffer all at once. This is highly desirable for extremely performance-sensitive applications, such as video games.

Apache Thrift

Apache Thrift (*https://thrift.apache.org*) is also similar to protobuf, in that it is a binary data format that includes an RPC framework, an interface definition language, and code generation tooling. However, while it was originally created at Facebook, it has since become an Apache project. Thrift and protobuf are typically seen as roughly equivalent in terms of performance (most comparisons have these two tied at first place). Thrift does offer a full RPC implementation, whereas protobuf generates only RPC stub functions that need to be implemented to be useful.

It's useful to be aware of these other formats, and each has its own benefits and drawbacks. However, as a network automation professional, the choice of which binary data format to use will almost always be made for you. A network platform will typically determine one of these and provide either message definitions for you to create your own code or a prebuilt library that you can simply consume.

Next, we'll cover data modeling, which allows us to place additional constraints on the data sent using one of these formats.

Data Modeling

So far in this chapter, we've discussed a variety of data formats. Text-based formats like YAML, XML, and JSON are great for representing data in a human-readable and portable way. Binary data formats like protobuf are useful when performance is a bit more important. All these formats have basic type systems so your program is able to understand that a given series of characters or bytes is a string, integer, or boolean. At the end of the day, all these formats are aimed at representing data in a way that can be serialized and deserialized, to facilitate things like API-based communication.

However, sometimes we need more than just simple serialization. Let's imagine that we are interacting with an API endpoint to update the hostname for a network device. The JSON payload for a request to this endpoint might look something like Example 8-13.

Example 8-13. Example JSON payload

```
{
  "hostname": ""
}
```

This JSON object has a single key, hostname, whose value is also a string—presumably representing the new hostname we want to use for this device. However, while it is a valid string, it is also empty. From a JSON formatting perspective, this is a perfectly valid syntax; any mature JSON parser will have no problem deserializing this document.

However, if we were to send this payload to the API endpoint in question, it could still cause problems. These problems would have nothing to do with the validity of the JSON document itself, but rather the downstream effects of sending an empty string as a parameter to the hostname update functionality that this API endpoint represents. Now, of course, the API server could include a check to ensure that this field is not empty; this might take the form of a conditional, as in Example 8-14.

Example 8-14. Explicit check for an empty string

```
req = json.loads(json_str)
if req["hostname"] == "":
    raise Exception("Hostname field must not be empty")
```

However, what about hostnames that are too long? What about special characters that might be supported in JSON but aren't supported by the actual network device? By the way, all these considerations apply only to this one hostname field; what about even moderately more complex JSON payloads? We may have many more types in this payload to think about like integers, arrays, or nested objects, each with its own specific validity concerns. We might want to ensure that a given JSON array is not empty, or contains no more than five elements, or doesn't contain any duplicates.

Writing server-side code to check for *all* these cases can quickly become unsustainable. Even if we could stay on top of all of them, such an approach would create an ugly experience for anyone writing code to consume such an API. If all these checks were built into the API server itself, clients would have great difficulty knowing how to send valid data to this API. The maintainers of the API would have to maintain detailed documentation about all of these checks and ensure that it was kept up-to-date manually (you can probably imagine how rarely this approach ends in success).

Data modeling is a set of tools and techniques for solving this problem. Whereas data formats allow you to serialize structured data generically, data modeling allows us to take this a step further and provide constraints that this structured data must adhere to. It gives us the opportunity to describe more specific rules and relationships that bring data into alignment with a specific use case or business process.

Typically, this is accomplished using some kind of data modeling language, which specializes in describing these constraints and relationships between data. These are often developed in conjunction with applications (i.e., an API server) designed to leverage that data model. Such an approach gives us key advantages and capabilities, especially within the network automation domain:

- Data models can often be language agnostic. Multiple applications can use the same model (e.g., a Python API client and a Go API server). In addition, you have only one place to see or update the data model.

- This approach focuses on the data, not the application. This makes it easier for nondevelopers (or developers who specialize in various languages) to understand the data model, without having to worry about language-specific syntax.

- Many data-modeling techniques provide a way to generate application code that enforces these constraints. This can be extremely useful for working with APIs; if you have the data model, you can automatically generate code to reliably produce a correct payload for an API call.

The canonical example of data modeling in practice is the *database schema*, which is used to describe the organization and structure of data within a database. These schemas allow you to describe tables of data, which include columns of a particular data type, but also allow you to specify relationships between data, and constraints like the uniqueness of a particular value. For example, in relational database systems the *primary key* is a special designation describing a column of values that can be used to uniquely identify the row to which those values belong. Primary keys often enforce such a uniqueness constraint; an attempt to insert a new row with a primary-key value that already exists for another row will be rejected.

It may seem like we're straying into software developer territory here. While it's true that some of these concepts may be more aligned with the day-to-day work of professional developers, it doesn't mean you'll never need to create your own data models (even simple ones), and it certainly doesn't mean that understanding the concepts behind data modeling, the technologies involved, or an existing data model aren't profoundly useful skills to have as a network automation professional.

That said, more goes into creating a solid data model than throwing a few fields together. It can often require a more in-depth understanding of relationships between data, cardinality, and data normalization (or in some cases, denormalization), which can be tough for even seasoned software developers to get right.

As a result, this section doesn't cover every aspect of data modeling, for every possible use case. Rather, we give you just enough insight into the important concepts involved with data models, some of the specific tools and techniques for creating and evolving them, and the most likely ways you'll need to use this knowledge in your work as a network automation engineer.

While we won't be diving into database schemas in this chapter, the idea of a schema as applied to the data formats we've discussed thus far is very much applicable. In its most general definition, a *schema* is just a way to describe the structure of data. As a result, we use the terms *data model* and *schema* somewhat interchangeably in this section, since they're both close enough approximations for accomplishing our goals.

Before getting started, here are a few key points to keep in mind as you read the remaining sections of this chapter:

- Data modeling involves the creation of a schema to which data must conform. This allows us to go beyond simple serialization and provide a more opinionated structure of the data that is relevant to our business logic or use case.

- Data-modeling languages and tools are not serialization formats. They are not used to carry information, but only to describe it. You won't see any of these modeling technologies in a packet capture or browser network trace.

- Some data-modeling technologies are specific to a corresponding serialization format (e.g., JSON and XML), and others are a bit more broadly applicable.

- We don't cover every data modeling tool in existence—only those that you're most likely to run into in your network automation journey.

Within the context of network automation, you can consider data models as analogous to a grammar textbook. It doesn't tell you the specific words to say to a friend during a conversation, only the rules you should follow to ensure that the two of you can have a conversation of any kind. When you speak, you don't regurgitate the textbook itself; rather, you use your own words that follow the rules from that textbook. In the same way, data models provide the specific rules and constraints that a particular communication mechanism must follow. Given that both sides are following the same "grammar textbook," they can communicate.

YANG

Without a doubt, the data-modeling technology you're most likely to run into during your network automation journey is YANG. Originally published as IETF RFC 6020 (*https://oreil.ly/bYaZ4*), YANG was created as a data-modeling language specific to the NETCONF protocol, which we cover in greater detail in Chapter 10. However, in the most recent version, which is defined in RFC 7950 (*https://oreil.ly/nXq81*), YANG has begun to decouple itself from NETCONF and XML so that other serialization formats like JSON, defined in RFC 7951 (*https://oreil.ly/T3enl*), can be used, as well as other APIs like RESTCONF (NETCONF over an HTTP transport). Regardless, the main purpose of YANG is to model configuration and operational state data such as that transmitted during NETCONF RPCs.

You may have heard that a given NOS or API is YANG-based, or model driven using YANG. This is a way of summarizing an architectural approach to building programmable network systems that places the data model at the center. This is usually a good thing; starting with the data model allows a vendor to automatically generate code from that model to implement API servers, clients, and internal systems. It's a much less fragile, less burdensome approach than building API bindings by hand.

One unfortunate by-product of condensing the YANG approach into such simple terms is that it almost sounds like YANG is used as a serialization format for APIs like RESTCONF or NETCONF. This is a popular misconception about YANG. YANG is not a serialization format like JSON or XML, and you won't see YANG syntax in a packet capture of an API request or response. In fact, APIs that leverage YANG for data modeling *usually* use XML as the serialization format when sending data between a server and a client. For this reason, many of the examples in this section use XML to show how data that is modeled in YANG can be serialized in an API request.

YANG enjoys broad adoption by many companies and organizations. Many network vendors use YANG to build their systems with a model-driven approach. End-user-led organizations like OpenConfig aim to create a common set of vendor-neutral data models. The IETF also has working groups for building its own set of vendor-neutral models.

Like other data-modeling technologies, YANG enables you to define the constraints of that data—such as those found in a network configuration or state table. You can specify, for instance, that VLAN IDs must be between 1 and 4094. You can enforce the operational state of an interface, in that it must be "up" or "down." Through these models, the behavior of data within and between network systems can be defined.

Various types of YANG models exist. Some of these YANG models were created by end users; others were created by vendors or open working groups:

- Industry standard models include those from groups like the IETF and the OpenConfig Working Group. These models are vendor and platform neutral. Each model produced by an open standards group is meant to provide a base set of options for a given feature.

- Of course, vendor-specific models also exist. Almost every vendor has its own solution for multichassis link aggregation groups (MC-LAGs), for example, each with its own variances in configuration and state data. As a result, each vendor would need to build a data model specific to these implementations.

- Even within a single vendor, variances arise in the way a given feature is implemented across product platforms and would similarly require unique models.

As you may recall from earlier in this chapter, XML closely resembles a tree structure. Since YANG was originally intended to model data serialized in XML, it makes sense that the primitives it offers also follow this pattern. In fact, one of the core concepts in YANG is `leaf`, which allows you to define a singular piece of data that contains a single value and has no children. Note also the `type` statement, which allows you to specify that this element is a `string`, but other types are supported:

```
leaf hostname {
    type string;
    mandatory true;
    config true;
    description "Hostname for the network device";
}
```

This maps neatly to the XML document in Example 8-15.

Example 8-15. XML document satisfying the YANG model

```
<hostname>sw01</hostname>
```

This `leaf` statement is fairly flexible but still enforces some constraints on the data being described. For example, the `mandatory true;` statement means this field cannot be empty or blank. If you had omitted the `sw01` text from Example 8-15, it would not validate against your YANG data model.

You may also remember that XML can contain multiple instances of the same element. A good example of this in practice is the list of configured DNS servers on a device. The `leaf-list` statement allows you to model this kind of data:

```
leaf-list name-server {
    type string;
    ordered-by user;
    description "List of DNS servers to query";
}
```

The `ordered-by` statement controls whether the order of elements within this data structure should be respected and maintained, or whether the implementation of the system can order the elements in the way it sees fit. The latter can be useful for things like VLAN definitions, as the order in which VLANs are defined doesn't really matter. However, for other things like DNS name servers or access-list entries, order is *extremely* important. As a result, the statement `ordered-by user;` is used.

Again, here's an example of XML data that adheres to this model:

```
<name-server>1.1.1.1</name-server>
<name-server>8.8.8.8</name-server>
```

Until now, we've been looking only at elements that don't include any nested data. In YANG parlance, these are leaves in the tree. However, as we've shown, a nested structure is usually a more practical way of representing data like this. For instance, a specific VLAN may have several fields to describe it: minimally, a VLAN ID and a human-readable name. These could be represented as children of a generic `vlan` element:

```
<vlan>
    <id>100</id>
    <name>web_vlan></name>
</vlan>
<vlan>
    <id>200</id>
    <name>app_vlan></name>
</vlan>
```

YANG provides another way of defining lists, but unlike the `leaf-list` statement, the `list` statement is used when the elements of that list are themselves parent elements—that is, they contain nested elements, as shown in Example 8-16.

Example 8-16. List statement in YANG

```
list vlan {
    key "id";
    unique "name";
    leaf id {
        type int16;
    }
    leaf name {
        type string;
    }
}
```

This is also where you get to see some useful constraints in action. This **key** statement indicates that the **id** field should be used as a unique identifier for elements in this list. This is roughly analogous to a primary key in database terms. The **unique** statement specifies that the **name** value within these list elements should also be unique. This is useful for values that may not be used as a key, but should still be unique; in this case, it's useful to ensure that the VLAN names are not duplicated.

However, you're missing an important constraint here. The type for the VLAN ID is **int16**—which is quite broad when you consider that VLAN IDs are only positive and can go up to only a value of 4094 (16-bit signed integers can represent values from −32,768 to 32,767). Unfortunately, an 8-bit integer would be too small for this purpose. So, what do you do?

You can define your own custom data type that helps enforce these kinds of constraints. Using the **typedef** statement, you can define a new type by name—say, **vlanid**:

```
typedef vlanid {
    type int16 {
      range "1 .. 4094";
    }
}
```

Within this block, you can specify that this new type definition inherits from the built-in type **int16**, but then also enforces a constraint that the value must be within the **range** 1 to 4094. As a result, any element that references this type must not only be a 16-bit integer, but also fit within this more specific range.

You can then amend the leaf node from Example 8-16 to use this new type definition:

```
list vlan {
    key "id";
    unique "name";
    leaf id {
        type vlanid;
    }
    leaf name {
        type string;
```

```
            }
        }
```

Of course, seeing a series of `vlan` elements at the root of an XML document would be strange. It's more likely that these would be nested within a parent element like `vlans`:

```
<vlans>
    <vlan>
        <id>100</id>
        <name>web_vlan></name>
    </vlan>
    <vlan>
        <id>200</id>
        <name>app_vlan></name>
    </vlan>
</vlans>
```

This can be specified in YANG by using the `container` statement:

```
container vlans {
    list vlan {
        key "id";
        unique "name";
        leaf id {
            type vlanid;
        }
        leaf name {
            type string;
        }
    }
}
```

This was just a taste of some of the more common primitives within YANG syntax. YANG has plenty of other terms and concepts that we don't have time to get into. The YANG RFCs are surprisingly readable and quite thorough, so these can be a reliable reference if you want to dive deeper. Numerous online resources are also available for YANG fundamentals and practical applications.

Before we end this section, however, it's useful to take a look at ways you can do something practical with a YANG model by using some of the tools in its ecosystem. One of the most popular of these is `pyang`, which is a Python-based library as well as command-line tool for working with YANG. With `pyang` and some plug-ins built for it, you can do things like validate that a given model is compliant with YANG RFCs, check whether a given XML document is valid against a given model, and even generate a Python class hierarchy from a model.

Once `pyang` is installed, you can use it from the bash command line to check that a given YANG model is valid:

```
~$ pyang config.yang
```

If any validation errors result from parsing this YANG model, this command would list them in the resulting output.

pyang also allows you to convert a YANG model to several supported output formats. One useful output is `tree`, which provides a nice tree-like map of the module and its statements and types:

```
~$ pyang config.yang -f tree
module: config
  +--rw hostname        string
  +--rw vlans
  |  +--rw vlan* [id]
  |     +--rw id      vlanid
  |     +--rw name?   string
  +--rw name-servers
     +--rw name-server*   string
```

Another useful output format is a sample XML skeleton:

```
~$ pyang config.yang -f sample-xml-skeleton
<?xml version='1.0' encoding='UTF-8'?>
<data xmlns="urn:ietf:params:xml:ns:netconf:base:1.0">
  <hostname xmlns="https://example.org/config"/>
  <vlans xmlns="https://example.org/config">
    <vlan>
      <id/>
      <name/>
    </vlan>
  </vlans>
  <name-servers xmlns="https://example.org/config">
    <name-server>
      <!-- # entries: 0.. -->
    </name-server>
  </name-servers>
</data>
```

pyangbind is a plug-in for pyang that allows you to automatically generate a Python module from a YANG model. This can then be used to serialize out to XML, JSON, etc. You reference the plug-in directory where pyangbind can be located, and then refer to this location with the `--plugindir` flag. This makes a new output format available, pybind:

```
~$ PYANG_PLUGIN_DIR=$(pwd)/venv/lib/python3.8/site-packages/pyangbind/plugin
~$ pyang --plugindir $PYANG_PLUGIN_DIR -f pybind -o yangconfig.py config.yang
```

These commands generate a Python file, *yangconfig.py*, which you can then import from a Python prompt at the same location. Within this module is a class called `config`, which you can instantiate into `cfg`:

```
from yangconfig import config
cfg = config()
```

As of now, `cfg` is basically the Python equivalent of our YANG data model but is also empty. You can start populating it with information that is compliant with the model—for instance, a hostname:

```
cfg.hostname = "sw01"
```

Since the name servers are stored as a leaf list, these must be appended:

```
cfg.name_servers.name_server.append("1.1.1.1")
cfg.name_servers.name_server.append("8.8.8.8")
```

The VLANs are a bit more complicated, since these are modeled as a plain `leaf`. This means you need to `add()` a new VLAN by specifying its key as a parameter (this is the VLAN ID in our model). Then you can refer to it via that same key to set the other attributes, like `name`:

```
cfg.vlans.vlan.add(100)
cfg.vlans.vlan[100].name = "VLAN_100"
```

Note that you use a custom type to describe the VLAN ID, which specifies that it must be an integer between 1 and 4094. If you try to add a VLAN with an ID outside this range, an exception is raised:

```
>>> cfg.vlans.vlan.add(5000)

(traceback omitted for brevity)

ValueError: 5000 does not match a restricted type
```

From here, you can serialize this into either XML or JSON. You can also use `pyang bind` to deserialize an existing XML or JSON document into this same class structure, and more. The `pyangbind` README file contains examples for these and other use cases.

As with most topics in this chapter, the preceding examples are really just a taste of what you can do with YANG. If you're interested in providing a more structured, model-based approach to thinking about network data, you could do worse than to start off with YANG. However, you also should be aware of other modeling languages, which we'll explore next.

JSON Schema

JSON is an incredibly popular data format, especially in the frontend (web) developer world. As a result, it also enjoys a healthy ecosystem of tools and related specifications. *JSON Schema* is a data-modeling technology that allows you to easily document and validate JSON documents. If you know you want to use JSON as a data format, JSON Schema is a safe choice for creating a model or schema for validating the data you're working with.

Like other data modeling technologies, JSON Schema includes a series of primitives and constraints for describing the layout of a set of data. As you might expect, its type system closely aligns with that of JSON itself; types like string, number, array, and object are all built right in. However, JSON Schema also provides a wide variety of other tools for describing the constraints within which those types should operate.

Let's start with an example similar to the one you worked with for YANG, but instead of XML, you'll use JSON; see Example 8-17.

Example 8-17. JSON document to model

```json
{
    "hostname": "sw01",
    "vlans": [
        {
            "id": 100,
            "name": "VLAN_100"
        },
        {
            "id": 200,
            "name": "VLAN_200"
        }
    ],
    "nameservers": [
        "1.1.1.1",
        "8.8.8.8"
    ]
}
```

This JSON document contains an object type, which includes three fields:

hostname
> This has a simple string value containing the device hostname.

nameservers
> An array of strings containing our name servers.

vlans
> An array of objects, which contain two fields, id and name. Each object represents a different VLAN.

As discussed in the previous section, you might want to make sure that the data shown in this example conforms to a few additional constraints beyond those imposed by the basic type system:

- The vlans and nameservers arrays must not be empty, and they must not contain duplicate entries.
- VLAN IDs must be between 1 and 4094.
- All three fields—hostname, vlans, and nameservers—must be present; they cannot be omitted from the document.

A JSON Schema document is actually written in JSON, using a set of predefined terms and fields. Creating a new JSON Schema document starts by defining the outer type. Since our configuration data is a JSON object, you can specify this by using the `type` property. You can also provide useful metadata like `title` and `description` for our schema. The `$schema` property specifies the version of JSON Schema you're using. This allows tools that use this schema to know which rules to use when parsing this schema and validating data with it. Example 8-18 shows a definition for a JSON schema.

Example 8-18. JSON Schema definition

```
{
    "$schema": "https://json-schema.org/draft/2020-12/schema",
    "title": "Config",
    "description": "A bit of configuration data for a network device",
    "type": "object",
    "properties": {
        ......omitted for brevity......
    },
    "required": ["hostname", "vlans", "nameservers"]
}
```

This definition includes two fields that you'll see a lot more of in the following examples. The `required` key references keys within the JSON document that are mandatory; they should be present for a JSON document to be considered valid. The `properties` property allows you to specify further constraints that should be applied to these keys. Let's now explore each property with specific examples (the following three examples are contained within `properties`).

The `hostname` key is fairly simple. You know it needs to be a string, but you also probably want to enforce a minimum and maximum length:

```
"hostname": {
    "type": "string",
    "minLength": 1,
    "maxLength": 20
}
```

The `nameservers` property is a bit more complex because it represents an array of values:

```
"nameservers": {
    "type": "array",
    "items": {
        "type": "string"
    },
    "minItems": 1,
    "uniqueItems": true
}
```

You need to not only specify the type `array` for this property but also use the `items` field to describe the type of the elements of that array—in this case, `string`. You can also specify that the array must have at least one item with the `minItems` field, and that the array shouldn't contain duplicates by setting `uniqueItems` to `true`.

Finally, `vlans` is quite a bit more complicated since it is an array of objects:

```json
"vlans": {
    "type": "array",
    "items": {
        "type": "object",
        "properties": {
            "id": {
                "type": "integer",
                "minimum": 1,
                "maximum": 4094
            },
            "name": {
                "type": "string"
            }
        },
        "required": ["id", "name"]
    },
    "minItems": 1,
    "uniqueItems": true
},
```

Fortunately, this part of the JSON document mostly uses terms you've already seen. The type of `vlans` is `array`, but its elements are of type `object`. Therefore, you also need to use the `properties` field to describe the properties of each object in the array. This is where you can use the `required` field again to specify that `id` and `name` are mandatory keys in each element. You can specify that `id` must not only be an integer, but also be between 1 and 4094.

Altogether, our JSON schema looks like this:

```json
{
    "$schema": "https://json-schema.org/draft/2020-12/schema",
    "title": "Config",
    "description": "A bit of configuration data for a network device",
    "type": "object",
    "properties": {
        "hostname": {
            "type": "string",
            "minLength": 1,
            "maxLength": 20
        },
        "vlans": {
            "type": "array",
            "items": {
                "type": "object",
                "properties": {
                    "id": {
                        "type": "integer",
                        "minimum": 1,
                        "maximum": 4094
```

```
            },
            "name": {
                "type": "string"
            }
        },
        "required": ["id", "name"]
    },
    "minItems": 1,
    "uniqueItems": true
},
"nameservers": {
    "type": "array",
    "items": {
        "type": "string"
    },
    "minItems": 1,
    "uniqueItems": true
}
},
"required": ["hostname", "vlans", "nameservers"]
}
```

You can store this schema as a JSON file, just as you can store the JSON document described in Example 8-18.

A plethora of tools exist for working with JSON Schema, in a variety of languages, for all kinds of use cases. One common use case is to simply validate that a JSON document adheres to a given schema. For instance, jsonschema (*https://oreil.ly/tsaCI*) is a popular Python-based tool for doing this. You can write Python scripts to use this library to perform validation, or you can use the command-line tool that comes with it to validate documents right on the bash command line:

```
~$ jsonschema --instance data.json schema.json
```

If there's no output, you have a valid JSON document. However, you can easily tweak your JSON document to include invalid data to ensure that you've written a well-thought-out schema. For instance, say your document includes an invalid VLAN ID:

```
~$ jsonschema --instance data.json schema.json
50000: 50000 is greater than the maximum of 4094
```

Or say you've omitted the nameservers property:

```
~$ jsonschema --instance data.json schema.json
{
    'hostname': 'sw01',
    'vlans': [
        {'id': 100, 'name': 'VLAN_100'},
        {'id': 200, 'name': 'VLAN_200'}
    ]
}: 'nameservers' is a required property
```

As you've seen, JSON Schema can be a powerful tool for validating JSON data, and is probably a good choice if you know you'll be working with JSON as a data format.

 Since YAML and JSON are close relatives, some tools allow you to seamlessly validate YAML data as if it were JSON. In addition, it's usually possible to convert a YAML document to JSON so that existing JSON-only tools can be used.

Next, we'll explore how to validate data formatted in XML.

XML Schema Definition

XML also has its own dedicated modeling language, known as *XML Schema Definition*, or *XSD* (*https://oreil.ly/ziWqv*). One popular use case for XSD (as with most modeling languages) is to generate source code data structures that match and enforce the schema described by that data model. You can then use that source code to automatically generate XML that is compliant with that schema, as opposed to writing out the XML by hand.

For a concrete example of how this is done in Python, let's look once more at our XML example:

```
<device>
  <vendor>Cisco</vendor>
  <model>Nexus 7700</model>
  <osver>NXOS 6.1</osver>
</device>
```

Your goal is to print this XML to the console by using some automatically generated code. You can do this by first creating an XSD document, and then using a third-party tool to generate Python code from that document. Then, that code can be used to print the XML you need.

Let's write an XSD schema file that describes the data you intend to write out:

```
<?xml version="1.0" encoding="utf-8"?>
<xs:schema elementFormDefault="qualified" xmlns:xs="http://www.w3.org/2001/
XMLSchema">
  <xs:element name="device">
  <xs:complexType>
    <xs:sequence>
      <xs:element name="vendor" type="xs:string"/>
      <xs:element name="model" type="xs:string"/>
      <xs:element name="osver" type="xs:string"/>
    </xs:sequence>
  </xs:complexType>
</xs:element>
</xs:schema>
```

In this schema document, you are describing that each <device> element can have three children and that the data in each child element must be a string. Not shown here but supported in the XSD specification is the ability to specify that child elements are required; in other words, you could specify that a <device> element *must* have a <vendor> child element present.

You can use a tool called PyXB (*https://oreil.ly/ko-4l*) at the bash command line to create a Python file that contains class object representations of this schema:

```
~$ pyxbgen -u schema.xsd -m schema
```

This creates *schema.py* in this directory. So, if you open a Python prompt at this point, you can import this schema file and work with it. In Example 8-19, you're creating an instance of the generated object, setting some properties on it, and then serializing it into XML by using the toxml() function.

Example 8-19. Generating XML from an XSD schema in Python

```
>>> import schema
>>> dev = schema.device()
>>> dev.vendor = "Cisco"
>>> dev.model = "Nexus"
>>> dev.osver = "6.1"
>>> dev.toxml("utf-8")
'<?xml version="1.0" encoding="utf-8"?><device><vendor>Cisco</vendor><model>Nexus
</model><osver>6.1</osver></device>'
```

Next, we'll explore how to validate data that uses protobuf.

Modeling and Validating Protocol Buffers

Protocol Buffers don't include any built-in data modeling or validation beyond their basic type system. If you want to do this, you need to look at third-party options. One popular choice is protoc-gen-validate (*https://oreil.ly/VyKz_*), which is a plug-in to the protobuf compiler protoc that is maintained as part of the Envoy Proxy project.

This plug-in allows you to specify validation rules within the protobuf definitions we explored earlier. Let's say you have a message Vlan with fields id and name:

```
message Vlan {
    int32 id = 1;
    string name = 2;
}
```

You can provide validation rules for this plug-in within brackets after the field number:

```
message Vlan {
    int32 id = 1 [(validate.rules).int32 = { gte: 1,  lte: 4094 }];
    string name = 2 [(validate.rules).message.required = true];
}
```

When compiled with this plug-in, the generated code will include validation methods on these types, such as `Vlan.Validate()`. This method can be used to determine whether a given class instance or struct adheres to the constraints described in these validation rules.

Summary

Data formats and data models are at the core of everything we do in network automation. Whether we're talking about configuration management, troubleshooting, or even just generating quick reports, a firm grasp on these fundamentals is essential to being successful on your automation journey. As you've seen, specific technologies come and go, but the need for structured data, and the ability to describe the layout of that data and the constraints to which it must adhere, will never change.

Here are some parting thoughts:

- Structured data is essential to a successful automation initiative. Unstructured data formats, while often ideal for humans to consume, are not designed to be easily parsed or understood by our automation systems and scripts.

- None of the languages or formats discussed in this chapter are perfect. They're all designed with specific trade-offs in mind; your job is to identify which trade-offs align best with your situation.

- New data-modeling methods and languages are emerging all the time. For instance, CUE (*https://oreil.ly/GPwfB*) has recently grown in popularity as a bit of a hybrid between a schema definition language and a templating system. Some technologies discussed in this chapter have also decreased in popularity over time. This is a natural and expected evolution; keep your head on a swivel and assess each new tool on its own merits and trade-offs and how they align with your goals.

In the next chapter, we'll use data from formats like those we've discussed here to drive the automatic creation of consistent, templated configurations.

## CHAPTER 9

Templates

Much of a network engineer's job involves the CLI, and much of this work requires syntax-specific keywords and phrases that are often repeated several times, depending on the change. This not only becomes inefficient over time but also is error prone. The way to configure a BGP neighbor relationship on Cisco IOS may be obvious, for instance, but what's not obvious at times are the smaller, "gotcha" configurations, like remembering to append the right BGP community configuration. Often in networking, there are many different ways to do the same thing—and this may be totally dependent on your organization.

One of the key benefits of network automation is *consistency*—being able to predictably and repeatably make changes to production network infrastructure and achieve a desired result. One of the best ways to accomplish this is by creating templates for all automated interaction with the network.

Creating templates for your network configurations means that you can standardize those configurations for your organization, while also allowing network administrators and *consumers* (help desk, network operations center, IT engineers) to dynamically fill in some values when needed. You get the benefits of speed, requiring much less information to make a change, but also consistency (and through this, safety) because the template contains all the necessary configuration commands that your policies dictate.

This chapter starts with an introduction to template tools in general, and then presents specific implementations and shows how to leverage these tools to create network configuration templates.

The Rise of Modern Template Languages

Template technologies have been around for a very, very long time. Just a basic web search for "template languages" shows a multitude of these, most often several options for every related programming language.

You may also notice that the majority of these languages have deep applications in the web development industry. This is because much of the web is based on templates! Instead of writing HTML files for every single user-profile page that a social media site may have, the developers will write one and insert dynamic values into that template, depending on the data being presented by the backend.

In short, template languages have a wide variety of relevant use cases. Their obvious roots are in web development, and of course we'll be talking about using them for network configuration in this chapter, but they have applications in just about any text-based medium, including documentation and reports.

So it's important to remember that using templates requires three steps. First, the templates have to be written. Second, you need some form of data, which will ultimately get rendered into the template to produce something meaningful like a network configuration. This leads us to the third step: something has to drive data into the template. This could be an automation tool like Ansible, which we cover in Chapter 12, or you could be doing it yourself with a language like Python, which we show later in this chapter. Templates are not very useful on their own.

 Most template languages aren't full-on programming languages in the purest sense. Most often, a template language is closely tied to another language that will drive data into the templates that you've built. As a result, each template language and its "parent" language have several similarities. A good example is one that we heavily discuss in this chapter: Jinja is a template language that came out of a Python-centric community, so Jinja has distinct similarities with Python. So if you're wondering which template language to use, it's probably best to decide which "real" language you're aligned with (either through writing your own code or by using an existing tool like Ansible) and go from there.

As mentioned previously, template languages aren't necessarily a new concept, but we are seeing new ideas and even entire languages make it into the ecosystem all the time. If you look at the history of template languages, many were created to serve as a crucial part of the web: dynamic content. This is easily taken for granted these days, but back when the web was just getting started and most websites were built from fairly static content, dynamically loading pieces of data into a page was a big step forward.

Using Templates for Web Development

Django (*https://www.djangoproject.com*), a Python-based web framework, significantly leverages the concept of templated documents. Django has a template language that allows the web developer to create web content in much the same way they normally would, but also offers a way to make portions of the page dynamic. Using Django's template language, the developer can designate portions of an otherwise static page to load dynamic data when the user requests a page.

Here's a simple example—note that this looks much like an HTML document, but with certain portions replaced with variables (indicated with {{ }} notation):

```
<h1>{{ title }}</h1>

{% for article in article_list %}
<h2>
  <a href="{{ article.get_absolute_url }}">
    {{ article.headline }}
  </a>
</h2>
{% endfor %}
```

This template can be rendered by Django when a user loads the page. The Django framework will populate the `title` and `article_list` variables, and the user will receive a page that's been fully populated with real data. The developer doesn't have to write a static HTML page for every possible thing the user wants to retrieve; this is managed by logic on the backend of this web application.

> The Django templating language is similar (but not identical) to the templating language Jinja (*https://oreil.ly/FdzuH*), which we discuss in depth in this chapter. Don't worry about the syntax; we'll get into that. For now, just focus on the concepts and the value that templates provide: consistency.

Detailing the multitude of other available template languages is outside the scope of this chapter, but you should be aware that they exist. Python alone has several options, such as the aforementioned Django and Jinja languages, but also Mako (*https://www.makotemplates.org*) and Genshi (*https://genshi.edgewall.org*). Other languages like Go (*https://oreil.ly/x0V40*) and Ruby (*https://oreil.ly/lUVr9*) have built-in template systems. Again, the point to remember is that the important work of populating a template with data is the role of one of these languages, like Python or Go, so this is the number-one factor in deciding which template language to use. More often than not, it's best to go with a template system built for that language.

Expanding On the Use of Templates

The concepts of templating, especially those discussed in this chapter, are not specific to any single use case and can be applied to nearly any text-based medium. At the end of the day, templates are just a way to transform data into a specific text format. Figure 9-1 illustrates this flow.

Figure 9-1. How templates are produced

All template technologies discussed in this chapter generally work this way. This makes templates useful for anything text based, including reports, configuration files, and configurations. Perhaps you're pulling data from a network device and want to be able to produce a nice report on this data and email it to coworkers. Example 9-1 shows a Jinja template for producing a report containing a list of VLANs.

 Full versions of the code examples in this chapter can be found in the book's GitHub repo at *https://github.com/oreilly-npa-book/exam ples/tree/v2/ch09-templates*.

Example 9-1. Basic report with Jinja

```
| VLAN ID | NAME | STATUS |
| ------- |------| -------|
{% for vlan in vlans %}
| {{ vlan.get('vlan_id') }} | {{ vlan.get('name') }} | {{ vlan.get('status') }} |
{% endfor %}
```

Because you're really just working with text, you can build a template for it. Keep the generic nature of templates in mind as you get into the details of specific use cases and particular template technologies like Jinja; templates have applications well beyond the narrow set of use cases presented in this chapter.

The Value of Templates in Network Automation

At this point, you might be wondering why we're talking about web development and how that could possibly help you on your network automation journey. It's important to understand the value behind templates in general, whether they're used for the web or not. Templates provide consistency—instead of handcrafting text files full of

HTML tags or entering CLI commands, templates enable you to declare which parts of your files need to remain static and which parts should be dynamic.

Every network engineer who has worked on a network long enough has had to prepare a configuration file for a new piece of network gear, like a switch or router. Maybe this has to be done for many switches—perhaps for a new data center build. To make the best use of time, it's useful to build these configurations ahead of time, so that when the switch is physically racked and cabled, the network engineer needs only to paste the configuration into a terminal.

Let's say you're in charge of a rollout like this—it's your job to come up with configurations for all switches going into the new data center being built for your organization. Obviously, each switch will need its own unique configuration file, but a large portion of the configuration will be similar among devices. For instance, you might have the same SNMP community strings, the same admin password, and the same VLAN configuration (at least for similar device types like ToR switches).

Then again, some parts of the configuration are probably unique to a single device. Routers or Layer 3 switches typically require unique addresses, and probably some fairly unique routing protocol configurations, depending on where that device exists in the topology. Deciding what parameters go to which switches can be time-consuming and likely to result in errors. Templates allow you to standardize on a common base configuration and help ensure that the right values get filled in for each device. Separating the template from the data that populates it is one of the best ways to simplify this process.

The primary value of templates for network engineers is achieving configuration consistency. Appropriately implemented, templates can reduce the likelihood of human errors caused when changing network configurations. There seems to be a lot of fear that making complex changes in an automated way in production is a bad idea, but if you follow good discipline and properly test your templates, you really can improve network operations. Templates don't automatically remove human error, but when used properly, they can greatly reduce it, resulting in fewer outages.

Using templates to aid the rollout of new network devices is a simple yet powerful way to demonstrate the value of templates, since it has the added benefit of saving a lot of time for the network engineer. However, don't think that this is the only place where templates can be used. In many network automation projects, templates are not even used by humans but by automation software like Ansible to push configuration changes to network devices—live, in production.

The following sections cover some of the most popular options for building template-based configurations and documents that exist for network automation.

Jinja

We mentioned Jinja in the introduction to this chapter, but it's time to dive in a little deeper. While we'll briefly explore a few other options in this chapter, you'll notice that we spend a lot more pages on Jinja. Currently, Jinja is still by far the most popular template language in the world of network automation because of broad support by many automation tools and languages, including Python.

Let's start with a basic example and write a template to configure a single switch interface. Here's an example switchport configuration that you want to convert to a template (so you can configure the hundreds of other switchports in your environment):

```
interface GigabitEthernet0/1
 description Server Port
 switchport access vlan 10
 switchport mode access
```

This kind of snippet is easy to write a template for—you need only decide which parts of this configuration need to stay the same and which need to be dynamic. Example 9-2 has removed the specific interface name and converted it into a variable that you'll populate when you render the template into an actual configuration.

Example 9-2. Parameterized interface name in a switchport config template

```
interface {{ interface_name }}
 description Server Port
 switchport access vlan 10
 switchport mode access
```

You can pass in the variable `interface_name` when rendering this template, and that spot will get filled in with the value associated with `interface_name`.

However, this template assumes that each network interface has an identical configuration. What if you want a different VLAN or a different interface description on some of the interfaces? In that case, you should also convert some of the other parts of the configuration into their own variables, as shown in Example 9-3.

Example 9-3. Several variables in the switchport config template

```
interface {{ interface_name }}
 description {{ interface_description }}
 switchport access vlan {{ interface_vlan }}
 switchport mode access
```

These are simple examples, but they're not very namespace-friendly.

It's common to leverage concepts like classes and dictionaries in a language like Python when rendering a template. This allows us to store multiple instances of data that we can loop over and write multiple times in our resulting configuration. We'll look at loops in a future section, but for now, Example 9-4 shows that same template rewritten to take advantage of something like a Python class or dictionary.

Example 9-4. Using a dictionary in a switchport config template

```
interface {{ interface.name }}
 description {{ interface.description }}
 switchport access vlan {{ interface.vlan }}
 switchport mode access
```

This is a minor change, but an important one. The `interface` object is passed to the template as a whole. If `interface` is a Python class, then `name`, `description`, and `vlan` are all properties of that class. The same is true if `interface` is a dictionary—the only difference is that they are all keys of this dictionary, and not properties, so the rendering engine would automatically place the corresponding values for those keys when rendering this template.

Rendering a Jinja Template File in Python

In the previous example, you created a basic Jinja template for a switchport configuration, but you didn't explore how that template is rendered or what drives data into the template to result in the final product. We'll explore that now by using Python and the Jinja2 library.

While the templating language itself is known as *Jinja*, the Python library for working with Jinja is called *Jinja2*.

Let's use the same template snippet from Example 9-4 and use Python to populate those fields with real data. We'll use the Python interpreter this time so you can walk through the example on your own machine.

The Jinja2 rendering engine in Python is not part of the standard library, so it is not installed by default. However, Jinja2 can be installed with `pip3`, through the command `pip3 install jinja2`, the same as any other Python package found on PyPI, as we covered in Chapter 6.

Once the Jinja2 library is installed, you should first import the required objects that you'll need in order to render your templates:

```
>>> from jinja2 import Environment, FileSystemLoader
```

Next, you need to set up the environment, so the renderer knows where to find the template:

```
>>> ENV = Environment(loader=FileSystemLoader('.'))
>>> template = ENV.get_template("template.jinja")
```

The first line sets up the Environment object, specifying a single dot (.) to indicate that the templates exist in the same directory in which you started the Python interpreter. The second line derives a template object from that environment by statically specifying the template name, *template.jinja*. The contents of this file are identical to Example 9-4.

Now that this is done, you need your data, which you'll specify using a dictionary. The keys for this dictionary correspond to the field names referenced in your template:

```
>>> interface_dict = {
...     "name": "GigabitEthernet0/1",
...     "description": "Server Port",
...     "vlan": 10,
...     "uplink": False
... }
```

 You probably won't have to manually create data structures in Python to populate a template with data. This is being done for illustrative purposes in this book. Typically, you'll want to pull data from an API or a file on disk, rather than declaring it statically in your program or script.

You now have everything you need to render your template. You'll call the render() function of your template object to pass data into the template engine, and use the print() function to output your rendered output to the screen:

```
>>> print(template.render(interface=interface_dict))
interface GigabitEthernet0/1
 description Server Port
 switchport access vlan 10
 switchport mode access
```

Note that you pass an argument to the render() function of your template object. Pay close attention to the name—the keyword argument interface corresponds to the references to interface within your Jinja template. This is how you get your interface dictionary into the template engine—when the template engine sees references to interface or its keys, it will use the dictionary passed here to satisfy that reference.

As you can see, the rendered output is as you expect. However, you don't have to use a Python dictionary. It's common to drive data from other Python libraries into a Jinja template, and this may take the form of a Python class.

Example 9-5 shows a Python program that's similar to the code you just went through, but instead of using a dictionary, you use a Python class.

Example 9-5. Using a Python class to populate a Jinja template

```python
from jinja2 import Environment, FileSystemLoader
ENV = Environment(loader=FileSystemLoader('.'))
template = ENV.get_template("template.jinja")

class NetworkInterface(object):
    def __init__(self, name, description, vlan, uplink=False):
        self.name = name
        self.description = description
        self.vlan = vlan
        self.uplink = uplink

interface_obj = NetworkInterface("GigabitEthernet0/1", "Server Port", 10)
print(template.render(interface=interface_obj))
```

The output from this program is identical to the previous output. Therefore, there really isn't one right way to populate a Jinja template with data—it depends on where that data comes from. Fortunately, the Python Jinja2 library allows for some flexibility here.

Using Conditionals and Loops

It's time to really make your templates work for you. The previous examples are useful for understanding how to insert dynamic data into a text file, but that's just part of the battle of scaling network templates up to properly automate network configuration.

 Jinja allows you to embed Python-esque logic into your template files in order to do things like make decisions or condense duplicate data into one chunk that is *unpacked* at render time via a for loop. While these tools are powerful, they can also be a slippery slope. Don't get too carried away with putting all kinds of advanced logic into your templates. Jinja has some really useful features, but it was never meant to be a full-blown programming language, so it's best to keep a healthy balance. Read the Jinja FAQ (*https://oreil.ly/ kKA8O*), specifically the section titled "Isn't It a Bad Idea to Put Logic in Templates?" for some tips.

Using conditional logic to create a switchport configuration

Let's continue our example of configuring a single switchport—but in this case, you want to decide what to render by using a conditional in the template file itself.

Often some switchport interfaces will be VLAN trunks, and others will be in *mode access*. A good example is an access layer switch, where two or more interfaces are the uplink ports that need to be configured to permit all VLANs. Our previous examples showed an `uplink` boolean property, set to `True` if the interface is an uplink and `False` if it is just an access port. You can check against this value in your template by using a conditional:

```
interface {{ interface.name }}
 description {{ interface.description }}
{% if interface.uplink %}
 switchport mode trunk
{% else %}
 switchport access vlan {{ interface.vlan }}
 switchport mode access
{% endif %}
```

If you run some of the examples in this section, you may notice extra whitespace, especially extra newlines between lines of rendered text. This is due to the way Jinja removes the template syntax when rendering the final text. You can use opt-in methods to manage this whitespace, such as placing a hyphen immediately following or preceding the substitution syntax (e.g., `{% for item in seq -%}`). This gives you the option to trim extra whitespace either before or after a given bit of Jinja logic. We've omitted these options to keep the examples simpler, but in practice you can and probably should use them to keep your rendered text cleaner, especially when rendering to formats where whitespace has a significant impact on the data being represented.

In short, if the `uplink` property of `interface` is `True`, you want to make this interface a VLAN trunk. Otherwise, let's make sure that it's set up with the appropriate access mode.

In the previous example, you also see a new syntax: the `{% ... %}` braces are a special Jinja tag that indicates some kind of logic. This template is built to configure `GigabitEthernet0/1` as a VLAN trunk, and any other interface will be placed in access mode, in VLAN 10.

Using a loop to create many switchport configurations

You've configured only a single interface at this point, so let's see if you can use Jinja loops to create configurations for many switchports. For this, you use a for loop that's extremely similar to the syntax you would normally have in Python:

```
{% for n in range(10) %}
interface GigabitEthernet0/{{ n+1 }}
 description {{ interface.description }}
 switchport access vlan {{ interface.vlan }}
 switchport mode access
{% endfor %}
```

Note that you're again using the {% ... %} syntax to contain all logic statements. In this template, you're calling the range() function to give a list of integers to iterate over, and for each iteration, you print the result of n+1 because range() starts at 0, and normally, switchports start at 1.

Using a loop and conditionals to create switchport configurations

This creates an identical configuration for 10 switchports—but what if you want a different configuration for some of them? Take the example about Jinja conditionals—perhaps the first port is a VLAN trunk. You can combine what you've learned about conditionals and loops to accomplish this:

```
{% for n in range(10) %}

interface GigabitEthernet0/{{ n+1 }}
 description {{ interface.description }}
{% if n+1 == 1 %}
 switchport mode trunk
{% else %}
 switchport access vlan {{ interface.vlan }}
 switchport mode access
{% endif %}

{% endfor %}
```

This results in GigabitEthernet0/1 being configured as a VLAN trunk, but Gigabit Ethernet0/2-10 is in access mode. Here is an example using simulated data for the interface descriptions:

```
interface GigabitEthernet0/1
 description TRUNK INTERFACE
 switchport mode trunk
interface GigabitEthernet0/2
 description ACCESS INTERFACE
 switchport mode access
interface GigabitEthernet0/3
 description ACCESS INTERFACE
 switchport mode access
 ...
```

Iterating over a dictionary to generate configurations

You were able to access keys in a dictionary in your Jinja template in the preceding section, but what if you want to iterate over dictionaries and lists by using a for loop? Let's imagine that you're passing the following list to your template as inter face_list. Here's the relevant Python:

```
intlist = [
    "GigabitEthernet0/1",
    "GigabitEthernet0/2",
    "GigabitEthernet0/3"
]
print(template.render(interface_list=intlist))
```

You then reference interface_list in your loop so that you can access its members and generate a switchport configuration for each one. Note that the nested conditional has also been modified, since your counter variable n no longer exists:

```
{% for iface in interface_list %}

interface {{ iface }}
{% if iface == "GigabitEthernet0/1" %}
 switchport mode trunk
{% else %}
 switchport access vlan 10
 switchport mode access
{% endif %}

{% endfor %}
```

You now simply refer to iface to retrieve the current item of that list for every iteration of the loop.

You can also do the same thing with dictionaries. Again, here's a relevant Python snippet for constructing and passing in a dictionary to this Jinja template. Let's keep it simple this time, and just pass a set of interface names as keys, with the corresponding port descriptions as values:

```
intdict = {
    "GigabitEthernet0/1": "Server port number one",
    "GigabitEthernet0/2": "Server port number two",
    "GigabitEthernet0/3": "Server port number three"
}
print(template.render(interface_dict=intdict))
```

You can modify your loop to iterate over this dictionary in much the same way you'd do in native Python:

```
{% for name, desc in interface_dict.items() %}
interface {{ name }}
  description {{ desc }}
{% endfor %}
```

The `for name, desc...` means that at each iteration of the loop, `name` will be a key in your dictionary, and `desc` will be the corresponding value for that key. Don't forget to add the `.items()` notation as shown here, to properly unpack these values.

This allows you to simply refer to `name` and `desc` in the body of the template, and the result is shown here:

```
interface GigabitEthernet0/1
  description Server port number one

interface GigabitEthernet0/2
  description Server port number two

interface GigabitEthernet0/3
  description Server port number three
```

 In previous versions of Python, the order in which these interfaces appear would not be guaranteed, as dictionaries were by nature an unordered data structure. However, as of Python 3.7, dictionaries preserve insertion order for literals like these.

Generating interface configurations from a list of dictionaries

In this section, you're going to combine using lists and dictionaries to really put this template to work for you. Each interface will have its own dictionary, and the keys will be attributes of each network interface, like `name`, `description`, or `uplink`. Each dictionary will be stored inside a list, which is what your template will iterate over to produce configuration.

First, here's the data structure in Python that we just described:

```python
interfaces = [
    {
        "name": "GigabitEthernet0/1",
        "desc": "uplink port",
        "uplink": True
    },
    {
        "name": "GigabitEthernet0/2",
        "desc": "Server port number one",
        "vlan": 10
    },
    {
        "name": "GigabitEthernet0/3",
        "desc": "Server port number two",
        "vlan": 10
    }
]
print(template.render(interface_list=interfaces))
```

This allows you to write a powerful template that iterates over this list, and for each list item, simply refers to keys found within that particular dictionary. Example 9-6 makes use of all the techniques you've learned about loops and conditionals.

Example 9-6. Iterating over a list of dictionaries in Jinja

```
{% for interface in interface_list %}
interface {{ interface.name }}
  description {{ interface.desc }}
  {% if interface.uplink %}
    switchport mode trunk
  {% else %}
    switchport access vlan {{ interface.vlan }}
    switchport mode access
  {% endif %}
{% endfor %}
```

 When using Jinja to access data in a dictionary, you can use the traditional Python syntax `dict['key']` or the shorthand form `dict.key` (as we've been showing). These two are identical. If you're trying to access a key that doesn't exist, a key error will be raised. However, you can also use the `get()` method in Jinja if it's an optional key or if you want to return another value if the key doesn't exist—for example, `dict.get(key, 'UNKNOWN')`.

As mentioned previously, it's bad form to embed data into your Python applications (see the `interfaces` list of dictionaries from the previous example). Instead, let's place that data into its own YAML file and rewrite our application to import this data before using it to render the template. This is a good practice, because it allows someone with no Python experience to edit the network configuration by simply changing this simple YAML file.

Example 9-7 shows a YAML file that is written to be identical to your `interfaces` list in Example 9-6.

Example 9-7. YAML file for switchport configurations

```
---
- name: GigabitEthernet0/1
  desc: uplink port
  uplink: true
- name: GigabitEthernet0/2
  desc: Server port number one
  vlan: 10
- name: GigabitEthernet0/3
  desc: Server port number two
  vlan: 10
```

As we explored in Chapter 8, importing a YAML file in Python is easy. As a refresher, here's our full Python application, but instead of the static, embedded list of dictionaries, you're simply importing a YAML file to get that data:

```python
from jinja2 import Environment, FileSystemLoader
import yaml

ENV = Environment(loader=FileSystemLoader('.'))

template = ENV.get_template("template.jinja")

with open("data.yml") as f:
    interfaces = yaml.safe_load(f)
    print(template.render(interface_list=interfaces))
```

You can reuse the same template from Example 9-6 and achieve the same result—but this time, the data that you're using to populate your template comes from an external YAML file, which is a bit easier to maintain. The Python file now contains only the logic of pulling in data and rendering a template. This makes for a more maintainable template-rendering system.

This covers the basics of loops and conditionals. In this section, we've explored only a portion of what's possible. Explore these concepts on your own and apply them to your own use cases.

Using Jinja Filters

The data structures (like lists and dictionaries) and basic logical constructs (like loops and conditionals) presented so far are useful, but sometimes something a little more advanced is warranted. What if you want to convert a given bit of input to uppercase before it's rendered out to the template? Or perhaps you want to reverse the characters in a string? Tasks like these can be prohibitively difficult or even impossible with what we've covered in this chapter up to this point.

Jinja filters provide an extremely powerful answer to these and many more problems. You can think of them like little modular functions you can call upon at any point in your templates. They generally work by taking in data or text as input (such as a variable you are passing in to the template environment), performing some kind of specialized task on that data, and then outputting the result.

The syntax for using filters in a Jinja template is simple. In the same way that you can pipe output from a command into another command in a terminal shell on a Linux distribution, you can take the result of a Jinja statement and pipe it into a filter. The resulting text will make it into the rendered output of your template.

Example 9-8 uses the familiar double-brace syntax to specify that you want to use a variable named hostname. However, before the contents of hostname are rendered into the final output for this template, they are first *piped* (using |) into the filter called myfilter. The output from that filter is then used to populate that portion of the template.

Example 9-8. Basic filter syntax in Jinja

```
{{ hostname|myfilter }}
```

This is a bit contrived, so let's move on to practical examples of Jinja filters in action.

Using the upper Jinja filter

Let's take the preceding template and use a built-in filter called upper to capitalize the descriptions for each interface configuration:

```
{% for interface in interface_list %}
interface {{ interface.name }}
  description {{ interface.desc|upper }}
  {% if interface.uplink %}
    switchport mode trunk
  {% else %}
    switchport access vlan {{ interface.vlan }}
    switchport mode access
  {% endif %}
{% endfor %}
```

This filter, built into the Jinja2 library for Python, capitalizes the text piped to it.

Chaining Jinja filters

You can also chain filters, in much the same way that you might pipe commands together in Linux. Let's use the reverse filter to take your capitalized text and print it backward:

```
{% for interface in interface_list %}
interface {{ interface.name }}
  description {{ interface.desc|upper|reverse }}
  {% if interface.uplink %}
    switchport mode trunk
  {% else %}
    switchport access vlan {{ interface.vlan }}
    switchport mode access
  {% endif %}
{% endfor %}
```

This results in the following output:

```
interface GigabitEthernet0/1
  description TROP KNILPU
  switchport mode trunk

interface GigabitEthernet0/2
  description ENO REBMUN TROP REVRES
  switchport access vlan 10
```

```
  switchport mode access

interface GigabitEthernet0/3
  description OWT REBMUN TROP REVRES
  switchport access vlan 10
  switchport mode access
```

To recap, our original description for GigabitEthernet0/1 was first uplink port, and then it was UPLINK PORT because of the upper filter, and then the reverse filter changed it to TROP KNILPU, before the final result was printed into the template instance.

Creating custom Jinja filters

This is all great, and tons of other great built-in filters are documented within the Jinja specification. But what if you want to create your own filter? Perhaps there's something specific to network automation that you would like to perform in your own custom filter that doesn't come with the Jinja2 library?

Fortunately, the library allows for this. Example 9-9 shows a full Python script defining a new function, get_interface_speed(). This function is simple—it looks for certain keywords like gigabit or fast in a provided string argument and returns the current Mbps value. It also loads all your template data from a YAML file, as shown in previous examples.

Example 9-9. Full Python script with custom Jinja filter

```
from jinja2 import Environment, FileSystemLoader      ❶
import yaml                                             ❶

ENV = Environment(loader=FileSystemLoader('.'))        ❷


def get_interface_speed(interface_name):
    """ get_interface_speed returns the default Mbps value for a given
        network interface by looking for certain keywords in the name
    """

    if 'gigabit' in interface_name.lower():
        return 1000
    if 'fast' in interface_name.lower():
        return 100

ENV.filters['get_interface_speed'] = get_interface_speed  ❸
template = ENV.get_template("template.jinja")

with open("data.yml") as f:                              ❹
    interfaces = yaml.safe_load(f)
    print(template.render(interface_list=interfaces))
```

❶ Imports the Jinja2 and PyYAML libraries.

❷ Declares the template environment.

❸ Filters are added to the ENV object after declaration. We're actually passing in the `get_interface_speed` function and not running it—the template engine will execute this function when we call `template.render()`.

❹ We load the YAML file and pass it in to the template when rendering it.

With a slight modification to our template, as shown in Example 9-10, we can leverage this filter by passing `interface.name` into the `get_interface_speed` filter. The resulting output will be whatever integer the function decides to return. Since all interface names are Gigabit Ethernet, the speed is set to `1000`.

Example 9-10. Updated Jinja template leveraging the custom filter

```
{% for interface in interface_list %}
interface {{ interface.name }}
  description {{ interface.desc|upper|reverse }}
  {% if interface.uplink %}
  switchport mode trunk
  {% else %}
  switchport access vlan {{ interface.vlan }}
  switchport mode access
  {% endif %}
  speed {{ interface.name|get_interface_speed }}
{% endfor %}
```

 You don't always have to create your own function to pass in as a Jinja filter. Plenty of libraries provide helpful functions that you can import and simply pass right into the Jinja2 environment.

Template Inheritance in Jinja

As you create bigger, more capable templates for your network configuration, you may want to be able to break templates into smaller, more specialized pieces. It's common to have a template for VLAN configuration, one for interfaces, and maybe another for a routing protocol. This kind of organizational tool, while optional, can allow for much more flexibility. The question is, how do you link these templates together in a meaningful way to form a full configuration?

Jinja allows you to perform inheritance in a template file, which is a handy solution to this problem. For instance, you may have a *vlans.jinja* file that contains only the

VLAN configuration, and you can inherit this file to produce a VLAN configuration in another template file. You might be writing a template for interface configuration, and you want to also produce a VLAN configuration from another template. Example 9-11 shows how this is done by using the `include` statement.

Example 9-11. Using `include` for Jinja template inheritance

```
{% include 'vlans.jinja' %}

{% for name, desc in interface_dict.items() %}
interface {{ name }}
  description {{ desc }}
{% endfor %}
```

This renders *vlans.jinja* and inserts the resulting text into the rendered output for the template that includes it. Using the `include` statement, template writers can compose switch configurations made up of modular parts. This is great for keeping multiple template files organized.

Another inheritance tool in Jinja is the `block` statement. This is a powerful but more complicated method of performing inheritance, as it mimics object inheritance in more formal languages like Python. Using blocks, you can specify portions of your template that may be overridden by a child template, if present. If a child template is not present, this portion of the rendered output will still contain some default text.

Example 9-12 shows how blocks are declared within a parent template.

Example 9-12. Jinja block definition

```
{% for interface in interface_list %}
interface {{ interface.name }}
  description {{ interface.desc }}
{% endfor %}
!
{% block http %}
  no ip http server
  no ip http secure-server
{% endblock %}
```

Call this template *no-http.jinja*, indicating that you'd like to normally turn off the embedded HTTP server in your switch. However, you can use blocks to provide greater flexibility here. You can create a child template called *yes-http.jinja* that is designed to override this block and output the configuration that enables the HTTP server if that's what you want; see Example 9-13.

Example 9-13. Jinja block reference

```
{% extends "no-http.jinja" %}
{% block http %}
  ip http server
  ip http secure-server
{% endblock %}
```

This allows you to enable the HTTP server simply by rendering the child template. The first line in Example 9-13 extends the parent template *no-http.jinja* so all of the interface configurations will still be present in the rendered output. However, because you've rendered the child template, the `http` block of the child overrides that of the parent. Using blocks in this way is useful for portions of the configuration that may need to change but aren't properly served by traditional variable substitution.

The Jinja documentation on template inheritance (*https://oreil.ly/RqRua*) goes into much more detail and is a great resource to keep bookmarked.

Variable Creation in Jinja

Jinja allows you to create variables within a template by using the `set` statement. A common use case is variable shortening. Sometimes you have to go through several nested dictionaries or Python objects to get what you want, and you may want to reuse this value several times in your template. Rather than repeat a long string of properties or keys, use the `set` statement to represent a particular value with a much smaller name:

```
{% set int_desc = sw01.config.interfaces['ge0/1']['description'] %}
{{ int_desc }}
```

While Jinja is clearly the dominant templating tool in network automation, it isn't the only one. At times another tool is more appropriate, and we cover a few of them in the following sections.

Extensible Stylesheet Language Transformations

As discussed in Chapter 8, XML is an extremely popular data format that's typically well supported by major NOSs for automation purposes and more. XML enjoys a rich ecosystem of tools surrounding it.

One of these is a fairly robust templating format called *Extensible Stylesheet Language Transformations* (*XSLT*). XSLT is typically used for applying transformations to XML data, such as to convert that data into XHTML or other XML documents. However, like Jinja, it can be used to create templates for any arbitrary document format, and given its affinity to the XML ecosystem, is an important option to have in your repertoire if you're going to be working with XML frequently.

As with XML itself, the XSLT specification is defined by W3C (*https://oreil.ly/vnjJl*).

Let's look at a practical example of populating an XSLT template with meaningful data in Python so that a resulting document can be achieved. The first thing you need is raw data to populate your template. This XML document will suffice:

```
<?xml version="1.0" encoding="UTF-8"?>
<authors>
    <author>
        <firstName>Christian</firstName>
        <lastName>Adell</lastName>
    </author>
    <author>
        <firstName>Scott</firstName>
        <lastName>Lowe</lastName>
    </author>
    <author>
        <firstName>Matt</firstName>
        <lastName>Oswalt</lastName>
    </author>
</authors>
```

This amounts to a list of authors, each with `<firstName>` and `<lastName>` elements. The goal is to use this data to generate an HTML table that displays these authors, via an XSLT document. An XSLT template to perform this task might look like Example 9-14.

Example 9-14. XSLT template

```
<xsl:stylesheet xmlns:xsl="http://www.w3.org/1999/XSL/Transform" version="1.0">
<xsl:output indent="yes"/>
<xsl:template match="/">
  <html>
  <body>
  <h2>Authors</h2>
    <table border="1">
      <tr bgcolor="#9acd32">
        <th style="text-align:left">First Name</th>
        <th style="text-align:left">Last Name</th>
      </tr>
      <xsl:for-each select="authors/author">
      <tr>
        <td><xsl:value-of select="firstName"/></td>
        <td><xsl:value-of select="lastName"/></td>
      </tr>
      </xsl:for-each>
    </table>
  </body>
```

```
    </html>
  </xsl:template>
</xsl:stylesheet>
```

A few notes on this:

- A basic for-each construct is embedded in what otherwise looks like valid HTML. This is a standard practice in template language—the static text remains static, and little bits of logic are placed where needed.

- The for-each statement uses a *coordinate argument* (listed as authors/author) to state exactly which part of your XML document contains the data you wish to use. This is called *XPath*, a syntax used within XML documents and tools to specify a location within an XML tree.

- You use the value-of statement to dynamically insert a value (like a variable in a Python program) as text from your XML data.

Assuming your XSLT template is saved as *template.xslt* and your data file as *data.xml*, you can return to your trusty Python interpreter to combine these two pieces and come up with the resulting HTML output:

```
from lxml import etree
xslRoot = etree.fromstring(bytes(open("template.xslt").read(), encoding='utf8'))
transform = etree.XSLT(xslRoot)

xmlRoot = etree.fromstring(bytes(open("data.xml").read(), encoding='utf8'))
transRoot = transform(xmlRoot)
```

This produces a valid HTML table, as shown in Figure 9-2.

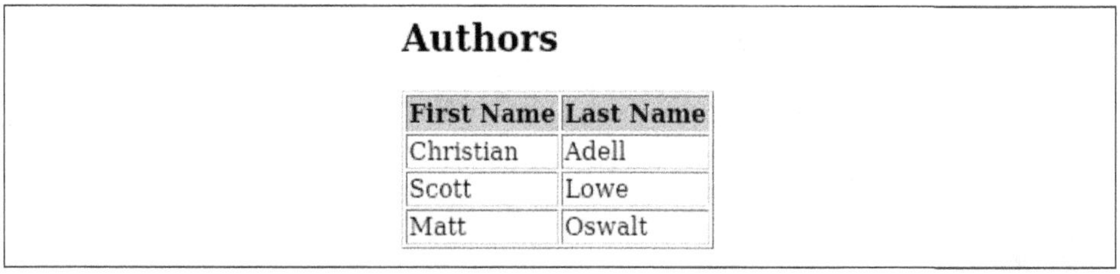

Authors

First Name	Last Name
Christian	Adell
Scott	Lowe
Matt	Oswalt

Figure 9-2. HTML table produced by XSLT

XSLT also provides additional logic statements:

\<if\>
   Output the given element(s) only if a certain condition is met.

\<sort\>
   Sort elements before writing them as output.

```
<choose>
```
A more advanced version of the if statement (allows else if or else style of logic).

You can take this example even further and use this concept to create a network configuration template using configuration data defined in XML; see Example 9-15.

Example 9-15. XML interface data

```
<?xml version="1.0" encoding="UTF-8"?>
<interfaces>
    <interface>
        <name>GigabitEthernet0/0</name>
        <ipv4addr>192.168.0.1 255.255.255.0</ipv4addr>
    </interface>
    <interface>
        <name>GigabitEthernet0/1</name>
        <ipv4addr>172.16.31.1 255.255.255.0</ipv4addr>
    </interface>
    <interface>
        <name>GigabitEthernet0/2</name>
        <ipv4addr>10.3.2.1 255.255.254.0</ipv4addr>
    </interface>
</interfaces>
```

Then, you can create an XSLT template to take this data and render it out into a new document that contains your valid network configuration, as shown in Example 9-16.

Example 9-16. XSLT template for router config

```
<xsl:stylesheet version="1.0" xmlns:xsl="http://www.w3.org/1999/XSL/Transform">
    <xsl:template match="/">
        <xsl:for-each select="interfaces/interface">
interface <xsl:value-of select="name"/>
    ip address <xsl:value-of select="ipv4addr"/>
        </xsl:for-each>
    </xsl:template>
</xsl:stylesheet>
```

With these XML and XSLT documents, you can get a rudimentary router configuration in the same way you generated an HTML page:

```
interface GigabitEthernet0/0
    ip address 192.168.0.1 255.255.255.0
interface GigabitEthernet0/1
    ip address 172.16.31.1 255.255.255.0
interface GigabitEthernet0/2
    ip address 10.3.2.1 255.255.254.0
```

As you can see, it's possible to produce a network configuration by using XSLT. However, it is admittedly a bit cumbersome. You will likely find Jinja a much more useful templating language for creating network configurations, as it has a lot of features that are conducive to network automation.

Go Templates

The Go programming language has a package for working with templates (*https:// oreil.ly/w1RS0*) in the standard library, importable as `text/template`. This package implements a template language that is tightly integrated with the Go programming language. So, if you're working with Go, this package is a strong choice for building and rendering templates.

While the template language implemented by this package is specific to Go, and therefore includes some familiar Go-esque keywords and syntax, it does share some familiar concepts with other template languages like Jinja. For instance, the actual text replacement syntax in Go templates also uses double braces: {{ }}.

To get started, you'll create a simple template using a string literal defined in your Go program, and print the results to the terminal; see Example 9-17.

Example 9-17. Simple Go template

```
package main

import (
  "os"
  "text/template"
)

func main() {
  // We can create an inline template using the Parse() method of the
  // template.Template type
  //
  // Note that simpleTemplate is just an arbitrary name chosen for this example.
  tmpl, err := template.New("simpleTemplate").Parse(`{{ "foobar" | print }}`)
  if err != nil {
    panic(err)
  }

  // We can render the template with Execute, passing in os.Stdout
  // as the first parameter, so we can see the results in our terminal
  err = tmpl.Execute(os.Stdout, nil)
  if err != nil {
    panic(err)
  }
}
```

Example 9-17 shows a full working Go template that can be run with go run, but the following examples are simplified to show only the most relevant code. Full working versions of the following examples can be found at *https://github.com/oreilly-npa-book/exam ples/tree/v2/ch09-templates*.

You're not even doing any variable substitution here. Go templates allow you to define string literals within the template itself, thus the escaped double quotes. So, this example simply results in the text foobar.

Also note that you don't have to send the results to stdout. Anything that satisfies io.Writer can be used as the first parameter to Execute(), including a file opened via os.Create(), as shown in Example 9-18.

Example 9-18. Rendering a template to a file

```
tmpl, err := template.New("simpleTemplate").Parse(`{{ "foobar" | print }}`) ❶
if err != nil {
  panic(err)
}

file, err := os.Create("./output.txt")                                        ❷
if err != nil {
  panic(err)
}

err = tmpl.Execute(file, nil)                                                 ❸
if err != nil {
  panic(err)
}
```

❶ Creates an inline template by using the Parse() method of the template .Template type.

❷ Creates the file to contain the output.

❸ Anything that satisfies io.Writer can be passed as the first parameter to Execute(), which includes the file returned by os.Create.

To keep the remaining examples simple, you'll continue to write to stdout.

Now, on to some more practical examples. As with Jinja, the chief use case for Go templates in network automation is to inject some kind of structured data into a predefined output format. This allows you to define the text that should more or less remain consistent within the template, and pass data retrieved from a user parameter or API call to "fill in" the parts of the template that require it.

For instance, you may have a `Switch` struct with the fields `Hostname` and `Interface Count` that you wish to use to pass data into your template; see Example 9-19.

Example 9-19. Passing data into a template via a struct

```
type Switch struct {                    ❶
  Hostname        string
  InterfaceCount uint
}

sw01 := Switch{"sw01", 48}              ❷

tmpl, err := template.New(
    "switchTemplate").Parse("Device {{.Hostname}} has {{.InterfaceCount}} interfaces\n"
)                                       ❸
if err != nil {
  panic(err)
}

err = tmpl.Execute(os.Stdout, sw01)  ❹
if err != nil {
  panic(err)
}
```

❶ First, we must define the struct that represents a switch.

❷ Then we instantiate this struct into a variable `sw01`.

❸ We can refer to the fields of the struct by using the `.field name` syntax.

❹ Our input struct is passed in as the second parameter to `Execute()`.

You may have noticed you were able to refer to the `Hostname` field of your struct via a leading dot (`.`). In the package documentation, this is literally referred to as *dot* and is a reference to whatever type is passed in to your template context. In this case, dot is a simple struct with fields you could refer to by name, but this doesn't have to always be the case, as you'll see in the next few examples.

This prints the following:

```
Device sw01 has 48 interfaces
```

Instead of a single struct, you can pass in a slice of multiple `Switch` elements and iterate over them using the `range` keyword:

```
type Switch struct {
  Hostname        string
  InterfaceCount uint
}
```

```
// switches is a slice that represents all our Switch instances
switches := []Switch{
    {"sw01", 48},
    {"sw02", 24},
    {"sw03", 48},
}

// As with Jinja, it's often better to define templates in a multiline string
// like tmplStr below, or in a separate file that is read in before rendering.
tmplStr := `
{{range $i, $switch := .}}
Device {{$switch.Hostname}} has {{$switch.InterfaceCount}} interfaces
{{end}}
`
```

In this case, dot represents your slice, and iterating over this slice in the template is done via `range $i, $switch := `. This is similar to iterating over a slice natively in Go, as the slice is to the right of the short variable declaration operator `:=`, and `i` and `switch` represent the index value of each element and a copy of the element itself, respectively.

Go templates support conditionals as well. You can optionally print a line based on the value of the `Enabled` boolean field:

```
type Switch struct {
    Hostname       string
    InterfaceCount uint
    Enabled        bool
}

// switches is a slice that represents all our Switch instances
switches := []Switch{
    {"sw01", 48, true},
    {"sw02", 24, true},
    {"sw03", 48, false},
}

tmplStr := `
{{range $i, $switch := .}}
{{if $switch.Enabled}}
Device {{$switch.Hostname}} has {{$switch.InterfaceCount}} interfaces
{{end}}
{{end}}
`
```

Your struct thus far has been fairly simple, and you might wonder if you can simplify it to a `map` and iterate over that. You can!

```
switches := map[string]int{
    "sw01": 48,
    "sw02": 24,
    "sw03": 48,
}
```

```
// Since we're now iterating over a map, the two created variables after the
// range keyword represent each key/value pair
tmplStr := `
{{range $hostname, $ifCount := .}}
Device {{$hostname}} has {{$ifCount}} interfaces
{{end}}
`
```

When discussing Jinja, we explored the use of filters to further manipulate data within the template and even defined our own custom filter. You can do the same in Go templates, albeit with a slightly different terminology. Go templates include a feature called *pipelines*, which can be a sequence of commands delimited by the pipe operator (|). Go has several built-in commands, but you'll see how to define your own. While the terms differ, the syntax is extremely similar to Jinja.

Let's go back to passing a `Switch` struct as the `data` parameter for your template, but instead of an integer field representing the number of interfaces, this struct can contain a slice of strings, so you can actually have the names of each interface. This will allow you to iterate over the interface names if you want to, but at the same time, you can also still print the total number of interfaces by passing that field through a pipeline, using the `len` command, as shown in Example 9-20.

Example 9-20. Go template pipelines

```
// A fairly small switch, indeed
sw01 := Switch{"sw01", []string{
  "ge-0/0/1",
  "ge-0/0/2",
  "ge-0/0/3",
  "ge-0/0/4",
}}

tmplStr := "Device {{.Hostname}} has {{ .Interfaces | len }} interfaces\n"
```

The built-in `len` command prints the length of the value passed to it, rather than the value itself. This results in the following:

```
Device sw01 has 4 interfaces
```

Other commands are available, such as `slice` for subslicing an argument, `and` and `or` for comparing two arguments for emptiness, and `call` for calling a function. However, you can create your own function and make it available to the template context on creation. For instance, you can create a function called `IfParse()` for parsing the speed and location details out of a string interface name:

```
type Interface struct {
  Speed int
  FPC   int
  PIC   int
  Port  int
```

```
        }

        func IfParse(ifaceStr string) Interface {

          iface := Interface{}

          ifSplit := strings.Split(ifaceStr, "-")

          speeds := map[string]int{
            "ge": 1,
            "xe": 10,
            "et": 40,
          }
          iface.Speed = speeds[ifSplit[0]]

          locSplit := strings.Split(ifSplit[1], "/")

          fpc, _ := strconv.Atoi(locSplit[0])
          iface.FPC = fpc

          pic, _ := strconv.Atoi(locSplit[1])
          iface.PIC = pic

          port, _ := strconv.Atoi(locSplit[2])
          iface.Port = port

          return iface
        }
```

To use this function, you must create a mapping between the function itself and a name you can refer to in your template. The `template` package has a function called `FuncMap()` you can use to create this. Then, you must remember to pass in this function map by using the `Funcs()` method of the template object, as shown in Example 9-21.

Example 9-21. Using custom functions in Go templates

```
fmap := template.FuncMap{"ifparse": IfParse}                    ❶

sw01 := Switch{"sw01", []string{
  "ge-0/0/1",
  "ge-0/0/2",
  "ge-0/0/3",
  "ge-0/0/4",
}}

tmplStr := `
{{range $i, $interface := .Interfaces}}
{{with $loc := $interface | ifparse}}
Interface {{$interface}}   port {{$loc.Port}}
{{end}}
{{end}}
`                                                              ❷
```

```
tmpl, err := template.New("switchTemplate").Funcs(fmap).Parse(tmplStr) ❸
if err != nil {
  panic(err)
}
```

❶ Creates a mapping of functions to names we can refer to in the template.

❷ In this template, we're first creating a new variable loc by pipelining $interface
   into the custom function ifparse. Since ifparse returns an Interface type, we
   can then refer to the fields of that struct directly!

❸ Don't forget to pass in the FuncMap by using the Funcs() method, as shown here.

This prints the following:

```
Interface ge-0/0/1    port 1
Interface ge-0/0/2    port 2
Interface ge-0/0/3    port 3
Interface ge-0/0/4    port 4
```

There is much more to explore with Go templates, but we've covered the basics.
Again, if you're working with Go and already familiar with the basic concepts we
previously discussed with Jinja, you could do worse than to skill up on Go templates.

Summary

You don't have to work directly with programming languages like Go and Python in
order to use templates, as we've done in this chapter. As we discuss in Chapter 12,
tools like Ansible and Nornir include native support for template languages like
Jinja2, allowing you to populate your templates with data available within those
platforms.

Here are a few parting thoughts on using templates for network automation:

- Keep the templates simple. Leveraging loops and conditionals to enhance your
  templates is fine, but don't go overboard. Jinja isn't as robust as a fully featured,
  general-purpose programming like Python, so keep the more advanced stuff out
  of the template.

- Leverage template inheritance to reuse portions of configurations that don't need
  to be duplicated.

- Remember, syntax and data should be handled separately. For instance, keep
  VLAN IDs in their own data file (maybe YAML) and the CLI syntax to implement those VLANs in a dedicated template.

- Templates are just text files, so you can and should use version control (i.e., Git)
  to track changes and collaborate with others. We discuss this in Chapter 11.

Working with Network APIs

From Python, Go, and data formats to configuration templating with Jinja, we've explored key foundational technologies and skills that will make you a better network engineer. In this chapter, you're going to put these skills to practical use and start to consume and communicate with various types of network device APIs to start automating your network.

As we introduced in Chapter 2, nowadays there are multiple options to interact with network platforms. Along with the traditional CLI and SNMP, we have new alternatives—from network-specific APIs (such as NETCONF, RESTCONF, and gNMI) to multipurpose APIs (such as HTTP-based ones or the Linux shell). Not every device supports all of these options, so understanding their capabilities will determine your automation options.

All interfaces are viable for automation, each one with its own pros and cons. The goal of this chapter is to introduce these APIs, showcasing how you can use them programmatically in Python and Go.

To best help you understand how to start interacting with networks programmatically, this chapter is organized into two sections:

Understanding network APIs
> We examine the architecture and foundation of APIs, including RESTful and non-RESTful HTTP-based APIs, NETCONF, RESTCONF, and gRPC/gNMI. In each case, we introduce common tools used for testing and show how to use each one.

Automating using network APIs
> We introduce some popular Python and Go libraries that allow you to start creating applications to interact with your network. We'll look at the Python Requests and Go HTTP libraries for consuming HTTP-based APIs (including

RESTCONF), the Python ncclient for interacting with NETCONF devices, the Go gNMIc for interacting with the gNMI interface, and the Python Netmiko library for automating devices over SSH.

As you read this chapter, keep in mind one thing: this chapter is *not* a comprehensive guide on any particular API and should not serve as API documentation. We provide examples using different vendor implementations of a given API, as it's common to be working in a multivendor environment. It's also important to see the common patterns and unique contrasts among APIs.

Understanding Network APIs

Our focus is on four of the most common types of APIs you'll find on network devices: HTTP-based APIs, NETCONF, RESTCONF, and gRPC/gNMI. We're going to start by looking at foundational concepts for each type of API; once we review them, we'll explore the consumption of these APIs with hands-on examples using multiple vendors.

 For each network API type, we have used one or two network platforms. This doesn't imply that each API is the only interface a platform supports. Actually, each platform usually supports multiple interfaces, but for illustrating multiple vendors and interfaces, we have used an arbitrary mapping to show diversity, without extra considerations.

As we start our journey of *consuming* and interacting with network APIs, in each API subsection, our focus is just like the focus we've had thus far throughout the book—on vendor-neutral tools and libraries. More specifically, we are going to look at tools such as cURL for working with HTTP-based APIs (RESTCONF included), NETCONF over SSH for working with NETCONF APIs, and gNMIc to interact with the gNMI interface.

It's important to note that this section is about *exploring* network APIs in that we showcase how to get started using and testing network APIs without writing any code. We want you to understand the concepts from each particular API type before putting them to use in the next section. This section is *not* about the tools and techniques you would use for automating production networks. Those types of tools and libraries are covered in "Using Network APIs for Automation" on page 451.

Let's get started by diving into HTTP-based APIs.

Getting Familiar with HTTP-Based APIs

HTTP-based APIs are not exclusively used for network management. They are one of the most common interprocess connection types; thus most of the concepts introduced in this section apply to general use cases. Within the context of network automation, you will learn how to use APIs to manage network services using HTTP APIs as the management interface. For instance, HTTP APIs are used in Chapter 12 to provision dynamic network infrastructure via Terraform providers. In the same chapter, HTTP APIs are used to fetch data from a source of truth (SoT) containing the network device inventory and to create a dynamic inventory for Nornir.

You should understand two types of HTTP-based APIs in the context of network APIs: RESTful HTTP-based APIs and non-RESTful HTTP-based APIs. To better understand them and what the term *RESTful* means, we are going to start by examining RESTful APIs. Once you understand RESTful architecture and principles, we'll move on and compare them with non-RESTful HTTP-based APIs.

Understanding RESTful APIs

RESTful APIs are becoming more popular and more commonly used in the networking industry, although they've been around since the early 2000s. Most of the APIs that exist today within network infrastructure are HTTP-based RESTful APIs. Therefore, when you hear about a RESTful API on a network device or SDN controller, it is an API that will be communicating between a client and a server.

The client is an application such as a Python script or web UI application, and the server is the network device or controller. Moreover, since HTTP is being used as transport, you'll perform some operations using URLs just as you do already as you browse the internet. Thus, if you understand that when you're browsing a website, HTTP GETs are performed, and when you're filling out a web form and clicking Submit, an HTTP POST is performed, you already understand the basics of working with RESTful APIs.

Let's look at examples of retrieving data from a website and retrieving data from a network device via a RESTful API. In both instances, an HTTP GET request is sent to the web server (see Figure 10-1).

In Figure 10-1, one of the primary differences is the data that is sent to and from the web server. When browsing the internet, you receive HTML data that your browser will interpret so that it can properly display the website. On the other hand, when issuing an HTTP GET request to a web server that is exposing a RESTful API (remember, it's exposing it via a URL), you receive data back that is mostly encoded using JSON or XML. This is where you'll use what we reviewed in Chapter 8. Since you receive data back in JSON/XML, the client application must understand how to interpret JSON and/or XML. Let's continue with the overview, so you have a more complete picture before we start to explore the use of RESTful HTTP APIs.

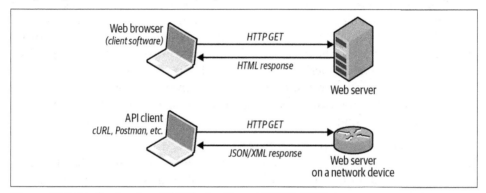

Figure 10-1. Understanding REST by looking at HTTP GET responses

Let's take our high-level overview one step further and look at the origins of RESTful APIs. The birth and structure of modern web-based RESTful APIs came from a PhD dissertation (*https://oreil.ly/1a9lz*) by Roy Fielding in 2000. In "Architectural Styles and the Design of Network-based Software Architectures," he defined the intricate detail of working with networked systems on the internet that use the architecture defined as REST.

An interface must conform to six architectural constraints in order to be considered RESTful. For the purposes of this chapter, we'll look at three:

Client-server
> This is a requirement to improve the usability of systems while simplifying the server requirements. Having a client-server architecture allows for the portability and changeability of client applications without the server components being changed. This means you could have different API clients (web UI, CLI) that consume the same server resources (backend API).

Stateless
> The communication between the client and server must be stateless. Clients that use stateless forms of communication must send all data required for the server to understand and perform the requested operation in a single request. This is in contrast to interfaces such as SSH, which have a persistent connection between a client and a server.

Uniform interface
> Individual resources in scope within an API call are identified in HTTP request messages. For example, in RESTful HTTP-based systems, the URL used references a particular resource. In the context of networking, the resource maps to a network device construct such as a hostname, interface, routing protocol

configuration, or any other *resource* that exists on the device. The uniform interface also states that the client should have enough information about a resource to create, modify, or delete a resource.

These are just three of the six core constraints of the REST architecture, but you likely can already see the similarity between RESTful systems and how you consume the internet through web browsing on a daily basis. Keep in mind that HTTP is the primary means of implementing RESTful APIs, although the transport type could, in theory, be something else. To really understand RESTful APIs, then, you must also understand the basics of HTTP.

Understanding HTTP request types. While every RESTful API you look at is an HTTP-based API, you will eventually look at HTTP-based APIs that do not adhere to the principles of REST and therefore are not RESTful. In either case, the APIs require an understanding of HTTP. Because these APIs are using HTTP as transport, you're going to be working with the same HTTP request types and response codes that are used on the internet already.

Common HTTP request types include GET, POST, PATCH, PUT, and DELETE. As you can imagine, GET requests are used to request data from the server, DELETE requests are used to delete a resource on the server, and the three Ps (POST, PATCH, PUT) are used to make a change on the server. In Table 10-1, we list each method's definition along with its meaning in the context of networking.

Table 10-1. HTTP request

Request type	Description	In networking context
GET	Retrieves a specified resource	Obtaining configuration or operational data
PUT	Creates or replaces a resource	Making a configuration change
PATCH	Creates or updates a resource object	Making a configuration change
POST	Creates a resource object	Making a configuration change
DELETE	Deletes a specified resource	Removing a particular configuration

Understanding HTTP response codes. Just as the request types are the same if you're using a web browser on the internet or using a RESTful API, the same is true for response codes.

Ever see a 401 Unauthorized message when you were trying to log in to a website and used invalid credentials? Well, you would receive the same response code if you were trying to log in to a system using a RESTful API and you sent the wrong credentials. The same is true for successful messages or if the server has an error of its own. Table 10-2 lists the common types of response codes you see when working with HTTP-based APIs. This list is not exclusive; others exist too.

Table 10-2. HTTP response codes

Response code	Description
1*XX*	Informational
2*XX*	Successful
3*XX*	Redirect
4*XX*	Client error
5*XX*	Server error

Remember, the response code types for HTTP-based APIs are no different from standard HTTP response codes. We are merely providing a list of the types and will leave it as an exercise for you to learn about individual responses.

Exploring HTTP-based APIs with cURL

cURL is a command-line tool for working with URLs. From the Linux command line, you can send HTTP requests by using the cURL program. While cURL uses URLs, it can communicate to servers using protocols besides HTTP, including FTP, SFTP, TFTP, Telnet, and many more. You can use the command man curl from the Linux command line to get an in-depth look at all the various options cURL supports.

 cURL isn't limited to Linux. It's available in multiple OSs such as macOS and Windows. For installation instructions, check *https://curl.se/docs/install.html*.

Multiple alternatives to cURL are available, either as command-line tools or GUIs, but all share the same concepts. Once you understand the basic ideas, you can apply them to the other tools. However, using a user-intuitive web GUI frontend, such as Postman (*https://www.postman.com*), could make it much easier to learn and test HTTP APIs. These GUI tools put the focus on using the API without worrying about writing code. You'll see an example shortly in Figure 10-2 to help you understand the look and feel.

We start our exploration of HTTP APIs by using cURL with the Cisco Meraki (*https://meraki.cisco.com*) RESTful API (Meraki's API documentation is available at *https://oreil.ly/zHOWy*). *Cisco Meraki* is a cloud networking controller that helps to illustrate how to interact with this type of network infrastructure. Many modern NOSs also offer REST APIs, usually (but not limited to) implementing the REST-CONF interfaces, covered in "Using RESTCONF" on page 425.

Using the HTTP GET method to retrieve information. As we're just getting started with RESTful APIs, we'll begin with a simple HTTP GET request to retrieve all *organizations* from the API, targeting the URL *https://api.meraki.com/api/v1/organizations*.

 Organization is an abstract concept from Cisco Meraki created to support multiple tenants for the same account. Each will contain different network resources.

In Example 10-1, we use a cURL statement to call the Cisco Meraki URL and retrieve a list of all the organizations.

 Full versions of the code examples in this chapter can be found in the book's GitHub repo at *https://github.com/oreilly-npa-book/exam ples/tree/v2/ch10-apis*.

Example 10-1. Retrieving Meraki organizations with cURL

```
$ curl 'https://api.meraki.com/api/v1/organizations' \        ❶ ❷
  -H 'X-Cisco-Meraki-API-Key: 6bec40cf957de430a6f1f2baa056b99a4fac9ea0' \  ❸
  -L                                                           ❹

# response omitted
```

❶ The URL is generic; it is shared by all Cisco Meraki customers. It's offered as IaaS, covered in Chapter 4.

❷ We have not defined any HTTP operation. Nevertheless, by default, cURL performs a GET operation. This behavior can be modified using the -X flag, as in next examples. You can see all the available cURL customizations via the command documentation: man cURL.

❸ The -H argument, or --header, is used to include HTTP headers in the HTTP request. HTTP headers are key-value pairs used to pass metadata to the server, useful for things like authentication.

❹ The -L flag, or --location, allows the client to follow any redirects issued by the server.

The Cisco Meraki API token used in Example 10-1 has been taken from Cisco Developer Hub (*https://oreil.ly/XVQfU*). You can use the same one if it is still active. If not, a new one will likely be available on this website, for API exploration.

Also, note that in the previous URL, the base URL path contains /v1/. This is an arbitrary way to indicate the targeted version of this API. As with any other application, the API can evolve over time, adding, changing, and removing resources. Using API versioning is a common pattern to offer a predictable behavior to consumer applications, without facing breaking changes (i.e., accessing a path that has been removed). In other APIs, the version may be specified via the api_version query parameter. This way, the URL path is not modified, and only the query parameter is appended; here's an example:

```
$ curl https://my_application.com/api/my_path?api_version=1.3
```

The omitted output from the cURL statement in Example 10-1 is an output word wrapped on the terminal, which is hard to read. Alternatively, as shown in Example 10-2, you can *pipe* the response to python3 -m json.tool to pretty-print the response object, making it much more human-readable.

Example 10-2. Using the Python json.tool to render a JSON response

```
$ curl 'https://api.meraki.com/api/v1/organizations' \
  -H 'X-Cisco-Meraki-API-Key: 6bec40cf957de430a6f1f2baa056b99a4fac9ea0' \
  -L \
  | python3 -m json.tool

[
  {
    "id": "573083052582915028",
    "name": "Next Meraki Org",
    "url": "https://n18.meraki.com/o/PoiDucs/manage/organization/overview",
    "api": {
      "enabled": true
    },
    "licensing": {
      "model": "co-term"
    },
    "cloud": {
      "region": {
          "name": "North America"
      }
    }
  },
  # other organizations omitted for brevity
]
```

The object retrieved is a JSON object, which converts to a list in Python because it begins and ends with square brackets. Each item in the list is a dictionary, representing an organization and all its attributes. The response media type (in this case, JSON), can be influenced by the Accept header (expressing the client wish), but in this case, it has no impact because JSON is the only media type supported by this API.

To compare the user experience from cURL to Postman, Figure 10-2 shows an equivalent HTTP GET request done via the Postman GUI.

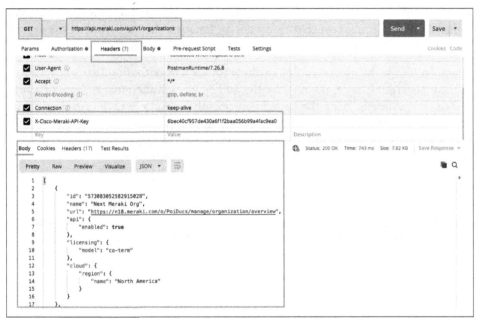

Figure 10-2. Postman GET request

 The UI you get from Postman may differ from the one in this book. UIs are evolving with the product, so it's likely to change over time. However, the concepts remain the same.

In Figure 10-2, you can appreciate the same request and output from Example 10-1, but in a better visual presentation. Following the same pattern, you could reproduce all the examples in this section in Postman.

Postman allows you to create and publish Postman Collections as common API examples to be reused (using variables for customization). These collections can serve as a good reference for common operations on APIs. As an example, Nick Russo maintains an interesting collection for several network APIs at *https://oreil.ly/ QBJmd*.

Commonly, behind a REST API, different resources are *related*. From Cisco Meraki documentation, we know that each organization can contain *networks*. So, similar to the previous API endpoint for organizations, there is one for networks: /api/v1/ organizations/{organizationId}/networks. Between the curly braces, the organi zationID must be replaced by the actual organization identifier.

This identifier is the most relevant attribute for each organization that you retrieved in Example 10-2. It is represented by the id key in each dictionary. Taking this ID, you can continue exploring the nested networks that belong to each organization. It's interesting to notice the nested nature of this API, so you can't list all the networks directly, but use the organizations they belong to as a reference. In Example 10-3, the organization ID is used to retrieve the networks that belong to it.

Example 10-3. Retrieving Meraki networks with cURL

```
$ curl 'https://api.meraki.com/api/v1/organizations/573083052582915028/networks' \ ❶
  -H 'X-Cisco-Meraki-API-Key: 6bec40cf957de430a6f1f2baa056b99a4fac9ea0' \
  -L \
  | python3 -m json.tool

[
  {                                                                              ❷
    "id": "L_573083052582989052",                                               ❸
    "organizationId": "573083052582915028",
    "name": "Long Island Office",
    "productTypes": [
      "appliance",
      "camera",
      "switch"
    ],
    "timeZone": "America/Los_Angeles",
    "tags": [
      "tag1",
      "tag2"
    ],
    "enrollmentString": null,
    "url": "https://n18.meraki.com/Long-Island-Offi/n/kWaHAbs/manage/usage/list",
    "notes": "Combined network for Long Island Office",
    "isBoundToConfigTemplate": false
  },
  # other networks removed for brevity
]
```

❶ The URL path contains the organization ID that limits the scope of the request to the networks belonging to that organization.

❷ The response is a list of dictionaries, each representing a network. And in each dictionary, we can find each network's attributes.

❸ Similar to the previous organization's example, the id key is used to uniquely identify the network.

Next, we continue exploring HTTP methods introduced in "Understanding HTTP request types" on page 401. In particular, we'll start with a method you can use to modify resources on the API: the POST.

Using the HTTP POST method to create a new resource. In Example 10-3, you retrieved the networks belonging to a specific organization. Now, for the same organization, you want to create a new network (Example 10-4).

Example 10-4. Creating a Meraki network with cURL

```
curl -X POST 'https://api.meraki.com/api/v1/organizations/573083052582915028/networks' \ ❶
  -H 'X-Cisco-Meraki-API-Key: 6bec40cf957de430a6f1f2baa056b99a4fac9ea0' \
  -L \
  -d '{"name": "my new automated network", "productTypes": ["switch"]}' \       ❷
  -H 'Content-Type: application/json' \                                          ❸
  | python3 -m json.tool

{
    "id": "N_573083052583237701",
    "organizationId": "573083052582915028",
    "productTypes": [
        "switch"
    ],
    "url": "https://n18.meraki.com/my-new-automated/n/mQ9KWds/manage/usage/list",
    "name": "my new automated network",
    "timeZone": "America/Los_Angeles",
    "enrollmentString": null,
    "tags": [],
    "notes": null,
    "isBoundToConfigTemplate": false
}
```

❶ The HTTP method to create new objects is POST, and it is specified with the -X flag. The POST method requires *data*.

❷ With the -d flag, or --data, we pass a JSON object with the attributes of the new network in the form of a key-value pair (name and productTypes).

❸ The Content-Type header is used to specify the data format. In this case, we are using JSON, but other formats are also supported (e.g., XML).

 Learning how to construct a proper API request requires becoming familiar with API documentation. The API documentation (the API definition and specs) defines what a given URL must be, the HTTP request type, headers, and what the body needs to be for a successful API call. For instance, in the previous example, we passed the required attributes for the POST request, but we could have also passed optional attributes, such as timeZone or tags. All these attributes are defined in the *API documentation*. Additionally, performing GET requests offers some hints of the required attributes, as you can see in the output of the networks GET (in Example 10-3) and the data used for the POST.

Now that you understand the principles of REST and HTTP, it's important to also take note of non-RESTful HTTP-based APIs.

Understanding non-RESTful HTTP-based APIs

RESTful APIs are the most popular HTTP-based APIs, and other HTTP-based APIs are not compliant with REST principles. In the network industry, during the adoption of newer interfaces, such as RESTful ones, some APIs were built on top of CLIs, meaning that the API call actually sends a command to the device versus sending native structured data. Obviously, the preferred approach is to have any modern network platform's CLI or web UI use the underlying API, but for legacy or preexisting systems that were built using commands, it is common to see the use of non-RESTful APIs, as it was easier to add an API this way rather than rearchitect the underlying system.

RESTful HTTP-based APIs and non-RESTful HTTP-based APIs have two major differences. RESTful APIs use particular verbs (e.g., GET, POST, PATCH, etc.) to dictate the type of change being requested of the target server. For example, in the context of networking, a configuration change would never occur if you're doing an HTTP GET, since you're simply retrieving data. However, systems that are HTTP based but do not follow RESTful principles could use the same HTTP verb for every API call. This means if you're retrieving data or making a configuration change, all API calls could be using a POST request. Another common difference is that non-RESTful HTTP-based APIs always use the same URL and do not allow you to access a specific resource via a URL change. You can see both characteristics in Example 10-5.

Within the non-REST HTTP-based APIs, there is one popular methodology, the RPC, which was available before the REST APIs become popular. An RPC is a simple calling to a function in a remote system, with a data payload containing a method, and some other attributes. Depending on how the data is codified, we could talk about XML-RPC or JSON-RPC. This command-and-action approach makes it more performant, but also more obscure in terms of predictability.

 Both types, REST and RPC, can coexist on the same API server, in different parts of the API, leveraging their benefits for different use cases. We will present more RPC use cases in "Using NETCONF" on page 410 and "Understanding gRPC" on page 434.

One example of a JSON-RPC API is the Arista eAPI. It offers an RPC endpoint (/command-api) to run CLI commands via the HTTP API. Example 10-5 uses cURL again to request the execution of the CLI commands providing the proper JSON payload.

Example 10-5. Running CLI commands via the Arista eAPI

```
$ curl --insecure \
  -H "Content-Type: application/json" \
  -X POST \                                               ❶
  -d '{"jsonrpc":"2.0", "method":"runCmds", "params":{ "version":1,
  "cmds":["show version"], "format":"text"}, "id":""}' \  ❷
  https://ntc:ntc123@eos-spine1/command-api \             ❸
  | python3 -m json.tool

{
    "jsonrpc": "2.0",
    "id": "",
    "result": [
        {                                                 ❹
            "output": " vEOS\nHardware version:    \nSerial number:       \n
            System MAC address:  5254. 0097.1b5e\n\nSoftware image version:
            4.22.4M\nArchitecture:           i686\nInternal build version:
            4.22.4M-15583082.4224M\nInternal build ID:
            08527907-ec51-458e-99dd-e3ad9c80cbbd\n\nUptime:
            15 weeks, 4 days, 13 hours and 22 minutes\nTotal memory:
            2014520 kB\nFree memory:          1335580 kB\n\n"
        }
    ]
}
```

❶ We are using the POST method to retrieve data. As we've commented, in non-REST APIs, the method is not meaningful. Actually, with the same method, depending on the CLI commands passed, we could be retrieving the state or changing it.

❷ We define the *operation* to be executed remotely with the method (runCmds), and the cmds parameter, which contains a list of all the commands to be executed.

❸ The authentication parameters (ntc:ntc123@) are passed in the URL that is equivalent to the standard HTTP Authorization header.

❹ The result key contains the output of the command executed—in this case, the output of the show version command without any formatting, simply the raw text (i.e., what we get via an SSH CLI access).

 Alternatives to RESTful APIs other than RPC have appeared. For instance, GraphQL was published in 2015 by Facebook. It defines a data query language that simplifies the way data is consumed, allowing clients to define the structure/filtering of the data required, which will be served by the server. This approach reduces the amount of data transferred but can impede caching of the results. GraphQL is especially useful for retrieving data from an SoT, collecting the relevant data from one object (including nested resources). We dig into this in more detail in Chapter 14.

As you start to use various types of HTTP-based APIs on network devices, keep in mind the following points:

- HTTP APIs can use XML or JSON for data encoding, but the device may implement only one or the other. The API's author determines what gets supported.

- Tools such as cURL and Postman are helpful as you get started with APIs, but to write code to interact with HTTP APIs, you need a library that *speaks* HTTP, such as the Python Requests library or Go net/http package (covered in "Using Network APIs for Automation" on page 451).

- Pay close attention to the HTTP verbs used when making configuration changes—using the wrong verb can have unintended consequences.

- You need to use API documentation to understand how to construct a proper API request. You'll need the URL, headers, HTTP method, and body.

Now that we've introduced HTTP-based APIs, let's shift our focus and introduce the NETCONF API.

Using NETCONF

NETCONF is a network configuration management protocol, defined in RFC 6241 (*https://oreil.ly/Bf8G4*) and designed from the ground up for configuration management and for retrieving configuration and operational state data from network devices. In this respect, NETCONF has a clear delineation between configuration and operational state; API requests are used to perform operations such as retrieving the configuration state, retrieving the operational state, and making configuration changes.

We stated in the previous section that RESTful APIs aren't new; they are merely new for network devices and SDN controllers. As we transition to looking at the NETCONF API, it's worth noting that NETCONF is also not new. NETCONF has been around for nearly two decades. In fact, it's an industry-standard protocol with its original RFC published in 2006. It's even been on various network devices for years, although often as a limited API rarely being used.

One of the core attributes of NETCONF is its ability to utilize various configuration data stores. Most network engineers are familiar with running configurations and startup configurations. These are thought of as two configuration files, but they are two configuration data stores in the context of NETCONF.

NETCONF implementations often tend to use a third data store called a *candidate configuration*. The candidate configuration data store holds configuration objects (CLI commands if you're using CLI for configuration) that are not yet applied to the device. As an example, if you enter a configuration on a device that supports candidate configurations, they do not take action immediately. Instead, they are held in the candidate configuration and applied to the device only when a *commit* operation is performed. When the commit is executed, the candidate configuration is written to the running configuration.

Candidate configuration data stores have been around for years as originally defined in the NETCONF RFC almost two decades ago. One of the issues the industry has faced is having usable implementations of NETCONF that offered this functionality. However, not all implementations have been unused—there have, in fact, been successful implementations. Juniper's Junos OS has had a robust NETCONF implementation for years, along with the capability of a candidate configuration; more recently, other products from vendors such as Cisco, Huawei, and Nokia have adopted support for the candidate configuration data store.

Always check your hardware and software platforms, even if they are from the same vendor. The capabilities they support likely differ. The support of a candidate configuration is just one example.

We stated that with a candidate configuration, you enter various configurations, and they aren't yet applied until a commit operation is performed. This leads us to another core attribute of NETCONF-enabled devices: configuration changes as a *transaction.* In our example, it means that all configuration objects (commands) are committed as a transaction. All commands succeed or are *not* applied. This is in contrast to the more common scenario of entering a series of commands and having a command somewhere in the middle fail, yielding a partial configuration.

Moreover, a unique feature of NETCONF (not available in any of the other interfaces) is the *network-wide* transaction. If a configuration change affects multiple devices—for example, provisioning a Layer 3 VPN (L3VPN) service end to end, updating the configuration of several network devices—all the changes need to succeed, or the whole operation is rolled back (which is called an *abort* phase).

The support of a candidate configuration and atomic transactions are just two features of NETCONF. Let's take a deeper dive into the underlying NETCONF protocol stack.

Learning the NETCONF protocol stack

Now we'll tackle the four basic layers in NETCONF: the content representation, the operation types, the messages, and the supported transport protocols, as outlined in Table 10-3. We are going to review each and show concrete examples of what they mean for the XML object being sent between the client and server.

Table 10-3. NETCONF protocol stack

Layer	Example
Content	XML representation of data models (YANG, XSD)
Operations	`get-config`, `get`, `copy-config`, `lock`, `unlock`, `edit-config`, `delete-config`, `kill-session`, `close-session`, `commit`, `validate`, ...
Messages	rpc, rpc-reply, hello
Transport	SSHv2, SOAP, TLS, BEEP

 NETCONF supports only XML for data encoding. On the other hand, remember that RESTful APIs *have the ability* to support JSON and/or XML.

Transport. NETCONF is commonly implemented using SSH as transport; it is its own SSH subsystem. While all of our examples use NETCONF over SSH, it is technically possible to implement NETCONF over SOAP, TLS, or any other protocol that meets the requirements of NETCONF.

A few of these requirements are as follows:

- It must be a connection-oriented session, and thus there must be a consistent connection between a client and a server.

- NETCONF sessions must provide a means for authentication, data integrity, confidentiality, and replay protection.

- Although NETCONF can be implemented with other transport protocols, each implementation *must* support SSH at a minimum.

With the popularity of RESTful APIs, instead of further developing NETCONF over other protocols, the brand-new RESTCONF interface was created to implement NETCONF functionalities using REST principles. We cover this approach in "Using RESTCONF" on page 425.

Messages. NETCONF messages are based on an RPC–based communication model, and each message is encoded in XML. Using an RPC-based model allows the XML messages to be used independent of the transport type. NETCONF supports three message types: <hello>, <rpc>, and <rpc-reply>. Viewing the actual XML-encoded object helps elucidate NETCONF, so let's take a look at a NETCONF RPC request.

The <hello> message is sent by the NETCONF server when the connection is established, exposing its *capabilities*—the data models and the actions supported:

```
<hello xmlns="urn:ietf:params:xml:ns:netconf:base:1.0">
  <capabilities>
    <capability>urn:ietf:params:netconf:base:1.1</capability>
    <!-- rest of request as XML... -->
  </capabilities>
</hello>
```

For a refresher on XML concepts, such as the XML namespace xmlns, see Chapter 8.

After the initial <hello>, the message types are always going to be <rpc> and <rpc-reply> and will always be the outermost XML tag in the encoded object:

```
<rpc message-id="101">
    <!-- rest of request as XML... -->
</rpc>
```

Every NETCONF <rpc> includes a required attribute called message-id. You can see this in the preceding example. It's an arbitrary string the client sends to the server.

The server reuses this ID in the response header so the client knows which message the server is responding to.

The other message type is `<rpc-reply>`. The NETCONF server responds with the `message-id` and any other attributes received from the client (e.g., XML namespaces):

```
<rpc-reply message-id="101" xmlns="urn:ietf:params:xml:ns:netconf:base:1.0">
  <data>
      <!-- XML content/response... -->
  </data>
</rpc-reply>
```

This `<rpc-reply>` example assumes that the XML namespace is in the `<rpc>` sent by the client. Note that the actual data response coming from the NETCONF server is embedded within the `<data>` tag.

Next, we'll show how the NETCONF request dictates which particular NETCONF operation (RPC) it's requesting of the server.

Operations. The outermost XML element is always the type of message being sent (e.g., `<rpc>` or `<rpc-reply>`). When you are sending a NETCONF request from the client to the server, the next element, or the child of the message type, is the requested NETCONF (RPC) operation. You saw a list of NETCONF operations in Table 10-3, and now we'll take a look at some of them.

The two primary operations we review in this chapter are `<get>` and `<edit-config>`. The `<get>` operation retrieves running configuration and device state information:

```
<rpc message-id="101" xmlns="urn:ietf:params:xml:ns:netconf:base:1.0">
  <get>
    <!-- XML content/response... -->
  </get>
</rpc>
```

Since `<get>` is the child element within the `<rpc>` message, this means the client is requesting a NETCONF `<get>` operation.

Within the `<get>` hierarchy, optional filter types allow you to selectively retrieve a portion of the running configuration—namely, subtree and XPath filters. Our initial focus is on *subtree* filters, which allow you to provide an XML document, which is a subtree of the complete XML tree hierarchy that you wish to retrieve in a given request. Later, in "Using ncclient with Cisco IOS XE" on page 475, we will use the *XPath* filter to inject the filter into the query path.

Example 10-6 references a specific XML data object by using the `<native>` element and the *http://cisco.com/ns/yang/cisco-ios-xe-native* URL. This data object is the XML representation of a specific data model that exists on the target device. This data model represents a full running configuration as XML, but in the example, we are requesting only the `<interface>` configuration hierarchy.

As shown throughout this chapter, the actual JSON and XML objects sent can be based on either standard or vendor-specific models (often under the "native" tag).

The next two examples, for the `<get>` operation, are XML requests from a Cisco IOS XE device.

Example 10-6. NETCONF GET interfaces config

```
<rpc message-id="101" xmlns="urn:ietf:params:xml:ns:netconf:base:1.0">
  <get>
    <filter type="subtree">
      <native xmlns="http://cisco.com/ns/yang/Cisco-IOS-XE-native"> ❶
        <interface></interface>
      </native>
    </filter>
  </get>
</rpc>
```

❶   The custom `xmlns`, under the Cisco custom domain, represents a vendor-specific data model.

 In this edition of the book, we've updated the vendor model reference because the custom vendor data model changed. This may happen again in the future, so it's necessary to always be aware of the supported capabilities.

You could add more elements to the filter's XML tree to narrow the response that comes back from the NETCONF server. You will now add two elements to the filter—so instead of receiving the configuration objects for all interfaces, you'll receive the configuration of only GigabitEthernet1:

```
<filter type="subtree">
  <native xmlns="http://cisco.com/ns/yang/Cisco-IOS-XE-native">
    <interface>
      <GigabitEthernet>
        <name>1</name>
      </GigabitEthernet>
    </interface>
  </native>
</filter>
```

The next most common NETCONF operation is `<edit-config>`. This operation is used to make a configuration change. Specifically, this operation loads a configuration into the specified configuration data store: running, startup, or candidate. In Example 10-7, you add a static route to the running configuration.

Example 10-7. NETCONF edit-config to add a static route

```
<rpc message-id="101" xmlns="urn:ietf:params:xml:ns:netconf:base:1.0">
  <edit-config> ❶
    <target>
      <running/>
    </target>
    <config>   ❷
      <configuration>
        <routing-options>
          <static>
            <route>
              <name>0.0.0.0/0</name>
              <next-hop>10.1.0.1</next-hop>
            </route>
          </static>
        </routing-options>
      </configuration>
    </config>
  </edit-config>
</rpc>
```

❶ The <edit-config> operation is used, setting the target configuration data store with the <target> tag. If not specified, it'll default to the *running* configuration.

❷ Within the <config> element, we define the data-model hierarchy that we want to load onto the target data store. This structure is based on the NETCONF capabilities that are supported on a given platform.

 Vendors can implement platform-specific options. Juniper Junos OS, for example, offers options for <edit-config>. Example 10-7 uses <config>, and requires XML configuration objects for adding a static route to a Junos OS device. Junos OS also supports <config-text> within <edit-config>, which allows you to include configuration elements using text format (curly brace or set syntax).

The <edit-config> operation also supports an attribute called operation that provides more flexibility in the way a device applies the configuration object. When the operation attribute is used, it can be set to one of five values: merge, replace, create, delete, or remove. The default value is merge. If you wanted to delete the route from the previous example, you could use delete or remove; the difference is that an error occurs if you use delete when the object doesn't exist. You could optionally use create, but an error is raised if the object already exists. Often merge is used for making configuration changes for this reason.

Finally, you could use the `replace` operation if you wanted to replace a given XML hierarchy in the configuration data object. In the static route example, you would use `replace` if you wanted to end up with *just* the default static route on the device; it would automatically remove all other configured static routes.

 If the `operation` options still seem a little confusing, don't worry. Once we start exploring and automating devices using NETCONF later in this section, you'll see even more examples that use various XML objects across device types for operations such as the NET-CONF `merge` and `replace`.

We've shown what XML documents look like when using `<get>` and `<edit-config>`. The following list describes the other base NETCONF operations:

`<get-config>`
Retrieves all or part of a specified configuration (e.g., running, candidate, or startup).

`<copy-config>`
Creates or replaces a configuration data store with the contents of another configuration data store. Using this operation requires the use of a full configuration.

`<delete-config>`
Deletes a configuration data store (note that the running configuration data store can't be deleted).

`<lock>`
Locks the configuration data-store system of a device being updated to ensure that no other systems (NETCONF clients) can make a change at the same time.

`<unlock>`
Unlocks a previously issued lock on a configuration data store.

`<close-session>`
Requests a graceful termination of a NETCONF session.

`<kill-session>`
Forcefully and immediately terminates a NETCONF session.

This is not an exhaustive list of NETCONF operations, but rather the core operations that each device must support in a NETCONF implementation. NETCONF servers can also support extended operations such as `<commit>` and `<validate>`. To support extended operations like these, the device must support required dependencies called *NETCONF capabilities*.

The <commit> operation commits the candidate configuration as the device's new running configuration. To support the <commit> operation, the device must support the candidate capability.

The <validate> operation validates the contents of the specified configuration (running, candidate, startup). Validation consists of checking a configuration for both syntax and semantics before applying the configuration to the device.

 We've mentioned NETCONF capabilities twice already, so let's give a bit more context. As you know now, NETCONF supports a base set of NETCONF RPC operations. These are defined by the device as NETCONF *capabilities*. NETCONF capabilities are exchanged between the client and the server during connection setup, and the capabilities supported are denoted by a URL/URI. For example, every device that supports NETCONF should support the base operation from the namespace: urn:ietf:params:xml:ns:net conf:base:1.0. Additional capabilities use the form urn:ietf:par ams:netconf:capability:{*name*}:1.*x*, where *name* is the name of the capability and the way it is usually identified (without the full namespace). When we start exploring the use of NETCONF from a hands-on perspective (in Example 10-8), you'll get to see all capabilities a given device supports.

Content. The last layer of the NETCONF protocol stack to understand is the *content*. This is the actual XML document that gets embedded within the RPC operation tag elements. We already showed examples of what the content could be for particular NETCONF operations.

In Example 10-6, you looked at the content that selectively requested configuration elements for the interfaces on a Cisco IOS XE device:

```
<native xmlns="http://cisco.com/ns/yang/cisco-ios-xe-native">
  <interface>
  </interface>
</native>
```

The most important point to understand about content is that it is the XML representation of a particular schema, or data model, that the device supports. We introduced schemas and data models in Chapter 8.

After this short introduction to the basic NETCONF concepts, you're ready to start exploring what a real NETCONF API interaction looks like.

Exploring NETCONF

As you learn new APIs, it's advantageous to learn about associated tooling that allows you to learn the API without writing any code. You saw this with cURL when learning how to use HTTP-based APIs. For NETCONF, we are going to cover how to use an SSH client that creates an interactive NETCONF session. You'll learn how to construct a proper NETCONF request while also seeing how the device responds to a given request, without writing any code.

 Using an interactive NETCONF over SSH session as we do here is useful for *learning* and *exploring* the use of NETCONF, but it is also unintuitive, unfriendly, and fragile. For any use case outside of learning and experimentation (*especially* for those dealing with production infrastructure), you should instead use higher-level libraries and tools that we'll explore later. These higher-level resources manage the minutiae of NETCONF operations and syntax much more effectively and predictably.

In the next two examples, we show you how NETCONF works on two platforms: Junos and Cisco IOS XE.

NETCONF with Junos. Let's start with Juniper vMX running Junos as an example. You connect to the device via SSH on port 830, the default port number for NETCONF. To connect to the device, you'll use a standard Linux ssh command:

```
$ ssh -p 830 ntc@vmx1 -s netconf
```

 Based on the vendor implementation, you may need to supply -s netconf as you SSH to the device. The -s denotes the SSH subsystem being used.

In Example 10-8, as soon as you connect and authenticate, the NETCONF server (the router) responds with a hello message that includes all of its supported NETCONF operations, capabilities, models/schemas, and a session ID.

Example 10-8. NETCONF hello response from server

```
<nc:hello xmlns:nc="urn:ietf:params:xml:ns:netconf:base:1.0">
  <nc:capabilities>
    <nc:capability>urn:ietf:params:netconf:base:1.0</nc:capability>
    <nc:capability>urn:ietf:params:netconf:capability:candidate:1.0</nc:capability>
    <nc:capability>urn:ietf:params:netconf:capability:confirmed-commit:1.0</nc:capability>
    <--- output omitted for brevity --->
    <nc:capability>http://xml.juniper.net/netconf/junos/1.0</nc:capability>
    <nc:capability>http://xml.juniper.net/dmi/system/1.0</nc:capability>
  </nc:capabilities>
  <nc:session-id>77470</nc:session-id>
</nc:hello>
]]>]]>
```

All these capabilities announce what you could do with the device via the NETCONF interface.

Once you receive the server's capabilities, the NETCONF connection setup process starts. The next step is to send our (client) capabilities. A capabilities exchange is required to be able to send any NETCONF requests to the server.

The `hello` object you're going to send to the device to complete the capabilities exchange is the following:

```
<?xml version="1.0" encoding="UTF-8"?>
<hello xmlns="urn:ietf:params:xml:ns:netconf:base:1.0">
  <capabilities>
    <capability>urn:ietf:params:netconf:base:1.0</capability>
    <capability>http://xml.juniper.net/netconf/junos/1.0</capability>
  </capabilities>
</hello>
]]>]]>
```

Note the last six characters in the preceding XML documents: `]]>]]>`. These characters denote that the request is complete and can be processed. NETCONF supports two types of message separators, depending on the supported capabilities:

`urn:ietf:params:netconf:base:1.0`

    Structured as `]]>]]>` plus a newline. We use this separator in all the NETCONF examples with Junos, such as in Example 10-8.

`urn:ietf:params:netconf:base:1.1`

    This chunked framing (*https://oreil.ly/pwhqB*) uses `<number>` and `#`. We use this separator in the examples in "NETCONF with Cisco IOS XE" on page 423.

However, the hello message always uses the `]]>]]>`, for backward compatibility.

> In an interactive NETCONF session, you need to explicitly use the separators; when you use a library, this low-level action is abstracted (and implicit).

As you start working with the SSH client, you'll realize it's not like a familiar interactive CLI, although it is an interactive session. No help menu or question mark help is available. There is no man page. It's common to think something is broken or the terminal is frozen. It's not. If you don't get any errors after you copy and paste XML documents into the session terminal, things are likely going well. To break out of the interactive session, you need to press Ctrl-C on your keyboard—there is no way to safely exit the interactive NETCONF session.

Once the client responds with its capabilities, you're ready to start sending NET-CONF requests. You can use a text editor to preconstruct your XML documents.

At this point, we've successfully connected to the device and exchanged capabilities, and we can now issue an actual NETCONF request. Our first example will query the device for the fxp0 interface configuration. In Example 10-9, we construct the XML document in a text editor and then copy and paste it into the interactive session.

Example 10-9. NETCONF GET operation in Junos

```
<?xml version="1.0" encoding="UTF-8"?>
<rpc message-id="101" xmlns="urn:ietf:params:xml:ns:netconf:base:1.0">
  <get>
    <filter type="subtree">
      <configuration>
        <interfaces>
          <interface>
            <name>fxp0</name>
          </interface>
        </interfaces>
      </configuration>
    </filter>
  </get>
</rpc>
]]>]]>
```

As soon as you hit Enter, the request is sent to the device. As presented in Example 10-10, you'd see the XML RPC reply from the device in near real time.

Example 10-10. NETCONF GET reply

```
<nc:rpc-reply xmlns:nc="urn:ietf:params:xml:ns:netconf:base:1.0"
  xmlns:junos="http://xml.juniper.net/junos/18.2R1/junos"
  message-id="101" xmlns="urn:ietf:params:xml:ns:netconf:base:1.0">
  <nc:data>
    <configuration xmlns="http://yang.juniper.net/junos/conf/root"
      junos:commit-seconds="1653021086"
      junos:commit-localtime="2022-05-20 04:31:26 UTC" junos:commit-user="ntc">
      <interfaces xmlns="http://yang.juniper.net/junos/conf/interfaces">
        <interface>
          <name>fxp0</name>
          <unit>
            <name>0</name>
            <description>MANAGEMENT_INTERFACE__DO_NOT_CHANGE</description>
            <family>
              <inet>
                <address>
                  <name>10.0.0.15/24</name>
                </address>
              </inet>
            </family>
          </unit>
```

```
      </interface>
    </interfaces>
   </configuration>
   <database-status-information></database-status-information>
  </nc:data>
</nc:rpc-reply>
]]>]]>
```

At this point, you may have successfully performed your first request to a network device via NETCONF and received a response. The point here isn't to do anything with it, just as you didn't do anything with data returned with cURL. The value is that you've tested and validated an XML request to retrieve the configuration for interface fxp0, and now know what the response looks like, to ease you into automating devices with Python or Go.

You've seen one example using NETCONF <get> operations to the device. Let's take a look at one example introducing how to use the <edit-config> operation, which is used to make a configuration change.

To see the proper way to construct an XML request for a configuration change, you are going to first issue a get request, since that will show you the structure of the complete object that needs to get sent back to the device. This is similar to knowing different CLI commands in an operating system.

 This example uses a vendor-specific data model for the interfaces instead of the standard urn:ietf:params:xml:ns:yang:ietf-interfaces because the standard one is not available. It is not present in the output of Example 10-8.

In Example 10-10, you can notice how an interface (fxp0) is configured. If you remove the inner filter part, you could get the rest of the interfaces' configurations. You can use the data structure used for the fxp0 interface as the foundation to modify the configurations on other interfaces, to simplify the process.

Let's make our first NETCONF configuration change by configuring the IP address of 192.0.2.1/24 on interface ge-0/0/0. To construct the object, you'll extract the required data from your get request in Example 10-10. The two items you need to update are as follows:

- Your returned object in the <data> tag will get enclosed in a <config> tag when you want to make a configuration change using the NETCONF <edit-config> operation.

- The constructed object needs to specify a *target* data store (i.e., running, startup, or candidate) based on what the target node supports.

These changes result in the XML message in Example 10-11.

Example 10-11. NETCONF edit-config to change IP and interface description

```xml
<?xml version="1.0" encoding="UTF-8"?>
<rpc message-id="101" xmlns="urn:ietf:params:xml:ns:netconf:base:1.0">
  <edit-config>
    <target>
      <running/>
    </target>
    <config>
      <configuration xmlns="http://yang.juniper.net/junos/conf/root">
        <interfaces xmlns="http://yang.juniper.net/junos/conf/interfaces">
          <interface>
            <name>ge-0/0/0</name>
            <unit>
              <name>0</name>
              <description>Interface with changed IP</description>
              <family>
                <inet>
                  <address>
                    <name>192.0.2.1/24</name>
                  </address>
                </inet>
              </family>
            </unit>
          </interface>
        </interfaces>
      </configuration>
    </config>
  </edit-config>
</rpc>
]]>]]>
```

Once this XML document is built in a text editor, it can easily be copied and pasted into an active NETCONF session.

All the examples have been successful NETCONF operations so far, but the reality is that it could take a bit to get used to the XML syntax and the data models used in each platform. Luckily, NETCONF provides a useful error message to help you fix the problem. For instance, in Example 10-11, you have targeted the *candidate* configuration data store to change. However, if you use another data store, such as *running*, the NETCONF operation will complain because it's not expected to change it directly on this platform. It requires the use of the *commit* operation.

NETCONF with Cisco IOS XE. To complement the Junos NETCONF example, it's interesting to see another NETCONF implementation—in this case, for Cisco IOS XE.

You establish the SSH NETCONF session, and receive the hello from the device, as in Example 10-8:

```
$ ssh -p 830 ntc@csr1 -s netconf
<?xml version="1.0" encoding="UTF-8"?>
<hello xmlns="urn:ietf:params:xml:ns:netconf:base:1.0">
<capabilities>
<capability>urn:ietf:params:netconf:base:1.0</capability>
<capability>urn:ietf:params:netconf:base:1.1</capability>
<capability>http://tail-f.com/ns/netconf/actions/1.0</capability>
<capability>http://cisco.com/ns/cisco-xe-ietf-ip-deviation?...
    revision=2016-08-10</capability>
<capability>http://openconfig.net/yang/policy-types?...
    revision=2016-05-12</capability>
<capability>urn:ietf:params:xml:ns:yang:smiv2:RFC-1212?module=RFC-1212</capability>
<--- output omitted for brevity --->
```

All these capabilities announce what you could do with each device via the NET-CONF interface. The first big difference, among platforms, is in the number of supported capabilities—there are many more in this case. This doesn't mean that the first is less *capable* than the second. It means only that both support different data models and features.

It's interesting to notice the different *organizations* being referenced in each output. As expected, both support the base IETF definitions for NETCONF operations, but each vendor has its own extensions. The Juniper one uses its own data models (xml.juniper.net), as does Cisco (cisco.com and tail-f.com). In this output, you can see that it also supports OpenConfig models (openconfig.net). And last, but not least, you can observe a lot of translated data models, from SMIv2 to YANG (defined in RFC 6643), to make available the same structure data used in SNMP, via NETCONF. We talk about the data models' definitions in "Comparing NETCONF, RESTCONF, and gNMI" on page 446.

In this case, you will send a hello message announcing your intention to use base:1.1 (which you did not use in the previous NETCONF examples with Junos) because it allows the chunked framing delineator that is the only one supported in this platform:

```
<hello xmlns="urn:ietf:params:xml:ns:netconf:base:1.0">
    <capabilities>
        <capability>urn:ietf:params:netconf:base:1.0</capability>
        <capability>urn:ietf:params:netconf:base:1.1</capability>
    </capabilities>
</hello>
]]>]]>
```

To run a get-config operation, you target the *source* data store and use the chunked framing delineator before and after the message (the number is arbitrary):

```
#200
<rpc xmlns="urn:ietf:params:xml:ns:netconf:base:1.0" message-id="101">
  <get-config>
    <source>
      <running/>
    </source>
  </get-config>
```

```
</rpc>
##
```

This code outputs the full *running* configuration in XML format. You could apply filters to narrow the desired data.

 We've stated this a few times already, but we're going to restate it because it's extremely important. As you get started using APIs, you need to know how to construct the proper request object. This is often challenging as you get started, but the hope is you can find *easy* ways to help figure out how to build these objects. This help could come from API documentation, tooling built to interface with the underlying schema definitions files such as XSDs or YANG modules, or even CLI commands on the device. For example, Cisco Nexus and Juniper Junos OS have CLI commands that show you exactly what the XML document needs to be for a given request.

As we wrap up the NETCONF section to move to other network management interfaces, keep in mind that NETCONF uses only XML encoding and SSH transport (you're going to find different options next), and it supports data-model-based operations like the other interfaces.

After this deep dive into NETCONF, let's continue with its *cousin*, RESTCONF.

Using RESTCONF

In "Getting Familiar with HTTP-Based APIs" on page 399, we explained how popular REST APIs work, and afterward, in "Using NETCONF" on page 410, we presented the benefits of exposing network management operations based on data models. The network automation community's demand to bring both together should not come as a surprise. The answer was RESTCONF, defined in RFC 8040 (*https://oreil.ly/Lnv9Y*), which has been adopted by many NOSs.

Adhering to REST principles implies some limitations and simplifications compared to NETCONF:

- RESTCONF doesn't support network-wide transactions because it requires stateful communications. So, the clients should manage failure scenarios in the system-by-system interactions.
- RESTCONF drops the data-store concept; only a single data store exists, equivalent to the *running* one.
- No locking operation is supported.

Don't consider NETCONF and RESTCONF as mutually exclusive; the truth is almost the opposite. Devices can provide both interfaces relying on the same backend functionalities, so it's up to the client to choose the most convenient one for particular use cases. However, dual interaction could lead to compatibility issues. For instance, locking a data store via NETCONF and accessing it via RESTCONF will raise an error.

As it's a combination of REST APIs and NETCONF concepts, RESTCONF assembles characteristics from both. RESTCONF uses HTTP with the standard requests: GET, PUT, PATCH, POST, and DELETE, corresponding to some NETCONF operations, as you can see in Table 10-4.

Table 10-4. RESTCONF-to-NETCONF operation mapping

RESTCONF	NETCONF
GET	`<get>`/`<get-config>`
POST	`<edit-config>>` (`nc:operation="create"`)
PUT	`<edit-config>>` (`nc:operation="create/replace"`)
PATCH	`<edit-config>>` (`nc:operation`, depends on the content)
DELETE	`<edit-config>>` (`nc:operation="delete"`)

RESTCONF supports JSON *and* XML encoding. As the network developer, you have the choice to work with whichever data format you prefer. The structure of the content data is defined using YANG models, like NETCONF.

Exploring RESTCONF in Cisco IOS XE

As in "Exploring HTTP-based APIs with cURL" on page 402, you'll continue using cURL to explore RESTCONF because it's just another REST API. In this section, we use the Cisco IOS XE platform to demonstrate basic RESTCONF interaction. Similar to NETCONF, you may need to activate the RESTCONF interface in your network device, if it's supported.

 A great resource to extend your knowledge about RESTCONF is the Cisco DevNet learning tracks (*https://oreil.ly/mXCrl*). You will also find content about the other interfaces covered in this chapter.

Before getting started, you can use a well-known path (`/.well-known/host-meta`) to discover the RESTCONF path within the API:

```
$ curl https://csr1/.well-known/host-meta -k -u 'ntc:ntc123' ❶

<XRD xmlns='http://docs.oasis-open.org/ns/xri/xrd-1.0'>       ❷
    <Link rel='restconf' href='/restconf'/>
</XRD>
```

❶ The -u (or user) cURL argument provides the user and password for Basic authentication. In Basic authentication, the user and password are sent in clear text over the network (Base64 encoded), so it's not a recommended method for production.

❷ By default, the API returns the response in XML. Remember, you could change this behavior by using the HTTP Accept header.

 A Base64-encoded string does *not* mean it has been encrypted. You can easily encode and decode Base64-encoded strings with Python using the base64 BY Python module:

```
>>> import base64
>>>
>>> encoded = base64.b64encode('ntc:ntc123')
>>> encoded
'bnRjOm50YzEyMw=='
>>>
>>> text = base64.b64decode(encoded)
>>> text
'ntc:ntc123'
>>>
```

Now, knowing that the RESTCONF API is located at /restconf, you are ready to start exploring it:

```
$ curl -k -X GET https://csr1/restconf \
    -H 'Accept: application/yang-data+json' \ ❶
    -u 'ntc:ntc123'

{
  "ietf-restconf:restconf": {
     "data":{},                                    ❷
     "operations":{},                              ❸
     "yang-library-version":"2016-06-21"
  }
}
```

❶ Using the Accept header with application/yang-data+json, the response comes in JSON format instead of the default XML.

❷ The data path will contain all data resources.

❸ The operations path will include the data-model-specific operations.

Then, similar to NETCONF, you can discover the *capabilities* offered via the REST-CONF interface. In Example 10-8, you can target the path /restconf/data/netconf-state/capabilities to obtain the very same list you got in "NETCONF with Cisco IOS XE" on page 423:

```
$ curl -k -X GET https://csr1/restconf/data/netconf-state/capabilities \
    -H 'Accept: application/yang-data+json' \
    -u 'ntc:ntc123'

{
  "ietf-netconf-monitoring:capabilities": {
    "capability": [
      "urn:ietf:params:netconf:base:1.0",
      "urn:ietf:params:netconf:base:1.1",
      "http://cisco.com/ns/yang/Cisco-IOS-XE-native?module=Cisco-IOS-XE-native&
        revision=2019-11-01",  ❶
      # output omitted for brevity
    ]
  }
}
```

❶ This model contains all the Cisco IOS XE native configuration models.

In Example 10-12, we explore Cisco-IOS-XE-native:native under the /restconf/data/ path.

Example 10-12. GET configuration with RESTCONF

```
$ curl -k -X GET https://csr1/restconf/data/Cisco-IOS-XE-native:native \
    -H 'Accept: application/yang-data+json' \
    -u 'ntc:ntc123'

{
  "Cisco-IOS-XE-native:native": {
    "version": "17.1",
    "memory": {
      "free": {
        "low-watermark": {
          "processor": 72107
        }
      }
    },
    # output omitted for brevity
  }
}
```

The next subsections explore the RESTCONF API in more detail, including updating the configuration (with PATCH and PUT operations) and executing operations.

Updating configuration via RESTCONF.   As in any other REST API, you can change the content of the API via POST, PATCH, PUT, and DELETE operations. In this case, you want to add two OSPF network statements to an existing OSPF configuration, so the PATCH operation will allow updating it starting from the current state.

As we've already said, when dealing with APIs, you need to know the expected data model structure that the API can understand. You can check the data model specification from the announced capabilities, but it's quicker to explore the data model with a GET operation (as in Example 10-12). In the previous output, you got the full configuration, but to check a specific section, you can append it to the previous path. For instance, by adding `router/` to the previous path, you get *only* the `router` section that contains the OSPF current configuration:

```
"router": {
  "Cisco-IOS-XE-ospf:router-ospf": {
    "ospf": {
      "process-id": [
        {
          "id": 10,
          "network": [
            {
              "ip": "192.0.2.0",
              "wildcard": "0.0.0.7",
              "area": 0
            },
            {
              "ip": "192.0.2.64",
              "wildcard": "0.0.0.7",
              "area": 0
            }
          ],
          "router-id": "192.0.2.1"
        }
      ]
    }
  }
}
```

Now, in Example 10-13, we request a PATCH operation with the data payload containing two new networks to update the OSPF configuration.

Example 10-13. RESTCONF PATCH to add OSFP statements

```
$ curl -k
    -X PATCH "https://csr1/restconf/data/Cisco-IOS-XE-native:native/router/router-ospf" \  ❶
    -H 'Content-Type: application/yang-data+json' \
    -H 'Accept: application/yang-data+json' \
    -u 'ntc:ntc123' \
    -d $'{
  "router-ospf": {
    "ospf": {
```

```
    "process-id": [
      {
        "id": 10,                                                    ❷
        "network": [
          {
            "ip": "192.0.2.128",
            "wildcard": "0.0.0.7",
            "area": 0
          },
          {
            "ip": "192.0.2.192",
            "wildcard": "0.0.0.7",
            "area": 0
          }
        ]
      }
    ]
  }
 }
}'
```

❶   We target the `router-ospf` leaf in the URL path.

❷   The `process-id` is the same as the previous one (`10`), so it will append the new
    networks to the existing ones. We can check it by repeating the previous GET
    operation, and it would show the four OSPF networks.

If instead of PATCH you use the PUT method, the whole `router-ospf` will be
replaced by the new one. This method allows much more efficient configuration
management than traditional CLI configuration. In the CLI, adding configurations
is trivial. However, removing or negating commands is complex. For example, what
if you have a single instance of OSPF running with 50 network statements, but
because of a change in design, you need only 2 network statements? You will have
to know which 48 statements need to be negated with a `no` command. This process
is arduous and mundane as you extrapolate the effort for all types of configurations
on a network device. For our example, wouldn't it be easier to take the opposite
approach—focus on the configuration that *should* exist on the network device? This is
a growing trend, becoming more possible thanks to newer APIs and ways of thinking.
This is called *declarative configuration*.

> In "Updating configuration via RESTCONF with net/http" on page
> 466, you can see an example of using the HTTP PUT method to
> update the configuration.

Understanding the YANG PATCH HTTP operation.   Following REST principles, RESTCONF
comes with two limitations when compared to NETCONF. First, HTTP calls should

not carry the state in between, so a transaction is limited to one HTTP call. Second, an HTTP request implements one type of create, read, update, and delete (CRUD) operation specified by the HTTP method (e.g., GET or POST). The second limitation can be overcome by a new `YANG PATCH` HTTP media type that allows combining various operation types on the same HTTP request.

Before you start using it, you need to validate that the feature (i.e., `urn:ietf:par ams:restconf:capability:yang-patch:1.0`) is supported in the target platform. You can look for this capability in the `restconf-state/capabilities` endpoint:

```
$ curl -k -X GET \
    https://csr1/restconf/data/ietf-restconf-monitoring:restconf-state/capabilities \
    -H 'Accept: application/yang-data+json' \
    -u 'ntc:ntc123'

{
  "ietf-restconf-monitoring:capabilities": {
    "capability": [
      # output omitted for brevity
      "urn:ietf:params:restconf:capability:yang-patch:1.0", ❶
    ]
  }
}
```

❶ Notice the `yang-patch` capability listed under the `restconf-state/capabili ties` endpoint.

To illustrate how YANG PATCH works, you will manage loopback interfaces, adding and removing them. With YANG PATCH, you will first create a `Loopback0`, and in a second request, you will remove it and add a new `Loopback1`.

In Example 10-14, you have the YANG PATCH payload necessary to create a new `Loopback0` interface. Remember, you need to know the expected data structure for the `value` before.

Example 10-14. YANG PATCH with one operation

```
<yang-patch xmlns="urn:ietf:params:xml:ns:yang:ietf-yang-patch">
  <patch-id>add-Loopback0-patch</patch-id> ❶
  <edit>                                     ❷
    <edit-id>edit1</edit-id>
    <operation>create</operation>           ❸
    <target>/Loopback=0</target>            ❹
    <value>                                 ❺
        <Loopback xmlns="http://cisco.com/ns/yang/Cisco-IOS-XE-native">
          <name>0</name>
        </Loopback>
    </value>
  </edit>
</yang-patch>
```

❶ Unique ID to identify the YANG PATCH request.

❷ A YANG PATCH is an *ordered* list of edits, each one with an identifier (`edit-id`).

❸ The type of operation: `create`, `delete`, `insert`, `merge`, `move`, `replace`, or `remove`.

❹ Specifies the target node the operation targets.

❺ This is optional (for example, a `move` operation doesn't need it), but for a `create` operation, it is the content to be *created* in the target.

Then, you can use this data payload with an HTTP PATCH operation with a special `Content-Type`, `application/yang-patch+xml`. The @ specifies using a file instead of a data payload directly:

```
$ curl -k -X PATCH "https://csr1/restconf/data/Cisco-IOS-XE-native:native/interface" \
    -H 'Content-Type: application/yang-patch+xml' \
    -H 'Accept: application/yang-data+xml' \
    -u 'ntc:ntc123' \
    -d '@create-loopback-0.xml'

<yang-patch-status xmlns="urn:ietf:params:xml:ns:yang:ietf-yang-patch">
  <patch-id>add-Loopback0-patch</patch-id>
  <ok/>
</yang-patch-status>
```

Remember that YANG PATCH is not an HTTP method but a media type.

Example 10-14 helps you understand the key parts of the YANG PATCH media type, but a single operation can be done without this special type. In Example 10-15, we add a new interface, Loopback1, and remove the previous one, Loopback0, in the same HTTP request.

Example 10-15. YANG PATCH with two operations

```
<yang-patch xmlns="urn:ietf:params:xml:ns:yang:ietf-yang-patch">
  <patch-id>add-remove-loopback-patch</patch-id>
  <edit>
    <edit-id>edit1</edit-id>
    <operation>create</operation>
    <target>/Loopback=1</target>
    <value>
        <Loopback xmlns="http://cisco.com/ns/yang/Cisco-IOS-XE-native">
          <name>1</name>
```

```
        </Loopback>
      </value>
    </edit>
    <edit>
      <edit-id>edit2</edit-id>
      <operation>remove</operation>
      <target>/Loopback=0</target>
    </edit>
</yang-patch>
```

> The order of the operations within a YANG PATCH payload is not
> relevant. What is important is the final configuration outcome state
> and its behavior as an atomic transaction, for one single device.
> Either *all* the operations work well or the whole set of changes is
> rejected.

The YANG PATCH media supersedes all HTTP methods. This means that you could
concentrate all your CRUD operations via YANG PATCH if you wish.

Discovering RESTCONF operations. RESTCONF, like NETCONF, supports managing
modeled *data* but also running *operations*. You can list the supported operations
in the /restconf/operations path:

```
$ curl -k -X GET https://csr1/restconf/operations \
    -u 'ntc:ntc123' \
    -H 'Accept: application/yang-data+json' \
    | python3 -m json.tool

{
    "ietf-restconf:operations": {
        "Cisco-IOS-XE-rpc:factory-reset":                    ❶
          "/restconf/operations/Cisco-IOS-XE-rpc:factory-reset",
        "ietf-event-notifications:establish-subscription": ❷
          "/restconf/operations/ietf-event-notifications:establish-subscription",
        "ietf-event-notifications:create-subscription":    ❷
          "/restconf/operations/ietf-event-notifications:create-subscription",
        # output omitted for brevity
    }
}
```

❶ Notice the various *sources*. Some are vendor specific, defined by Cisco in this
case.

❷ Other operations are defined by the IETF.

With this, we conclude the exploration of the RESTCONF interface. In "The Go
net/http Package" on page 464, we will come back to RESTCONF, but will use the
Go net/http package to automate it. After NETCONF and RESTCONF, it's time to
explore another network management interface: gNMI.

Using gRPC and gNMI

The gRPC Network Management Interface (gNMI) is, as its name indicates, a network management interface built on top of gRPC. It tries to overcome some limitations seen in the network management space, from SNMP to NETCONF, solving the two network management goals—configuration management and state retrieval—in a data-model-oriented way. Like NETCONF or RESTCONF, gNMI is a data model interface. However, it has characteristics that make it different:

- It uses gRPC as the transport protocol, instead of SSH or HTTP, and protobuf for encoding.
- It is defined and maintained by the OpenConfig consortium, led by Google. In contrast, NETCONF and RESTCONF are IETF standards.

gNMI is an alternative to other network management protocols that has gained popularity because of a fast initial development, and a capable and simple feature set. Most popular NOSs support it: Nokia Service Router Operating System (SROS) and SR Linux; Cisco IOS XR, IOS XE, and NX-OS; Arista EOS; Junos OS; and SONiC. We compare gNMI and the other data model interfaces in more detail in "Comparing NETCONF, RESTCONF, and gNMI" on page 446.

Complementary to gNMI, the gRPC Network Operations Interface (gNOI) (*https:// oreil.ly/tzy4x*), defines operational commands on network devices (e.g., ping or reboot). We don't cover gNOI in this book, but it follows the same principles as gNMI.

But before getting into the gNMI capabilities, we need to introduce the framework that makes it possible: gRPC.

Understanding gRPC

gRPC (initially called *Stubby*) was created by Google and evolved into a public project within the CNCF (*https://www.cncf.io*). Before getting into the characteristics of gRPC, let's understand the motivations behind its creation.

Google's application stack is built around distributed microservices. Each application can be implemented in a different programming language and requires high performing communications to execute RPC operations. gRPC was designed to support these requirements by being useful in multiple environments, including intra-data-center and end-user applications. gRPC offers low latency and extensibility to add extra features, such as load balancing or tracing.

gRPC design embraces several principles (*https://oreil.ly/q_lBT*), and the following are a few of the most significant ones:

High performance
> Fast and efficient communication between services is one core principle of gRPC design. For example, one significant change versus REST APIs is the use of static paths instead of dynamic ones. Dynamic paths include query parameters that need to be parsed before processing the call, which makes it slower and more complex. In gRPC, everything is part of the message body.

Payload agnostic
> The framework supports multiple content types for data serialization and encoding, such as Protocol Buffers, JSON, and XML. Because of the high-performance requirement, the most common one is Protocol Buffers. In this section, we will use this data format, introduced in Chapter 8.

Several communication patterns
> gRPC allows various communication patterns, from traditional request/response (*unary*) to unidirectional and bidirectional streaming. Also, it can work in asynchronous or synchronous mode to enable scalability and streaming processing.

Language independent
> gRPC clients and servers can be built in multiple popular languages, such as Python and Go, and also in cross-platform environments. In "A gRPC example" on page 435, we demonstrate this by implementing the client in Python, and the server in Go.

You can extend your gRPC knowledge at *https://grpc.io*.

Using gRPC as a transport protocol brings a lot of flexibility. It works over TCP without a predefined port—the port is defined by each application. Also, it comes without any predefined calls and messages. It's up to each application to define them. You will see a specific implementation for network management in "Understanding the gNMI interface" on page 440.

The best way to understand a protocol like gRPC is via an example, so let's dig in.

A gRPC example

Figure 10-3 shows a gRPC service example using a Python client and a Go server. The gRPC service is defined by the protobuf file from Example 8-12. All the files for these examples are located at *https://github.com/oreilly-npa-book/examples/tree/v2/ch10-apis/grpc*.

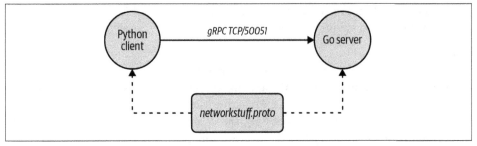

Figure 10-3. gRPC communication

The protobuf file (*networkstuff.proto*, defined in Chapter 8) contains the definition of the messages (the data types) and the service (the RPC operation). The only addition in comparison to Example 8-12 is the option go_package = "./network stuff"; to enable auto-generation of code for Go.

Running a gRPC server in Go.   One key feature of gRPC is its ability to create code bindings from the protobuf definition. This means that the messages and services will be transformed into type structures and functions, respectively. In the directory, the files have been autogenerated, so you don't need to do it. The only Go file manually defined is *server.go*; the rest of Go files in the folder are autogenerated by the protobuf compiler.

 To autogenerate gRPC bindings, you need to install the protocol buffer compiler. The installation for various platforms is described at *https://oreil.ly/1NtLG*.

We define and initialize a new Go module, grpc_example, that uses the autogenerated module networkstuff. The *server.go* file (part of the grpc_example module) uses the generated bindings to expose the gRPC service, which we analyze here in three parts.

Example 10-16 contains the beginning of the *server.go* file that will perform as the gRPC server.

Example 10-16. gRPC Go server.go, part 1

```
package main

import (
    "context"
    "encoding/json"
    "fmt"
    "log"
    "net"
```

```
    // implementation of gRPC for Go maintained by Google
    "google.golang.org/grpc"

    // our own package that was built before, and updated to point
    // to ./networkstuff via a replacement in the go.mod file
    pb "github.com/pkg/networkstuff"
)

// custom struct extending the pb.RouterServiceServer plus a
// local cache of Routers
type routerServiceServer struct {
    pb.UnimplementedRouterServiceServer
    localRouters []*pb.Router
}

// method necessary to match the interface definition for
// pb.RouterServiceServer, with the same signature
func (s *routerServiceServer) GetRouter(ctx context.Context,
    router_request *pb.RouterRequest) (*pb.Router, error) {
    // Use the local cache of Routers to match by the
    // router identifier
    for _, router := range s.localRouters {
        if router.Id == router_request.Id {
            return router, nil
        }
    }
    // No router was found, return a nameless router
    return &pb.Router{}, nil
}

// -> continues to part 2
```

The first part of the file contains the necessary imports, with special attention given to grpc and networkstuff. Then, the file defines the routerServiceServer struct, which is implementing the RouterServiceServer interface (from *network-stuff_grpc.pb.go*), plus a list of Routers objects to serve as a poor-man data store. The GetRouter method is required by the interface (Chapter 7 provides more details about implementing struct interfaces), and it returns the corresponding element from the localRouters list.

The gRPC package is part of Go included packages at *https://oreil.ly/7LeGx*, but it can also be found at *https://oreil.ly/WTNma*.

Continuing with the *server.go* file, Example 10-17 includes a server variable with all the data that the gRPC server will serve. The data could have been loaded from an external database or a JSON file, but we decided to directly initialize the objects.

Example 10-17. gRPC Go server.go, part 2

```
// -> comes from part 1
// server contains the data to expose via grpc
var server = &routerServiceServer{
    localRouters: []*pb.Router{
        &pb.Router{
            Id:       1,
            Hostname: "Router A",
            Interfaces: []*pb.Interface{
                &pb.Interface{
                    Id:          1000,
                    Description: "Gi 0/0/0",
                },
                &pb.Interface{
                    Id:          1001,
                    Description: "Gi 0/0/1",
                },
            },
        },
    // omitted for brevity
    },
}
// -> continues to part 3
```

Finally, in Example 10-18, a new TCP socket is defined and initialized to start serving TCP connections.

Example 10-18. gRPC Go server.go, part 3

```
// -> comes from part 2

func main() {
    // Create a TCP server listener in 50051 port
    lis, err := net.Listen("tcp", fmt.Sprintf("localhost:%d", 50051))
    // This is the common Go Pattern to handle errors
    if err != nil {
        log.Fatalf("failed to listen: %v", err)
    }
    // Bootstrap a gRPC server with defaults
    var opts []grpc.ServerOption
    grpcServer := grpc.NewServer(opts...)

    // Register the custom RouterServiceServer implementation to
    // the gRPC server
    pb.RegisterRouterServiceServer(grpcServer, server)
    // Attach the gRPC server to the TCP port 50051 opened before
    // to start serving requests.
    grpcServer.Serve(lis)
}
```

With the *server.go* file ready, you can start the gRPC server and move to another terminal while the server is listening for gRPC connections:

```
ch10-apis/grpc$ go run server.go
```

Running a gRPC client in Python.   gRPC can generate code bindings in multiple languages, so to complete the gRPC example, you will use Python to run the client gRPC requests. First, as we did for Go, it's necessary to autogenerate the Python bindings with the libraries grpcio and grpcio-tools. Using these libraries, we already generated the Python files that are available in the examples located at *https:// github.com/oreilly-npa-book/examples/tree/v2/ch10-apis/grpc*.

In Example 10-19, we demonstrate in the Python interpreter how to use the generated gRPC code to establish a client request toward the gRPC server (running in the other terminal).

Example 10-19. Python gRPC client usage

```
>>> import grpc                                            ❶
>>> import networkstuff_pb2_grpc as pb2_grpc               ❶
>>> import networkstuff_pb2 as pb2                         ❶
>>> channel = grpc.insecure_channel("localhost:50051")    ❷
>>> stub = pb2_grpc.RouterServiceStub(channel)            ❸
>>> router_request = pb2.RouterRequest(id=1)              ❹
>>> result = stub.GetRouter(router_request)              ❺
>>> type(result)
<class 'networkstuff_pb2.Router'>
>>> result                                                ❻
id: 1
hostname: "Router A"
interfaces {
  id: 1000
  description: "Gi 0/0/0"
}
interfaces {
  id: 1001
  description: "Gi 0/0/1"
}
```

❶ Imports the grpc library and the autogenerated bindings from the protobuf.

❷ Establishes a grpc *insecure* channel (a TCP connection) without certificate validation.

❸ Defines a stub (a single gRPC client on top of the TCP connection) by using the protobuf specification.

❹ Creates a proper request by using the protobuf specs embedded in a Python class and the id of the router to check.

❺ Using the stub and the router_request, we can call the predefined GetRouter method.

❻ Finally, we check that the response serialized with the protobuf specs and is of type Router.

We leave to you the exercise to create other gRPC requests, with existing IDs (id=2) or with nonexistent ones, to see how the client behaves. The expectations are to get Router B, or an empty router for another ID.

After this quick overview of gRPC, we start digging into the gNMI interface, which uses gRPC for network management.

Understanding the gNMI interface

gNMI defines a small set of gRPC operations: CapabilityRequest, GetRequest, SetRequest, and SubscribeRequest. These operations are defined in the *gnmi.proto* file, which is part of the OpenConfig project and can be found at *https://oreil.ly/pul-l*.

In "Comparing NETCONF, RESTCONF, and gNMI" on page 446, we dive into the differences between gNMI versus NETCONF and RESTCONF, but all these data-model-oriented interfaces share a lot of similarities, as you can see in Table 10-5, which compares the NETCONF and gNMI basic operations. More details about available gNMI operations can be found at the gNMI specification documentation (*https://oreil.ly/nc9Tm*).

Table 10-5. Mapping gNMI operations to NETCONF

gNMI	NETCONF
CapabilityRequest	hello
GetRequest	get/get-config
SetRequest	edit-config
SubscribeRequest	establish-subscription

gNMI has gained a lot of popularity in the industry because of the open source contributions by the OpenConfig consortium (mostly by Google), and in the observability realm because it provided the first implementation of dial-in streaming telemetry. You'll learn more about this in "Understanding model-driven telemetry" on page 448.

After this short introduction to gNMI, let's get hands-on and explore it.

Exploring gNMI with gNMIc

To explore gNMI, you will use the gNMIc CLI client. This open source client has been adopted under the OpenConfig umbrella and can be found at *https://oreil.ly/ d343N*.

In this section, you use the gNMIc CLI version, but in "The Open-Config gNMIc Go Package" on page 477, you will use the base Go package to create network automation scripts for interacting with gNMI.

First, you need to install gNMIc. You can use a downloaded bash script for macOS or Linux (or you could use gNMIc as a Docker container). For more information, check *https://gnmic.open config.net/install*; here's the command:

```
$ bash -c "$(curl -sL https://get-gnmic.openconfig.net)"
```

We use an Arista switch to explore gNMI. Because there is no standard TCP port for gNMI, the first thing to double-check is the TCP port being used (you can check it in the platform documentation or directly on the platform settings). The default port for Arista is TCP/6030, but you can change it if necessary.

Then, in Example 10-20, you can check which data models are supported behind the gNMI interface, using the `CapabilityRequest` operation (`capabilities`), equivalent to the NETCONF `hello`.

Example 10-20. gNMI capabilities

```
$ gnmic -a eos-spine1:6030 -u ntc -p ntc123 --insecure capabilities
gNMI version: 0.7.0
supported models:
  - openconfig-network-instance-types, OpenConfig working group, 0.9.3
  - iana-if-type, IANA,
  - openconfig-vlan, OpenConfig working group, 3.2.1
  - arista-vlan-deviations, Arista Networks <http://arista.com/>, 1.0.2
  - ietf-yang-types, IETF NETMOD (NETCONF Data Modeling Language) Working Group,
  // omitted models for brevity
supported encodings:
  - JSON
  - JSON_IETF
  - ASCII
```

Example 10-20 introduces two important topics to discuss:

Supported data models

    The supported data models define what can be changed/retrieved from the network device. In the output, you can notice data models coming from standards bodies (IANA and IETF), the OpenConfig consortium, and the vendor itself. Also, notice the versioning, relevant to understand the status of its definition.

Supported encoding

This is the encoding of the payload (not the transport encoding, which is proto-buf). It supports JSON and JSON_IETF (to support some serialization of YANG models), which allow structured data. It also supports ASCII encoding, used for semistructured CLI configuration, depending on the gNMI backend implementation.

You can find more information about these two topics at the gNMI specification on GitHub (*https://oreil.ly/YxUnw*).

gNMI GetRequest.   Once you know the interface capabilities, you can do your first gNMI Get operation. You can retrieve the actual configuration state from the running configuration, targeting the config container in an OpenConfig data model: /inter faces/interface/config. gNMI paths are a simplified variant of the XPath syntax. These paths can be obtained by observing the YANG data models or by using tools to extract paths from them—e.g., Cisco YANG Suite (*https://oreil.ly/WlojA*).

OpenConfig and IETF advocated for different styles of data model organization. In OpenConfig, a model node has two containers, *config* and *state*, to represent the intended and the operational state, respectively. In contrast, The IETF proposed to split both configurations into different data stores. There is more information in Rob Shakir's blog post "OpenConfig and IETF YANG Models: Can they converge?" (*https://rob.sh/post/215/*).

In Example 10-21, the configuration contains only a few *leaves* (mtu, name, and type), because only a few items are configured (the defaults are not shown). This is something that depends on each data-model specification.

Example 10-21. Get config interface with gNMIc

```
$ gnmic -a eos-spine1:6030 -u ntc -p ntc123 --insecure  --gzip \
    get \
    --path '/interfaces/interface/config'

[
  {
    "source": "eos-spine1:6030",
    "timestamp": 1664428366933949209,
    "time": "2022-09-29T05:12:46.933949209Z",
    "updates": [
      {
        "Path": "interfaces/interface[name=Management0]/config",
```

```
      "values": {
        "interfaces/interface/config": {
          "openconfig-interfaces:mtu": 0,
          "openconfig-interfaces:name": "Management0",
          "openconfig-interfaces:type": "iana-if-type:ethernetCsmacd"
        }
      }
    }
  ]
}
]
```

In this example, you see only one interface, Management0. If more were present, you could get the same behavior using XPath (filtering by the interface name) and target this specific interface with the path interfaces/interface[name=Management0]/config.

Now, instead of targeting the *config* container, we target the *state* one. Besides the interface configuration (with default values), the interface stats will be returned:

```
$ gnmic -a eos-spine1:6030 -u ntc -p ntc123 --insecure --gzip \
    get \
    --path '/interfaces/interface/state'
[
  {
    "source": "eos-spine1:6030",
    "timestamp": 1664428346403170400,
    "time": "2022-09-29T05:12:26.4031704Z",
    "updates": [
      {
        "Path": "interfaces/interface[name=Management0]/state",
        "values": {
          "interfaces/interface/state": {
            "arista-intf-augments:inactive": false,
            "openconfig-interfaces:admin-status": "UP",
            "openconfig-interfaces:counters": {
              "in-unicast-pkts": "1694",
              "out-unicast-pkts": "4410"
              // omitted output for brevity
            },
            "openconfig-interfaces:ifindex": 999999,
            "openconfig-interfaces:last-change": "1664343413005553920",
            "openconfig-interfaces:mtu": 0,
            "openconfig-interfaces:name": "Management0",
            "openconfig-interfaces:oper-status": "UP",
            "openconfig-interfaces:type": "iana-if-type:ethernetCsmacd"
          }
        }
      }
    ]
  }
]
```

gNMI SetRequest. Next, use the SetRequest operation to change the configuration of the interface. As you did in NETCONF and RESTCONF, when updating data-model-based configurations, you need to understand the data model. You can check the OpenConfig interfaces data model (*https://oreil.ly/ibP6F*), and you will discover that it supports a description attribute that was not retrieved in the previous Get examples because it was not set yet, and there is no default value. Our goal is to define the interface description to New Description:

```
$ gnmic -a eos-spine1:6030 -u ntc -p ntc123 --insecure --gzip \
    set \
    --update-path '/interfaces/interface[name=Management0]/config/description' \
    --update-value 'New Description'
```

Notice the use of set instead of get and the new parameters: update-path and update-value. In this case, we use XPath filtering to target a specific interface (if not, you would be updating *all* the interfaces with the same description) and the corresponding value. When the SetRequest is executed successfully, you receive a response confirming the operation.

Now, if you retrieve the configuration as you did in Example 10-21, the new attribute will show up:

```
[
  {
    "source": "eos-spine1:6030",
    "timestamp": 1664428969195249733,
    "time": "2022-09-29T05:22:49.195249733Z",
    "updates": [
      {
        "Path": "interfaces/interface[name=Management0]/config",
        "values": {
          "interfaces/interface/config": {
            "openconfig-interfaces:description": "New Description",
            "openconfig-interfaces:mtu": 0,
            "openconfig-interfaces:name": "Management0",
            "openconfig-interfaces:type": "iana-if-type:ethernetCsmacd"
          }
        }
      }
    ]
  }
]
```

However, not all the attributes are configurable because of dependencies on the platform. For instance, the mtu attribute is not configurable in this Arista platform, and if you try to update it, you will receive an error, as you can see next:

```
$ gnmic -a eos-spine1:6030 -u ntc -p ntc123 --insecure --gzip \
    set \
    --update-path '/interfaces/interface[name=Management0]/config/mtu' \
    --update-value '1400'
```

```
target "eos-spine1:6030" set request failed: target "eos-spine1:6030" SetRequest failed:
  rpc error: code = Aborted desc = failed to apply: Unavailable command (not supported
  on this hardware platform) (at token 1: 'mtu'): CLI command 3 of 5 'l2 mtu 1400'
  failed: invalid command
CLI Commands:
1 interface Management0
2 l2 mtu 1400
3 exit

Error: one or more requests failed
```

> This error message also shows something interesting—what is hap-
> pening behind the scenes. Every platform implements the RPC
> operations differently. In this case, you see from the CLI com-
> mands executed that the device is translating the YANG data model
> changes into CLI commands.

gNMI Subscribe. gNMI was the first data-model interface to support data-model-
driven telemetry (dial-in) with the subscribe operation. We go deep on telemetry in
"Understanding model-driven telemetry" on page 448, but here you have an example
of subscribing to the interface counters, targeting the counters' *path* in the prefix:

```
$ gnmic -a eos-spine1:6030 -u ntc -p ntc123  --insecure \
  subscribe \
  --path "/interfaces/interface/state/counters"

{
  "source": "eos-spine1:6030",
  "subscription-name": "default-1664428777",
  "timestamp": 1664428707256105665,
  "time": "2022-09-29T05:18:27.256105665Z",
  "prefix": "interfaces/interface[name=Management0]/state/counters",
  "updates": [
    {
      "Path": "in-octets",
      "values": {
        "in-octets": 141271
      }
    },
    {
      "Path": "in-unicast-pkts",
      "values": {
        "in-unicast-pkts": 1779
      }
    }
  ]
}
# other outputs omitted for brevity
```

The subscribe operation keeps a session established, from the client, to get updates
on the data model. In this case, we are subscribed to updates on the interface

counters, but you could also subscribe to the interface operational status or the BGP session establishment, and so on. The updates can be sampled periodically or triggered when the value changes, so you get notified only when something happens.

As you may have already concluded after reviewing NETCONF, RESTCONF, and gNMI, these protocols and interfaces share common concepts but also have differences. To make this content easier to digest, we spell out the differences next.

Comparing NETCONF, RESTCONF, and gNMI

At this point, you likely have questions about the differences between the three interfaces using a data-model-driven approach (NETCONF, RESTCONF, and gNMI). In this section, we want to give you more insight into how they are related.

Everything started with NETCONF (the first RFC published in 2006) trying to address the limitations of SNMP to manage network configurations. At that moment, SNMP was widely used to monitor network's operational state, but it was not adopted for network management. Because of this, as we explained in "Using NETCONF" on page 410, new ideas were introduced: multiple data stores, RPC operations, effective config management in transactions, and the use of data models to update/retrieve configuration data and retrieve operational data.

Notice that we stress configuration management as the primary use case for NET-CONF. Implicitly, it was acknowledging that the SNMP monitoring approach, ported to NETCONF, was good enough. However, later, new concerns about a better way to retrieve operational data appeared, and the IETF started (around 2014–2015) to get requirements to implement streaming telemetry (a continuous and customized stream of data from a YANG data store), which we present in "Understanding model-driven telemetry" on page 448.

Around the same time (2014), the OpenConfig consortium was founded and led by Google, focused on implementing streaming telemetry as one of the main drivers of gNMI, a new network management interface defined as an open source project (with the first commit in 2017), instead of an internet standard. For the rest of the functionalities, it used NETCONF ideas as a reference with a simpler implementation.

More or less in parallel (2017), the IETF created the RESTCONF interface that brought together the NETCONF approach and the simpler, well-known RESTful API paradigm to promote more adoption of data-model-driven management when not all the NETCONF requirements are needed.

Table 10-6 compares the three interfaces by focusing on their main differences.

Table 10-6. *Comparing data-model-driven interfaces*

	NETCONF	RESTCONF	gNMI
Encoding	XML	JSON or XML	protobuf or JSON
Transport	SSH	HTTP/TLS	gRPC over HTTP/2
Transaction scope	Network-wide	Single-target, single-shot	Single-target, single-shot, sequenced

Let's take a closer look at these three main differences:

Encoding

NETCONF used the most popular encoding when it was defined (XML), and RESTCONF, even though still supporting XML (likely for reusability from NET-CONF scripts), promoted JSON as a more popular encoding (and easier to read). However, gNMI chose protobuf because this binary encoding reduced the payload when compared to XML. Streaming operational data was an important use case for this interface, and this creates a lot of network traffic.

Transport

NETCONF can support multiple transport protocols, but the most common one when it was defined was SSH, and it became the de facto one. RESTCONF lever-aged HTTP to become yet another REST API, and gNMI adopted the Google internal protocol gRPC to support protobuf encoding.

Transaction scope

NETCONF came from operator best practices whereby the network itself is used to test and deploy configurations that can affect multiple devices, so the network-wide transaction scope was implemented. RESTCONF, to adhere to REST principles, doesn't support state and can deal with only one target at a time, without any relevant operation sequence. gNMI is the simplest of all, assuming a specific order of all the operations. This simple approach comes from software-oriented teams managing infrastructure, where the configuration validation is most likely done out of the box, in a development environment.

Next, so you can better understand the interfaces, we compare the development lifecycle of the organizations behind them, which are also developing vendor-neutral data models.

Network interfaces development lifecycle

NETCONF and RESTCONF are defined and promoted by the IETF (*https://www.ietf.org*). On the other side, gNMI is developed under the umbrella of the Open-Config community (*https://www.openconfig.net*). Each group has a completely differ-ent way of working, which affects how these protocols and interfaces are defined, developed, and adopted:

IETF

Its mission—defined in RFC 3936 (*https://oreil.ly/XtEg7*)—is to develop technical recommendations to design, use, and manage the internet. This is done via an open process, with volunteers, and rough consensus from multiple parts.

OpenConfig

This working group of network operators and vendors is focused on building a vendor-independent software layer for managing network devices. It operates as an open source project, with direct contributions.

Both have the common goal to create better ways to manage networks. However, the difference is in the way they achieve it. IETF's process of proposal, approval, and implementation usually takes longer than the same process under OpenConfig. In open source projects with strong leadership, the proposal, review, and adoption process leads to a faster release cycle. A standard addresses diverse use cases and will be stable for a while, but when you work on an open source project, you can move quickly to solve more concrete use cases and leave the door open for future changes. This capacity to deliver, especially for streaming telemetry, was one of the key factors for the adoption and popularity of the gNMI interface.

Having multiple options to solve a problem is nothing new in the networking world. Successful nonstandard solutions have been adopted multiple times, and afterward, these solutions (with small differences) were adopted by IETF (e.g., NetFlow and Internet Protocol Flow Information Export, or IPFIX). The experience says that both could likely coexist, solving different usage approaches.

OpenConfig and IETF are working on more than network management interfaces. A main focus of both organizations is to implement the right data models to describe the network information needed for configuration and operational validation. These models should work well under any of the interfaces—for instance, using an Open-Config data model under the NETCONF interface, as you saw in "NETCONF with Cisco IOS XE" on page 423. However, as we mentioned, the structure of the data models differ in how the intended and operational data is organized.

Last, we will delve into streaming telemetry.

Understanding model-driven telemetry

Current large-scale network architectures have uncovered the operational limitations of SNMP for network monitoring. Even though SNMP is still in use, its model to retrieve data via a *poll* method, with the management server *asking* for data every time, was adding delay and extra processing to get data continuously.

These performance limitations, together with the adoption of data-model manage-ment (e.g., NETCONF or gNMI), led to the definition of *model-driven telemetry*. It adopts a *push* model to stream data from network devices continuously, providing near real-time access to operational data. Now, instead of *asking* for data, the man-agement applications can *subscribe* to specific data from the supported data models defined with YANG. The retrieved data is structured and can be published at a defined cadence or as it changes.

With model-driven telemetry, you decide which data you need, when you need it, and where to send (or receive) it. You can subscribe to telemetry streams in two ways: dial-in and dial-out (represented in Figure 10-4).

Dial-in
    This is a dynamic model: an external application opens a session to the network device and establishes one or more subscriptions (to different parts of the data store) over the same session. The network devices send operation data for as long as the session stays up.

Dial-out
    This is a configured model: the subscriptions are configured on the network device in advance using any of the available interfaces, and it's up to the device to open a telemetry session to the receiver. If this session goes down, the network device will open a new one.

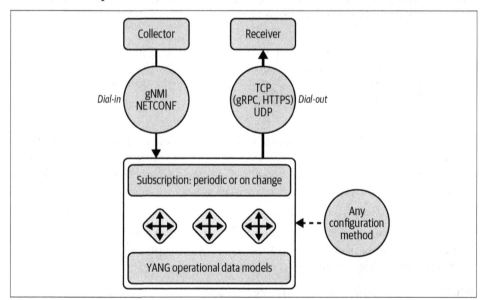

Figure 10-4. Model-driven telemetry

gNMI implemented the first streaming telemetry via the dial-in model, and it's still the most widely adopted one. However, the dial-out model adds some benefits:

- Reduces a network device's exposure to external threats as the connection is initiated from the device itself and avoids firewall configurations to let access in.

- Collectors can be stateless; they need to only listen and store the collected data. The control is on the configuration management system that created the subscription on the network device.

Nowadays, both NETCONF and gNMI support the dial-in model. Dial-out mode is simply a configuration setting, which can be done via any configuration interface (including CLI), and the data is exported over a transport protocol (TCP or UDP).

The first model-driven telemetry implementation was the gNMI `SubscribeRequest` operation, a dial-in mode. This has been, for a long time, one of the key benefits of gNMI versus NETCONF, which took more time to come up with its implementation definition. At the time of this writing, the adoption of streaming telemetry is much more mature in gNMI, which is widely adopted by most vendors. NETCONF dial-in and dial-out are still in their early stages.

Dial-out telemetry has some incipient implementations—for instance, by Cisco and Juniper, using gRPC as the transport protocol. In parallel, the IETF is working on standards grouped as YANG Push, UDP and HTTPS/TCP transport options, and support for JSON and CBOR encoding.

Concise Binary Object Representation or CBOR (*https://cbor.io*) standardized in RFC 8949 (*https://oreil.ly/UFjnD*), is a binary data format based on JSON that supports schema definition directly with the YANG language.

Model-driven telemetry has prioritized TCP as a transport protocol over UDP (used by SNMP) for providing more reliable data transfer, and with nonrepudiation. However, UDP support provides some benefits in highly intense event traffic, such as in sampling mode when TCP benefits are not mandatory.

As we will explore in Chapter 14 when discussing the role of model-driven telemetry in a network automation strategy, telemetry is usually combined with message brokers to distribute data from the collectors, adding some features such as data schema validation, versioning, or routing.

Which solution will prevail is hard to predict. gNMI is well established and supported by a lot of vendors. On the other side, YANG Push supports more use cases (e.g., more encoding options) and comes from a standardization body (IETF) that is important for some network industry actors (e.g., service providers).

Now that we've explained the API interfaces available to manage network devices and controllers, you must understand how to automate them via these APIs. We'll now take a look at using Python and Go to automate these interfaces, and also SSH.

Using Network APIs for Automation

As we've stated, the tools for *exploring* and *learning* to use an API differ from the tools used to *consume* an API within a programmatic solution. Thus far, we've looked at cURL for exploring HTTP-based APIs, an interactive NETCONF over SSH session for exploring the use of NETCONF, and gNMIc for exploring gNMI. In this part of the chapter, we'll look at how to use Python and Go to automate network devices, using some popular libraries:

Python Requests
> An intuitive and popular HTTP library for Python. This is the library we will use for automating devices and controllers with both RESTful HTTP-based APIs and non-RESTful HTTP-based APIs.

Go net/http
> A built-in package to serve as an HTTP client or server. Introduced in Chapter 7, it's similar to Python Requests, and we will use it to demonstrate how to interact with RESTCONF.

Python ncclient
> This is a NETCONF client for Python, so we will use it for automating devices using NETCONF.

Go OpenConfig gNMIc
> We used this gNMI client as a CLI in the previous section. Here, we will use the package directly in Go applications to interact via the gNMI interface.

Python Netmiko
> This is a network-first SSH client for Python. This is the library we will use for automating devices via native SSH for devices without programmatic APIs.

 Even though we cover multiple APIs in this chapter, it is meant to be read from start to finish and not as API documentation for any given API. All the scripts created in this chapter have loose error handling because we are prioritizing simplicity to show the ideas instead of creating production-ready code. Be aware that the examples shown depend on the library's version. The syntax and signature can change from one version to another.

Let's start by looking at the Requests library and communicating with HTTP-based APIs.

The Python Requests Library

You've seen how to make HTTP-based API calls from the command line with cURL, or maybe you used the Postman GUI. These are great mechanisms for learning how to use a given API—but realistically, to write a script or a program that helps automate network devices, you need to be able to make API calls from within a script or program. In this section, we introduce the Python Requests library, which simplifies working with web-based APIs.

To enable an easy mapping between the previous section and this one, we reuse the same examples from "Exploring HTTP-based APIs with cURL" on page 402, the Cisco Meraki API, and the Arista eAPI. This section is meant to be read from start to finish, as the core focus is getting started with using the Requests library.

> To install Requests, you can use `pip3` within your virtual environment. Remember that you can review basic Python concepts in Chapter 6. Here's the installation command:
>
> ```
> $ pip3 install requests
> $ pip3 list | grep requests
> requests                  2.26.0
> ```

Automating the Meraki API with Requests

Let's dive in and take a look at our first example using Requests. We're going to create a complete Python script to retrieve the first network, from the first organization, from a Cisco Meraki account. We've already executed this same GET request with cURL in Examples 10-2 and 10-3. Remember to check the Meraki API documentation (*https://oreil.ly/rzR5F*) if needed.

Now, in Example 10-22, we focus on the first part of a script to retrieve the organizations available in Cisco Meraki.

Example 10-22. Using Requests to get Meraki organizations

```
#!/usr/bin/env python3

# The Python Requests library is used to issue and work HTTP-based systems.
import requests

# This executes if our script is being run directly.
if __name__ == "__main__":
    # This token is taken from Cisco Developer Hub to experiment with the API
    my_token = "6bec40cf957de430a6f1f2baa056b99a4fac9ea0"

    # This statement creates a Python dictionary for the HTTP request
    # headers that are going to use in the API calls.  The first two
    # headers we are setting are Content-Type and Accept.
    # The last one uses a custom Meraki header for authentication
```

```
headers = {
    "Accept": "application/json",
    "Content-Type": "application/json",
    "X-Cisco-Meraki-API-Key": my_token,
}

# The URL is saved as a variable called base_url to modularize our
# code and simplify the next statement.
base_url = "https://api.meraki.com/api/v1"

# In the Requests library, there is a function per HTTP verb, and in
# this example we are issuing a GET request, so we are therefore
# using the get function. We pass two objects into the get function.
# The first  object passed in must be the URL, and the others should be
# keyword arguments (key=value pairs). Then, we pass the proper headers.
response = requests.get(f"{base_url}/organizations", headers=headers)
```

At the end of this Python script, the `response` variable contains the response from the Meraki API. You could reproduce the same steps in an interactive Python session, as noted in Chapter 6. Actually, it's a great idea to try this to better understand the content of the `response` variable. So, let's run the previous script in the interactive interpreter, using the `-i` flag. It is a great way to test and troubleshoot:

```
ch10-apis/python_requests$ python3 -i get_networks.py
# The interactive execution leave us at the end of our script, after the
# response = requests.get(f"{base_url}/organizations", headers=headers)
>>> response
<Response [200]>
```

The `response` variable contains a 200 HTTP response, so you should assume everything worked as expected. Indeed, one important piece of data is missing: where is the content of the response, containing the *organizations*?

Being in the Python interactive interpreter session, you can inspect the `response` with `dir()`, displaying all attributes and methods of a given object:

```
>>> dir(response)
[ # output omitted for brevity
 'apparent_encoding', 'close', 'connection', 'content',
 'cookies', 'elapsed', 'encoding', 'headers', 'history',
 'json', 'links', 'next', 'ok', 'raise_for_status', 'raw', 'reason',
 'request', 'status_code', 'text', 'url']
```

From all the attributes and methods available in the `response`, we will review two: `status_code` and `json`.

The `status_code` attribute gives us access to the HTTP response code as an integer:

```
>>> print(response.status_code)
200
```

The `json()` method returns the response content as a `dict`, decoding the JSON contained in the `text` attribute (which stores the actual response):

```
>>> response.json()
[
  {
    'id': '573083052582915028',
    'name': 'Next Meraki Org',
    'url': 'https://n18.meraki.com/o/PoiDucs/manage/organization/overview',
    'api': {
      'enabled': True
    },
    'licensing': {
      'model': 'co-term'
    },
    'cloud': {
      'region': {
        'name': 'North America'
      }
    }
  },
  # other entries omitted for brevity
]
>>>
```

You can start using this output by saving it as a variable and extracting the value of the name key from the first organization:

```
>>> organizations = response.json()
>>> type(organizations)
<type 'list'>
>>> organizations[0]["name"]
'Next Meraki Org'
```

In our script, we also store the response data in an `organizations` variable, and you can resume the script that will get the *networks* from a given organization, as shown in Example 10-23.

Example 10-23. Using Requests to get Meraki networks

```
# Continues from the previous code snippet

# We pick the id from the first organization to later gather the related networks
first_organization_id = organizations[0]["id"]  ❶

# Similar get request, composing the URL with the organization id
response = requests.get(
    f"{base_url}/organizations/{first_organization_id}/networks", headers=headers
)

networks = response.json()                        ❷
```

❶ We pick the identifier from the first available organization, accessing the 0 index in the list of organizations.

❷ If we explore the content of `networks`, we will see another dictionary—this time containing the network data from the Meraki API.

Let's continue to build on this; you are now going to create a new network (within an organization) by using Requests, as in Example 10-4. As you may guess, you need to only extend the previous script, adding the same content used in the cURL example: update the URL, update the HTTP request type, and send data in the body of the request, as we do in Example 10-24.

Example 10-24. Using Requests to create a Meraki network

```
# Continues from the previous code snippet
# first_organization_id comes from the previous script

# json library is used to encode a dictionary object as a JSON string
import json

# Payload contains the data necessary to define the expected
# data to create a new network in the API
payload = {
    "name": "my brand new automated network",
    "productTypes": ["switch"],
}

# Using the post method instead of get to create an object
response = requests.post( ❶
    f"{base_url}/organizations/{first_organization_id}/networks",
    headers=headers,
    data=json.dumps(payload)
)

print(response.json())
```

❶ Pay attention to the HTTP verb being used. This particular request uses the `post()` function as a resource is being created. To update a resource, you'd use the `patch()` function, and to replace a resource, you'd use `put()`. You'll see these functions in more examples later in the chapter.

Let's focus on how to send data in the body of the HTTP request. This is where you need to differentiate between a Python dictionary and a JSON string. While you work with dictionaries in Python to construct the required body, this is sent over the wire as a JSON string. To convert the dictionary to a well-formed JSON string, you use the `dumps()` function from the `json` module. This function takes a dictionary and converts it to a JSON string. You finally take the string object and pass it over the wire by assigning it to the `data` key being passed to the `post()` function.

We typically know which payload data is required to create/update an API resource by checking the API documentation. Some of the attributes will use some defaults, but for the rest, we need to provide some data. In the example, name looks like an obvious mandatory piece of data. But productTypes could be missed, assuming that it could be a default product type. In these cases, the API response should provide a useful error message to guide you, pointing out what is missing in the request payload.

Finally, when running the script, you get a response (from the POST). It provides a new network with the name and the productTypes defined before, plus the rest of the parameters automatically assigned in creation:

```
ch10-apis/python_requests$ python3 create_network.py
{
    'id': 'N_573083052583238204',
    'organizationId': '573083052582915028',
    'productTypes': ['switch'],
    'url': 'https://n18.meraki.com/my-brand-new-aut/n/vAQKbcs/manage/usage/list',
    'name': 'my brand new automated network',
    'timeZone': 'America/Los_Angeles',
    'enrollmentString': None,
    'tags': [],
    'notes': None,
    'isBoundToConfigTemplate': False
}
```

You have learned about using the Python Requests library for the Cisco Meraki API. Next, we continue exploring Requests but for the Arista eAPI (as in the cURL examples).

Consuming eAPI in a Python script

We're now going to look at Arista's eAPI. As you learned in "Understanding non-RESTful HTTP-based APIs" on page 408, as you go through the next examples with eAPI, keep the following points in mind:

- eAPI is a non-RESTful HTTP-based API. In other words, it's an HTTP-based API that doesn't follow all the principles of REST. An HTTP POST is used no matter which operation is being performed—even if show commands are used, a POST is still used. Specifically, it uses the JSON-RPC protocol to communicate between you (the client) and the switch (the server).

- Remember POST requests require data to be sent in the data payload of the request. This is where solid API tools and documentation come into play.

- The URL format for eAPI API calls is always *http(s)://<ip-address-eos>/command-api*.

Arista switches have a built-in tool called the *Command Explorer* that you could leverage to learn the required structure of the payload object. The API documentation provides details about this tool.

We start with a basic Python script in Example 10-25. This code uses the Requests library to communicate to the Arista API (eAPI), executing the show vlan brief CLI command. This command should return the VLAN information with the device. At the end of the script, the code will output the response and the HTTP status code.

Example 10-25. Using Python Requests with Arista eAPI

```
import json
import sys
import requests
from requests.auth import HTTPBasicAuth

if __name__ == "__main__":

    # requests class to create the basic authentication header
    auth = HTTPBasicAuth('ntc', 'ntc123') ❶

    url = 'http://eos-spine1/command-api' ❷

    # payload expected by the API
    payload = {
        "jsonrpc": "2.0",
        "method": "runCmds",
        "params": {
            "format": "json",
            "timestamps": False,
            "cmds": [
                "show vlan brief"
            ],
            "version": 1
        },
        "id": "EapiExplorer-1"
    }

    # Even though we retrieve data with the "show vlan brief",
    # the API uses the POST method
    response = requests.post(url, data=json.dumps(payload), auth=auth) ❸

    # Helper output onscreen to show the status code, and the response
    print(f'STATUS CODE: {response.status_code}')
    print(f'RESPONSE: {json.dumps(response.json(), indent=4)}')
```

❶ HTTPBasicAuth class, from the Requests library, to create the basic authentication format (using a Base64 encoding).

❷ Using an *http* endpoint is not recommended for production. If we use a self-signed certificate or unverified HTTPS connection (adding `verify=False` to the requests method), we will receive a warning, which can be disabled with `requests.packages.urllib3.disable_warnings()`.

❸ Even though we are *retrieving* data, the HTTP method used is POST. So, it requires a *payload*, which defines several parameters required by the API.

When you execute the script, it should give a similar output:

```
ch10-apis/python_requests$ python3 eapi-requests.py
STATUS CODE: 200
RESPONSE:
{                    ❶
    "jsonrpc": "2.0",
    "id": "EapiExplorer-1",
    "result": [ ❷
        {
            "sourceDetail": "",
            "vlans": {
                "1": {
                    "status": "active",
                    "name": "default",
                    "interfaces": {
                        "Ethernet1": {
                            "privatePromoted": false
                        },
                        # Omitted other interfaces for brevity
                    },
                    "dynamic": false
                },
                "20": {
                    "status": "active",
                    "name": "VLAN0020",
                    "interfaces": {},
                    "dynamic": false
                },
                "30": {
                    "status": "active",
                    "name": "VLAN0030",
                    "interfaces": {},
                    "dynamic": false
                }
            }
        }
    ]
}
```

❶ The response is a nested JSON object, as expected.

❷ The output of the commands (only one in this example) is a list of dictionaries. There would be a list element for each command executed.

It's noticeable that, even though you send a CLI command (show vlan brief), the format of the response content is JSON. This makes it much easier to interact with the API programmatically. However, if you are interested in the traditional text CLI output, you can specify it with "format": "text" in the payload, and the response would contain an output key with a string:

```
RESPONSE: {
    "jsonrpc": "2.0",
    "id": "EapiExplorer-1",
    "result": [
        {
            "output": "VLAN  Name                              Status     Ports\n
            ---- -------------------------------- --------- -------------------"
            # output omitted for brevity
        }
    ]
}
```

Next, we go a bit further with a more elaborate example to show the potential of automating the network via API-based scripts.

Using eAPI to autoconfigure interface descriptions based on LLDP data.
Let's continue to use eAPI to build something a little more useful. How about a Python script that auto-configures interface descriptions for Ethernet interfaces based on LLDP neighbors for two Arista spine switches?

To do this, you *should* modularize the script to support multiple devices as well as have a simple way to send multiple API calls without requiring multiple payload objects in the script. Our goal is to autoconfigure interface descriptions such that they will look like the following (this is an example, and you will see the actual LLDP data and the final description later):

```
interface Ethernet2
    description Connects to interface Ethernet2 on neighbor eos-leaf1.ntc.com
    no switchport
!
interface Ethernet3
    description Connects to interface Ethernet2 on neighbor eos-leaf2.ntc.com
    no switchport
!
```

To easily digest the code, we split it into three parts so you can progressively understand the complete example.

First, in Example 10-26, you create the issue_request() function, which takes two arguments: the target device and the commands. The data is the only data in the requests' operation. So, with this helper function, you could later pass different target devices and different commands to obtain the response (already converted from

JSON to a Python object). This is a good example of the Don't Repeat Yourself (DRY) software development principle.

Example 10-26. Wrapping requests in a helper function

```python
import json
import sys
import requests
from requests.auth import HTTPBasicAuth

# Helper method to issue "commands" to a "device", and return the result
def issue_request(device, commands):  ❶
    """Make API request to EOS device returning JSON response."""
    payload = {
        "jsonrpc": "2.0",
        "method": "runCmds",
        "params": {
            "format": "json",
            "timestamps": False,
            "cmds": commands,
            "version": 1
        },
        "id": "EapiExplorer-1"
    }

    response = requests.post(
        'http://{}/command-api'.format(device),
        data=json.dumps(payload),
        auth=HTTPBasicAuth('ntc', 'ntc123')
    )

    return response.json()

# continues in the next example
```

❶ The code of this function is exactly the same as Example 10-25, but has been modularized for reusability.

Next, in Example 10-27, we leverage the `issue_request()` function to get the specific information we want from the API response (in this case, `lldpNeighbors`). This implies knowledge of the data structure from the response, which you can get by experience or from the documentation.

Example 10-27. Extracting LLDP neighbors from the response

```python
# continues from the previous example

def get_lldp_neighbors(device):
    """Get list of neighbors

    Sample response for a single neighbor:
```

```
    {
      "ttl": 120,
      "neighborDevice": "eos-spine2.ntc.com",
      "neighborPort": "Ethernet2",
      "port": "Ethernet2"
    }
    """
    # Define the target methods
    commands = ['show lldp neighbors']
    response = issue_request(device, commands)
    # Extract the neighbors' data from the result of the first and only command
    # and return it as a list of dictionaries
    return response['result'][0]['lldpNeighbors']

# continues in the next example
```

Creating readable code takes practice, but in Example 10-27 you can observe two useful approaches:

- Using self-descriptive naming: get_lldp_neighbors clearly defines its intent
- Leveraging function docstrings to explain the function's purpose—in this case, the format of the response

Finally, in Example 10-28, we add another helper function, configure_inter faces(), and the main function to run the script. The configure_interfaces() function does exactly what it describes: takes the list of neighbors, and with *configuration* commands, updates the description of the interfaces. In the main function, you define all the target devices to iterate on and perform two operations: get the LLDP information, and configure the interfaces description accordingly.

Example 10-28. Configuring the interfaces description with LLDP information

```
# continues from the previous example

def configure_interfaces(device, neighbors):
    """Configure interfaces in a single API call per device."""
    command_list = ['enable', 'configure']
    for neighbor in neighbors:
        local_interface = neighbor['port']
        if local_interface.startswith('Eth'):
            # Excluding Management as it has multiple neighbors
            description = (
              f"Connects to interface {neighbor['neighborPort']} on neighbor "
              f"{neighbor['neighborDevice']}"
            )
            description = 'description ' + description
            interface = f'interface {local_interface}'
            # Extending the list of commands, in the proper order
            command_list.extend([interface, description])
```

```
    # Retrieve the output from the commands created from the neighbors
    response = issue_request(device, command_list)

if __name__ == "__main__":
    # device names are FQDNs
    devices = ['eos-spine1', 'eos-spine2']
    for device in devices:
        neighbors = get_lldp_neighbors(device)
        configure_interfaces(device, neighbors)
        print('Auto-configured Interfaces for {}'.format(device))
```

 Going through this example, you may be wondering if you could have organized the code differently. Maybe you could combine `get_lldp_neighbors` with the `configure_interfaces()` function, to get a bigger one. Or you could call `issue_request` out of the other functions, in the main code. The point here is that you have a myriad of options to create valid code. Choose one, experiment with it, and look for better patterns toward reusability and readability, while keeping it simple.

Let's run the script that will update the interfaces' descriptions according to the LLDP neighbor:

```
ch10-apis/python_requests$ python3 eapi-autoconfigure-lldp.py
Auto-configured Interfaces for eos-spine1
Auto-configured Interfaces for eos-spine2
```

Using the Requests Python library is an easy way to interact with APIs in your Python applications. However, to make it even simpler, some APIs provide their own libraries, the SDKs. We will give a quick glance at SDKs next.

Using API SDKs

An *API SDK* is a software package that abstracts access to an API by using functions, methods, and/or classes. It allows faster development because it comes with all the common conventions implemented. Therefore, you don't need to reinvent the wheel every time, reducing development time. The SDK makes the code simpler and more readable. On the other hand, it could introduce some constraints due to non-implemented features available in the API or introduce library dependencies, increasing the footprint of your application.

Most API platforms offer SDKs in the most popular languages in their user community. Both APIs explored in the previous section offer Python SDKs:

- Cisco Meraki (*https://oreil.ly/YCfkp*)
- Arista eAPI (*https://oreil.ly/retLy*)

It's not the purpose of this book to document using any specific SDK, but showing how an SDK is used enables you to see what one looks like. For detailed information about an SDK, check its reference docs page.

Exploring the Meraki API SDK. Using the Meraki API SDK instead of the Requests library, you will get the same output as in Example 10-22 without having to know about some API conventions. For instance, you don't need to know about the custom authentication header the API expects. This is also useful for maintainability because if this header key changes, you don't need to update your code.

Use `pip3` to install the Meraki API SDK:

```
$ pip3 install meraki
$ pip3 list | grep meraki
meraki                     1.25.0
```

After importing the library, you have to instantiate the class `meraki.DashboardAPI`, which contains all the methods to interact with the API. This initialization requires only the API key used before, but not the URL or the authentication header key, as these are implicitly defined by the library:

```
>>> import meraki
>>>
>>> meraki_client = meraki.DashboardAPI(
...     api_key="6bec40cf957de430a6f1f2baa056b99a4fac9ea0")
2022-10-01 16:18:28 meraki: INFO > Meraki dashboard API session initialized with ...
# output omitted for brevity
>>>
```

Then you can retrieve the organization, as you did in Example 10-22. Instead of crafting the HTTP request, you use the `getOrganizations()` method in `meraki_client.organizations`:

```
>>> my_orgs = meraki_client.organizations.getOrganizations()
2022-10-01 16:18:49 meraki: INFO > GET https://api.meraki.com/api/v1/organizations
2022-10-01 16:18:50 meraki: INFO > GET https://n392.meraki.com/api/v1/organizations
2022-10-01 16:18:50 meraki: INFO > organizations, getOrganizations - 200 OK
>>>
>>> my_orgs[0]
{
  'id': '5730083052582915028',
  'name': 'Next Meraki Org',
  'url': 'https://n18.meraki.com/o/PoiDucs/manage/organization/overview',
  'api': {'enabled': True},
  'licensing': {'model': 'co-term'},
  'cloud': {'region': {'name': 'North America'}}
}
>>>
```

By now, you're likely feeling comfortable interacting with HTTP APIs with Python. You've interacted with a native RESTful HTTP API, Cisco Meraki, and a non-RESTful one, Arista eAPI. As a reminder, every request to eAPI is an HTTP POST, and the URL is the same for every request, whereas a truly RESTful API using HTTP as its transport has a different URL based on the resource in question (e.g., organization, network, or routes in Cisco Meraki API).

Next, we will use the other programming language covered in the book, Go, to explore a specific HTTP API, the RESTCONF interface.

The Go net/http Package

In the previous section, you learned how to use the Python Requests library to interact with HTTP APIs. Here, we will use the Go net/http package to interact with HTTP APIs (focusing specifically on the RESTCONF interface—in this case, exposed by a Cisco IOS XE). Chapter 7 introduced the net/http package, and here we'll show a few examples of interacting with the RESTCONF interface.

Using net/http with RESTCONF

First, let's start with the same operation as in "Exploring RESTCONF in Cisco IOS XE" on page 426 to obtain the full native configuration. In Example 10-29, the main differences from the net/http example in Chapter 7 are the use of the basic http.NewRequest to create a GET request and the Authorization header.

Example 10-29. Using Go net/http to retrieve the configuration

```
package main

import (
    "crypto/tls"
    "encoding/base64"
    "fmt"
    "io/ioutil"
    "log"
    "net/http"
)

// helper method to construct the expected format of
// the basic authentication string, encoded in base64
func basicAuth(username, password string) string {
    auth := username + ":" + password
    return base64.StdEncoding.EncodeToString([]byte(auth))
}

// helper method to implement the error-checking pattern
func checkError(err error) {
    if err != nil {
        log.Fatal(err)
```

```
        }
    }

func main() {
    transCfg := &http.Transport{
        // ignore expired SSL certificates
        TLSClientConfig: &tls.Config{InsecureSkipVerify: true},
    }
    // create a new HTTP client, with the previously defined transport config
    client := &http.Client{Transport: transCfg}

    // create a new HTTP request, with the method, url, and headers
    request, err := http.NewRequest("GET",
        "https://csr1/restconf/data/Cisco-IOS-XE-native:native", nil)
    checkError(err)
    request.Header.Set("Accept", "application/yang-data+json")
    request.Header.Add("Authorization", "Basic "+basicAuth("ntc", "ntc123"))

    // perform the HTTP request, defined before, and store it in result
    result, err := client.Do(request)
    checkError(err)
    // read the body content from the response
    body, err := ioutil.ReadAll(result.Body)
    checkError(err)
    result.Body.Close()
    fmt.Printf("%s", body)
}
```

Running the code (go run get_config.go) will return the very same output obtained in "Exploring RESTCONF in Cisco IOS XE" on page 426. However, you could narrow the output by extending the path in the NewRequest with a specific data model and including filtering.

For instance, you can retrieve a specific interface configuration by using URI-encoded path expressions. In get_config_interface_g1.go, we use the URI-encoded path expression interface=GigabitEthernet1 to retrieve the config-uration of the GigabitEthernet1 interface: restconf/data/ietf-interfaces:inter faces/interface=GigabitEthernet1. This matches the identifier field (name) of the interface in the YANG model and gets you only the configuration of the specified interface:

```
ch10-apis/go_http$ go run get_config_interface_g1.go
{
  "ietf-interfaces:interface": {
    "name": "GigabitEthernet1",
    "description": "MANAGEMENT_DO_NOT_CHANGE",
    "type": "iana-if-type:ethernetCsmacd",
    "enabled": true,
    "ietf-ip:ipv4": {
      "address": [
        {
          "ip": "10.0.0.15",
          "netmask": "255.255.255.0"
```

```
        }
      ]
    },
    "ietf-ip:ipv6": {
    }
  }
}
```

Updating configuration via RESTCONF with net/http

You can also use net/http to run HTTP requests to change the configuration state. In "Exploring RESTCONF in Cisco IOS XE" on page 426, we used a PATCH request to update the existing OSPF configuration, and we mentioned that with a PUT request, you could apply the *declarative configuration* approach that defines the final state without considering the current one.

In Example 10-30, you can see the most relevant code from `update_ospf_config.go` that *replaces* the OSPF configuration with a new one. The HTTP request takes a JSON payload with the expected data structure and uses it in the PUT request.

Example 10-30. Using Go net/http to update the OSPF config

```
// Omitted code

func main() {
  // Omitted code

  // JSON payload for HTTP request
  var jsonStr = []byte(`{
  "router-ospf": {
    "ospf": {
      "process-id": [
        {
          "id": 10,
          "network": [
            {
              "ip": "203.0.113.0",
              "wildcard": "0.0.0.7",
              "area": 0
            },
            {
              "ip": "203.0.113.64",
              "wildcard": "0.0.0.7",
              "area": 0
            }
          ],
          "router-id": "203.0.113.1"
        }
      ]
    }
  }
}'`)
```

```
// create a new HTTP request, with PUT method, new URL,
// the payload, and new headers
request, err := http.NewRequest("PUT",
  "https://csr1/restconf/data/Cisco-IOS-XE-native:native/router/
  Cisco-IOS-XE-ospf:router-ospf", bytes.NewBuffer(jsonStr))
checkError(err)
request.Header.Set("Accept", "application/yang-data+json")
request.Header.Set("Authorization","Basic " + basicAuth("ntc","ntc123"))
request.Header.Set("Content-Type", "application/yang-data+json")

// Omitted code
}
```

In a real example, you would get the payload from an external file or a database, but we used a JSON object directly to simplify the script.

After these changes, you run the script, and voilà! The new OSPF configuration is in place. You can check it by repeating the GET request to the OSPF configuration node in the router.

With RESTful APIs that offer this type of power and control, you need to ensure you have a good process for making changes. As you can see, if you are trying to make only a small change or addition and happen to send a PUT request, catastrophic consequences can result. From an overall adoption perspective of this particular API, you may want to start using PATCH requests and gradually migrate to the point where you can indeed use PUT to declaratively manage specific sections of the configuration.

Example 10-30, using the PUT declaratively, configures everything under the ospf key. But if you targeted the router key, this key change would technically eliminate all other routing protocol configurations too. That's not a good thing. However, we chose to show the power and potential danger if it's not used and understood properly.

Now that we've shown how to start automating devices that have HTTP-based APIs by using Python and Go, let's look at the same approach by using the Python ncclient for automating devices with the NETCONF interface.

The Python ncclient Library

The Python ncclient is a popular NETCONF client for Python. It is client software that is built to communicate programmatically with NETCONF servers. Remember, in our case, a NETCONF server is going to be a network device. We'll walk through a vMX Juniper example, but the same approach will work for other platforms.

To install ncclient, you can use pip3:

```
$ pip3 install ncclient
$ pip3 list | grep ncclient
ncclient                    0.6.13
```

Once ncclient is installed, you can start to issue NETCONF API calls to network devices. Let's walk through this while in the Python interactive interpreter.

ncclient is not the only Python library offering NETCONF capabilities. Vendor-specific ones exist, such as PyEZ (*https://oreil.ly/8Cz23*) for Junos, as well as other generalist ones such as scrapli-netconf (*https://oreil.ly/sdPcl*) and netconf-client (*https://oreil.ly/XG6pK*).

When you enter the Python interpreter, your first step is to import the manager module within the ncclient Python package:

```
>>> from ncclient import manager
```

The basic function we are going to use within the manager module is responsible for establishing a persistent connection to the device. Keep in mind that since NET-CONF runs over SSH, this connection is stateful and persistent (as compared to RESTful APIs being stateless). This function is called connect() and accepts several parameters such as hostname/IP address, port number, and credentials. You'll see in the following example that other parameters will remain unchanged that map back to the underlying SSH configuration and properties:

```
>>> device = manager.connect(
...     host='vmx1', port=830, username='ntc',
...     password='ntc123', hostkey_verify=False,
... )
```

As soon as the connect() function is called, a NETCONF session is established to the network device, and an object is returned and saved as device, an instance of a ncclient Manager object. This object exposes the methods to interact with NETCONF RPC operations.

Understanding the Manager object

First, let's look at the `device` capabilities, as in Example 10-8, and get exactly the same output, but in a different format (a Python list):

```
>>> list(device.client_capabilities)
[
  'urn:ietf:params:netconf:base:1.0',
  'urn:ietf:params:netconf:base:1.1',
  'urn:ietf:params:netconf:capability:writable-running:1.0',
  'urn:ietf:params:netconf:capability:candidate:1.0',
  'urn:ietf:params:netconf:capability:confirmed-commit:1.0',
  # output omitted for brevity
]
```

Retrieving Juniper vMX device configurations with ncclient

In Example 10-9, when exploring the use of NETCONF over an SSH session, you used the complete `<get>` XML RPC operation to query the vMX router for the `fxp0` interface configuration. Now, you reuse the subtree filtering, defined as a string:

```
>>> get_filter = """
...     <configuration xmlns="urn:ietf:params:xml:ns:netconf:base:1.0">
...         <interfaces>
...             <interface>
...                 <name>fxp0</name>
...             </interface>
...         </interfaces>
...     </configuration>
...     """
```

Remember that triple quotes in Python denote a multiline comment and can be used to create a multiline string that can be used as a value of a variable.

Once the filter is defined, you pass that as a parameter to the `get()` method, specifying the subfilter `subtree` type. Without the filter, you would get the full configuration:

```
>>> nc_get_reply = device.get(('subtree', get_filter))
```

At this point, after the NETCONF GET request to the device, the result is stored in `nc_get_reply` and matches the result in Example 10-10.

The ncclient supports *XPath* filters. But, this support depends on the NETCONF capabilities of the platform. All filters used with Junos vMX examples are *subtree* filters because this platform doesn't support XPath for `get` operations. You can see how to use XPath filters in "Using ncclient with Cisco IOS XE" on page 475.

While our examples use XML strings as the filters, it is also possible to use native XML objects (etree objects). We are using string objects because they are much more human-readable and easier to use when getting started. You may want to use native etree objects if you need to dynamically build a filter object.

The `data` attribute in `nc_get_reply` contains the native XML object from the `lxml` Python library (lxml is covered in more detail in Chapter 8). For instance, the `etree.tostring()` method converts a native XML object to a string:

```
>>> from lxml import etree
>>>
>>> as_string = etree.tostring(nc_get_reply.data)
>>> print(as_string)
b'<rpc-reply message-id="urn:uuid:e2c1daa0-8556-4e6b-84dc-e72e90809f73"><data>
<configuration commit-seconds="1653021086" commit-localtime="2022-05-20 04:31:26
UTC" commit-user="ntc"><interfaces><interface><name>fxp0</name><unit><name>0
</name><description>MANAGEMENT_INTERFACE__DO_NOT_CHANGE</description><family>
<inet><address><name>10.0.0.15/24</name></address></inet></family></unit>
</interface></interfaces></configuration><database-status-information>\n
</database-status-information></data></rpc-reply>'
```

In the output of `nc_get_reply`, you can observe the IP address and mask for the `fxp0` interface (`10.0.0.15/24`). If this is the information you are interested in, you should parse the XML tags that contain this information: `<address>` and `<name>`.

To *find* a specific tag in an `lxml.etree` object, you can use the `find()` method. It provides a simple way to search a full XML object for a given XML tag when using the expression denoted by `.//`. Since you want to extract the `<address>` object and its children, you could try the following example:

```
>>> address = nc_get_reply.data.find('.//address')
```

Unfortunately, it doesn't work. What's wrong here? The statement tries to extract the XML element with the `<address>` tag. However, when XML namespaces are used, the tag name must include the namespace concatenated—in other words, `{namespace}tag`. In this case, `{http://yang.juniper.net/junos/conf/inter faces}address`. Alternatively, if an XML namespace *alias* is defined, it can be used as `alias:tag`.

 Our example has multiple namespaces. You can gradually print one child object at a time to see which namespace is used. In the example, the default namespace is `urn:ietf:params:xml:ns:net conf:base:1.0`, but when you print a single object, you see only one. The next namespace in the hierarchy is overriding the default namespace for all children of the `<configuration>` element.

To properly extract the IP address and mask, we'll follow three steps. First, we extract the `<address>` object that contains an inner `<name>` XML tag, then we extract the content of the <name> tag with the prefix and mask combined, and finally, we save it as a string by using text:

```
>>> address = nc_get_reply.data.find(
>>>     './/{http://yang.juniper.net/junos/conf/interfaces}address'
>>> )
>>> ip_address = address.find(
>>>     './/{http://yang.juniper.net/junos/conf/interfaces}name' ❶
>>> )
>>> ip_address.text
'10.0.0.15/24'
```

❶ We can't look for <name> directly because we would hit the *interface* name, which is first in the hierarchy.

You may be thinking, "Extracting values based on the namespaces is tedious." You are absolutely right. Parsing XML is not easy, and it is even more difficult when namespaces are involved. But, in the end, once you know the namespace, you just need to concatenate two strings. Also, it's possible to strip namespaces from an XML object before doing XML parsing, further simplifying the process.

By now, you should be getting the hang of issuing NETCONF <get> requests. Let's look at one more, but this time, working with the SNMP configuration to use the findall() method.

Using findall() to retrieve multiple XML objects.   On our Juniper vMX, we currently have two SNMP read-only community strings configured. For verification, this is the output after we issue the show snmp command while in configuration mode:

```
ntc@vmx1# show snmp
location EMEA-IE;
contact Scott_Grady;
community public123 {
    authorization read-only;
}
community supersecure {
    authorization read-write;
}
[edit]
```

Our goal is to extract the name of each community string and the authorization level for each. Juniper has functionality in its CLI such that you can see the expected XML response as well when you pipe the command to display xml (for instance, show snmp | display xml).

When you know the data returned from the NETCONF request, you can more easily write the associated Python code. Whenever you are issuing a NETCONF get request to a Junos device, <configuration> needs to be the outermost XML tag when you're collecting configuration state information. Within that element, you can build the appropriate filter, which can be gleaned from the XML text found while on the CLI. The filter string to request SNMP configuration looks like this:

```
get_filter = """
... <configuration>
...   <snmp>
...   </snmp>
... </configuration>
... """
```

The next step, in Example 10-31, is to make the request, just as we've done already. After the request is made, we'll verify the output, printing the XML string to the terminal.

Example 10-31. ncclient get SNMP configuration

```
>>> nc_get_reply = device.get(('subtree', get_filter))
>>> print(nc_get_reply)
<rpc-reply message-id="urn:uuid:c3170685-e275-4db1-855d-bb1a56404d55">
  <data>
    <configuration commit-seconds="1653021086"
    commit-localtime="2022-05-20 04:31:26 UTC" commit-user="ntc">
      <snmp>
        <location>EMEA-IE</location>
        <contact>Scott_Grady</contact>
        <community>
          <name>public123</name>
          <authorization>read-only</authorization>
        </community>
        # output omitted for brevity
  </data>
</rpc-reply>
```

As we stated, our goal is to parse the response, saving the community string and authorization type for each community. Rather than just print these to the terminal, let's save them as a list of Python dictionaries. To do this, you'll follow the same steps used earlier in Example 10-32.

Example 10-32. Using findall() to iterate over multiple XML objects

```
>>> snmp_list = []
>>> xmlns = "http://yang.juniper.net/junos/conf/snmp"
>>> communities = nc_get_reply.data.findall(f'.//{{{xmlns}}}community')      ❶
>>> for community in communities:                                           ❷
...     temp = {}
...     temp['name'] = community.find(f'.//{{{xmlns}}}name').text           ❸
...     temp['auth'] = community.find(f'.//{{{xmlns}}}authorization').text  ❸
...     snmp_list.append(temp)
...
```

```
>>>
>>> print(snmp_list)
[
  {'auth': 'read-only', 'name': 'public123'},
  {'auth': 'read-write', 'name': 'supersecure'}
]
```

❶ Instead of using `find()`, youwe use the `findall()` method, which allows extracting multiple elements of the same type instead of only the first match. Using a string formation option, such as f-strings, simplifies xmlns management.

❷ `communities` contains a list of objects, not only the first match.

❸ Because we need to output the curly brackets in the output within the f-string, we need to escape them via doubling: `{{{`.

You've seen how to issue NETCONF requests to obtain configuration data, but now we are going to transition a bit and show how to make configuration changes via NETCONF by using the `<edit-config>` operation.

Making Junos vMX configuration changes with ncclient

To illustrate how to use ncclient to change the configuration via NETCONF, we will use the `edit_config()` method of the `device` object, which maps directly to the `<edit-config>` NETCONF operation. Following the previous example, now we're going to configure a new SNMP community string.

The ncclient `edit_config()` method takes two mandatory arguments. The first one, called `<target>`, defines which configuration data store is going to get modified in the request. Valid data stores are running, startup, and candidate. The second parameter, called `<config>`, needs to be an XML string or object that defines the requested configuration changes.

Therefore, we need to construct the `<config>` that matches the expected format. The easiest way to get an understanding of the expected data structure is to use it from the `get` request, as shown in Example 10-31. Then, with this reference, we can construct a new XML configuration object. Let's add a new community string called `myNewCommunity` that has `read-only` privileges:

```
>>> config_filter = """
... <config>
...   <configuration>
...     <snmp>
...       <community>
...         <name>myNewCommunity</name>
...         <authorization>read-only</authorization>
...       </community>
...     </snmp>
```

```
...    </configuration>
...    </config>
...    """
```

 You need to encapsulate this document in one final tag: <config>. This is often required when you're using the <edit-config> operation, as covered in "Using NETCONF" on page 410.

To change the candidate data store with the new SNMP community, you call the edit_config() method:

```
>>> response = device.edit_config(target='candidate', config=config_filter)
>>> print(response)
<rpc-reply message-id="urn:uuid:56584f09-24d2-4e28-aa55-e583bf9d2ff2">
  <ok/>
</rpc-reply>
```

If you check the configuration via the CLI or make a get request, you'll see a new community string on the device.

Performing NETCONF delete/replace operations with the ncclient. You've seen how to make a configuration change on the device by using the <edit-config> operation. The default edit operation is merge. However, more operations are available via the XML operation attribute.

After adding the SNMP community myNewCommunity, we are going to remove it by using the delete operation. In this case, we need to construct the new <config> with operation="delete" in the <community> tag. Notice that only the <name> tag is required to identify the object:

```
>>> config_filter = """
... <config>
...    <configuration>
...       <snmp>
...          <community operation="delete">
...             <name>myNewCommunity</name>
...          </community>
...       </snmp>
...    </configuration>
... </config>
... """
>>> response = device.edit_config(target='candidate', config=config_filter)
```

The merge and delete operations allow managing the configuration from its current state. But what if you want to implement a declarative approach, in which you don't need to care about the current state, but only the final one?

There are a few ways to go about *replacing* a given hierarchy of XML configuration. One option is to make an API call to configure all desired SNMP community strings, and then retrieve all currently configured SNMP communities in another API call, loop over the response, and issue a `delete` operation per community for any not desired. While this approach is not terrible, NETCONF offers a better way—as you already know, of course.

With NETCONF, you can use the `replace` operation instead of `merge` or `delete`. This is the same as doing a PUT with RESTCONF. You define the `replace` operation (`<snmp operation="replace">`) and then define the desired SNMP community name and privilege.

When you start experimenting with the `delete` and `replace` operations, you need to be extremely careful. The `merge` operation is the default for a very good reason—it enables you to only add or update a configuration. More importantly, if you put the `operation="delete"` line at the wrong place in the XML hierarchy, it could have a catastrophic effect on the network. For instance, placing the `replace` operation as an attribute in the `<snmp>` tag replaces the *full* configuration of SNMP. As we said with RESTCONF PUT, the same is true with NETCONF `replace` operations; be aware of their power.

 Always make sure to test in a lab or sandbox environment first. Do *not* test full `replace` operations in production!

Now, after exploring NETCONF automation with Juniper vMX, we want to give a glimpse into using it for Cisco IOS XE to show another implementation.

Using ncclient with Cisco IOS XE

To illustrate the usage of the XPath filter instead of the subfilter one, we will use Cisco IOS XE, which implements this *capability*. In this example, we want to extract the configuration for a specific interface (`GigabitEthernet1`).

```
>>> from ncclient import manager
>>> device = manager.connect(
>>>     host='csr1', port=830, username='ntc',
>>>     password='ntc123', hostkey_verify=False,
>>> )
>>> nc_get_reply = device.get(
...     ('xpath', '/interfaces/interface[name="GigabitEthernet1"]/config')  ❶
... )
```

❶ The XPath filter injects `[name="GigabitEthernet1"]` in the path.

Now, as in Example 10-32, you use `find()` to traverse the XML structure to locate the data you are interested in. In this case, let's extract the `description` of the interface `GigabitEthernet1`:

```
>>> description = nc_get_reply.data.find(
...     './/{http://openconfig.net/yang/interfaces}description')
>>> interface.text
'MANAGEMENT_DO_NOT_CHANGE'
```

As more vendors and operating systems support vendor-neutral data models, you'll be able to issue the same exact API call against those devices, simplifying working with various device types. Until that point comes, you'll need to understand the XML objects supported per NOS.

Understanding vendor-specific NETCONF operations

We have been focusing on the two most commonly used methods in ncclient—namely, `<edit-config>` and `<get>`. However, as you may have noticed earlier in this chapter, many more methods are available when working with NETCONF and ncclient. Here are a few of those:

`commit()`
Commits a candidate configuration to the active running configuration.

`copy_config()` *and* `delete_config()`
Creates or replaces, and deletes, respectively, an entire configuration data store with the contents of another complete configuration data store.

`lock()` *and* `unlock()`
For a production environment, you may want to lock the configuration data store before changes are made so that no other person or system can make changes during your NETCONF session. When it's complete, you can unlock the configuration.

Everything we focused on with the Python-based ncclient was vendor neutral and would work across vendors, assuming you understand how to build the proper XML objects. However, you should understand that not every vendor implements NETCONF the same way even though it is an industry-standard protocol. For example, particular vendors have created their own platform-specific NETCONF operations or created their own methods for ncclient to simplify performing common operations. This is in contrast to NETCONF standard operations such as `<edit-config>`, `<get>`, `<lock>`, `<unlock>`, and `<commit>`.

To use these vendor-specific options when using ncclient, you need to specify the correct platform in the `device_params` parameter when instantiating a device object.

Every example we showed used device_params={} because we used industry-standard operations within ncclient. If you choose the vendor-specific methods and operations, you would set the device_params parameter to its required value. If you append device_params={"name": "junos"} in the connect() method, you will find out some custom Juniper RPC operations:

```
>>> device = manager.connect(
...   host='vmx1', port=830, username='ntc',password='ntc123',
...   hostkey_verify=False,device_params={"name": "junos"}
... )
>>> device._vendor_operations.keys()
dict_keys(['rpc', 'get_configuration', 'load_configuration', 'compare_configuration',
'command', 'reboot', 'halt', 'commit', 'rollback'])
```

 Juniper has developed custom methods within ncclient such as load_configuration(), get_configuration(), compare_configuration(), and command(), just to name a few. Several of Juniper's methods are wrappers to simplify performing common tasks with standard NETCONF operations, and others use Juniper-specific NETCONF RPC operations.

For instance, using the commit() method, the candidate configuration can be moved to the running one, making the changes active:

```
>>> response = device.commit()
>>> print(response)
<rpc-reply message-id="urn:uuid:12a2bea3-7aa3-48dd-bfe8-569ccd84d61d">
  <ok/>
</rpc-reply>
```

After this complete overview of NETCONF (using the ncclient library), we will use the gNMIc Go package, the same we used in its CLI form before, to interact via the gNMI interface programmatically.

The OpenConfig gNMIc Go Package

In "Exploring gNMI with gNMIc" on page 441, you already used OpenConfig gNMIc to explore gNMI, but via CLI. Here, you will use the inner Go package to build Go scripts, emulating the same operations as before with an Arista EOS switch.

In the Python world, the most popular library for gNMI management is pyGNMI (*https://oreil.ly/VKcTa*), which offers a similar interaction with gNMI methods as ncclient offers for NETCONF. This is an example of performing a `GetRequest` to a specific path with the pyGNMI library:

```
from pygnmi.client import gNMIclient

with gNMIclient(
    target=('eos-spine1', '6030'), username='ntc',
    password='ntc123', insecure=True
) as gnmi_client:
    result = gnmi_client.get(path=[
        'openconfig-interfaces:interfaces', 'openconfig-acl:acl'])
```

As we did in "gNMI GetRequest" on page 442, we will start first with a GetRequest operation.

Using OpenConfig gNMIc to perform a gNMI Get operation

In this example, we create a basic programmatic script with gNMI. It contains the base program structure to interact with the gNMI interface that we will reuse in later examples. To extend your understanding of the gNMIc package, see the online documentation (*https://oreil.ly/Wtarm*).

To use the OpenConfig gNMIc package, you need to get and install the package first, or manage the Go module dependencies with go mod:

```
$ go get github.com/openconfig/gnmic/api
go: downloading github.com/openconfig/gnmic v0.27.1
go: added github.com/openconfig/gnmic v0.27.1
```

Example 10-33 defines the necessary imports. The most important ones are the `openconfig/gnmic` that offers access to the gNMI interface, and the protobuf that is used to manage the data serialization.

Example 10-33. gNMIc script, part 1

```
package main

import (
  "context"
  "fmt"
  "log"

  // gnmic package
  "github.com/openconfig/gnmic/api"
```

```
  // prototext marshals and unmarshals protocol buffer messages
  // as the textproto format, which offers generic support for text-based
  // request/response protocols
  "google.golang.org/protobuf/encoding/prototext"
)

// helper method to implement the error-checking pattern
func checkError(err error) {
  if err != nil {
    log.Fatal(err)
  }
}

// continues to part 2
```

Continuing the script, in Example 10-34, the five steps to retrieve the device configuration are defined.

Example 10-34. gNMIc script, part 2

```
// -> comes from previous

func main() {
  // create a gnmic target
  tg, err := api.NewTarget(
      api.Name("gnmi example"),
      api.Address("eos-spine1:6030"),
      api.Username("admin"),
      api.Password("admin"),
      api.Insecure(true),
  )
  checkError(err)

  // cancelable context releases the associated resources, as soon as the
  // operation is completed or canceled.
  ctx, cancel := context.WithCancel(context.Background())
  defer cancel()

  // create a new gNMI client within the base target, using the previous context
  err = tg.CreateGNMIClient(ctx)
  checkError(err)
  defer tg.Close()

  // create a GetRequest
  getReq, err := api.NewGetRequest(
      // Retrieve the full path, all the configuration
      api.Path("/"),
      // Define the expected payload encoding
      api.Encoding("json_ietf"))
  checkError(err)
  fmt.Println(prototext.Format(getReq))

  // send the created gNMI GetRequest to the gnmic target
  getResp, err := tg.Get(ctx, getReq)
```

```
  checkError(err)
  fmt.Println(prototext.Format(getResp))
}
```

 Notice the common Go pattern for error checking after each operation, wrapped in the checkError() function.

Then, it's time to run the script and check its output:

```
ch10-apis/go_gnmic$ go run get_config.go
path: {}
encoding: JSON_IETF

notification:  {
  timestamp:  1664733418878706841
  update:  {
    path:  {}
    val:  {
      json_ietf_val:  "{\"openconfig-acl:acl\":{\"state\":
      {\"counter-capability\":\"AGGREGATE_ONLY\"}},
      \"arista-exp-eos:arista\":{\"eos\":
      {\"arista-exp-eos-igmpsnooping:bridging\":
      {\"igmpsnooping\":{\"config\":{}}},\"arista-exp-eos-mlag:mlag\":
      {\"config\":{\"dual-primary-action\":\"action-none\"
        "
      # omitted a VERY LONG output
    }
  }
}
```

In this initial example, we targeted the full data set with the / path. Now, as in
Example 10-21, we narrow the scope to get the only interfaces' data section—in
particular, its configuration.

The only change from the previous script is changing the Path to filter the
section /interfaces/interface/config, as defined in go_gnmic/get_interface_
config.go:

```
getReq, err := api.NewGetRequest(
  // Narrow the scope to the interfaces config
  api.Path("/interfaces/interface/config"),
  api.Encoding("json_ietf")
)
```

If you run the script with the path change, you get a filtered output:

```
ch10-apis/go_gnmic$ go run get_interfaces_config.go
path:  # omitted path
encoding:  JSON_IETF

notification: {
```

```
timestamp: 1664771809792522887
update: {
  path: {
    # omitted path
  }
  val: {
    json_ietf_val: "{ ❶
      \"openconfig-interfaces:description\":\"New Description\",
      \"openconfig-interfaces:mtu\":0,
      \"openconfig-interfaces:name\":\"Management0\",
      \"openconfig-interfaces:type\":\"iana-if-type:ethernetCsmacd\"}"
  }
}
}
```

❶ The interface's configuration values, with the JSON_IETF encoding

The next step is to interact with the output of the Get operation, which we saved in the getResp variable.

Evolving from the previous script, in Example 10-35 (part of the example script *get_interfaces_description.go*), you narrow the path to the description leaf with /interfaces/interface/config/description. Then, you need only to extract its value and start using it.

Example 10-35. Using value from the gNMI response

```
descriptionGnmiValue := getResp.GetNotification()[0].GetUpdate()[0].GetVal()  ❶
myCurrentDescriptionValue, err := value.ToScalar(descriptionGnmiValue)        ❷
checkError(err)

myCurrentDescriptionStr := myCurrentDescriptionValue.(string)                 ❸
fmt.Println("This is my current description: " + myCurrentDescriptionStr)
```

❶ Extracts json_ietf_val into the descriptionGnmiValue variable

❷ Converts the variable value into a scalar value

❸ Casts it into a string, and we are ready to use it

If you run the script, you can see how the interface description is retrieved and printed in the screen output:

```
ch10-apis/go_gnmic$ go run get_interfaces_description.go
# omitted previous output

This is my current description: New Description
```

With the current description, we will reuse part of the previous code to update the interface's description with a new value.

Using OpenConfig gNMIc to perform a gNMI Set operation

As in "gNMI SetRequest" on page 444 via CLI, in Example 10-36, you will update the interface description for the Management0 interface, but programmatically.

Example 10-36. gNMIc script to update configuration

```
myNewDescription := myCurrentDescriptionStr + "_something_else"  ❶

// create a gNMI SetRequest
setReq, err := api.NewSetRequest(
    api.Update(                                                  ❷
        // Use XPath to target the description for Management0 interface
        api.Path("interfaces/interface[name=Management0]/config/description"),
        // Define the value to update
        api.Value(myNewDescription, "json_ietf")
    ),
)
checkError(err)

// send the created gNMI SetRequest to the created target
setResp, err := tg.Set(ctx, setReq)                             ❸
checkError(err)
fmt.Println(prototext.Format(setResp))
```

❶ We use the previous description value, stored in `myCurrentDescriptionStr`, to create a new description.

❷ The `SetRequest` type contains an `Update` object with the path and the value. gNMI supports two `Set` operation modes: update and replace (similar to a PUT versus PATCH in REST APIs).

❸ We perform a `Set` operation in the gNMIc target, instead of a `Get`.

We run the script and receive confirmation that the update operation has been performed successfully:

```
ch10-apis/go_gnmic$ go run set_interfaces_description.go
# omitted previous output
response: {
  path: {
    # path omitted
  }
  op: UPDATE
}
timestamp: 1664863404149182568
```

If you retrieve the interface description configuration again, as before, you will see the new description updated.

Using OpenConfig gNMIc to subscribe to events

As we explained in "Understanding model-driven telemetry" on page 448, gNMI's support for streaming telemetry via the subscribe operation was, and still is, one of the main drivers for its adoption. In Example 10-37, the goal is to subscribe to interface counters as you did in "gNMI Subscribe" on page 445 via the CLI.

Example 10-37. gNMIc subscription to interface counters

```
// create a gNMI subscribeRequest
subReq, err := api.NewSubscribeRequest(
  api.Encoding("json_ietf"),
  // Select the stream mode, instead of poll
  api.SubscriptionListMode("stream"),
  // Define the subscription scope
  api.Subscription(              ❶
    // Data container to retrieve
    api.Path("/interfaces/interface/state/counters"),
    // Define the subscription method. Others are on_change and target_defined
    api.SubscriptionMode("sample"),
    // For the sample mode, the sample interval is defined
    api.SampleInterval(10*time.Second),
  ))
checkError(err)
fmt.Println(prototext.Format(subReq))

// start the subscription, identified as sub1, in a new goroutine
go tg.Subscribe(ctx, subReq, "sub1") ❷

// start a goroutine that will stop the subscription after 30 seconds
go func() {                    ❸
  select {
  case <-ctx.Done():
    return
  case <-time.After(30 * time.Second):
    // If the context is not stopped before, after 30 seconds
    // in this goroutine, it will stop the subscription defined
    // as sub1
    tg.StopSubscription("sub1")
  }
}()

// In the main process, starts creating two subscriptions, creating two channels
// that are read in an infinite loop, until the subscriptions are closed
// by the other goroutines
subRspChan, subErrChan := tg.ReadSubscriptions()
for {                          ❹
  select {
  case rsp := <-subRspChan:
    fmt.Println(prototext.Format(rsp.Response))
  case tgErr := <-subErrChan:
    log.Fatalf("subscription %q stopped: %v", tgErr.SubscriptionName, tgErr.Err)
```

```
  }
}
```

❶ `SubscribeRequest` is a *sampling* type, and it targets the `state`, not the `config` container.

❷ The `Subscribe()` method is run in a different goroutine (notice the `go` before). This will keep it running while you progress in the script.

❸ This goroutine is in charge to stop the subscription after 30 seconds. The identifier (`sub1`) connects the dots.

❹ The main process will keep reading the subscription responses and errors (via two Go channels) until the subscription is stopped.

 Example 10-37 shows how three flows are executed and communicated to Go. The main one (initializing and printing the output received via channels) is the one managing the subscription, and the one to stop the subscription after a specified number of seconds.

When running the script, you will see the operation summary at the top, with the mode (`SAMPLE`), its interval (10 seconds), and the encoding. Remember that there is another mode type, `on-change`, which only sends data when there is a change in the data source. You can see the output here:

```
ch10-apis/go_gnmic$ go run subscribe_int_counters.go
subscribe: {
  subscription: {
    path: {
      # path omitted
    }
    mode: SAMPLE
    sample_interval: 10000000000
  }
  encoding: JSON_IETF
}

update: {
  timestamp: 1664944947620748134
  prefix: {
    # prefix omitted
  }
  update: {
    path: {
      elem: {
        name: "out-octets"
      }
    }
```

```
    val:  {
      uint_val:  6243543
    }
  }
  update:  {
    path:  {
      elem:  {
        name:  "out-unicast-pkts"
      }
    }
    val:  {
      uint_val:  31339
    }
  }
  # output omitted for brevity
}
```

We've now provided an introduction to using the Python and Go libraries to communicate with modern programmatic network APIs. Now, we are going to shift gears
and talk about using SSH in Python, as SSH is still the most widely deployed interface
on network devices.

The Netmiko Python Library

Using CLI commands, SSH has been the de facto way network engineers and
operators manage their infrastructure. Commands are passed over a persistent SSH
connection to a network device, the device interprets them, and it responds with text
that is viewable by a human on a terminal window. SSH does not use structured
encoded data such as XML or JSON over the wire. While SSH is not a modern or a
programmatic API, it is important to have an understanding of how to use Python to
automate network operations with SSH for three reasons:

- Not all devices support a programmatic API.
- You may want to automate the turning on of the API.
- Even if you're automating a device with an API:
  — It's good to have a backup plan.
  — Not all operations of a device may be supported with the API. This is not
    ideal, as it shows immaturity in the underlying API.

In this section, we show how to get started with a popular open source SSH client
for Python called *Netmiko*. Netmiko's purpose is to simplify SSH device management
specifically for network devices.

Do not underestimate the utility of the SSH Netmiko library, as it's proven useful in providing a smooth transition from traditional network CLI management to network automation, and it's heavily used and developed, as you can see in the Netmiko GitHub Contributors page (*https://oreil.ly/xmpee*).

We're focused on Netmiko, as it provides a lower barrier to entry and already understands how to communicate with many network device types. Netmiko has varied support for dozens of device types, including those from Arista, Brocade, Cisco, Dell, HPE, Juniper, Palo Alto Networks, Linux, and many more; check the documentation (*https://oreil.ly/PI_q1*) for updated information. The great thing about Netmiko is that the overall usage is common across vendors. Only the commands used are specific to each platform.

To install Netmiko, you can use `pip3`:

```
$ pip3 install netmiko
$ pip3 list | grep netmiko
netmiko                    3.4.0
```

The first thing you need to do is import the proper Netmiko device object. This object handles the SSH connection setup, teardown, and the sending of commands to the device. You used a similar approach with ncclient:

```
>>> from netmiko import ConnectHandler
```

You're now ready to establish an SSH connection to the network device and create a Netmiko device object. The `ConnectHandler` object handles the SSH connection to the network device:

```
>>> device = ConnectHandler(
...     host='nxos-spine1',
...     username='admin',
...     password='admin',
...     device_type='cisco_nxos'
... )
```

At this point, there is an active SSH connection from Python using Netmiko with a Cisco NX-OS switch. Because each platform supports different commands and handles SSH differently, you must provide the `device_type` parameter when instantiating an instance of the `ConnectHandler` object.

Let's check the available methods for our new device object called `device` by using the `dir()` function:

```
>>> dir(device)
[
  # methods removed for brevity
  'cleanup', 'clear_buffer', 'close_session_log', 'commit', 'config_mode',
```

```
    'conn_timeout', 'device_type', 'disable_paging', 'disconnect', 'enable',
    'encoding', 'establish_connection', 'exit_config_mode', 'exit_enable_mode',
    'select_delay_factor', 'send_command', 'send_command_expect',
    'send_command_timing', 'send_config_from_file', 'send_config_set',
]
```

As a network engineer, you should feel pretty comfortable with many of the attributes shown from the dir() function, as they are very network centric. We'll walk through a few of them now.

Verifying the device prompt

Use the find_prompt() method to check the prompt string of the device:

```
>>> device.find_prompt()
'nxos-spine1#'
```

Entering configuration mode

Because Netmiko understands multiple vendors and what configuration mode means, it has a method to go into configuration mode that works across vendors; of course, the commands Netmiko uses under the covers may be different per OS:

```
>>> device.config_mode()
>>>
>>> device.find_prompt()
'nxos-spine1(config)#'
```

 Some NOSs could fail to enter config_mode() if there is already a CLI session in this mode.

Sending commands

The most common operation you're going to perform with Netmiko is sending commands to a device. Let's look at a few methods to do this.

To simply send a single command to a device, you can use one of three methods:

send_command_expect()
> This method is used for long-running commands that may take a while for the device to process (show run on a larger chassis, show tech, etc.). By default, this method waits for the same prompt string to return before completing. Optionally, you can pass what the new prompt string is going to be should it change based on the commands being sent.

```
send_command_timing()
```
This method is for short-running commands; it is timing based and does not check the prompt string.

```
send_command()
```
This is an older method in Netmiko, which now acts as a wrapper for calling `send_command_expect()`. Thus, `send_command()` and `send_command_expect()` perform the same operation.

Let's look at a few examples. Here you're gathering a show run and printing out the first 176 characters for verification:

```
>>> show_run_output = device.send_command('show run')
>>>
>>> print(show_run_output[:176])

!Command: show running-config
!Running configuration last done at: Wed Oct  5 04:18:12 2022
!Time: Wed Oct  5 04:23:22 2022

version 9.3(3) Bios:version
hostname nxos-spine1
```

Send a command that changes the prompt string—remember you're still in configuration mode when you enter `device.config_mode()`—as follows:

```
>>> output = device.send_command_expect('end')
Traceback (most recent call last):
  File "<stdin>", line 1, in <module>
  File "/usr/local/lib/python3.8/site-packages/netmiko/base_connection.py",
  line 1582, in send_command_expect
    return self.send_command(*args, **kwargs)
  File "/usr/local/lib/python3.8/site-packages/netmiko/utilities.py", line 500,
  in wrapper_decorator
    return func(self, *args, **kwargs)
  File "/usr/local/lib/python3.8/site-packages/netmiko/base_connection.py",
  line 1535, in send_command
    raise IOError()
OSError: Search pattern never detected in send_command: nxos\-spine1\(config\)\#
>>>
```

The stack trace shown is expected, as `send_command_expect()` expects to see the same prompt string by default. Since you are in config mode with the current prompt string of `nxos-spine1(config)#`, when you type the command end, the new prompt string is going to be `nxos-spine1#`.

To execute a command that changes the prompt string, you have two options. First, you can use the `expect_string` parameter that defines the new and expected prompt string:

```
>>> output = device.send_command_expect('end', expect_string='nxos-spine1#')
>>>
```

Second, you can use the send_command_timing() method, which is timing based and doesn't expect a particular prompt string to be found again:

```
>>> output = device.send_command_timing('end')
>>>
```

You've shown three methods thus far on how to send commands with Netmiko. Let's look at two more useful ones, as you may want to send several commands at once instead of one at a time.

Netmiko also supports a method called send_config_set() that takes a parameter that must be iterable. We'll show this using a Python list, but you can also use a Python set:

```
>>> commands = [
    'interface Ethernet1/1',
    'description configured by netmiko',
    'shutdown'
]
>>>
>>> output = device.send_config_set(config_commands=commands)
>>>
>>> print(output)
nxos-spine1(config)# interface Ethernet1/1
nxos-spine1(config-if)# description configured by netmiko
nxos-spine1(config-if)# shutdown
nxos-spine1(config-if)# end
nxos-spine1#
```

This method checks whether you're already in configuration mode. If you aren't, it goes into config mode, executes the commands, and by default, exits configuration mode. You can verify this by viewing the returned output, as shown in the previous example.

Finally, Netmiko has a method that can execute commands from a file. This allows you to do something like create a Jinja template, render it with variable data, write the data to a file, and then execute those commands from the file with the Netmiko method send_config_from_file(). Building on what we covered in Chapters 6 and 9, let's see how to perform this workflow in Example 10-38.

Example 10-38. Sending commands from a file with Netmiko

```
from netmiko import ConnectHandler
from jinja2 import Environment, FileSystemLoader

device = ConnectHandler(
    ...
)

interface_dict = {
    "name": "Ethernet1/2",
```

```
    "description": "Server Port",
    "vlan": 10,
    "uplink": False
}

# Create the custom commands, combining the Jinja config.j2 template
# with the data defined in interface_dict
ENV = Environment(loader=FileSystemLoader('.'))
template = ENV.get_template("config.j2")
commands = template.render(interface=interface_dict)

# Store the CLI commands in a local file
filename = 'nxos.conf'
with open(filename, 'w') as config_file:
    config_file.writelines(commands)

# Send CLI commands directly from the file
output = device.send_config_from_file(filename)

# Use show commands to verify that the change succeeded
verification = device.send_command(f'show run interface {interface_dict["name"]}')
print(verification)

device.disconnect()
```

Everything shown in this example was covered in prior chapters. Note that *config.j2* must be created for this to work, and for this example, that the Jinja template is stored in the same directory from where we entered the Python interpreter. The content of the template is from Example 9-3, and is as follows:

```
interface {{ interface.name }}
  description {{ interface.description }}
  switchport access vlan {{ interface.vlan }}
  switchport mode access
```

Finally, when you're done working with Netmiko, you can gracefully disconnect from the device by using the disconnect() method. If we run the script, we will see the verification of the new interface configuration according to the template:

```
ch10-apis/python_netmiko$ python3 send_commands_from_file.py

!Command: show running-config interface Ethernet1/2
!Running configuration last done at: Wed Oct  5 04:38:54 2022
!Time: Wed Oct  5 04:38:55 2022

version 9.3(3) Bios:version

interface Ethernet1/2
  description Server Port
  switchport access vlan 10
```

Context managers in Python help manage setup and teardown operations. For an SSH library such as Netmiko, a context manager seems ideal. Thus, Netmiko provides one, netmiko.ConnectHandler, that will take care of establishing the SSH session at the beginning, and tearing it down when exiting it (so you don't leave open SSH connections):

```
with netmiko.ConnectHandler(**device_config) as device:
    device.send_command("show run")
```

So far, you have shown the benefits of Netmiko, allowing interaction with a traditional CLI interface programmatically. Unfortunately, the unstructured data used in the CLI output is a big drawback in the automation journey. Hopefully, we have some helpers available.

Empowering Netmiko with TextFSM and NTC Templates

TextFSM (*https://oreil.ly/cVuCh*) is an open source project built by Google that converts semiformatted text (the CLI output) to structured data, using templates. So, for each CLI output, you need to provide a specific template that NTC Templates solves.

NTC Templates (*https://oreil.ly/A1svX*) is an open source project sponsored by Network to Code that provides a large collection of TextFSM templates for a lot of network vendors (*https://oreil.ly/IhLYy*).

 You don't need to install TextFSM or NTC Templates because they are dependencies of Netmiko, so they are already installed.

In Example 10-39, we demonstrate how to use NTC Templates in two steps:

1. Get raw CLI output from Netmiko and store it as a string.
2. Use the NTC Templates parser to transform the raw output into structured data.

Example 10-39. Using NTC Templates to get structured data from Netmiko output

```
>>> from netmiko import ConnectHandler
>>> device = ConnectHandler(
...     host='nxos-spine1',
...     username='admin',
...     password='admin',
...     device_type='cisco_nxos'
... )
>>> show_interfaces_raw = device.send_command('show int brief')
>>> show_interfaces_raw[:150]
```

```
'\n----------------------------------------------------------------------------\n
Port   VRF        Status IP Address                                S'
>>>
>>> from ntc_templates.parse import parse_output
>>> show_interfaces_parsed = parse_output(
...     platform="cisco_nxos",        ❶
...     command="show int brief",      ❷
...     data=show_interfaces_raw,       ❸
... )
>>> show_interfaces_parsed[0]
{
  'interface': 'mgmt0', 'vrf': '--', 'status': 'up', 'ip': '10.0.0.15',
  'speed': '1000', 'mtu': '1500', 'vlan': '', 'type': '', 'mode': '',
  'reason': '', 'portch': '', 'description': ''
}
```

❶ Indicates the reference platform. Each will have different parsers.

❷ Identifies the specific template within a platform because each CLI command may have different data.

❸ The raw input data to be parsed.

Luckily, since its 2.0.0 release, Netmiko has the implicit support of NTC Templates, simply using the use_textfsm argument:

```
>>> show_interfaces_parsed_directly = device.send_command(
...     'show int brief',
...     use_textfsm=True,
... )
>>> show_interfaces_parsed == show_interfaces_parsed_directly
True
```

This functionality is just combining the two steps presented in Example 10-39.

Netmiko is also used as the primary SSH driver for devices within NAPALM, a robust and multivendor network Python library for configuring devices and retrieving data. We cover NAPALM in Chapter 12.

This concludes using Netmiko to automate SSH-based network devices. You've now seen how to automate various types of network devices across a range of API types, no matter the device or API type you need to work with.

Summary

This chapter introduced the available types of APIs in the context of networking: HTTP-based APIs (both RESTful and non-RESTful), NETCONF, RESTCONF, and gNMI. After an introduction using command-line tools, we went through how these interfaces can be leveraged with the Go and Python programming languages. All these programmatic interfaces allow a much more efficient automation pattern than the traditional CLI with unstructured data. However, even nowadays, a lot of network devices are still out there where the main interface is still an SSH connection. Because of this, we also covered the Netmiko Python library.

At this point, you may be wondering, "Which network interface should I use?" The answer is, it depends. It depends on the device you are trying to automate—including the interfaces it supports and the capabilities you need to use. Another important factor is the tooling you prefer. Having tools that allow effective and efficient automation is key to success. One way or another, all the data-model interfaces share one big challenge that slows their adoption: the translation between standard or community data models to the device models does not always cover all the features or may not be fully supported. In the end, the goal is to change the data in the device's data store, and these data models come with inertia. This is the reason text-based configurations are still the main interface for many network devices.

As you continue your journey automating network devices with various types of APIs, remember that there is no magic here—you need to perform due diligence to understand how to use any given API and to know which options each platform offers over each interface.

In the next chapter, we shift gears and introduce the importance of using source code control to support network automation and programmability.

## CHAPTER 11

Source Control with Git

So far in this book, we've shown you lots of ways to add automation to your toolbox, whether via scripting languages like Python (see Chapter 6) or via templating languages like Jinja (see Chapter 9). The increased use of Python-based scripts or Jinja templates means that managing these artifacts is important (and by *artifacts* we mean the files that make up these scripts, templates, and other automation tools you're employing). In particular, managing the *changes* to these artifacts has significant value (we'll explain why shortly).

In this chapter, we're going to show you how to use a *source control* tool—that is, a tool designed to manage the artifacts you're creating and using in your network automation processes. The use of a source control tool lets you avoid messy and error-prone approaches like appending date- and timestamps to the end of filenames, and keeps you from running into accidentally deleted or overwritten files.

To start, let's take a closer look at the idea of source control. We'll keep the discussion fairly generic for now and delve into a specific source control tool known as Git later in the chapter. The generic qualities discussed in the next section are not specific to any particular source control tool.

Use Cases for Source Control

Simply put, *source control* is a way of tracking files and the changes made to those files over time (source control is also known as *version control* or *revision control*). We know that's a really generic description, so let's look at some specific use cases:

- If you're a developer writing code as part of a larger software development project, you could track the code you're writing by using source control tools. This is probably the most well-known use case, and the one most people immediately think about when we mention source control.

- Let's say you're part of a team of administrators managing network devices. You could take the device configuration files and track them by using source control tools.

- Suppose you're responsible for maintaining documentation for portions of your organization's IT infrastructure. You could use source control tools to track the documentation.

In each of these cases, source control is tracking files (network configurations, documentation, software source code). By *tracking* these files, we mean that the source control tool is keeping a record of the files, the changes made to the files over time, and who made each set of changes. If a change to one of the files being tracked breaks something, you can revert, or roll back, to a previous version of the file, undoing the changes and getting back to a known good state. In some cases (depending on the tool being used), source control tools might enable you to more easily collaborate with coworkers in a distributed fashion.

Benefits of Source Control

The previous section indirectly outlined some of the benefits of using a source control tool, but let's pull out a few specific benefits that come from the use of source control.

Change Tracking

First, you're able to track the changes to the files stored in the source control tool over time. You can see the state of the files at any given point, and therefore you're able to relatively easily see exactly *what* changed. This is an often overlooked benefit. When you're working with lengthy network configuration files, wouldn't it be helpful to be able to see *exactly* what changed from one version to the next?

Further, most source control tools also have the ability to add metadata about the change, such as why a change was made or a reference back to an issue or trouble ticket. This additional metadata can also prove quite useful in troubleshooting.

Accountability

Not only do source control tools track changes over time, but they also track *who* made the changes. Every change is logged with who made that particular change. In a team environment, where multiple team members might be working together to manage network configurations or server configuration files, this is extraordinarily useful. Never again will you have to ask, "Who made this change?" The source control tool will already have that information.

Process and Workflow

Using source control tools also helps you and your organization enforce a healthy process and workflow. We'll get into this more in Chapter 13, but for now think about the requirement that all changes must be logged in source control *before* being pushed to production. This gives you a linear history of changes, along with a log of the individual responsible for each set of changes, and enables you to enforce things like review (having someone else review your changes before they get put into production) or testing (having automated tests performed against the files in the source control system).

Benefits of Source Control for Networking

Although source control is most typically associated with software development, it has clear benefits for networking professionals. Here are just a few examples:

- Python scripts (such as the ones you will be able to write after reading this book!) that interact with network devices can be placed in source control, so that versions of the script can be more easily managed.

- Network device configurations can be placed in source control, enabling you to see the state of a network device configuration at any point in time. A really well-known tool called RANCID uses this approach for storing network device configuration backups.

- It's easy to highlight the changes between versions of network device configurations, allowing you and your team to easily verify that only the desired changes are in place (e.g., that you didn't accidentally prune a VLAN from the wrong 802.1Q trunk).

- Configuration templates can be placed in source control, ensuring that you and your team can track changes to these templates *before* they are used to generate network device configurations or reports.

- You can use source control with network documentation.

- All changes to any of these types of files are captured along with the person responsible for the changes—no more "playing the blame game."

Now that you have an idea of the benefits that source control can bring to you, your organization, and your workflow, let's take a look at a specific source control tool that is widely used: Git (*https://git-scm.com*).

Enter Git

Git, the latest in a long series of source control tools, has emerged as the de facto source control tool for most open source projects. (It doesn't hurt that Git manages the source code for the Linux kernel.) For that reason, we'll focus our discussion of source control tools on Git, but keep in mind that other tools do exist. They are, unfortunately, beyond the scope of this book.

Let's start with a brief history of how and why Git appeared.

Brief History of Git

As we've mentioned, Git is the source control tool used to manage the source code for the Linux kernel. Git was launched by Linus Torvalds, the creator of the Linux kernel, in early April 2005 in response to a disagreement between the Linux kernel developer community and the proprietary system they were using at the time (a system called BitKeeper).

Torvalds had a few key design goals when he set out to create Git:

Speed
> Torvalds needed Git to be able to rapidly apply patches to the Linux source code.

Simplicity
> The design for Git needed to be as simple as possible.

Strong support for nonlinear development
> The Linux kernel developers needed a system that could handle lots of parallel branches. Thus, this new system (Git) needed to support rapid branching and merging, and branches needed to be as lightweight as possible.

Support for fully distributed operation
> Every developer needed a full copy of the entire source code and its history.

Scalability
> Git needed to be scalable enough to handle large projects, like the Linux kernel.

Development of Git was fast. Within a few days of its launch, Git was self-hosted (meaning that the source code for Git was being managed by Git). The first merge of multiple branches occurred just a couple of weeks later. At the end of April—just a few weeks after its launch—Git was benchmarked at applying patches to the Linux kernel tree at 6.7 patches per second. In June 2005, Git managed the 2.6.12 release of the Linux kernel, and the 1.0 release of Git occurred in late December 2005.

As of this writing, the most recent release of Git is version 2.41.0, and versions of Git are available for all major desktop operating systems (Linux, Windows, and macOS). Notable open source projects using Git include the Linux kernel (as we've already mentioned), Perl, the GNOME desktop environment, Android, KDE, and the X.Org implementation of the X Window System. Additionally, some very popular online source control services are based on Git, including GitHub (*https://github.com*), Bitbucket (*https://bitbucket.org*), and GitLab (*https://about.gitlab.com*). Some of these services also offer on-premises implementations. You'll get the opportunity to look more closely at GitLab in Chapter 13, when we discuss continuous integration.

Git Terminology

Before we progress any further, let's be sure that we've properly defined the terminology. Some of these terms we may have used before, but we include them here for the sake of completeness:

Repository
> In Git, a repository is a database that contains all of a project's information (files and metadata) and history. (We're using the term *project* here to refer to an arbitrary grouping of files for a particular purpose or effort.) A repository is a complete copy of all the files and information associated with a project throughout its lifetime. After data is added to a repository, it is immutable; that is, it can't be changed once added. This *isn't* to say that you can't make changes to files stored in a repository, just that the repository stores and tracks these files in such a way that changes to a file create a new entry in the repository (specifically, Git uses SHA-1 hashes to create content-addressable objects in the repository).

Working directory
> This is the directory where you, as the user of Git, will modify the files contained in the repository. The working directory is *not* the same as the repository. Note that the term *working directory* is also used for other purposes on Linux/Unix/macOS systems (to refer to the current directory, as output by the `pwd` command). Git's working directory is *not* the same as the current directory, and specifically refers to the directory where the *.git* repository is stored.

Index
> The index describes the repository's directory structure and content at a point in time. The index is a dynamic binary file maintained by Git and modified as you stage changes and commit them to the repository.

Commit
> A commit is an entry in the Git repository, recording metadata for each change introduced to the repository. This metadata includes the author, the date of the commit, and a commit message (a description of the change introduced to the repository). Additionally, a commit captures the state of the entire repository at the time the commit was performed. Keep in mind that when we say "a change to the repository," this might mean multiple changes to multiple files; Git allows you

to lump changes to multiple files together as a single commit. (We discuss this in a bit more detail later in this chapter.)

Overview of Git's Architecture

With the terminology from the previous section in mind, we can now provide an overview of Git's architecture. We'll limit our discussion of Git's architecture to keep it relatively high-level but detailed enough to help with your understanding of how Git operates.

For a more in-depth discussion of Git's architecture, we recommend *Version Control with Git*, 3rd Edition, by Prem Kumar Ponuthorai and Jon Loeliger (O'Reilly).

As we described earlier, a Git *repository* is a database that contains all the information about a project: the files contained in the project, the changes made to the project over time, and the metadata about those changes (who made the change, when the change was made, etc.). By default, this information is stored in a directory named *.git* in the root of your working directory (this behavior can be changed). For example, here's a file listing of a newly initialized Git repository's working directory, showing the *.git* directory where the actual repository data is found:

```
macbookpro:npab-examples slowe (main)$ ls -la
total 0
drwxr-xr-x   3 slowe   staff  102 May 11 15:37 .
drwxr-xr-x  16 slowe   staff  544 May 11 15:37 ..
drwxr-xr-x  10 slowe   staff  340 May 11 15:37 .git
macbookpro:npab-examples slowe (main)$
```

Although the preceding directory listing came from a MacBook Pro laptop, throughout this chapter we'll primarily be using three different Linux distributions to show the output of various `git` commands and subcommands: Debian 11, Ubuntu 20.04, and Amazon Linux 2. We've customized the prompts shown here to clearly show the name of each distribution in the prompt; your prompt will quite likely look different.

As you can tell from this prompt, this directory listing is from the directory *npab-examples*. In this example, the *working directory* is the *npab-examples* directory, and the Git *repository* is in *npab-examples/.git*. This is why we said earlier that the working directory and the repository aren't the same. It's common for new users to refer to the working directory as the repository, but keep in mind that the actual repository is in the *.git* subdirectory.

Within the *.git* directory you'll find all the various components that make up a Git repository:

- The index—which we defined earlier as representing the repository's directory structure and content at a given point in time—is found at *.git/index*.
- The files contained within a Git repository are treated as content-addressable objects and stored in subdirectories in *.git/objects*.
- Any repository-specific configuration details are found in *.git/config*.
- Metadata about the repository, the changes stored in the repository, and the objects in the repository can be found in *.git/logs*.

All the information stored in the *.git* directory is maintained by Git—you should never need to directly interact with the contents of this directory. Over the course of this chapter, we'll share with you the various commands for interacting with the repository to add files, commit changes, revert changes, and more. In fact, that leads us directly into our next section, which will show you how to work with Git.

Working with Git

Now that you have an idea of what Git's architecture looks like, let's shift our focus to something a bit more practical: actually *working* with Git.

Throughout this discussion, we're going to use a (hopefully) practical example. Let's assume that you are a network engineer responsible for rolling out some network automation tools in your environment. During this process, you're going to end up creating Python scripts, Jinja templates, and other files. You'd like to use Git to manage these files so that you can take advantage of all the benefits of source control.

The following sections walk you through each of the major steps in getting started using Git to manage the files created as part of your network automation effort.

Installing Git

The steps for installing Git are extremely well documented, so we won't go through them here. Git is often preinstalled in various distributions of Linux; if not, Git is almost always available to install via the Linux distribution's package manager (such as dnf for RHEL/CentOS/Fedora or apt for Debian/Ubuntu). Installers are available for macOS and Windows that make it easy to install Git. Detailed instructions and options for installing Git are also available on the Git website (*https://oreil.ly/1IxBe*).

Creating a Repository

Once Git is installed, the first step is to create a directory where the repository will be stored. Assuming you're using a Debian GNU/Linux system, the command might look something like this (and would be similar, if not identical, on other Linux distributions or on macOS):

```
admin@debian11:~$ mkdir ~/net-auto
```

Then you can change into this directory and create the empty repository by using the `git init` command:

```
admin@debian11:~$ cd net-auto
admin@debian11:~/net-auto$ git init
hint: Using 'master' as the name for the initial branch. This default branch name
hint: is subject to change. To configure the initial branch name to use in all
hint: of your new repositories, which will suppress this warning, call:
hint:
hint:   git config --global init.defaultBranch <name>
hint:
hint: Names commonly chosen instead of 'master' are 'main', 'trunk' and
hint: 'development'. The just-created branch can be renamed via this command:
hint:
hint:   git branch -m <name>
Initialized empty Git repository in /home/admin/net-auto/.git
```

The `git init` command is responsible for *initializing*, or creating, a new Git repository. This involves creating the *.git* directory and all the subdirectories and contents found within them as well as setting up the initial branch (you'll learn more on branches in "Branching in Git" on page 527).

The preceding message regarding the name of the initial branch was added in Git 2.28, released on July 27, 2020. Linux distributions and operating systems released after this time will most likely ship with or make available a version of Git that is at least 2.28 or higher. The preceding output was taken from a Debian 11 system, which provides Git 2.30.2. Ubuntu 20.04.3, which ships with Git 2.25.1, does not display the same output.

 The `git` commands described throughout this chapter should be nearly identical across all systems on which Git runs. We'll use various Linux distributions (as reflected in the shell prompts in the examples), but using Git on macOS should be the same as on Linux. Using Git on Windows should be similar, but syntactical differences may exist here and there because of the differences in the underlying operating systems.

If you were now to run `ls -la` in the *net-auto* directory, you'd see the *.git* directory that stores the empty Git repository created by the `git init` command. The repository is now ready for you to start adding content. You add content to a repository by adding files.

Adding Files to a Repository

Adding files to a repository is a multistage process:

1. Add the files to the repository's working directory.
2. Stage the files to the repository's index.
3. Commit the staged files to the repository.

Let's go back to our example. You've created your new Git repository to store files created as part of your network automation project, and some of the first files you'd like to add to the repository are the current configuration files from your network devices. You already have three configuration files: *sw1.txt*, *sw2.txt*, and *sw3.txt*, that contain the current configurations for three switches.

First, copy the files into the working directory (in our example, */home/admin/net-auto*). More generically, remember that the working directory is the parent directory of the *.git* directory (which holds the actual Git repository). On a Linux or macOS system, copying files into the working directory would involve the cp command; on a Windows-based machine, you'd use the copy command.

The files are now in the working directory but are *not* in the repository itself. This means that Git is not tracking the files or their content, and therefore you can't track changes, know who made the changes, or roll back to an earlier version.

You can verify this by running the git status command, which in this example produces output that looks like this:

```
admin@debian11:~/net-auto$ git status
On branch main

No commits yet

Untracked files:
  (use "git add <file>..." to include in what will be committed)

    sw1.txt
    sw2.txt
    sw3.txt

nothing added to commit but untracked files present (use "git add" to track)
```

The output of the git status command tells you that untracked files are present in the working directory and that nothing has been added to the repository. As the output indicates, you need to use the git add command to add these untracked files to the repository, like this:

```
admin@debian11:~/net-auto$ git add sw1.txt
admin@debian11:~/net-auto$ git add sw2.txt
admin@debian11:~/net-auto$ git add sw3.txt
```

You could also use shell globbing to add multiple files at the same time. For example, you could use `git add sw*.txt` to add all three switch configurations with a single command. On systems running bash, you could also use brace expansion, as in `git add sw{1,2,3}.txt`, to stage multiple files.

After you've used `git add` to add the files to the staging area, you can run `git status` again to see the current status:

```
admin@debian11:~/net-auto$ git status
On branch main

No commits yet

Changes to be committed:
  (use "git rm --cached <file>..." to unstage)

        new file:   sw1.txt
        new file:   sw2.txt
        new file:   sw3.txt
```

At this point, the files have been *staged* into Git's index; Git's index and the working directory are in sync. Technically speaking, the files have been added as objects to Git's object store as well, but there is no point-in-time reference to these objects. To create that point-in-time reference, you must first *commit* the staged changes.

Committing Changes to a Repository

Before you're ready to commit changes to a repository, you need to be sure that you've done a couple of things. Recall that one of the benefits of using Git as a source control tool is that you're able to not only track the changes made to the files stored in the repository, but also know who made each set of changes. To obtain that information, you first need to provide it to Git. (You could also do this right after installing Git; it's not necessary to create a repository first.) This configuration is also important when it comes to collaborating with others using Git, as you'll see in "Collaborating with Git" on page 545.

Providing user information to Git

Git has a series of configuration options; some are repository-specific, some are user-specific, and some are system-wide. Recall from earlier that Git stores repository-specific configuration information in *.git/config*. In this particular case—where we need to provide the user's name and email address so Git can track who made each set of changes—it's the user-specific configuration we need to modify, not the repository-specific configuration.

So where are these values stored? These settings are found in the *.gitconfig* file in your home directory. This file is an INI-style file, and you can edit it by using either your favorite text editor or the `git config` command. In this case, we'll show you how to use `git config` to set this information.

To set your name and email address, use the following commands:

```
ubuntu@ubuntu2004:~/net-auto$ git config --global user.name "John Smith"
ubuntu@ubuntu2004:~/net-auto$ git config --global user.email
"john.smith@networktocode.com"
```

You use the `--global` option here to set it as a user-specific value; if you want to set a different username and/or email address as a repository-specific value, just omit the `--global` flag (but be sure you're in the working directory of an active repository first; Git will report an error otherwise). With the `--global` flag, `git config` modifies the *.gitconfig* file in your home directory; without it, `git config` modifies the *.git/config* file of the current repository.

Committing changes

When Git has been configured with your identity, you're ready to *commit* the changes you've made to the files into the repository. Remember that before you can commit changes into the repository, you must first *stage* the files by using the `git add` command; this is true both for newly created files as well as modified files that were already in the repository (we'll review that scenario shortly). Since you've already staged the changes (via the `git add` command earlier) and verified that (via the `git status` command, which shows the files are staged), then you're ready to commit.

Committing changes to a repository is as simple as using the `git commit` command:

```
ubuntu@ubuntu2004:~/net-auto$ git commit -m "First commit to new repository"
[main (root-commit) 9547063] First commit to new repository
 3 files changed, 24 insertions(+)
 create mode 100644 sw1.txt
 create mode 100644 sw2.txt
 create mode 100644 sw3.txt
```

 If you omit the `-m` parameter to `git commit`, Git will launch the default text editor so you can provide a commit message. The text editor that Git launches is configurable (via `git config` or editing *.gitconfig* in your home directory). You could, for example, configure Git to use Visual Studio Code (*https://code.visualstudio.com*), Sublime Text (*https://www.sublimetext.com*), or another graphical text editor.

So what's happening when you commit the changes to the repository? When you add the files via `git add`, objects representing the files (and the files' content) are added to Git's object database. Specifically, Git creates *blobs* (binary large objects) to represent the files' content, and *tree objects* to represent the files and their directory structure.

When you commit the changes via `git commit`, you're adding another type of object to the Git database (a *commit object*) that references the tree objects, which in turn reference the blobs. With a commit object, you now have a point-in-time reference to the entire state of the repository.

At this point, your repository has a single commit, and you can see that commit by using the `git log` command:

```
[ec2-user@amazonlinux2 net-auto]$ git log
commit 8d18465d697de11ebe34494f33d0cad42e01e076 (HEAD -> main)
Author: John Smith <john.smith@networktocode.com>
Date:   Wed Feb 9 02:24:24 2022 +0000

    First commit to new repository
[ec2-user@amazonlinux2 net-auto]$
```

The `git log` command shows the various commits—or checkpoints, if you will—you created over the lifetime of the repository. Every time you commit changes, you create a commit object, and that commit object references the state of the repository at the time it was created. This means you can view the state of the repository and its contents only at the time of a commit. Commits, therefore, become the checkpoints by which you can move backward (or forward) through the history of the repository.

Recommendations for committing changes

Understanding how commits work leads to a few recommendations around committing your changes to a repository:

Commit frequently
> You can view the state of the repository only at the time when changes are committed (via a commit object). If you make changes, save the files, make more changes, and then save and commit, you won't be able to view the state of the repository at the first set of changes (because you didn't commit).

Commit at logical points
> Don't commit every time you save changes to a file in the repository. We know this sounds like a contradiction to the previous bullet, but it makes sense to commit changes only when they are complete. For example, committing changes when you're only halfway through updating a switch's configuration doesn't make sense; you wouldn't want to roll back to a half-completed switch configuration. Instead, commit when you've finished the switch configuration.

Use helpful commit messages
> As you can see from the previous `git log` output, commit messages help you understand the changes contained in that commit. Try to make your commit messages helpful and straightforward—in six months, the commit message will likely be the only clue to help you decipher what you were doing at that time.

Before we move on to the next section, we need to discuss one more topic. We've explained that objects in a Git repository are immutable, and that changes to an object (like a file) result in the creation of a new object (addressed by the SHA-1 hash of the object's content). This is true for all objects in the Git repository, including blobs (file content), tree objects, and commit objects.

What if, though, you make a commit and realize the commit contains errors? Maybe you have some typos in your network configuration, or the commit message is wrong. In this case, Git allows you to modify (or *amend*) the last commit.

Amending commits

If the last commit is incorrect for some reason, it is possible to *amend* the commit via the `--amend` flag to `git commit`. Note that you could just make another commit instead of amending the previous commit; both approaches are valid, and each approach has its advantages and disadvantages, which we'll discuss shortly. First, though, let's show you how to amend a commit.

To amend a commit, you follow the same set of steps as with a "normal" commit:

1. Make whatever changes you need to make.
2. Stage the changes.
3. Run `git commit --amend` to commit the changes, marking it as an amendment.

Under the hood, Git is actually creating new objects—which is in line with Git's philosophy and approach of content-addressable immutable objects—but in the history of the repository, you'll see *only* the amended commit, not the original commit. This results in a "cleaner" history, although some purists may argue that simply making another commit (instead of using `--amend`) is a better approach.

Which approach is best? That is mostly decided by you, the user, but there are a couple of considerations. If you're collaborating with others via Git and a shared repository, using `--amend` to amend commits already sent to the shared repository is generally a bad idea. The one exception is in an environment using Gerrit, where amended commits are used extensively. We talk more about Gerrit in Chapter 13, and we cover collaborating with Git in "Collaborating with Git" on page 545.

Changing and Committing Tracked Files

You've created a repository, added new files, and committed changes to the repository. Now, though, you need to make some changes to the files that are already in the repository. How does that work?

Fortunately, the process for committing modified versions of files into a repository looks pretty much identical to what we've shown you already:

1. Modify the file(s) in the working directory.

2. Stage the change(s) to the index by using `git add`. This puts the index in sync with the working directory.

3. Commit the changes by using `git commit`. This puts the repository in sync with the index, and creates a point-in-time reference to the state of the repository.

Let's review this in a bit more detail. Suppose you need to modify one of the files, *sw1.txt*, because the switch's configuration has changed (or perhaps because you're enforcing that configurations can be deployed only *after* they've been checked into source control). After a tracked file (a file about which Git already knows and is tracking) is modified, `git status` will show that changes are present:

```
ubuntu@ubuntu2004:~/net-auto$ git status
On branch main
Changes not staged for commit:
  (use "git add <file>..." to update what will be committed)
  (use "git restore <file>..." to discard changes in working directory)

        modified:   sw1.txt

no changes added to commit (use "git add" and/or "git commit -a")
```

Note the difference between this status message and the status message we showed you earlier. In this case, Git knows about the *sw1.txt* file (it's already been added to the repository), so the status message is different. The status message changes if you add another switch configuration file, *sw4.txt*, to the working directory:

```
ubuntu@ubuntu2004:~/net-auto$ git status
On branch main
Changes not staged for commit:
  (use "git add <file>..." to update what will be committed)
  (use "git restore <file>..." to discard changes in working directory)

        modified:   sw1.txt

Untracked files:
  (use "git add <file>..." to include in what will be committed)

        sw4.txt

no changes added to commit (use "git add" and/or "git commit -a")
```

Again, Git provides a clear distinction between tracking changes to an already known file and detecting untracked (not previously added) files to the working directory. Either way, though, the process for getting these changes (modified file and new file) into the repository is exactly the same, as you can see in the output of the `git status` command: just use the `git add` command and then the `git commit` command:

```
admin@debian11:~/net-auto$ git add sw1.txt
admin@debian11:~/net-auto$ git add sw4.txt
admin@debian11:~/net-auto$ git status
On branch main
Changes to be committed:
  (use "git restore --staged <file>..." to unstage)

    modified:   sw1.txt
    new file:   sw4.txt

admin@debian11:~/net-auto$ git commit -m "Update sw1, add sw4"
[main 679c41c] Update sw1, add sw4
 2 files changed, 9 insertions(+)
 create mode 100644 sw4.txt
```

In the output of the `git status` commands, you may have noticed a reference to `git commit -a`. The `-a` option simply tells Git to add all changes from all known files. If you're only committing changes to known files *and* you are OK with committing all the changes together in a single commit, then using `git commit -a` allows you to avoid using the `git add` command first.

If, however, you want to break up changes to multiple files into separate commits, you need to use `git add` followed by `git commit` instead. Why might you want to do this?

- You might want to limit the scope of changes in a single commit so that it's less impactful to revert to an earlier version.

- You may want to limit the scope of changes in a single commit so that others can review your changes more easily. (We'll discuss this in more detail in Chapter 13.)

- When collaborating with others, it's often considered a best practice to limit commits to a single logical change, which means you may include some changes in a commit but not others. We discuss general guidelines for collaborating with Git in "Collaborating with Git" on page 545.

You'll also notice that we've been using `git commit -m` in our examples. The `-m` option allows the user to include a commit message on the command line. If you don't include the `-m`, Git will open your default editor so that you can supply a commit message. Commit messages are required, and as we mentioned earlier, we recommend that you make your commit messages as informative as possible. (You'll be thankful for informative commit messages when reviewing the output of `git log` in the future.) You can also combine both the `-a` and `-m` options, as in `git commit -am "Committing all changes to tracked files"`.

For more information on the various options to any of the git commands, just type **git help** *command*, like git help commit or git help add. This opens the man page for that part of Git's documentation. If you like to use the man command instead, you can do that; just put a dash into the git command. Thus, to see the man page for git commit, you'd enter **man git-commit**.

Now that you've committed another set of changes to the repository, let's look at the output of git log:

```
[ec2-user@amazonlinux2 net-auto]$ git log
commit f3a00e6596878faffbfb169063cafba67833323c (HEAD -> main)
Author: John Smith <john.smith@networktocode.com>
Date:   Wed Feb 9 02:34:26 2022 +0000

    Update sw1, add sw4

commit 8d18465d697de11ebe34494f33d0cad42e01e076
Author: John Smith <john.smith@networktocode.com>
Date:   Wed Feb 9 02:24:24 2022 +0000

    First commit to new repository
[ec2-user@amazonlinux2 net-auto]$
```

Your repository now has two commits. Before we explore how to view a repository at a particular point in time (at a particular commit), let's first review a few other commands and make some additional commits to the repository.

Unstaging Files

If you've been following along, your repository now has four switch configuration files (*sw1.txt* through *sw4.txt*) and two commits. Let's say you need to add a fifth switch configuration file (named *sw5.txt*, of course). You already know the process:

1. Copy the file *sw5.txt* into the working directory.

2. Use git add to stage the file from the working directory into the index.

At this point, running git status will report that *sw5.txt* has been staged and is ready to commit to the repository:

```
[ec2-user@amazonlinux2 net-auto]$ git status
On branch main
Changes to be committed:
  (use "git restore --staged <file>..." to unstage)

    new file:   sw5.txt

[ec2-user@amazonlinux2 net-auto]$
```

However, you realize after staging the file that you aren't ready to commit it in its current state. Maybe the file isn't complete, or perhaps it doesn't accurately reflect the actual configuration of sw5 on the network. In such a situation, the best approach is to *unstage* the file.

The command to unstage the file—that is, to remove it from the index so the working directory and the index are no longer synchronized—has already been given to you by Git. If you refer to the output of git status shared just a couple paragraphs ago, you'll see Git telling you how to unstage the file. The command looks like this:

```
git restore --staged file
```

In earlier versions of Git, the command was git reset HEAD *file*. Newer versions of Git added the git restore command you see here. The older version actually gives a clue as to what's happening when you run this command, but to explain what's happening, we first need to explain what *HEAD* is.

HEAD is a pointer referencing the last commit you made (or the last commit you checked out into the working directory, but we haven't gotten to that point yet). Recall that when you stage a file (using git add), you are taking content from the working directory into the index. When you commit (using git commit), you are creating a point-in-time reference—a commit—to the content. Every time you commit, Git updates HEAD to point to the latest commit.

 HEAD also plays a strong role when you start working with multiple Git branches. You'll learn more when we discuss branches in "Branching in Git" on page 527.

Here's a quick way to help illustrate updating HEAD. If you've been following along with this chapter's examples, you can use these commands as well (just keep in mind that the SHA-1 checksums shown here will differ from your own SHA-1 checksums).

First, use cat to show the contents of *.git/HEAD*:

```
[ec2-user@amazonlinux2 net-auto]$ cat .git/HEAD
ref: refs/heads/main
[ec2-user@amazonlinux2 net-auto]$
```

You'll see that HEAD is a pointer to the file *refs/heads/main*. If you cat that file, you'll see this:

```
[ec2-user@amazonlinux2 net-auto]$ cat .git/refs/heads/main
f3a00e6596878faffbfb169063cafba67833323c
[ec2-user@amazonlinux2 net-auto]$
```

The content of *.git/refs/heads/main* is a SHA-1 checksum. Now run git log, and compare the SHA-1 checksum of the latest commit against that value:

```
[ec2-user@amazonlinux2 net-auto]$ git log
commit f3a00e6596878faffbfb169063cafba67833323c (HEAD -> main)
Author: John Smith <john.smith@networktocode.com>
Date:   Wed Feb 9 02:34:26 2022 +0000

    Update sw1, add sw4

commit 8d18465d697de11ebe34494f33d0cad42e01e076
Author: John Smith <john.smith@networktocode.com>
Date:   Wed Feb 9 02:24:24 2022 +0000

    First commit to new repository
[ec2-user@amazonlinux2 net-auto]$
```

You'll note that the SHA-1 checksum of the last commit matches the value of HEAD (which points to *refs/heads/main*), illustrating that HEAD is a pointer to the latest commit. Later in this chapter, we'll show how HEAD also incorporates branches and how it changes when you check out content to your working directory.

For now, though, let's get back to git reset as way of unstaging a file. This command is powerful, but fortunately it has some sane defaults. When used in this way —that is, without any flags and when given a filename or path—the only thing git reset will do is make the index look like the content referenced by HEAD (which you now know references a particular commit—by default, the latest commit).

Recall that git add makes the index look like the working directory, which is how you stage a file. The git reset HEAD *file* command is the exact opposite, making the index look like the content referenced by HEAD. It *undoes* changes to the index made by git add, thus *unstaging* files.

The git restore command works in the same fashion: it restores the specified paths with the content from a restore source. When used with the --staged parameter, it will (by default) restore from HEAD, just exactly as git reset HEAD *file* does. You can find out more about the git restore command by running man git-restore.

Let's see this command in action. You've already staged *sw5.txt* in preparation for committing it to the repository, so git status shows the file listed in the Changes to be committed: section. Now run git restore:

```
[ec2-user@amazonlinux2 net-auto]$ git restore --staged sw5.txt
[ec2-user@amazonlinux2 net-auto]$ git status
On branch main
Untracked files:
  (use "git add <file>..." to include in what will be committed)

    sw5.txt

nothing added to commit but untracked files present (use "git add" to track)
[ec2-user@amazonlinux2 net-auto]$
```

You can see that *sw5.txt* is no longer listed as a change to be committed and is instead shown as an untracked file (it's no longer in the index). Now you can continue working on the content of *sw5.txt* and committing a version of it to the repository when you're ready.

We've shown you how to create a repository, add files (both new and existing), commit changes, and unstage files. What if you have files that need to be colocated with other files in the repository but shouldn't be tracked by Git? This is where file exclusions come into play.

Excluding Files from a Repository

Sometimes you might need to store files in the working directory—the "scratch space" for a Git repository—that you don't want included in the repository. Fortunately, Git provides a way to exclude certain files or filename patterns from inclusion in the repository.

Going back to our example, you've created a repository in which to store network automation artifacts. Let's suppose you have a Python script that connects to your network switches in order to gather information from them. An example of one such Python script—in this case, one written to connect to an Arista switch and gather information—might look like this:

```python
#!/usr/bin/env python

from pyeapi.client import Node as EOS
from pyeapi import connect
import yaml

def main():

    creds = yaml.load(open('credentials.yml'))

    un = creds['username']
    pwd = creds['password']

    conn = connect(host='eos-npab', username=un, password=pwd)
    device = EOS(conn)

    output = device.enable('show version')
    result = output[0]['result']

    print('Arista Switch Summary:')
    print('---------------------')
    print('OS Version:' + result['version'])
    print('Model:' + result['modelName'])
    print('System MAC:' + result['systemMacAddress'])
```

```
if __name__ == "__main__":
    main()
```

Part of the way this script operates is via the use of authentication credentials stored in a separate file (in this case, a YAML file named *credentials.yml*). Now, you need these credentials to be stored with the Python script, but you don't necessarily want the credentials to be tracked and managed by the repository.

 Whether to include secrets—information like passwords, SSH keys, or the like—into a Git repository depends greatly on the way the repository is being used. For a strictly private repository where per-user secrets are not needed, including secrets in the repository is probably fine. For repositories where per-user secrets should be used or for repositories that may at some point be shared publicly, you'll likely want to exclude secrets from the repository by using the mechanisms outlined in this section.

Fortunately, Git provides a couple of ways to exclude files from being tracked as part of a repository. In "Committing Changes to a Repository" on page 504, we noted that Git configuration can be handled on a repository-specific, user-specific, or system-wide basis. Excluding files from Git repositories is similar in that there are ways to exclude files per repository or per user.

Excluding files per repository

Let's start with the per-repository method. The most common way of excluding (or ignoring) files is to use a *.gitignore* file stored in the repository itself. Like any other content in the repository, the *.gitignore* file must be staged into the index and committed to the repository anytime changes are made. The advantage of this approach is that the *.gitignore* file is then distributed as part of the repository, which is useful when you are part of a team whose members are all using Git as a distributed version control system (DVCS).

The content of the *.gitignore* file is simply a list of filenames or filename patterns, one on each line. To create your own list of files for Git to ignore, you simply create the file named *.gitignore* in the working directory, edit it to add the filenames or filename patterns you want ignored, and then add/commit it to the repository.

Looking at our Python script from earlier, you can see that it looks for its credentials in the file named *credentials.yml*. Let's create *.gitignore* (if you don't already have one) to ignore this file:

1. Create an empty file by using touch .gitignore.

2. Edit *.gitignore*, using the text editor of your choice, to add *credentials.yml* on a single line in the file.

At this point, if you run git status, you'll see that Git has noticed the addition of the *.gitignore* file, but the *credentials.yml* file is *not* listed:

```
ubuntu@ubuntu2004:~/net-auto$ git status
On branch main
Untracked files:
  (use "git add <file>..." to include in what will be committed)

    .gitignore

nothing added to commit but untracked files present (use "git add" to track)
```

You can now stage and commit the *.gitignore* file into the repository by using git add . and git commit -m "Adding .gitignore file".

Now, if you create the *credentials.yml* file for the Python script, Git will politely ignore the file. For example, here you can see the file exists in the working directory, but git status reports no changes or untracked files:

```
ubuntu@ubuntu2004:~/net-auto$ ls -la
total 40
drwxrwxr-x 3 ubuntu ubuntu 4096 May 31 16:32 .
drwxr-xr-x 5 ubuntu ubuntu 4096 May 12 17:18 ..
drwxrwxr-x 8 ubuntu ubuntu 4096 May 31 16:34 .git
-rw-rw-r-- 1 ubuntu ubuntu    8 May 31 16:27 .gitignore
-rw-rw-r-- 1 ubuntu ubuntu   15 May 31 16:32 credentials.yml
-rwxrwxr-x 1 ubuntu ubuntu    0 May 31 16:32 script.py
-rw-rw-r-- 1 ubuntu ubuntu   98 May 12 20:22 sw1.txt
-rw-rw-r-- 1 ubuntu ubuntu   84 May 12 17:17 sw2.txt
-rw-rw-r-- 1 ubuntu ubuntu   84 May 12 17:17 sw3.txt
-rw-rw-r-- 1 ubuntu ubuntu   84 May 12 20:33 sw4.txt
-rw-rw-r-- 1 ubuntu ubuntu  135 May 31 14:56 sw5.txt
ubuntu@ubuntu2004:~/net-auto$ git status
On branch main
nothing to commit, working directory clean
```

If you're really paying attention, you might note that the fact Git reports nothing to commit isn't necessarily a guarantee that the file has been ignored. Let's use a few more git commands to verify it. First, we'll use git log to show the history of commits:

```
ubuntu@ubuntu2004:~/net-auto$ git log --oneline
554b084 (HEAD -> main) Adding .gitignore file
ee7e7bf Add Python script to talk to network switches
d40fe74 Add configuration for sw5
dd61e7b Update sw1, add sw4
6b9b6cd First commit to new repository
```

Next, let's interrogate Git to see the contents of the repository at these various points in time. You'll use the `git ls-tree` command along with the SHA-1 hash of the commit you want to inspect. You've probably noticed by now that Git often uses just the first seven characters of a SHA-1 hash, as in the preceding output of the `git log --oneline` command (Git will automatically use more characters to keep the hashes unique as needed). In almost every case (an exception may be out there somewhere!), that's true for commands you enter that require a SHA-1 hash. For example, to see what was in the repository at the time of the next-to-last commit (whose SHA-1 hash starts with `ee7e7bf`), you could do this:

```
ubuntu@ubuntu2004:~/net-auto$ git ls-tree ee7e7bf
100755 blob e69de29bb2d1d6434b8b29ae775ad8c2e48c5391    script.py
100644 blob 2567e072ca607963292d73e3acd49a5388305c53    sw1.txt
100644 blob 02df3d404d59d72c98439f44df673c6038352a27    sw2.txt
100644 blob 02df3d404d59d72c98439f44df673c6038352a27    sw3.txt
100644 blob 02df3d404d59d72c98439f44df673c6038352a27    sw4.txt
100644 blob 88b23c7f60dc91f7d5bfeb094df9ed28996daeeb    sw5.txt
```

You can see that *credentials.yml* does not exist in the repository as of this commit. What about the latest commit?

```
ubuntu@ubuntu2004:~/net-auto$ git ls-tree 554b084
100644 blob 2c1817fdecc27ccb3f7bce3f6bbad1896c9737fc    .gitignore
100755 blob e69de29bb2d1d6434b8b29ae775ad8c2e48c5391    script.py
100644 blob 2567e072ca607963292d73e3acd49a5388305c53    sw1.txt
100644 blob 02df3d404d59d72c98439f44df673c6038352a27    sw2.txt
100644 blob 02df3d404d59d72c98439f44df673c6038352a27    sw3.txt
100644 blob 02df3d404d59d72c98439f44df673c6038352a27    sw4.txt
100644 blob 88b23c7f60dc91f7d5bfeb094df9ed28996daeeb    sw5.txt
```

(We'll leave it as an exercise for you to review the rest of the commits in order to verify that the *credentials.yml* file is *not* present in any commit.)

Excluding files globally

In addition to excluding files per repository by using a *.gitignore* file in the repository's working directory, you can also create a global file for excluding files for all repositories on your computer. Just create a *.gitignore_global* file in your home directory and add exclusions to that file. You may also want to run this command to ensure that Git is configured to use this new *.gitignore_global* file in your home directory:

```
git config --global core.excludesfile /path/to/.gitignore_global
```

If you placed *.gitignore_global* in your home directory, the path to the file would typically be noted as *~/.gitignore_global*.

The use of `git log` and `git ls-tree` naturally leads us into a discussion of how to view more information about a repository, its history, and its content.

Viewing More Information About a Repository

When it comes to viewing more information about a repository, we've already shown you one command that you'll use quite a bit: `git log`. The `git log` command has already been used on numerous occasions, which should give you some indicator of just how useful it is.

Viewing basic log information

The most basic form of `git log` shows the history of commits up to HEAD, so just running `git log` shows you all the commits over the history of the repository. Here's the output of `git log` for this chapter's example repository:

```
admin@debian11:~/net-auto$ git log
commit 045c1aa80b2a75f304eff4f001c77dfba23935e7 (HEAD -> main)
Author: John Smith <john.smith@networktocode.com>
Date:   Wed Feb 9 03:02:43 2022 +0000

    Adding .gitignore file

commit dcddb60add227e99c7ece91d22aa7f9e2001c268
Author: John Smith <john.smith@networktocode.com>
Date:   Wed Feb 9 02:58:42 2022 +0000

    Add Python script to talk to network switches

commit 097bbd348c5148d2f788ee00a8d59c7462e7e836
Author: John Smith <john.smith@networktocode.com>
Date:   Wed Feb 9 02:54:14 2022 +0000

    Add configuration for sw5

commit 0bc86eb847083a38e5cffedd780fd0a5217a90db
Author: John Smith <john.smith@networktocode.com>
Date:   Wed Feb 9 02:34:24 2022 +0000

    Update sw1, add sw4

commit 3121e674be42b59e0af4bcfbb30ad5d61dd45fdd
Author: John Smith <john.smith@networktocode.com>
Date:   Wed Feb 9 02:24:11 2022 +0000

    First commit to new repository
```

Viewing brief log information

The `git log` command has multiple options—too many to cover here. One of the more useful options that we've already shown you, the `--oneline` option, would produce the following output for the same example repository:

```
admin@debian11:~/net-auto$ git log --oneline
045c1aa (HEAD -> main) Adding .gitignore file
dcddb60 Add Python script to talk to network switches
```

```
097bbd3 Add configuration for sw5
0bc86eb Update sw1, add sw4
3121e67 First commit to new repository
```

As you can see from this output, `--oneline` abbreviates the SHA-1 hash and lists only the commit message. For repositories with a lengthy history, it may be most helpful to start with `git log --oneline` and then drill into the details of a specific commit.

 Disabling Git's default behavior to pipe output through a pager can make finding things via the use of `grep` possible. To disable Git's pager functionality, use the `--no-pager` option, as in `git --no-pager log --oneline`.

To drill into the details of a specific commit, you have a few options. First, you can use the `git log` command and supply a range of commits to show. The syntax is `git log start SHA..end SHA`. So, if you want to show more details on the last couple of commits in our example repository, you run a command that looks like this (if you're wondering where the SHA-1 values came from, refer to the output of `git log --oneline` from earlier in this section, and recall that you need to supply only the first seven characters of the SHA-1 hash):

```
admin@debian11:~/net-auto$ git log dcddb60..045c1aa
commit 045c1aa80b2a75f304eff4f001c77dfba23935e7 (HEAD -> main)
Author: John Smith <john.smith@networktocode.com>
Date:   Wed Feb 9 03:02:43 2022 +0000

    Adding .gitignore file
```

Git also has symbolic names that you can use in commands like `git log` (and others). We've already reviewed HEAD. If you want to use the commit just before HEAD, you reference that symbolically as `HEAD~1`. If you want to refer to the commit two places back from HEAD, you use `HEAD~2`; for three commits back, it's `HEAD~3`. (You can probably spot the pattern.) In this case, with this particular repository, this command produces the same results as the previous command we showed you:

```
admin@debian11:~/net-auto$ git log HEAD~1..HEAD
commit 045c1aa80b2a75f304eff4f001c77dfba23935e7 (HEAD -> main)
Author: John Smith <john.smith@networktocode.com>
Date:   Wed Feb 9 03:02:43 2022 +0000

    Adding .gitignore file
```

When we expand our discussion of HEAD later in this chapter, you'll understand why we said "in this case, with this particular repository" that the two `git log` commands would produce the same output.

Drilling into information on specific commits

Another way to drill into the details of a particular commit is to use the git cat-file command. Git, like so many other Unix/Linux tools, treats everything as a file. Thus, commits can be treated as a file and their "contents" shown on screen. This is what the git cat-file command does. So, taking the abbreviated SHA-1 from a particular commit, you can look at more details about that commit with a command like this:

```
admin@debian11:~/net-auto$ git cat-file -p 097bbd3
tree b289b034cab1ca9a95de8604d8576c5a752ae601
parent 0bc86eb847083a38e5cffedd780fd0a5217a90db
author John Smith <john.smith@networktocode.com> 1644375254 +0000
committer John Smith <john.smith@networktocode.com> 1644375254 +0000

Add configuration for sw5
```

(The -p option to git cat-file, by the way, just does some formatting of the output based on the type of file. The man page for git cat-file will provide more details on this and other switches.)

You'll note this output contains a couple of pieces of information that the default git log output doesn't show: the parent commit SHA-1 and the tree object SHA-1. You can use the parent commit SHA-1 to see this commit's parent commit. Every commit has a parent commit that lets you follow the chain of commits all the way back to the initial one, which is the only commit in a repository without a parent. The tree object SHA-1 captures the files that are in the repository at the time of a given commit; we used this earlier with the git ls-tree command, like this:

```
[ec2-user@amazonlinux2 net-auto]$ git ls-tree c703cdf
100644 blob 0835e4f9714005ed591f68d306eea0d6d2ae8fd7    sw1.txt
100644 blob e69de29bb2d1d6434b8b29ae775ad8c2e48c5391    sw2.txt
100644 blob e69de29bb2d1d6434b8b29ae775ad8c2e48c5391    sw3.txt
100644 blob e69de29bb2d1d6434b8b29ae775ad8c2e48c5391    sw4.txt
100644 blob e69de29bb2d1d6434b8b29ae775ad8c2e48c5391    sw5.txt
[ec2-user@amazonlinux2 net-auto]$
```

Using the SHA-1 checksums listed here, you could then use the git cat-file command to view the content of one of these files at that particular time (as of that particular commit).

Let's see how that works. In the following set of commands, you first use git log --oneline to show the history of commits to a repository. Then you use git cat-file and git ls-tree with the appropriate seven-character SHA-1 hashes to display the contents of a particular file at two different points in time (as of two commits):

```
ubuntu@ubuntu2004:~/net-auto$ git log --oneline
554b084 (HEAD -> main) Adding .gitignore file
ee7e7bf Add Python script to talk to network switches
d40fe74 Add configuration for sw5
dd61e7b Update sw1, add sw4
```

```
6b9b6cd First commit to new repository
ubuntu@ubuntu2004:~/net-auto$ git cat-file -p 6b9b6cd
tree cdba8229f6ffb6fec5364ea3ec083e513b029d8a
author John Smith <john.smith@networktocode.com> 1644373442 +0000
committer John Smith <john.smith@networktocode.com> 1644373442 +0000

First commit to new repository
ubuntu@ubuntu2004:~/net-auto$ git ls-tree 6b9b6cd
100644 blob 02df3d404d59d72c98439f44df673c6038352a27    sw1.txt
100644 blob 02df3d404d59d72c98439f44df673c6038352a27    sw2.txt
100644 blob 02df3d404d59d72c98439f44df673c6038352a27    sw3.txt
ubuntu@ubuntu2004:~/net-auto$ git cat-file -p 02df3d
interface ethernet0

interface ethernet1

interface ethernet2

interface ethernet3
```

This shows you the contents of *sw1.txt* as of the initial commit. Now, let's repeat the same process for the second commit:

```
ubuntu@ubuntu2004:~/net-auto$ git log --oneline
554b084 (HEAD -> main) Adding .gitignore file
ee7e7bf Add Python script to talk to network switches
d40fe74 Add configuration for sw5
dd61e7b Update sw1, add sw4
6b9b6cd First commit to new repository
ubuntu@ubuntu2004:~/net-auto$ git cat-file -p dd61e7b
tree a0b53a7d568b0d46d87edd50fd3b553b5b414258
parent 6b9b6cd6a05ae85c22f870c6319b3158808d379c
author John Smith <john.smith@networktocode.com> 1644374061 +0000
committer John Smith <john.smith@networktocode.com> 1644374061 +0000

Update sw1, add sw4
ubuntu@ubuntu2004:~/net-auto$ git ls-tree dd61e7b
100644 blob 0835e4f9714005ed591f68d306eea0d6d2ae8fd7    sw1.txt
100644 blob e69de29bb2d1d6434b8b29ae775ad8c2e48c5391    sw2.txt
100644 blob e69de29bb2d1d6434b8b29ae775ad8c2e48c5391    sw3.txt
100644 blob e69de29bb2d1d6434b8b29ae775ad8c2e48c5391    sw4.txt
ubuntu@ubuntu2004:~/net-auto$ git cat-file -p 0835e4f
interface ethernet0
  duplex auto

interface ethernet1

interface ethernet2

interface ethernet3
```

Ah, note that the contents of the *sw1.txt* file have changed! However, this is a bit laborious—wouldn't it be nice if there were an easier way to show the differences between two versions of a file within a repository? This is where the `git diff` command comes in handy.

Distilling Differences Between Versions of Files

We mentioned at the start of this chapter that one of the benefits of using version control for network automation artifacts (switch configurations, Python scripts, Jinja templates, etc.) is being able to see the differences between versions of files over time. In the previous section, we showed you a manual method of doing so; now we're going to show you the easy way: the `git diff` command.

 Git also supports integration with third-party diff tools, including graphical diff tools. In such cases, you would use `git difftool` instead of `git diff`.

Examining differences between commits

The `git diff` command shows the differences between versions of a file (the differences between a file at two points in time). You just need to supply the two commits and the file to be compared. Here's an example. First, you list the history by using `git log`, and then you use `git diff` to compare two versions of a file:

```
[ec2-user@amazonlinux2 net-auto]$ git log --oneline
9c66592 (HEAD -> main) Adding .gitignore file
b67c1dd Add Python script to talk to network switches
c703cdf Add configuration for sw5
f3a00e6 Update sw1, add sw4
8d18465 First commit to new repository
[ec2-user@amazonlinux2 net-auto]$ git diff 8d18465..f3a00e6 sw1.txt
diff --git a/sw1.txt b/sw1.txt
index 02df3d4..2567e07 100644
--- a/sw1.txt
+++ b/sw1.txt
@@ -1,4 +1,5 @@
 interface ethernet0
+   duplex auto

 interface ethernet1

[ec2-user@amazonlinux2 net-auto]$
```

The format in which `git diff` shows the differences between the files can be a bit confusing at first. The key in deciphering the output lies in the lines just after the `index...` line. There, `git diff` tells you that dashes will be used to represent file *a* (`--- a/sw1.txt`), and pluses will be used to represent file *b* (`+++ b/sw1.txt`). Following that is the representation of the differences in the files—lines that exist in file *a* are preceded by a dash, while lines that exist in file *b* are preceded by a plus. Lines that are the same in both files are preceded by a space.

Thus, in this example, you can see that in the later commit, represented by the hash f3a00e6, the line duplex auto was added. Obviously, this is a simple example, but hopefully you can begin to see just how useful this is.

> If you omit the filename with the git diff command (for example, if you enter git diff *start SHA..end SHA*), then Git will show a diff for *all* the files changed in that commit, rather than just a specific file referenced on the command line. Adding the filename to the git diff command allows you to focus on the changes in a specific file.

Viewing other types of differences

Let's change the configuration file for *sw1.txt* so that the diff is a bit more complex, and then we'll also show how you can use git diff in other ways.

First, you'll make some changes to *sw1.txt* by using the text editor of your choice. It doesn't really matter what the changes are; you'll run git status to confirm that changes exist in the working directory. However, *before* you stage the changes, let's see if you can use git diff again:

```
admin@debian11:~/net-auto$ git status
On branch main
Changes not staged for commit:
  (use "git add <file>..." to update what will be committed)
  (use "git restore <file>..." to discard changes in working directory)

        modified:   sw1.txt

no changes added to commit (use "git add" and/or "git commit -a")
admin@debian11:~/net-auto$ git diff
diff --git a/sw1.txt b/sw1.txt
index 2567e07..7005dc6 100644
--- a/sw1.txt
+++ b/sw1.txt
@@ -1,9 +1,11 @@
 interface ethernet0
-  duplex auto
+  switchport mode access vlan 101

 interface ethernet1
+  switchport mode trunk

 interface ethernet2
+  switchport mode access vlan 102

 interface ethernet3
```

```
-
+  switchport mode trunk
```

Running `git diff` like this—without any parameters or options—shows you the differences between your working tree and the index. That is, it shows you the changes that have not yet been staged for the next commit.

Now, let's stage the changes in preparation for the next commit and then see if there's another way to use `git diff`:

```
admin@debian11:~/net-auto$ git add sw1.txt
admin@debian11:~/net-auto$ git status
On branch main
Changes to be committed:
  (use "git restore --staged <file>..." to unstage)

    modified:   sw1.txt

admin@debian11:~/net-auto$ git diff
admin@debian11:~/net-auto$ git diff --cached
diff --git a/sw1.txt b/sw1.txt
index 2567e07..f3b5ad5 100644
--- a/sw1.txt
+++ b/sw1.txt
@@ -1,9 +1,11 @@
 interface ethernet0
-  duplex auto
+  switchport mode access vlan 101

 interface ethernet1
+  switchport mode trunk

 interface ethernet2
+  switchport mode access vlan 102

 interface ethernet3
-
+  switchport mode trunk
```

You can see that the first `git diff` command returns no results, which makes sense—there are no changes that *aren't* staged for the next commit. However, when you add the `--cached` parameter, it tells `git diff` to show the differences between the index and HEAD. In other words, this form of `git diff` shows the differences between the index and the last commit.

Once you finally commit this last set of changes, you can circle back around to your original use of `git diff`, which allows you to see the changes between two arbitrary commits:

```
admin@debian11:~/net-auto$ git commit -m "Defined VLANs on sw1"
[main 3588c31] Defined VLANs on sw1
 1 file changed, 4 insertions(+), 2 deletions(-)
admin@debian11:~/net-auto$ git status
```

```
On branch main
nothing to commit, working directory clean
admin@debian11:~/net-auto$ git log --oneline
ead6f37 (HEAD -> main) Defined VLANs on sw1
045c1aa Adding .gitignore file
dcddb60 Add Python script to talk to network switches
097bbd3 Add configuration for sw5
0bc86eb Update sw1, add sw4
3121e67 First commit to new repository
admin@debian11:~/net-auto$ git diff 0bc86eb..ead6f37 sw1.txt
diff --git a/sw1.txt b/sw1.txt
index 2567e07..f3b5ad5 100644
--- a/sw1.txt
+++ b/sw1.txt
@@ -1,9 +1,11 @@
 interface ethernet0
-  duplex auto
+  switchport mode access vlan 101

 interface ethernet1
+  switchport mode trunk

 interface ethernet2
+  switchport mode access vlan 102

 interface ethernet3
-
+  switchport mode trunk
```

In several of the commands we've shown you thus far, you've had to reference a specific commit's SHA-1 hash (at least, the first seven characters of it). That's not a significant problem when your repository has a relatively small number of commits; you can fairly easily use git log --oneline to see the list of commits and find the one you want.

What if your repository has thousands of commits? What if you're collaborating with others on a repository, so you're not familiar with the commits listed by git log? Is there an easier way to find an important commit you might need later? In fact, there is. The next section discusses Git's tagging functionality, which makes it easy to mark and refer back to important commits in your repository's commit history.

Tagging Commits in Git

Tags are essentially pointers to a specific commit. As such, they can be used in place of a commit hash. At first glance, this may not seem enormously useful, but let's consider the current state of our repository as viewed using git log --oneline:

```
ubuntu@ubuntu2004:~/net-auto$ git log --oneline
d268c37 (HEAD -> main) Defined VLANs on sw1
554b084 Adding .gitignore file
ee7e7bf Add Python script to talk to network switches
d40fe74 Add configuration for sw5
```

```
dd61e7b Update sw1, add sw4
6b9b6cd First commit to new repository
```

Now, let's say that commit d40fe74 represents some sort of significant milestone in the development of the repository, like the state of the repository when the network initially went live. You can *tag* this commit with a user-friendly name—perhaps something like golive or v1.0—and then refer to this user-friendly name instead of having to remember the SHA-1 hash. So, if you want to compare the state of a file now versus at the time of initial roll-out using git diff, the command would be something like git diff HEAD..golive sw1.txt instead of the more esoteric git diff HEAD..d40fe74.

The process for tagging a commit involves the use of the git tag *name commit-hash*. If you omit the commit hash, the tag will be added to the latest commit, aka HEAD. This means that it is easy to tag commits after the fact, if necessary, so let's add a couple of tags to our repository by using git tag:

```
ubuntu@ubuntu2004:~/net-auto$ git tag golive d40fe74
ubuntu@ubuntu2004:~/net-auto$ git log --oneline
d268c37 (HEAD -> main) Defined VLANs on sw1
554b084 Adding .gitignore file
ee7e7bf Add Python script to talk to network switches
d40fe74 (tag: golive) Add configuration for sw5
dd61e7b Update sw1, add sw4
6b9b6cd First commit to new repository
```

Note the addition of the tag to the specific commit in the output of git log. You can verify that the tag refers to the commit fairly easily by using git show, once referencing the tag and once referencing the specific commit hash:

```
ubuntu@ubuntu2004:~/net-auto$ git show golive
commit d40fe743568a82b89c93ca58279855762f091305 (tag: golive)
Author: John Smith <john.smith@networktocode.com>
Date:   Wed Feb 9 02:54:18 2022 +0000

    Add configuration for sw5

diff --git a/sw5.txt b/sw5.txt
new file mode 100644
index 0000000..e69de29
ubuntu@ubuntu2004:~/net-auto$ git show d40fe74
commit d40fe743568a82b89c93ca58279855762f091305 (tag: golive)
Author: John Smith <john.smith@networktocode.com>
Date:   Wed Feb 9 02:54:18 2022 +0000

    Add configuration for sw5

diff --git a/sw5.txt b/sw5.txt
new file mode 100644
index 0000000..e69de29
```

This is an example of what Git calls a *lightweight tag*. It is only a pointer to the commit. Git also supports *annotated tags*, which are full objects in the repository and have their own metadata. To create an annotated tag, you'll add the `-a` flag to the `git tag` command. Let's create an annotated tag in our repository:

```
ubuntu@ubuntu2004:~/net-auto$ git tag -a v1.0 d268c37 -m "Version 1.0 release"
ubuntu@ubuntu2004:~/net-auto$ git log --oneline
d268c37 (HEAD -> main, tag: v1.0) Defined VLANs on sw1
554b084 Adding .gitignore file
ee7e7bf Add Python script to talk to network switches
d40fe74 (tag: golive) Add configuration for sw5
dd61e7b Update sw1, add sw4
6b9b6cd First commit to new repository
```

Like the `git commit` command, using `git tag` to create an annotated tag supports the use of `-m` to add a tag message (lightweight tags don't require tag messages). If you don't specify one, Git will open your default editor so you can supply a tag message. That tag message is then displayed when users run `git show` against the tag name, like this:

```
ubuntu@ubuntu2004:~/net-auto$ git show v1.0
tag v1.0
Tagger: John Smith <john.smith@networktocode.com>
Date:   Sat Mar 5 21:35:53 2022 +0000

Version 1.0 of network automation tools

commit d268c37b57c01962b0829df946fe19c67e4da448 (tag: v1.0)
Author: John Smith <john.smith@networktocode.com>
Date:   Thu Feb 10 05:04:47 2022 +0000

    Defined VLANs on sw1

diff --git a/sw1.txt b/sw1.txt
index 0835e4f..58d8b7d 100644
--- a/sw1.txt
+++ b/sw1.txt
@@ -1 +1,12 @@
-change
+interface ethernet0
+ duplex auto
+ switchport mode access vlan 101
+
+interface ethernet1
+ switchport mode trunk
+
+interface ethernet2
+ switchport mode access vlan 102
+
+interface ethernet3
+ switchport mode trunk
```

To list all the tags found in a Git repository, just use `git tag` or `git tag --list`. Any tag listed in the output can be used in place of a commit hash in commands like `git diff` or others. To delete a tag, use `git tag -d` *tag-name*.

 When should you use annotated tags versus lightweight tags? The generally accepted practice is that annotated tags should be used for any long-term purposes, such as for version/release management. In such instances, you will want the ability to store additional metadata about the tag, and possibly even cryptographically sign the tag using GNU Privacy Guard (GnuPG). Lightweight tags, on the other hand, are primarily intended for temporary object labels.

Before we move on to our next topic—branches in Git—let's take a moment to review what you've done so far:

- Staged changes (using `git add`) and committed them to the repository (using `git commit`)
- Modified the configuration of Git (using `git config`)
- Unstaged changes that weren't yet ready to be committed (using `git restore` or the previous `git reset` method)
- Excluded files from inclusion in the repository (using `.gitignore`)
- Reviewed the history of the repository (using `git log`)
- Compared different versions of files within the repository to see the changes in each version (using `git diff`)
- Bookmarked specific commits in a repository (using `git tag`)

In the next section, we expand our discussion of Git to cover what is, arguably, one of Git's most powerful features: branching.

Branching in Git

As we've stated previously, one of the primary design goals for Git was strong support for nonlinear development. That's a fancy way of saying that Git needed to support multiple developers working on the same thing at the same time. So how is this accomplished? Git does it through the use of branches.

A *branch* in Git is a pointer to a commit. Now, that might not sound too powerful, so let's use some illustrations to help better explain the concept of a branch and why nonlinear development in Git can be powerful.

First, recall from "Overview of Git's Architecture" on page 500 that Git uses a series of objects: blobs (representing the content of files in the repository), trees (representing the file and directory structure of the repository), and commits (representing a point-in-time snapshot of the repository, its structure, and its content). You can visualize this as shown in Figure 11-1.

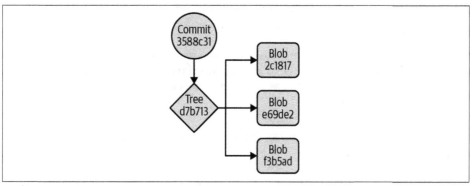

Figure 11-1. Objects in a Git repository

Each of these objects is identified by the SHA-1 hash of its contents. You've seen how commits are referenced via their SHA-1 hash, and you've seen how to use the git ls-tree or git cat-file commands to see the contents of tree and blob objects, respectively, by referencing their SHA-1 hash.

As you make changes and commit them to the repository, you create more commit objects (more snapshots), each of which points back at the previous commit (referred to as its *parent* commit; you saw this in "Viewing More Information About a Repository" on page 517). After a few commits, you can visualize it like Figure 11-2 (we've omitted the blobs to simplify the diagram).

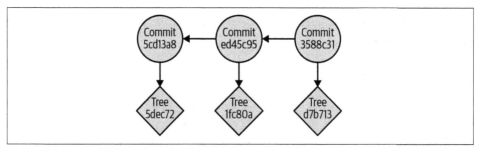

Figure 11-2. A chain of commits in a Git repository

Each commit points to a tree object, and each tree object points to blobs that represent the contents of the repository at the time of the commit. Using the reference to the tree object and the associated blobs, you can re-create the state of the repository at any given commit—hence why we refer to commits as point-in-time snapshots of the repository.

This is all well and good—and helps to explain Git's architecture a bit more fully—but what does it have to do with branching in Git? To answer that question (and we *will* answer it, we promise!), we need to revisit the concept of HEAD. Previously, we defined HEAD as a pointer to the latest commit, or to the commit we've checked out into the working directory. You visualize HEAD as something like Figure 11-3.

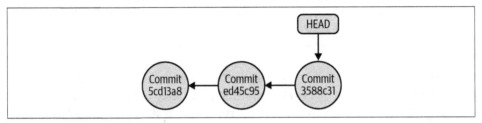

Figure 11-3. HEAD pointing to the latest commit

You can verify this using a procedure outlined earlier in this chapter (this assumes you haven't checked out a different branch or different commit, something we'll discuss shortly):

1. From the repository's working directory, run **cat .git/refs/heads/main**. Note the value displayed.

2. Compare the value of the previous command to the value of the last commit from the output of `git log --oneline`. You should see the same value in both places, indicating that HEAD points to the latest commit.

By default, *every* Git repository starts out with a single branch, named *master* (by default; this is configurable). As a branch is just a reference to a commit, this is illustrated graphically in Figure 11-4.

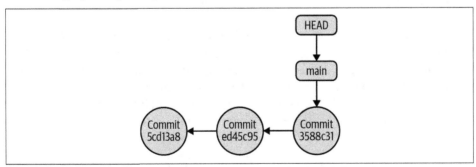

Figure 11-4. HEAD pointing to the latest commit in the default branch

You can see that the branch reference points to a commit, and that HEAD points to the branch reference.

 To avoid cultural insensitivity, numerous Git-based online services have moved away from the use of *master* to denote the default branch and have started using *main* instead (GitHub is one example). Users can use `git config --global init.defaultBranch` *<name>* to tell Git to use a different name, like *main*, for the initial default branch. See "Creating a Repository" on page 501 for more information on creating a Git repository. We are using *main* as the name for the default branch in this chapter.

However, you're not limited to only a single branch in a Git repository. In fact, because branches are so lightweight (a reference to a commit), you're strongly encouraged to use multiple branches. So, when you create a new branch—let's call this new branch *testing*, though the name doesn't really matter—the organization of the Git objects now looks something like Figure 11-5.

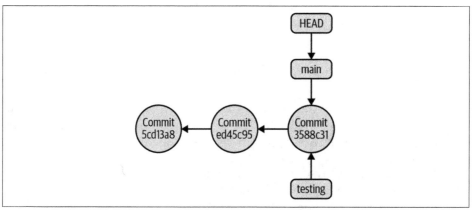

Figure 11-5. New branch created in a Git repository

So, you've created the new branch—we'll show you the commands to do that shortly—and the new branch now references a particular commit. However, HEAD hasn't moved. HEAD gets moved when you check out content in the repository, so to move HEAD to the new branch, you first have to *check out* the new branch. Similarly, if you want to work with the repository at an earlier point in time (at an earlier commit) you need to check out that particular commit. Once you check out a branch, HEAD now points to the new branch, as in Figure 11-6.

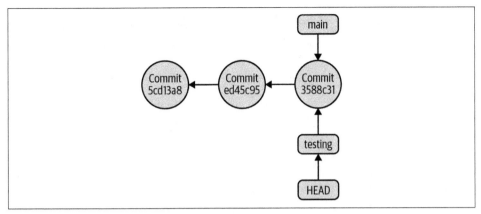

Figure 11-6. HEAD pointing to a checked-out branch

At this point, you can start making changes and committing them to the repository. This is where branches start to really show their power: they *isolate new changes from other branches.* Let's assume you've made some changes to the testing branch and have committed those changes to the repository. The graphical view of the objects and relationships inside the repository now looks like Figure 11-7.

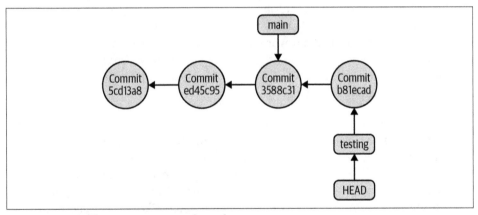

Figure 11-7. Adding a commit to a branch

You'll note that the testing branch—and HEAD—move forward to represent the latest commit, but the default branch remains *untouched.* At any point, you can check out the default branch and be right back where you were before you created the new branch and made the changes. This diagram shows how multiple branches can evolve over time and allow for the development of hotfixes, new features, and new releases without affecting other branches.

Figure 11-8 is a complicated example of branches, but it gives an idea of how branches *might* be used in a typical software development environment.

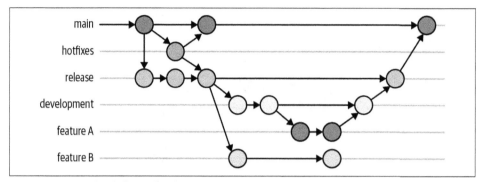

Figure 11-8. Multiple branches in a development cycle

Hopefully, the wheels in your head are turning, and you're starting to think about the possibilities that branches create:

- You can create a new branch when you want to try something new or different, without affecting what's in the default (or main) branch. If it doesn't work out, no big deal—the content in other branches, including the default branch, remains untouched.

- Branches form the basis for collaborating with other authors on the same repository. If you're working in branch A and your coworker is working in branch B, then you're assured that you won't affect each other's changes. (Now, you might have some issues when it comes time to bring the changes from the two branches together in a *merge*, but that's a different story—one we tackle in "Merging and Deleting Branches" on page 539.)

We've mentioned the default branch several times in this section. While, strictly speaking, Git has no concept of a default branch, there must always be at least one branch, and if you haven't explicitly created one, Git will create one for you. We think of this as the *default branch*. We also mentioned that most open source communities and many Git-based online services are moving away from the use of *master* as the name for the default branch, and switching to something like *main* or *default* instead. Before we turn our attention to actually working with Git branches, we'd like to first show you how to rename the default branch.

Renaming the Default Branch

For now, before we get into collaborating with Git (in "Collaborating with Git" on page 545), you can rename the default branch on your Git repository with one simple command: git branch -m *old_name* *new_name*. In fact, you can use this command to rename *any* branch.

If you didn't set the `init.defaultBranch` configuration setting with `git config` and end up with a *master* branch after running `git init`, you can use this command to easily change the name of the branch to *main* or *default* or whatever you'd like.

The process for renaming branches gets a little more complicated once you start adding Git remotes—which we cover in the collaboration section—but until then it's pretty straightforward to rename a branch.

Now let's turn our attention to the practical side of working with Git branches, where you can see the theory we've been describing in practice.

Creating a Branch

To create a Git branch—which, again, is just a reference to a commit—you use the `git branch` command. So, to create the testing branch we discussed in the previous section, you'd simply run `git branch testing`. The command doesn't produce any output, but there *is* a way you can verify that it actually did something.

First, look in the *.git/refs/heads* directory, and you'll see a new entry named after your newly created branch. If you run `cat` on that new file, you'll see that it points to the commit referenced by HEAD when you created the branch. Let's see that in action:

```
ubuntu@ubuntu2004:~/net-auto$ git branch testing
ubuntu@ubuntu2004:~/net-auto$ ls -la .git/refs/heads
total 16
drwxrwxr-x 2 ubuntu ubuntu 4096 Feb 10 05:19 .
drwxrwxr-x 4 ubuntu ubuntu 4096 Feb  9 02:20 ..
-rw-rw-r-- 1 ubuntu ubuntu   41 Feb 10 05:18 main
-rw-rw-r-- 1 ubuntu ubuntu   41 Feb 10 05:19 testing
ubuntu@ubuntu2004:~/net-auto$ cat .git/refs/heads/testing
d268c37b57c01962b0829df946fe19c67e4da448
ubuntu@ubuntu2004:~/net-auto$ git log --oneline
d268c37 (HEAD -> main, testing) Defined VLANs on sw1
554b084 Adding .gitignore file
ee7e7bf Add Python script to talk to network switches
d40fe74 Add configuration for sw5
dd61e7b Update sw1, add sw4
6b9b6cd First commit to new repository
```

The presence of the *testing* file in *.git/refs/heads*, along with the content of the file referencing the latest commit as of the time of creation, shows that the branch has been created. You can also verify this by simply running `git branch`, which will output the list of branches. The active branch—the branch that is *checked out* for use in the working directory—will have an asterisk before it (and, if colors are enabled in your terminal, may be listed in a different color). This shows you that your testing branch has been created, but not checked out—the main branch is still active.

To switch the active branch, you must first check out the branch.

Checking Out a Branch

To *check out* a branch means to make it the active branch, the branch that will be available in the working directory for you to edit/modify. To check out a branch, use git checkout, supplying the name of the branch you'd like to check out:

```
admin@debian11:~/net-auto$ git branch
* main
  testing
admin@debian11:~/net-auto$ git checkout testing
Switched to branch 'testing'
```

 You can create a branch and check it out at the same time by using git checkout -b *branch name*.

Let's make a simple change to the repository—say, let's add a file—and then switch back to the main branch to see how Git handles this. First, we'll stage *sw6.txt* to the repository and commit it to the testing branch:

```
[ec2-user@amazonlinux2 net-auto]$ git add sw6.txt
[ec2-user@amazonlinux2 net-auto]$ git commit -m "Add sw6 configuration"
[testing 3a6f8cb] Add sw6 configuration
 1 file changed, 7 insertions(+)
 create mode 100644 sw6.txt
[ec2-user@amazonlinux2 net-auto]$
```

Note that the response from Git when you commit the change includes the branch name and the SHA-1 hash of the commit ([testing 3a6f8cb]). A quick git log --oneline will verify that the latest commit has the same hash as reported by the git commit command. Likewise, a quick cat .git/HEAD will show that you're on the testing branch (because it points to *.git/refs/heads/testing*), and cat .git/refs/heads/testing will also show the latest commit SHA-1 hash. This shows that HEAD points to the latest commit in the checked-out branch.

Viewing Git Branch Information in the Prompt

When you're working with multiple branches in a Git repository, it can sometimes be challenging to know *which* branch is currently active (checked out). To help address this, most distributions of Git since version 1.8 have included support to allow bash—the shell most Linux distributions use by default—to display the currently active Git branch in the bash prompt.

On Debian and Debian derivatives like Ubuntu, this file is named *git-sh-prompt* and is found in the */usr/lib/git-core* directory. On RHEL-like distributions like Fedora and Amazon Linux 2, the file is named *git-prompt.sh* and is found in the */usr/share/*

---

git-core/contrib/completion directory. On macOS, the file is installed as part of the Xcode command-line tools, is named *git-prompt.sh,* and is found in the */Library/ Developer/CommandLineTools/usr/share/git-core* directory. The instructions for using this functionality are found at the top of the appropriate file for your OS.

Now, let's switch back to the main branch and see the working directory:

```
[ec2-user@amazonlinux2 net-auto]$ git checkout main
Switched to branch 'main'
[ec2-user@amazonlinux2 net-auto]$ ls -la
total 12
drwxrwxr-x 3 ec2-user ec2-user 151 Feb 11 05:04 .
drwx------ 4 ec2-user ec2-user 145 Feb 11 04:56 ..
-rw-rw-r-- 1 ec2-user ec2-user   0 Feb  9 03:00 credentials.yml
drwxrwxr-x 8 ec2-user ec2-user 166 Feb 11 05:04 .git
-rw-rw-r-- 1 ec2-user ec2-user  16 Feb  9 03:00 .gitignore
-rw-rw-r-- 1 ec2-user ec2-user 634 Feb  9 02:56 script.py
-rw-rw-r-- 1 ec2-user ec2-user 213 Feb 10 05:04 sw1.txt
-rw-rw-r-- 1 ec2-user ec2-user   0 Feb  9 02:22 sw2.txt
-rw-rw-r-- 1 ec2-user ec2-user   0 Feb  9 02:22 sw3.txt
-rw-rw-r-- 1 ec2-user ec2-user   0 Feb  9 02:32 sw4.txt
-rw-rw-r-- 1 ec2-user ec2-user   0 Feb  9 02:37 sw5.txt
[ec2-user@amazonlinux2 net-auto]$
```

Wait—the *sw6.txt* file is *gone!* What happened? Not to worry, you haven't lost anything. Recall that checking out a branch makes it the active branch, and therefore the branch that will be present in the working directory for you to modify. The *sw6.txt* file isn't in the main branch, it's in the testing branch, so when you switched to main by using git checkout main, that file was removed from the working directory. Recall also that the working directory *isn't* the same as the repository—even though the file has been removed from the working directory, it's *still* in the repository, as you can easily verify:

```
[ec2-user@amazonlinux2 net-auto]$ git checkout testing
Switched to branch 'testing'
[ec2-user@amazonlinux2 net-auto]$ ls -la
total 16
drwxrwxr-x 3 ec2-user ec2-user 166 Feb 11 05:05 .
drwx------ 4 ec2-user ec2-user 145 Feb 11 04:56 ..
-rw-rw-r-- 1 ec2-user ec2-user   0 Feb  9 03:00 credentials.yml
drwxrwxr-x 8 ec2-user ec2-user 166 Feb 11 05:05 .git
-rw-rw-r-- 1 ec2-user ec2-user  16 Feb  9 03:00 .gitignore
-rw-rw-r-- 1 ec2-user ec2-user 634 Feb  9 02:56 script.py
-rw-rw-r-- 1 ec2-user ec2-user 213 Feb 10 05:04 sw1.txt
-rw-rw-r-- 1 ec2-user ec2-user   0 Feb  9 02:22 sw2.txt
-rw-rw-r-- 1 ec2-user ec2-user   0 Feb  9 02:22 sw3.txt
-rw-rw-r-- 1 ec2-user ec2-user   0 Feb  9 02:32 sw4.txt
-rw-rw-r-- 1 ec2-user ec2-user   0 Feb  9 02:37 sw5.txt
-rw-rw-r-- 1 ec2-user ec2-user  83 Feb 11 05:05 sw6.txt
[ec2-user@amazonlinux2 net-auto]$
```

This illustrates how branches help isolate changes from the main branch, a key benefit of using branches. Using a branch, you can make some changes, test those changes, and then discard them if necessary—all while knowing that your main branch remains safe and untouched.

The preceding example shows what happens to committed changes and how the working directory changes when you switch branches, but what happens to uncommitted changes when you switch branches?

- For untracked files (files that don't already exist in the repository), changes are left in the working directory. This is easy to demonstrate: create a new, untracked file in the working directory and then switch to a new branch. You'll still see the untracked file in the working directory, and git status will report the file as an untracked file in either branch. The contents of the untracked file won't change as you switch branches.

- For tracked files, uncommitted changes are saved into a temporary area called a *stash*, and the contents of the tracked file are restored to what's stored in the commit referenced by the branch to which you switched.

Before looking at merging branches, we'd like to first review stashing in a bit more detail. Knowing how to stash uncommitted changes is useful when working with multiple branches.

Stashing Uncommitted Changes

Stashing changes places those changes into a temporary storage area so that you can recall them later. There are numerous use cases for stashing; the one you've seen so far is capturing uncommitted changes so you can switch branches, but we'll mention others as we progress through the chapter.

Here's one example: say you need to add switch configuration changes to your network automation repository, so you start hacking away on the updated configuration only to realize at some point later than you forgot to create a branch in which to store these changes. Now what? The easiest thing for you to do is stash your changes, create a branch for your changes, and then apply the stash to the branch. Effectively, this allows you to move uncommitted changes from one branch to another.

Stashing in Git is handled via the git stash command, which has subcommands to add changes to the stash (git stash push), to list the stashed changes (git stash list), to examine the stashed changes (git stash show), and to take the changes from the stash and put them back into the working directory (git stash pop).

Using the preceding situation as our example—you've made changes with the wrong branch checked out, and you realized your mistake before committing the changes— we'll walk through using the various git stash commands.

First, let's make sure that the main branch is checked out:

```
ubuntu@ubuntu2004:~/net-auto$ git branch
* main
```

Great. Now we're going to make some changes on the main branch, which—especially when working with others in a single repository—is generally not recommended (the changes should be isolated on their own branch). For example, let's make some changes to *sw5.txt*, and then run `git status`:

```
ubuntu@ubuntu2004:~/net-auto$ git status
On branch main

Changes not staged for commit:
  (use "git add <file>..." to update what will be committed)
  (use "git restore <file>..." to discard changes in working directory)
        modified:   sw5.txt

no changes added to commit (use "git add" and/or "git commit -a")
```

When you review the output of `git status`, you realize that you're on the main branch instead of in a feature branch. This is where using `git stash` comes into play. The first step is to push the changes onto the stash:

```
ubuntu@ubuntu2004:~/net-auto$ git stash push -m "Updated changes for sw5"
Saved working directory and index state On main: Updated changes for sw5
ubuntu@ubuntu2004:~/net-auto$ git status
On branch main
nothing to commit, working tree clean
ubuntu@ubuntu2004:~/net-auto$ git stash list
stash@{0}: On main: Updated changes for sw5
```

The `git stash push` command pushes changes into (or onto) the stash. It supports the `-m` parameter to add a message; if you omit a message, the command will use the commit message from the last commit as the description. In our experience, this often isn't very helpful, so we recommend using `-m` to add a stash-specific message to help you understand the contents of the stash. Once the changes are pushed into the stash, Git restores the working directory to match HEAD, as illustrated by the output of `git status`.

The `git stash list` command shows that the stash was created and shows the syntax for how Git refers to stashes (`stash@{0}` in this case).

To see what's in this stash, you can use the `git stash show` command:

```
ubuntu@ubuntu2004:~/net-auto$ git stash show stash@{0}
 sw5.txt | 9 +++++++++
 1 file changed, 9 insertions(+)
```

The output of `git stash show` shows the changes in the stash as a diff (similar to how `git diff` works). The diff is between the stashed contents and the commit when the stash entry was first created.

Next, create a new branch, and then use the `git stash pop` command to apply the changes from the stash to the new branch:

```
ubuntu@ubuntu2004:~/net-auto$ git checkout -b sw5-updates
Switched to a new branch 'sw5-updates'
ubuntu@ubuntu2004:~/net-auto$ git status
On branch sw5-updates
nothing to commit, working tree clean
ubuntu@ubuntu2004:~/net-auto$ git stash pop stash@{0}
On branch sw5-updates
Changes not staged for commit:
  (use "git add <file>..." to update what will be committed)
  (use "git restore <file>..." to discard changes in working directory)
        modified:   sw5.txt

no changes added to commit (use "git add" and/or "git commit -a")
Dropped stash@{0} (cf8fab0f7083feb5a817ab5933e9028bd64407d1)
ubuntu@ubuntu2004:~/net-auto$ git stash list
```

The `git stash pop` command takes the changes from a stash, applies them to the checked-out branch, and then drops the stash. As a result of dropping the stash, `git stash list` no longer shows it in the list of stashes. After the changes in the stash are applied to the checked-out branch, `git status` shows there are now unstaged changes in the working directory, and in the correct branch this time!

The `git stash` command has a pop as well as an apply subcommand. Both take changes from the specified stash and apply them against the working directory of the checked-out branch, but they aren't the same! The `git stash pop` command drops the stash afterward, assuming no conflicts were encountered. However, `git stash apply` does not drop the stash afterward; you have to use `git stash drop` manually to drop the stash.

To summarize:

- Use `git stash push` to take uncommitted changes and stash them away, restoring the working directory to HEAD.
- Use `git stash list` to see the list of stashed changes.
- The `git stash show` command shows the stashed changes as a diff against the commit when the stash was created.
- Changes in a stash can be used with the `git stash pop` command.

Although our example scenario leveraged only a single stash entry, it is possible to have multiple stash entries. When you have multiple stash entries, be sure to append the appropriate stash name when using `git stash show` or `git stash pop`.

It's now time to circle back to our discussion of Git branches. Stashes are useful in preserving uncommitted changes when switching between branches, or perhaps even to move uncommitted changes from one branch to another. Branches themselves are useful for isolating committed changes away from other branches. What about when you're ready to make committed changes a permanent part of your repository? Perhaps you create a branch to try out a new Jinja template, and it works perfectly so you want to keep it. What's the next step? This is where *merging* branches comes into play.

Merging and Deleting Branches

Before we get into merging branches, let's revisit the contents of a commit object in Git. In our example repository, you'll examine the contents of the latest commit object for the testing branch:

```
admin@debian11:~/net-auto$ git checkout testing
Switched to branch 'testing'
admin@debian11:~/net-auto$ git cat-file -p 2e6fced
tree e895cac9760eba8d16b85a57ee8fff6fe9c590db
parent ead6f372effce74de8d96deade198a09558a5432
author John Smith <john.smith@networktocode.com> 1644556039 +0000
committer John Smith <john.smith@networktocode.com> 1644556039 +0000

Add sw6 configuration
```

What does this tell you?

1. This particular commit references the tree object with the hash 2e6fced.
2. The author and committer of this commit is John Smith.
3. The commit message indicates that this commit captures the addition of the configuration for sw6.
4. This commit has a parent commit with a hash of ead6f37.

We've mentioned before that every commit (except the very first commit) has a pointer to a parent commit. This is illustrated in Figures 11-2 through 11-7, where the commit objects point "backward in time" to the previous commit.

When you merge branches, Git is going to create a new commit object—called a *merge commit* object—that will actually have *two* parents. Each parent represents the two branches that were brought together as part of the merge process. In so doing, Git maintains the link back to previous commits so that you can always roll back to previous versions.

At a high level, the merge process looks like this:

1. Switch to the branch into which the other branch should be merged. If you're merging back into main, check out (switch to) main.

2. Run the `git merge` command, specifying the name of the branch to be merged into main.

3. Supply a message (a commit message for the merge commit) describing the changes being merged.

Reviewing fast-forward merges

Let's see this in action. Let's take the testing branch, which has a new switch configuration (*sw6.txt*) that isn't present in the main branch, and merge it back into main.

First, let's ensure you are on the main branch:

```
ubuntu@ubuntu2004:~/net-auto$ git branch
  main
* testing
ubuntu@ubuntu2004:~/net-auto$ git checkout main
Switched to branch 'main'
```

Next, let's actually merge the testing branch into the main branch:

```
ubuntu@ubuntu2004:~/net-auto$ git merge testing
Updating d268c37..e70f353
Fast-forward
 sw6.txt | 7 +++++++
 1 file changed, 7 insertions(+)
 create mode 100644 sw6.txt
```

Note the `Fast-forward` in the response from Git; this indicates that it was possible to merge the branches by simply replaying the same set of changes to the main branch as was performed on the branch being merged. In situations like this—a simple merge—you won't see an additional merge commit:

```
ubuntu@ubuntu2004:~/net-auto$ git log --oneline
e70f353 (HEAD -> main, testing) Add sw6 configuration
d268c37 Defined VLANs on sw1
554b084 Adding .gitignore file
ee7e7bf Add Python script to talk to network switches
d40fe74 Add configuration for sw5
dd61e7b Update sw1, add sw4
6b9b6cd First commit to new repository
ubuntu@ubuntu2004:~/net-auto$ ls -la sw6.txt
-rw-rw-r-- 1 ubuntu ubuntu 221 Jun  7 20:53 sw6.txt
```

Deleting a branch

Once a branch (and its changes) have been merged, you can delete the branch by using `git branch -d+ branch-name`. You generally shouldn't delete a branch before it's been merged; otherwise, you'll lose the changes stored in that branch (Git will prompt you if you try to delete a branch that hasn't been merged). Once a branch has been merged, though, its changes are safely stored in another branch (typically the main branch, but not always), and it's therefore now safe to delete.

Reviewing merges with a merge commit

Now, let's look at a more complex example. First, let's create a new branch to store some changes you'll make relative to the configuration for sw4. To do that, you'll simply run `git checkout -b sw4`. This creates the new branch *and* checks it out so it's the active branch. Once you've made some changes to *sw4.txt*, use `git add` and `git commit` to stage and commit the changes.

Next, let's switch back to main (using `git checkout main`) and make changes to a *different* switch configuration. Stage and commit the changes to the main branch. Now what happens when you try to merge the sw4 branch into main?

Before we answer that question, let's explore the commit objects a bit. Here are the contents of the last commit object in the sw4 branch:

```
admin@debian11:~/net-auto$ git checkout sw4
Switched to branch 'sw4'
admin@debian11:~/net-auto$ git log --oneline HEAD~2..HEAD
1bae927 (HEAD -> sw4) Update sw4 configuration
2e6fced (main) Add sw6 configuration
admin@debian11:~/net-auto$ git cat-file -p 1bae927
tree 72f0533c16734939d15624fbc41d47f33b54f7f9
parent 2e6fced00c8aad171d54a279232a569dec392f69
author John Smith <john.smith@networktocode.com> 1644556917 +0000
committer John Smith <john.smith@networktocode.com> 1644556917 +0000

Update sw4 configuration
```

The `git log --oneline HEAD~2..HEAD` command shows just the last two commits leading up to HEAD (which points to the last commit on the active branch). As you can see, this commit object points to a parent commit of `2e6fced`.

Here's the last commit on the main branch:

```
admin@debian11:~/net-auto$ git checkout main
Switched to branch 'main'
admin@debian11:~/net-auto$ git log --oneline HEAD~2..HEAD
e222171 (HEAD -> main) Fix sw3 configuration for hypervisor
2e6fced Add sw6 configuration
admin@debian11:~/net-auto$ git cat-file -p e222171
tree c0c8034ab09379d350d718d8f1a63f1dbd033706
parent 2e6fced00c8aad171d54a279232a569dec392f69
author John Smith <john.smith@networktocode.com> 1644557833 +0000
committer John Smith <john.smith@networktocode.com> 1644557833 +0000

Fix sw3 configuration for hypervisor
```

This commit, the latest in the main branch, *also* points to the same parent commit—showing that the two branches diverge.

Now let's run the merge. First, you'll verify you have the main branch checked out; then you'll use `git merge` to actually perform the merge:

```
admin@debian11:~/net-auto$ git branch
* main
  sw4
admin@debian11:~/net-auto$ git merge sw4
(default Git editor opens to allow user to provide commit message)
Merge made by the 'recursive' strategy.
 sw4.txt | 9 +++++++++
 1 file changed, 9 insertions(+)
admin@debian11:~/net-auto$ git log --oneline HEAD~3..HEAD
8c34005 (HEAD -> main) Merge branch 'sw4'
e222171 Fix sw3 configuration for hypervisor
1bae927 (sw4) Update sw4 configuration
2e6fced Add sw6 configuration
```

In this instance, changes on *both* branches need to be reconciled when merging the branches. It isn't possible to just "replay" the changes from the sw4 branch to main, because main has some changes of its own. Thus, Git creates a *merge commit*. Let's look at that file real quick:

```
admin@debian11:~/net-auto$ git cat-file -p 8c34005
tree bff23ea7763a583586c0cf82e7651e35a7aa58fd
parent e2221715da5229e33ffd981c81d5874bb12957b7
parent 1bae92734368fc68a570539696aa4435c5ab5517
author John Smith <john.smith@networktocode.com> 1644558317 +0000
committer John Smith <john.smith@networktocode.com> 1644558317 +0000

Merge branch 'sw4'
```

Note the presence of *two* parent commits, which—if you look—represent the commits you made to each branch before merging the sw4 branch into main. This is how Git knows that the branches have converged and how Git maintains the relationship between commits over time.

Now that the commits in the sw4 branch have been merged into the main branch, you can just delete the sw4 branch by using `git branch -d sw4`:

```
admin@debian11:~/net-auto$ git branch -d sw4
Deleted branch sw4 (was 1bae927).
admin@debian11:~/net-auto$ git branch
* main
```

 It's possible to delete an unmerged branch by using `git branch -D` *branch*. However, in such situations, you will *lose* the changes in that branch, so tread carefully.

Rebasing to avoid merge commits

In the previous section, we showed how to use `git merge` to merge two branches that had diverged (in other words, changes on both branches needed to be reconciled). In such cases, Git uses a merge commit to show that the two branches were brought together. However, merge commits are sometimes frowned upon; in 2021, Linus Torvalds took a Linux kernel contributor to task for what he called "useless merge commits." Is there a way to avoid merge commits? Often, yes, and it involves something known as rebasing.

Rebasing is taking changes committed on one branch and replaying (applying) them to another branch. Let's go back to the example from the previous section, where you made changes to both the sw4 and main branches. This could be illustrated as shown in Figure 11-9.

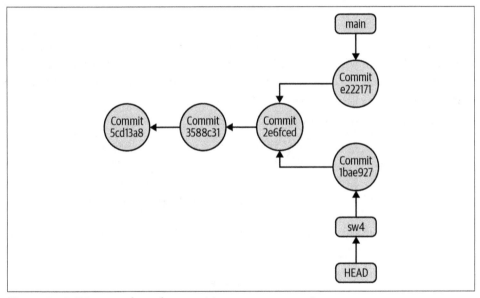

Figure 11-9. Divergent branches requiring a merge commit

However, rebasing the sw4 branch to include the changes from the main branch would change it to look like Figure 11-10.

This sort of situation would allow you to use a fast-forward merge and avoid a merge commit, keeping a "cleaner" commit history.

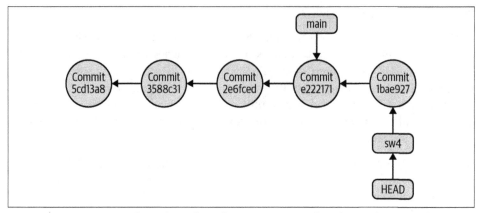

Figure 11-10. Divergent branches after rebasing can use a fast-forward merge

You can rebase a branch by using the git rebase command, which has the syntax git rebase *upstream*, where *upstream* is the name of the branch onto which the changes in the current branch should be replayed. In our example, if you wanted to avoid using a merge commit to merge the changes in the sw4 and main branches together, you'd first need to rebase sw4 on main:

```
ubuntu@ubuntu2004:~/net-auto$ git checkout sw4
Switched to branch 'sw4'
ubuntu@ubuntu2004:~/net-auto$ git branch
  main
* sw4
ubuntu@ubuntu2004:~/net-auto$ git rebase main
First, rewinding head to replay your work on top of it...
Applying: Update sw4 configuration
```

At this point, you could now merge sw4 into main with a fast-forward merge. We'll leave that as an exercise for you. So, to recap:

- To create a branch, use git branch *new branch name*.
- To check out a branch, use git checkout *branch*.
- To create a new branch and check it out in one step, use git checkout -b *new branch name*.
- To merge a branch into main, run git merge *branch* while the main branch is checked out.
- To delete a branch after its changes have been merged, use git branch -d *branch name*.
- To rebase a branch, use git rebase *upstream branch*.

Let's now turn our attention to using Git's distributed nature to collaborate with others via Git.

Collaborating with Git

As we discussed in "Brief History of Git" on page 498, one of the key design goals for Git was that it was a fully distributed system. Thus, every developer needed to be able to work from a full copy of the source code stored in the repository as well as the repository's full history. When you combine this fully distributed nature with Git's other key design goals—speed, simplicity, scalability, and strong support for nonlinear development via lightweight branches—you can see why Git has become a leading option for users needing a collaborative version control system.

On its own, Git can act as a "server" and provides mechanisms for communications between systems running Git. Git supports a variety of transport protocols, including SSH, HTTPS, and Git's own protocol (using TCP port 9418). If you're simply using Git on a couple of systems and need to keep repositories in sync, you can do this with no additional software.

Further, Git's distributed nature has enabled online services based on Git to appear. Many Git users take advantage of online Git-based services such as GitHub (*https://github.com*) and Bitbucket (*https://bitbucket.org*). A wide variety of open source projects facilitate collaboration via Git, such as GitLab (*https://about.gitlab.com*), Gitblit (*https://gitblit.com*), and Djacket (*https://djacket.github.io*), which, somewhat ironically, is hosted on GitHub. As you can see, there's no shortage of ways to collaborate with others by using Git and Git-based tools.

In this section, we explore how to collaborate using Git. That collaboration might be as simple as keeping repositories in sync on multiple systems, but we also cover using public Git-based services (focusing on GitHub). Along the way, you'll learn about cloning repositories; Git remotes; pushing, fetching, and pulling changes from other repositories; and using branches when collaborating.

Let's start with exploring a simple scenario involving multiple systems running Git, where you need to share/sync one or more repositories between these systems.

Collaborating Between Multiple Systems Running Git

So far in this chapter, you've been building your collection of network configurations, scripts, and templates in a Git repository on a single system. What happens when you need or want to be able to access this repository from a separate system? Maybe you have a desktop system at work and a laptop that you use for travel and at home. How do you use your network automation repository from both systems? Fortunately, because of Git's fully distributed design, this is pretty straightforward.

Can it be as simple as copying files? Let's see what happens when you copy a repository and its working directory to a new location on the same system. First, run `git log --oneline HEAD~2..HEAD` in the existing repository:

```
ubuntu@ubuntu2004:~/net-auto$ git log --oneline HEAD~2..HEAD
829764b (HEAD -> main) Merge branch 'sw4' into main
53e3c45 Fix sw3 configuration for hypervisor
3ab27f8 Update sw4 configuration
```

Now, let's copy the repository and working directory to a new location on the same system, run the same `git log` command, and see what you get:

```
ubuntu@ubuntu2004:~$ cp -ar net-auto netauto2
ubuntu@ubuntu2004:~$ cd netauto2
ubuntu@ubuntu2004:~/netauto2$ git log --oneline HEAD~2..HEAD
829764b (HEAD -> main) Merge branch 'sw4' into main
53e3c45 Fix sw3 configuration for hypervisor
3ab27f8 Update sw4 configuration
```

Looks like the contents are identical! If you were to continue to explore the contents of the repository at *~/netauto2* by using `git ls-tree`, `git cat-file`, or other commands, you'd find that the two repositories are, in fact, identical. Why is this? Recall that Git uses SHA-1 hashes to identify all content: blobs, tree objects, and commit objects. A key property of SHA-1 hashes is that *identical content produces identical hashes*. Recall also that the contents of the Git repository are immutable (once created, they can't be modified). The combination of these attributes and Git's architecture means that it's possible to copy a repository by using simple tools like `cp` and end up with an intact version of the repository. It's this ability to copy repositories—with all data and metadata intact—that is a key factor in Git's fully distributed nature.

Note there's no link between the copies, so changes made in one copy *won't* be automatically reflected in the other copy, or vice versa. (You can verify this, if you'd like, by making a commit in either copy and then using `git log` in both repositories.) To create a link between copies, you need something known as a *remote*.

Linking repositories with remotes

A Git *remote* is really nothing more than a reference to another repository. Git uses lightweight references pretty extensively—you've seen this already in the use of branches and HEAD—and in this case, remotes are similar. A remote is a lightweight reference to another repository, specified by a location.

Let's add a remote to the *netauto2* repository that refers back to the original repository in *net-auto*. To do this, you use the `git remote` command:

```
admin@debian11:~/netauto2$ git remote
admin@debian11:~/netauto2$ git remote add first ~/net-auto
admin@debian11:~/netauto2$ git remote
first
```

When you use git remote with no parameters, it simply lists any existing remotes. In this case, there are none (yet). So you next run the git remote add command, which takes two parameters:

- The name of the remote repository. This name is purely symbolic—it can be whatever makes sense to you. In this case, you use first as the name for the remote.
- The location of the remote repository. In this case, the remote repository is on the same system (for now), so the location is simply a filesystem path.

Finally, running git remote again shows that the new remote has been added.

With the remote in place, you now have an asymmetric link between the two remotes: *netauto2* has a reference to *net-auto*, but the reverse is *not* true. Via this asymmetric link, you can exchange information between Git repositories. Let's see how this works.

First, let's list the branches available in our *netauto2* repository. You'll add the -a parameter here, which we'll explain in more detail shortly:

```
vagrant@trusty:~/netauto2$ git branch -a
* main
```

Now, let's fetch—and we're using the term *fetch* here intentionally, for reasons that will be evident later in this section—information from the remote repository, which you configured earlier. You'll update the information by using the git remote update command and then run git branch -a again:

```
admin@debian11:~/netauto2$ git remote update first
Fetching first
From /home/admin/net-auto
 * [new branch]      main     -> first/main
admin@debian11:~/netauto2$ git branch -a
* main
  remotes/first/main
```

Now a new branch is listed here. This is a special kind of branch known as a *remote tracking branch.* You won't make changes or commits to this branch, as it is only a reference to the branch that exists in the remote repository. You'll notice the first in the name of the branch; this refers to the symbolic name you gave the Git remote when you added it. You have to use the -a parameter to git branch in order to show remote tracking branches, which aren't listed by default.

 Instead of the two-step git remote add followed by git remote update, you can fetch information from a remote repository when you add the remote by using the syntax git remote add -f *name location.*

So what does this new remote tracking branch allow us to do? It allows us to *transfer* information between repositories in order to keep two repositories up-to-date. We'll show you how this works in the next section.

Fetching and merging information from remote repositories

Once a remote has been configured for a repository, information has been retrieved from the configured remote, and remote tracking branches have been created, it's possible to start to transfer information between remotes by using various git commands. You could use these commands to keep branches of repositories or entire repositories in sync.

To see this in action, you'll want to change one of the two repositories on your system (the *net-auto* repository) and see how to get that information into the *netauto2* repository.

First, in the *net-auto* repository, let's make a change to the *sw2.txt* configuration file and commit that change to the repository. (We won't go through all the steps here, as we've covered them previously. Need a hint? Edit the file, use git add, then git commit.)

Verify that you can see the new commit in the *net-auto* directory by using git log --oneline HEAD~1..HEAD; then switch to the *netauto2* repository and run the same git log command. The commit(s) listed will be different.

To get the updated information from *net-auto* over to *netauto2*, you have a few options:

- You can run git remote update *name*, which updates *only* the specified remote.
- You can run git remote update (without a remote's name), which updates *all* remotes for this repository.
- You can run git fetch *name*, which will update (or *fetch*) information from the specified remote repository. In this respect, git fetch is a lot like git remote update, although the syntax is slightly different (again, we refer you to the man pages or the help screens for specific details). Note that git fetch is considered the conventional way of retrieving information from a remote, as opposed to using git remote update as we did earlier.

So, let's run **git fetch first**, which will pull information from the repository named *first*. You'll see output that looks something like this (the SHA-1 hashes will differ, of course):

```
remote: Enumerating objects: 3, done.
remote: Counting objects: 100% (3/3), done.
remote: Compressing objects: 100% (2/2), done.
```

```
remote: Total 2 (delta 1), reused 0 (delta 0)
Unpacking objects: 100% (2/2), 245 bytes | 245.00 KiB/s, done.
From /home/ubuntu/net-auto
   829764b..3267a4a  main          -> first/main
```

OK, so you've retrieved information from *first/main* (the main branch of the remote named *first*). Why, then, does `git log` in `netauto2` not show this? This is because you've only *fetched* (updated) the information from the remote repository; you haven't actually made it part of the current repository.

 We caution you against using the word "pull" when referring to simply retrieving information from a remote repository. In Git, the idea of "pulling" from a remote repository has a specific meaning and its own command (both of which we'll discuss shortly). Try to train yourself to use "fetching" or "retrieving" when referring to the act of getting information from a remote repository.

So if you've only fetched the changes across but not made them a part of the current repository, how do you do that? The changes in the remote repository are stored in their own branch, which means they are kept separate from other branches of the current repository. How do you get changes from one branch to another branch? That's right—you *merge* the changes:

```
ubuntu@ubuntu2004:~/netauto2$ git checkout main
Already on 'main'
ubuntu@ubuntu2004:~/netauto2$ git merge first/main
Updating 829764b..3267a4a
Fast-forward
 sw2.txt | 7 +++++++
 1 file changed, 7 insertions(+)
```

As you can see from Git's output, it has taken the changes applied to *first/main* (the main branch of the remote repository named *first*) and merged them—via a fast-forward—into the main branch of the current repository. Because this is a fast-forward, there will not be a merge commit, and now both repositories are in sync.

 If you noted that the use of `git fetch` and `git merge` on the main branch of two repositories doesn't necessarily keep the repositories in sync, then you are *really* paying attention! In fact, only the main branches of the two repositories are in sync. To keep the entire repositories in sync, you'd need to perform this operation on all branches.

Pulling information from remote repositories

Why the two-step process of first git fetch and then git merge? The primary reason is you might want to be able to review the changes from the remote repository *before* you merge them, in the event that you aren't ready for those changes to be applied to the current repository.

As with so many things in Git, though, there is a shortcut. If you'd like to fetch changes and merge them in a single operation, you can use git pull *name*, where *name* is the name of the remote from which you'd like to get and merge changes into the current branch. The git pull command is simply combining the git fetch and git merge operations.

So you've seen how to get changes from *net-auto* to *netauto2*, but what about the reverse? We mentioned that adding a remote to *netauto2* is an asymmetric relationship in that *netauto2* now knows about *net-auto*, but the reverse is not true. In a situation such as we've described here—where you, as a single user, want to keep repositories in sync on separate systems—the best approach is to add a remote from *net-auto* to *netauto2*, and then use git fetch and git merge to move changes in either direction. Graphically, this looks something like Figure 11-11.

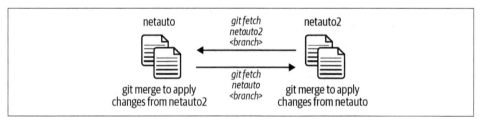

Figure 11-11. Using git fetch and git merge between repositories

 Git almost always offers multiple ways to do something, which can be both useful (in that it is very flexible) and frustrating (in that there's no "one way" to do something). Two-way transfer of information between Git repositories as we've described in this section is one of these areas where there's more than one way to get the job done. For new users of Git, this is probably the easiest way to handle it.

We started this section asking the question, "How do I use my network automation repository from multiple systems?" We've shown you how to make a copy of a repository, how to use Git remotes to link repositories, and how to use various Git commands to transfer data between repositories. In the next two sections, we're going to show you a simpler, easier way of copying and linking repositories, and we'll extend our working model across multiple systems, respectively.

Cloning repositories

In the previous sections, we showed that you could simply copy a repository from one location to another and then use `git remote` to create a remote that would allow you to transfer information between repositories.

This process isn't difficult, but what if there were an even easier way? There is, and it's called *cloning* a repository via the `git clone` command. Let's see how this works.

The general syntax of this command is `git clone` *repository directory*. In this command, *repository* is the location of the repository you're cloning and *directory* is the (optional) directory where you'd like to place the cloned repository. If you omit *directory*, Git will place the cloned repository into a directory with the same name as the repository. Adding the *directory* parameter to the `git clone` command gives you some flexibility in where you'd like to place the cloned repository.

To illustrate how `git clone` works, let's kill the *netauto2* repository. It shouldn't have any changes in it, but if it does, you should know how to get those changes back into the original *net-auto* repository. Need a hint? Add a remote, fetch changes, and merge the changes:

```
ubuntu@ubuntu2004:~$ rm -rf netauto2
ubuntu@ubuntu2004:~$ git clone ~/net-auto na-clone
Cloning into 'na-clone'...
done.
ubuntu@ubuntu2004:~$ cd na-clone
ubuntu@ubuntu2004:~/na-clone$ git log --oneline HEAD~2..HEAD
3267a4a (HEAD -> main, origin/main, origin/HEAD) Update sw2 configuration
829764b Merge branch 'sw4' into main
3ab27f8 Update sw4 configuration
```

This example illustrates how `git clone` makes a copy of the repository, just as you did manually in the previous section. There's more, though—now run `git remote` in this new cloned repository:

```
ubuntu@ubuntu2004:~/na-clone$ git remote
origin
```

Here's the advantage of using `git clone` over the manual steps we showed you earlier—it *automatically* creates a remote pointing back to the original repository from which this repository was cloned. Further, it *automatically* creates remote tracking branches for you (you can verify this by using `git branch -a` or `git branch -r`). Because it handles these extra steps for you, `git clone` should be your preferred mechanism for cloning a repository.

Before we move on, let's talk a bit about the `origin` remote that was automatically created by `git clone`. While the name of a remote is strictly symbolic, origin does have special significance for Git. You can think of it as a default remote name. When you have multiple remotes (yes, this is definitely possible!) and you run a `git fetch` without specifying a remote, Git will default to origin. Aside from this behavior, though, no special attributes are given to the remote named origin.

As an example of using multiple remotes, this book was written using Git and multiple Git remotes. One Git remote was GitHub; the other was O'Reilly's repository. Here's the output of `git remote -v` from one author's repository:

```
oreilly   git@git.atlas.oreilly.com:oreillymedia/network-automation.git (fetch)
oreilly   git@git.atlas.oreilly.com:oreillymedia/network-automation.git (push)
origin    https://github.com/jedelman8/network-automation-book.git (fetch)
origin    https://github.com/jedelman8/network-automation-book.git (fetch)
```

Now we're finally ready to tackle the last step, which is taking everything you've learned so far and applying it to extend our Git working model with repositories across multiple systems.

Extending our working model across multiple systems

When we discussed the idea of creating a Git remote (see "Linking repositories with remotes" on page 546), we said that a remote has two attributes: the name (symbolic in nature) and the location. So far, you've seen only remotes on the same system, but Git natively supports remotes on *different* systems across a variety of protocols.

For example, a remote on the same system uses a location like this:

```
/path/to/git/repository
file:///path/to/git/repository
```

However, a remote could also use various network protocols to reach a repository on a separate system:

```
git://host.domain.com/path/to/git/repository
ssh:/[user@]host.domain.com/path/to/git/repository
http://host.domain.com/path/to/git/repository
https://host.domain.com/path/to/git/repository
```

The `git://` syntax references Git's native protocol, which is unauthenticated and therefore used for anonymous access (generally read-only access). The `ssh://` syntax refers to Secure Shell; this is actually Git's protocol tunneled over SSH for authenticated access. Finally, you have HTTP and HTTPS variants as well.

This means that you could take the working model we've described throughout this section and *easily* extend it to multiple systems, using whatever network protocol best suits your needs. In this section, we focus on the use of SSH, and later in this chapter we'll show you examples of using HTTPS with public Git hosting services.

Going back to our example, let's say you need to be able to work on your network automation repository from both your desktop system and a laptop that you take with you. Let's assume that both systems support SSH (i.e., they are running Linux, macOS, or some other Unix variant). The first step is to configure passwordless authentication for SSH, generally using SSH keys. This will allow the various git commands to work without prompting for a password. Configuring SSH falls outside the scope of this book, but it's well documented online.

The next step is then to create the necessary Git remotes. The repository already exists on your desktop (for the purposes of this example, we'll use our Ubuntu 20.04.3 Focal Fossa system to represent your desktop), but it doesn't exist on your laptop (which we'll represent with our Debian 11 Bullseye system). So, you need to clone the repository over to the laptop:

```
admin@debian11:~$ git clone ssh://ubuntu/~/net-auto net-auto
Cloning into 'net-auto'...
remote: Counting objects: 32, done.
remote: Compressing objects: 100% (30/30), done.
remote: Total 32 (delta 12), reused 0 (delta 0)
Receiving objects: 100% (32/32), 2.99 KiB | 0 bytes/s, done.
Resolving deltas: 100% (12/12), done.
Checking connectivity... done.
```

This copies the repository from your desktop (*ubuntu*, defined using an SSH configuration file) to your laptop (placing it in the directory specified; in this case, *net-auto*), creates a Git remote named origin pointing back to the original, and creates remote tracking branches. You can verify all this by using git remote to see the remote and git branch -r to see remote tracking branches.

If you prefer to have a remote name that more clearly identifies where the remote is found, you can rename the remote from the default name, origin. Let's rename the remote to reflect that it's coming from our desktop system:

```
admin@debian11:~/net-auto$ git remote
origin
admin@debian11:~/net-auto$ git remote rename origin desktop
admin@debian11:~/net-auto$ git remote
desktop
```

Now, back on the Ubuntu system, you need to create a remote to the repository on the Debian laptop. The repository already exists here, so you can't use git clone; instead, you need to add the remote manually and then fetch information from the remote to create the remote tracking branches:

```
ubuntu@ubuntu2004:~/net-auto$ git remote add laptop ssh://debian11/~/net-auto
ubuntu@ubuntu2004:~/net-auto$ git remote
laptop
ubuntu@ubuntu2004:~$ git fetch laptop
From ssh://debian11/~/net-auto
 * [new branch]      main       -> laptop/main
ubuntu@ubuntu2004:~/net-auto$ git branch -r
  laptop/main
```

Great—now you have the repository on both systems, a remote on each system pointing back to the other, and remote tracking branches created on each side. From here, the workflow is exactly as we described in earlier sections:

1. Make changes on either system (not both at the same time!) and commit those changes to the repository. Ideally, you should work *exclusively* in branches other than the main branch.

2. When you get back to the other system, run a `git fetch` and `git merge` to fetch and merge changes from remote branches into local branches. (If you don't care to review the changes before merging, you can use `git pull`.) Be sure to do this *before* you get started working!

3. Repeat as needed to keep branches on both systems up-to-date with each other.

With regard to using `git pull` to fetch and merge from a remote repository in a single step, there may be a configuration setting you need to turn on. Newer versions of Git ask the user to reconcile divergent branches, as shown in this output in response to running `git pull`:

```
admin@debian11:~/na-shared$ git pull origin main
hint: Pulling without specifying how to reconcile divergent branches is
hint: discouraged. You can squelch this message by running one of the following
hint: commands sometime before your next pull:
hint:
hint:   git config pull.rebase false  # merge (the default strategy)
hint:   git config pull.rebase true   # rebase
hint:   git config pull.ff only       # fast-forward only
hint:
hint: You can replace "git config" with "git config --global" to set a default
hint: preference for all repositories. You can also pass --rebase, --no-rebase,
hint: or --ff-only on the command line to override the configured default per
hint: invocation.
```

We touched on rebasing briefly earlier in "Rebasing to avoid merge commits" on page 543, but there is a lot more to rebasing. However, it is well documented online. For now, it's probably safe to go ahead and run `git config pull.rebase false`, which is noted in the preceding hint as the default strategy.

The approach we've shown you so far works fairly well for a single developer on two systems, but what about more than one developer? While it's possible to build a full mesh of Git remotes and remote tracking branches, this can quickly become unwieldy. Using a shared repository in cases like this greatly simplifies using Git across multiple systems.

Using a shared repository

If you've been poking around Git remotes with the `git remote` command, you may have discovered the `-v` switch, which enables more verbose output. For example, running `git remote -v` from one of the two systems configured in the previous section shows this:

```
admin@debian11:~/na-shared$ git remote -v
desktop  ssh://ubuntu/~/net-auto (fetch)
desktop  ssh://ubuntu/~/net-auto (push)
```

This is useful, as it shows the full location of the remote repository. We've discussed the use of `git fetch` to retrieve information from the remote repository, but what's this push?

So far we've discussed only retrieving information from a remote repository to your local repository through the use of commands like `git remote update`, `git fetch`, and `git pull`. It is possible, though, to send (Git uses the term *push*) changes to a remote repository from your local repository. However, in such cases, it is strongly recommended that the remote repository should be a bare repository.

What is a bare repository? Put simply, a *bare repository* is a Git repository without a working directory. (Recall that *working directory* has a specific definition in Git and shouldn't be taken to mean the same as the *current directory*.) All the discussions of Git repositories so far have assumed the presence of a working directory, because someone—a user like you—was going to be working on the repository. You, as the user of the repository, needed a way of interacting with the content in the repository, and the working directory was the way Git provided that method of interaction.

The reason you are strongly recommended against pushing to a nonbare repository (a repository with a working directory) is that a push doesn't reset the working directory. Let's go back to our previous example—two systems configured with remotes and remote tracking branches pointing to the other system—and see how this might cause problems:

1. Let's say you're being a really good Git citizen and working from a branch. We'll call this branch *new-feature*. You've got new-feature checked out on your first system, so it's the contents of the new-feature branch that are in the working directory. As the day ends, you still have a few unfinished changes left in the working directory, but you commit a few other changes.

2. From your second system, you fetch the changes, review them, merge them into the local new-feature branch, and continue working. You know that you can't see the uncommitted changes in the working directory on your first system, but that's no problem. All is well so far.

3. It's the end of the evening now, and you've just completed some work. You decide to push your changes to your work system's new-feature branch.

4. The next day, you come into work and decide to get started. Your uncommitted changes are still in the working directory, but you don't see the changes you pushed last night. What's going on here?

This is the issue with pushing to a nonbare repository: the changes were pushed to the remote repository, but the working directory was not updated. That's why you can't see the changes. To be able to see the changes, you'll have to run `git reset --hard HEAD`, which will *throw away* the changes in the working directory in order to show the pushed changes. Not a good situation, right?

Using a bare repository eliminates these problems but also eliminates the possibility of being able to interactively work with the repository. This is probably perfectly fine for a shared repository being used by multiple developers, though.

To create a new, bare repository, simply add the `--bare` option to `git init`:

```
[ec2-user@amazonlinux2 ~]$ git init --bare shared-repo.git
Initialized empty Git repository in /home/ec2-user/shared-repo.git/
[ec2-user@amazonlinux2 ~]$ git init non-bare-repo
Initialized empty Git repository in /home/ec2-user/non-bare-repo/.git/
```

Note the difference in the output of Git when `--bare` is used and when it is not used. In a non-bare repository, the actual Git repository is in the *.git* subdirectory, and Git's response indicates this. In a bare repository, though, there's no working directory, so the Git repository sits *directly* at the root of the directory specified.

 Although not required, it is accepted convention to end the name of a bare repository in *.git*.

In this case, you have an *existing* repository, and you need to somehow transition that into a bare repository that you can now share among multiple users. Git is prepared for such a scenario: you can use `git clone` to clone an existing repository into a new bare repository:

```
ubuntu@ubuntu2004:~$ git clone --bare net-auto na-shared.git
Cloning into bare repository 'na-shared.git'...
done.
```

When you use `git clone --bare`, Git does not add any remotes or remote tracking branches. This makes sense if you think about it; generally, remotes and remote tracking branches are useful only when you are directly interacting with the repository. With a bare repository, you aren't interacting directly; you'll use a clone on another system, which will have remotes and remote tracking branches.

Let's take our two-system setup (with the repository on the Ubuntu desktop system and the Debian laptop system and remotes pointing back to each other) and transition it into a shared, bare repository on a third system. We'll introduce our third system, a system running Amazon Linux 2 (AL2), to serve as the shared repository.

First, you need to get the repository onto the AL2 system. Here's where `git clone --bare` comes into play:

```
[ec2-user@amazonlinux2 ~]$ git clone --bare ssh://ubuntu/~/net-auto
na-shared.git
Cloning into bare repository 'na-shared.git'...
remote: Counting objects: 32, done.
remote: Compressing objects: 100% (30/30), done.
Receiving objects: 100% (32/32), done.
remote: Total 32 (delta 12), reused 0 (delta 0)
Resolving deltas: 100% (12/12), done.
```

Now you can clone this bare repository onto your two work systems. First, the Ubuntu desktop system:

```
ubuntu@ubuntu2004:~$ git clone ssh://amzn2/~/na-shared.git
na-shared
Cloning into 'na-shared'...
remote: Counting objects: 32, done.
remote: Compressing objects: 100% (18/18), done.
remote: Total 32 (delta 12), reused 32 (delta 12)
Receiving objects: 100% (32/32), done.
Resolving deltas: 100% (12/12), done.
Checking connectivity... done.
ubuntu@ubuntu2004:~$ cd na-shared
ubuntu@ubuntu2004:~/na-shared$ git remote -v
origin  ssh://amzn2/~/na-shared.git (fetch)
origin  ssh://amzn2/~/na-shared.git (push)
ubuntu@ubuntu2004:~/na-shared$ git branch -r
  origin/HEAD -> origin/main
  origin/main
ubuntu@ubuntu2004:~/na-shared$ git log --oneline HEAD~2..HEAD
3267a4a (HEAD -> main, origin/main, origin/HEAD) Update sw2 configuration
829764b Merge branch 'sw4' into main
3ab27f8 Update sw4 configuration
```

You can see that the `git clone` into the bare repository and subsequently back down to your Ubuntu system preserves all the data and metadata in the repository, and automatically creates Git remotes and remote tracking branches. (You can verify the Git history, if you'd like, by running `git log` in the new `na-shared` repository as well as in the old `net-auto` repository still on your system.)

Next, you perform the same steps on the Debian laptop system:

```
admin@debian11:~$ git clone ssh://amzn2/~/na-shared.git
na-shared
Cloning into 'na-shared'...
remote: Counting objects: 32, done.
remote: Compressing objects: 100% (18/18), done.
```

```
remote: Total 32 (delta 12), reused 32 (delta 12)
Receiving objects: 100% (32/32), done.
Resolving deltas: 100% (12/12), done.
Checking connectivity... done.
admin@debian11:~$ cd na-shared
admin@debian11:~/na-shared$ git remote -v
origin  ssh://amzn2/~/na-shared.git (fetch)
origin  ssh://amzn2/~/na-shared.git (push)
admin@debian11:~/na-shared$ git branch -r
  origin/HEAD -> origin/main
  origin/main
```

Now that you have the new *na-shared* repository on all your systems, you can simply remove the old *net-auto* repository with `rm -rf net-auto`.

What does the workflow look like now?

1. You'll still want to work almost exclusively in branches other than the main branch. This becomes particularly important when working with other users in the same shared repository.

2. Before starting work on the local clone on any system, run `git fetch` to retrieve any changes present on the shared repository but not in your local clone. Merge the changes into local branches as needed with `git merge`.

3. Make changes in the local repository and commit them to your local clone.

4. Push the changes up to the shared repository by using `git push`.

We've mentioned pushing changes a few times in this chapter, but this probably warrants additional explanation. To that end, let's dive into the `git push` command to see this concept in action.

Pushing changes to a shared repository

Now that you have a bare repository, you can push changes to the remote by using `git push`. The general syntax is `git push remote branch`, where *remote* is the name of the Git remote, and *branch* is the name of the branch to which these changes should be pushed.

To illustrate this in action, let's make changes to the network automation repository on our Debian system. You'll add a Jinja template, *hv-tor-config.j2*, that represents the base configuration for a ToR switch to which hypervisors are connected.

First, because you don't want to work off the main branch, you create a new branch to hold your changes:

```
admin@debian11:~/na-shared$ git checkout -b add-sw-tmpl
Switched to a new branch 'add-sw-tmpl'
```

After you add the file to the working directory (by creating it from scratch or by copying it from elsewhere), you stage and commit the changes:

```
admin@debian11:~/na-shared$ git add hv-tor-config.j2
admin@debian11:~/na-shared$ git commit -m "Add Jinja template for TOR config"
[add-sw-tmpl 8cbbe6f] Add Jinja template for TOR config
 1 file changed, 15 insertions(+)
 create mode 100644 hv-tor-config.j2
```

Now, you push the changes to the origin remote, which points to our shared (bare) repository on the AL2 system:

```
admin@debian11:~/na-shared$ git push origin add-sw-tmpl
Enumerating objects: 4, done.
Counting objects: 100% (4/4), done.
Delta compression using up to 2 threads
Compressing objects: 100% (3/3), done.
Writing objects: 100% (3/3), 426 bytes | 426.00 KiB/s, done.
Total 3 (delta 1), reused 0 (delta 0), pack-reused 0
To ssh://amzn2/~/na-shared.git
 * [new branch]      add-sw-tmpl -> add-sw-tmpl
```

This allows coworkers and others with whom you are collaborating to then fetch the changes on their systems. They would just use git fetch to retrieve the changes, make a local branch corresponding to the remote tracking branch, and then review the changes by using whatever methods they wanted. Here, we'll show git diff, which isn't terribly useful considering the only change is adding a single new file:

```
ubuntu@ubuntu2004:~/na-shared$ git fetch origin
remote: Enumerating objects: 4, done.
remote: Counting objects: 100% (4/4), done.
remote: Compressing objects: 100% (3/3), done.
remote: Total 3 (delta 1), reused 0 (delta 0), pack-reused 0
Unpacking objects: 100% (3/3), 406 bytes | 406.00 KiB/s, done.
From ssh://amzn2/~/na-shared
 * [new branch]      add-sw-tmpl -> origin/add-sw-tmpl
ubuntu@ubuntu2004:~/na-shared$ git checkout --track -b add-sw-tmpl origin/add-sw-tmpl
Branch add-sw-tmpl set up to track remote branch add-sw-tmpl from origin.
Switched to a new branch 'add-sw-tmpl'
ubuntu@ubuntu2004:~/na-shared$ git diff main..HEAD
diff --git a/hv-tor-config.j2 b/hv-tor-config.j2
new file mode 100644
index 0000000..8de9181
--- /dev/null
+++ b/hv-tor-config.j2
@@ -0,0 +1,13 @@
+interface ethernet0
+ description Mgmt interface for hypervisor
+ switchport mode access
+ switchport mode access vlan {{ mgmt_vlan_id }}
+
+interface ethernet1
+ switchport mode {{ modeSelection }}
+
+interface ethernet2
```

```
+   switchport mode {{ modeSelection }}
+
+interface ethernet3
+   switchport mode {{ modeSelection }}
+
```

Once everyone agrees that the changes are OK, you can merge the changes into the
main branch. First, perform the merge locally:

```
admin@debian11:~/na-shared$ git checkout main
Switched to branch 'main'
Your branch is up-to-date with 'origin/main'
admin@debian11:~/na-shared$ git merge add-sw-tmpl
Updating 3267a4a..01616d1
Fast-forward
 hv-tor-config.j2 | 13 +++++++++++++
 1 file changed, 13 insertions(+)
 create mode 100644 hv-tor-config.j2
```

This a fast-forward, so there's no commit merge. Now push the changes to the shared
repository:

```
admin@debian11:~/na-shared$ git push origin main
Total 0 (delta 0), reused 0 (delta 0), pack-reused 0
To ssh://amzn2/~/na-shared.git
   3267a4a..01616d1  main -> main
```

Finally, delete your branch (also frequently referred to as a *feature branch* or a *topic
branch*) and push that change to the shared repository:

```
admin@debian11:~/na-shared$ git branch -d add-sw-tmpl
Deleted branch add-sw-tmpl (was 01616d1).
admin@debian11:~/na-shared$ git push origin --delete add-sw-tmpl
To ssh://amzn2/~/na-shared.git
 - [deleted]         add-sw-tmpl
```

Your collaborators can then get the changes that were merged into the main branch,
delete the local branch they created, and then delete the remote tracking branch that
is no longer needed by using the git fetch --prune command:

```
ubuntu@ubuntu2004:~/na-shared$ git pull origin main
From ssh://amzn2/~/na-shared
 * branch            main       -> FETCH_HEAD
   3267a4a..01616d1  main       -> origin/main
Updating 3267a4a..01616d1
Fast-forward
 hv-tor-config.j2 | 13 +++++++++++++
 1 file changed, 13 insertions(+)
 create mode 100644 hv-tor-config.j2
ubuntu@ubuntu2004:~/na-shared$ git fetch --prune origin
From ssh://amzn2/~/na-shared
 - [deleted]         (none)     -> origin/add-sw-tmpl
ubuntu@ubuntu2004:~/na-shared$ git branch -d add-sw-tmpl
Deleted branch add-sw-tmpl (was 01616d1).
```

The `git fetch --prune` command is new; it's used to delete a remote tracking branch when the branch no longer exists on the remote. In this particular case, you're removing the remote tracking branch for *origin/add-sw-tmpl*, as noted in the output of the command.

 We know that all this may sound complicated if you're new to Git. It's OK—everyone was new to Git at some point (except maybe Linus). Take it slow and be patient with yourself. After a little while of using Git, the commands will start to feel more natural. Until then, you might find it handy to have a Git cheat sheet nearby to remind you of some of the commands and their syntax.

Before we move on to our final topic—collaborating using Git-based online services—let's recap what we've discussed in this section:

- Git uses *remotes* to create links between repositories. You'll use the `git remote` command to manipulate remotes. A remote can point to a filesystem location as well as to a location across the network, such as another system via SSH.

- To retrieve changes from a remote repository into your local repository, use `git fetch remote`.

- Git relies heavily on branches when working with remote repositories. Special branches known as *remote tracking branches* are automatically created when you use `git fetch` to retrieve changes.

- Changes retrieved from a remote repository can be merged into your local repository just like any other branch merge by using `git merge`.

- If you don't want to follow the two-step `git fetch` followed by `git merge`, you can use `git pull`.

- You'll use `git push` to push changes to a remote repository, but this remote repository should be a bare repository.

- Using a bare repository as a central, shared repository can enable multiple users to collaborate on a single repository. Changes are exchanged via branches and through the use of `git push`, `git fetch`, `git merge`, and `git pull`.

Our last section in this chapter builds on everything we've shown you so far and focuses on using Git-based online services to collaborate with other users.

Collaborating via Git-Based Online Services

Fundamentally, collaborating with other users by using a Git-based online service will look and feel much like what we described in the previous section. All the same concepts apply—using clones to make copies of repositories, using remotes and remote tracking branches, and working in branches to exchange changes with other users in the same repository. You'll even continue to use the same commands: git fetch, git push, git merge, and git pull.

All that being said, we'd like to cover a few differences. For the sake of brevity, we focus on the use of GitHub as our Git-based online service for collaborating. The topics covered in this section are as follows:

- Forking repositories
- Pull requests

Ready? Let's start with forking repositories.

Forking repositories

Forking a GitHub project is essentially the same as *cloning* a Git repository. (We use the terms *project* and *repository* somewhat interchangeably in this section.) When you fork a GitHub repository, you are issuing a command to GitHub's servers to clone the repository into your user account. At the time of creation, your fork will be a full and complete copy of the original repository, including all the content and the commit history. Once the repository has been forked into your account, it's just as if you'd issued a git clone from the command line—links are maintained back to the original project, much like a Git remote. (These remotes are not exposed to the user, though.) The key difference here is that forking a repository on GitHub does *not* create a local copy of the repository; you'll still need to use git clone to clone the forked copy down to your local system, as we'll show you shortly.

So why fork a repository? In the case of a large online service such as GitHub, hundreds of thousands of repositories are hosted there. Each repository is associated with a GitHub user ID, and that user ID is allowed to control who may or may not contribute to the repository.

What if you find a repository to which you want to contribute? The owner of that repository may not know you (a likely situation) and may not trust your ability to contribute to their repository. However, if you had your own copy of the repository, you could make the contributions you wanted to make and then let the owner of the original decide if such contributions were worthwhile.

So, instead of trying to get approval to contribute directly to a repository, you instead *fork* (clone) the repository to your own account, where you can work with it. At some point later, you can (optionally) see if the original repository wants to include your changes moving forward (we discuss this in "Creating pull requests" on page 565).

To fork a GitHub repository, just follow these steps:

1. Log into GitHub, using your security credentials.

2. Locate the repository you'd like to fork into your own account and then click the Fork button in the upper-right corner of the screen.

3. If you are a member of any GitHub organizations, you may be prompted for the user account or organization where you'd like this repository to be forked. Choose your own user account unless you know you need a different option.

That's it! GitHub will fork (clone) the repository into your user account.

Because GitHub repositories are bare repositories, you generally need to then clone this bare repository down to your local system to work with it. (GitHub provides web-based tools to create files, edit files, make commits, and similar.) To clone a GitHub repository out of your account, you just use the `git clone` command, followed by the URL of the GitHub repository. For example, here's the URL of one of the author's GitHub repositories: *https://github.com/scottslowe/learning-tools.git*.

Let's say your GitHub username is npabook (this user did not exist at the time of this writing). If you were to fork the preceding repository, it would make a full and complete copy of the repository into your user account, just as if you'd used `git clone`. At this point, the URL for your forked repository would be *https://github.com/npabook/learning-tools.git*.

If you ran `git clone https://github.com/npabook/learning-tools.git` from your local system, Git would clone the repository down to your local system, create a remote named origin that points back to your forked repository on GitHub, and create remote tracking branches—just as `git clone` worked in our earlier examples.

Once you have a clone of the repository on your local system, working with your forked GitHub repository is *exactly* as we described in the previous section:

1. Create new feature/topic branches locally to isolate changes away from the main branch.

2. Use `git push` to push those changes to the remote GitHub repository.

3. Merge the changes into the main branch via `git merge` whenever you're ready.

4. Use `git fetch` followed by `git merge` to pull down the changes to the main branch, or combine those steps by using `git pull`.

5. Delete the local feature/topic branch and the remote branch on the GitHub repository.

So far, this should all seem pretty straightforward—we haven't really shown anything different from what we described earlier. One situation, though, requires some discussion: how do you keep your fork in sync with the original?

Keeping forked repositories in sync

Although GitHub maintains links back to the original repository when you fork it into your user account, GitHub does not provide a way to keep the two repositories synchronized. Why is it important to keep your fork synchronized with the original? Suppose you want to contribute to an ongoing project. Over time, your forked copy will fall hopelessly behind the original as development continues, branches are merged, and changes committed to the original. To be able to contribute useful changes, you need your fork to be up-to-date with the original.

To keep your forked repository up-to-date, you use multiple remotes. (We did say earlier that multiple remotes are definitely something you might need to use with Git.) Let's walk through how this works. We'll assume you've already forked the repository in GitHub.

First, clone the forked repository down to your system by using `git clone`. The command looks something like this:

```
git clone https://username@github.com/username/repository-name.git
```

This clones the repository down to your local system, creates a remote named origin that points back to the URL specified before, and creates remote tracking branches. At this point, if you run `git remote` in this repository, you'll see a single remote named origin (remember that `git remote -v` will also show the location of the remote—in this case, the HTTPS URL).

Next, add a *second* remote that points to the original repository. The command looks something like this:

```
git remote upstream add https://github.com/original-user/repository-name.git
```

The name `upstream` here is strictly symbolic, but we like to use it as this reminds us that the remote points to the upstream (or original) project. (We've also found that `upstream` is commonly used, so it may make sense to use the same remote name that others use for consistency.) Your local repository now has two remotes: origin, which points to your forked repository, and upstream, which points to the original repository.

Now, follow these steps to keep your repository up-to-date with the original (all these steps are taken from within the cloned Git repository on your local system):

1. Check out the main branch via `git checkout main`.

---

2. Get the changes from the original repository. You can use a combination of `git fetch upstream main` followed by `git merge upstream/main`, or you can use `git pull upstream main` (which combines the steps). Your local, cloned repository is now in sync with the original repository.

3. Push the changes from your local repository to the forked repository, using `git push origin main`. Now your forked repository is up-to-date with the original.

This process doesn't keep any feature/topic branches up-to-date, but that's generally not a problem—most of the time, you'll want to keep main synchronized only between the original and the forked repository. If you do want to keep a different branch up-to-date between the original repository and your fork, substitute the correct branch name for the commands in the preceding list. The process is the same.

In the next section, you'll learn how to let the owner of a repository know that you have changes you'd like them to consider including in their repository.

Creating pull requests

Let's quickly recap the recommended process for working with a shared repository such as that offered by GitHub:

1. Create a local branch—called a *feature* or *topic* branch—in which to store the changes you're going to make.

2. Stage and commit the changes to the new local branch.

3. Push the local branch to the remote repository via `git push remote branch`.

That gets the changes into your forked repository, but how does the owner of the original repository know that you've pushed changes up to your forked copy? In short: they *don't*. Why? Well, for one, it's entirely possible that you are truly forking—creating a divergent codebase—and don't want or need the original author(s) to know about your changes. Second, what if the changes you commit don't include *all* the changes you want the original authors to consider? How would Git or GitHub know when you are ready? In short: it *can't*. Only you can know when your code is ready for the original authors to review for inclusion, and that's the purpose of a pull request.

A *pull request* is a notification to the authors of the original repository that you have changes you'd like them to consider including in their repository. Creating a pull request comes after step 3 in the preceding list. Once you've pushed your changes into a branch in your forked repository, you can create a pull request against the original repository. (Note that other Git-based platforms, such as GitLab, may use terms like *merge request* instead of pull request. The basic idea and workflow are much the same.)

To create a pull request after pushing a branch up to GitHub, go to the original repository. Just under the line listing the commits, branches, releases, and contributors, a new line will appear with a button labeled "Compare & pull request." This is illustrated in Figure 11-12.

Figure 11-12. Creating a new pull request in GitHub

Click that button, and GitHub will open a screen to create the pull request. The base fork, base branch, head fork, and comparison branch will all be automatically filled in for you, and the notes in the pull request will be taken from the last commit message. Make any changes as needed; then click the green "Create pull request" button.

The owners of the original repository then have to decide if the changes found in your branch can and should be merged into their repository. If they agree—or if you are the one receiving the pull request—then you can merge the changes in GitHub's web interface.

Once the changes have been merged into the original repository, you can update your fork's main branch from the original (using `git fetch` and `git merge`, or the one-step `git pull`). Since the changes from your feature/topic branch are now found in the main branch, you can then delete the branch (as well as any remote tracking branches for your forked repository), as it is no longer needed.

As you can see, aside from a few minor differences, the general workflow for collaborating via GitHub is very similar to the workflow for collaborating using only a shared (bare) repository. By and large, the same terms, concepts, and commands are used in both cases, which makes it easier for you to collaborate with others using Git.

Summary

In this chapter, we've provided an introduction to Git, a widely used version control system. Git is a fully distributed version control system that provides strong support for nonlinear development with branches. Like other version control systems, Git offers accountability (who made what changes) and change tracking (knowing the changes that were made). These attributes are just as applicable in networking-centric use cases as they are in developer-centric use cases. Branches are a key part of collaborating with Git. To help with Git collaboration, online services (such as GitHub and Bitbucket) have appeared, allowing users across organizations to collaborate on repositories with relative ease.

## CHAPTER 12

Automation Tools

No discussion of network automation would be complete without evaluating the role that automation tools—like Red Hat Ansible, Nornir, and HashiCorp Terraform—play in a network automation context.

Traditionally, this tooling has been more focused on the server automation use case. This was understandable given that some of these tools had their origins in automating server operating systems and managing OS and/or application configurations. In recent years, though, multiple companies have expended a great deal of effort to enhance the network automation functionality of their products. These enhancements make these products much more useful and powerful for network automation.

Automated configuration management was the primary use case in the beginning. But with the advent of dynamic infrastructure services offered mainly by public cloud providers, tooling has evolved and new actors have entered the playground to enable the IaC paradigm.

This chapter introduces how to use some popular open source automation tools in the context of network automation:

- Ansible
- Nornir
- Terraform

Before we get into the details and examples of using these tools for network automation, let's take a quick look at an overview of them.

Reviewing Automation Tools

While all of these tools are focused on automation, each has its own architecture and approaches automation in a slightly different way. This gives each tool its own set of strengths and weaknesses. In this section, we quickly review each of the tools so that you can begin to see how they might be used in your environment.

At a high level, some of the major architectural/conceptual differences among the tools include the following:

Configuration management versus infrastructure provisioning
> Infrastructure provisioning is the process used to create infrastructure—network services, virtual machines, databases, etc. Configuration management is the process of automating the installation of software components and performing configuration management tasks. So, you could understand infrastructure provisioning as a day 0 activity and configuration management as a day 1 activity. In spite of most automation tools being able to achieve both, this chapter will help you understand where each one shines.

Agent-based versus agentless
> Some tools require an agent—a piece of software—to be running on the system or device being managed. In a network automation use case, this could prove to be a problem, as not every NOS supports running agents on a network device. If a NOS doesn't support running an agent natively on the device, there are sometimes workarounds involving a proxy agent. Agentless tools, obviously, don't require an agent and may be more applicable in network automation use cases.

Centralized versus decentralized
> Agent-based architectures often also require a centralized master server. Some agentless products also use a master server, but most are decentralized.

Custom protocol versus standards-based protocol
> Some tools use a custom protocol; this is often tied to agent-based architectures. Other tools leverage SSH. Given the ubiquity of SSH in network devices, tools leveraging SSH as their transport protocol may be better suited to network automation use cases.

DSL versus standards-based data formats and general-purpose languages
> Some tools have their own domain-specific language (DSL); users of these tools must create the appropriate files in that DSL to be consumed by the automation tool. A DSL is a language purpose-built for a specific domain (or tool). For organizations that aren't already familiar with the DSL, this might create an additional learning curve. Other tools leverage YAML, which is considered a

general-purpose language in this context. Remember, we discussed YAML in Chapter 8.

Declarative versus imperative

Some tools use a declarative approach to define the final state of the infrastructure: independent of the definition order, the proper dependencies and tasks will be inferred and executed to enforce the target state. Other tools use the imperative approach: each step is a procedure to be performed, and the definition order determines the execution order.

Extensibility

Most of these automation tools allow you to add or extend functionality via high-level scripting languages, such as Python or Go.

Push versus pull versus event-driven

Some automation tools operate in a push model: information is pushed from one place out to the devices or systems being managed. Others operate in a pull model, typically pulling configuration information or instructions (often on some sort of scheduled basis). Finally, event-driven tools perform an action in response to another event or trigger.

Mutable versus immutable

Traditionally, when you needed to change an infrastructure's configuration, you simply *mutated* its state by applying changes to the current state. This process is known as the *mutable approach* and is how configuration management tools work. In contrast, in an *immutable* approach, you need to *replace/restart* the infrastructure with a new one to change its state. Even the smallest change, such as changing a server's hostname, would then require you to reprovision that server and start from scratch. Depending on the focus, some tools are more suited than others for each case.

State management

Configuration management tools don't manage the lifecycle of the remote infrastructure. You can gather the state at each step, but it's not implicitly tracked. Conversely, the tools based on the immutable pattern need to decide when it's necessary to re-create an infrastructure component, so they usually keep the state of the remote infrastructure that was provisioned by them.

With this high-level set of architectural differences in mind, let's take a quick look at the three tools covered in this chapter:

Ansible

Ansible uses a decentralized, agentless architecture with SSH as the underlying transport protocol. It is typically operated in a push model, though it also supports a pull model. Ansible is built using Python and leverages Python for extensibility. Ansible supports templating using the Jinja templating language. Ansible originally targeted a way to run ad hoc commands on servers, but has since evolved into task orchestration using *playbooks* that perform idempotent tasks on target systems. Playbooks can be written in standard YAML or an Ansible derivation of YAML.

Nornir

Nornir is a lightweight Python framework (not a CLI) designed for network automation that can be extended via plug-ins adding new features (e.g., tasks or inventory sources) without having to write them from scratch. It is an alternative to automation tools like Ansible because, being pure Python, it gives you full control of the logic and direct access to all the libraries and tools available. Nornir comes with a few Python constructs that make it easy to use the inventory of hosts, run tasks, and process the results, everything in a structured way. And, by default, Nornir uses multithreading, so the tasks are performed in parallel per host.

Terraform

Terraform takes a dramatically different approach from the other tools listed here. Terraform is focused on infrastructure provisioning instead of configuration management, and lets you define your infrastructure (and manage its lifecycle) in human-readable and declarative configuration files, using a Terraform configuration language. It is agnostic to the infrastructure providers and easy to extend via providers, becoming the most relevant tool in the IaaS ecosystem.

 Other popular network automation tools are not covered in this book because of space constraints. However, at *https://oreilly-npa-book.github.io*, you have available content from the first edition of this book, covering two extra tools:

- Salt (*https://oreil.ly/06QkX*) can use either an agent-based architecture or an agentless architecture. Salt started as a tool for remote server management, like Ansible, with idempotent configuration management via Salt States, written in YAML. One distinction to make with Salt is that it is also a platform for event-driven automation (using a message bus) beyond general configuration management.

- StackStorm (*https://oreil.ly/2piMv*) focuses on event-driven automation; tasks are performed in response to events. StackStorm leverages Python to build sensors that emit events or actions to trigger a task.

Now, let's dive a bit deeper into how Ansible, Nornir, and Terraform can be used for network automation. We've arranged the in-depth discussion of the products in alphabetical order, so we'll start with Ansible.

Using Ansible

Ansible takes months (or more) to master. Our goal in this section is to provide enough information that you can start automating common tasks immediately. To facilitate this jump start, we've divided this section into seven major areas:

- Discovering the Ansible framework
- Understanding how Ansible works
- Constructing an inventory file
- Executing an Ansible playbook
- Understanding variable files
- Writing Ansible playbooks for network automation
- Using third-party collections and modules

 Ansible is constantly evolving and adding new features to the framework. A newer one, not covered in this book, is the Event-Driven Ansible (*https://oreil.ly/mDzbW*) automation that, at a glance, introduces the capacity to subscribe to an event source (e.g., Kafka) to trigger workflows (implementing *if this, then that* instructions) and generate scheduled events.

By the time you complete this section, you'll have a solid foundation on Ansible, the different types of network automation you can accomplish using Ansible, and most importantly, enough to continue on your automation journey. We'll start by presenting the various projects under the Ansible umbrella.

Discovering the Ansible Framework

Ansible is an open source community project sponsored by Red Hat, and since version 2.9, it's been split into two main components: Ansible Core (`ansible-core`) and the Ansible community (`ansible`) packages:

Ansible Core package
This core building block of the Ansible framework contains all the functionalities (language, runtime, and built-in plug-ins). It's useful for a minimal installation footprint and development environments.

Ansible community package

This package includes a range of community-curated collections with hundreds of modules (you'll learn more about modules in "Getting familiar with Ansible tasks and modules" on page 583). It requires the `ansible-core` package.

You can install both packages via PyPI by executing `pip3 install ansible`, as shown in Example 12-1.

 Full versions of the code examples in this chapter can be found in the book's GitHub repo at *https://github.com/oreilly-npa-book/exam ples/tree/v2/ch12-automationtools*.

Example 12-1. Getting the Ansible version

```
$ pip3 install ansible
# omitted output

$ pip3 list | grep ansible
ansible      4.8.0   ❶
ansible-core 2.11.6  ❶

$ ansible --version  ❷
ansible [core 2.11.6]
  config file = /etc/ansible/ansible.cfg
  configured module search path = ['/etc/ntc/ansible/library']
  ansible python module location =
    /usr/local/lib/python3.8/site-packages/ansible
  ansible collection location =
    /home/ntc/.ansible/collections:/usr/share/ansible/collections
  executable location = /usr/local/bin/ansible
  python version = 3.8.12 (default, Oct 13 2021, 09:22:51) [GCC 8.3.0]
  jinja version = 3.0.2
  libyaml = True
```

❶ Installs two packages, `ansible` and `ansible-core`, which are the versions used in this book

❷ Displays more details about the Ansible installation

 AWX (*https://oreil.ly/C0KDM*) is another open source project in the Ansible ecosystem. This project helps build more sophisticated network automated solutions on top of Ansible. AWX provides a web-based UI, REST API, and a task engine, so it could work as the orchestrator and workflow executor of multiple Ansible tasks. It is also worth noting that Red Hat does sell a commercial product with enterprise support called Ansible Automation Platform (*https://oreil.ly/WwG5N*).

Now that you're aware of the components, it's time to understand how Ansible works.

Understanding How Ansible Works

The first thing we're going to review is how Ansible works from an architectural perspective when automating not only network devices but also Linux servers. Subtle but important differences exist in these two options, and these differences are ultimately reflected in the automation workflows we create with Ansible.

Automating Linux servers

When Ansible is used to automate Linux servers, it operates in a distributed fashion. The Ansible control host, the machine that has Ansible installed, connects via SSH to each server being automated. The control host subsequently copies Python code to each server—this code is what performs the automation task at hand.

These tasks include anything from restarting a Linux process and installing Linux packages to updating text files, pulling updates down from a Git repository, or simply running a bash script on the target Linux hosts being automated. If 100 Linux servers are being automated, 100 servers execute the Ansible code (or modules) to perform the task.

Ansible can also be used to automate Windows servers, but the context here is to describe the origins and most common use of Ansible and how that compares to automating networking devices.

Automating network devices

How Ansible works when automating network devices is a little different: it works in a local, or centralized mode. When automating network devices, the Ansible control host gets configured to run in *local* mode. When Ansible runs in local mode, Ansible does not connect to each device via SSH *and* copy Python code to each network device. In fact, when running in local mode, Ansible actually connects to itself and executes the Python code *locally*.

The Python code that runs locally may still connect to the network device via SSH, but it may also be via an API (or Telnet or SNMP). However, even when Ansible connects via SSH for network devices, Python files are not copied to the device, and CLI commands are simply sent over an SSH connection. From an extremely high-level view, this becomes analogous to executing Python scripts on a server and automating multiple network devices in parallel.

It is possible to have network modules not operate in local mode, but it requires updates to many NOSs. To support this, the network device must permit you to SSH into the device, copy Python files to a temp directory, and then execute those files with a Python execution engine. With the rise of Linux-based NOSs, running Python code inside the box is getting more and more common.

Now that you understand how Ansible operates differently for network devices as compared to Linux hosts (which is what Ansible was initially built for), let's review some Ansible vernacular that's critical to getting started.

Constructing an Inventory File

The first Ansible file we're going to look at is the Ansible inventory file. The *inventory file* is one of two files required to start automating network devices with Ansible. The second, which we cover next, is the playbook.

Traditionally, the inventory file has been defined as an INI-like file that contains the devices that will be automated with Ansible. Example 12-2 shows a basic Ansible inventory file.

Example 12-2. Basic Ansible inventory INI file

```
10.1.100.10
10.5.10.10
nyc-lf01
```

This example is one of the simplest inventory files you can have. It has three lines in it, one per device. As you can see, by default you can use either IP addresses or hostnames (which are fully qualified domain names).

Alternatively, you could also define the inventory file by using the YAML syntax. In Example 12-3, you get the same result as in Example 12-2.

Example 12-3. Basic Ansible inventory YAML file

```
all:
  hosts:
    "10.1.100.10":
    "10.5.10.10":
    nyc-lf01:
```

You can notice two new dictionary keys, all and hosts (we elaborate on them in the following sections). So, the YAML format is a bit more verbose and even more precise. Both options are valid and easy to write and read, but for consistency we use only one through the chapter, the INI notation.

While an inventory file can seem basic, you can gradually add more structure and data to it as you start doing more with Ansible. If you're testing and getting started with only a few devices, the previous example may suffice. However, you need to consider more realistic scenarios such as having larger quantities of devices, having different types of devices, and deploying those devices in different parts of a network (e.g., data center, DMZ, WAN, or access, just to name a few). The upcoming examples introduce how to create groups and define variables in the inventory file.

Let's walk through building out an inventory file that will represent the devices for two regions, *EMEA* and *AMERS*, and two device roles, *dc* and *cpe* (see Figure 12-1). Each device role per region comprises different types of network equipment, as you can see in the diagram.

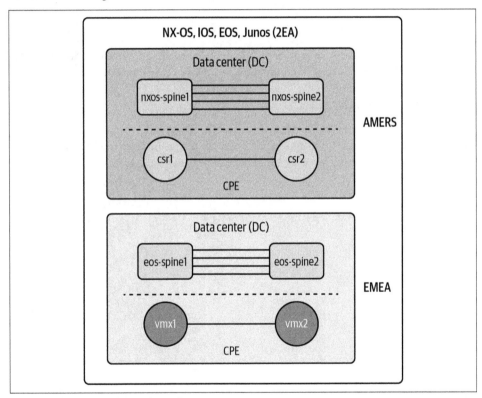

Figure 12-1. Network topology diagram

Working with inventory groups

As you can see, you have two core geographic locations, the AMERS and EMEA regions, with different device types. You'll create different groups so you can easily automate all devices of a certain type, for a certain operating system, or within a given location.

We start in Example 12-4 by creating two groups for the devices in the AMERS region called `amers-cpe` and `amers-dc`. Each group will have two devices. The cpe group will have two Cisco IOSXE devices, and the dc group will have two Cisco NXOS switches. Instead of using IP addresses, we use the router fully qualified domain name (FQDN) defined in your local */etc/hosts* file.

Example 12-4. Ansible inventory file with groups

```
[amers-cpe]
csr1
csr2

[amers-dc]
nxos-spine1
nxos-spine2
```

The bracket [ ] syntax creates logical groups within the inventory file. You'll see later how to reference these groups in a playbook so they are easily automated.

Using nested groups in an inventory file

You can also create groups of groups, or *nested groups*, in an inventory file. For example, you may want to automate all devices in the AMERS region. To do this, you'll add a group called `amers` that contains `amers-cpe` and `amers-dc`, as shown in Example 12-5.

Example 12-5. Ansible inventory file with groups for AMERS

```
[amers:children]
amers-cpe
amers-dc

[amers-cpe]
csr1
csr2

[amers-dc]
nxos-spine1
nxos-spine2
```

When creating nested groups, you must use `:children` in the group name definition. After you've added the `amers` group, your inventory file has three explicitly defined groups: `amers`, `amers-cpe`, and `amers-dc`.

Using the same approach, you can build out the inventory for the EMEA region as shown in Example 12-6.

Example 12-6. Ansible inventory file with groups for EMEA

```
[emea:children]
emea-cpe
emea-dc

[emea-cpe]
vmx1
vmx2

[emea-dc]
eos-spine1
eos-spine2
```

You may also want to create groups to automate all devices of a particular role in the network, such as all CPE devices or all DC devices. To do this, you can create additional groups, as shown in Example 12-7.

Example 12-7. Ansible inventory file with groups for device roles

```
[all-cpe:children]
amers-cpe
emea-cpe

[all-dc:children]
amers-dc
emea-dc
```

As you're seeing, inventory files can be extremely basic when you're just getting started but can quickly expand based on how you want to automate your network devices.

After getting your group structure defined and into your desired state, it's good to know that you can even define variables within your inventory file.

Using variables in Ansible

You can define two types of variables in your Ansible inventory file:

- Group variables
- Host variables

Managing group variables. *Group variables* are assigned at the group level. For example, you may define a variable such as the NTP Server IP address to use for all devices in the AMERS region and then another NTP IP address for devices in EMEA. This is reflected in an inventory, as shown in Example 12-8.

Example 12-8. Group variables

```
[amers:vars]
ntp_server=10.1.200.11

[emea:vars]
ntp_server=10.10.200.11
```

As you can see, when you define group variables, you create a new section in the inventory file with the name of the group and append :vars. In this section, you define group-based variables. Our example creates a single variable called ntp_server. When you're automating devices in the AMERS group and reference this variable, the value of 10.1.200.11 is used, and when automating devices in the EMEA group, the value of 10.10.200.11 is used.

 There is no specific requirement around the ordering of groups and variables in your inventory file. You can have all groups and then all variables, or group 1, group 1 variables, group 2, group 2 variables, and so on.

Managing host variables. You can also define *host variables* that are specific to a given device in the inventory file. To define a host variable, you put the variable on the same line as the host. One scenario, given our NTP example, is that there is a dedicated NTP server per region. But what if there is a device called nxos-spine1 that *must* use a different address? This is accomplished as shown in Example 12-9.

Example 12-9. Host variables

```
[amers-dc]
nxos-spine1  ntp_server=10.1.200.200
nxos-spine2
```

Adding *variable=value* on the same line as the device is how you add host-specific variables within the inventory file. You can also add multiple variables on the same line, such as in Example 12-10.

Example 12-10. Defining multiple host variables

```
[amers-dc]
nxos-spine1  ntp_server=10.1.200.200  syslog_server=10.1.200.201
nxos-spine2
```

Understanding variable priority. More-specific variables have priority, so if you have nested groups such as `amers` and `amers-cpe`, a group variable in `amers-cpe` will override the same variable if defined as an `amers` group variable. If there was a host-specific variable for a device in `amers-cpe`, that would then have higher priority and override the `amers-cpe` group variable.

Ansible provides many more ways to use variables than this book outlines. Although variable priority may not seem like an issue when you're getting started, it's a much more significant topic to consider in large Ansible projects. Variable precedence is well defined in Ansible's documentation (*https://oreil.ly/XvTD7*), with more than 20 possibilities!

Getting familiar with the all group. Be aware that there is an implicit group that always exists, called `all`. This group is used to automate all devices in an inventory file. Example 12-11 shows how you can also assign group variables in the `all` group.

Example 12-11. Group-based variables in the `all` group

```
[all:vars]
ntp_server=10.1.200.199
syslog_server=10.1.200.201
```

Variables defined in the `all` group end up being defaults and are used only if the given variable isn't defined in a more specific group or as a host-based variable.

 You need to know how group and host-based variables work, but the inventory file is not the proper place to define all your variables for a given project. Dedicated files are recommended for defining variables—these files are covered in "Managing host variables" on page 578.

If you're testing along as you're reading, you may want to add a few more groups and variables to the inventory file, as shown in Example 12-12.

Example 12-12. Creating groups per OS

```
[nxos]
nxos-spine1
nxos-spine2

[nxos:vars]
ansible_network_os=nxos

[eos]
eos-spine1
eos-spine2
```

```
[eos:vars]
ansible_network_os=eos

[iosxe]
csr1
csr2

[iosxe:vars]
ansible_network_os=ios

[junos]
vmx1
vmx2

[junos:vars]
ansible_network_os=junos
```

The reason we've added groups and group-based variables for each OS is that in many cases this information is required to automate a given device because many modules either (a) only work for a particular device OS or (b) are multivendor and still require knowing the OS up front.

After combining the previous inventory snippets, you get a full inventory. You can check it in the Ansible folder in the examples repository, in the inventory file (*https://github.com/oreilly-npa-book/examples/blob/v2/ch12-automationtools/ansible/inventory*).

The easiest and most common way to get started with inventory is to use the inventory file. However, if you happen to work in a very dynamic or large environment, or have an existing configuration management database (CMDB) or network management system (NMS) that contains inventory data, Ansible can be integrated with those systems. Ansible supports dynamic inventory scripts such that an inventory file is replaced with a script. The script queries your CMDB/NMS, normalizes the data, and then returns valid JSON in the structure Ansible requires as defined in its docs (out of scope for this book). You can also return variables in the dynamic inventory script such that if you're a large enterprise, all you'd manage are playbooks—all inventory and variables are then returned dynamically as you execute your playbook.

Earlier we stated that the Ansible inventory file is one of two files required to start automating network devices with Ansible. The second file is the Ansible playbook—this is what we'll dive into next.

Executing an Ansible Playbook

The Ansible playbook (*https://oreil.ly/Rmn2e*) is a file that contains your automation instructions. In other words, playbooks contain the individual tasks and workflows that you want to use to automate your network. The playbook itself is written in YAML. This is when being familiar with YAML, as covered in Chapter 8, will come in handy.

The term *playbook* comes from a sports analogy, and thus each playbook file contains one or more plays. And if we expand on that, each play contains one or more tasks.

Let's take a look at a playbook in Example 12-13 to better understand its structure and associated terminology. We are going to review plays, tasks, modules, and using variables in a playbook, as well as the link from the playbook to the inventory file.

Example 12-13. Ansible playbook (ch12-automationtools/ansible/snmp-intro.yml)

```
---                                              ❶
- name: "PLAY 1 - ISSUE SNMP COMMANDS"           ❷
  hosts: "iosxe"                                 ❸
  gather_facts: "no"                             ❹
  connection: "ansible.netcommon.network_cli"    ❺

  tasks:                                         ❻
    - name: "TASK1 - SHOW SNMP CONFIG"
      ios_command:
        commands:
          - "show run | inc snmp"

    - name: "TASK 2 - DEPLOY SNMP COMMANDS"
      cisco.ios.ios_config:
        commands:
          - "snmp-server chassis-id {{ inventory_hostname }}"
```

❶ A playbook is a YAML file that defines a list of *plays*. Every *play* is a dictionary that includes several key-value pairs. Being familiar with the basics of YAML and indentation from Chapter 8 should help you to manage it (remember to avoid indentation issues, or Ansible will complain). YAML files generally start with ---, although it isn't, strictly speaking, required. It's required only when multiple YAML documents are within a single file.

❷ name is optional but recommended. This is used to define what the play is for and what task is being performed. In other words, it's arbitrary text.

❸ hosts specifies which devices we want to automate. We can specify a host, group, multiple of each, or even expressions that refer to names in our inventory file. For example, if we want to automate all devices in EMEA by using our previous inventory file, we can use `hosts: emea`; or for devices that are EOS and Junos groups, we could use `hosts: eos,junos` denoting a comma-separated list.

❹ `gather_facts` allows getting facts from the device running Ansible, but because we're automating network devices, we run Ansible locally, so we are not getting facts. If we were running Ansible out of the box to automate Linux servers, Ansible would by default collect facts from each node, including items such as OS type, OS version, vendor, IPv4 addresses, and much more.

❺ `connection` defines the connection type a play uses. We use `Ansible.netcommon.network_cli` to provide a CLI shell connection to remote devices over SSH, implicitly using the *local* mode. The `netcommon` collection (we explain Ansible collections in "Using Third-Party Collections and Modules" on page 611) also contains other modules to use other network connections, such as `netconf` or `httpapi`.

❻ Within `tasks`, we define a list of tasks that will be executed sequentially by the playbook.

 Most network Ansible modules (such as `ios_command`) implemented a `provider` parameter used together with `connection: local`, for the same purpose as `Ansible.netcommon.network_cli`. However, this option is now being deprecated in favor of `network_cli`, used at the play level.

It is important to notice that a module (such as `Ansible.netcommon.network_cli` or `ios_command`), can take several parameters to tune its behavior. Some are mandatory, and others are optional (they come with a default value), but they may be tuned in three ways: Ansible variables, environment variables, or Ansible configuration options. For instance, in `Ansible.netcommon.network_cli`, the parameter `host_key_checking` defaults to `Yes` but can be changed via any of the following:

- Ansible configuration file, with the `host_key_checking` key
- Environment variables: `ANSIBLE_HOST_KEY_CHECKING` and `ANSIBLE_HOST_KEY_CHECKING`
- Ansible variables: `ansible_host_key_checking` and `ansible_ssh_host_key_checking`

We explain more about using these tuning options in "Executing a playbook" on page 584.

We recommend checking the Ansible module documentation (*https://oreil.ly/OLQOe*) to understand each module's implicit configuration. It could save you a lot of surprises when running your playbooks and will help you better define the data population strategy.

Next, we'll take a look at tasks and how they relate to modules.

Getting familiar with Ansible tasks and modules

After you define the high-level attributes of your play, such as the connection type and the hosts you want to automate, you need to define tasks. Each task runs an Ansible module, which is performing some form of automation. Our example has two tasks, denoted by the task names.

On the same indent level as name in both tasks, you'll see ios_command and cisco.ios.ios_config. Called Ansible *modules*, these perform a specific operation. In particular, ios_command issues exec-level commands to Cisco IOS devices, and cisco.ios.ios_config sends configuration-level commands. We'll cover many more modules in this section as we walk through example playbooks.

You may be also wondering why we refer to one module as simply ios_command, but the ios_config module includes a cisco.ios prefix. The reason is that the ios_command module existed prior to the introduction of the *collections* feature in Ansible. With collections, modules are grouped into namespaces, and in the case of the ios_config module, located within the cisco.ios namespace. The old syntax is kept for backward compatibility with old playbooks, serving as an alias to the actual new collection syntax.

 Ansible has over 750+ modules, grouped in collections, that allow you to automate Linux servers, network devices, Windows servers, public cloud environments, and much more. You can get an index to all these modules in the Ansible documentation (*https://oreil.ly/hRj3O*).

Let's focus on the first task in Example 12-14, which uses the ios_command module.

Example 12-14. Getting the SNMP config with Ansible

```
tasks:                              ❶
  - name: "TASK1 - SHOW SNMP CONFIG"  ❷
    ios_command:                      ❸
      commands:                       ❹
        - "show run | inc snmp"
        - "show snmp"                 ❺
```

❶ A task is a dictionary in the tasks list, within a play.

❷ The task name is optional but helpful to follow tasks' execution.

❸ ios_command is the module we use to run this task. It takes several parameters that will be passed into the module, similar to passing variables or key-value pairs into a Python function.

❹ commands indicates a list of strings (CLI commands) that will be executed in the device. It's important to understand YAML data types because you will find them everywhere, including strings, integers, or dictionaries.

❺ Because this is a list, we can concatenate commands as desired.

Now, in Example 12-15, we focus on the second task, to configure SNMP settings.

Example 12-15. Deploying SNMP commands with Ansible

```
- name: "TASK 2 - DEPLOY SNMP COMMANDS"
  cisco.ios.ios_config:                                    ❶
    commands:
      - "snmp-server chassis-id {{ inventory_hostname }}"   ❷
```

❶ In this case, we are using the long module syntax that resolves to the same module as the ios_command in Example 12-14.

❷ We are using an Ansible variable—more specifically, a Jinja variable. You should recognize this from the Jinja configuration templates in Chapter 9. This particular variable, inventory_hostname, is a built-in Ansible variable that is equal to the device name as defined in the inventory file. In our example playbook, we're automating all devices in the group called iosxe, which is two Cisco routers: csr1 and csr2. For all devices in that group, both tasks are executed by Ansible. When the device being automated is csr1, inventory_hostname is equal to csr1; when the device being automated is csr2, inventory_hostname is equal to csr2.

We've now provided a high-level overview of how to construct a playbook. As this section progresses, we'll continue to dive into more detail on how certain modules work and cover much more about Ansible and automating network devices.

Executing a playbook

As we've stated, the two files required to get started with Ansible are the inventory file and the playbook. We've reviewed both and are ready to execute a playbook against a set of network devices.

In our example, we saved the inventory file as *inventory* and the playbook as *snmp-intro.yml*. Both filenames are arbitrary and user defined.

To execute a playbook, you use `ansible-playbook` and the playbook file. Along with these two basic components, you can customize the execution, defining a specific inventory file by using the `-i` flag, or passing Ansible variables with the `-e` flag.

In Example 12-16, you run your first playbook with a *full* command to specify all the options that you want this playbook to take into account, and you will simplify it later.

Example 12-16. Executing an Ansible playbook

```
$ ansible-playbook snmp-intro.yml \
    -i inventory \
    -e ansible_user="ntc" \
    -e ansible_password="ntc123"

PLAY [PLAY 1 - ISSUE SNMP COMMANDS] *****************************************

TASK [TASK1 - SHOW SNMP COMMANDS] *******************************************
ok: [csr2]
ok: [csr1]

TASK [TASK 2- DEPLOY SNMP COMMANDS] *****************************************
changed: [csr2]
changed: [csr1]

PLAY RECAP *****************************************************************
csr1              : ok=2    changed=1    unreachable=0    failed=0
skipped=0    rescued=0    ignored=0
csr2              : ok=2    changed=1    unreachable=0    failed=0
skipped=0    rescued=0    ignored=0
```

In the playbook execution output, you can observe a global PLAY section, with TASK_ sections inside. In each task, you identify the hosts, the tasks that have been executed, and the result. Using the `ios_commands`, you have not actually changed the configuration, but by using `ios_config`, you can check that the result is showing a changed state. At the end, you can see the summary of the play execution.

You also have the option to not specify the inventory file every time you execute a playbook. To do this, you can either use the default inventory file */etc/ansible/hosts*, set the `ANSIBLE_INVENTORY` environment variable, or define it in the *ansible.cfg* file. In Example 12-17, we show how to use the environment variable.

Example 12-17. Setting the ANSIBLE_INVENTORY environment variable

```
$ export ANSIBLE_INVENTORY=inventory
$ ansible-playbook snmp-intro.yml -e ansible_password="ntc" -e ansible_user="ntc123"
```

Depending on the scenario, when connecting to the network devices, you may want to disable host_key_checking for the SSH connections. This is the case in our demo scenario, where security is not critical. So far, you have not seen how to disable this option; it is enabled by default. We have chosen to update the Ansible configuration file (see Example 12-18), but we could have used an environment variable.

Example 12-18. Ansible configuration file

```
$ cat /etc/ansible/ansible.cfg

[defaults]
host_key_checking = False

# omitted other options
```

You may have already noticed that Ansible has several options for tuning execution: configuration file, command-line arguments, or environment variables. Choose what works better for your case.

You have already simplified the playbook execution command, but there are still two variables. These are implicitly used by network_cli to authenticate to the devices (ansible_user and ansible_password) that we are passing in the command line because, being secrets, they should not be stored in the clear-text inventory file. Luckily, Ansible offers different options to gather secrets, one of which we'll explore next.

Using Secrets

The simplest way to define secrets in Ansible is by using Ansible Vault (installed with the Ansible package), which provides content encryption and decryption capabilities. We define our secrets in a clear-text file that then is encrypted for storage and decrypted when we need to use it.

In Example 12-19, you see how from an initial unencrypted file (*secrets.enc*), you create an encrypted one that we can use next.

Example 12-19. Using secrets in Ansible Vault

```
$ cat secrets.enc
ansible_user: ntc
ansible_password: ntc123
$
$ ansible-vault encrypt secrets.enc
New Vault password:
Confirm New Vault password:
Encryption successful
$
$ cat secrets.enc
$ANSIBLE_VAULT;1.1;AES256
653036373563373465333334333439353235393730373165343838383532623665303961 64613363
653737343433323134396164303761313739336639616137 0a313532303132653663656163373539
363930346639656165373037366634373362386330376136656333531306536343962653866333863
3033663062663837380a653931653031646136663063046537666339931363635663766 3630343030
313530613435396563623766161 37333963636466346063433483830393536643939643431 33361383833
3933363863316333663362383435663361306234373036303933
```

With *secrets.enc* from Example 12-19, you need to use only the file in your playbook execution with the -e argument option:

```
$ ansible-playbook snmp-intro.yml -e @secrets.enc --ask-vault-pass
Vault password:
```

When using --ask-vault-pass, you will be prompted to enter the password used to encrypt the file. This is OK(ish) when running playbooks manually, but in an automated environment, it would be better to use --vault-password-file, which can take the password from a file that will be created on the fly.

> When working with secrets, even if you have them encrypted at rest, do not forget to protect them from being accidentally leaked in the Ansible log file—for instance, when using the extra *verbose* level of execution (see "Understanding check mode, verbosity, and limit" on page 597). When your task *could* output secrets, use no_log: True to avoid it.

Ansible Vault is only one of the several options for improving the security posture of your playbook execution. If you have another secrets manager backend, an integration option would likely be available.

After this brief introduction to secrets, we go deep into how to customize regular variables for each individual/group from the inventory.

Using Variable Files

If you understand how to construct an inventory file with groups and variables and the basics of writing playbooks, you can accomplish quite a bit with Ansible. However, the inventory file is not the recommended place to keep many variables. It's quick and easy for testing, but when managing a production implementation, you should use variable files (when not using dynamic inventory and a CMDB).

Using variable files requires that you understand their naming. The concept of using variables is no different from group- and host-based variables in the inventory file— the only difference is that they are stored in YAML files.

Group-based variable files

To store group variables in YAML files, you must store them in a directory called *group_vars*, often in the same directory as your playbooks for basic projects. This is a special and unique name for Ansible—this directory *must* be called *group_vars*.

In the *group_vars* directory, you have two options. The first and most common for getting started with Ansible is to have YAML files that are equal to the group names as they're defined in the inventory file. When constructing our inventory file, you had explicitly defined groups such as `emea`, `amers`, and `iosxe`, but also the implicitly defined group called `all`. To define variables in these files, you'd need files named *emea.yml*, *amers.yml*, *iosxe.yml*, and *all.yml*. These files are required only if you need to define group variables for that specific group.

Example 12-20 defines group variables for the `amers` group.

Example 12-20. AMERS group variables

```
$ cat group_vars/amers.yml
---
snmp:
  contact: Joe Smith
  location: AMERICAS-NJ
  communities:
    - community: public
      type: ro
    - community: public123
      type: ro
    - community: private
      type: rw
    - community: secure
      type: rw
```

You would do the same for each group you need to define variables for.

As you define more variables for a given group, it may seem logical to want to have particular variables in their own files—for example, AAA variables in their own, NTP in their own, and so on. This is the second option.

In this option, you create a subdirectory equal to the group name, and in it, you put multiple files named whatever you like. Here is an example showing both options:

```
$ tree group_vars
.
├── amers.yml
└── emea
    ├── aaa.yml
    ├── interfaces.yml
    └── ntp.yml

1 directory, 4 files
```

Host-based variable files

Using host-based variable files is exactly like using group variables, but the directory is called *host_vars*, and files (or directories) need to match the device name as defined in the inventory file.

This is an example showing both options, analogous to the previous group variables example:

```
$ tree host_vars
.
├── csr1.yml
├── csr2.yml
└── vmx1
    ├── interfaces.yml
    └── ntp.yml

1 directory, 4 files
```

Now that we've covered variables and how to use them in a more robust manner, it's time to move on to writing more useful Ansible playbooks.

Writing Ansible Playbooks for Network Automation

At this point, we've presented the Ansible architecture, reviewed the Ansible inventory file and playbook, and introduced common Ansible terminology such as *plays*, *tasks*, *modules*, *parameters*, and *variables*. In this section, we introduce more Ansible modules and specific Ansible functionality while highlighting what is possible with Ansible, specifically for network automation. Our focus is on showing how Ansible is used to automate the following tasks:

- Creating multivendor configuration templates and autogenerating configurations
- Deploying configurations and ensuring that a given configuration exists

- Gathering data from network devices
- Performing compliance checks
- Generating reports

Breaking down common core network modules

Before we walk through the aforementioned tasks and examples, we need to review the set of modules that Ansible has for many network vendors and operating systems. Understanding these modules is critical, as they are included with the Ansible package and all operate similarly. Ansible has three types of common network modules:

command
: Sends exec-level commands to network devices. These are implemented and named as *xos*_command (e.g., `ios_command`, `eos_command`, `junos_command`).

config
: Sends configuration commands to network devices. These are implemented and named as *xos*_config (e.g., `ios_config`, `eos_config`, `junos_config`).

facts
: Gathers information from network devices such as OS version, hardware platform, serial number, hostname, neighbors, and much more. These are implemented and named as *xos*_facts (e.g., `ios_facts`, `eos_facts`, `junos_facts`).

With these three modules per network OS, you can accomplish quite a bit with Ansible for network automation. Each module does have parameters, such as `commands`, which we previously looked at (as well as a number of others). We'll review a few more of these in our upcoming examples.

> To see which parameters a given module supports, along with a few examples, you can use the `ansible-doc` utility. For example, to learn how to use `eos_config`, you can enter the following command at your Linux bash prompt:
> ```
> $ ansible-doc eos_config
> > ARISTA.EOS.EOS_CONFIG  (/usr/local/lib/python3.8/
>     site-packages/ansible_collections/arista/eos/plugins/
>     modules/eos_config.py)
> ```
> Notice that the `eos_config` module is a shortcut to `arista.eos.eos_config`, part of the `arista.eos` collection. You can use the short or the long format.

Since the introduction of Ansible collections (you'll learn more details in "Using Third-Party Collections and Modules" on page 611), each collection is defined by a *namespace*. Some vendors have their own namespaces (such as `cisco.nxos` and `arista.eos`), and others are nested under `community.network` (such as Nokia SR modules in `community.network.sros_***`).

Now that you understand the more common network modules, we'll walk through our first real network example.

Creating and using configuration templates

In our first example, the goal is to show that you can use Ansible to autogenerate SNMP configurations, provided you have SNMP configuration templates and the associated input data.

The following SNMP CLI commands for IOS are what we want to deploy for IOS, but the goal is to deploy the same *data* across Arista EOS, Cisco NX-OS, and Juniper Junos too. You need to consider this when building out an Ansible project. Here are the commands:

```
snmp-server location AMERICAS-NJ
snmp-server contact Joe Smith
snmp-server community public RO
snmp-server community public123 RO
snmp-server community private RW
snmp-server community secure RW
```

At this point, you need to deconstruct the CLI commands into configuration templates by using Jinja and YAML files that will store our inputs as variables—more specifically, group-based variable files.

Since the goal is to support four operating systems, you're going to need a Jinja template per network OS. You also need to consider that there could be different input data for a given geography, which our example happens to have. We are going to show how to use the same template, but use different data since we have different SNMP community strings, contacts, and locations per region.

Creating variable files. First, we'll show our data variables in each respective group variables file. We already defined the SNMP data for the devices in the AMERS region in Example 12-20. In Example 12-21, we'll use the same structure for the data required for the EMEA region.

Example 12-21. EMEA group variables

```
$ cat group_vars/emea.yml
---
snmp:
  contact: Scott Grady
  location: EMEA-IE
  communities:
    - community: public123
```

```
    type: ro
- community: supersecure
    type: rw
```

 We aren't spending time covering the details or data types of a given YAML variable and how to consume that in Jinja, as this has already been covered in Chapters 8 and 9.

If you need data to apply to all devices in our inventory, you could use the *group_vars/all.yml* file to store it.

Creating Jinja templates. The SNMP data is now defined that'll be used for configuration inputs. Next, the associated Jinja templates need to be created. Ansible automatically looks for templates in the directory your playbooks are executed from and in a directory called *templates* relative to the same path. You are going to store the SNMP templates in *./templates/snmp*.

You can prebuild our files per platform as shown here:

```
$ tree templates/
templates/
└── snmp
    ├── eos.j2
    ├── ios.j2
    ├── junos.j2
    └── nxos.j2
```

Example 12-22 is the template that was constructed in *ios.j2*.

Example 12-22. IOS SNMP Jinja template

```
snmp-server location {{ snmp.location }}
snmp-server contact {{ snmp.contact }}
{% for community in snmp.communities %}
snmp-server community {{ community.community }} {{ community.type | upper }} ❶
{% endfor %}
```

❶ The IOS template is straightforward; however, it does show the use of the Jinja filter called upper, which capitalizes the type we've defined as ro or rw in the YAML data file. While both work on the IOS CLI, the upper filler translates to RO and RW when entered into the configuration.

Filters are a Jinja feature; refer to Chapter 9 for details. Ansible comes with extra built-in filters and with an extensible option to create new custom filters as Ansible plug-ins.

Ansible plug-ins augment Ansible's core functionality via Python code and serve several purposes, including filtering, connection, callback, or inventory, among others. For instance, inventory plug-ins allow dynamic inventories, integrating with external data sources. We don't cover plug-in development in this book, but you can get more details from the Ansible docs (*https://oreil.ly/AQM9V*).

Example 12-23 shows the Juniper template to configure the SNMP data on a Junos device, stored in *junos.j2*.

Example 12-23. Junos SNMP Jinja template

```
set snmp location {{ snmp.location }}
set snmp contact {{ snmp.contact | replace(' ', '_') }} ❶
{% for community in snmp.communities %}
{%   if community.type | lower == "rw" %}        ❷ ❸
set snmp community {{ community.community }} authorization read-write
{%   elif community.type | lower == "ro" %}      ❷
set snmp community {{ community.community }} authorization read-only
{%   endif %}
{% endfor %}
```

❶ The `replace` filter is used since Junos doesn't support spaces in its contact. The other option is to change the data itself, but we want to show how a template for one OS compares to a template for another OS.

❷ The `lower` filter normalizes the community type to lowercase for a convenient comparison.

❸ A conditional is added because `ro` and `rw` aren't used in Junos commands, and we need to map our data to the right Junos commands.

The previous Jinja templates, and the EOS and NX-OS ones, are all available at *https://github.com/oreilly-npa-book/examples/tree/v2/ch12-automationtools/ansible/templates/snmp*.

Generating network configuration files. Now that the data variables and templates are in place, the final step prior to deployment is to generate the SNMP configuration files. To do this, you'll use the Ansible module called `template`. This module automates the creation of files by rendering input data (variables) with Jinja templates.

Example 12-24 shows how to use the `template` module. It uses the `src` and `dest` parameters. The `src` parameter references the proper template you want to use, and the `dest` parameter points to the location where you want the final rendered config to be stored.

Example 12-24. Generating SNMP configurations by using the `template` module

```
---
- name: "PLAY 1 - GENERATE SNMP CONFIGURATIONS"
  hosts: "all"
  connection: "local"  ❶
  gather_facts: no

  tasks:
    - name: "GENERATE CONFIGS FOR EACH OS"
      template:
        src: "./templates/snmp/{{ ansible_network_os }}.j2"
        dest: "./configs/snmp/{{ inventory_hostname }}.cfg"
```

❶ Uses the `local` connection instead of `ansible.netcommon.network_cli`, because we don't actually need to connect to any device. Everything is happening locally to the computer running the playbook.

 In our test environment, we manually created the *configs* directory and the *snmp* subdirectory. You could have also automated this with Ansible by using the `file` module.

Note in the previous example that you can also use variables within paths, values, or anywhere else within a playbook. That way, within a single task in a playbook, you can autogenerate the required configurations for any number of devices regardless of OS type.

 Remember that you added `ansible_network_os` as a group-based variable when constructing the inventory file earlier in this section. This variable name was selected on purpose to be also implicitly reused by the `ansible.netcommon.network_cli` connection.

At this point, the playbook is ready to be executed to generate the desired configs. This is shown in Example 12-25.

Example 12-25. Executing the SNMP playbook to generate configurations

```
$ ansible-playbook snmp.yml -e @secrets.enc --ask-vault-pass

PLAY [PLAY 1 - GENERATE SNMP CONFIGURATIONS] **********************************

TASK [GENERATE CONFIGS FOR EACH OS] **********************************************
changed: [nxos-spine1]
changed: [eos-spine1]
changed: [csr1]
changed: [eos-spine2]
changed: [csr2]
changed: [vmx2]
changed: [vmx1]

# omitted some output
```

After the playbook is executed, you end up with the following files automatically created by inserting the proper data variables into the respective Jinja templates. You can validate the existence of the files by checking the content in the *configs/snmp* folder:

```
$ tree configs/snmp/
configs/snmp/
├── csr1.cfg
├── csr2.cfg
├── eos-spine1.cfg
├── eos-spine2.cfg
├── nxos-spine1.cfg
├── nxos-spine2.cfg
├── vmx1.cfg
└── vmx2.cfg

0 directories, 8 files
```

To validate that each of the YAML data variables was inserted correctly, let's see the outputs for one device in AMERS (csr1), and one device in EMEA (vmx1):

```
$ cat configs/snmp/csr1.cfg
snmp-server location AMERICAS-NJ
snmp-server contact Joe Smith
snmp-server community public RO
snmp-server community public123 RO
snmp-server community private RW
snmp-server community secure RW

$ cat configs/snmp/vmx1.cfg
set snmp location EMEA-IE
set snmp contact Scott_Grady
set snmp community public123 authorization read-only
set snmp community supersecure authorization read-write
```

Creating templates, variables, and a single-task playbook is one of the common ways to get started with Ansible, as it doesn't require access to the network devices. It allows you to gradually hone your Jinja and YAML skills while building and standardizing network device configurations.

Ensuring that a configuration exists

The previous example automatically generated eight configurations. In this example, you're going to deploy those configurations and ensure that they exist on each device.

Understanding idempotency. As you go through this example, pay attention to the words and phrases being used, such as *configuring SNMP* versus *ensuring that the SNMP configuration exists*. A traditional Python script may send the SNMP commands every time you execute it. With Ansible, like many DevOps configuration management tools, the approach for configuration management is to be idempotent, meaning to make the change only if needed. In the context of networking modules, each module has added intelligence to ensure that configuration commands are sent to the device only if they are needed to get the device into its desired state.

From a high level, modules accomplish this by always first collecting the existing configuration of the device. The commands that you want to exist on the device are compared against the current state (running configuration). Only if the desired commands do not exist in the current configuration are they sent to the device. This is safer in that the module runs a playbook *N* times and sends the commands to the device only once.

This is exactly how the `config` modules work within Ansible. By default, they obtain a `show run`, and the commands within the playbook are sent to the device only if they don't exist within `show run`.

Using the config module. Now, let's extend Example 12-24 into a complete SNMP provisioning playbook example (*snmp.yml*). In Example 12-26, you start using the `arista.eos.eos_config` module to deploy the SNMP configuration file for the Arista EOS devices.

Example 12-26. Deploying SNMP commands for Arista devices

```
- name: "PLAY 2 - ENSURE EOS SNMP CONFIGS ARE DEPLOYED"   ❶
  hosts: "eos"                                             ❷
  connection: local
  gather_facts: no

  tasks:
    - name: "DEPLOY CONFIGS FOR EOS"
      arista.eos.eos_config:
        src: "./configs/snmp/{{ inventory_hostname }}.cfg"  ❸
```

```
        provider:                              ❷
          username: "{{ ansible_user }}"
          password: "{{ ansible_password }}"
          host: "{{ inventory_hostname }}"
```

❶ This play was added to the existing playbook that generated the configurations as shown here, denoted by PLAY 2; we also could have created a new playbook strictly for deploying configurations.

❷ This play contains its own configuration, with a specific scope defined with hosts: eos and using the local connection in combination with the provider parameter within the eos_config module. This method is being deprecated, but it serves to illustrate that we can combine different connection types per play in the same playbook.

❸ The config modules accept multiple parameters, while the previous task simply uses src. The src parameter can reference a config file or a Jinja template directly. As you can see, you're referencing the exact file that was generated in the first play.

The following are other common parameters used in the config modules:

commands
> Mutually exclusive with src; rather than reference a template or configuration file, it allows you to embed a list of commands directly in the playbook.

parents
> List of parent commands that identify the hierarchy that commands should be evaluated against (required when you're using commands and configuring a device with commands that go outside global configuration mode). For instance, an example parent is ['interface Eth1'] and the commands list is ['duplex full'] when you're trying to configure duplex on Eth1.

Even more parameters are available for the config modules, such as those that allow you to issue a particular command before and after issuing the commands from parents and commands. Remember to use ansible-doc <os>_config to see all parameters supported and more examples.

Understanding check mode, verbosity, and limit. Before executing the playbook that'll create the configurations and deploy them, let's review a few other features you need to know when running Ansible playbooks:

Check mode

This is the ability to run playbooks in *dry run* mode—the ability to know if changes *will* occur. It does everything as you'd expect when running a task, but does not actually make the given change. To use check mode, add the `--check` flag when executing your playbook. Check mode is a feature of individual modules.

Verbosity

Every module returns JSON data. This JSON data contains metadata about the task at hand. For the `config` modules, the data contains the commands being sent to the device; for `command` modules, it contains the response from the device. To run a playbook in verbose mode and see the JSON data returned from each module, add the `-v` flag when executing the playbook. You can use up to four v's (`-vvvv`) when troubleshooting.

Limit

The common place to change the devices being automated is in the play definitions of a playbook by using `hosts`, such as `hosts: all`. If you want to automate just `junos` devices, one option is to change the playbook scope to `hosts: junos`. Of course, this depends on having `junos` defined in your inventory file. Another option is to use the `--limit` flag when executing a playbook, such as `--limit junos`. What you pass in with the `--limit` flag must be *in* the group or groups defined already within the `hosts` key in the playbook. You can also pass in a single device, group, or multiple of each, as in `--limit junos,eos,csr1`.

Example 12-27 shows how you can use all three of these flags when running a single playbook. Using check mode in conjunction with verbose mode is valuable when deploying configurations—because it shows exactly which commands *will* get sent to the device but does not actually deploy them.

Example 12-27. Using limit, check mode, and verbose mode

```
$ ansible-playbook snmp.yml -e @secrets.enc --ask-vault-pass \
    --limit eos-spine1 --check -v

PLAY [PLAY 1 - GENERATE SNMP CONFIGURATIONS] ***********************************

TASK [GENERATE CONFIGS FOR EACH OS] *******************************************
ok: [eos-spine1] => {"changed": false,
"checksum": "fd14c0ad92649fd73793162415504295516f62b81",
"dest": "./configs/snmp/eos-spine1.cfg", "gid": 0, "group": "root",
"mode": "0644", "owner": "ntc", "path": "./configs/snmp/eos-spine1.cfg",
 "size": 133, "state": "file", "uid": 1000}

PLAY [PLAY 2 - ENSURE EOS SNMP CONFIGS ARE DEPLOYED] **************************
```

```
TASK [DEPLOY CONFIGS FOR EOS] ***************************************************
changed: [eos-spine1] => {"changed": true,
"commands": ["snmp-server location EMEA-IE", "snmp-server contact Scott Grady",
"snmp-server community public123 ro", "snmp-server community supersecure rw"],
"session": "ansible_1650603615", "updates": ["snmp-server location EMEA-IE",
"snmp-server contact Scott Grady", "snmp-server community public123 ro",
"snmp-server community supersecure rw"]}

PLAY RECAP *********************************************************************
eos-spine1                 : ok=2    changed=1    unreachable=0    failed=0
skipped=0    rescued=0    ignored=0
```

As you can see, much more output is displayed because the example is executed in verbose mode; this allows us to see the JSON data returned by each task and module.

One other important point in reading playbook output is to understand what ok and changed are referring to. In the previous example, the last line states ok=2 changed=1. This tells us that two tasks successfully executed but only one made a change (since this was run in check mode). If you are running a fully idempotent playbook for the second or more time, you'll always have changed=0, as no changes would occur.

You can now easily add subsequent plays that'll deploy the SNMP per OS. Example 12-28 deploys commands for Junos.

Example 12-28. Deploying SNMP commands for Juniper devices

```
- name: "PLAY 3 - ENSURE JUNOS SNMP CONFIGS ARE DEPLOYED"
  hosts: junos
  connection: "ansible.netcommon.netconf"  ❶
  gather_facts: no

  tasks:
    - name: "DEPLOY CONFIGS FOR JUNOS"
      junipernetworks.junos.junos_config:
        src: "./configs/snmp/{{ inventory_hostname }}.cfg"
```

❶ We use the ansible.netcommon.netconf connection because the junos_config module supports only this connection type. Ansible modules have their own requirements and should provide useful error messages to guide you in their usage. This limitation is not for all the junipernetworks.junos collection modules. Other modules, such as junos_commands, can work with the network_cli connection.

Then, to complete the SNMP provisioning example, you are missing only Cisco devices, which you'll deploy next.

Filtering tasks with when

In Example 12-29, you use a single play for both Cisco platforms (hosts: "iosxe,nxos"), so all the play parameters are used for all the *tasks*. In this case, you use the same connection type.

Example 12-29. Deploying SNMP commands for Cisco devices

```
- name: "PLAY 4 - ENSURE CISCO (IOS,NXOS) SNMP CONFIGS ARE DEPLOYED"
  hosts: "iosxe,nxos"
  connection: "ansible.netcommon.network_cli"
  gather_facts: no

  tasks:
    - name: "DEPLOY CONFIGS FOR IOS"
      cisco.ios.ios_config:                    ❶
        src: "./configs/snmp/{{ inventory_hostname }}.cfg"
        when: ansible_network_os == 'ios'    ❷

    - name: "DEPLOY CONFIGS FOR NXOS"
      cisco.nxos.nxos_config:                  ❶
        src: "./configs/snmp/{{ inventory_hostname }}.cfg"
        when: ansible_network_os == 'nxos'   ❷
```

❶ Even though both Cisco platforms support the same connection type, we have to use the proper Ansible module for each platform, ios or nxos. Each module is specialized for one platform type or the other, and running the module on a different platform could generate errors.

❷ To allow conditional execution of tasks, we can use the when parameter. We use the ansible_network_os variable, coming from the inventory, to use the proper module for each NOS.

When executing the playbook, notice that for PLAY 4, you are still targeting all the hosts (in the iosxe and nxos inventory groups) for each task, but when running each task, the network devices that do not match the condition will be *skipped*, as you can see in Example 12-30.

Example 12-30. Playbook output when filtering out hosts

```
$ ansible-playbook snmp.yml -e @secrets.enc --ask-vault-pass

# omitted some output

PLAY [PLAY 4 - ENSURE CISCO (IOS,NXOS) SNMP CONFIGS ARE DEPLOYED] *************

TASK [DEPLOY CONFIGS FOR IOS] ************************************************
skipping: [nxos-spine1]
skipping: [nxos-spine2]
```

```
ok: [csr1]
ok: [csr2]

TASK [DEPLOY CONFIGS FOR NXOS] ***************************************************
skipping: [csr1]
skipping: [csr2]
ok: [nxos-spine2]
ok: [nxos-spine1]
```

Gathering and viewing network data

Ansible, like many automation tools, is often used to deploy configurations. However, Ansible also makes it possible to automate the collection of data from network devices. We're going to focus on two key methods for gathering data: using the core `facts` modules and issuing arbitrary `show` commands with the `command` module.

Using the core facts modules.   Core `facts` modules return the data in Table 12-1 as JSON.

Table 12-1. Core facts modules for automating data collection from network devices

Core facts module	Result
ansible_net_model	The model name returned from the device
ansible_net_serialnum	The serial number of the remote device
ansible_net_version	The OS version running on the remote device
ansible_net_hostname	The configured hostname of the device
ansible_net_config	The current active config from the device
ansible_net_all_ipv4_addresses	All IPv4 addresses configured on the device
ansible_net_all_ipv6_addresses	All IPv6 addresses configured on the device
ansible_net_interfaces	A hash of all interfaces running on the system
ansible_net_neighbors	The list of LLDP neighbors from the remote device

After running a task to gather facts, you can access each of the previous keys directly in a playbook or a Jinja template, just like any other variable (usually with double curly braces). Let's take a look at Example 12-31, defined in *collect.yml*.

Example 12-31. Using the `ios_facts` and `debug` modules

```
---
- name: "PLAY 1 - COLLECT FACTS FOR IOS"
  hosts: iosxe
  connection: "ansible.netcommon.network_cli"
  gather_facts: no

    tasks:
      - name: "COLLECT FACTS FOR EOS"
```

```
        cisco.ios.ios_facts:

    - name: "DEBUG OS VERSION"
      debug:
        var: ansible_net_version

    - name: "DEBUG HOSTNAME"
      debug:
        var: ansible_net_hostname
```

You could optionally add more plays to gather facts per device type based on the OS.

Running the `ios_facts` module task alone, without *verbose* mode, will not produce any output. However, adding the `-v` when running it will allow you to see all the data collected in the form of a dictionary. To show the relevant data in the playbook output, you use the next module: *debug*.

Using the debug module.   To view the facts being returned from the module, you can run the playbook in verbose mode or simply use the `debug` module with the `var` parameter while referencing a valid facts key, as shown here:

```
# play definition omitted
    - name: "DEBUG OS VERSION"
      debug:
        var: ansible_net_version

    - name: "DEBUG HOSTNAME"
      debug:
        var: ansible_net_hostname
```

 You usually reference variables with double curly braces within a playbook and Jinja template. Using the `debug` module with the `var` parameter is one of the times you do not use the curly brace notation! And remember, any variable in the playbook is also accessible in a Jinja template.

Running the *collect.yml* playbook with the task shown before, and limited to only `iosxe` devices, produces the output in Example 12-32.

Example 12-32. Viewing facts with the debug module

```
$ ansible-playbook collect.yml -e @secrets.enc --ask-vault-pass

PLAY [PLAY 1 - COLLECT FACTS FOR IOS] ****************************************

TASK [COLLECT FACTS FOR IOS] ************************************************
ok: [csr2]
ok: [csr1]
```

```
TASK [DEBUG OS VERSION] ********************************************************
ok: [csr2] => {
    "ansible_net_version": "17.01.01"
}
ok: [csr1] => {
    "ansible_net_version": "17.01.01"
}

TASK [DEBUG HOSTNAME] **********************************************************
ok: [csr2] => {
    "ansible_net_hostname": "csr2"
}
ok: [csr1] => {
    "ansible_net_hostname": "csr1"
}
```

Note the playbook output and the exact variables being referenced in the debug statements.

Issuing show commands and writing data to a file

You now know how to gather facts and debug the data being returned. In this section, we perform the same operation, but with the core command module. We'll show how to issue show commands, debug the response, and then subsequently write the show command output to a file.

Remember that one way to view JSON response data from a task is simply executing the playbook in verbose mode. There is another way that allows you to use the debug module—to use this approach, you must first save the JSON response from the module as a variable and then debug that variable. Note that you don't need to save facts as a variable since facts are available to use natively within Ansible.

Using the register task attribute. To save the JSON output that is returned from a module, you use the register task attribute. This allows you to save the JSON response data as a variable of the dictionary data type.

A task attribute gets inserted on the same indent level as the module name. In this example, you'll use the ios_command module, and thus you'll use the register attribute as a key on the same indent level as ios_command; register's associated value is the variable you want to save the data in. This is shown in the following snippet from the *snmp-debug.yml* example:

```
        - name: "ISSUE SHOW COMMAND"
          cisco.ios.ios_command:
            commands:
              - "show run | inc snmp-server community"
          register: snmp_data
```

After the playbook is executed, the value of snmp_data is the JSON object returned by the ios_command module, which you also see when running the playbook in *verbose* mode.

Since the snmp_data variable is now created, or *registered*, the debug module can be used to view the data. In Example 12-33, you see the playbook output for the previous task after the playbook was executed in verbose mode.

Example 12-33. Viewing the response data from ios_command, limited to csr1

```
$ ansible-playbook snmp-debug.yml -e @secrets.enc --ask-vault-pass --limit csr1

TASK [TASK1 - SHOW SNMP CONFIG] ************************************************
ok: [csr1] => {
  "changed": false,
  "stdout": [
    "snmp-server community ntc-public RO\nsnmp-server community ntc-private
    RW\nsnmp-server community public RO\nsnmp-server community public123 RO\n
    snmp-server community private RW\nsnmp-server community secure RW"
  ],
  "stdout_lines": [
    [
      "snmp-server community ntc-public RO",
      "snmp-server community ntc-private RW",
      "snmp-server community public RO",
      "snmp-server community public123 RO",
      "snmp-server community private RW",
      "snmp-server community secure RW"
    ]
  ]
}

# omitted some output
```

When you run the playbook in verbose mode, you can understand the data structure of the task output, as well as how to access the data desired, to be used in subsequent tasks. For example, command modules return keys such as stdout and stdout_lines. Each of those respective values is a list. The stdout key is a list of command responses with a list length equal to the quantity of commands sent to the device, and each element is the command response for that particular ordered command. The stdout_lines key is a nested object: the outer object is a list, and the inner object changes based on the transport being used—a list for CLI/SSH or a dictionary for API (such as eAPI). Our focus is on using stdout.

As you can see, using register along with the debug module provides a way to save and view the response data. This means if you want to debug *only* the actual response as a string, you need to use one of the debug statements in Example 12-34.

Example 12-34. Using debug with output from `register`

```
- name: "DEBUG COMMAND STRING RESPONSE WITH JINJA SHORTHAND SYNTAX"
  debug:
    var: snmp_data.stdout.0

- name: "DEBUG COMMAND STRING RESPONSE WITH STANDARD PYTHON SYNTAX"
  debug:
    var: snmp_data['stdout'][0]
```

Additionally, as we've said, any variable in a playbook is also accessible in a template, so if you want to write the data to a file, you can use the `template` module with a basic template like the following:

```
{{ snmp_data['stdout'][0] }}
```

You can then use a single task to write the data to a file using the previously defined template:

```
- name: "WRITE DATA TO FILE"
  template:
    src: "basic.j2"
    # this template was saved in the templates directory, so there is
    # no need to add the implicit ./templates/ folder
    dest: "./commands/snmp/{{ inventory_hostname }}.txt"
    # the commands and snmp directories were created manually
```

It's critical to understand that every module returns JSON, and that data is saved with the `register` task attribute. This approach is used not only for debugging data or writing data to file, but also for performing compliance checks and generating reports, which we cover next.

Performing compliance checks

Compliance checks are quite often done manually by SSHing into devices and verifying something is either enabled or disabled, or configured or not configured, in order to satisfy a given network or security requirement. Automating these types of checks streamlines the process of ensuring that the configuration and operational state is always as expected. These checks are always helpful for security engineers too—for example, when they're looking to validate that devices are hardened per requirements.

To perform compliance checks with Ansible, we need to first cover two more concepts:

set_fact
    This module creates an ad hoc variable out of another complex set of data. For example, if you already registered a new variable that is a large dictionary, you may care only about a single key-value pair in that object. Using `set_fact` allows you to save one of those values as a new fact or variable.

assert

It's common in software development to use `assert` statements for testing to ensure that a given condition is `True` or `False`. In Ansible, you can use the `assert` module to ensure that a condition is `True` or `False`.

Let's take a look at an example of *asserting* that VLAN 20 is configured on our two Arista EOS switches. The example consists of the following tasks:

1. Gather VLAN data.
2. Save VLAN data as `vlan_data`.
3. Print (debug) all VLAN data to see what's being returned.
4. Extract just the VLAN IDs from the full response.
5. Print just the VLAN IDs (validate that the extraction worked as expected).
6. Finally, perform the assertion that VLAN 20 is in the list of VLANs.

Example 12-35 is the associated playbook, defined in *compliance.yml*.

Example 12-35. Performing a compliance check with `assert`

```
---
- name: "PLAY 1 - VLAN COMPLIANCE"
  hosts: eos
  connection: "ansible.netcommon.network_cli"
  gather_facts: no

  tasks:
    - name: "RETRIEVE VLANS JSON RESPONSE"
      arista.eos.eos_command:
        commands:
          - "show vlan brief | json"
      register: vlan_data

    - name: "DEBUG VLANS AS JSON"
      debug:
        var: vlan_data

    - name: "CREATE EXISTING_VLANS FACT TO SIMPLIFY ACCESSING VLANS"
      set_fact:
        existing_vlan_ids: "{{ vlan_data.stdout.0.vlans.keys() }}"

    - name: "DEBUG EXISTING VLAN IDs"
      debug:
        var: existing_vlan_ids

    - name: "PERFORM COMPLIANCE CHECKS"
      assert:
        that:
          - "'20' in existing_vlan_ids"
```

Running this playbook produces the output (Example 12-36) for the last task, showing that the VLAN is configured on eos-spine1 (we did it manually before), but not on eos-spine2.

Example 12-36. Playbook output from the assert task

```
$ ansible-playbook compliance.yml -e @secrets.enc --ask-vault-pass --limit eos

# omitted some output

TASK [PERFORM COMPLIANCE CHECKS] *********************************************
fatal: [eos-spine2]: FAILED! => {
    "assertion": "'20' in existing_vlan_ids",
    "changed": false,
    "evaluated_to": false,
    "msg": "Assertion failed"
}
ok: [eos-spine1] => {
    "changed": false,
    "msg": "All assertions passed"
}
```

Once you understand what data is being returned from a given task and show command, you can perform an endless number of assertions based on your exact need. Next, we'll show how to autogenerate reports from data coming back from devices too.

Generating reports

This section continues to build on the topic of gathering data. We first showed how to gather data about device facts, issue show commands, register the data, write the data to a file, and finally perform assertions. In this section, we're going to refocus on writing data to a file, but in the context of generating a report.

Earlier, we showed how to gather facts via the core facts modules. Now, in Example 12-37, you'll build three tasks in a single playbook that gathers facts via eos_facts, ios_facts, and nxos_facts, filtering per NOS, and finally autogenerates a facts report.

> While our report is for device facts, the same approach can be taken for *any* data returned from show commands or from any other variable that exists in an Ansible project.

Example 12-37. Generating an automated report

```
---
- name: "PLAY 1 - CREATE REPORTS"
  hosts: "iosxe,eos,nxos"                                    ❶
  connection: "ansible.netcommon.network_cli"
  gather_facts: no

  tasks:
    - name: "COLLECT FACTS FOR EOS"
      arista.eos.eos_facts:
      when: ansible_network_os == "eos"

    - name: "COLLECT FACTS FOR IOS"
      cisco.ios.ios_facts:
      when: ansible_network_os == "ios"

    - name: "COLLECT FACTS FOR NXOS"
      cisco.nxos.nxos_facts:
      when: ansible_network_os == "nxos"

    - name: "GENERATE DEVICE SPECIFIC REPORTS"
      template:
        src: "./reports/facts.j2"
        dest: "./reports/facts/{{ inventory_hostname }}.md"  ❷

    - name: "CREATE MAIN REPORT"
      assemble:                                              ❸
        src: "./reports/facts/"
        dest: "./reports/main-report.md"
        delimiter: "---"                                     ❹
      run_once: "true"                                       ❺
```

❶ Denotes that this example is automating three groups of devices from the inventory file.

❷ The template task generates a Markdown-based (*.md*) report per device.

❸ The assemble module assembles all the individual reports into a single master report.

❹ The `---` in Markdown is a horizontal bar across the page. This is being used as a device delimiter as the individual reports are combined into the master report.

❺ run_once is, technically, not needed; but remember, we have several hosts being automated in this play and need only *one* master report. So we simply tell Ansible to run the task only for the *first* device that happens to get automated—since the module is idempotent, even running it N times without run_once wouldn't adversely impact the system.

To build on this, we could also include the task attribute called `delegate_to` and use the line `delegate_to: localhost` so the task is run in the system (localhost) versus running once on the first host automated. At this point, the choice is not important because both options work and solve the problem.

Example 12-38 shows the template used to generate the facts report.

Example 12-38. Viewing the facts report template, facts.j2

```
# {{ inventory_hostname }}

## Facts

Serial Number: {{ ansible_net_serialnum }}
OS Version:    {{ ansible_net_version }}

## Neighbors

| Device | Local Interface | Neighbor | Neighbor Interface |
|--------|-----------------|----------|--------------------|
{% for interface, neighbors in ansible_net_neighbors.items() %}
{%   for neighbor in neighbors %}
| {{ inventory_hostname }} | {{ interface }} | {{ neighbor.host }} |
{{ neighbor.port }} |
{%   endfor %}
{% endfor %}

## Interface List
{% for interface in ansible_net_interfaces.keys() %}
  - {{ interface }}
{% endfor %}
```

This syntax builds a Markdown-based table. This renders as an HTML-like table if you push it to GitHub, view it on Visual Studio Code (covered in Chapter 5), or use a Markdown viewer.

Most web browsers have plug-ins for viewing Markdown files; you can also easily try a Markdown editor such as StackEdit (*https://stackedit.io/app*).

Viewing the rendered text output for a single device is shown in Example 12-39.

Example 12-39. Generated report as text

```
# csr1

## Facts

Serial Number: 9SAGBHTUEE9
OS Version: 17.01.01

## Neighbors
```

```
| Device | Local Interface  | Neighbor            | Neighbor Interface |
| ------ | ---------------- | ------------------- | ------------------ |
| csr1   | GigabitEthernet4 | csr2.ntc.com        | GigabitEthernet4   |
| csr1   | GigabitEthernet1 | csr2.ntc.com        | GigabitEthernet1   |
| csr1   | GigabitEthernet1 | eos-spine1.ntc.com  | Management1        |
| csr1   | GigabitEthernet1 | vmx1                | fxp0               |
| csr1   | GigabitEthernet1 | eos-spine2.ntc.com  | Management1        |
| csr1   | GigabitEthernet1 | vmx2                | fxp0               |

## Interface List
  - GigabitEthernet4
  - GigabitEthernet1
  - GigabitEthernet2
  - GigabitEthernet3
```

After pushing the rendered Markdown file to GitHub, you can see how it renders when viewing it in Visual Studio Code (see Figure 12-2).

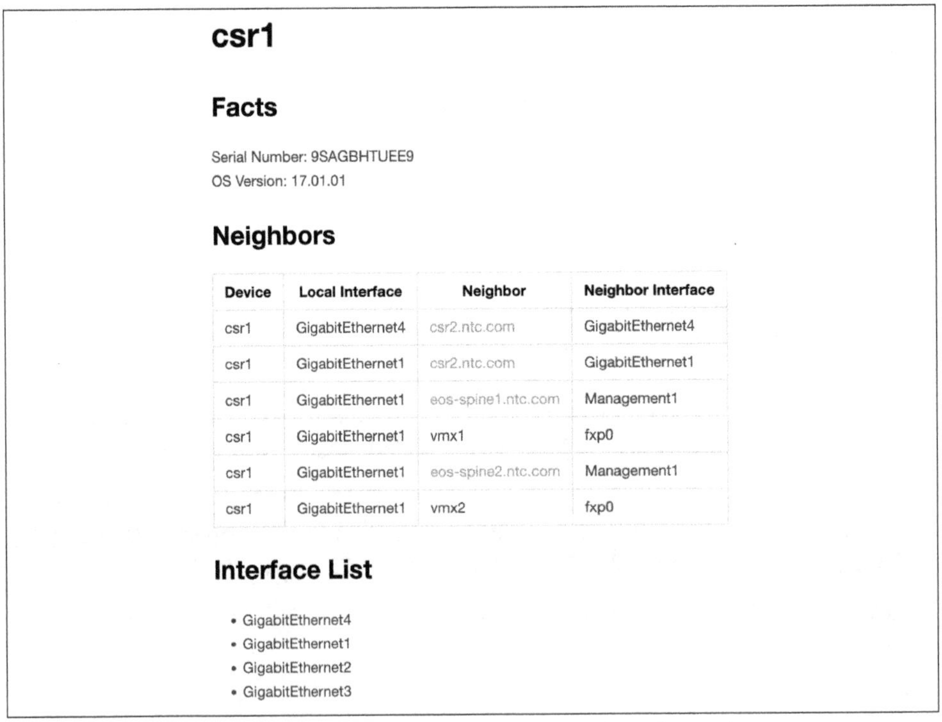

csr1

Facts

Serial Number: 9SAGBHTUEE9
OS Version: 17.01.01

Neighbors

Device	Local Interface	Neighbor	Neighbor Interface
csr1	GigabitEthernet4	csr2.ntc.com	GigabitEthernet4
csr1	GigabitEthernet1	csr2.ntc.com	GigabitEthernet1
csr1	GigabitEthernet1	eos-spine1.ntc.com	Management1
csr1	GigabitEthernet1	vmx1	fxp0
csr1	GigabitEthernet1	eos-spine2.ntc.com	Management1
csr1	GigabitEthernet1	vmx2	fxp0

Interface List

  • GigabitEthernet4
  • GigabitEthernet1
  • GigabitEthernet2
  • GigabitEthernet3

Figure 12-2. Viewing the Facts generated report in Visual Studio Code

You can create any kind of templates desired: we've looked at configuration templates and Markdown templates, but you can just as easily create HTML templates too for ever greater customization.

Ansible Roles

In this introductory section to Ansible, we have run simple playbooks, but as your network automation complexity grows, keeping all the tasks together in one file will become difficult to manage. To give you the flexibility to enable task composition, you can use *roles*. Ansible roles are organized in folders containing their own tasks, variables, templates, and other information. Thus, you can imagine them as capsules that you can combine as needed.

Let's imagine that you create a role for each configuration feature (e.g., SNMP, BGP, and ACLs) so that in each directory, all the necessary tasks are properly encapsulated, and you don't end up with a hundred lines in a YAML file. Then you can simply compose your playbooks by using the proper roles, depending on your inventory groups. For instance, you can create a playbook summarizing the configuration management task, reusing roles as needed:

```
---
- hosts: "amers-dc,emea-dc"
  roles:
     - snmp
     - bgp

- hosts: "emea-cpe,amers-cpe"
  roles:
     - snmp
     - bgp
     - acl
```

So far, you have used Ansible collections and modules in your playbooks, but now let's focus on using others that don't come by default with the Ansible package.

Using Third-Party Collections and Modules

One of the biggest benefits of Ansible is its active community and how easy is to reuse others' work in your own playbooks. While you've always been able to import and use others' modules, the Ansible 2.9 release (in 2019) introduced a new distributing artifact, *Ansible collections*, which can pack together playbooks, roles, modules, and plug-ins. This packaging facilitates reusing Ansible content within an organization and also with the community.

The simplest place to find these collections is the Ansible Galaxy hub (*https://galaxy.ansible.com*). Ansible Galaxy hosts collections from the community, and everyone can contribute with their own collection, following the contributor guide.

By default, some collections come auto-installed with the Ansible package, but you can always install a new one or get the latest version of a preinstalled collection. To help you with this, Ansible comes with an `ansible-galaxy` CLI tool. It helps by installing roles directly from Ansible Galaxy, but also from other sources (such as Git or a local folder). For instance, you can update the general community collection:

```
$ ansible-galaxy collection install community.general --upgrade
```

You can build and distribute your own private collections without leveraging Ansible Galaxy (you could run your own galaxy server), but the hub is the place to go if you're looking to make your collections available to the broader Ansible community.

All the examples we've reviewed in this chapter have used Ansible modules included in the Ansible package. You can accomplish a tremendous amount with these modules, from configuration to compliance checks to generating reports, as you've seen. However, there is an active community for third-party Ansible modules/collections relevant to network automation that are not part of the main Ansible package. In this section, you'll install third-party collections/modules and review two core sets of open source third-party modules.

Getting familiar with NAPALM modules

As you will see in "Understanding NAPALM" on page 624, the NAPALM project (*https://oreil.ly/wVQy-*) is a well-established open source community supporting multivendor network automation integrations.

The NAPALM collection is available at Ansible Galaxy, so you need to use only the `ansible-galaxy` client, as shown in Example 12-40.

Example 12-40. Installing the Ansible NAPALM collection

```
$ pip3 install napalm
# omitted output

$ ansible-galaxy collection install napalm.napalm
```

 Ansible Galaxy takes care of installing collection dependencies if they are defined in the collection `dependencies` metadata. If not, you will need to install them manually (in this case, the `napalm` Python library).

Then, you can list all the available modules, filtering for the NAPALM collection:

```
$ ansible-doc -l | grep napalm.napalm
# omitted deprecation warnings
napalm.napalm.napalm_cli            Executes network device CLI commands and...
napalm.napalm.napalm_diff_yang      Return diff of tw...
napalm.napalm.napalm_get_facts      Gathers facts from a network dev...
napalm.napalm.napalm_install_config Installs the configuration taken from a ...
napalm.napalm.napalm_parse_yang     Parse native config/state from a f...
napalm.napalm.napalm_ping           Executes ping on the device and returns...
```

```
napalm.napalm.napalm_translate_yang  Translate a YANG object to native...
napalm.napalm.napalm_validate        Performs deployment validat...
```

The NAPALM Ansible modules (*https://oreil.ly/9tVjS*) use the features offered by the library, mainly for configuration management (e.g., the `napalm_install_config` module) and obtaining configuration and operational state from devices (e.g., the `napalm_get_facts` module).

Getting familiar with NTC modules

The company Network to Code made several multivendor Ansible modules open source a few years ago. Now often referred to as NTC modules (*https://oreil.ly/diGPo*), they are available at Ansible Galaxy as the netauto collection. To install and use NTC modules, you need to follow the same steps you used with the NAPALM collection when installing the pyntc library for backend logic.

This suite of modules is most commonly used for two primary reasons:

Automatic parsing of raw text output from legacy devices using prebuilt TextFSM templates
> TextFSM simplifies performing regular expressions on command output. All templates are also open source on GitHub (*https://oreil.ly/Wm_u1*). This parsing is accomplished with the `ntc_show_command` module, which is merely a wrapper for Netmiko and TextFSM. The module also has an offline mode that allows you to use `command` modules, write the data to a file, and still parse that data with this module.

Issuing commands on devices not yet supported by Ansible modules
> Because `ntc_show_command` and `ntc_config_command` use Netmiko internally, you can automate any device Netmiko supports (all via SSH). The Netmiko library supports almost a hundred device types, so the support for these modules is robust.

Other features are available, such as NOS upgrade management, validation of data using the JSON schema, or leveraging the jdiff library to examine and compare structured data.

> Both NTC and NAPALM modules are multivendor, and the modules themselves have a parameter that dictates the OS of the device being automated. There is not a module per OS as in the previous examples with a module per vendor.

Installing third-party collections and modules

As noted earlier, the collection or module you need is likely already available in Galaxy, so installation should be straightforward (as in Example 12-40), with `ansible-galaxy collection install` *name_of_the_collection*.

However, you could use collections or modules not available in the Galaxy hub, including self-developed ones. The installation for third-party open source or custom collections or modules is also straightforward. Only a few steps are required:

1. Choose a path on your Linux system where you want to store all your third-party collections or modules (or use the one already defined).

2. Navigate to that path and perform a `git clone` on each repository that has collections or modules you want to use.

3. If you chose a different path than the default, you have to update the Ansible config file (*ansible.cfg*) and update your collection, or module paths, with the directory where you performed your clones. As we did in Example 12-1, you can get all this information with `ansible --version`. You may find the `collec tions_paths` for collections and the `library` for modules. If not defined, define `collections_paths` to point to your target path.

4. Install any dependencies the collections/modules have. These should be documented on each project's GitHub site and probably require a few packages to be installed via `pip`. If you're using Python Virtualenv or a system with several Python versions, you may need to use the `ansible_python_interpreter` variable within Ansible.

> If the collection is packaged as a *tar.gz*, you can install it from the source, defining the destination path:
>
> ```
> $ ansible-galaxy collection install /path/to/collection \
>     -p ./your-collections-folder
> ```

Ansible Summary

As you've now seen, Ansible is a robust and versatile option for network automation, from compliance checks and reports to more general configuration management and automation. Its agentless architecture enables Ansible to have a lower barrier to entry for network automation. Note that we only scratched the surface by showing what's possible when using Ansible. For more information, check out *https://docs.ansible.com*.

Next, we are going to take a look at Nornir, which takes a different approach to task automation.

Automating with Nornir

Nornir (https://oreil.ly/pGR6O) is a Python automation framework born as an alternative to low-code automation frameworks driven by DSLs, such as Ansible or Salt. While simple ancillary files like configuration and inventory files still use YAML, the workflows themselves are defined in Python. This is in contrast to other frameworks, which define workflow steps (playbooks) in a YAML-based DSL.

 Nornir has a Go version, Gornir (*https://oreil.ly/f2JvQ*), but we focus on the Python version in this section because it has more available options (plug-ins) to extend it.

Defining all the logic directly in Python comes with four main differences as compared to the DSL-based automation frameworks:

The barrier of entry
As a network engineer without experience in a programming language, DSL languages like YAML (covered in Chapter 8) lower the barrier to getting started versus learning a programming language (e.g., Python) to run Nornir. This makes tools like Ansible easier to adopt for network engineers coming into automation. However, there is no need to be an expert Python developer, because Nornir comes with well-defined abstractions ready to use. After getting started with Python in Chapter 6, you are ready to go!

Debugging
Once you feel comfortable with a programming language, being able to use the language debugging tools (e.g. pdb in Python) eases a lot of the development process. In contrast, a DSL (e.g., YAML) that is being interpreted by another engine can offer only limited options for debugging (e.g., the Ansible debug module).

Speed
Nornir comes with less overhead than other automation frameworks that need to serialize DSL definitions (e.g., Ansible YAML playbooks) to the automation engine (e.g., Python in Ansible). Also, Nornir is really minimalist, so the overhead is much less than in more opinionated automation frameworks.

Sophisticated logic
Even though automation frameworks using DSLs support some logic customization (e.g., when or loop keywords in Ansible), the reality is that complex logic is harder to define in a DSL than in a programming language. Nornir is also easier to extend, adding new functionalities that can't be achieved directly with DSLs in other automation frameworks.

As opposed to Ansible and Terraform (community-based tools with commercial support by Red Hat and HashiCorp, respectively), Nornir is a pure community project; thus only community-based support is available.

In this section, we explain how Nornir works; then we will illustrate how you can use Nornir with other libraries (NAPALM, in this case) to create capable network automation solutions.

Getting Started with Nornir

Nornir, a really minimalist and nonopinionated framework, has a few constructs that we introduce in this section progressively, with examples. You'll learn to use Nornir to directly automate your networks via Python code.

The first step, as with other Python libraries, is to install the Nornir package via `pip`:

```
$ pip3 install nornir
$ pip3 list | grep nornir
nornir                    3.3.0
```

Initializing Nornir

Nornir comes with the `InitNornir` class to bootstrap Nornir and define how it will behave (Example 12-44 provides more details). Before getting there, Example 12-41 defines a YAML configuration file for Nornir settings. You could define these settings directly using a Python dictionary.

The following YAML files, and the final Python script, are available in the examples repository at *https://github.com/oreilly-npa-book/ examples/tree/v2/ch12-automationtools/nornir*.

Example 12-41. Nornir configuration

```
---
inventory:                          ❶
    plugin: "SimpleInventory"       ❷
    options:
        host_file: "inventory/hosts.yaml"
        group_file: "inventory/groups.yaml"
runner:                             ❸
    plugin: "threaded"              ❹
    options:
        num_workers: 20
```

❶ The `inventory` section defines how Nornir will build its inventory. The inventory, similar to an Ansible inventory file, is the reference to the target objects (e.g., network devices) with all their related data.

❷ Nornir can be extended via various plug-in types. `SimpleInventory` implements an *inventory* that uses local files to define the *host*, *group*, and *default* values. Every plug-in type comes with different available options.

❸ The `runner` section defines how the Nornir tasks will be executed.

❹ The default, and most popular, runner option is `threaded`, which leverages Python multithreading capabilities to run tasks in multiple threads (`num_workers` defines the number of threads to be used in parallel). The actual implementation is almost identical to the one used in Example 6-11.

 Using inventory plug-ins, you can easily integrate Nornir with external inventory systems that allow fetching data dynamically without storing it statically in a file. A Nornir inventory plug-in connects to external APIs and translates the data to Nornir constructs. "Extending Nornir with plug-ins" on page 622 provides examples of available inventory plug-ins along with other plug-in types.

Defining the inventory

Using `SimpleInventory`, you define two files: one for the hosts and another for the groups. Comparing these files to those in Ansible, the host file would match the Ansible inventory and *host_vars*, and the groups file would match *group_vars*.

host_file. The *host_file* file contains a dictionary with all the hosts and with extended data, such as the platform, access credentials, or any other relevant data per device.

In this section, we reuse exactly the same network scenario from Figure 12-1 to facilitate the comparison with the Ansible example. An equivalent *host_file* is shown in Example 12-42.

Example 12-42. Nornir host_file

```
---
csr1:                ❶
  hostname: "csr1"
  platform: "ios" ❷
  groups:          ❸
    - "amers-cpe"
vmx1:
```

```
    hostname: "vmx1"
    platform: "junos"
    groups:
      - "emea-cpe"
eos-spine1:
    hostname: "eos-spine1"
    platform: "eos"
    groups:
      - "emea-dc"
nxos-spine1:
    hostname: "nxos-spine1"
    platform: "nxos"
    groups:
      - "amers-dc"
    data:            ❹
      ntp_server: "10.1.200.200"
      syslog_server: "10.1.200.201"
# omitted one device per type for brevity
```

❶ This YAML file represents a dictionary in which every item is a network device in the topology. This key will be used in Nornir to identify each host. The value of the items is another dictionary. In this inner dictionary, the hostname is a mandatory key, as it represents the target IP or FQDN.

❷ The platform is convenient to help the connection libraries choose the right driver when using plug-in *connections*.

❸ This optional key contains a list of the group names to which a host belongs. Groups help reuse data across multiple hosts by defining them only once.

❹ data is also optional and contains whatever extra information this host relates to.

In this *host_file* some basic information is missing on purpose. You may have noticed that the hosts don't have any data related to their credentials. This information could have been defined here, but because all the devices use the same credentials, using groups makes it simpler.

group_file. The *group_file* file should match the groups referenced in *host_file*. So, in *host_file*, for the host csr1, you define the amers-cpe group. This group should be defined here (if not matching, Nornir will complain when initializing).

You may be asking, which groups make sense to define? Well, this depends a lot on every environment. Let's examine our implementation in Example 12-43.

Example 12-43. Nornir group_file

```
---
amers-cpe:     ❶
  groups:
    - "global"
emea-cpe:
  groups:
    - "global"
  data:        ❷
    syslog_server: "10.9.1.1"
amers-dc:
  groups:
    - "global"
emea-dc:
  groups:
    - "global"
global:        ❸
  data:
    ntp_server: "10.1.200.199"
    syslog_server: "10.1.200.201"
  username: "ntc"
  password: "ntc123"
```

❶ In the proposed network topology, the network devices are grouped into four roles. The amers-cpe group does not contain, for now, any relevant data, but it is already referencing another group: global.

❷ The emea-cpe group, aside from referencing the global group, has a more specific syslog_server.

❸ All the groups are referencing a global one that contains the general data and device credentials (the same for all the devices).

With so many options for merging data, you may be wondering which is the final state of the data for a given host. If your intuition tells you that the more specific wins, you're right. But there's nothing better than checking it in a real example. Let's get hands-on with Nornir (Example 12-44) using the Python interpreter!

Example 12-44. Reviewing the Nornir inventory

```
>>> from nornir import InitNornir
>>> nr = InitNornir(config_file="config.yaml")     ❶
>>> nr.inventory.hosts                              ❷
{'csr1': Host: csr1, 'csr2': Host: csr2, 'vmx1': Host: vmx1, 'vmx2': Host: vmx2,
 'eos-spine1': Host: eos-spine1, 'eos-spine2': Host: eos-spine2,
 'nxos-spine1': Host: nxos-spine1, 'nxos-spine2': Host: nxos-spine2}
>>> nr.inventory.groups
```

```
{'global': Group: global, 'csr': Group: csr, 'vmx': Group: vmx,
'eos-spine': Group: eos-spine, 'nxos-spine': Group: nxos-spine,
'amers-cpe': Group: amers-cpe, 'emea-cpe': Group: emea-cpe,
'amers-dc': Group: amers-dc, 'emea-dc': Group: emea-dc}
>>> nr.inventory.hosts["nxos-spine1"].platform ❸
'nxos'
>>> nr.inventory.hosts["nxos-spine1"]["syslog_server"]
'10.1.200.201'                                            ❹
>>> nr.inventory.hosts["vmx1"]["syslog_server"]
'10.9.1.1'
>>> nr.filter(platform="ios").inventory.hosts ❺
{'csr1': Host: csr1, 'csr2': Host: csr2}
```

❶ InitNornir initializes Nornir. We are using *config_file*, but we could do it directly with a Python dictionary. Using the configuration from Example 12-41, Nornir knows how to build the inventory and which runner to use.

❷ Once Nornir is initialized in nr, we can access the defined Hosts and Groups. This would also be valid for a dynamic inventory instead of a statically defined one.

❸ Within the inventory, we can navigate the hosts as a Python dictionary and check which are the attributes—for instance, the platform or the data values (accessed as a Python dictionary).

❹ When multiple values are available for a host (because of group inheritance), the merge order is from more specific to more general. For nxos-spine1, the value of syslog_server is the one defined in *hosts.yaml*. For vmx1, because the group emea-cpe has a value and also inherits from the global group, the more specific (the emea-cpe one) wins.

❺ A useful feature of the Nornir inventory is the filter option, which helps narrow the scope of Nornir. In the example, only the hosts with the ios platform are selected, so any related task will be applicable to these devices.

Once the inventory is in place, the fun part begins: running Nornir tasks!

Executing tasks

Apart from the inventory, the other two key constructs in Nornir are *tasks* and *results*. The implementation follows a simple pattern: you define a function that takes as an attribute the Task (and other arguments) and returns a Result. A Task is a wrapper around a function that takes a callable (a function) as an argument, together with other parameters for this function. The task contains a host attribute containing a Host object from the Nornir inventory, with all its related data. The most important method implemented is run(), which runs the wrapped function for a specific host and returns the `Result` containing some attributes such as the *diff* (the difference between the state of the system before/after running the task) or the *result* that is the output of the task function.

Example 12-45 defines a simple Nornir task. It does not contain any complex logic at all (but it could have) but will help you understand how to build Nornir tasks.

Example 12-45. Defining Nornir tasks

```
>>> from nornir.core.task import Task, Result          ❶
>>> import time
>>> def check_config(task: Task, feature: str) -> Result:
...     # here you could do whatever logic suits to you
...     time.sleep(5)                                    ❷
...     data_key = f"{feature}_server"
...     message = f"{task.host.name} {feature} is {task.host[data_key]}"  ❸
...     return Result(                                   ❹
...         host=task.host,
...         result=message,
...     )
```

❶ The `Task` and `Result` classes are imported from Nornir, and a new function is created using them. Notice that we are using Python typing hints to inform about the expected types.

❷ Adding a sleep time will help to understand task parallelization when running the task in Example 12-46.

❸ The function can implement any complex logic we decide. We have access to the `Task` object that contains all the inventory data related to the host.

❹ Finally, a `Result` object is returned to the Nornir runner.

Once the task is defined, it is time to use it. In Example 12-46, you use the previously defined task `check_config` via the `run()` method.

Example 12-46. Nornir run() tasks

```
>>> result = nr.run(task=check_config, feature="ntp")   ❶
>>> result["csr1"][0].result                             ❷
'csr1 ntp is 10.1.200.199'
>>>
>>> from nornir_utils.plugins.functions import print_result  ❸
>>> print_result(result)                                 ❸
check_config********************************************************************
* csr1 ** changed : False ******************************************************
vvvv check_config ** changed : False vvvvvvvvvvvvvvvvvvvvvvvvvvvvvvvvvvvvvvvvvvvvv INFO
csr1 ntp is 10.1.200.199                                 ❹
```

```
^^^^ END check_config ^^^^^^^^^^^^^^^^^^^^^^^^^^^^^^^^^^^^^^^^^^^^^^^^^^^^^^^^^^^^^^^^
* csr2 ** changed : False *********************************************************
vvvv check_config ** changed : False vvvvvvvvvvvvvvvvvvvvvvvvvvvvvvvvvvvvvvvvvvvv INFO
csr2 ntp is 10.1.200.199                                            ❹
^^^^ END check_config ^^^^^^^^^^^^^^^^^^^^^^^^^^^^^^^^^^^^^^^^^^^^^^^^^^^^^^^^^^^^^^^^
# omitted the other devices for brevity
* nxos-spine1 ** changed : False *************************************************
vvvv check_config ** changed : False vvvvvvvvvvvvvvvvvvvvvvvvvvvvvvvvvvvvvvvvvvvv INFO
nxos-spine1 ntp is 10.1.200.200                                     ❹
^^^^ END check_config ^^^^^^^^^^^^^^^^^^^^^^^^^^^^^^^^^^^^^^^^^^^^^^^^^^^^^^^^^^^^^^^^
```

❶ The run() method takes as input the function defined and any extra arguments
to this function. Notice that the Nornir object contains the full inventory, and
if the filter method is not used, a task per device will be executed, producing
as many results. Even with the 5 seconds of sleep time inserted in the task (in
Example 12-45), the overall execution time, for the 8 devices, is 5 seconds. In
a serial execution, the overall time would be 40 seconds but, by default, Nornir
runs the tasks in parallel.

❷ Once the Nornir run ends, the result contains one result per inventory host.
Notice that the index 0 is used, because a task could have multiple subtasks (see
Example 12-50).

❸ Nornir has an extra package, nornir-utils, with helper methods such as
print_result, which provides a nice output format. Remember to install it
before using it (pip3 install nornir-utils).

❹ You can observe in the output that every host would use the actual data extracted
from the inventory, after merging all the data available at the host and group
levels.

Extending Nornir with plug-ins

Nornir includes, by default, minimum features but can be easily extended with
third-party plug-ins, such as those available at nornir.tech (*https://oreil.ly/UnVJh*).

Different types of plug-ins implement different feature types:

Functions
    Helper methods around Nornir constructs.

Connection
    Defines how to connect to a network device implementing two methods: open()
    and close().

Inventory
    Creates the inventory objects: hosts, groups, and defaults.

Processors

Manipulates task results to adapt to different outcomes.

Tasks

Defines tasks to be used directly in the Nornir run() method. Usually, these tasks are simple wrappers around a library, exposing the library methods as Nornir tasks.

Runners

Determines *how* the tasks will be executed—for instance, you could add a retry logic if necessary.

To give a glimpse of what you can do with plug-ins, let's take a look at the Nornir Nautobot plug-in (*https://oreil.ly/xj3F8*) that offers dynamic inventory, task, and processor features. Install it with pip3 install nornir-nautobot, and you get access to the plug-in extensions.

Example 12-47 shows how the inventory is *pulled* from an external source—in this case, a publicly available Nautobot instance (you'll learn more info about Nautobot and other sources of truth in Chapter 14). Finally, with a more complex inventory, we will demonstrate some advanced filtering options.

Example 12-47. Nornir Nautobot inventory plug-in

```
>>> nr = InitNornir(
...     inventory={
...         "plugin": "NautobotInventory",          ❶
...         "options": {                            ❷
...             "nautobot_url": "https://demo.nautobot.com",
...             "nautobot_token": "a" * 40,
...         },
...     },
... )
>>> len(nr.inventory.hosts)
393
>>> from nornir.core.filter import F                ❸
>>> len(nr.filter(F(platform__contains="arista")).inventory.hosts)   ❹
345
>>> len(nr.
...     filter(F(platform__contains="arista")).
...     filter(F(data__pynautobot_dictionary__device_role__slug="edge")).   ❺
...     inventory.hosts
... )
72
```

❶ NautobotInventory (instead of SimpleInventory) loads the Nautobot inventory plug-in.

❷ The Nautobot inventory plug-in comes with options: mandatory ones, like the URL and token, and optional ones, such as `filter_parameters` to limit the scope of devices to load, to narrow the loaded inventory scope (also reducing the loading time).

❸ The F class allows some advanced filtering patterns, using filter operators (e.g., `contains` or accessing host data).

❹ With `__contains`, we get all the hosts whose platform contains the word `arista`.

❺ Nornir filters can be *stacked*, or filtered on a previous filter. In this case, we limit the scope to only the device with the `edge` role for Arista devices.

In the next section, you will learn about `nornir-napalm`, a Nornir plug-in for the popular NAPALM library. This plug-in provides tasks for interacting with network devices from multiple platforms in a homogeneous way.

Using NAPALM with Nornir

This section brings together Nornir with NAPALM to illustrate how to use Nornir with predefined tasks in a really straightforward way. But, we can't get to the mixed example without going a bit deeper with NAPALM first.

In this section, we first cover basic NAPALM concepts while retrieving information from network devices. Second, we focus on the configuration management feature of NAPALM combined with the Nornir framework.

Understanding NAPALM

NAPALM (*https://oreil.ly/AIEji*), which stands for *Network Automation and Programmability Abstraction Layer with Multivendor support*, is a Python library that offers a robust set of operations for managing network devices via a common set of Python objects, regardless of *how* each operation is performed for a given device type. In NAPALM, note that performing any given operation is the same, which vendor or OS you're working with, as long as there is a supported NAPALM driver and feature for the given operation.

NAPALM supports many device vendors and uses various APIs to communicate with each. For example, Cisco Nexus uses NX-API and SSH, Arista EOS uses eAPI, Cisco IOS uses SSH, and the Juniper Junos drivers use NETCONF. When evaluating NAPALM, you should be aware of which API is required for the device(s) you're working with. The core library comes with the support of the most popular APIs, but you can find extensions for other platforms at the NAPALM Automation Community Drivers repository on GitHub (*https://oreil.ly/xr0LC*). Not all drivers have full feature parity, so it's important to review each driver's capabilities to understand what can be done for each platform.

For more details on supported APIs and devices, as well as on topics not covered in this section, consult the NAPALM documentation (*https://oreil.ly/s5TAS*). For now, we'll start by looking at retrieving operational data with NAPALM.

Retrieving operational data with NAPALM

The most common NAPALM feature, when getting started with it, is its capability to retrieve information from network devices in a uniform fashion. Any data returned from NAPALM is normalized for all devices in a consistent way.

As you may recall, when we looked at various APIs in Chapter 10, each vendor or device returns vendor-specific key-value pairs. This is even more relevant when the information is available only via text from a CLI. Some devices might support vendor-neutral data models such as YANG models from the IETF or OpenConfig working group mentioned in Chapter 8, but this is not fully adopted across all platforms and vendors yet. Thus, NAPALM data normalization helps you with this heterogeneity.

You can easily install NAPALM via pip:

```
$ pip3 install napalm
pip3 list | grep napalm
napalm                    4.0.0
```

Getting started with NAPALM is straightforward: select the platform driver, initialize it, and connect to the device to establish a connection, as shown in Example 12-48.

Example 12-48. Initializing NAPALM

```
>>> from napalm import get_network_driver
>>> driver = get_network_driver('eos')     ❶
>>> device = driver(                        ❷
...     hostname='eos-spine1',
...     username='ntc',
...     password='ntc123'
... )
>>> device.open()                           ❸
```

❶ The get_network_driver() function returns the proper object depending on the driver identifier (eos corresponds to Arista EOS).

❷ driver is the object that is instantiated with parameters to establish the connection properly. It accepts optional_args to customize it as needed.

❸ With the open() method, the connection is established and we are ready to interact with the network device.

At this point, device is a NAPALM device object. Let's use the dir() function, which we originally introduced way back in Chapter 6, to see the methods that the NAPALM device object supports:

```
>>> dir(device)
[...omitted methods..., 'commit_config', 'compare_config', 'compliance_report',
'config_session', 'confirm_commit', 'connection_tests', 'device', 'discard_config',
'eapi_kwargs', 'get_arp_table', 'get_bgp_config', 'get_bgp_neighbors', 'get_config',
'get_environment', 'get_facts', 'get_firewall_policies', 'get_interfaces',
'get_interfaces_counters', 'get_interfaces_ip', 'get_lldp_neighbors',
'load_merge_candidate', 'load_replace_candidate', 'load_template', 'lock_disable',
'locked', 'open', 'password', 'ping', 'rollback', 'traceroute']
>>>
```

In this list, you can see some methods for configuration management—e.g., load_merge_candidate() and load_replace_candidate())—but most of the methods are get_ methods used to retrieve information from network devices. We're going to use a few of these now.

The first one we'll look at is get_facts(). This retrieves common information from the device, such as OS, uptime, interfaces, vendor, model, hostname, and FQDN:

```
>>> device.get_facts()
{'hostname': 'eos-spine1', 'fqdn': 'eos-spine1.ntc.com', 'vendor': 'Arista',
'model': 'vEOS', 'serial_number': '', 'os_version': '4.22.4M-15583082.4224M',
'uptime': 389825.1441075802, 'interface_list': ['Ethernet1', 'Ethernet2',
'Ethernet3', 'Ethernet4', ...omitted some interfaces..., 'Management1']}
>>>
```

The great thing about the data returned is that it's structured exactly the same no matter which vendor you're using within NAPALM. In this case, NAPALM is normalizing and doing the heavy lifting, making it so you don't need to integrate/translate each vendor you're working with. NAPALM is already doing that for you.

Let's take a look at a few more examples. The get_snmp_information() function retrieves a dictionary that summarizes the SNMP configuration present on a device:

```
>>> device.get_snmp_information()
{
  'chassis_id': '', 'location': '', 'contact': '',
  'community': {'networktocode': {'acl': '', 'mode': 'ro'}}
}
>>>
```

The get_lldp_neighbors() function provides a dictionary that summarizes a list of currently seen LLDP neighbors on a per-interface basis:

```
>>> device.get_lldp_neighbors()
{
  'Ethernet2': [{'hostname': 'eos-leaf1.ntc.com', 'port': 'Ethernet2'}],
  'Ethernet3': [{'hostname': 'eos-leaf2.ntc.com', 'port': 'Ethernet2'}],
  'Ethernet4': [{'hostname': 'vmx1', 'port': 'ge-0/0/3'}]
}
>>>
```

All these functions return a dictionary. We can create a small script to consume and print the LLDP neighbors dictionary in a human-friendly format:

```
>>> for interface, neighbors in device.get_lldp_neighbors().items():
...     print(f"INTERFACE: {interface}")
...     print("NEIGHBORS: ")
...     for neighbor in neighbors:
...         print(f"  - {neighbor["hostname"]}")
...
INTERFACE: Ethernet2
NEIGHBORS:
  - eos-leaf1.ntc.com
INTERFACE: Ethernet3
NEIGHBORS:
  - eos-leaf2.ntc.com
INTERFACE: Ethernet4
NEIGHBORS:
  - vmx1
>>>
```

Now, we shift gears to, finally, combine NAPALM with Nornir to solve configuration management challenges *at scale*.

Configuration management at scale

NAPALM offers two flavors for managing device configurations:

Configuration merge operation
> This takes a partial configuration or just a few device commands and *ensures* that they exist on the target network device. This works fine for all types of platforms, including traditional ones.

Configuration replacement operation
> Also known as *declarative configuration management*, the sole focus is on what you want the device configuration to be. This is in stark contrast to worrying about what it is, and how to go from what it is to what you want it to be. While this is a major benefit and feature of NAPALM, it's actually a by-product of particular features that exist on the network devices. A few of these device-centric features include candidate configurations with Juniper, configuration sessions with Arista, and the `config replace` feature with Cisco IOS. In essence, we are declaring what the configuration should be, not worrying about any no or `delete` commands.

A configuration replacement requires pushing the *full* active configuration. Being able to render a full *intended* configuration requires an advanced maturity level of your automation and a capable source of truth, as we explain in Chapter 14. For this reason, a configuration merge is usually adopted first in brownfield network environments and eventually, if supported by the network infrastructure and the configuration rendering is complete, there is a shift toward a configuration replacement. This shifting approach is more realistic for those just starting their automation journey to manage specific features.

The goal in this configuration management example is to configure a new SNMP community (`secret123`) in all Arista devices. Example 12-49 shows how to leverage Nornir and the NAPALM `napalm_configure` task, which support both configuration modes (using the `replace` argument to choose). Before using the Nornir NAPALM plug-in, install it with `pip3 install nornir-napalm`.

Example 12-49. Configuring devices with `napalm_configure`

```
>>> from nornir_napalm.plugins.tasks import napalm_configure
>>> from nornir import InitNornir
>>> nr = InitNornir(config_file="config.yaml")
>>> results = nr.filter(platform="eos").run(              ❶
...     task=napalm_configure,                            ❷
...     dry_run=False,                                    ❸
...     replace=False,
...     configuration="snmp-server community secret123 rw" ❹
... )
...
>>> print(results["eos-spine1"].diff)                     ❺
@@ -8,6 +8,7 @@
 ip domain-name ntc.com
 !
 snmp-server community networktocode ro
+snmp-server community secret123 rw
 !
 spanning-tree mode mstp
 !
```

❶ Using the Nornir `filter` option, we limit the scope to the Arista EOS devices.

❷ The `napalm_configure` task is passed as the Nornir task, which will perform a configuration operation.

❸ The extra options available in Nornir allow a `dry_run` operation to not commit the changes. The `replace` option is set to `False` by default, but we want to explicitly define that this is a merge operation.

❹ The `configuration` argument allows passing a string of CLI commands. Alternatively, it also accepts the `filename` to pass a file directly.

❺ By accessing the `diff` attribute, we can review the changes in the configuration.

Using the NAPALM object (`device`) from Example 12-48, or connecting via SSH, you can verify that the new SNMP community is there:

```
>>> device.get_snmp_information()
{
  'chassis_id': '', 'location': '', 'contact': '',
  'community': {
    'networktocode': {'acl': '', 'mode': 'ro'},
    'secret123': {'acl': '', 'mode': 'rw'}
  }
}
```

A configuration merge does not purge any commands or specific configuration hierarchy in a declarative fashion. However, if you know how NAPALM is functioning for a specific device driver, you can use that information to your advantage to manage a specific feature declaratively.

> Several other plug-ins offer *tasks* to connect to network devices: nornir_netmiko, nornir_scrapli, nornir_paramiko, nornir_netconf, and many more. Check the updated list of Nornir plug-ins (*https://oreil.ly/fXG1W*).

With all the Nornir features you have learned and your Python skills, you're ready to combine them and build more sophisticated workflows. For instance, in Example 12-50, a Python script uses Nornir to render configuration from the inventory data and configure the proper NTP settings for each device. Remember, this example is available in the book examples repository.

> The Jinja tasks in Nornir are available in the nornir-jinja2 plug-in that can be installed with `pip3 install nornir-jinja2`.

Example 12-50. Nornir complete example

```
from nornir import InitNornir
from nornir.core.task import Result, Task
from nornir_jinja2.plugins.tasks import template_string
from nornir_napalm.plugins.tasks import napalm_configure
from nornir_utils.plugins.functions import print_result
```

```
# TEMPLATE represents an option to manage multiple templates per platform
TEMPLATE = {
  "eos": "ntp server {{ host['ntp_server'] }}",
  "ios": "ntp server {{ host['ntp_server'] }}",
  "nxos": "ntp server {{  host['ntp_server'] }}",
  "junos": "set system ntp server {{  host['ntp_server'] }}",
}

def config_task(task: Task, template) -> Result:
    """Nornir task that combines two subtasks:
        - Render a configuration from a Jinja template
        - Push the rendered configuration to the device
    """
    render_result = task.run(
      task=template_string,
      # The right template per platform is selected
      template=template[task.host.platform],
    )

    config_result = task.run(
      task=napalm_configure,
      # The rendered configuration from the previous subtask is used
      # as the configuration input
      configuration=render_result.result,
      # dry_run means the changes without applying them
      dry_run=True,
    )

    return Result(host=task.host, result=config_result)

# Initialize Nornir inventory from a file
nr = InitNornir(config_file="config.yaml")
# The "config_task" will aggregate two subtasks
result = nr.run(
  task=config_task,
  template=TEMPLATE,
)

print_result(result)
```

In the output of this script, you can observe that the main Nornir task executes two subtasks (and its outputs) per host—one to render the proper configuration per device, and another to push it to show the potential changes (dry_run is set to True). Notice how the proper NTP server IP, from our inventory definition, is used in the configuration rendered here:

```
$ python example.py
# only showing one output per platform type, others omitted
config_task***************************************************************
* csr1 ** changed : True ************************************************
vvvv config_task ** changed : False vvvvvvvvvvvvvvvvvvvvvvvvvvvvvvvvvvvvvvvvvvvv INFO
MultiResult: [Result: "napalm_configure"]
---- template_string ** changed : False ------------------------------------- INFO
ntp server 10.1.200.199
```

```
---- napalm_configure ** changed : True ------------------------------------- INFO
+ntp server 10.1.200.199
^^^^ END config_task ^^^^^^^^^^^^^^^^^^^^^^^^^^^^^^^^^^^^^^^^^^^^^^^^^^^^^^^^^^^
* eos-spine1 ** changed : True ***********************************************
vvvv config_task ** changed : False vvvvvvvvvvvvvvvvvvvvvvvvvvvvvvvvvvvvvvvvvvv INFO
MultiResult: [Result: "napalm_configure"]
---- template_string ** changed : False ------------------------------------- INFO
ntp server 10.1.200.199
---- napalm_configure ** changed : True ------------------------------------- INFO
@@ -6,6 +6,8 @@
 !
 hostname eos-spine1
 ip domain-name ntc.com
+!
+ntp server 10.1.200.199
 !
 snmp-server community networktocode ro
 snmp-server community secret123 rw
^^^^ END config_task ^^^^^^^^^^^^^^^^^^^^^^^^^^^^^^^^^^^^^^^^^^^^^^^^^^^^^^^^^^^
* nxos-spine1 ** changed : True **********************************************
vvvv config_task ** changed : False vvvvvvvvvvvvvvvvvvvvvvvvvvvvvvvvvvvvvvvvvvv INFO
MultiResult: [Result: "napalm_configure"]
---- template_string ** changed : False ------------------------------------- INFO
ntp server 10.1.200.200
---- napalm_configure ** changed : True ------------------------------------- INFO
ntp server 10.1.200.200
^^^^ END config_task ^^^^^^^^^^^^^^^^^^^^^^^^^^^^^^^^^^^^^^^^^^^^^^^^^^^^^^^^^^^
* vmx1 ** changed : True *****************************************************
vvvv config_task ** changed : False vvvvvvvvvvvvvvvvvvvvvvvvvvvvvvvvvvvvvvvvvvv INFO
MultiResult: [Result: "napalm_configure"]
---- template_string ** changed : False ------------------------------------- INFO
set system ntp server 10.1.200.199
---- napalm_configure ** changed : True ------------------------------------- INFO
[edit system]
+   ntp {
+       server 10.1.200.199;
+   }
^^^^ END config_task ^^^^^^^^^^^^^^^^^^^^^^^^^^^^^^^^^^^^^^^^^^^^^^^^^^^^^^^^^^^
```

Nornir Summary

In this section, we covered the basic Nornir concepts—including building an inventory, defining and running tasks (in a multithread execution), and working with the results. These are the basic constructs needed to build complex network automation tasks.

Moreover, the true power of Nornir comes from its extensibility via plug-ins, as you saw with the NAPALM one. The NAPALM library by itself gives a useful abstraction of multiple network interfaces and vendors to gain a consistent experience, both for retrieving the operational state and for changing it. Even though using Python directly could seem a bit overwhelming when getting started, when you gain confidence with it, Nornir is a great option for giving you full control of your network automation tasks.

Finally, in the last section of the chapter, we review how Terraform approaches infrastructure automation, using a declarative approach.

Managing Dynamic Infrastructure with Terraform

As introduced in Chapter 1, during the 2010s, cloud infrastructure adoption became mainstream and changed the way we manage IT infrastructure. Now, infrastructure resources are *dynamic* and can be spun up on demand and consumed *as a service*. In plain language, if we want a MySQL database, we no longer need to physically install and connect the server and then apply the proper OS configuration to, finally, set up the MySQL service. In the cloud, you simply do a REST API call to provision a MySQL service, with some parametrization in the data payload, and in a few seconds or minutes, your MySQL database will be ready to consume.

The API is, usually, the main entry point for infrastructure management in the cloud, and the rest of the interfaces, such as CLI, SDKs, or GUIs, are built on top of it. This new paradigm enables *infrastructure as code* (IaC): you define in code how your infrastructure should look, and then tooling interprets it, translating it to API calls. This is a perfect match for the declarative approach. We define *what* we want, not *how* to get into it as we do with the *imperative* approach.

 The declarative and imperative approaches can still work together. In some cases, creating a new service is not enough to use it, and post-provisioning configuration is required. This is how Terraform and Ansible can complement each other. For instance, Terraform creates a virtual server, and Ansible connects, once ready, to complete its configuration and move the server to the desired state. Recently, an official Terraform integration for Ansible has been announced (*https://oreil.ly/pd0z1*), so now you can provision your IaC via Terraform, and the resulting objects are added to the Ansible inventory to automate the configuration or additional post-provisioning tasks.

To provide easier use of these APIs, some cloud providers came out with their own tools to implement this IaC, but as you may guess, with limited coverage for other infrastructure providers. For instance, AWS, the dominant public cloud provider at the time of this writing, created AWS CloudFormation, which interprets YAML or JSON to interact with the proper AWS APIs.

In this context, Terraform was created in 2014 by HashiCorp with the aim to manage any dynamic infrastructure behind an API. This scope includes any cloud or on-premises resources that can be managed via APIs. It started with support for some of the most common providers, but its extensibility and easy usage has spread its adoption as the single tool for managing IaC. Terraform supports more cloud providers than any other IaC tool and has community-driven extensions for more than 1,700 providers!

This section covers Terraform key concepts and how they apply in various cases. We'll walk through networking-related examples divided into these five areas:

- Understanding Terraform architecture
- Provisioning your first resource with Terraform
- Extending Terraform execution
- Managing Terraform at scale
- Using Terraform out of its comfort zone

We'll start with an overview of Terraform's configuration language and then present the Terraform components and workflow to illustrate the Terraform fundamentals.

Understanding Terraform Architecture

Terraform, like other tooling, introduces new terminology and concepts, and even a new configuration language, which is our first stop in this journey.

Terraform configuration language

Terraform uses a DSL, the HashiCorp Configuration Language (HCL), like the other HashiCorp products. It was created as a trade-off between other serialization formats used to define configurations, such as JSON and YAML, and traditional programming languages. This combination helps create more sophisticated configurations, leveraging the declarative pattern.

 Even though the HCL DSL is the most popular way to use Terraform, if you prefer to use a regular programming language, such as Go or Python, you can use Cloud Development Kit for Terraform, or CDKTF (*https://oreil.ly/N9F6F*). The use of programming languages, instead of learning specific DSLs, is preferred for developers who are familiar with some of these programming languages. This also allows reusing all the same toolchains and features they are used to playing with. Other alternative IaC solutions use this approach, such as AWS CDK (*https://oreil.ly/K4cxC*) and Pulumi (*https://oreil.ly/kQ2IQ*).

From all the HCL features, we will focus solely on the most relevant for its use in Terraform. HCL has a *native syntax*, intended to be pleasant to read and write for humans, and a *JSON-based variant*, easier for machines to generate and parse. Because we're humans, our examples use the *native syntax*.

The two basic syntax constructs are arguments and blocks.

An *argument* assigns a value to a particular name or variable, and depending on the context where it is defined, will determine which value types are valid. For instance, when you learn later about *resources*, you will find out that each resource has a schema for its arguments, and it is enforced when assigning the values. In this example, we are using a string value "192.0.2.0/24" to an argument with the name cidr_block:

```
cidr_block = "192.0.2.0/24"
```

 The Terraform documentation uses the term *argument*, whereas the HCL documentation uses *attribute*. In this section, we use *argument* for the inputs.

A *block* is a container for other content, and its extensibility converts Terraform into a powerful tool to declare complex dynamic infrastructure. HCL supports several block *types*. In the following example, the type is resource. The next label, aws_vpc, specifies the exact resource component, from all the available ones in this context. This combination, resource and aws_vpc, is what defines the arguments, or other nested *blocks*, mandatory or optional. Each has its own definition:

```
resource "aws_vpc" "my_vpc" {
  cidr_block = "192.0.2.0/24"
}
```

Besides arguments and blocks, HCL also has identifiers, used to identify the arguments, blocks, and other Terraform constructs that you will discover in this section. *Identifiers* are the argument names (cidr_block), block type names (aws_vpc), and block names (my_vpc). They allow the configuration files to reuse all these components in multiple places. For instance, you could use the my_vpc identifier to connect other resources to it.

Finally, as most languages do, HCL provides support for comments. It has three syntaxes: # and // for single-line comments, and /* ... */ for multiline ones:

```
# This argument defines the CIDR for our Amazon VPC
// And the next one is for multiple lines
/*
  This is a multiline comment
*/
cidr_block = "192.0.2.0/24"
```

After this brief introduction to the basic concepts of HCL, let's dive into Terraform's own terminology of key concepts.

Terraform in a nutshell

The Terraform process is built on top of basic components that you will discover, progressively, throughout this section. In Figure 12-3, we give you a 1,000-foot overview to help you visualize them, and, afterward, a short description.

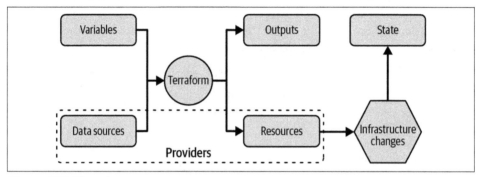

Figure 12-3. Terraform components

Let's walk through each Terraform component used in the Terraform configuration file to define the expected status of the IaC:

Providers
> Plug-ins created to interact with the APIs from dynamic infrastructure providers. They can be in *read* mode (*data sources*) or *write* mode (*resources*).

Variables
> Parameters with values for customizing the behavior of Terraform configurations.

Terraform
> Software providing the commands to implement the Terraform workflow that manages the dynamic infrastructure.

Outputs
> Explicit information exposed after Terraform execution. It can be used as input variables for other Terraform executions.

State
> Binds the Terraform definition to the infrastructure. The state includes *reading* from the actual infrastructure plus *tracking* the new services added in order to maintain a mapping between the plan and the reality. Then, when Terraform runs again, it doesn't start from scratch and can be aware of already existing services that may need to be updated (instead of created from scratch).

Infrastructure changes

The infrastructure services created in the target dynamic infrastructure provider.

Next, you need to understand the Terraform workflow to manage the whole dynamic infrastructure lifecycle.

Terraform workflow

Terraform has a simple and well-defined workflow, from writing the configuration to deploying the dynamic infrastructure. In the official documentation, the *core* Terraform workflow is composed of three steps (write, plan, and apply), but we extend it to five here to better explain the whole cycle (Figure 12-4).

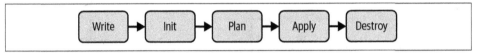

Figure 12-4. Terraform workflow

The five workflow steps are as follows:

Write
Define the desired infrastructure state by using the Terraform configuration language. This stage also contains the information required to initialize Terraform.

Init
Initialize the environment, installing the necessary plug-ins, modules, and backends, according to the configuration defined in the *write* step.

Plan
Create an execution plan, in *dry-run* mode, describing all the changes that your configuration will translate into the target infrastructure.

Apply
Enforce the desired state in the real infrastructure. This step is the same as *plan*, but not in dry-run mode.

Destroy
Deprovision the managed infrastructure.

Except for *write*, the rest of the workflow steps map to Terraform main commands. Actually, we could map the write step to the `validate` command, used to review the written configuration.

Make sure you have Terraform installed to continue progressing in this section. Instructions can be found at *https://oreil.ly/pMgds*. All these examples have been run using Terraform v1.2.0.

You can check these main commands with `terraform -help`:

```
$ terraform -help
Usage: terraform [global options] <subcommand> [args]

The available commands for execution are listed below.
The primary workflow commands are given first, followed by
less common or more advanced commands.

Main commands:
  init       Prepare your working directory for other commands
  validate   Check whether the configuration is valid
  plan       Show changes required by the current configuration
  apply      Create or update infrastructure
  destroy    Destroy previously-created infrastructure
```

With this overall understanding in place, it is time for the hands-on part of the section, where you will learn all the key Terraform concepts through a concrete networking example.

Provisioning Your First Resource with Terraform

There is no better way to understand how Terraform works than actually using it. Following the leitmotif of the book, we will use a cloud networking–related example (Chapter 4 provides more details) to illustrate the use of Terraform. From the multiple available options, we choose AWS as our cloud provider because it is the most popular public cloud (generally available) and offers great documentation for both API and Terraform. However, the same concepts and approach could be used in any other provider supported in Terraform—for instance, other public clouds, such as Microsoft Azure or GCP, or private ones, such as VMware or OpenStack.

To get started, you will create a basic networking setup: a virtual network and two subnets, as depicted in Figure 12-5. In the AWS platform, a virtual network is named Amazon Virtual Private Cloud (VPC).

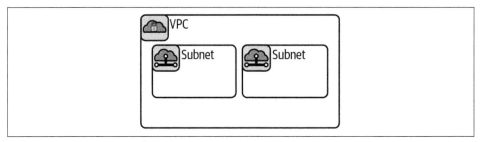

Figure 12-5. AWS network scenario

Setting up an AWS free account

You can use any AWS account, but if you don't have one, you can create a free account at AWS Free Tier (*https://aws.amazon.com/free*).

To interact with the AWS platform and to check the resulting infrastructure managed by Terraform, we will use the AWS CLI. However, the very same outcomes could be seen in the GUI, if you choose to use it.

First, in Example 12-51, you install the AWS CLI (*https://aws.amazon.com/cli*) for your particular OS, and configure it by running aws configure.

Example 12-51. Configuring the AWS CLI

```
$ aws configure
AWS Access Key ID [None]: Your Access Key ID
AWS Secret Access Key [None]: Your Secret Access Key
Default region name [None]: us-west-1
Default output format [None]:
```

The requested *access key ID* and *secret access key* are the security credentials to identify your account and get programmatic access. Keep in mind that these credentials have to be managed properly, following security measures (e.g., rotating and encrypting). You can use any credentials you already created or create new ones in the AWS GUI:

```
"Identity and Access Management (IAM)" -> "Dashboard" -> "Manage access keys"
```

From now on, you can review the status of our AWS infrastructure via the AWS CLI. To double-check that the setup is right, you can run the aws sts get-caller-identity command, and it will return your account information:

```
$ aws sts get-caller-identity
{
    "UserId":  "123456789012",
    "Account": "123456789012",
    "Arn": "arn:aws:iam::123456789012:root"
}
```

For this example, we used a root account for a personal account for simplicity. This is strongly discouraged in a proper AWS environment; following the principle of least privilege, a user with the minimum required access should be used.

Now that your AWS CLI is ready to go, you can start writing your first Terraform configuration snippet.

Using Terraform providers

Following the steps in "Terraform workflow" on page 636, the initial stage is to write the configuration, declaring the infrastructure you want to provision. In our example, you will start first with the Amazon VPC because it's the logical step for later including subnets.

To write the configuration, you need one or more files. In Terraform, the directory from where we are running determines the context, and all the files with the extension *.tf, in the top-level directory, will be seen as part of the Terraform configuration. The name of these files is not relevant, so you can name them as desired. This folder is also used to store other relevant files related to Terraform execution, as you will discover later.

Terraform configuration can be written in native syntax, for humans, or also in a JSON variant. In JSON, the extension of the configuration files is *.tf.json.

Then, you create a new directory and a new Terraform file (for instance, *01-create-vpc/create_vpc.tf*), where you will start defining the Terraform configuration:

```
$ tree
.
└── 1-create-vpc
    └── create_vpc.tf
```

For simplicity, we keep all the Terraform configurations in one file. But, in real scenarios, it's common to have different files, serving different purposes.

The first configuration you need in Terraform is for the provider. Terraform providers implement all the logic to translate from HCL to each infrastructure platform API. Selecting one provider or another in the configuration will allow you to use its resources and data sources in the configuration. Because we want to provision an Amazon VPC, we have to use the `aws` Terraform provider. The same approach applies to other providers: you define the Terraform providers in the configuration, depending on the platforms you have to manage.

Luckily, most dynamic infrastructure providers have officially supported Terraform providers, published in the Terraform Registry (*https://oreil.ly/O9iCJ*). There, you can also find documentation about how to use its configuration blocks and arguments.

The Terraform provider configuration is composed of two parts.

First, under the global `terraform` block (used to configure Terraform's own behavior), a nested block, `required_providers`, defines a mapping between the local name of the provider (in this case, `aws`) and the location where it can be found, with the `source` argument (in this case, the Terraform Registry `hashicorp/aws`). Finally, to pin a specific version, you set the `version` argument with the proper version number.

Then, in a second block, `provider`, you configure the provider defined in the first block. Here, you have access to the arguments described in this specific provider. For instance, for `hashicorp/aws`, it is necessary to define only one argument, the `region`. Example 12-52 shows both blocks combined.

Example 12-52. Defining and configuring the AWS Terraform provider

```
# Configure Terraform to find the right Provider
terraform {
  required_providers {
    aws = {
      source  = "hashicorp/aws"
      version = "~> 3.0"
    }
  }
}

# Configure the aws Provider
provider "aws" {
  region = "eu-west-3"
}
```

You can compare Terraform providers with Ansible modules or Nornir plug-ins. They extend Terraform's functionality to be able to work with a particular dynamic infrastructure provider.

In Terraform, providers are written in Go. Defining custom providers, or extending them, is doable but likely not something you will need to do. Typically, cloud providers create and evolve these plug-ins to make them available to everyone, to ease the consumption of their services.

The providers block in the configuration has a big impact on the rest of the configuration. When you reference a provider in the Terraform file, you get access to the related resources. Also, note that you can have multiple providers in the same Terraform configuration. This will be the case when multiple cloud environments are provisioned from the same configuration file.

With this initial setup, you have written the foundations of your configuration. However, during the initial *write* stage, there is always the chance for a syntax error. Even though the configuration is correct, you will learn next how to discover errors during this early stage.

Validating the Terraform syntax

To check the correctness of the Terraform configuration syntax, Terraform offers the `validate` command, which explores your configuration files, checking for inconsistent definitions. For instance, if in Example 12-52 you remove the ending curly brace in the last line and execute the `terraform validation` command, you will see an error and the reason for it:

```
$ terraform validate
│
│ Error: Unclosed configuration block
│
│   on create_vpc.tf line 11, in provider "aws":
│   11: provider "aws" {
│
│ There is no closing brace for this block before the end of the file. This
│ may be caused by incorrect brace nesting elsewhere in this file.
```

Now, if you put the curly brace back in, your code will have the correct syntax. However, if you execute `terraform validate` again, you will find an unexpected error. The configuration requires a Terraform provider that it is not yet available:

```
$ terraform validate
│
│ Error: Missing required provider
│
│ This configuration requires provider registry.terraform.io/hashicorp/aws,
│ but that provider isn't available. You may be able to install it
│ automatically by running:
│   terraform init
│
```

You receive this error because, in the configuration, you pointed to a provider from the registry—but not one locally available. Solving this validation error is the point of the next stage in the Terraform workflow, the *init*.

Initializing the Terraform environment

In the configuration, you have defined the Terraform provider to use, but this just provides the intent; you have not yet made it available locally. You can compare this to using a Python library: to run the code, it's not enough to *import* the library. You need to install the library locally to make it available to the interpreter.

Example 12-53 installs Terraform providers by running the `terraform init` command, which reads the configuration defined under the `required_providers` nested block and downloads all the necessary dependencies.

Example 12-53. Initializing the Terraform configuration

```
$ terraform init

Initializing the backend...                                                ❶

Initializing provider plugins...
- Finding hashicorp/aws versions matching "~> 3.0"...                       ❷
- Installing hashicorp/aws v3.75.2...
- Installed hashicorp/aws v3.75.2 (signed by HashiCorp)

Terraform has created a lock file .terraform.lock.hcl to record the provider ❸
selections it made above. Include this file in your version control repository
so that Terraform can guarantee to make the same selections by default when
you run "terraform init" in the future.

Terraform has been successfully initialized!
# some output trimmed
```

❶ The backend has been initialized. The *backend*, in Terraform, is the place to store the Terraform `State`, which you will learn more about later. By default, if not defined differently, it is the local directory from where you run Terraform commands.

❷ The Terraform provider plug-in, `hashicorp/aws`, has been found and installed using the version specified.

❸ A lock file, *.terraform.lock.hcl*, has been created to lock the pinned version of the plug-in.

 Pinning Terraform provider versions ensures the behavior of subsequent Terraform runs. Without pinning, the provider version could change when a newer one is available and still compatible with the definition (in the example, we get version 3.75.2, compatible with 3.*), and with it the actual outcome of our Terraform configuration.

You can check all the changes mentioned in the output, listing the files and folders in the local directory, including the hidden ones:

```
$ tree -la
.
├── .terraform
│   └── providers
│       └── registry.terraform.io
│           └── hashicorp
│               └── aws
│                   └── 3.75.2
│                       └── darwin_amd64
│                           └── terraform-provider-aws_v3.75.2_x5
├── .terraform.lock.hcl
└── create_vpc.tf
```

You can see the initial Terraform configuration file, which we named *create_vpc.tf*, and the versioning lock file *.terraform.lock.hcl*. Then, within the *.terraform* directory, the provider that has been installed locally uses version 3.75.2.

After initializing the environment, according to the Terraform configuration, you are in a good spot to get a successful validation, so let's check it:

```
$ terraform validate
Success! The configuration is valid.
```

Nice! You have a valid Terraform configuration, properly initialized. So, you are ready to jump into the next Terraform workflow stage, the *plan*.

Getting insights into Terraform changes

The `terraform plan` command checks whether the desired state of the infrastructure, described in our Terraform configuration, matches the actual state.

Even though you have not already defined the configuration for the Amazon VPC, you can try the command, to validate the proper access to the target infrastructure provider API:

```
$ terraform plan

No changes. Your infrastructure matches the configuration.

Terraform has compared your real infrastructure against your configuration and
found no differences, so no changes are needed.
```

As expected, no changes are required. This is due to having a Terraform configuration that defines only the Terraform provider to use but not any infrastructure element to provision, and that has no reference state. You will learn about the Terraform state later.

However, `terraform plan` is giving you an important implicit validation. Terraform connects to the target infrastructure provider API, and this connection requires proper authentication. So, running `terraform plan` successfully is, at least, validating that you have access to the platform.

In the example, we have not explicitly provided any authentication credentials to the provider configuration block. This is because the AWS Terraform provider implicitly uses the same authentication used by the AWS CLI, which we initialized in Example 12-51.

At this point, you are ready to start defining the infrastructure. So, the next concept to introduce is the Terraform resource. A *resource* defines an object that you are declaring *should* exist in the target infrastructure. It is defined using the resource Terraform block type and the syntax used in Example 12-54.

Example 12-54. Terraform resource definition

```
resource resource_name resource_identifier { ❶ ❷
  ...
}
```

❶ Name of the resource as defined in the Terraform provider, which should be properly initialized. Its usage should be detailed in the provider documentation, explaining all the available arguments.

❷ Identifier of this resource in the Terraform configuration, so we can reference this specific resource later.

To create the Amazon VPC, you write a new resource block of type aws_vpc and an identifier—for instance, my_vpc. From the multiple arguments available, let's define the cidr_block, because it's the only one mandatory. As noted previously, for simplicity, you can use the same file where the provider is configured:

```
...
# Create a VPC
resource "aws_vpc" "my_vpc" {
  cidr_block = "192.0.2.0/24"
}
```

Looks simple, no? To create an Amazon VPC, using the Terraform declarative approach, you define its final state with only one parameter! This is possible because of hiding the low-level details and exposing only the key attributes necessary to define the final state of the infrastructure service.

Now, the Terraform configuration contains the *intent* to have an Amazon VPC. Thus, it's time to run terraform plan again in Example 12-55 and check the outcome of its execution. In this output, you can observe the expected changes in the infrastructure due to applying this configuration.

Example 12-55. terraform plan with changes

```
$ terraform plan

Terraform used the selected providers to generate the following execution plan.
Resource actions are indicated with the following symbols:
  + create

Terraform will perform the following actions:

  # aws_vpc.my_vpc will be created
  + resource "aws_vpc" "my_vpc" {                                ❶
      + arn                                   = (known after apply) ❷
      + cidr_block                            = "192.0.2.0/24"
      + default_network_acl_id                = (known after apply)
      + default_route_table_id                = (known after apply)
      + default_security_group_id             = (known after apply)
      + dhcp_options_id                       = (known after apply)
      + enable_classiclink                    = (known after apply)
      + enable_classiclink_dns_support        = (known after apply)
      + enable_dns_hostnames                  = (known after apply)
      + enable_dns_support                    = true                ❸
      + id                                    = (known after apply)
      + instance_tenancy                      = "default"
      + ipv6_association_id                   = (known after apply)
      + ipv6_cidr_block                       = (known after apply)
      + ipv6_cidr_block_network_border_group  = (known after apply)
      + main_route_table_id                   = (known after apply)
      + owner_id                              = (known after apply)
      + tags_all                              = (known after apply)
    }

Plan: 1 to add, 0 to change, 0 to destroy.                         ❹
```

_____

```
Note: You didn't use the -out option to save this plan, so Terraform can't
guarantee to take exactly these actions if you run "terraform apply" now.
```

❶ The list contains all the arguments supported by this resource in the Terraform provider implementation.

❷ Several attributes are set to known after apply. This is because these values are not known until the resource is created. For instance, the value generated to identify the object in AWS, named arn, is available only after it's created; we're only planning at this point.

❸ Remember that we provided only the cidr_block but, in this output, you can see other attributes taking a default value, such as enable_dns_support with the default value true.

❹ When we apply this Terraform configuration with the current target infrastructure state, a new resource, defined as `aws_vpc`, will be added.

The *plan* step is really useful to understand what is going to change, before actually changing the infrastructure state. This step can give you good insight into the impact of the configuration so you can take the necessary actions to adapt it to your real intent. However, as the last `Note` in the plan output suggests, it can't guarantee that the state of the target infrastructure will be exactly the same when you move to the next step, *apply*. This is the reason that when you run `terraform apply`, you are implicitly running a `terraform plan` before, and a manual confirmation is, by default, requested.

However, you can skip the manual confirmation when *applying* if you use, as a reference, the output of a plan generated using the option `-out` *name_of_plan*. This output reference skips the prompt to confirm because it has a reference, to understand whether the plan output is the expected one and proceed, or a different one and abort. Example 12-56 shows how to use `-out`.

Example 12-56. `terraform plan` using `-out`

```
$ terraform plan -out my_plan
# output trimmed, same as above

Saved the plan to: my_plan

To perform exactly these actions, run the following command to apply:
    terraform apply "my_plan"
```

The result of the `-out` option is a binary file created in the Terraform backend—in our case, the local directory. It contains all the information needed to compare against another plan output later.

Now, understanding the role of the plan in the Terraform workflow, you can move to the next step, *apply*, which will, finally, provision the dynamic infrastructure in the target platform.

Applying the Terraform configuration

Managing the dynamic infrastructure state is the main purpose of Terraform: moving from a configuration written in a declarative approach to actual infrastructure services provisioned in the cloud platform. The Terraform command for this purpose is `terraform apply`. This command runs a plan before, showing what would change, and then prompts for a manual confirmation, which you will decline for now by answering "No" to the prompt:

```
$ terraform apply
# output trimmed, similar to plan

Plan: 1 to add, 0 to change, 0 to destroy.

Do you want to perform these actions?
  Terraform will perform the actions described above.
  Only 'yes' will be accepted to approve.
```

As expected, the output of the plan is the same as that from `terraform plan`. Because we have not provided a reference plan, we are prompted for manual approval. This works fine for development, but when automating Terraform, you will want to skip the user interaction—and that's where the reference plan you created in Example 12-56 comes in. Now, you can use the `my_plan` reference in the `terraform apply` command to skip the output of the plan, and be able to compare the current planned output with the previously generated output. If both plans match, the `apply` action is executed (Example 12-57).

Example 12-57. `terraform apply` with a plan reference

```
$ terraform apply "my_plan"
aws_vpc.my_vpc: Creating...
aws_vpc.my_vpc: Creation complete after 3s [id=vpc-04f21f46af099b516]

Apply complete! Resources: 1 added, 0 changed, 0 destroyed.
```

Voilà! You've created your first resource via Terraform, an Amazon VPC! At least, this is what Terraform says in its output. You can see the AWS identifier for the new resource, the `id`. Using this `id`, you can verify that the infrastructure service has been created in the AWS cloud platform.

In Example 12-58, we use the `aws ec2 describe-vpcs` CLI command, specifying the VPC `id` from the previous output and the `region` to look for. The `region` is the only argument we specified in the `aws` provider configuration, and it's a concept in AWS used to create isolated infrastructure domains behind the same API interface.

Example 12-58. Verifying the creation of the Amazon VPC

```
$ aws ec2 describe-vpcs --region eu-west-3 --vpc-ids vpc-04f21f46af099b516
{
    "Vpcs": [
        {
            "CidrBlock": "192.0.2.0/24",
            "DhcpOptionsId": "dopt-4f17a126",
            "State": "available",
            "VpcId": "vpc-04f21f46af099b516",
            "OwnerId": "123456789012",
            "InstanceTenancy": "default",
            "CidrBlockAssociationSet": [
```

```
        {
            "AssociationId": "vpc-cidr-assoc-04285027d194e35c3",
            "CidrBlock": "192.0.2.0/24",
            "CidrBlockState": {
                "State": "associated"
            }
        }
    ],
    "IsDefault": false
    }
]
}
```

From the AWS CLI command output information, you can see the proper IP prefix in place, as well as other information not specified in the configuration. Especially noticeable are the references to other objects, such as DhcpOptionsId and CidrBlock AssociationSet. These are other infrastructure objects required by the VPC, but this was abstracted by the AWS API and not explicitly defined.

You can also check that now, after the applying step, the Terraform configuration is fully in sync with the target infrastructure. You can validate this by running terraform plan again and discovering that No changes are pending:

```
$ terraform plan
aws_vpc.my_vpc: Refreshing state... [id=vpc-04f21f46af099b516]

No changes. Your infrastructure matches the configuration.

Terraform has compared your real infrastructure against your configuration and
  found no differences, so no changes are needed.
```

You might notice something relevant in this output. The conclusion of no changes comes after reviewing the state. An important component in Terraform architecture, the Terraform state keeps track of the relationship between its configuration and the actual infrastructure, and this is our next topic.

Understanding Terraform state

The *Terraform state* is a mapping between the Terraform configuration and the real-world resources created from it. This information helps Terraform understand the resources it is managing, without impacting other resources that may be running in the remote infrastructure that could have been created via GUI, API, or from another Terraform configuration.

The Terraform state is stored in the *terraform.tfstate* file using a custom JSON format. This file contains metadata. The resources key, a list of all the resources managed by Terraform, is especially relevant. This list includes not only created resources but also others that may have been imported, as you will see later. The bindings between the real objects and the resources defined in the configuration are done via both identifiers, the Terraform and the remote infrastructure ones.

In the `resource` configuration, you used two identifiers for the Amazon VPC, the resource type and the name: `resource "aws_vpc" "my_vpc"`. These identifiers are two keys in the `resource` dictionary, and under the `instances` key, we find the reference to the actual infrastructure object created in AWS, with its own `id`:

```
# some output trimmed
{
  "resources": [
    {
      "mode": "managed",
      "type": "aws_vpc",
      "name": "my_vpc",
      "provider": "provider[\"registry.terraform.io/hashicorp/aws\"]",
      "instances": [
        {
          "attributes": {
            "id": "vpc-04f21f46af099b516",
  ...
```

As you can imagine, this state is a onetime picture of the infrastructure. Terraform can't rely 100% on it, because since it was generated, the actual state could have changed for many reasons. So, before every Terraform operation, *plan* or *apply*, a `refresh` step is executed, updating the state before running. You can also validate the state with the sole `terraform refresh` command, which will check for any difference between the actual infrastructure and the backend state:

```
$ terraform refresh
aws_vpc.my_vpc: Refreshing state... [id=vpc-04f21f46af099b516]
```

Without a state reference, as happens when you do the first apply, Terraform doesn't have any reference mapping between its configuration and the infrastructure state, so it will try to provision all the resources. You can test this behavior by running `terraform apply` twice, removing the state between the apply commands. You will end up with two resources with a duplicated configuration. With this simple exercise, you can understand how critical it is to ensure the Terraform state integrity, so the state reflects the changes that the Terraform configuration has done in the infrastructure provider.

But integrity is not enough. You also need to make the state available for all the potential Terraform actors that could intervene in the workflow execution. In production environments—for instance, during a pipeline execution that would spin up a process in a virtual server or container—it's common practice to run Terraform from different places. These different actors need to share access to the same state, so both know about the other changes.

However, providing availability and integrity at the same time is difficult. Let's imagine that two Terraform processes, sharing the same state, want to update it. This puts the integrity of the state at risk. Luckily, Terraform offers a locking mechanism to avoid potential race conditions. In the local environment, when you run a Terraform command, it *locks* the file, so other concurrent processes will complain about locking if trying to update the state.

Finally, the other key aspect of the Terraform state is security. State files are stored in plain text. But this file can include resources storing sensitive data—for instance, a database user and password. We should consider protecting the state, via encryption, in transit and in rest.

One common approach when starting with Terraform is to store the state in a version control system (e.g., Git), together with the Terraform configuration. This provides some level of availability. However, this is not a recommended option because it doesn't grant integrity and security.

To solve all these requirements together, Terraform introduces the concept of *backends* to store its state. A Terraform backend can be implemented in multiple ways, using distributed systems that offer availability with locking mechanisms, and encryption in transit and at rest. The default backend is the local directory, and it's the one you have been using in this book. Many other options are available, but we don't cover them in detail here. Check the Terraform documentation (*https://oreil.ly/UIeKO*) for detailed information.

Even still, despite taking all the precautions, you could lose the Terraform state of your configuration. However, even in that case, not everything would be lost for our infrastructure. Terraform offers a remediation option: the import command.

Remediating Terraform state

If you have lost your Terraform state or start managing an infrastructure that was provisioned outside your Terraform configuration, you can re-create the state mapping between the configuration and the real infrastructure.

The terraform import command serves to *connect*, via a mapping in the state, a real infrastructure object and a Terraform resource. The logic necessary to establish this mapping is also specific for each provider.

Following our example, you could have provisioned the Amazon VPC and then lost or removed the state. To reimport the state, you need to know only both identifiers, the infrastructure and Terraform. In the Amazon VPC example, on one side we have the VPC id, and on the other the resource with the *type* and the configuration *identifier*:

```
terraform import aws_vpc.my_vpc vpc-04f21f46af099b516
aws_vpc.my_vpc: Importing from ID "vpc-04f21f46af099b516"...
aws_vpc.my_vpc: Import prepared!
  Prepared aws_vpc for import
aws_vpc.my_vpc: Refreshing state... [id=vpc-04f21f46af099b516]

Import successful!
```

> The resources that were imported are shown above. These resources are now in
> your Terraform state and will henceforth be managed by Terraform.

After running `terraform import`, you can see how the state file has been created,
or updated, accordingly. Then you can continue managing this resource from Terraform, as it was created by Terraform itself.

To complete the infrastructure management lifecycle, after provisioning, there will
be deprovisioning. The dynamic infrastructure has, because of its nature, a shorter
lifecycle than the traditional one, and the last Terraform workflow stage is for this.

Cleaning up infrastructure with Terraform

In the same way that you use Terraform to provision new infrastructure services,
you can also use it to deprovision them when they're no longer relevant. This is a
common practice in dynamic infrastructure environments, where you pay as you use
the infrastructure. Terraform provides a destroy command to help you to clean up
your infrastructure.

> To keep your costs down, always clean up your infrastructure when
> not using it. You will always be able to re-create it, in the very
> same state, later, when you need it. Obviously, if you need data
> persistence, keep the data well-preserved in another place where
> you can get it later.

The `terraform destroy` command is the antagonist to `terraform apply`. As in
the provisioning flow, you can also use the plan command before actually changing
things, with `-destroy`, as shown in Example 12-59.

Example 12-59. Terraform destroy plan

```
$ terraform plan -destroy -out destroy_my_plan
aws_vpc.my_vpc: Refreshing state... [id=vpc-04f21f46af099b516]

Terraform used the selected providers to generate the following execution plan.
Resource actions are indicated with the following symbols:
  - destroy

Terraform will perform the following actions:

  # aws_vpc.my_vpc will be destroyed
  - resource "aws_vpc" "my_vpc" { ❶
    - arn                              =
      "arn:aws:ec2:eu-west-3:1:vpc/vpc-04f21f46af099b516" -> null
    - assign_generated_ipv6_cidr_block = false -> null
    - cidr_block                       = "192.0.2.0/24" -> null
    - default_network_acl_id           = "acl-03c818f415777e9c3" -> null
    - default_route_table_id           = "rtb-06b8f1263d440dfaa" -> null
```

```
    - default_security_group_id     = "sg-08378207f8f073a85" -> null
    - dhcp_options_id                = "dopt-4f17a126" -> null
    - enable_classiclink             = false -> null
    - enable_classiclink_dns_support = false -> null
    - enable_dns_hostnames           = false -> null
    - enable_dns_support             = true -> null
    - id                             = "vpc-04f21f46af099b516" -> null
    - instance_tenancy               = "default" -> null
    - ipv6_netmask_length            = 0 -> null
    - main_route_table_id            = "rtb-06b8f1263d440dfaa" -> null
    - owner_id                       = "1" -> null
    - tags                           = {} -> null
    - tags_all                       = {} -> null
  }

Plan: 0 to add, 0 to change, 1 to destroy.
```

```
Saved the plan to: destroy_my_plan

To perform exactly these actions, run the following command to apply:
    terraform apply "destroy_my_plan"
```

❶ All the lines with the hyphen (-), at the resource and attribute level, mean that they will be removed.

To execute the destroy action, you run `terraform apply -destroy`, which then creates a plan to destroy and asks for manual approval. But, as you did before when provisioning, you can use a plan reference taken from the `-out` option, and skip the approval for the destroy command:

```
$ terraform apply "destroy_my_plan"
aws_vpc.my_vpc: Destroying... [id=vpc-04f21f46af099b516]
aws_vpc.my_vpc: Destruction complete after 0s

Apply complete! Resources: 0 added, 0 changed, 1 destroyed.
```

After this, even though you still have a *terraform.tfstate* file, it has no `resources`. Terraform has removed the remote infrastructure, the state references to it, and the Terraform configuration.

> The command `terraform destroy` is a convenience alias for `terra form apply -destroy`. However, you can't use `terraform destroy` together with the `-out` option, which we recommend, so we opt to use `apply` in both cases.

To be sure that the infrastructure is deprovisioned, you can use `aws ec2 describe-vpcs` as before, and check that the Amazon VPC is no longer present:

```
$ aws ec2 describe-vpcs --region eu-west-3 --vpc-ids vpc-04f21f46af099b516

An error occurred (InvalidVpcID.NotFound) when calling the DescribeVpcs
operation: The vpc ID 'vpc-04f21f46af099b516' does not exist
```

 Terraform doesn't automatically destroy infrastructure. When you're done playing with this chapter, don't forget to run the destroy command at the end so you don't get a surprise bill.

After working on the Amazon VPC example, you should understand the basics of Terraform and its workflow. Now it's time to go further with our scenario, adding the subnets, while learning how to extend Terraform resource usage.

Extending Terraform Execution

This Terraform section continues our journey through the scenario introduced in Figure 12-5, adding two Amazon subnets within the previously created VPC. In this process, you will discover new functionalities of Terraform and learn how to use them to support advanced infrastructure designs.

The first step is to *connect* infrastructure elements—for instance, the Amazon VPC and a subnet.

Adding resource dependencies

To create a new Terraform resource, you simply add a new configuration snippet by using a new AWS provider resource type, aws_subnet. Notice you will start creating only *one* subnet (my_subnet_1), not the *two* you will get at the end of this subsection.

For the aws_subnet resource type, you provide two required arguments cidr_block and vpc_id. The cidr_block argument is another IP prefix, a subprefix (192.0.2.0/25) of the cidr_block used for the VPC before (192.0.2.0/24). The other one, vpc_id, is a reference to another Terraform resource. To create Terraform configuration references, you use the syntax resource_type.resource_name.attribute. This syntax works for Terraform resources, but also for any other Terraform object, such as variables, as you will discover later.

 To keep examples self-contained, you can copy the previous configuration file to a new directory (for instance, *2-create-vpc-and-subnet*) and then add the new resource there.

The new resource configuration snippet in Example 12-60 looks similar to the previous one, with the special reference to the VPC resource.

Example 12-60. Creating an AWS subnet

```
...
# Create a Subnet
resource "aws_subnet" "my_subnet_1" {
  vpc_id    = aws_vpc.my_vpc.id ❶
  cidr_block = "192.0.2.0/25"
}
```

❶ The id is a special attribute from the aws_vpc resource. Its value can't be known before its provisioning, as it is computed by AWS when the object is created. However, in Terraform, we can reference attributes that will be eventually available and establish a dependency between these two resources. With this configuration, we implicitly say that the subnet needs the VPC before it can be created.

 Sometimes, hidden dependencies exist that Terraform cannot automatically infer—for instance, when a Terraform resource depends on another but is not using any of its attributes. For this case, Terraform offers a depends_on meta-argument to list the dependencies that Terraform will take care of establishing in the proper provisioning order.

Now, in this new folder, you initialize Terraform again with terraform init (remember, the context depends on the folder where you run the Terraform commands), and you will be ready to test the new configuration with terraform plan. In Example 12-61, having no state yet in this directory, you will see the same output as in Example 12-55, plus the subnet part.

Example 12-61. Planning the VPC and subnet provisioning

```
$ terraform plan -out vpc_and_subnet
  # aws_subnet.my_subnet_1 will be created
  + resource "aws_subnet" "my_subnet_1" {
      + arn                                            = (known after apply)
      + assign_ipv6_address_on_creation                = false
      + availability_zone                              = (known after apply)
      + availability_zone_id                           = (known after apply)
      + cidr_block                                     = "192.0.1.0/25"
      + enable_dns64                                   = false
      + enable_resource_name_dns_a_record_on_launch    = false
      + enable_resource_name_dns_aaaa_record_on_launch = false
      + id                                             = (known after apply)
      + ipv6_cidr_block_association_id                 = (known after apply)
      + ipv6_native                                    = false
```

```
    + map_public_ip_on_launch                   = false
    + owner_id                                   = (known after apply)
    + private_dns_hostname_type_on_launch        = (known after apply)
    + tags_all                                   = (known after apply)
    + vpc_id                                      = (known after apply)
  }

# trimmed output for the aws_vpc.my_vpc part
```

The plan output looks as expected, as you can see two objects ready to be created: the VPC and the subnet. As noted previously, the vpc_id attribute from the subnet, taken from the VPC id, is not known during the plan but will be automatically populated during the apply execution.

This configuration would provision the desired VPC and subnet in AWS. However, instead of applying it straightaway, let's hold on for a moment and focus on understanding an important aspect of any programming language: how to handle wrong data input.

Handling data validation

Even though the Terraform configuration syntax may look good, and terraform validate might not complain, sometimes the value of the arguments you are using may be not consistent with the real expectations of the infrastructure platform.

An example case is using a value that is not complying with the data validation defined in the provider definition for a specific argument. For instance, when setting the value of cidr_block, you can't use a nonvalid IP prefix, such as abcd, because the schema validation and the terraform plan execution would catch it. Notice that the validation is not simply by the value type, string, but takes into account other extra validation:

```
$ terraform plan
|
| Error: "abcd" is not a valid CIDR block: invalid CIDR address: abcd
|
|   with aws_subnet.my_subnet_1,
|   on create_vpc_and_subnet.tf line 23, in resource "aws_subnet" "my_subnet_1":
|   23:   cidr_block = "abcd"
```

 You will learn about defining your custom validation for Terraform *variables* later in this section.

However, in some cases, even though the data passes the schema validation, it doesn't actually make sense for the target infrastructure implementation. Following the same cidr_block example, if you set a proper IP prefix, but it does not belong to the parent

VPC prefix, the Terraform validation (using the provider rules) will succeed but will raise a validation issue when Terraform tries to apply the changes:

```
...
# Create a Subnet
resource "aws_subnet" "my_subnet_1" {
  vpc_id    = aws_vpc.my_vpc.id
  cidr_block = "198.51.100.0/24"
}
```

You, as network engineer, can spot that this configuration is inconsistent, because the reference VPC has the prefix `192.0.2.0/24`, and you are using a CIDR value that's not part of this reference prefix. However, this "advanced" data validation is not coded in the Terraform provider and is left to the cloud provider API backend. Thus, Terraform won't detect any issues when validating this plan.

If you run `terraform plan` again, the output will look exactly the same as in Example 12-61, except for the subnet `cidr_block` value. Terraform considers that this plan makes sense and can't spot the issue.

However, as expected, if you try `terraform apply` after the plan, the validation will complain, as shown in Example 12-62.

Example 12-62. Using an inconsistent subnet prefix

```
$ terraform apply "vpc_and_subnet"
aws_vpc.my_vpc: Creating...
aws_vpc.my_vpc: Creation complete after 2s [id=vpc-0c6fa4fb8c521970c]
aws_subnet.my_subnet_1: Creating...
|
| Error: error creating EC2 Subnet: InvalidSubnet.Range: The CIDR ❶
|       '198.51.100.0/24' is invalid.
|       status code: 400, request id: 80d332ce-c5fa-4e17-bfa0-055a98dcdf8f
|
|   with aws_subnet.my_subnet_1,
|   on create_vpc_and_subnet.tf line 21, in resource "aws_subnet" "my_subnet_1":
|   21: resource "aws_subnet" "my_subnet_1" {
```

❶ The AWS API complains with the error `InvalidSubnet.Range`. It was not possible to apply this configuration, even though it looked good in the eyes of Terraform. This should make us aware that simply having a successful Terraform plan is not a guarantee for successful provisioning.

Furthermore, this error in the Terraform execution reveals another important behavior of Terraform execution. Even though an error is raised in the subnet creation step, Terraform creates the VPC in the first step, and this is not undone. Terraform execution is *not atomic*: it is a sequential execution of declarative tasks, and an issue in one task stops the execution, but the actions executed are not rolled back. You can check that an Amazon VPC is created by following Example 12-58, matching the VPC ID from the apply output, or checking the content of the *terraform.tfstate* file.

 We strongly recommend using development environments to help you to test the Terraform configuration in apply mode, before actually running the code in the production environment.

To solve the data consistency issue and other data transformation problems, you will learn about Terraform functions next.

Using Terraform functions

The Terraform language comes with built-in functions you can use in your configuration, within expressions or to manipulate values. We do not cover all the Terraform functions, but you will learn about one to understand how you can leverage them.

In our example, it would be convenient to calculate the subnet CIDR from the VPC one. This would reduce the chances of using the wrong one and would reduce the amount of user data required. Luckily, Terraform has the cidrsubnet() function to calculate prefixes from a parent. The function's syntax is cidrsubnet(*prefix, newbits, netnum*), where *prefix* is the referenced prefix, *newbits* is the number of mask bits taken for the subprefixes, and *netnum* is an index on the resulting prefixes list.

To see how a function works, you will use an interesting Terraform tool: its interactive console. You can access it with terraform console and experiment with Terraform expressions before using it in the static Terraform configuration:

```
$ terraform console
>
```

Once in the console, you can play with the cidrsubnet() function. For instance, in Example 12-60, we decided to use the prefix mask /25, so take 1 bit from the parent prefix mask, /24. Translating this to the cidrsubnet() argument, we set the original prefix as the *prefix* and 1 for the *newbits*. Finally, in Example 12-63, playing with the *netnum* index, you will get the different prefixes.

Example 12-63. Getting subnet prefixes with cidrsubnet()

```
> cidrsubnet("192.0.2.0/24", 1, 0)
"192.0.2.0/25"
> cidrsubnet("192.0.2.0/24", 1, 1)
"192.0.2.128/25"
```

The function raises an error when the usage is not appropriate. For example, using only 1 bit for subnetting produces only two child prefixes, so you can't access a third item, index 2:

```
> cidrsubnet("192.0.2.0/24", 1, 2)

| Error: Error in function call
|
|   on <console-input> line 1:
|   (source code not available)
|
| Call to function "cidrsubnet" failed: prefix extension of 1 does not
| accommodate a subnet numbered 2.
|
```

 Terraform does not support user-defined functions (at the time of writing), so only built-in functions are available. You can check the function documentation (*https://oreil.ly/vbUgV*) to get a detailed list of all the available ones and how to use them. Knowing some of the most common Terraform functions will help you develop better and simpler Terraform configurations.

Now, it is time to use the cidrsubnet() function in the Terraform configuration. You call the function with the my_vpc resource and its cidr_block (this value matches the *prefix* argument from the function signature). In this case, the value is manually defined, but the same would apply to data available only during provisioning time:

```
...
# Create a Subnet
resource "aws_subnet" "my_subnet_1" {
  vpc_id    = aws_vpc.my_vpc.id
  cidr_block = cidrsubnet(aws_vpc.my_vpc.cidr_block, 1, 0)
}
```

Finally, in Example 12-64, you are ready to validate the function applying the Terraform configuration to create one AWS subnet.

Example 12-64. Creating an AWS subnet

```
$ terraform apply
aws_vpc.my_vpc: Refreshing state... [id=vpc-0c6fa4fb8c521970c]

Terraform used the selected providers to generate the following execution plan.
Resource actions are indicated with the following symbols:
  + create

Terraform will perform the following actions:

  # aws_subnet.my_subnet_1 will be created
  + resource "aws_subnet" "my_subnet_1" {
```

```
    + arn                                                   = (known after apply)
    + assign_ipv6_address_on_creation                       = false
    + availability_zone                                     = (known after apply)
    + availability_zone_id                                  = (known after apply)
    + cidr_block                                            = "192.0.2.0/25"            ❶
    + enable_dns64                                          = false
    + enable_resource_name_dns_a_record_on_launch           = false
    + enable_resource_name_dns_aaaa_record_on_launch        = false
    + id                                                    = (known after apply)
    + ipv6_cidr_block_association_id                        = (known after apply)
    + ipv6_native                                           = false
    + map_public_ip_on_launch                               = false
    + owner_id                                              = (known after apply)
    + private_dns_hostname_type_on_launch                   = (known after apply)
    + tags_all                                              = (known after apply)
    + vpc_id                                                = "vpc-0c6fa4fb8c521970c"  ❷
  }

Plan: 1 to add, 0 to change, 0 to destroy.

# some output omitted

aws_subnet.my_subnet_1: Creating...
aws_subnet.my_subnet_1: Creation complete after 6s [id=subnet-0502b7df8a948edda]

Apply complete! Resources: 1 added, 0 changed, 0 destroyed.
```

❶ The `cidrsubnet()` function generates the expected prefix, as you can see in the approved plan, and the subnet is finally created.

❷ In this output, the `vpc_id` is already available. This is because of the partial creation in Example 12-62.

As you did in Example 12-58 to check the Amazon VPC status, in Example 12-65 you check the status of the subnet in the target infrastructure with `aws ec2 describe-subnets`.

Example 12-65. Validating the AWS subnet status

```
$ aws ec2 describe-subnets --region eu-west-3 --subnet-ids subnet-0502b7df8a948edda
{
    "Subnets": [
        {
            "AvailabilityZone": "eu-west-3b",
            "AvailabilityZoneId": "euw3-az2",
            "AvailableIpAddressCount": 123,
            "CidrBlock": "192.0.2.0/25",
            "State": "available",
            "SubnetId": "subnet-0502b7df8a948edda",
            "VpcId": "vpc-0c6fa4fb8c521970c",
            # omitted output for brevity
        }
```

```
    ]
}
```

You have created one Amazon subnet but our example scenario has two subnets. One simple way to create the second one is to add another resource block with the new subnet definition and use another prefix. You simply use a different identifier, my_subnet_2, and instead of using the index 0 for cidrsubnet(), you choose the 1:

```
resource "aws_subnet" "my_subnet_2" {
    vpc_id    = aws_vpc.my_vpc.id
    cidr_block = cidrsubnet(aws_vpc.my_vpc.cidr_block, 1, 1)
}
```

However, one of the key principles when writing code is DRY. And, if you compare this configuration snippet with the one used before, you can see a lot of repeated code. Programming languages offer various functionalities to help you with the DRY principle. And Terraform is no exception. Let's find out how Terraform helps you create multiple resources in only one resource block.

Creating multiple resources in a loop

The most common approach for running code multiple times is *looping*. Terraform offers several options to implement loops: count, for loop, and for_each. Each has different use cases. In this case, where you don't have any data to iterate over, the simplest approach is to use count to iterate over a range:

```
resource "aws_subnet" "my_subnets" {
    count     = 2
    vpc_id    = aws_vpc.my_vpc.id
    cidr_block = cidrsubnet(aws_vpc.my_vpc.cidr_block, 1, count.index)
}
```

The count meta-argument takes an integer to define how many elements of a block type will be created. Then it leverages count.index to select the proper prefix in cidrsubnet(). Neat and simple. In Example 12-66, we apply this configuration to create two subnets.

Example 12-66. Creating a VPC and two subnets with Terraform

```
$ terraform apply

# omitted validation output

aws_vpc.my_vpc: Creating...
aws_vpc.my_vpc: Creation complete after 3s [id=vpc-0b3c91f2bf747a857]        ❶
aws_subnet.my_subnets[0]: Creating...                                        ❷
aws_subnet.my_subnets[1]: Creating...
aws_subnet.my_subnets[1]: Creation complete after 1s [id=subnet-09616706925ea65e2] ❶
aws_subnet.my_subnets[0]: Creation complete after 1s [id=subnet-016160ea148e1e0de] ❶
```

```
Apply complete! Resources: 3 added, 0 changed, 0 destroyed.
```

❶ Three infrastructure objects are provisioned with their identifiers.

❷ The my_subnets resource block is now a *list*, containing two infrastructure elements.

 The output of your execution and the examples provided could differ because of the actual state in each case. You can always start from a blank state by destroying the previous infrastructure.

You have reached the desired scenario output! The network design is now described as IaC, using Terraform configuration. Now you can easily tear up and down this infrastructure at any time, with terraform apply and destroy. Take a second to think about how easy (and fast) it is for you to manage your dynamic infrastructure while keeping a consistent approach.

However, your Terraform journey doesn't end here. You have learned the basics, but using Terraform in real environments still requires mastering a few more concepts.

Managing Terraform at Scale

When you use Terraform in real production environments, you will face challenges that require advanced Terraform concepts. In this section, you will tackle some of them, starting with a common problem: how to deal with dependencies on infrastructure that you don't directly manage.

Using data sources to get data from nonmanaged infrastructure

So far, you have managed a self-contained infrastructure. Your Terraform configuration contains the definition of all the resources required. You don't have any dependencies on other objects that are not configured in the Terraform configuration. However, this is not always the reality. For instance, some companies have teams managing shared infrastructure services that others teams depend on.

Terraform *data sources* allow you to import information from the target infrastructure, even those not managed by the present Terraform configuration. Maybe these resources were provisioned by another Terraform plan or, directly, via API or GUI. Data sources are defined in the providers, like the resources, and use a different block type, data.

In our example, let's imagine that Team A manages the VPCs and Team B the subnets. If you put yourself in the shoes of Team B, you have the challenge to solve in the subnet configuration: how could you know about the vpc_id and cidr_block, from the Amazon VPC?

Example 12-67 shows how to use the data block. You can reference an object in the target infrastructure, and then use this reference in the rest of the configuration. The information will be retrieved in the *refresh* step when running Terraform.

Example 12-67. Terraform data source for an Amazon VPC

```
# provider configuration omitted

data "aws_vpc" "my_vpc" {
  id = "vpc-0da120f2568c06c33"
}

# Create two subnets
resource "aws_subnet" "my_subnets" {
  count      = 2
  vpc_id     = data.aws_vpc.my_vpc.id
  cidr_block = cidrsubnet(data.aws_vpc.my_vpc.cidr_block, 1, count.index)
}
```

Note that in the data block you need arguments to identify the target VPC so Terraform can import the related information. Our example uses the resource identifier (id), but each provider implementation could use a different argument (or multiple). For instance, a common practice when referencing objects, without knowing their identifiers, is to use metadata, such as labels or tags.

In this example, you use the aws_vpc data resource to get data from a VPC previously created. You could create a standalone VPC via Terraform, as you did in Example 12-57. Then, in another directory (for instance, 3-use-data), you can add this configuration snippet with the proper VPC id. Once you have defined the data source, you can use its reference, prepending data (data.aws_vpc.my_vpc.id).

When using references in Terraform, you add a prefix with the type of the object. This is true except for resources, which is implicit.

```
$ terraform apply
data.aws_vpc.my_vpc: Reading...
data.aws_vpc.my_vpc: Read complete after 1s [id=vpc-0da120f2568c06c33]

# omitted the rest of the plan

aws_subnet.my_subnets[0]: Creating...
aws_subnet.my_subnets[1]: Creating...
```

```
aws_subnet.my_subnets[1]: Creation complete after 1s [id=subnet-02bc291334d87cd1c]
aws_subnet.my_subnets[0]: Creation complete after 1s [id=subnet-0f1b499937a2cbd98]
```

Curiously, this execution takes longer that the ones before. Why? The data gathering process, which you can identify in the output as Reading..., imports all the data from the target infrastructure, and this takes longer than using the Terraform state.

Note that this Terraform execution owns only the provisioning of the subnets. This applies to both the apply and the destroy steps. So, if you use the same configuration to destroy, only the subnets will be destroyed, not the *data* used as the reference.

One drawback in this example is its use of hardcoded data, the VPC id. The same challenge applies to other input data that could customize the output of a Terraform configuration. So, let's discover how Terraform helps with input data management.

Using Terraform variables

Terraform *variables*, or input variables, are used to customize the outcome of a Terraform configuration, without changing its source code. Variables are code references to a value that will be provided in Terraform execution time. Then, in the configuration, you can use this reference when configuring your data sources, resources, or others.

In Example 12-67, we set the VPC ID directly in the code. If you decide to change this ID, you should update the configuration file, but doing so is cumbersome when the data changes often.

The alternative is to declare a Terraform variable, which you could call vpc_id. When writing the configuration, this variable doesn't contain a value yet, but you can reference it in the code, prepending the var. prefix. In the example, you can assign the reference to the variable vpc_id by setting the argument id in the data block to var.vpc_id:

```
variable "vpc_id" {
  type = string
}

data "aws_vpc" "my_vpc" {
  id = var.vpc_id
}
```

Variables have meta-arguments to tune their behavior. The type meta-argument defines the type of the variable—for example, string or integer. The type enforces an implicit validation, but a validation block also can enforce a more sophisticated validation on the variable's content. In Example 12-68, you can see condition enforcing the vpc_id variable to start with vpc- as well as the error message to be raised if the validation fails.

Example 12-68. Validating Terraform variables

```
variable "vpc_id" {
  type        = string
  description = "The id of the vpc_id."
  sensitive   = true

  validation {
    condition     = length(var.vpc_id) > 4 && substr(var.vpc_id, 0, 4) == "vpc-"
    error_message = "The vpc_id must be a valid VPC id, starting with \"vpc-\"."
  }
}
```

Other common meta-arguments for variables are `description`, to provide a helper message before submitting the input value, and `sensitive`, to hide the variable's value from the output.

Also, the `default` option indicates a reference value for the variable. If there is no `default` value, and Terraform can't obtain the value via other means, as you will learn soon, it will prompt you to enter the value of the variable. In this case, it will ask you about the value of `var.vpc_id`, with the extra helper message from the `description`. You can check that the validation rule is working properly by entering the wrong VPC ID—for instance, abcd:

```
$ terraform plan
var.vpc_id
  The id of the vpc_id.

  Enter a value: abcd

│
│ Error: Invalid value for variable
│
│   on use-data.tf line 15:
│   15: variable "vpc_id" {
│      ├────────────────
│      │ var.vpc_id is "abcd"
│
│ The vpc_id must be a valid VPC id, starting with "vpc-".
│
│ This was checked by the validation rule at use-data.tf:20,3-13.
```

As expected, Terraform execution complains about the variable value not complying with the validation criteria. It's always recommended, not only in Terraform, to enforce user input validation. It will save time and prevent other issues when finally executing the code or configuration.

Now, after you have seen the validation in action, you can run it again using a proper variable input (the same you hardcoded in Example 12-67), and the Terraform plan should succeed:

```
$ terraform plan
var.vpc_id
  Enter a value: vpc-0da120f2568c06c33

data.aws_vpc.my_vpc: Reading...
data.aws_vpc.my_vpc: Read complete after 0s [id=vpc-0da120f2568c06c33]

# omitted other plan output
```

Terraform variables help keep your code reusable via customization. However, this clearly is not a good programmatic practice, because human interaction is required. In most cases, Terraform execution is automated, so it requires a programmatic way to get the variables' input.

Defining variables programmatically

Terraform has various ways to gather input data via nonhuman interaction. One common approach is to define the variables in files, along with the Terraform configuration variables.

Terraform, by default, reads from the file *terraform.tfvars* when executing a `terraform plan` or `apply` (there is an example on this book's GitHub page (*https://oreil.ly/ct-FQ*)). Thus, you need only to assign the variables' values in this file and they will be automatically available:

```
vpc_id = "vpc-0da120f2568c06c33"
```

You can also use custom filenames by adding the `-var-file=filename` option in the Terraform command. Or, if you don't want to write the value to a file, you can assign a variable value in the command line with `-var 'foo=bar'`.

Now, if you run `terraform plan` again, with the variable `vpc_id` defined, you will see how the plan is executed without prompting you for input. Nevertheless, the same variable `validation` criteria still apply.

This simple approach of storing the variables in code files works well in some cases, but not when the content is sensitive. You shouldn't store sensitive values in clear text, for security reasons.

One mitigation option is to use environmental variables that are stored only in process memory, not persisted. Terraform implicitly imports environmental variables into its execution environment, following a specific naming convention. You can use any environmental variable with the `TF_VAR_` prefix plus the name of the variable, and it will be automatically available for Terraform.

Following our example, if you export `TF_VAR_vpc_id` as an environment variable, the variable `vpc_id` will take the value from it, and you will not get the input prompt:

```
$ export TF_VAR_vpc_id="vpc-0da120f2568c06c33"
```

Finally, you can also get variables to Terraform via external sources—such a source of truth that stores the data defining the intended state of your infrastructure (Chapter 14 provides more details)—and get content from them. This is similar to the Ansible or Nornir dynamic inventory. Needless to say, you will need to install and use the proper Terraform provider that exposes the data sources. For example, to get the VPC CIDR prefix, you could retrieve it from an IPAM system, getting the proper one according to the network plan.

> If you have sensitive variables, also known as *secrets*, you can use a secrets manager (which organizes your secrets via best security practices) such as the HashiCorp Vault provider (*https://oreil.ly/mFCcG*).

Now that you understand how to use variables in Terraform, let's see how to manage different environments from the same configuration.

Using workspaces

Terraform understands the context of the execution—configuration and state—from the path where Terraform is executed. However, when you want to reuse the same Terraform configuration to define multiple environments (for instance, development and production), you need a mechanism to isolate the different states, similar to *namespaces*. Terraform uses *workspaces* for this purpose.

By default, you are already using workspaces. Specifically, you are using the `default` one, as you can see when listing the workspaces with `terraform workspace list`:

```
$ terraform workspace list
* default
```

Workspaces help you reuse the same Terraform configuration to manage multiple environments. You can define the same infrastructure for multiple environments by changing the credentials pointing to one or another account from the cloud provider.

> Terraform workspaces are not supported by all Terraform *state* backends. Check the documentation. The `local` backend supports workspaces.

In this example, you will create two workspaces, A and B, and each will match one of two different AWS profiles. An *AWS profile* is a combination of account credentials and other user settings (for instance, different accounts in the same region or the same account in different regions).

In our example, we simply use two regions for the same AWS account, both having the same network setup used in our example (a VPC and two subnets) but different CIDR prefixes. However, the same principle applies to different accounts. This approach is commonly used to isolate different environments, such as testing and production.

 An AWS profile can be added in the *credentials* file, which was created in Example 12-51, by simply adding two new entries, A and B in .aws/credentials and .aws/config (in your user home directory). We suggest you keep the same credentials for all the profiles and simply change the region. This way, you don't need to create more AWS accounts. Here's the code:

.aws/credentials

```
[default]
aws_access_key_id = YOUR_AWS_KEY_ID
aws_secret_access_key = YOUR_AWS_SECRET_KEY
[A]
... similar as default ...
[B]
... similar as default ...
```

.aws/config

```
[default]
region = eu-west-3
output = json
[A]
... similar as default ...
[B]
... similar as default ...
```

The first step is to create a new workspace via `terraform workspace new A`. This command initializes the workspace and activates it:

```
$ terraform workspace new A
Created and switched to workspace "A"!

You're now in a new, empty workspace. Workspaces isolate their state,
so if you run "terraform plan" Terraform will not see any existing state
for this configuration.
```

Now, if you list the workspaces, you'll see a new one, with the asterisk (*) indicating it is the active workspace:

```
$ terraform workspace list
  default
* A
```

In the configuration, you can use `terraform.workspace`, which contains the string value of the workspace name. Using this reference will help you select the right data for each execution. This could be done in different ways. One that works well when there are relatively few variables is using `map` type variables and using the Terraform workspace as the key (Example 12-69).

Example 12-69. Terraform configuration for workspaces

```
terraform {
  required_providers {
    aws = {
      source  = "hashicorp/aws"
      version = "~> 3.0"
    }
  }
}

# Configure the AWS Provider
provider "aws" {
  profile = terraform.workspace            ❶
}

variable "cidr" {                          ❷
  type = map(string)

  default = {
    A = "198.51.100.0/24"
    B = "203.0.113.0/24"
  }
}

# Create a VPC
resource "aws_vpc" "my_vpc" {
  cidr_block = var.cidr[terraform.workspace] ❸
}

# Create two subnets
resource "aws_subnet" "my_subnets" {
  count      = 2
  vpc_id     = aws_vpc.my_vpc.id
  cidr_block = cidrsubnet(aws_vpc.my_vpc.cidr_block, 1, count.index)
}
```

❶   In the `provider` block, we set the `profile` argument with the workspace name, instead of the `region` that we used before. As we've mentioned, in the example this points to the same account in different regions, using AWS profiles.

❷   We define a variable of type `map(string)` which, in the `default`, contains a map for each workspace name. This map is similar to a *dict* in Python, but keys are only of `string` type.

❸ We can access one CIDR value or another, using a different key, with `var.cidr[terraform.workspace]`. So, when we run `terraform plan`, having the workspace A activated, Terraform will use the `198.51.100.0/24` prefix.

To complete the example, you can create the other workspace B, with `terraform workspace new B`. If you run `terraform plan` again, you will see the other prefix being used.

Another difference when using workspaces is the way Terraform stores the state. In the `local` backend, notice that there won't be the file *terraform.tfstate*. Instead, now you have a directory *terraform.tfstate.d*, which contains a folder for each workspace, with the corresponding state:

```
$ tree terraform.tfstate.d
terraform.tfstate.d
├── A
│   ├── terraform.tfstate
│   └── terraform.tfstate.backup
└── B
    ├── terraform.tfstate
    └── terraform.tfstate.backup
```

Terraform workspaces help you reuse the same configuration to manage multiple environments. But to improve reusability between configurations, you need to learn about Terraform modules.

Using modules to improve reusability

Throughout this section, you may have inferred the potential of Terraform to manage dynamic infrastructure via its declarative approach. However, you can also foresee how complex this configuration could become in real environments. You need some way to break this configuration into different reusable parts. Terraform modules are the answer.

A *module* is a container of Terraform resources that are grouped together. You can imagine it as a package in other programming languages, which you can import and use from other code.

Going back again to the VPC and subnets example, you will now create two modules: one for the VPC and another for the subnet. You start in a new directory (for instance, *6-modules*) with a Terraform configuration file (*main.tf*), which will reference the modules. Notice that the filename is arbitrary; it could be anything with the *.tf* extension. For the two modules, it's necessary to create two nested folders, such as *subnet* and *vpc*, which will contain the Terraform configuration needed for each case. These folders don't need to be nested; the location could be any other reachable source.

You will end up with a folder structure like that in Example 12-70.

Example 12-70. Terraform module structure

```
$ tree 6-modules
.
├── main.tf
├── subnet
│   └── subnet.tf
└── vpc
    └── vpc.tf
```

 Modules are usually composed of multiple files, to represent the different objects: variables, resources, and outputs. In the example, for simplicity, we used only one Terraform file.

In Example 12-71, using a top-down approach, first, you create the *main.tf* configuration, containing the overall Terraform configuration plus the call to the two modules, named my_vpc_module and my_subnet_module.

Example 12-71. Terraform module composition

```
# Omitted AWS Terraform provider reference
# Omitted AWS Provider config

variable "base_cidr" {                                              ❶
  default = "192.0.2.0/24"
}

module "my_vpc_module" {                                           ❷
  source      = "./vpc"                                           ❸
  cidr_for_vpc = var.base_cidr
}

module "my_subnet_module" {
  source         = "./subnet"                                     ❸
  count          = 2                                              ❹
  vpc_id         = module.my_vpc_module.id                        ❺
  vpc_cidr_block = cidrsubnet(module.my_vpc_module.cidr_block, 1, count.index) ❺
}
```

❶ The *main.tf* configuration contains the provider definition plus the variable base_cidr (with a default value) that we will use when calling the modules. You should imagine this configuration file as the entry point of the Terraform plan, so it's the place where the global input variables will be defined. The modules will have their own input variables, but these won't be exposed to the caller.

❷ To use a module, we simply define the block module and provide the arguments that it requires. The source meta-argument is necessary because it points to the module's location. In this case, we are using the nested local path, but it could be an HTTP URL, a GitHub repository, or a reference to Terraform Registry, and many more. The modules, like the providers, are initialized during `terraform init`, so the modules, if not local, are retrieved and installed in the *.terraform* folder.

❸ The other arguments used to call the module from *main.tf* are input variables defined by the module. For instance, when using the module `./vpc`, we set the argument `cidr_for_vpc`. This means that in the `vpc` module, there is an input variable with this name. The same applies to the `./subnet` module, with the `vpc_id` and `vpc_cidr_block` arguments.

❹ The `count` meta-argument for `my_subnet_module` creates two objects from the same module, similar to what we did with the subnet resources in Example 12-71.

❺ Another difference is the use of the `module` prefix in the references to these configuration blocks: `module.my_vpc_module.id` and `module.my_vpc_mod ule.cidr_block`. You have already seen this syntax (for instance, in Example 12-60) with the type of the resource, the identifier, and the argument. To be more precise, this argument we reference is actually a Terraform *output*, which indicates the values Terraform exposes at the end of the execution, via the command-line output, or programmatically to other Terraform code.

Let's review each module definition, starting with the VPC in Example 12-72.

Example 12-72. Terraform VPC module

```
variable "my_cidr" {}

resource "aws_vpc" "my_vpc" {
  cidr_block = var.my_cidr
}

output "cidr_block" {
  value = aws_vpc.my_vpc.cidr_block
}

output "id" {
  value = aws_vpc.my_vpc.id
}
```

As we mentioned, we defined the input variable `my_cidr`, which becomes a mandatory input because it has no `default` argument (which would define the value of `my_cidr` in its absence). Then, internally in this module, the variable is used in the `aws_vpc` resource, as in previous examples.

The newcomers in this configuration are the *outputs*, cidr_block and id. The most important argument is value, which in this case references outputs from resource. Other options to tune its behavior exist, such as sensitive to suppress the values in the CLI output, and depends_on to define dependencies that are not explicit. Notice that the output identifiers are exactly the ones we referenced in *main.tf*.

You can notice a similarity between a Terraform module and a programming language function. Here, we have input variables instead of function arguments, followed by some code, and finally, some outputs returned instead of return values.

 You could use Terraform outputs not only to pass data between modules but to simply expose special values on the Terraform CLI.

The subnet module configuration is even simpler than in previous examples because the multiple object creation logic is left to *main.tf*, using the count meta-argument. In this case, this module is focused on creating only one subnet and setting the two arguments it needs:

```
variable "vpc_id" {}
variable "vpc_cidr_block" {}

resource "aws_subnet" "my_subnet" {
  vpc_id          = var.vpc_id
  vpc_cidr_block = var.cidr_block
}
```

Notice that this code includes only an input variable definition, matching the arguments calling the module from *main.tf*. The code includes no outputs because we don't need to use outputs from this module as inputs for other modules nor to render in the CLI.

Applying this Terraform configuration produces exactly the same infrastructure as the previous examples: one Amazon VPC and two subnets. However, with this setup, the two modules created could be reused for other Terraform configurations. It's a common practice to define infrastructure stacks—for instance, all the base networking components in one module (which could be itself composing other modules)—and then reuse this module from multiple application deployments. So, the DevOps teams don't need to reinvent the wheel for every infrastructure deployment, but can simply reuse what's understood as the best practice.

You have now completed your introductory journey through Terraform! You learned how to manage dynamic infrastructure, focusing on network services and using a declarative approach. However, Terraform could be used in other ways, with limitations, as you will see next.

Terraform Out of Its Comfort Zone

Throughout this section, you have seen how to use Terraform canonically, using a declarative approach and managing dynamic infrastructure services. However, as it happens when a tool becomes mainstream, other options have been added to extend its usage.

Even though the declarative approach is where Terraform shines, it also supports an *imperative* approach via Terraform provisioners. Next, you'll see how Terraform provisioners can cover certain use cases that can't be represented in the native Terraform's declarative model.

Using Terraform provisioners

You may be wondering, "Why do we need to tweak Terraform to support the imperative approach if other tools exist for this purpose?" The reason is to keep all the infrastructure management within one tool, for operational simplicity.

This approach addresses some use cases, such as provisioning compute resources, that require configuration changes to do their job. Not all Terraform providers support this functionality, but the most popular ones do. For instance, Amazon EC2 instances support the `user_data` argument to provide custom data to the instance, to be run at launch time (for instance, passing commands to customize the instance status).

However, if the Terraform resource does not provide a specific option to customize the bootstrap of the infrastructure, you still have the option to provision a resource after a state change: the Terraform provisioner. The `provisioner` block, within the `resource` block, supports three provisioner types:

`local-exec`
An executable is invoked *locally*, after the resource is created.

`remote-exec`
An executable is invoked *remotely* in the remote resource after the resource is created. This option requires a remote connection to the resource.

`file`
It copies files or directories to the new resource, via a remote connection.

`local-exec` and `remote-exec` have security concerns that should be taken into account: excessive privileges and execution in clear text. To mitigate these concerns, we recommend minimizing their use, and using them only following best practices for securing credentials and managing SSH access. Alternatively, using Ansible as a provisioner is a more robust option; using Terraform and Ansible where each tool shines is a good idea and is especially easier now with the new Terraform Provider for Ansible (*https:// oreil.ly/Gaib2*).

Example 12-73 uses a `local-exec` provisioner that simply takes a `command`. This command will be executed in the local computer running Terraform when the resource, the AWS instance, is created.

Example 12-73. Terraform provisioner

```
resource "aws_instance" "server" {
  # some config omitted
  provisioner "local-exec" {
    command = "echo The server IP is ${self.private_ip}"
  }
}
```

Terraform provisioners can help you simplify infrastructure management in one tool. However, this approach adds complexity and uncertainty, and should be used only as a last resort.

For example, thoughout this Terraform section, we have shown how useful it is to rely on `terraform plan` execution to foresee the final status of the infrastructure. The actions from provisioners can't be modeled, so their potential effects are not taken into account in the feedback from the dry-run execution.

Keep this in mind: just because you can, doesn't mean you should. You can use other tools, such as Ansible or Nornir, to manage configurations, as you learned in this chapter. Or, using the immutable approach, you could use other tooling, like HashiCorp Packer (*https://www.packer.io*), to create server images with all the proper configurations in place before provisioning them.

Lastly, pushing Terraform out of its common uses, let's discuss its potential for managing network devices.

Using Terraform to manage network devices

Terraform has progressively been adopted by network operations teams to manage cloud network services in general-purpose clouds, network-centric clouds (such as OpenStack, Arista CloudVision, Cisco ACI or Multi-Site Orchestrator (MSO), VMware NSX), and multicloud solutions (such as Alkira and Aviatrix).

In parallel to these natural use cases, in early 2022, experimental initiatives started to manage network devices using Terraform providers. The new network management interfaces, using REST APIs and structured data (Chapter 10 provides more info), make it easier to build Terraform providers. The same rationale used for provisioners applies here, using the same tool to manage the whole infrastructure.

However, managing network devices is different from provisioning network services behind a controller. The network APIs are used to change the state of the configuration as a whole and per feature. This doesn't completely match the declarative approach Terraform is used to.

At the time of writing, this trend has two experimental examples: the Junos Terraform Automation Network, or JTAF (*https://oreil.ly/B9Twl*), and the IOS XE provider (*https://oreil.ly/DvYBR*). These two options offer generic arguments to wrap the inner behavior of their network management interfaces. For instance, as you will see in Example 12-75, with the IOS XE provider, the resource arguments are simply the URL path and the data payload.

Even though it's not clear whether this approach will gain traction over time, it's interesting to observe the differences between our previous main example and this use case, using the IOS XE Terraform provider leveraging the RESTCONF API interface.

First, as in every Terraform configuration, you define the `required_provider`, referencing the provider in the Terraform Registry, and then the specific `provider` block configuration (see Example 12-74). You could use any IOS XE device available, taking into account the required OS version. But, as an easy alternative, you can use an always-on IOS XE instance from Cisco DevNet. The `host` and credentials used in the example are pointing to this sandbox.

Example 12-74. IOS XE Terraform provider configuration

```
terraform {
  required_providers {
    iosxe = {
      source  = "CiscoDevNet/iosxe"
      version = "0.1.1"
    }
  }
}

provider "iosxe" {
  host            = "https://sandbox-iosxe-latest-1.cisco.com"
  device_username = "developer"
  device_password = "C1sco12345"
}
```

If the host or credentials provided don't work, check the parameters on the official DevNet page (*https://oreil.ly/juxty*).

This provider consists of one resource and one *data source*, both named `iosxe_rest`. Both are simple wrappers of the REST API. First, in Example 12-75, you will use the data source, referencing the full device configuration with the `path`, and finally outputting it in the CLI output.

Example 12-75. IOS XE Terraform provider data source

```
# omitted provider configuration

data "iosxe_rest" "full_config" {
  path = "/data/Cisco-IOS-XE-native:native"
}

output "response" {
  value = data.iosxe_rest.full_config
}
```

Executing `terraform apply`, you will output the full configuration and store it in the Terraform state. This is the configuration, in YANG format, from the IOS XE instance:

```
$ terraform apply
data.iosxe_rest.full_config: Reading...
data.iosxe_rest.full_config: Read complete after 2s [id=1844435120]

Changes to Outputs:
  + response = {
      + id       = "1844435120"
      + path     = "/data/Cisco-IOS-XE-native:native"
      + response = jsonencode(
            {
              + "Cisco-IOS-XE-native:native" = {
                  + "Cisco-IOS-XE-diagnostics:diagnostic" = {
                      + bootup = {
                          + level = "minimal"
                        }
                    }
                  + banner                              = {
                      + motd = {
                          + banner = <<-EOT

                            Welcome to the DevNet Sandbox for CSR1000v and IOS XE

# output trimmed for brevity
```

You can see how this Terraform provider is just an adapter to the RESTCONF API. The data source performs a GET to the path, and the returned data is structured in YANG.

The next step is to modify some parts of the configuration and understand how the provider works with resources. You are, again, using the resource iosxe_rest. Here, you can notice the different types of usage, as compared to previous AWS resources, where the low-level details are hidden and only the key arguments are requested. In this case, you need to know and specify the full YANG path as the path argument value, instead of having a different resource for each network feature:

```
# omitted provider configuration

resource "iosxe_rest" "snmp_example_chassis_id" {
  method = "PUT"
  path   = "/data/Cisco-IOS-XE-native:native/snmp-server/chassis-id"
  payload = jsonencode(
    {
      "Cisco-IOS-XE-snmp:chassis-id" : "a_new_chassis_id"
    }
  )
}
```

When you apply the Terraform configuration, as shown in Example 12-76, the new configuration will be applied in the YANG path specified.

Example 12-76. Creating an IOS XE configuration with Terraform

```
$ terraform apply -auto-approve
data.iosxe_rest.full_config: Reading...
data.iosxe_rest.full_config: Read complete after 1s [id=1844435120]

Terraform used the selected providers to generate the following execution plan.
Resource actions are indicated with the following symbols:
  + create

Terraform will perform the following actions:

  # iosxe_rest.snmp_example_chassis_id will be created
  + resource "iosxe_rest" "snmp_example_chassis_id" {
      + id      = (known after apply)
      + method  = "PUT"
      + path    = "/data/Cisco-IOS-XE-native:native/snmp-server/chassis-id"
      + payload = jsonencode(
            {
              + "Cisco-IOS-XE-snmp:chassis-id" = "a_new_chassis_id"
            }
        )
      + response = (known after apply)
    }

Plan: 1 to add, 0 to change, 0 to destroy.
```

```
iosxe_rest.snmp_example_chassis_id: Creating...
iosxe_rest.snmp_example_chassis_id: Creation complete after 1s [id=772450073]

Apply complete! Resources: 1 added, 0 changed, 0 destroyed.

# Omitted output
```

In this case, the new configuration is *added* with the + symbol because no previous configuration was present before.

 If you use -auto-approve, you don't get the user-prompt confirmation, even without a plan reference.

Finally, you can connect to the IOS XE device and validate that the configuration has been applied:

```
csr1000v-1#sh running-config | include snmp
snmp-server chassis-id a_new_chassis_id
```

Now, you can change the chassis-id to another one and validate how the plan would look when a previous chassis-id is defined:

```
$ terraform plan
iosxe_rest.snmp_example_chassis_id: Refreshing state... [id=772450073]
data.iosxe_rest.full_config: Reading...
data.iosxe_rest.full_config: Read complete after 1s [id=1844435120]

Terraform used the selected providers to generate the following execution plan.
Resource actions are indicated with the following symbols:
  ~ update in-place

Terraform will perform the following actions:

  # iosxe_rest.snmp_example_chassis_id will be updated in-place
  ~ resource "iosxe_rest" "snmp_example_chassis_id" {
        id      = "772450073"
      ~ payload = jsonencode(
          ~ {
              ~ "Cisco-IOS-XE-snmp:chassis-id" = "a_new_chassis_id"
                                              -> "another_chassis_id"
            }
        )
        # (2 unchanged attributes hidden)
    }

Plan: 0 to add, 1 to change, 0 to destroy.
```

In this case, you can see the ~ symbol, pointing out that it's not adding, but changing, the content of this configuration leaf. This is an improvement over the provisioner approach because you can determine the difference in the plan before actually performing the changes in the configuration.

As you can see, today there is a big difference between using Terraform to manage network devices versus using cloud or controller-based network services, but only time will tell if this new approach will become adopted to consolidate operations.

Terraform Summary

In this section, you've seen the different approach that Terraform brings to infrastructure management—the declarative approach—which makes it a good choice to provision dynamic infrastructure, especially exposed *as a service*. Terraform's flexibility to adapt to multiple APIs has raised its popularity and positioned it as the default choice as the IaC tools when working with various cloud platforms.

Also keep in mind that Terraform is not incompatible with other configuration management tools, like the ones presented in this chapter. For instance, when working with raw infrastructure as a service, you could use Terraform to provision the dynamic infrastructure (for instance, a VM), and then run a provisioner that will call an Ansible playbook to configure it. You should choose the solutions that suit better in each case.

You can refer to the Terraform documentation (*https://www.terraform.io/docs*) to find more details about Terraform usage and more advanced use cases.

Summary

In this chapter, we discussed how some automation tools—like Ansible, Nornir, and Terraform—can be put to work in network automation. We provided example use cases and discussed the advantages and disadvantages of each product along the way. In Table 12-2, we provide a high-level comparison of each tool for your reference.

Table 12-2. Automation tools summary

Tool	Approach	Language	Logic customization	State tracking
Ansible	Imperative	YAML	Moderate	No
Nornir	Imperative	Python	High	No
Terraform	Declarative	HCL[a]	Moderate	Yes

[a] CDKTF allows multiple programming languages.

With all these tools and other technologies from previous chapters, the next chapter will show you how to apply the software development best practices of continuous integration to the network automation domain.

## CHAPTER 13

Continuous Integration

In this chapter, we're going to change direction a little bit. Until now, this book has provided details on specific tools and technologies that you can learn, all for the purpose of applying them toward network automation. However, it would be improper to assume that network automation is all about shiny new tools—in fact, that's only one piece of the bigger picture.

This chapter instead focuses much more on optimizing the processes around network management and operations. Armed with knowledge of the specific tools and technologies mentioned in previous chapters, you can use this chapter as a guide for using those tools to solve the *real*, challenging problems that network operators at any scale are facing. This chapter answers questions like these:

- How can I use network automation to produce a more stable, more available network?
- How can I help the network move as quickly as the rest of the business demands, without compromising on availability?
- What kind of software or tools can I use to help me implement better processes around my network?

Networking touches *every* other area of IT, and any outages, policy changes, or impediments to efficient process will impact any technology connected to the network. In modern times, these impacts are felt by every other technology discipline. This has caused the rest of IT and the business at large to view the network as something that should "get out of the way" and "just work." These days, the network is called upon to be always accessible and be more flexible at a more rapid pace than ever before, ensuring that it supports any service or application the business requires.

The reality is there is no magic bullet here; accomplishing these goals requires discipline as well as a disruption of your existing processes and communication silos. It also takes a significant amount of work, learning, and new tools. That work may seem like you're just adding more complexity, but it will pay off in the long run by adding both stability and speed to your network operations processes.

One common underlying theme is the removal of humans from the direct control path of the network. You would be right to be skeptical of this idea, since we've talked about automating humans out of a job for a long time. However, removal of humans from direct control is not the same thing as removing humans entirely. Today, humans maintain direct control over the network by forming a manual, human pipeline for making changes to the network, as illustrated in Figure 13-1.

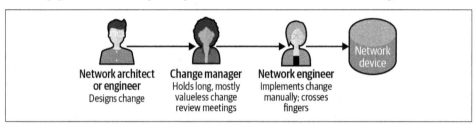

Figure 13-1. Humans in the direct path of a network

This technique has proven to be slow and arduous, while also not providing much, if any, additional reliability to making changes on the network. This method mostly just gets in the way, while providing the illusion of safety around making changes.

When we talk about removing humans from the direct path, we're talking about *continuous integration (CI)*—that is, automating the discrete tasks that should be taking place when we are managing infrastructure change, and freeing technical resources to sit above that pipeline, improving it and making it more efficient (Figure 13-2).

As a result of this fundamental shift toward CI, we can introduce real protections against human error in network operations instead of the "Change Management Theater" that we've relied on historically.

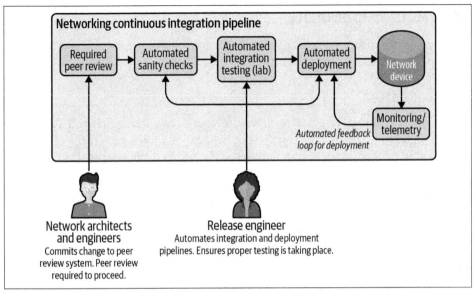

Figure 13-2. Automated change with continuous integration

 As shown in Figure 13-2, some organizations hire specialists called *release engineers* to manage the CI pipeline. They're skilled with tools like Git, testing tools, build servers, and peer review systems. They maintain the pipeline's integrity so the developers don't have to. Ultimately, their goal is to automate the process, from laptop to production (thus, *release* engineer).

These days, developers are expected to take more responsibility for the code they write, including deployment and ongoing operations (such as participating in an on-call rotation). An engineer or team may still be responsible for managing the CI/CD pipeline infrastructure, but the role of building a pipeline that produces well-tested, well-vetted code is being distributed to the developers themselves. For this reason, your organization may not have dedicated release engineers, particularly those focused on one team's development processes.

Important Prerequisites

To maximize your success in using the concepts in this chapter, you need to keep a few things in mind, as outlined in this section.

Simple Is Better

One of the best things you can do to enable your network automation has nothing to do with learning to code or using a hot new automation tool—it's all about your network design. Stay away from snowflakes and strive to deploy network services in a cookie-cutter fashion.

In other words, you may decide you want to deploy network configurations driven by templates, such as those we discussed at length in Chapter 9. If each of your network devices has a unique configuration with a wide variety of features, it's going to be fairly difficult to build templates for a large group of devices.

The more thought you put into making your network design simpler and more consistent, the less work you'll have to do when it comes time to automate network tasks. Often this means staying away from vendor-specific features, or bypassing embedded features entirely and implementing network services right at the compute layer.

People, Process, and Technology

In the previous chapters, we've discussed several great technologies and tools, but a lot more serious challenges face the network industry today—challenges of process and of working with other IT teams that may not share your primary skill set.

We've addressed specific technologies and tools that you can use to build efficient systems for network automation. A multitude of technologies can be used for automation—many of which may be new to many network engineers—and it's important to be aware of them. It's also important to improve and change the ways that we communicate with other areas of IT and the business at large.

In this chapter, however, we're going to discuss process enhancements that software developers have used for quite some time to improve the way they make changes to applications. The ultimate goal is to make such changes quickly and push them into production while minimizing the risk of negative impact. There are many important lessons here that can be learned by the network engineering community, especially when considering network automation.

Learn to Code

First, you don't have to be a software developer to leverage the concepts in this chapter. In fact, this chapter primarily exists to convey that message. However, you will likely find that no one tool (or even set of tools) will solve all your problems.

You'll likely have to fill some gaps in your CI journey by writing a custom solution, like a script. Use this as an opportunity to broaden your skill set. As discussed in previous chapters, both Python (Chapter 6) and Go (Chapter 7) are easy to start with and powerful enough to suit the vast majority of network automation use cases.

Introduction to Continuous Integration

Before we dive into how CI is useful within a network automation context, let's talk about its origins and its value to software development teams.

When we talk about implementing CI, we're looking to accomplish two primary objectives:

Improve reliability
> Learn from old lessons, and improve quality and stability of the overall system.

Move faster
> Be able to respond to the changing needs of the business more quickly.

Before CI, changes to software were often made in large batches, and sometimes it took months for developers to see their features make it into production. This made for incredibly long feedback loops, and if there were any serious issues or new features/requirements, it took a very long time for issues to be addressed. This inefficiency meant not only that new features took much longer to get developed but also that software quality suffered.

Naturally, it would be great if developers could simply make changes and push them directly to production, right? It would certainly solve the speed problem—and developers would be able to see the results of their changes more quickly. However, as you might expect, this is incredibly risky. In this model, it's easy to introduce bugs into production, which could seriously impact the bottom line for many businesses.

CI (when combined with continuous delivery, which we explore later in this chapter) is the best of both worlds. In this model, we're quickly pushing changes to production—but we're doing so within a context that tests and validates these changes, to be more confident that they're not going to cause problems when they're manifested in production.

In the sections to come, we discuss some of the components of and concepts related to CI, and then look at how we can apply these concepts to our network automation journey.

Basics of Continuous Integration

You've probably heard horror stories about software teams with insufficient processes deploying code to production directly from their laptops (Figure 13-3)—or even editing code live on a server. Such changes *may* be peer reviewed, but even in this case, there's little to no formal guarantee that the change will even work. Nevertheless, we hear about deployments like this being made, usually in the name of "it just needs to get done quickly" or "it's not a very risky change."

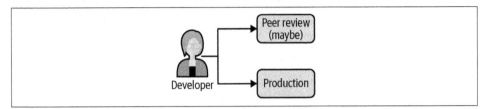

Figure 13-3. Deploying software directly to production

Stories like this are thankfully becoming increasingly rare. The expectations on any online service to maintain a high uptime have never been higher, and the processes for reliably shipping code to production have now been around for decades. In the world of software, there's really no legitimate excuse for deploying code directly to production without a formal testing and peer-review process.

In contrast, network engineers do this kind of thing all the time. Yet, logging in to an SSH session to a router to make config changes is no less risky than editing the source code of an application live in production. In many ways, it's even more risky: a developer who screws up a deployment might bring down that application, but a network engineer who screws up a configuration change can cause reverberating effects throughout not only the entire organization's network, but even the entire internet—e.g., via BGP route leaking (*https://oreil.ly/HVqgR*).

Software teams have moved toward a much more rigorous process for deploying code to production. While there is more than one name for this process, one extremely common and important component used in many organizations goes by the name of *continuous integration*. In short, CI is all about being able to merge changes to a source code repository at any time. A team of developers, no matter when they're working, can integrate changes to a shared repository at any time because tools are in place that allow the team to know—in an automated fashion—that those changes are not going to break the functionality of the overall system.

You might have heard the term *pipeline* used when discussing CI. This is because CI is not one particular technology, but usually a suite of tools and technologies used together to accomplish the goal. Changes to a codebase flow through these tools in a predetermined way, which forms a *CI pipeline*. All changes must go through this pipeline in its entirety before moving on to deployment, as shown in Figure 13-4.

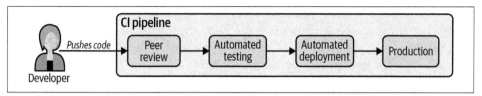

Figure 13-4. Deploying software to a CI pipeline

This process may seem like it makes deploying harder and slower. In contrast, it provides a foundation for continuously learning from (and ideally preventing) mistakes, so the deployments that do make it through are much more likely to succeed, which means far less wasted time on rollbacks and troubleshooting. This model has worked well to not slow, but actually accelerate, velocity for software teams to become more agile and provide value more quickly for their organizations. Many of these same benefits can be realized within the network infrastructure domain.

We've talked about the basics of CI, so now let's dive into some of the components and related concepts and technologies you might encounter along the way.

Continuous Delivery

Continuous delivery (CD) is another term closely related to CI that you may have heard. In a CD approach, the software team is continuously providing software that could be deployed into production; they are *delivering* working software in the form of an always-deployable codebase.

 Continuous deployment tends to imply that you're always pushing new code to production immediately. The industry has lately been using the term *continuous delivery* instead. This term generally means that your code is always in a condition where it *could* be deployed at any time, but doesn't have to be. Your organization may still wish to keep deployments on a set schedule, such as on a nightly or weekly basis.

CI is fairly easy to apply to network automation (as you'll see in upcoming sections), but CD requires a bit more thought. The rest of this chapter may blur the lines between CI and CD with respect to network automation, so keep in mind these two questions:

- *What* am I deploying?
- *To what/whom* am I deploying it?

These are important questions to address because they determine your delivery model. For instance, some network teams may perform all their automation with in-house Python applications. This is fairly simple since they are essentially a software development shop within the infrastructure team.

On the other hand is the canonical network automation example: provide some kind of configuration artifact (say, a YAML file) into a Git repository, and have the CI/CD pipeline take it through basic sanity checks before finally calling it with a tool like Ansible, resulting in actual and immediate changes to network devices in production. This may work for some organizations, but this is analogous to a software development team deploying each and every software patch to production immediately—and this is not always desired.

Consider, perhaps, a staging environment to which these changes can be continuously delivered, and whenever the business requires that those changes are finally deployed to production, they can be moved from staging, where (hopefully) they've been tested. At the time of this writing, many network vendors have heard our demands for providing virtual images of their platforms, so this is much easier to do than it used to be.

 While virtual appliances work great for testing automation, not all are meant to carry production network traffic. Refer to your vendor's documentation for clarity on this.

You also need to think about rollback procedures. Are you periodically taking the configurations that are in your production Git repository and using them to overwrite the current production configurations, or at least comparing the two? If you're not, even if you roll back the repository, the production deployment of those configurations may not get rolled back. What will be the impact, based on whether you're using Ansible or Puppet, or maybe custom Python programs, if you roll back the Git repository? You need to own that layer of your software stack and understand how your tools and software will react (if at all) when your production configurations get rolled back.

The truth is, you'll likely have to address the CD question on your own. What works for one organization probably won't work for yours, because of the many tools and languages available for solving network automation problems. However, this chapter should at least provide a starting point and ideas for properly delivering changes to your network in an automated fashion.

Test-Driven Development

It's also important to discuss yet another software development paradigm that has seen a growing amount of adoption: *test-driven development* (*TDD*).

Let's say you're working as a software developer tasked with creating a new feature in your project. Naturally, you might first gather basic requirements, put together a minimal design, and then move forward with building the feature (Figure 13-5). We'll even say that you're on board with CI, so you will then build unit tests to validate the functionality you've built.

Unfortunately, it doesn't always happen this way. In reality, building tests after the feature has been built is often difficult to justify, or at the very least, deemed less important than the feature itself.

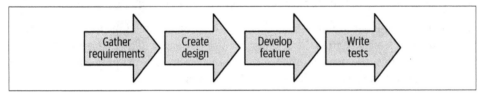

Figure 13-5. Software development lifecycle before test-driven development

In practice, this can easily lead to the accumulation of *technical debt*: if you don't build your tests first, there's always a temptation to not build them immediately after you develop the desired feature, or to not build them at all. This inevitably leads to gaps in test coverage, and on large projects, this gap only increases over time.

TDD turns this idea on its head. When using TDD, after going through requirements gathering and putting together a basic design, you write a test for that feature *before* the feature is even implemented (Figure 13-6). Naturally, this means the test will fail, since there's no code to test against. So, the final validation of this feature is to write code that passes that test (or tests).

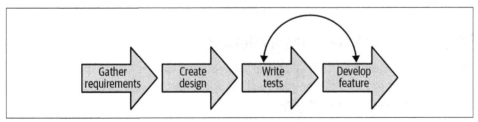

Figure 13-6. Software development lifecycle after test-driven development

Why use a test-driven approach? The most immediate benefit is the reduction of technical debt; if the tests are built before the feature, there's no temptation to let test coverage fall behind while the shiny new feature takes priority. However, a bit of a conceptual difference also exists. By writing tests first, the developer must have a strong grasp of how their software is being used—since they're writing tests to do just that. This is widely believed to improve software quality.

When you apply these concepts to network automation, you begin to realize numerous parallels. The network is as much of a business resource as the applications that flow on top of it. Therefore, it's important to have adequate testing in place that not only validates any changes made on the network, but also helps warn of any problems ahead of time (capacity planning). Are you gathering detailed statistics about the applications flowing on your network—not just what the SNMP service on your network devices is telling you—but from the perspective of the applications themselves? It's important as network engineers to learn the lesson that TDD is teaching software developers: understanding how our network is used, and further codifying this understanding into automated testing, is crucial.

Regardless of whether this testing takes the form of an existing off-the-shelf tool, a custom set of tests written in a programming language like Python or Go, or a mixture of the two, the two reasons we care about doing testing apply equally and are the same reasons software developers test their systems:

- We care enough about the quality of our network automation system, our network's uptime, and the positive experience of our users and applications to ensure that our system is properly tested.

- Enforcing a test-first methodology ensures we maintain a firm understanding of the key metrics and behaviors of our network. This allows us to continue to add new functionality quickly, without compromising on our existing obligations.

By adopting a methodology similar to TDD, we are not only helping to put the applications first, but also building a repeatable process by which we can constantly be *sure* that our network is serving the needs of the application, despite changes to configuration or environment. Later in this chapter, we discuss specific tools and technologies that we can use to accomplish these goals.

Why Continuous Integration for Networking?

So far, we've discussed CI and TDD, and how they provide value to software development teams. From now on, however, we'll be applying concepts like these exclusively to our network automation journey.

Why are we doing this? What value could CI or TDD have to network engineers? Remember the goals of CI:

Improve reliability
> Learn from old lessons, and improve quality and stability of the overall system.

Move faster
> Be able to respond to the changing needs of the business more quickly.

These goals, which have driven results for more stable software and more agile development teams, can also help us create a *more* reliable network—not less. Automation that compromises on either of these two goals is pointless.

For a long time, we've thought about and administered our networks as black boxes that happen to be connected to one another, and this mindset isn't conducive to the practices and concepts implemented in CI. So the first thing to do is start to think about your network as a pool of resources and fluid configurations—a system with ever-changing environments and requirements. Such a mindset requires a change in the way we deploy changes to production.

CI for networking means a lot of the same things as the canonical software example—creating a single point where changes to network infrastructure are performed, and testing and reviewing those changes is automated and nonoptional.

A Continuous Integration Pipeline for Networking

At this point, it's time to put the high-level CI concepts we've discussed into practice. In this section, we'll go through a few practical examples and tools for helping us achieve the goals we've outlined within the context of network automation.

While reading the following examples, keep these tips in mind:

- The tools used in this section are just examples. In every category, you have choices beyond what's presented here. We encourage you to evaluate the tools available in each category and determine whether they fit your needs.

- This section comes after the previous section for a reason. Implementing these tools without fixing the bad process that has plagued many organizations for years will accomplish nothing.

 The tools in this section also can be configured in a variety of ways. Only one approach is presented in this section, so remember the fundamental concepts here and adopt the right configuration to realize the same benefits within your organization.

Our CI pipeline for networking has five main components:

- Peer review
- Build automation
- Deployment validation and testing
- Test/dev/staging environment
- Deployment tools and strategies

To illustrate the concepts in this chapter, we'll use a project called Templatizer, which renders Jinja templates into network device configurations based on data found in YAML data files. Many of the examples center on the Templatizer Git repository hosted on our private Git server.

Figure 13-7 serves as a useful illustrative example for our CI journey.

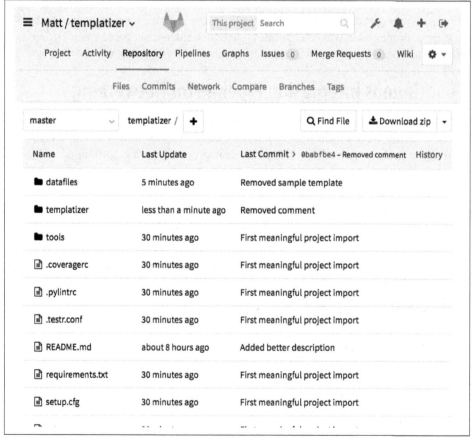

Figure 13-7. Templatizer project

The concepts in this chapter are generic and apply well beyond the Templatizer project we're using as a contrived, illustrative example. That said, if you want to obtain a copy of the files that make up this project, you can find them at *https://github.com/oreilly-npa-book/ examples/tree/v2/ch13-cicd*.

Peer Review

When we talk about peer review in a traditional software sense, we're typically talking about source code for an application. A developer submits a patch containing diffs to source code files, that patch is posted to the code review system in some way, and a reviewer (or reviewers) looks at the patch and provides comments or approval.

When adapting this portion of the pipeline for network automation, we're not that far off from this example. Chapters 8 and 9 have advocated an IaC approach with network automation, whereby any and all relevant configuration information is treated in the same way a developer would treat source code. In our case, instead of Java code, we might have YAML files or Jinja templates. They're all just text files, and we can run automated tests on them just the same.

Another related term you may have heard in recent years is *GitOps*. GitOps shares a lot of similar ideas with IaC. Both emphasize the use of a version control system like Git to store configuration files and scripts used to manage infrastructure. Whereas IaC can in some circles be thought of as applying to only the infrastructure domain (servers, networking, storage, cloud, etc.), GitOps takes a more holistic approach, using Git as the interface through which all operations professionals manage their platforms, including the application stack.

We're going to be building on the knowledge you gained about version control in Chapter 11 by using Git to not only control the versions of our various configuration artifacts like YAML files, but also leverage the first stage of this pipeline—peer review—to get an additional pair of eyes on our change to make sure we're doing the right thing.

If you've maintained any form of production IT infrastructure, you've likely taken part in change advisory board (CAB) meetings. Perhaps you were responsible for filling out a form describing the configuration change you want to make, and then attending long conference calls to say a few quick words that were carefully constructed to appease the approvers and get them out of your way. This process has deep roots in modern IT, but it doesn't do much to *actually* minimize risk or provide transparency among related technical teams. This is the old way of doing things.

When we talk about using CI for networking, we start with the idea of peer review, and although it might seem similar to what was just described, fundamental differences exist. In CI, if you want to make the change, you simply cut a new branch in Git and *make the change*. By having our configurations performed in a Git repository that is part of a CI pipeline, we don't have to ask for permission before doing the work in a branch, because that work is not actually pushed through production until it has been reviewed and merged to main.

This new model has some attractive benefits. With respect to peer review, you no longer need to describe the change you want to make and then hope you get it right when it comes time to implement—now, the description of the change is the same as the change itself. There is no ambiguity about what you're going to do because it's displayed right in the peer review system being used. To put your change into production, the approver(s) will simply merge your working branch into main.

When it comes to code review platforms, you have a few options. Here is a non-exhaustive list:

GitHub
Popular SaaS offering for reviewing and displaying source code (enterprise edition also available for a cost).

GitLab
Community edition is open source and free to download and run behind your firewall. There is also a tiered SaaS offering, as well as a closed-source enterprise edition.

Gerrit
Open source, complicated, but lots of integrations available, and a popular choice for some very large open source projects.

Bitbucket
Atlassian's code review and CI/CD platform. Useful if your organization already uses other Atlassian products like Jira or Confluence.

All these options leverage Git for the actual version control portion (and Git is therefore the way that you will interface with them when submitting code), but on top of Git, they all have subtle differences when it comes to their workflow. For instance, with GitHub, you can submit additional changes by simply pushing more commits to the same branch, but with Gerrit, the submitter must always work with the same commit (meaning additional changes require the `--amend` flag).

We'll be using GitLab throughout this chapter, primarily because it offers a lot for free, and we don't have to fuss around with setup too much. Know, however, that the other systems may work out better for you.

At this point in the book, you should be familiar with not only Jinja templates (Chapter 11) and YAML (Chapter 8), but also how to work with a Git repository (Chapter 11). All three are extremely common components of any CI pipeline for network automation. Additionally, the tools discussed in Chapter 5 will make a reappearance later in this chapter, so it's a good idea to at least be aware of these. If you skipped over these chapters, you're encouraged to revisit these concepts, as the remainder of this chapter won't make much sense otherwise.

As an example, we'll add some Jinja templates and YAML files so the Templatizer project is able to create configurations for network device interfaces. These examples assume that the Templatizer Git repository has already been cloned to the local filesystem. We'll start by creating a new Git branch for committing our changes in Example 13-1.

 Full versions of the code examples in this chapter can be found in the book's GitHub repo at *https://github.com/oreilly-npa-book/exam ples/tree/v2/ch13-cicd/templatizer*.

Example 13-1. Cutting a new branch

```
~$ git checkout -b "add-interface-template"

Switched to a new branch 'add-interface-template'
```

We're on a branch that is only on your machine (we haven't run `git push` yet) and it's on a nonmain branch. So we simply make the change. No waiting for approval before we get started—we do the work first, and let the work speak for itself when the time comes for approval.

After we've added the template and YAML file, Git should notify us that two new files are present but untracked, as shown in Example 13-2.

Example 13-2. Making a change to the Templatizer project

```
~$ git status

On branch add-interface-template
Untracked files:
  (use "git add <file>..." to include in what will be committed)

    datafiles/interfaces.yml
    templatizer/templates/interfaces.j2

nothing added to commit but untracked files present (use "git add" to track)
```

We need only make a commit and push to our origin remote (as shown in Example 13-3), which in this case is the GitLab repository shown earlier.

Example 13-3. Committing and pushing the change to Templatizer

```
~$ git add datafiles/ templatizer/

~$ git commit -s -m "Added template and datafile for device interfaces"
[add-interface-template 4121bfa] Added template and datafile for device interfaces
 2 files changed, 10 insertions(+)
 create mode 100644 datafiles/interfaces.yml
 create mode 100644 templatizer/templates/interfaces.j2

~$ git push origin add-interface-template
Counting objects: 7, done.
Delta compression using up to 8 threads.
Compressing objects: 100% (7/7), done.
Writing objects: 100% (7/7), 718 bytes | 0 bytes/s, done.
Total 7 (delta 2), reused 0 (delta 0)
To http://gitlab/Matt/templatizer.git
 * [new branch]      add-interface-template -> add-interface-template
```

The next step is to log in to our code review system (GitLab) and initiate the step that would kick off a peer review. Every code review system has its own workflow, but ultimately they all accomplish the same thing. For instance, Gerrit uses terminology like *change* and *patchset*, and GitHub uses *pull requests*. In short, these tools are a way of saying, "I have a change, and I'd like it to be merged into the main branch" (usually main).

GitLab uses a concept similar to GitHub pull requests called *merge requests*. Now that we've pushed our changes to a branch, we can specify in the merge request creation wizard that we'd like to merge the commit we made on add-interface-template to the main branch, which is considered stable for this project (Figure 13-8).

After we click through to the follow-up confirmation screen, our merge request is created. Keep in mind that this is still just that—a request. There has still been zero impact to the main branch, and as a result, the current stable version of the Templatizer project. This is just a proposal we've made, and will serve as a point of reference for the upcoming peer review.

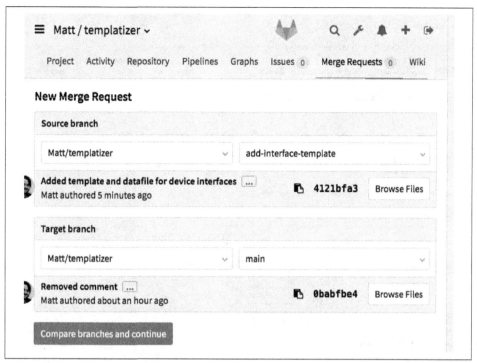

Figure 13-8. Creating a merge request

So the next step is to get our merge request reviewed by someone in authority. This part of the workflow can differ based on the culture of the team, as well as the review platform. Some teams restrict access to the main branch so that only certain senior members can accept merge requests, while other teams use the honor system and ask that each merge request is reviewed by at least one other team member. A common convention is to refrain from merging any changes until someone gives a +1, which is a way of saying, "From my perspective, this change is ready to be merged." This may happen right away, or a reviewer may have some comments or pointers before they're ready to give their +1.

Our imaginary teammate Fred is on hand to review our Templatizer change, and we can engage him in any number of ways. Most code review tools have a way of adding a reviewer, which should notify them by email, or you can message them directly. Either way, Figure 13-9 shows what Fred will see when reviewing our change in GitLab.

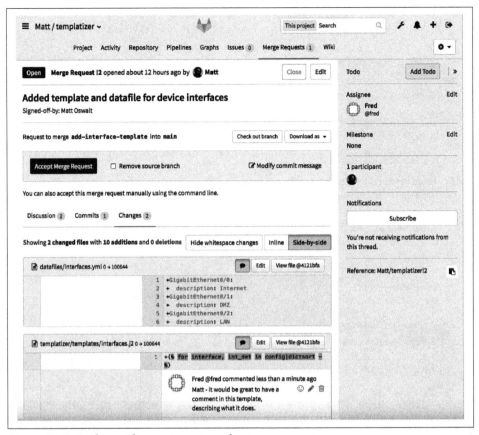

Figure 13-9. Fred providing comments to the merge request

As you can see, Fred leaves a message indicating he feels we should add a comment to our template, explaining how it works. It's not uncommon for a change to go through multiple iterations before being merged, and most platforms have facilities for this. With GitLab, we need to only add another commit to this branch and push to GitLab, and the new commit will be added to this merge request. Fred can easily see these additional changes, and once he is satisfied that this change is ready to be merged, he can do so.

Figure 13-10 shows us how GitLab can track this entire event stream for anyone who may want to see the status of this change.

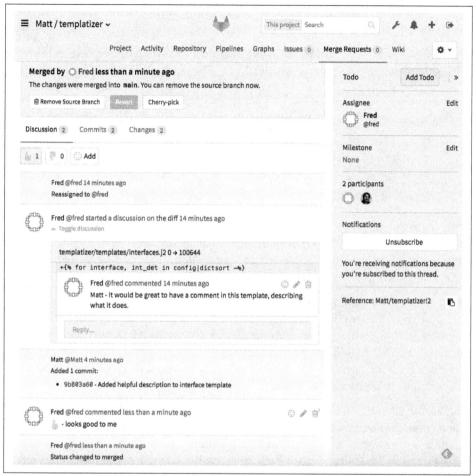

Figure 13-10. Change accepted and merged

Build Automation

Next up is an extremely important topic: *build automation*. This term largely stems from the use of CI tooling as a way of automatically compiling or installing software in order to test it. For instance, a program written in C must be compiled before it can be run in a test environment.

We may not necessarily be compiling software in our pipeline, but we can reuse many of the tasks that software developers will want to automatically perform on every proposed change to the repository. For instance, a pipeline for a Python project may perform static code analysis to ensure that the code conforms to Python's style guide, PEP 8. In a network automation context, we may only be making changes to YAML files, but we can perform similar checks to automate some of the simple stuff that we don't want human reviewers to deal with, including verifying that the file is in fact valid YAML (ensuring indentation is correct)!

This is the crux of what makes build automation so valuable. Before even bothering a human reviewer, we can automatically do numerous things to ensure that the reviewer is providing useful comments:

- Static code analysis (checking for proper syntax and adherence to any style guides)
- Unit testing (unit tests, parsing of data files or templates, etc.)
- Integration testing (checking whether a change breaks any existing functionality in the whole system)

With these out of the way, the reviewer can leave comments like "this needs to be more readable," instead of "add a space here." For this reason, these automated steps usually take place immediately when a change is submitted (our merge request from the previous example), and a reviewer is engaged only when these checks pass.

This process saves time for both the submitter and the reviewer, since the submitter gets close to immediate feedback if their change breaks something, and the reviewer knows that if a change passes these basic tests, they won't be wasting their time with simple comments. This approach also produces repeatable, more stable changes to network automation efforts—when a bug is discovered, it can be added to these automated tests to ensure that it doesn't happen again.

Numerous solutions are available for build automation, which we discuss later in this section. Fortunately, GitLab includes some build automation features natively, so the next few examples stick with that. In addition, much of the automation can be done by scripts in the repository itself, keeping the dependence on the build server to a minimum, and providing a lot of transparency for anyone working with the repository. This is yet another example where IaC is a powerful ally.

Let's say we make a minor change to our new *interfaces.yml* file, and Fred reviews it. Everything looks good to him, so he gives a +1 and merges the change to the main branch (Figure 13-11).

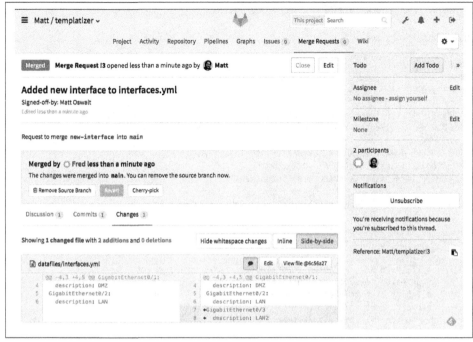

Figure 13-11. Minor change to YAML

However, we have a problem. This change produces invalid YAML, which shows when we try to run our Templatizer program (Example 13-4).

Example 13-4. Error parsing YAML

```
File "/Users/mierdin/Code/Python/templatizer/lib/python3.8/.../scanner.py", line 289,
  in stale_possible_simple_keys "could not found expected ':'", self.get_mark())
yaml.scanner.ScannerError: while scanning a simple key
  in "datafiles/interfaces.yml", line 7, column 1
could not found expected ':'
  in "datafiles/interfaces.yml", line 8, column 14
```

This was a minor change, but Fred is still a human being and overlooks typos like this, just as Matt did. When multiple files undergo multiple changes, this kind of mistake can be an even more common occurrence.

On the other hand, it should be trivial to write a script that checks for this error and provides feedback to our build system (Example 13-5). If we can do this, and configure our automated build system to check for this on all future patches, we should avoid this problem in the future.

Example 13-5. Python script to check valid YAML

```
#!/usr/bin/env python3

import os
import sys
import yaml

# YAML_DIR is the location of the directory where the YAML files are kept
YAML_DIR = "%s/../datafiles/" % os.path.dirname(os.path.abspath(__file__))

# Let's loop over the YAML files and try to load them
for filename in os.listdir(YAML_DIR):
    yaml_file = "%s%s" % (YAML_DIR, filename)

    if os.path.isfile(yaml_file) and ".yml" in yaml_file:
        try:
            with open(yaml_file) as yamlfile:
                configdata = yaml.load(yamlfile)

        # If there was a problem importing the YAML, we can print
        # an error message, and quit with a nonzero error code
        # (which will trigger our CI system to indicate failure)
        except Exception:
            print("%s failed YAML import" % yaml_file)
            sys.exit(1)

sys.exit(0)
```

 Example 13-5 shows a simple script that only checks for valid YAML. Chapter 8 introduced a few tools that can perform much more comprehensive validation for a variety of data formats. Including tools like these in your CI/CD pipeline is strongly encouraged.

Once we've committed that script to our *tools* directory in the repo, we also need to modify the CI configuration file *.gitlab-ci.yml* since we're running GitLab (as shown in Example 13-6).

Example 13-6. Configuring the CI environment to run the YAML validation script

```
test:
  script:
  - cd tools/ && python validate_yaml.py
```

GitLab will run this script every time a change is proposed. Now that this validator script is in place, let's take a look at what Fred sees when Matt proposes another change with invalid YAML (Figure 13-12).

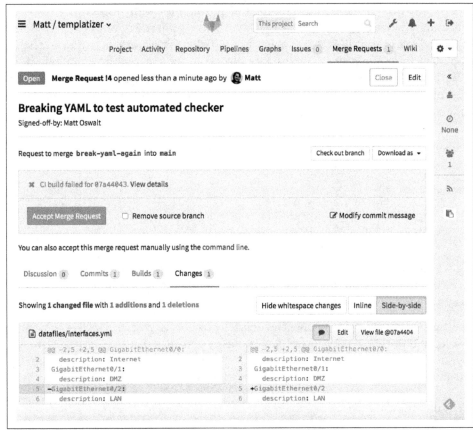

Figure 13-12. CI build fails because of invalid YAML

Both Matt and Fred can plainly see that a problem occurred during automated testing. They can also click through to see the details, including a full console log that shows the output of the script, indicating which file had the issue (Figure 13-13).

Figure 13-13. YAML validation script output

This is just one example in a multitude of possibilities with respect to automated validation and testing. Templatizer is also a Python project, so we can explore some of the tooling present in that ecosystem to run Python-specific validation and testing as part of this CI pipeline. For instance, Tox is a popular tool for doing all kinds of automated testing within a Python project. The OpenStack community uses Tox to simplify the CI process by summarizing a slew of tasks within a small list of commands; see Example 13-7.

Example 13-7. Adding Tox to the CI configuration

```
test:
  script:
  - cd tools/ && python validate_yaml.py
  - tox -epep8  # Checks for PEP8 compliance with Python files
  - tox -epy38  # Runs unit tests
  - tox -ecover # Checks for unit test coverage
```

Again, all these commands must pass without error in order to "pass" the build process. When a reviewer receives a merge request that shows that these checks were passed, they know it's ready for a real review.

The build automation component of the CI pipeline is crucial and is a great way to keep the workflow efficient, while also helping ensure that past mistakes are not repeated. Here are some additional ideas that may be useful at this stage in the pipeline—explore each in your own journey toward network automation:

- Unit testing any code (e.g., Python)
- Integration testing to ensure that any code can interoperate with other projects and APIs
- Syntax and style validation (both source code as well as data formats like YAML)

In the preceding examples, we used GitLab's included build automation features. However, you may not be using GitLab, and even if you are, you might wonder if other solutions exist for build automation. There are, in fact, quite a few, and each comes with its own pros and cons. These are some popular general-purpose solutions:

Jenkins
This open source build server has been around for long enough that just about anyone who is a true expert in CI will have experience with it.

GitLab
We covered GitLab while talking about code review options. GitLab is open source (but has a hosted option) and is one of few options containing both code review/repository functionality and build server functionality in one platform.

GitHub Actions

A more recent entrant into the build automation space, this extremely powerful, highly customizable workflow engine is cloud based and obviously tied to Git-Hub.

CircleCI

Also cloud-based, and able to work with a wide variety of version control systems and platforms.

You'll also find niche players focused on particular aspects of CI. For instance, Codecov is a cloud-based platform for reporting on test coverage in your projects. You can set up rules in your pipeline that reject any new contributions that don't at least maintain the current percentage of test coverage, for example. You can use a multitude of more focused platforms and tools like this, so you don't have to reinvent the wheel.

The good news is, you don't have to spend months researching all possible options before selecting "the one" that will meet your needs. You can start with a handful and evaluate them over time. And you should not expect to have all your needs met by a single solution, but likely a combination of them, including both off-the-shelf and custom build steps. The reason we refer to the collection of these tools as a *pipeline* is that there's really no one-size-fits-all approach, and the needs of your team will differ from the needs of another.

Deployment Validation and Testing

Earlier in this chapter, we talked a lot about the influence that TDD can have on network automation. CI is one place where such an approach can have tremendous benefits on our ability to deploy new changes in an automated way, but with height-ened confidence that this change will not negatively impact our production systems.

When we have rigorous, automated tests defined for not only asserting the validity of the configurations that make up our network elements (roughly analogous to unit tests in the software development world), but also the end-to-end UX over our net-work (validating things like base-level connectivity, expected link/flow performance, etc.), it gives us an incredible safety net that we can use to test changes both before and after we hit production. This forms a feedback loop that we can use to quickly drive further iteration (Figure 13-14).

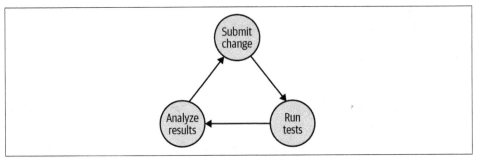

Figure 13-14. Continuously testing automated changes

Traditionally, such an approach is rare. We've all been in the situation where the best thing we can do to validate that our change didn't break production is a long-running ping that we watch very carefully while we wait for our commit operation to succeed. Fortunately, modern tools have evolved to provide other options.

The methods and tools for validating changes—automated or otherwise—depend on the type and scope of validation you're pursuing. For instance, if all you're after is some basic checks that your configuration is valid, maybe a simple Python script that loads a YAML file and renders a template is good enough. As we'll explore in the next section, you could extend this by uploading this configuration to a virtual topology and verify that at least a virtual instance of your intended network device accepts the configuration as valid.

However, static validation of configuration—especially within the context of a single network device—is often insufficient on its own. After all, the operational state of a device doesn't always match the configuration. Beyond this, our networks are much more than a collection of isolated boxes; they must all work together as part of a cohesive distributed system to provide a reliable service. To that end, a few other aspects are important to consider as part of your deployment validation strategy:

Operational state
Do your network devices have the operational state (e.g., number of active BGP peers) you would expect, given their configuration?

Basic connectivity
Can the users on your network access the applications they need?

End-to-end performance
Does the network have the bandwidth and latency characteristics you would expect? Has a recent change impacted these characteristics?

As we've discussed in the previous sections, not every tool in your pipeline needs to solve all your problems. Using a combination of tools is usually necessary to ensure that you're able to hit all the layers of validation we've just described. Open source tools like NAPALM (*https://oreil.ly/aBhv1*) and Batfish (*https://www.batfish.org*) as well as commercial tools like Forward Networks (*https://www.forwardnetworks.com*) enable you to not only check, but provide ongoing assurance on, operational state and basic connectivity of your network. Other commercial solutions like NetBeez (*https://netbeez.net*) and ThousandEyes (*https://www.thousandeyes.com*), which is part of Cisco, can give you visibility into the end-to-end performance characteristics of your network. These are just examples; tools are falling in and out of favor all the time.

The important point to consider is how well solutions like these can be integrated with your CI/CD pipeline. Here are good questions to ask of these projects or products:

- How programmable is this solution? Is it designed to fit into a pipeline or only for human interaction (e.g., through the GUI)?
- Are there existing integrations with build systems like Jenkins or GitHub Actions that can be used off the shelf, or do I need to build my own?

Tools like these can provide additional value during failover testing, such as the simulation of a data center failure. Failover testing is an underappreciated activity when it comes to network infrastructure. Often, it's hard to get the approval to run such a test, and in the rare cases when such approval is obtained, it's even more difficult to determine how the network and the connected applications are performing. Using these and other tools, we can gather a baseline of what "normal" connectivity and performance looks like, and by running the same tests after a failover, we can have greater confidence that we have sufficient capacity to keep the business running.

 As discussed in Chapter 10, the rise of model-driven telemetry, especially streaming/push-style telemetry, has made it easier than ever before to maintain constant awareness of how well the network is fulfilling its obligations. Using conventionally standardized data models allows us to do this with multiple vendors. Integrating tools that take advantage of these new technologies is something you should consider as part of your pipeline's validation steps.

The importance of validation as part of not only your pre-deployment checks but also your post-deployment and continuous assurance cannot be overstated. Downloading or buying a solution in isolation is not enough, though; integrating it into your pipeline raises the quality of every change that makes it into production.

Test/Dev/Staging Environment

In addition to the validation/testing methodologies we've discussed thus far, it's usually desirable to run more real-world testing on the changes we make to our automation solution, before pushing the change to our production systems. For Templatizer, we might want to render real configurations using the Jinja templates and YAML files against virtual devices that mimic the real production devices we'd like to eventually target.

In this case, some of the tools we discussed in Chapter 5 for developing automation solutions against a virtual topology of network devices can be particularly helpful. For instance, tools for creating simulated network topologies give us the ability to develop and quickly iterate on our workflows in as close to a production context as possible, but without the inherent risk that would come from developing these workflows against real, production infrastructure.

It's common for a virtual reference topology to be reused for both development and testing purposes, as shown in Figure 13-15.

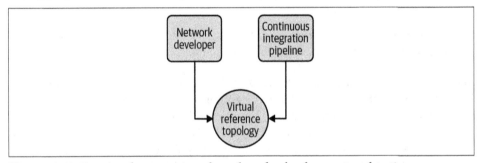

Figure 13-15. Reusing the same virtual topology for development and testing

This reuse allows automation solutions to be vetted much earlier in the development lifecycle. While this can be a valuable approach to creating more reliability in your automation journey, virtual topologies are not a panacea. Here are some factors to be aware of:

- Virtual testing can get you only so far. Some features are simply not possible to test in a virtual NOS, and even those that are often have vastly different performance characteristics than their hardware counterparts.

- As with any test suite or fixture, a virtual topology meant to mimic production is in a perpetual state of entropy. It will take work to ensure that this topology continues to appropriately mirror production and remain a useful ally against deploying bad changes.

In Chapters 5 and 12, we discussed several tools that are essential for developing network automation solutions. Three tools we explored in those chapters have additional utility in this regard:

Vagrant
> Sets up an automated topology of connected VMs, with support for a wide variety of hypervisors.

Containerlab
> Creates container-based networking labs using a simple, YAML-based configuration model.

Terraform
> This embodiment of IaC allows you to declare resources (both cloud and on-premises) that are then programmatically managed.

All three of these tools have strong support for the IaC methodology we've been discussing in this chapter, and are therefore ideal to be used within a CI/CD pipeline for network automation. The same commands used to instantiate a virtual topology on your laptop can be embedded into a workflow within one of the build systems we've discussed. With this, you can run a series of automated tests against that topology, in conjunction with your Ansible playbook or Python script. If everything works out, the build passes, and your change is permitted to continue in the pipeline.

Having a reliable, accurate test environment isn't something you should overlook in your pipeline. Piecemeal testing of individual configs or state tables can get you only so far. Networks are complicated distributed systems, and some failure scenarios can happen only in such a system. Replicating this environment virtually may be your only safety net against causing production outages, and putting it in the pipeline means every change is vetted equally.

Deployment Tools and Strategies

Earlier in the chapter, we discussed the importance of understanding *what* you're deploying in a CI/CD pipeline. This knowledge has a big impact on the tools you use to actually deploy the changes you make.

For instance, if you're writing Python code to automate tasks around your network, you should consider treating it like a full-fledged software project. Regardless of the size, production code is production code. Even a bug in a small script can cripple your infrastructure, so you apply the same rigorous process to it as any large-scale web project.

In addition to the important testing and peer review discussed earlier, you may find it useful to explore the delivery mechanisms that software developers are starting to use. You may be able to learn from (and even copy) the cloud deployment processes and tools that other teams in your organization use to deploy their changes.

It's also becoming increasingly popular to deploy software in Docker containers. You could instruct your CI pipeline to automatically build a Docker image after a new change is reviewed and merged. This image can be deployed to a Docker Swarm or Kubernetes cluster in production.

On the other hand, sometimes we're not deploying custom software; sometimes our Git repositories are used simply to store configuration artifacts like YAML or Jinja templates. This is common for network automation efforts that use configuration management tools like Ansible to push network device configurations onto the infrastructure. However, while the method of deployment may differ between network engineers and software developers, CI plays a vital role (Figure 13-16).

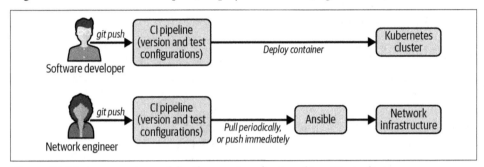

Figure 13-16. A comparison of development and networking CI pipelines

In this case, it's important to understand how these configurations are going to be used in production, as well as how rollbacks will be handled. This is important for deciding not only how Ansible will run in production but also how the configuration templates themselves are constructed. For instance, you might consider running an Ansible playbook to deploy configuration templates onto a set of network devices every time a new change is merged to the main branch—but what impact will that have on the configuration? Will the configuration always be overwritten? If so, will that overwrite a crucial part of the configuration that you didn't intend?

Some vendors provide options to help solve this problem; for example, when pushing an XML-based configuration to a Junos device, you can use the `operation` flag with a value of `replace` to specify that you want to replace an entire section of configuration. The following example shows a Jinja template for a Junos configuration that uses this option:

```
<configuration>
  <protocols>
    <bgp operation="replace">
      {% for groupname, grouplist in bgp.groups.iteritems() %}
      <group>
        <name>{{ groupname }}</name>
        <type>external</type>
        {% for neighbor in grouplist %}
        <neighbor>
          <name>{{ neighbor.addr }}</name>
          <peer-as>{{ neighbor.as }}</peer-as>
```

```
            </neighbor>
            {% endfor %}
        </group>
        {% endfor %}
      </bgp>
    </protocols>
  </configuration>
```

Unfortunately, not all vendors allow for this, but in this particular case, you could simply overwrite entire sections of configuration for each new patch in the CI pipeline to ensure that *what it should be* (WISB) always equals *what it really is* (WIRI).

This is another area with no silver bullet. The answer to the deployment question depends largely on what you are deploying and how often. It's best to first settle on a strategy for network automation; decide if you want to invest in some developers and write more formalized software, or if you want to leverage existing open source or commercial tools to deploy simple scripts and templates. This will guide you toward the appropriate deployment model.

However, deployment should *never* take place until the aforementioned concepts like peer review and automated testing have taken place. A network automation effort that does not prioritize quality and stability above all is doomed to failure.

Thinking a bit more broadly, how might we approach deploying a change to our entire network from a CI/CD context—not just to a single device at a time? A few deployment strategies have become popular for deploying applications, particularly in the cloud era, and it's important to consider what we can learn from them:

Deploy in place
    Just make the change blindly to all infrastructure nodes at once.

Rolling
    Slowly roll a change to one infrastructure element at a time, until complete.

Canary
    Roll a change out to a relatively small percentage of production infrastructure, pausing to evaluate success/failure.

Blue/green
    Create a new environment to contain the change—in parallel to the old—and migrate traffic from old to new using routing or load balancing.

While these work well for the application domain, especially in environments where the application infrastructure is relatively homogenous, it may not be obvious how these map to the network domain. After all, networks are a series of interconnected and interrelated infrastructure elements; often it's not possible to simply make a change on one network device at a time.

However, there are still lessons we can learn. Here's some food for thought:

- Blue/green deployments may not seem possible at first; we can't necessarily spin up a parallel network for every change we want to make. But often we can create parallel virtual resources like VRFs or routing adjacencies. Although this causes a bit more complication in the moment (making a change in place rather than duplicating configuration is always going to be "easier"), it not only can make the change itself easier, but also has a much simpler rollback model.

- Canary deployments work best when production infrastructure is well modularized and homogenous. You have to be able to make a change in a way that's well contained (perhaps a single data-center row) but that is also a valid production environment (deploying to a network that's used only for testing is not a valid canary deployment). This is why simple, repeatable network design is so critical for network automation success.

Summary

Your organization, especially if it's a large enterprise, might have some kind of in-house software development shop, or at least interact with third-party contractors for projects that require some custom software to be built. Reach out to those teams and ask about their processes. If they're using CI, there's a chance they'd be willing to let you use some of their existing tooling to accomplish similar goals with network automation.

In this chapter, we talked about a lot of process improvements (as well as tooling to help enforce these processes), but the real linchpin to all of this is a culture that understands the costs and benefits of this approach. If you don't have buy-in from the business to make these improvements, they will not last.

It's also important to remember that a big part of CI/CD is continuously learning. Continuously challenge the status quo, and ask yourself if the current model of managing and monitoring your network is *really* sufficient. Application requirements change often, so the answer to this question is often "no." Try to stay plugged in to the application and software development communities so you can get ahead of these requirements and build a pipeline that can respond to these changes quickly.

## CHAPTER 14

Network Automation Architecture

This book has covered and introduced many concepts, technologies, and tools for network automation. However, there is a big leap from learning a new technology or concept to stitching them together to create a plan that can be used to drive enterprise adoption of network automation. This chapter aims to give you a comprehensive strategy to start building network automation solutions, including the ones described in Chapter 2.

It is common to build network automation solutions to address an specific domain (e.g., Campus, Data Center, Security, and Cloud), but this isolation adds complexity and doesn't help in breaking down silos and reusing automation among teams. To mitigate this, we dare to propose a *network automation architecture* to help you organize the tasks to be automated in an easy-to-understand and easy-to-apply way. This architecture will provide you with a structured view to ease the definition of requirements and dependencies, which will lead to better decisions when choosing how to design and implement each task that will be automated by the network automation solution with a holistic approach.

This chapter starts by presenting a structured approach to a network automation architecture, followed by a deep dive into each component within this architecture. Finally, an example of how to apply this methodology in a real use case will show you how you can leverage it.

 In this chapter, you will find many references to other chapters in this book. We are aiming to connect the dots, to help you understand how each topic plays its role in the big picture of network automation.

Without further delay, let's get to know the network automation architecture.

Introducing the Network Automation Architecture

Even though every network automation solution may have different implementations or tools, all of them end up sharing some common patterns. Being able to identify and classify these patterns will help you adopt a systematic approach to building new solutions and evolving them while keeping them aligned to their specific functionalities. This is the goal of the network automation architecture proposed here.

Figure 14-1 depicts the six components of the network automation solution. Each component in the architecture has one or more functional goals (based on implementation), and connects with the other components to achieve the desired goals of the solution. By understanding each component, you will be able to determine where to map each action required to implement a network operational workflow, and easily identify the challenges to address and the available options for implementation.

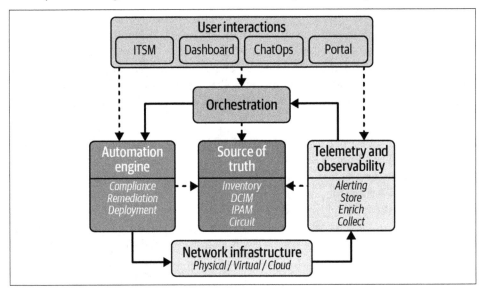

Figure 14-1. Network automation architecture

To get started, the following provides a short introduction to each architecture component:

Network infrastructure

Chapter 1 presented the new trends in network infrastructure (e.g., NFV and cloud/controller-based services). All of them, including traditional network physical devices, are contained in the scope of the *network infrastructure*. This component has already been covered throughout the book: exploring the available management interfaces in Chapter 10, discovering new networking paradigms in Chapter 4, and emulating them in Chapter 5.

User interactions

One way or another, human beings will interact with the network automation solution. You may be interfacing with Git if you're adopting a GitOps workflow; you may interface via a ticketing system if you've adopted self-service for non-technical users. Each use case requires a proper *interface*, and choosing the right one for each case will have a big impact on the solution's adoption. Getting this right is extremely important. The user interactions align culture and people to network automation. The worst thing that can happen is to expose an interface that does not end up getting used. In "User Interactions" on page 718, we describe various forms it can take, such as service portals, dashboards, and messaging applications.

Source of truth

Every network automation solution needs data to act upon it. In simple solutions that are not persistently managing a network, data can be provided ad hoc. For instance, a user could trigger a script to do a small automation task. However, when the network automation solution has to constantly manage the network state, that solution requires reference data that we define as the *intended* state (the state you want your network to be in). As you will see in "Source of Truth" on page 727, describing the network state could include multiple data use cases that are required to deploy and manage a network—like IP addressing, VLANs, routing protocols, ACLs, and much more. Moreover, to properly implement a source of truth, you need to understand the constraints and trade-offs around data management.

Automation engine

This component includes all the tasks related to changing the state of (or more generally, interacting with) the network infrastructure. It takes data from user interactions and/or from the source of truth as input in order to interact with the network via the proper interfaces. As you will see in "Automation Engine" on page 745, the automation engine includes all the aspects related to configuration management and other operational tasks (e.g., a device reboot). In this section, you will identify the role of the tools introduced in Chapter 12 or of scripts using libraries from Chapter 10.

Telemetry and observability

Contrary to the automation engine, the telemetry and observability component is focused only on retrieving (*read-only*) the network's operational state. In "Telemetry and Observability" on page 751, you will learn about how to collect, store, and consume this state, providing a proper visualization or alerting to trigger other automation tasks when the actual state of the network doesn't meet the expectations defined in the source of truth.

Orchestration

This component implements the glue between the other components, defining the logic to chain tasks to create orchestrated workflows. Most automation solutions don't have a single execution path. Depending on success, failure, or approval, different paths will be traversed. As an example, the orchestration would kick off a task in the automation engine when an alert from the observability is received, enabling closed-loop solutions. In "Orchestration" on page 771, you will go over the characteristics of a workflow engine and how it can enable event-driven automation solutions.

> Even though not explicit in the architecture (depicted as dotted arrows in Figure 14-1), every component implements APIs to facilitate communications with other components within the architecture, as well as external services. Depending on the complexity of your API implementation, you may need to implement advanced API architectures (e.g., API gateways), but these are not covered in this book.

This reference model could be generalized to any infrastructure automation solution, only replacing the network infrastructure block with a more generic one. However, because of the unique characteristics of the networking domain, with its own unique interfaces and use cases, we are focusing only on describing how to use this architecture to build network automation solutions.

It is important to know that this architecture and framework arose from years of experience designing and implementing network automation solutions. This architecture helps map tasks into high-level building blocks in order to better understand their purpose and their interconnections. We believe it will help you better understand how to apply all the concepts introduced in this book to build complete solutions.

> There are other available architectures, with more low-level details. A recent initiative by the IETF is the Intent-Based Networking informational RFC 9315 (*https://oreil.ly/AecOb*). If you read it, you will find a lot of familiar ideas because *intent-based networking* has its root in the concept of the "source of truth," and the implementation follows closed-loop automation, as does the one proposed here.

You should not overlook the fact that a network automation solution is just another software solution. Therefore, when you build it, you should consider all the architectural factors that apply when building and running software applications. Your final solution could be composed of commercial tools, open source software, and possibly custom extensions or add-ons. Each should be carefully integrated into the overall system.

How to build your own software components is beyond the scope of this book (many other books cover this topic), but in short, we strongly recommend following software development best practices to consolidate and deploy your applications, as introduced in Chapters 11 and 13, respectively. Likewise, for the sake of brevity, we don't cover considerations about the scalability, resiliency, or security of the implemented solutions. However, you should take these into account when building your real solutions.

Before getting started with the components deep dive, let's stress a key rule about approaching automation. Network automation is about transforming and improving existing operational workflows. But *you can't automate what you don't understand*. Therefore, the first step will always be to understand the current process. One way to adopt this mindset is described in "Understanding the Architecture with an Example" on page 775.

Now, it's time to go deeper into each one of the architecture components.

Overview of the Architecture Components

With the overall view of the network automation architecture (Figure 14-1), you hopefully have a basic understanding of the role of each component. In this section, you will learn more about the purpose, features, common use cases, and related challenges of each.

As commented before, we don't cover the network infrastructure component here because it has already been covered throughout Chapters 1, 4, 5, and 10. However, we want to stress that all types of networks are in the scope of the architecture.

Throughout this section, we explain how the components are interrelated and also give some references about products and tooling that can be leveraged to implement them. As you will see, most of the tools cover multiple components of the architecture, but we classify them by their main and most common role. For instance, Ansible (see Chapter 12) as a configuration management tool is referenced in the *automation engine* component, but it also comes with a CLI that could be a valid *user interaction* tool in some use cases.

Moreover, you will find references to tools that provide you with most of the features you would need to implement your solution. In some cases, you would add some configuration (e.g., defining your own Ansible playbooks) or add a small code extension. Reusing, if possible, is always preferred because of the resources needed to build and maintain a solution versus leveraging external solutions. However, you may end up building your own application when your requirements can't be addressed. This dilemma is named *build versus buy*. In the case of *build*, always consider the consequences for your company, in the present and future.

 When working on any architecture design, it's strongly recommended that you document your decision-making process, in order to help others understand your conclusion and the constraints you took into account. A good reference in this area is the Architectural Decision Record process (*https://adr.github.io*) used by GitHub.

The ultimate goal of this section is to provide a reference of the key points to tackle when designing a network automation solution and materializing them into a concrete implementation. The first step is understanding how users will interact with the solution.

User Interactions

Even though we are building automation solutions, we shouldn't forget that an end user is always interacting with them. Understanding each persona's role (skills and motivation) is a crucial part of choosing the right interface in order to tailor the user's experience and improve the solution's adoption.

For example, imagine you are managing an internet content provider with myriad points of presence (PoPs) and BGP peerings to sustain your network. In your organization, the network operations team would likely be fond of a CLI-like interface that could offer a well-known way to troubleshoot any issue. On the other side, the network capacity team would be more comfortable interacting with a dashboard offering easy-to-consume data. Only changing the UI can transform the UX without changing the underlying system.

One unstoppable trend transforming the way consumers are interacting with network services is consuming the *network as a service*. Nowadays, with the massive adoption of cloud-based solutions, everyone has gotten used to consuming infrastructure in almost real time. So, being able to offer a similar experience for the network service will match users' expectations and remove friction on its adoption. Without a doubt, creating a network as a service is a complex challenge with many facets, but user interaction is the front end of the solution, and it needs to be ready to allow the proper UX.

To give you an overview of the alternatives for this component, we cover both graphical and text-based interfaces. In both cases, you will find options for managing the network state or simply observing it. In addition, the knowledge share (or documentation) solutions are covered because of their relevance to understanding, operating, and extending the network automation solution.

Most of the user interactions we introduce next won't be new for you. You have likely used some of them before. However, the trick here is to leverage these tools to their full potential so that they are no longer simply human-facing interfaces but the first line of network automation. Tailoring them to match the expectations from both sides—the user and the automation—makes the process smoother and prevents wasting time. As we mentioned earlier, users are looking for a self-service experience when consuming any IT service, and this aligns with a more efficient use of time from the network engineering team.

One common challenge for all the user interactions is defining the data in both directions, data in and data out:

Data in
The data ingested by the user should match the expectations of the other architecture components. From the beginning, the data must adhere to well-known schemas to enforce data quality. The data will conform to a structure, and its content could follow validation rules. Suppose that the input data contains a host IPv6 address; the UI can't accept any format not compliant with the RFC defining the IPv6 address format.

On top of that, another important aspect is simplicity: request only the minimum data needed by the user and leave data extension for an automated process. It makes the data input process less tedious and minimizes human errors. As an example, if there is a request to provision a new device in a location, and the device's name follows a naming convention, the user would not need the option to set the device name but rely on automation to auto-define it.

 Data quality is not the sole responsibility of user interactions but a shared responsibility. Following the previous IPv6 example, in a later stage of the network automation process, other validation steps could raise an issue because the IP address is already in use or does not match the routing design.

Data out
Every user needs information, but depending on their role in the automation process, the best data content and format will vary. To illustrate, if the workflow starts via a ticketing system, the data out will likely be an update on the ticket. The data should contain all the relevant information required to understand the outcome of the executed task and use text, hyperlinks, and images as required.

However, do not understand data out as the final workflow execution output. During automated workflow execution, multiple data elements can be exposed to the user to indicate progress or to ask for interaction (for example, a task approval request).

After this brief overview of user interactions, we begin with the description of graphical user interfaces.

Graphical user interfaces

Graphical user interfaces (*GUIs*) serve a myriad of purposes, every one with its own characteristics. In this section, we review three of the most popular GUIs: IT service management systems to make service requests, dashboards to observe the services, and ChatOps to allow human language interactivity.

However, as we go over the architecture's components described in Figure 14-1, you will realize that a lot of other tools also offer GUIs, even though their main goal is not to interact with the end user but to offer a low-barrier interface to interact with their functionalities. Most tools offer capable UIs for network engineers but may not be suitable for all end users. Always take into account the end user's point of view to pick the right tool.

IT service management. *IT service management* (*ITSM*) systems, also known as *self-service portals*, offer an entry point to request any type of service available in the organization's *service catalog*. Every service has a definition of how it will be delivered, containing multiple stages in the process. The simplest implementation performs as a ticketing system that manages the request lifecycle (including approvals, traceability, and notifications).

Naturally, network service offerings have been moving to ITSM services because of its advantages versus other communication systems that make coordination harder, like email loops. But this is just the first step. Using an ITSM doesn't imply any automation per se. You can manually implement all the steps in the service delivery. The goal of a network automation strategy is to transform the service management steps into tasks that can be performed by a machine. Through the automation journey, you will incrementally improve the process, adding more and more automated tasks. However, it's not all or none. Sometimes it makes sense to leave some manual tasks or human judgment gates throughout the process.

Modern ITSM platforms come with a lot of features to promote automation because it optimizes delivery time and resource efficiency. Some key ITSM features that support automation are as follows:

- Configurable data input, with validation and conversion to structured data. Keeping simplicity in mind, the user should provide the relevant data needed to deliver the service, and this data should conform to custom conventions that match the expectations of the next steps in the workflow.

- Input integrations to fetch data from several sources to help users. For example, if the user has to enter a location to deliver a service, being able to retrieve the available location from a facility management system makes the input process simpler and more reliable.

- Triggering integrations with external components (via APIs). Automated tasks often require starting an external process, and this process is not going to be completed immediately. The requested system, when done, should be able to notify the ITSM of the operation result and resume the process.

- Notification systems to interact with humans participating in the service delivery—for instance, requesting approval from a qualified team member.

In Figure 14-2, a screenshot from an ITSM (ServiceNow) ticket shows a new VLAN that has been requested by a user and, once accepted, the change is scheduled and an external Ansible playbook is triggered to execute the change. These kinds of tools, with proper integrations, facilitate user interaction with network automation.

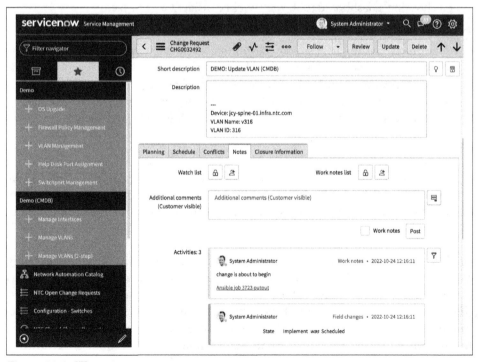

Figure 14-2. IT service management

Change management is a subject of its own. We encourage you to get a good understanding of your organization's change management process to build network automation solutions that fit well into it.

Dashboards. On the other side of ITSMs, *dashboards* offer read-only visualization to present a large amount of information in a condensed and effective format. The information may come from a myriad of sources and take multiple forms, depending on the needs of each use case.

In "Telemetry and Observability" on page 751, we cover in more detail the use of dashboards to visualize the operational state collected from the network infrastructure. There, you will learn the importance of leveraging normalized and enriched data in order to perform advanced queries to obtain relevant information.

For each purpose, you can find specialized tooling. For instance, in the business intelligence area, you have commercial products like Tableau (*https://www.tableau.com*) and Microsoft Power BI (*https://oreil.ly/zw0GJ*). IT engineering has its own multiple flavors, and two popular open source projects that have gained a lot of traction lately are Grafana (*https://oreil.ly/IYL46*) and Kibana (*https://oreil.ly/cyPyG*).

When choosing a dashboard tool, you should consider two key factors:

Data source integrations
> How many existing data source integrations exist? How easy is it to develop new ones? The first point is especially relevant if you have limited capacity in house to develop your integrations, but the reality is that it's unlikely that integrations would be available for all your data sources. Thus, it's important that the tooling offers an easy way to develop new integrations (via APIs) when needed.

Dashboard customization
> Once you have data connected, understanding the options to visualize it can make its use more effective. Typical dashboard types are bar/line charts, histograms, heatmaps, and Sankey diagrams. Another important feature is the ability to define these diagrams as code, to make their management more effective and efficient.

ChatOps. Nowadays, almost every organization has adopted instant messaging applications. These solutions—including Slack (*https://slack.com*), Microsoft Teams (*https://oreil.ly/EJoAY*), Cisco Webex (*https://www.webex.com*), and Mattermost (*https://mattermost.com*)—support asynchronous communication between people. But you can replace a person with a *bot* and expose, in a low-barrier way, some functionalities of the network automation solution. This is commonly known as *ChatOps*.

In a ChatOps bot, you can wrap multiple types of operations, including triggering a workflow, updating the source of truth, or getting the actual state of the network to support troubleshooting while sharing with the rest of the team. This occurs all without exposing all the complexity and simplifies its usability and effectiveness.

In Figure 14-3, the output of a ChatOps command from the Nautobot ChatOps application (*https://oreil.ly/1LxPh*) locates the switch and interface where an IP/MAC address is connected, using the command /netops find ip 10.1.1.3. It's a conversation that starts with a message, and the automation handles the rest. This is a simple example, but every command can be crafted to the needs of every network team and evolve over time with improvements contributed by the whole team.

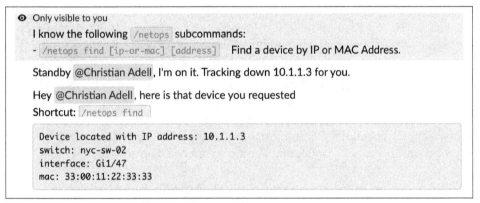

Figure 14-3. ChatOps example

 An interesting benefit of using ChatOps for network operations is the cumulative effect. Your commands will keep improving over time as more and more experience and knowledge are contributed back to the logic. As an example, you may have created an MPLS troubleshooting script that other engineers have been adding more features to over time. Furthermore, if some of these engineers leave the company, their knowledge will persist.

Chat-based interfaces like these could be further augmented with advances in artificial intelligence and natural language processing to provide a more organic, conversational UX in interacting with network automation architectures. For instance, the recently popular ChatGPT (by OpenAI) offers access to a large language model (LLM) that enables humans to "converse" with the model, which generates, word by word, a response according to the context.

This could allow for many impactful features, such as analyzing logs to propose a root cause, translating network device configurations to other platforms, performing configuration compliance analysis, or generating code snippets in any programming language to solve a specific need. On top of that, you can integrate plug-ins that allow interaction with other sources of information via APIs (for example, getting real-time operational data from the network or fetching the network intent from a source of truth).

Even though GUIs are really useful for user interactions, text-based interactions are convenient for some use cases and/or personas. We explore them next.

Text-based interactions

As with GUIs, you have multiple text-based UIs to consider. Let's start with an old friend for network engineers: the command-line interface (CLI).

If you have been in network engineering for more than five years, you've likely used CLIs to interact with network devices. Even though, as you've noticed throughout this book, the trend is to move away from them, CLIs can be a useful way to interact with your network automation solutions because a lot of your network automation users (other network engineers) feel comfortable with them. Actually, if you recap the tools described in Chapter 12, Ansible and Terraform offer a CLI too.

 You can also build your own CLI. You can use popular libraries for Python (such as Click (*https://oreil.ly/RbouD*) or Rich (*https://oreil.ly/Q-xCZ*)) or libraries for Go such as Cobra (*https://oreil.ly/VqHqg*).

Finally, let's look at how network automation can create documents and reports for various types of users.

Documentation and reporting

Each user has different requirements regarding documentation and reporting. Network engineers are used to understanding network designs in diagrams. Leadership members are interested in compliance reports to validate that standards are implemented. Without automation, generating each type of document can be costly, and once created, those documents are instantly outdated because networks are constantly changing. This is when automation comes to the rescue.

In Chapter 12, we showed an example of how to create a report taking actual data, using the Markdown language to be rendered later to HTML. Markdown is not the only markup language that can be used to generate user-friendly documentation. Alternatives include AsciiDoc (*https://oreil.ly/X8f2b*) and reStructuredText (*https://oreil.ly/Q0WPP*), popular languages to generate documentation *as code*. The final documentation is rendered in the desired format (e.g., HTML, PDF, DOCX, etc.). Other languages are focused on generating diagrams and graphs: Structurizr (*https:// oreil.ly/X7UXa*) for C4 modeling and Mermaid (*https://oreil.ly/Iayo1*) for complex diagrams.

 This book was written in AsciiDoc format.

Let's generate a network diagram as code with Mermaid. This could come from a network inventory system or the network state (e.g., LLDP). Imagine that you have a network with two spines and two leaves, and you want to generate a diagram with the network topology and the servers connected to the leaf switches. In the source of truth, the data could look like this:

```
---
connections:
    - side_a: sw1-spine
      side_b: sw1-leaf
      ip_prefix: 192.0.2.0/29
    - side_a: sw1-spine
      side_b: sw2-leaf
      ip_prefix: 192.0.2.8/29
    - side_a: sw2-spine
      side_b: sw2-leaf
      ip_prefix: 192.0.2.4/29
    - side_a: sw2-spine
      side_b: sw1-leaf
      ip_prefix: 192.0.2.12/29
    - side_a: sw1-leaf
      side_b: serverA
      ip_prefix: 10.0.0.0/29
    - side_a: sw2-leaf
      side_b: serverA
      ip_prefix: 10.0.0.4/29
```

And, using the Jinja syntax you learned in Chapter 9, you can define the following template:

```
graph TD
{% for connection in connections %}
{{ connection.side_a }}({{ connection.side_a }}) ---|{{ connection.ip_prefix }}|
    {{ connection.side_b }}({{ connection.side_b }})
{% endfor %}
```

Bringing both together, you can render the following Mermaid snippet (which can be included in a Markdown document). This code generates the diagram in Figure 14-4:

```
graph TD
sw1-spine(sw1-spine) ---|192.0.2.0/29| sw1-leaf(sw1-leaf)
sw1-spine(sw1-spine) ---|192.0.2.8/29| sw2-leaf(sw2-leaf)
sw2-spine(sw2-spine) ---|192.0.2.4/29| sw2-leaf(sw2-leaf)
sw2-spine(sw2-spine) ---|192.0.2.12/29| sw1-leaf(sw1-leaf)
sw1-leaf(sw1-leaf) ---|10.0.0.0/29| serverA(serverA)
sw2-leaf(sw2-leaf) ---|10.0.0.4/29| serverA(serverA)
```

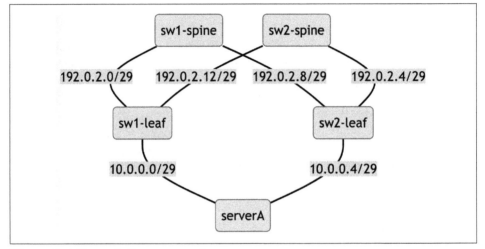

Figure 14-4. Network diagram as code

You can render Mermaid diagrams with the live editor available at *https://oreil.ly/3ihAv*.

Being able to generate *live* documentation provides access to data in almost real time and in a consistent format that can be reproduced and adapted as needed—moreover, with much less effort. You define the logic once, and you get the outcome many times. Because the data used can be provided from either the desired or the actual state, you can easily provide snapshots of one or the other. Therefore, you can generate the desired network design (from the source of truth) or represent the actual network status (from the operational state).

After reviewing some basic characteristics of user interfaces, we transition next to the cornerstone of any network automation solution: defining *how* the network should be.

Source of Truth

In this book, we have mentioned several times how every automation solution must be built on top of structured data. However, this is not a new idea. As you will see in "Data use cases" on page 730, concepts such as data center infrastructure management and IP address management have been around for a while. The big shift now is that data is no longer used only for documentation or as a representation of what is deployed. When network automation kicks in, the data will drive the network operations.

The *source of truth* (*SoT*) is a broadly accepted concept in the industry that indicates the *intended* state of the network. Even though the name *source of truth* is singular, it's an abstract concept that may be implemented by one or more systems. However, as you will see in "Data quality" on page 728, it should *behave* as one consistent data set.

Adopting the SoT as the pillar of network operations is likely the biggest mental shift for a network engineer. We have been used to describing the network design in documents or diagrams. However, as introduced in "Documentation and reporting" on page 724, the paradigm changes and the authoritative reference becomes the SoT that later renders into the most appropriate format to consume the data. Only after adopting an SoT strategy that defines the intended state of the network can you successfully deploy network automation.

The role of the network engineer in an automated network includes managing data in an SoT. They define what the network state *should be* as the intent. And this intent is represented as *structured data*. If you are already defining YAML fines in a Git repository, you may have already started deploying an SoT strategy without knowing it. The data will be used by other architecture components to change and validate the operational state.

 A data-first strategy to drive network management will save you a lot of manual work and unexpected errors while translating from the network design to the actual configuration artifacts.

As the scope of automation grows, the SoT also grows. What initially starts as data populated by humans, or as one-time import scripts, could eventually incorporate data managed by third-party systems that must be integrated to have a consolidated representation of the intended state of the network. Like any data management process that collects, normalizes, and persists data (also known as extract-transform-load, or ETL), it must be carefully designed to keep the SoT's data in good shape. For example, you may have in the SoT all the interfaces and circuits described, but the intent of these circuits may vary over time because of scheduled maintenance.

Including the circuit provider's intent in your SoT will provide more educated data to operate the network.

In this section, we cover several aspects to take into account when designing and implementing an SoT strategy:

Data quality
> The SoT is all about data, and it's going to be as good as the data it manages. Even though the definition of data quality may have several interpretations, we explain the basic dimensions to assess.

Data use cases
> The SoT concept applies to any IaC solution. Focusing on network-related data use cases would give you a more concrete example in this domain.

Data modeling
> Maybe one of the most critical aspects when working with data is to define the right data models. These should be good enough to define the network intent but simple enough to facilitate data operation.

Persistence
> To keep our network working without disruptions, the data that defines its state must persist. We have several options, with pros and cons to consider.

Data population
> To finally use the SoT requires populating data into it. We will comment on the most common approaches.

Distributed SoT
> As we introduced previously, the SoT may be composed of many data systems that require integration to provide a consistent network intent as a whole.

Let's start with defining what we understand as *good data*.

Data quality

In any automation solution, data is king. It is the data that is going to be used by the automation engine to ensure that the network intent is applied to the network infrastructure. Therefore, this network infrastructure state will be as good as the data used. You must ensure that the data adheres to quality principles to be considered reliable. This is what we understand as *data quality*.

Even though its definition may vary among data domains, we recommend keeping the following questions in mind to help you understand whether your data complies with basic quality principles. As an example reference, let's assume your goal is to generate a BGP configuration for a network device; the questions are as follows:

Completeness

Does this data cover all the necessary information to fulfill the network operation needs? Are all the BGP attributes defined so the final configuration is complete?

Consistency

Is the data holistically providing a consistent view, or do conflicts exist? If the BGP attributes are coming from two data sets, one containing the BGP peerings and the other the IP addresses, a one-to-one mapping should exist between them, without overlaps.

Validity

Is the data adhering to the business rules and in the proper format? If the BGP neighbor is defined as an IP address, that data should adhere to the expected format and values. A value of 300.1.1.1 should not be accepted as an IPv4 address.

Usability

Is the data easy to modify and consume? Your system may need to expose via API the addition of BGP peers, and then use the data to render the proper configuration.

Relevance

Is the data relevant at the right moment in time? Past, present, and future? Maybe you want to deprovision a BGP peer, so the data should express the desired status now and also be available to expose the previous status for reporting.

Accuracy

How well does this data reflect the network intent? Are there any gaps between the design and the data models storing it? To improve the accuracy of the BGP peer IPs, you could add a validation of the peer IPs and the ASN to check whether both belong to the same entity.

You can delve deeper into data quality with the following books: *Data Quality Fundamentals* by Barr Moses et al. (O'Reilly) or *Fundamentals of Data Engineering* by Joe Reis and Matt Housley (O'Reilly).

Next, before exploring the challenges of data management in the SoT, we present the common data use cases in a network SoT.

Data use cases

The data models you need for describing your network's intended state have likely already been defined by someone else. Unless you have very specific needs, we recommend getting started with solutions that already come with battle-tested models and easy extensibility to adapt to your needs.

In this space and as open source projects, some tools address only one use case—for example, NIPAP (*https://oreil.ly/LDAGI*) to manage IP addresses or Peering Manager (*https://oreil.ly/NdZJ4*) to manage BGP peerings. Others try to cover more data use cases in one tool, such as Nautobot (*https://oreil.ly/c18X_*) and NetBox (*https://oreil.ly/Gs224*). In all these cases, you get out-of-the-box opinionated data models ready to use.

> In this section, we use the Nautobot public demo instance, available at *https://demo.nautobot.com*, to illustrate the content type examples because it covers all of them, but you could get similar data models from other projects.
>
> We will explore a few Nautobot network models via its REST API. You could complement this exploration via the GUI to get a more visual representation. With this code snippet, you are ready to start interacting via the Python Requests library using the demo token:

```
>>> import requests, json
>>> url = "https://demo.nautobot.com"
>>> token = "a" * 40
>>> headers = {"Authorization": f"Token {token}"}
```

We start with the network inventory, or more generally, infrastructure inventory. It must contain all the devices under the scope of automation, and it serves as the reference for the rest of the data use cases.

Network inventory.   As you may recall from our Ansible, Nornir, and Terraform coverage in Chapter 12, the inventory data is fundamental. In Ansible and Nornir, it comes with connection details and extra variables attached to each element. On the other side, for Terraform, the inventory is defined as the variable data to provision the infrastructure resources.

There is no strict definition of what an inventory item contains, but the following list is a good summary of the most common attributes:

Name
   A human-friendly identifier of the device.

Location
   Where the device is placed. For example, in an on-premises environment, it could be a rack within a data center, and in a cloud platform, the region.

Type

Which type of network service/platform? It could be the device model or the type of network cloud service.

Connection details

How to connect to manage the device. If it's a standalone device, the details would be its IP or FQDN, and if it's a cloud service, a well-known API. Proper credentials must be provided to get the right level of access to the management.

Status

To represent the intended state of the object. For instance, whether it's *active* or *planned*.

In Example 14-1, the Nautobot REST API retrieves the *devices* that in Nautobot represent part of the inventory (other options exist, but we leave them out for simplicity).

Example 14-1. Exploring a Nautobot device as inventory

```
>>> response = requests.get(f"{url}/api/dcim/devices", headers=headers) ❶
>>> devices = response.json()["results"]
>>> print(json.dumps(devices[1], indent=4))
>>>
{
    "device_role": {"name": "edge"},
    "device_type": {"model": "DCS-7280CR2-60"},
    "id": "9d512f81-5523-456d-8508-506da78fe6e2",
    "name": "ams01-edge-01",
    "platform": {"name": "Arista EOS"},
    "primary_ip": {
        "id": "6983eaad-3b82-46c8-8533-ffa382508895",
        "address": "10.11.128.1/32",
    }
    "site": {"name": "AMS01"},
    "status": {"value": "active"},
    # Output trimmed for brevity
}
```

❶ It uses the `url` and `headers` variables defined previously.

In Example 14-1, you can observe (some of) the attributes of a device exposed via the REST API. If you explore the result by yourself, you will see much more data that is aggregated from other data use cases related to this device model as the anchor reference.

REST API Versus GraphQL

REST APIs, explained in Chapter 10, are the most popular way to interact program-matically with applications. However, other API protocols can be extremely helpful when data needs to be aggregated and customized by the client. *GraphQL*, developed by Meta (formerly Facebook), can achieve in one single API call what would require several when using REST.

In this example, you can easily compare how to get the same data. The GraphQL API allows embedding a *query* that defines exactly what needs to be returned. Using the REST API, you need to access multiple REST API endpoints one by one (green/dot-ted lines) and, finally, combine the data in the client. On the other side, in GraphQL, the client accesses only one endpoint (red/dashed lines) with a *query* that defines exactly which information is needed.

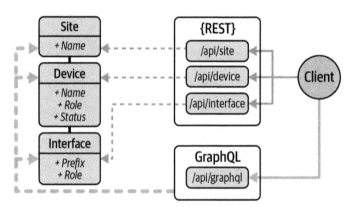

Figure 14-5. REST versus GraphQL APIs

Let's reproduce Example 14-1 but using a *query* definition that gets passed to the API path via the POST method. The query may contain filters with variables, and the nested attribute selection within connected models (e.g., select the `name` under `platform`):

```
>>> query = """
... query {
...   devices (name: "ams01-edge-01"){
...     name
...     platform {
...       name
...     }
...   }
... }
... """
>>> response = requests.post(
...     f"{url}/api/graphql/",
...     json={"query": query},
```

```
...        headers=headers,
... )
>>> print(json.dumps(response.json(), indent=4))
{
    "data": {
        "devices": [
            {
                "name": "ams01-edge-01",
                "platform": {
                    "name": "Arista EOS"
                }
            }
        ]
    }
}
```

We don't cover GraphQL in detail here, but hopefully this brief comparison has shown you some of its unique benefits in contrast to REST APIs. GraphQL can allow you to be more *effective* in retrieving the data you want, while also being more *efficient*, requiring far fewer requests to retrieve the data. You can extend your knowledge through the official GraphQL learning page (*https://graphql.org/learn*).

Once the inventory is in place, it's time to enrich the data with other related content.

Data center infrastructure management. In physical network environments, *data center infrastructure management* (*DCIM*) defines how the network devices should be placed and connected. It may include information about the racks, device hardware, power feeds, cables, circuits, or any other details required to build the network physically.

Example 14-2 uses the device from Example 14-1 to retrieve the *intended* cable tracing, from its first interface to another device.

Example 14-2. Exploring Nautobot cable tracing

```
>>> device_id = '9d512f81-5523-456d-8508-506da78fe6e2'
>>> response = requests.get(
>>>     f"{url}/api/dcim/interfaces/?device_id={device_id}", headers=headers)       ❶
>>> interfaces = response.json()["results"]
>>> response = requests.get(
>>>     f"{url}/api/dcim/interfaces/{interfaces[0]['id']}/trace", headers=headers)   ❷
>>> trace = response.json()                                                          ❸
>>> print(json.dumps(trace, indent=4))
[
    [
        {
            "device": {"name": "ams01-edge-01"},
            "name": "Ethernet1/1",
            "cable": "e1472be1-056b-4b4d-b135-e5c287d9b570"
        },
```

```
        {"status": {"value": "connected",},},
        {
            "device": {"name": "ams01-edge-02"},
            "name": "Ethernet1/1",
            "cable": "e1472be1-056b-4b4d-b135-e5c287d9b570"
        }
        # Output trimmed for brevity
    ]
]
```

❶ We retrieve the interfaces for a specific device using its ID.

❷ For a specific interface ID, we retrieve the trace for the cable.

❸ The trace information contains both ends and other information such as the state.

The DCIM data can be used for multiple purposes, from providing accurate guidance for on-field engineers to serving as the reference to validate the network topology by comparing it with the state. If the retrieved LLDP information from a connected interface shows different information than the intent, for example, we know that a mismatch needs to be solved.

> Even though this content type could seem irrelevant for cloud-based network services because there are no racks, console cables, or cables (exposed to the consumer), some of this content can be reused and adapted as *virtual* concepts—for example, virtual interfaces or virtual circuits.

IP address management. Tools for managing IP address objects have been around for a while because of the conflicts that an IP address/prefix overlap may cause. IPAM solutions have usually been wrapped as DDI platforms: DNS, DHCP, and IPAM, because all three typically share common relationships.

In Example 14-3, we reuse the `primary_ip` identifier from the device to explore, in more detail, all the attributes contained in the IP address model such as the DNS name, the attached VRF, or the NAT mapping.

Example 14-3. Exploring the Nautobot IP address

```
>>> ip_address_id = "6983eaad-3b82-46c8-8533-ffa382508895"
>>> response = requests.get(
>>>     f"{url}/api/ipam/ip-addresses/{ip_address_id}/", headers=headers)
>>> print(json.dumps(response.json(), indent=4))
{
    "family": {
        "value": 4,
        "label": "IPv4"
    },
    "address": "10.11.128.1/32",
    "assigned_object_type": "dcim.interface",
    "assigned_object": {
        "device": {
            "name": "ams01-edge-01"
        },
        "name": "Loopback0",
        "cable": null
    },
    "dns_name": "edge-01.ams01.atc.nautobot.com",
    # Output trimmed for brevity
}
```

Network properties. This category includes any other network-related data that is required to define the intent of your network. These properties will differ depending on each network design. In this group, we can find VLANs, ACLs, VRFs, BGP, OSPF, or any network services, including DNS or NTP.

The myriad network protocols and features are more specialized than the previous ones that are common in all the networks. Because of this, there are fewer predefined data models available in the general-purpose SoT projects, but it is evolving as network automation adoption is becoming mainstream.

> Don't confuse the data models defined in the SoT with the data models used by model-driven protocols (e.g., NETCONF or gNMI). Both are data models but with different purposes. The latter should be complete and cover all the potential use cases a network device supports. But in the SoT, the data model should be as simple as possible to improve manageability while addressing your network design needs. We provide more details in "Data modeling" on page 737.

Still exploring Nautobot, in Example 14-4, you can see how a BGP peer endpoint is modeled.

Example 14-4. Exploring a Nautobot BGP model

```
>>> response = requests.get(
>>>     f"{url}/api/plugins/bgp/peer-endpoints", headers=headers) ❶
>>> bgp_peer_endpoints = response.json()["results"]
>>> print(json.dumps(bgp_peer_endpoints[0], indent=4))
{
    "routing_instance": {
        "display": "dfw01-edge-02 - AS 65535",
    },
    "source_ip": {
        "address": "10.9.192.10/32"
    },
    "autonomous_system": null,
    "peer_group": {
        "name": "EDGE-to-LEAF",
    },
    "peer": {
        "display": "dfw01-leaf-02",
    },
    "import_policy": "",
    "export_policy": "",
    "secret": null,
    # Output trimmed for brevity
}
```

❶ The BGP model is not included in the core application but as extensions under the /api/plugin endpoint.

It may happen that you can't find a preexisting data model for the network services you are interested in. Don't stress; you can always craft your own data models, either extending existing solutions on top of databases (as in Example 14-4) or simply using structured data (JSON or YAML) and storing it in Git. You will understand the implications of each approach in "Data modeling" on page 737.

Configuration templates. The data represented in the SoT should be agnostic to the platforms where the network services will be running. The data should work well for different vendors, versions, or network interfaces. Thus, at this level of abstraction, the data can't be directly used to configure the network infrastructure. If you can use it directly, then, the data model is likely so specific that it could not be reused for other platforms.

To fill the gap between the data in the SoT and the required configuration artifact syntax for each platform and interface (e.g., CLI, XML, or JSON), you can use configuration templates. As you learned in Chapter 9, you can use Jinja templates or equivalent solutions to *render* the configuration artifacts that you will put into action in "Configuration management" on page 746.

Because of their nature (they don't get too much benefit from database features), configuration templates are usually stored in version control systems such as Git. This allows a peer-review process and continuous integration (to validate the syntax and/or the expected operational state) to enforce that the rendered configuration is consistent with the network infrastructure expectations.

 When testing configuration templates, keep the template's input data and expected output consistent, avoiding testing two aspects at a time.

After covering the most representative data use cases in the networking area, next we review recommendations for creating *good* data models to represent them.

Data modeling

The SoT data models must be capable of describing the intended network state, but, at the same time, they should provide the right level of accuracy, completeness, validity, and usability. You need to find the right balance.

Defining data models requires the ability to translate a network design into data structures that can represent it. As already covered in detail in Chapter 8, data formats (e.g., JSON or YAML) allow us to serialize structured data, and data modeling languages (e.g., YANG) let us define the rules and relationships of the data regarding a specific use case.

The data modeling can leverage group-based design to simplify the amount of data. Suppose that all the upstream interfaces use a common set of attributes (e.g., MTUs and VLANs); these attributes can be grouped in a role type that applies to multiple interfaces at the same time.

Luckily for you, you won't always need to create your own data models. If you are using an existing SoT project, like Nautobot or NetBox, they come with opinionated models that have worked well for other networks. However, you would likely need some customization to represent your own network design. This is where options for extending existing data models, with new attributes or links to other data use cases, would be helpful.

If you don't find a capable data model, your last resort is to create it from scratch. You can use data models from other SoT projects or complete data models used as configuration artifacts, such as the models defined in YANG by the OpenConfig consortium or the IETF.

A structured approach. Coming up with a final data model to support your network design may take a while, and usually an incremental and iterative approach is recommended (especially in brownfield network environments). The following steps may help you structure this process:

1. Understand your network design.

    Find out which configuration items are static or variable, and identify patterns at different levels to reduce the amount of data required. Having a simple network design will make things easier.

2. Define the scope.

    Limit the network environment to model, and use it as your inventory. You don't need to automate the whole network at once.

3. Choose some part of the configuration.

    Modeling a full configuration may be a complicated task. But you can start small and model only some configuration sections to get started and show value.

4. Sketch the data model.

    Define the data structures required to track the variable data of the configuration part (you will use representative configuration snippets from the selected inventory), understanding where the data will be stored. The static data will go into configuration templates.

5. Create the configuration templates.

    Establish the configuration templates to create the configuration artifacts using the variable data coming from the data model. To support multiple network platforms and interfaces, you will verify that the data model is capable of solving various use cases.

6. Start using the model.

    Get started with low-risk tasks, such as validating configuration compliance (more in "Configuration management" on page 746), that will show the value of using the SoT as the north star of the network automation.

Data modeling example. Let's do a small exercise to help you understand what data modeling looks like in a real scenario.

First, you get the actual interface configuration snippets from various vendors and for some network devices (the scope):

Cisco IOS

```
interface gigabitethernet 1/0/2
 ip address 192.0.2.1/24
 switchport mode access
 switchport access vlan 123
```

Juniper Junos

```
set interfaces ge-1/0/2 native-vlan-id 123
set interfaces ge-1/0/2 unit 0 family inet address 192.0.2.1/24
set interfaces ge-1/0/2 enabled
```

From the configuration, you observe that each interface configuration has some values that change (the interface name, IP address, and VLAN ID) and others that remain constant (the mode access and the *enabled* mode).

Sketching the *interface* data model using YAML format, covering multiple interfaces, results in the following:

```
interfaces:
  - name: "gigabitethernet 1/0/2"
    vlan: 123
    address: "192.0.2.1/24"
```

Notice that the data model works well for both vendors. Then it's time to define the Jinja templates that work well with the data model, as you have seen in Chapters 9 and 12:

Cisco IOS

```
{% for interface in interfaces %}
interface {{ interface["name"] }}
 ip address {{ addr["address"] }}
 switchport mode access
 switchport access vlan {{ interface["vlan"] }}
{% endfor %}
```

Juniper Junos

```
{% for interface in interfaces %}
set interfaces {{ interface["name"] }} native-vlan-id {{ interface["vlan"] }}
set interfaces {{ interface["name"] }} unit 0 family inet
  address {{ interface["address"] }}
set interfaces {{ interface["name"] }} enabled
{% endfor %}
```

And, combining both, you are ready to re-create your intended configuration from the SoT. It's important to note that both the data model and the templates work together to create the configuration artifacts, and when data does not change, it is stored in the templates.

As you may guess, the data in the SoT must be persisted, and choosing one option or another will come with different trade-offs.

Data Persistence

Defining a data structure and saving its content in memory is only the first step to storing the network intent. This data must be available at any point in time, even though the ingestion system goes down.

We have several options to persist the data, and deciding one way or another will come with different features and constraints. We focus on two popular options to store the SoT data:

Version control system
> Storing files in a version control system like Git (covered in Chapter 11) is more accessible for collaboration, and offers great historical traceability and rollback functionality.

Database
> Storing data in a proper database gives us a structured, schema-driven way to store and organize our data, and guarantee scalable and efficient consumption of that data.

> Most of the time, the final SoT solution will be composed of different persistence options, taking the best of each type. We go deeper into this topic in "Distributed source of truth" on page 743.

Beyond the scope of this book but worth mentioning is the a set of properties known as ACID (*https://oreil.ly/HLlR3*) that define how a data transaction should behave. With that noted, let's do a quick overview of the characteristics of these two common persistency options.

Version control systems. From Chapter 11, you are already aware of the benefits of using version control systems to manage files. This approach empowers the collaboration of multiple engineers working on the same files and introduces requirements to *merge* their work. These files can contain any kind of data: a script, a Jinja template, or structured data (e.g., YAML or JSON).

Using a version control system makes integration with CI pipelines easier (as seen in Chapter 13). This integration facilitates running validation tests on any change in the data. For example, a version control system can check whether the result of rendering the data with the templates is creating a valid configuration artifact. Finally, via peer review, you can make sure that any update on the SoT has been reviewed and accepted by more than one engineer. Also, because the *history* comes for free, it's trivial to check who added a new ACL entry a few months ago.

Using Git to manage infrastructure operations is known as *GitOps*. Integrating code with pipelines enables powerful collaboration and automation, such as kicking off a configuration deployment process (see "Configuration deployment" on page 750).

However, this ingestion process, which works well for updating some types of data or configuration templates, can become cumbersome when the SoT is updated frequently or is integrated with other data sources, such as a service portal. Also, data consumption is limited to managing structured data files, without a query language that could provide convenient data manipulation for read and write operations. You can't use relationships as in databases, and the only option is to create static references between objects in the structured data files.

You should not forget about enforcing data validation when using structured data documents. As mentioned in Chapter 8, every one of these formats has available some schema validation tools, like JSON Schema, to make sure that the data conforms to predefined rules. Using schema definitions will save errors on data ingestion (running in during the CI pipeline) or on data consumption (fetching data from an external source).

Databases.   Databases are the most popular ways to store and consume data. The most popular type, the *relational* database, organizes data in *tables* (representing an object type), and every *column* represents an attribute or an interconnection to other tables via *relationships*. Using the database *schema*, you can enforce constraints such as uniqueness or type of attributes. In Example 14-1, you can infer that the *device* and *site* are stored in different tables, with a relationship between them (for example, Nautobot and NetBox use a relational database). To consume the data, SQL allows sophisticated queries to read or write exactly the data you want. Many open source SQL databases exist, such as MySQL (*https://oreil.ly/NPIoV*), PostgreSQL (*https://oreil.ly/C8bmn*), and MariaDB (*https://oreil.ly/w__yL*).

 Learning SQL is not mandatory at all for a network engineer. You will find multiple frameworks that allow using SQL via a programming language. However, if you want to apply advanced features, we recommend reading *Learning SQL*, 3rd Edition, by Alan Beaulieu (O'Reilly).

Nowadays, we have other types of databases, known as *NoSQL* databases. Without the *relational* characteristic, there is more flexibility to define the data models, optimizing for different aspects such as scalability or performance. It's beyond the scope of this book to provide a detailed analysis of these types. Regarding the SoT or IaC, the *Graph* databases offer a more intuitive representation between entities (nodes) and the properties of these relationships (edges). Two examples of this type are Neo4j (*https://oreil.ly/V-ntH*) and EdgeDB (*https://oreil.ly/pPSYk*).

When to use Git or a database.   There is no simple answer when you're trying to decide between using Git or a database. *It depends.* The most common scenario, in complex network automation solutions, is to have a mix of both to get the best of both worlds.

The rule of thumb is to store data that doesn't change often (usually coming from the network architecture team) in Git, and store information that changes frequently (usually coming from the users or the network operations team) in databases.

For example, say you need to create an automated solution for managing firewall rules exposed to the user (which you'll see in "Understanding the Architecture with an Example" on page 775). The firewall rules will go into the database, enforcing valid attributes, because frequent changes are likely expected. In parallel, in Git, you may have an *acceptable* firewall policy defined and maintained by the security team and used to validate that the firewall rules adhere to it before deploying them.

 The dilemma of choosing between Git and a database is something that new databases are trying to solve by offering a Git-like operation on top of SQL. One example of this approach is Dolt (*https://oreil.ly/y2yXc*), an SQL database with documentation describing it as "Git versions files, Dolt versions tables. It's like Git and MySQL had a baby."

So far, you have learned how to define data models ("Data modeling" on page 737) and how to store them to build an SoT. The next step is to get data in.

Data population

Once your SoT is ready to use, it's time to populate the data that defines your network intent. As introduced in "Data use cases" on page 730, you'll have different types of content to define. You need to set up the inventory first and then, incrementally, enrich it with more data as required by your network automation solution.

How to get started depends mostly on whether your network is already running (a brownfield environment) or only planned and will be provisioned afterward (a greenfield environment).

Brownfield environments.   In a brownfield environment, the network is already up and running. A reasonable assumption is to take the actual operational state as the *initial* intended state. To import this state, a common approach is to define a one-time operation (per device) to retrieve the configuration from the network devices (with a predefined list of devices or via auto-discovery) and convert it into the SoT data models.

You may argue that retrieving the configuration from network devices is *never a one-time operation*. Well, the idea is to trust the actual configuration state then, and from now on, always give precedence to the data present in the SoT. So, later configuration retrievals will be used to compare and understand whether a drift has occurred.

However, this import process requires curation. Assuming that no automation was in place before, the configuration across the network likely won't be 100% consistent, so you can't trust all the data as valid. For instance, the VLANs in an interface may include some leftover ones. When your import process detects issues, it could try to autocorrect them, follow some rules, or raise a warning to manually correct them.

After this first load, you must flip the paradigm (if not, you will be in an endless loop). From now on, the SoT data represents the desired state, and any subsequent changes should be reflected there first. This applies only to the configuration defined from the SoT. In brownfield environments, it's common to start with only some coverage and leave some configuration out of the SoT in the initial stage, to import later after automation has been working.

Greenfield environments. In a greenfield environment, you might start by defining the network intent in the SoT and configure the network afterward. Defining this intent may require you to manually input a lot of data, to represent all the configuration aspects your network requires. This may become a tedious process.

To make things easier and more consistent, we recommend you use automated processes to generate all the necessary data from the minimum input data. To show you what we mean, to create a complete leaf-and-spine data center architecture, the automation could require only the location and the number of leaves. Automatically, using design logic, an automated process would create the required definition of leaf and spine devices, their interface configuration and cable interconnection, IP addresses, routing protocol setup, and any other necessary data.

 Automating data generation for new deployments lowers the adoption barrier of the SoT strategy and allows enforcing a consistent network design.

Finally, the last topic to cover is how to operate with a distributed SoT.

Distributed source of truth

Throughout this chapter, we refer to the SoT as a single entity. The reality proves to be slightly different. Most organizations maintain data relevant to network management in different data sources. For instance, the network inventory data may be part of the company-wide asset management system, and the IP addresses may be defined together with DHCP and DNS configuration.

The data management strategy may need to align with organizational (e.g., allowing domain-specific policies) or technical (e.g., representing specific data use cases) constraints—and in this case, both must be taken into account when designing this part of your network automation architecture. However, the goal of the SoT remains the same: to represent a consistent network intent. Thus, a key aspect is to identify which data store owns each data set, also known as the *authoritative source* or a *system of record (SoR)*. Honoring data ownership is crucial to avoid data inconsistencies.

Designing a data management solution that includes a distributed SoT can be done in several ways:

Establish integrations with every data store
> The SoT consumer defines and manages integrations with every data source. This decentralized approach offers higher flexibility than a centralized approach, but implies more complexity on the customer side because it has to implement data validation and normalization and define the logic to interconnect data coming from each source. Furthermore, the complexity of this full-mesh integration (between consumers and data sources) grows exponentially.

Consolidate data into a single SoT
> The strategy here is aggregating data from multiple data stores into a single entity that adapts and combines the data in a centralized fashion. This makes the clients' implementation and data management much simpler. Also, it allows source data enrichment, extending the original model with extra information available in the central source of truth. Sometimes this aggregation means decommissioning the original source, and other times, the source remains as the SoR, so the aggregated data is only read-only (to keep consistency). In this second case, we have to keep in mind the implications of data being temporarily out of sync for a while (during the time between the sync and the present).

Aggregate data stores behind one facade
> This approach offers a single pane of glass for the network intent, but data is not stored in a single place but aggregated on-the-fly. It's a similar pattern to API gateways, which aggregate multiple APIs behind a single one. This aggregation enforces data validation and normalization in each integration and takes the data directly from the SoR. However, it is more complicated to enrich the data and fulfill custom needs because the process requires creating new properties to extend the original objects.

In our experience, in the distributed SoT environments, the most sustainable strategies are consolidating and/or aggregating data stores, simplifying the client-side implementation, and offering a central place to control the SoT.

Once the network intent is defined in the SoT, it's time to start using it. This is the role of the automation engine component.

Automation Engine

The automation engine encompasses the operations to manage the network state and perform network tasks such as upgrades. You learned about tools to build automation engine tasks in several chapters. In Chapter 12, you learned about tools to manage infrastructure, including Ansible, Terraform, and Nornir. In Chapter 10, you learned about the most popular interfaces and libraries for interacting with network infrastructure (e.g., NETCONF, RESTCONF, gNMI).

The first thing to recall, from Figure 14-1, is that this block interacts with the network infrastructure, together with the telemetry and observability blocks. However, there is a big distinction. While the latter focus on data collection, the automation engine *impacts* the network state, so you should proceed carefully. We have two key recommendations:

- Get started by implementing dry-run tasks to gain confidence in the automation. This execution mode should provide a detailed report of what would change in the network infrastructure before it actually happens.

- Leverage continuous integration (Chapter 13) and emulation solutions (Chapter 5) to validate the effect of changes before deploying in production.

This section will help you understand, at a high level, the key functions of this architecture component. It can be split into two main groups: configuration management and operations. Other tasks may not fall into these categories, but most of them do.

Choosing the best solution(s) depends on several factors (remember to always consider the *buy versus build* dilemma):

Supported network interfaces
  The network infrastructure in use strongly influences the available options. However, usually you will have several options, each with the characteristics mentioned in Chapter 10.

Existing tooling
> If you are not starting from scratch (some automation is already in place), you should always assess reusing existing tools before adopting new ones.

Team skills
> Any automation solution requires you to set it up, maintain it, and operate it. Choose the solution that better fits your team by considering questions like programming language versus data formats.

Integrations
> Via either user interaction or APIs, it's important to define how automation users or automated processes (respectively) will interact with the automation engine tools.

> Don't overthink your tooling choices. If the goal and scope are well-defined, jumping from one to another will be easy when needed.

Configuration management

The main goal of most network automation solutions is to automatically manage the network state. But, zooming in, you can identify four stages that can be incrementally adopted to fulfill a complete configuration management solution; see Figure 14-6.

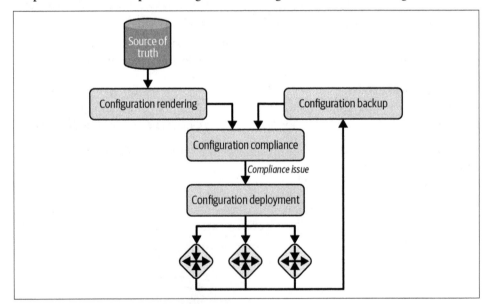

Figure 14-6. Configuration management

The four stages are as follows:

Configuration backup

Retrieves and persists the configuration state of the network, to be used as the reference of the actual state. The configuration backup can also be used to return the network to a previous state (e.g., via a rollback operation).

Configuration rendering

Creates the proper configuration artifacts (per interface), combining the data and templates from the SoT.

Configuration compliance

Compares the actual configuration (from configuration backup) with the intended one (from configuration rendering), and calculates the drift between them.

Configuration deployment

Updates the state of the network infrastructure using the proper configuration artifacts generated in the configuration rendering. It may include some processing to move the configuration state from where it is to where it should be.

 A few open source solutions offer all four configuration management features together. Nautobot Golden Config (*https://oreil.ly/lo6br*) provides a framework to implement all but the deployment stage (at the time of writing).

Configuration backup. Configuration backup and archiving have been around for a long time. You may be familiar with RANCID (*https://oreil.ly/CQAF6*), a popular tool for maintaining router configuration files in Git or Subversion. This and similar solutions have been used long before network automation was a trend, with the main purpose to retrieve and store configurations from devices. These configuration files were used to compare the state between specified moments in time and to roll back configurations to a *stable* point when an undesired behavior was observed.

Example 14-5 compares two configuration outputs by using versioning capabilities to spot the differences.

Example 14-5. Configuration backup diff

```
$ git diff
diff --git a/nyc/nyc-leaf-02.infra.ntc.com.cfg b/nyc/nyc-leaf-02.infra.ntc.com.cfg
index 0f3fa95..4e14e60 100644
--- a/nyc/nyc-leaf-02.infra.ntc.com.cfg
+++ b/nyc/nyc-leaf-02.infra.ntc.com.cfg
@@ -189,9 +189,9 @@ ip route 0.0.0.0/0 10.0.0.2
```

```
router bgp 65255
    router-id 10.0.20.7
    neighbor 10.11.11.17 remote-as 65253
-   neighbor 10.11.11.17 maximum-routes 12000
+   neighbor 10.11.11.17 maximum-routes 14000 ❶
    neighbor 10.11.11.25 remote-as 65253
```

❶ The BGP maximum-routes parameter changed.

Using version control systems is the most common way to store backup configurations because of the features around file versioning and comparison. But if you are storing your backup configuration files in clear text, be sure to remove any secret before persisting it—for instance, the BGP MD5 keys or the user (hashed) passwords.

 Comparing configuration artifacts (we are not talking only about CLI) is useful to understand changes between configuration states, but keep in mind that the intended configuration is always the one coming from the rendering of data from the SoT. Use it as your reference.

Configuration rendering. A solid network automation solution defines the intended state in the SoT (see "Source of Truth" on page 727). But this intent is useless if we can't translate it into actual configurations, adapted to each networking platform. This is exactly the role of the configuration rendering. It combines data (explained in "Data modeling" on page 737) with templates (covered in Chapter 9), both part of the SoT, to create the configuration artifacts expected by the network infrastructure (see Chapter 12 for a configuration rendering example with Ansible).

The configuration rendering uses the inventory as the starting point and extends the data with related data—for example, IP addresses, interfaces, circuits, and any other relevant content types, as expected by the template. This data manipulation process usually involves a hierarchy for combining and merging the data. Imagine you have global NTP servers, but for some locations, you may have different servers. When incorporating the NTP servers into the device data, you should take the more specific ones. This is the rule of thumb—the more specific wins—but in some cases, you may want to use *weights* to have more control over the logic.

Every network can embrace automation. However, the effort and complexity in automating a *standardized* network versus one without clear patterns (also known as a *snowflake*) differ significantly. If every device has its own configuration knobs and custom design, the number of statements in your automation solution would result in spaghetti code that's hard to maintain and extend. We strongly recommend that before starting the configuration management journey, you take a while to reflect on your standard network design and the exceptions that need to be corrected eventually. This will make your automation effort more efficient and robust.

Being able to render the *intended* configurations, partial or complete, is a great step toward commanding your network from the SoT. In brownfield environments, it makes sense to start with only a subset of the configuration to gain confidence incrementally. In new network deployments, configuration rendering is an opportunity to build the full configuration from scratch, to drive the network from the beginning.

Configuration compliance. Once you have the actual configuration (from backup) and the intended one (from rendering), you are ready to see whether the configuration state is in sync or some deviation exists. This is the goal of configuration compliance.

Becoming aware of configuration inconsistencies (the first step in a *network assurance strategy*) opens the door to, eventually, remediating them. The final goal is to automate the process end to end, but getting started on the automated configuration management is helpful, as this read-only operation is low-hanging fruit. We strongly recommend checking configuration compliance regularly to detect deviations (maybe introduced by a manual intervention), to bring the network back to matching the network's intended state.

Configuration compliance applies to all types of configuration artifacts: CLI-based or API payloads (JSON, XML, YANG). Indeed, comparing structured data is easier, but when the configuration is not structured (CLI), parsing it is still possible with tools such as Batfish (*https://oreil.ly/sK1Y8*), Cisco pyATS/Genie (*https://oreil.ly/t7N9p*), or NTC Templates (*https://oreil.ly/baeb9*); see Chapter 10 for an example.

Even though CLI-based configurations are harder to manage (expect some vendor formatting weirdness, including reordering of lines), the reality is that they are still common in 2023.

Configuration deployment. The final step in configuration management is to change the state of the network infrastructure to match the intended one. This change may be a complete configuration deployment or a partial one, targeting only a specific part of the configuration. Both options are valid, and using one or the other will depend on how far along you are on the configuration management journey. In the early stages, you focus only on managing the state of network features that are especially relevant for you (e.g., managing the BGP state on a neighbor when the circuit is expected to enter a maintenance period). Later, you can increase the coverage while your automation experience evolves.

In the scope of configuration deployment, configuration *remediation* changes the network state starting from the current state, and calculates the changes to move to the desired state. You need to provide the configuration elements in a particular order to achieve the final state using an *imperative* mode; in contrast, the *declarative* approach defines the target state independent of the current one.

In both cases, implicit in changing the configuration is being ready to return to a stable state when things go wrong. This is known as configuration *rollback*. In Chapter 10, we mentioned the native support in NETCONF, but in general, you will need to create a plan to return the configuration to a previous state when needed. Features like *commit-confirm*, which requires validating a change after deploying it, are a first safeguard to avoid losing access permanently to a device because of a configuration change.

You have many options to implement configuration deployment, depending on the type of network infrastructure being automated:

- Custom applications using multiplatform libraries (e.g., Netmiko, NAPALM, ncclient, Scrapli, gNMIc), specific vendor SDKs (e.g., Cisco Meraki SDK, Juniper Networks Junos PyEZ, AWS Boto3), or directly via APIs calls

- Multipurpose open source tooling (e.g., Terraform, Ansible)

- Vendor platforms (e.g., Cisco Crosswork Network Services Orchestrator, or NSO, and Juniper Apstra)

Unattended network changes may sound scary for some operation teams, especially for those with little understanding of what's going on behind the scenes of automation. We recommend first testing the changes in dry-run mode to increase awareness, and then start with a lab environment or less critical infrastructure before eventually targeting critical ones.

You should never underestimate the risks of automated configuration deployment and should add the protection mechanism that makes you feel in control. Pre-deployment tests, change review processes and approvals, or deploying changes via one of the deployment strategies covered in Chapter 13 are all recommended to help manage this risk. It's a common practice to connect configuration deployment with the observability component of the automation architecture for a post-validation of the network infrastructure state after the configuration changes have been deployed. This validation can be composed of multiple checks to validate that the operational state after the change matches the expectations defined in the SoT. Sometimes validation simply entails checking that the state hasn't changed since the configuration change. Test frameworks like PyATS (*https://oreil.ly/3n4iI*) or the Robot Framework (*https://robotframework.org*) can help implement this validation.

Another common use case in this area is *zero touch provisioning* (*ZTP*). Here, a network device is automatically configured from scratch when it is connected to the network. You still need to render the intended configuration, but the difference is that you need a discovery mechanism in the device (e.g., DHCP) to find out where to pull the configuration from, self-identifying via its MAC address or serial number.

Operations

Still, in the automation engine scope, there are network operations that are not related to configuration management. These operations have been exposed, traditionally, via a CLI, but as introduced in Chapter 10, the new programmatic interfaces offer access to RPC operations (e.g., gNOI or NETCONF).

Some common operations in networking are system reboot, ping and traceroute, file transfer, NOS activation, and certificate management. Using only these operations, without configuration management, you can implement several network automation solutions. As an example, a NOS upgrade solution could encompass the following tasks:

1. Pre-validate that the device has enough space to store the NOS files.
2. Make a local copy of the configuration for rollback.
3. Transfer the new NOS files.
4. Activate the new NOS and reboot.
5. Post-validate the device status with a ping and a traceroute.

Next, we focus on the antagonist of the automation engine, the one focused on retrieving the operational state, not changing it.

Telemetry and Observability

In networking, we have been doing network monitoring (or network performance management) since the beginning (SNMPv1 was standardized in 1990). The need for more insight into the state of network services has motivated a continuous evolution that brings us to the present moment. Nowadays, the DevOps approach, where development and operations work side by side, requires better understanding of networking performance within the whole context of IT services.

Thus, the *telemetry and observability* component, within the network automation architecture, goes further than the previous network monitoring scope. Knowing *what* is wrong is not enough; this component has to point out *why* it is wrong (so it can be mitigated) and how it connects to the business impacting the user experience. In other words, telemetry and observability have to provide *network assurance* or verification that the network state matches the intended one (coming from the SoT) and correlate that with how it impacts any applications running on top. If drift occurs, this component can trigger a closed-loop automation process (via orchestration) to remediate the drift, or at least support troubleshooting efforts.

Most of the concepts in this section are not networking specific but apply to all types of IT services.

The key characteristics of these solutions are as follows:

- Convergence of multiple data sources, with optimized and higher-performing retrieval
- Flexible data manipulation and enrichment
- API-driven data consumption with powerful query languages
- Scale-out capacity and easy service composability

With these features, you will get better capacity planning and anomaly detection or advanced alerting decisions to trigger other automation workflows (implementing closed-loop solutions). Also, because of the extensibility of the stack, it is possible to connect new solutions, such as analytic ones (based on artificial intelligence), to enhance the capabilities.

However, all these benefits come with the challenges of more complex architecture and orchestration. To better tackle these challenges, we propose a stack reference, covered in "Telemetry and observability stack" on page 761, to help you understand the role of each component and its design.

But before getting into the stack, it's worth doing a quick recap of the type of data we would collect and its source.

Operational state data

Automation is about data. As presented in the "Source of Truth" on page 727, you need to use structured data to express the intent of your network design. Here, data is king again, because it's going to *tell* you about what is going on in the network and the surrounding automation solutions (don't forget that automation becomes an indistinguishable part of your network).

In this section, we provide a high-level description of the various data use cases that a telemetry and observability solution could take into account. And the data will come from multiple sources and formats. However, as you may guess, the same data quality principles (introduced in "Data quality" on page 728) are still valid here. Therefore, the data will be transformed and normalized to make it comparable.

Next, we describe several data types you should consider in scope. Don't feel pressured to use all of them on day one; choose wisely where to start and evolve from there. We start with the common ones in IT: metrics, logs, and traces. Then we also look at network-specific ones: flows and packet traces.

> In Chapter 4, The Three Pillars of Observability (*https://oreil.ly/ dso_ch4*), from *Distributed Systems Observability* by Cindy Sridharan (O'Reilly), you will find a more detailed description of metrics, logs, and traces.

Metrics. *Metrics* are the simplest type of data, only a number. However, metrics are really useful to represent network state—for instance, the amount of received/sent octets in an interface, the observed latency on an ICMP echo/reply, or the state of a BGP session (where each state maps to an integer). This information is the raw data used to create other metrics by mathematically processing it. From the difference, in a period of time, of received octets, you can obtain the incoming bits per second rate.

> Metrics are a numeric representation of data measured over intervals of time.
>
> —*Distributed Systems Observability*, Cindy Sridharan

Everything about the network state can be expressed as metrics. In networking, most of these metrics are well-defined using SNMP MIBs or YANG models, but you can define any metric you consider relevant for your use case, including the applications running on top of the network. For example, you can define a metric that tracks how many automated firewall rules have been created to track the activity in an automated firewall rule process.

One historical limitation of metrics for monitoring has been the lack of *context* around a *sample* (a metric value at a concrete moment). Modern metric storage systems allow enriching metrics with extra metadata along with the sample. Figure 14-7 shows the four parts of a metric in the Prometheus metric format (you'll learn more about Prometheus and other TSDBs in "Storage" on page 767). Notice how the contextual information can enrich the metrics with data you consider relevant (usually taken from the SoT).

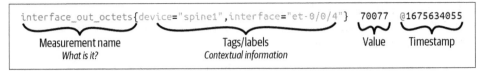

Figure 14-7. Prometheus metric format

In Example 14-6, three samples from Prometheus indicate the attributes illustrated in Figure 14-7.

Example 14-6. Prometheus metric

```
bgp_sessions_prefixes_sent{collection_method="execd",device="ceos-01",     ❶
device_platform="arista",device_role="router",host="telegraf-01",local_as="65111",
neighbor_address="10.1.7.2",net_os="eos",peer_as="65222",peer_type="external",
region="lab",router_id="10.17.17.1",session_state="active",site="lab-site-01"} ❷

0 @1671966244.39                                                             ❸ ❹
3 @1671966247.39
2 @1671966250.39
```

❶ `bgp_sessions_prefixes_sent` is the name of the metric.

❷ The key-value pairs are the labels or metadata associated with the metric. We could later consume the metric using it.

❸ `0`, `3`, and `2` are the values of the metric at three specific times.

❹ `1671966244.39`, `1671966247.39`, and `1671966250.39` are the metric sampling times as timestamps.

 In heterogeneous network environments, you would get data from different sources but with the same meaning. Being able to transform all to the same format would ease later comparison and consumption.

Logs. *Logs* are produced by the network infrastructure and network automation applications to notify of any activity that deserves attention. Syslog is the de facto logging protocol, available in almost every network device.

> An event log is an immutable, timestamped record of discrete events that happened over time.
>
> —*Distributed Systems Observability*, Cindy Sridharan

The syslog message contains five main components: the message (the content), the facility (type of the system originating the message), the priority (severity of

---

the message), the source IP, and the timestamp. However, this information comes unstructured in free-form text that varies from vendor to vendor. To make use of the data programmatically, it must be parsed and converted into structured data.

Almost every log collector provides parsers that help define the rules to *interpret* the syslog message. For example, the Logstash log collector (*https://oreil.ly/yPDFT*) has the grok filter to define the parsing logic in the templates to extract the data fields.

In Example 14-7, a log message is transformed into a structured object.

Example 14-7. Log parsing

Raw log message:

```
Sep 20 08:01:13: <10.0.0.10> %LINEPROTO-5-UPDOWN: Line protocol on Interface
GigabitEthernet0/5, changed state to up
```

Structured data output:

```
{
  "source_ip": "10.0.0.10",
  "severity": "5",
  "facility": "LINEPROTO",
  "facility_process": "UPDOWN",
  "message": "Line protocol on Interface GigabitEthernet0/5, changed state to up",
} 1663660873000
```

 Log patterns are likely available to match the messages you are interested in. Furthermore, the napalm-logs library (*https://oreil.ly/ 3uM0Q*) comes with predefined parsers for some popular platforms (*https://oreil.ly/zM3DX*), providing a structured output following the OpenConfig or IETF YANG models.

Structured logs are an example of *high-dimensional structured data*. By definition, this type of observed data contains multiple features. For instance, the log entry from Example 14-7 has a timestamp, a facility, an IP, etc., versus being a raw string (as it was originally before structuring it). The network automation realm has other high-dimensional structured data: traces, flows, and packet captures.

 Having more data dimensions offers many advanced options for analyzing it. However, this increment requires extra effort for its processing and/or analysis (sometimes exponential). This trade-off was named the *curse of dimensionality* by mathematician Richard E. Bellman.

Traces. Maybe they're not commonly related to networking operations, but with software entering into the networking space as a control plane or automation, traces are becoming important for understanding how the network-related applications are behaving. *Traces* are used extensively in distributed applications to track process executions, such as a request traversing several services. This is especially relevant for microservice architectures, to understand the end-to-end processing, and capturing relevant data in multiple control points, like the time spent in each stage.

Newer than metrics and logs, traces have been the main factor in promoting a standardized format to ease integration between senders and receivers. In 2019, the OpenTelemetry project was created at the CNCF (*https://www.cncf.io*). The project's goal is to provide standardized vendor-agnostic SDKs, APIs, and tools for ingesting, transforming, and sending observability data. Its scope is not only traces but also metrics and logs. The solutions to analyze traces are commonly named application performance management (APM), and examples include Cisco AppDynamics (*https://www.appdynamics.com*), Elastic Observability (*https://oreil.ly/WJ_SR*), and Honeycomb (*https://www.honeycomb.io*).

Flows.   A specific high-dimensional structured data type for networking is the *flow* that describes communication between two IP addresses. Nowadays, several formats coexist. It started with NetFlow, developed by Cisco in the late 1990s. NetFlow v9 served as the basis for the standard version of Internet Protocol Flow Information Export (IPFIX). Another protocol in use is sFlow, developed by InMon Corp. and supported by the sFlow consortium (*https://sflow.org*), which also offers packet data capturing (which has been added to IPFIX too).

With its own format specifics, a flow contains some common information: the source and destination IP address and TCP/UDP port, the packet/byte count, plus other information. This data is useful for capacity planning, flow-based billing, security monitoring, or application discovery, for example. The following is a simplified representation of a flow:

```
| Timestamp   | Src IP    | Src Port | Dst IP    | Dst Port | Intf  | Prot | Bytes |
| 1671966244  | 192.0.2.1 | 32541    | 192.0.2.2 | 443      | Gi0/0 | TCP  | 1234  |
```

 Keep in mind the extra cost of flow export because it's a computational task. Capturing flows in all your network ports or using aggressive sampling could impact your network devices.

Packet capture.   Yet another source of operational network data is *packet captures*. Networks move packets, so these packets provide the most detailed information about their behavior. Like flows, packet captures also require a lot of resources, especially on memory (depending on how much information from a packet is persisted).

You are likely aware of popular tools like Linux tcpdump (*https://www.tcpdump.org*) and Wireshark (*https://www.wireshark.org*), using the libpcap/Npcap libraries to capture network data. The following example shows the two packets (only summary data) for a ping conversation (ICMP request and reply):

```
18:48:46.439907 IP 192.2.0.2 > 192.2.0.1: ICMP echo request, id 31, seq 0, length 64
18:48:46.455567 IP 192.2.0.1 > 192.2.0.2: ICMP echo reply, id 31, seq 0, length 64
```

You could argue that the preceding example is not structured data, and you would be right. To get structured data, you need to interact with the libraries or parse the output as we did for the logs.

These data sources offer different information that can be relevant for different purposes. Choosing which data sources are needed, and how those have to be aggregated to correlate information, is part of your architectural decisions.

Options to collect network operational data

The next question to solve is, how to obtain the data? In addition to the mechanisms we already mentioned (syslog for logs or NetFlow for flows), in this part, we discuss other common ways to collect operational state from the network.

SNMP. SNMP has been the king of network monitoring for years. It works well for device monitoring and has been widely adopted by all vendors, which makes it a reliable way to retrieve data. It exposes the data structured in MIBs and implements a *pull* approach: the client *asks* for data every time it needs it. However, SNMP comes with limited support for *push* notifications (called *traps*).

MIB structure adds complexity that requires correlation to obtain relevant information. For example, to create the metric `interface_out_octets{interface="Gigabi tEthernet0/1"} 1234` (again, using Prometheus syntax), you need to combine two pieces of data because the index, 3, doesn't provide enough context:

```
interfaces.ifTable.ifEntry.ifOutOctets.3 = Counter32: 1234
  corresponds to
interfaces.ifTable.ifEntry.ifDescr.3 = GigabitEthernet0/1
```

Syslog and flow exporters. Even though syslog and flow protocols deal with different data, both share similar patterns. They run directly on a process in the network device, and they send the data via UDP to a target (the collector). In both cases, the information is sent without a guarantee of reception.

Each one has its own basic configuration options. For syslog, you select the *facilities* (processes) and the *severity* level of the messages. And, for flow exporters, the key configuration is the interfaces under observation and the packet sampling (the percentage of actual packets exported).

CLI. The other traditional way to get network state is the CLI. Network engineers have used it for troubleshooting, and sometimes it provides information that is not available via other interfaces. However, CLI data comes unstructured and must be retrieved as text and parsed. In this example, you can observe how much relevant BGP information can be obtained from the CLI output, but it would require parsing it to extract the data and allow its consumption:

```
Router# show ip bgp 192.0.2.3 255.255.255.255

BGP routing table entry for 192.0.2.3/32, version 35
Paths: (2 available, best #2, table default)
Multipath: eBGP
Flag: 0x860
  Advertised to update-groups:
    1
  200
    203.0.113.166 from 203.0.113.166 (192.168.0.102)
      Origin incomplete, localpref 100, valid, external, backup/repair
      Only allowed to recurse through connected route
  200
    203.0.113.165 from 203.0.113.165 (192.168.0.102)
      Origin incomplete, localpref 100, weight 100, valid, external, best
      Only allowed to recurse through connected route
```

 As we've mentioned several times throughout this book, retrieving data by scraping text from a CLI is error prone, slow, and requires fragile and difficult-to-maintain parsing logic. It should be avoided if at all possible. That said, sometimes scraping is the only option, and even with all these caveats, it can still be integrated with a telemetry and observability solution.

Model-driven telemetry. As introduced in Chapter 10, model-driven management protocols (NETCONF, RESTCONF, and gNMI) offer an alternative for configuration management and operational state retrieval, overcoming the limitations of existing interfaces (SNMP and CLI). Regarding the state retrieval, they come with a meaningful data structure (using YANG models) and a *streaming telemetry* to improve the time to detect a change. You can review the model-driven telemetry features in Chapter 10, but as a reminder, this is the output of a telemetry subscription on the interface counters of a specific interface:

```
{
  "source": "eos-spine1:6030",
  "subscription-name": "default-1664428777",
  "timestamp": 1664428775338387214,
  "time": "2022-09-29T05:19:35.338387214Z",
```

```
    "prefix": "interfaces/interface[name=Management0]/state/counters",
    "updates": [
      {
        "Path": "out-octets",
        "values": {
          "out-octets": 723727
        }
      },
      {
        "Path": "out-unicast-pkts",
        "values": {
          "out-unicast-pkts": 4500
        }
      }
    ]
}
```

REST API. As introduced in Chapter 1, network infrastructure is served as a service behind cloud- or controller-based platforms. These services are usually managed via REST APIs. Each has its own data model that covers the features offered by the service, in a simplified fashion compared with the level of control over NOSs.

As an example, documentation of the VPN service offered by AWS offers the following information via its REST API, mixing configuration and operational state (under the VgwTelemetry key):

```
{
    "VpnConnections": [
        {
            "CustomerGatewayId": "cgw-01234567abcde1234",
            "Category": "VPN",
            "State": "available",
            "Type": "ipsec.1",
            "VpnConnectionId": "vpn-1122334455aabbccd",
            "TransitGatewayId": "tgw-00112233445566aab",
            "Options": {
                "StaticRoutesOnly": true,
                "LocalIpv4NetworkCidr": "0.0.0.0/0",
                "RemoteIpv4NetworkCidr": "0.0.0.0/0",
                "TunnelInsideIpVersion": "ipv4"
            },
            "VgwTelemetry": [
                {
                    "AcceptedRouteCount": 0,
                    "LastStatusChange": "2023-07-29T10:35:11.000Z",
                    "OutsideIpAddress": "203.0.113.3",
                    "Status": "DOWN",
                    "StatusMessage": ""
                }
            ]
            // some information omitted for brevity
        }
    ]
}
```

Network protocols. Another option to get network operational data is to participate in distributed routing protocols. For instance, running a process that speaks OSPF or BGP would give access to the inner information exchanged by these protocols. Extensions can provide more information, including the BGP Monitoring Protocol (BMP) to monitor BGP updates from the sender's point of view.

Several open source projects (*https://oreil.ly/qGFxn*) allow interacting with network protocols or simply receiving and replying with crafted messages, such as ExaBGP (*https://oreil.ly/YYG7E*). To illustrate, using ExaBGP (from its documentation), you can obtain structured BGP data:

```
{
    "exabgp": "4.0.1",
    "time": 1560371099.404008,
    "host" : "2.113.0.203.in-addr.arpa",
    "pid" : 37750,
    "ppid" : 10834,
    "counter": 1,
    "type": "update",
    "neighbor": {
        "address": { "local": "127.0.0.1", "peer": "127.0.0.1" },
        "asn": { "local": 1, "peer": 1 } ,
        "direction": "in",
        "message": {
            "update": {
                "attribute": { "origin": "igp", "med": 200, "local-preference": 100 },
                "announce": {
                    "ipv4 unicast": {
                        "198.51.100.1": [
                            { "nlri": "192.0.2.0/32", "path-information": "0.0.0.0" }
                        ]
                    }
                }
            }
        }
    }
}
```

Synthetic monitoring. All the previous information is about observing the operational state without any *direct* interaction. It does not take into account the user's perspective. Synthetic monitoring tries to emulate the user's experience to understand how the network is behaving, from this specific point of view.

The overall idea is simple. Inject data in one point of the network and compare it with the data outputting at the other end. The outcome may be a success (with information about the delay) or a partial/total loss of information.

Here, the key point is to reproduce as well as possible the communication pattern you want to observe. It can be as simple as doing ICMP or TCP/UDP tests from your network gear (e.g., IP SLA in Cisco or Juniper probes) to distributed solutions running agents that work coordinately to reproduce the interesting traffic under observation (e.g., DNS, SSL, gRPC).

> The internet ecosystem has an interesting initiative, RIPE Atlas (*https://atlas.ripe.net*), that gives you community insights about internet connectivity and allows performing customized measurements to simulate the end user's experience.

After this general overview of the various types of data under the scope of the telemetry and observability solution, it's time to present the building blocks of a modern stack implementation.

Telemetry and observability stack

The takeaway from the previous section should be that retrieving data is not a simple task. You have many options to collect data, so network monitoring solutions should be flexible enough to integrate multiple systems to store and consume that data. However, traditional monitoring systems took the form of a monolith, integrating all the features into one tool.

This makes getting started easier but constrains the system's evolution and adaptability. The best option would be to have orchestration solutions to ease the integration and configuration of the components. Lucky for us, this is an ongoing trend in the whole IT community, and many options are available nowadays.

> You can build capable monolithic solutions, but you will be constrained to choose the best tool for a purpose or to scale only parts of the stack.

To be able to choose the right tool, you need a clear understanding of the components of a modern telemetry and observability solution for network monitoring. Figure 14-8 depicts the main components of a modern monitoring stack.

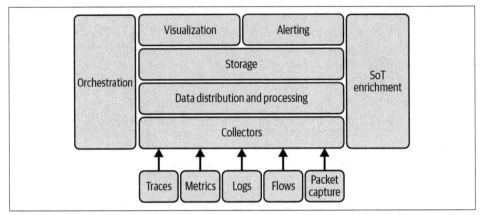

Figure 14-8. Telemetry and observability stack

As an overview, these are the seven functions of the stack:

Collector
Gathers the data, any type of data required

Data distribution and processing
Helps move collected data around to allow scaling complex scenarios

Storage
Persists the data, and offers a consumption interface

Visualization
Renders the data in the form of graphs or reports to be interpreted

Alerting
Raises alerts to trigger actions when data matches expectations

SoT enrichment
Adds extra metadata to the data, allowing more attributes to query data

Orchestration
Manages how all the telemetry stack components are configured and operated sustainably

Through this section, we will go step by step, explaining the relevant challenges that must be addressed and how to approach them. But before getting into each one, you should consider some general questions as a clear guide on making decisions:

- What is the data to be collected? (see "Operational state data" on page 752)

- How much data is expected?

- What is the extensibility and scalability of the designed system?

- Who will consume the data (and how)? (Capacity Planning team? NOC?)
- What is the required level of automation to orchestrate the stack? How will the organization deploy new applications?
- How will the system's load be distributed? (Regional pods?)

Some well-known stacks have tools that usually work together. Table 14-1 lists some of the most adopted. It is just a simplified example; all of them could incorporate other tools to extend their functionalities.

Table 14-1. Popular telemetry and observability stacks

Function	TPG[a]	TIG[b]	ELK[c]
Visualization	Grafana (*https://oreil.ly/dDJUd*)	Grafana	Kibana (*https://oreil.ly/V84Me*)
Storage	Prometheus (*https://oreil.ly/KcED3*)	InfluxDB (*https://oreil.ly/cW4hB*)	Elasticsearch (*https://oreil.ly/Hr1t-*)
Collector	Telegraf (*https://oreil.ly/0uRn_*)	Telegraf	Logstash (*https://oreil.ly/9T77s*)

[a] Telegraf/Prometheus/Grafana
[b] Telegraf/InfluxDB/Grafana
[c] Elasticsearch/Logstash/Kibana

> In this book, we do not cover how to set up a telemetry stack in detail. A good reference is *Open Source Network Management* by Josh VanDeraa (Leanpub), which covers the TPG option.

While some tools implement all the components to offer complete solutions, no tool is likely to cover 100% of your needs. Thus, being able to integrate with other tools is key. Composability in all the layers of the stack allows you to extend the features as needed without the constraints of a monolithic solution. As an example, a specialized open source tool for network state observability is Suzieq (*https://oreil.ly/lkxF2*), which offers the capacity to collect network data (e.g., LLDP, routing table, ARP/ND table, BGP), and analyze it to verify the state of the network's protocols. Suzieq exposes a GUI and a CLI, but also a REST API or Python objects to interact with and integrate with other components of your observability stack.

Now it's time to dig into the components depicted in Figure 14-8, starting with the first one in the process, the collector.

Collector

Everything starts with the *collector*, as it retrieves the observed data, either from the network infrastructure or from other sources (e.g., synthetic monitoring). But first you must determine which data you are interested in and how you can get it. In "Operational state data" on page 752 and "Options to collect network operational data" on page 757, you have the most relevant options, respectively. This decision comes from the needs of the network automation solution—which data is required to validate the outcome of the workflow? Naturally, as more workflows are incorporated into the solution, these needs will evolve, and you'll need to consider more and more options.

Processing and storing observability data come with a cost. We recommend adding data only as needed to keep focus and save resources (and money)!

You will always be able to extend the types of collected data later, but focusing initially on a certain type helps to get started. Later you will extend the coverage to other data types, supported by the network infrastructure, that are relevant to you. Once you determine the data type (e.g., metrics), you need to choose the proper interface to collect it (e.g., SNMP, NETCONF, gNMI, REST API, or CLI).

Determining how to retrieve the data may vary among network infrastructure providers. Some legacy devices may support only SNMP and CLI, while more modern ones offer newer options like gNMI. In either case, take care to avoid duplicating your data sources.

Traditionally, in networking, collectors have been deployed *externally* to the network device, because running user applications on the NOS wasn't possible. This has changed since vendors started opening their NOSs to allow running user processes (such as collectors), as happens on any server. External deployment is still the only option for cloud- or controller-based services. Both options work, so use the one that better suits your environment.

Once the collector retrieves the data, the first task is to *structure* it (if it's not already). For instance, whether it's a raw log message or a CLI output, the collector should parse it and give every part of the data some meaning (according to a template strategy).

The next step is data *normalization*, to make it comparable among sources (and formats). In Figure 14-9, the same metric data coming from SNMP or gNMI is homogenized into a compatible format, using the same metric name. In the example, the data from SNMP (`interface_ifHCInOctets`) and the data from gNMI (`in_octets`) is renamed to `interface_in_octets`.

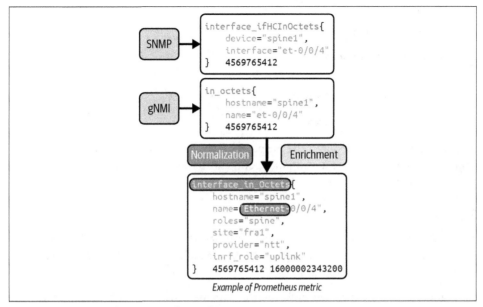

Example of Prometheus metric

Figure 14-9. Normalization and enrichment

You have many options for collectors available today; note that they're also sometimes known as *agents*. Some specialize in different data types and have multiple output options available (where data is sent after being collected). One of the key factors in choosing a collector is its extensibility to adapt to different collector methods.

Here is a summary (not exhaustive at all) of some popular open source projects:

Metrics
>   Telegraf (*https://oreil.ly/DWqAn*)

Logs
>   Logstash (*https://oreil.ly/MOZ4H*)
>
>   Fluentd (*https://oreil.ly/gWyBJ*)
>
>   Promtail (*https://oreil.ly/fnhnn*)

Flows
>   pmacct (*https://oreil.ly/PvNcy*)
>
>   GoFlow (*https://oreil.ly/uwspn*)
>
>   GoFlow2 (*https://oreil.ly/aUn7Q*)
>
>   Pktvisor (*https://oreil.ly/WXqVZ*)

Packet capture
> libpcap (*https://oreil.ly/Rt_Cs*)
>
> pktvisor (*https://oreil.ly/eyyub*)

Traces
> Jaeger (*https://oreil.ly/Z3uuG*)
>
> Zipkin (*https://oreil.ly/dNXkT*)

The collector may also have the responsibility of *enriching* the data. This is an important step, as it allows adding more context to the data, which will be useful later when visualizing or querying it.

SoT enrichment

We can't forget that, within a network automation architecture, a lot of potential exists to add contextual data from the SoT to the collected data, to add more dimensionalities for later consumption.

In Figure 14-9, you can see how metrics can be enriched with extra labels—for example, adding the role and site of the device or the provider of the circuit. This metadata can be used later when grouping or filtering the data by these labels. We might, for instance, visualize all the packet loss statistics for the interfaces belonging to a specific network service provider.

This enrichment or processing can happen in the same place where the data is collected or in a specific process for this purpose. This disaggregation leads us to the next stage: data distribution.

Data distribution and processing

Even though, for most use cases, the collector agent can collapse most functions before sending the data to the storage layer, some complex use cases require an extra layer. This is the case for highly distributed environments with high scalability needs.

In those cases, between the collector and the storage is a distribution layer. Its key aspect is the scalability to support high-throughput rates without stressing any component of the stack. These solutions are called *message queues* or *message brokers*, and implement a publish-subscribe paradigm. These transport mechanisms provide advanced features such as predefined schema validation for safer data consumption.

> Message queues are used for many machine-to-machine use cases, where scalability and asynchronous communications are required.

Several open source projects exist in this area: Apache Kafka (*https://oreil.ly/HFXfd*), RabbitMQ (*https://oreil.ly/8dloG*), EMQX (*https://oreil.ly/EueiM*), and Eclipse Mosquitto (*https://oreil.ly/lq1JB*). The last ones implement the MQTT (an ISO standard), which is a lightweight format especially suited for telemetry and Internet of Things (IoT) use cases.

Storage

In "Databases" on page 741, we presented some databases for storing the network intent. Here, in the context of operational data, a new attribute gains extra relevance: *time*. In the SoT, the network intent is something more or less stable; it is not changing every second. But, regarding the observed state, time is everything.

 In the SoT, being able to attach a time to intent is important too. You may want to define an intent in the future—for example, defining a maintenance window for next week.

In traditional network monitoring, it was common to store data in the Round Robin Database Tool, or RRDtool (*https://oss.oetiker.ch/rrdtool*). It handles time-series data by using a circular buffer database that keeps the storage size constant over time. This tool is the backend of classic network monitoring projects including Cacti (*https://www.cacti.net*) and Multi Router Traffic Grapher, or MRTG (*https://oreil.ly/VtB0K*).

Modern telemetry uses new time-series databases (TSDBs) to overcome the limitations of the RRDtool. TSDBs have the following:

- High transaction volumes to support a high rate of data ingestion and persistence over time.

- A flexible data schema so the user can define how data is organized and how to scale data via sharding and replication.

- A powerful consumption language, accessible via the API. Every TSDB comes with its own language and features. InfluxDB (*https://oreil.ly/1BxVa*) has InfluxQL, Prometheus (*https://oreil.ly/x-w4o*) has PromQL, and TimescaleDB (*https://oreil.ly/4ZwOu*) uses full SQL (based in PostgreSQL).

As an example, this is what a PromQL query looks like:

```
rate(interface_in_octets{device_role="backbone"}[2m])*8
```

The inner part of this function filters the metrics that belong to a specific `device_role` (actually, a label enriched from the SoT in the collector process). Then it creates a *rate* (in 2 minutes), and finally, the result is converted to bits multiplied by 8. You could use this same query in a dashboard, an alerting system, or a script.

An important consideration when choosing the right TSDB is the type of data it can store. For example, Graphite and Prometheus support only numeric data, InfluxDB supports numeric data and strings, and TimescaleDB supports any type (supported by PostgreSQL).

TSDBs work really well for metrics, but not for high-dimensional data like logs or flows. In these cases, other databases suit better. Search engines are NoSQL databases dedicated to searching for data content. They allow searching for complex expressions or full text, and then grouping the results. They are also optimized for stemming (identifying words based on their grammatical stem) or for distributing searches to support high scalability. The most popular open source search engine is Elasticsearch (*https://oreil.ly/Snl2j*), which offers a SQL-like query language accessible via a REST API.

Another challenge in the persistency layer is the high volume of data for long-term storage that requires scale-out and easy consumption capabilities. Some projects on top of the previous TSDBs provide these functionalities. As a reference, for Prometheus, you have Grafana Mimir (*https://oreil.ly/5h5B6*) or Thanos (*https://oreil.ly/e8y5H*).

Determining your storage requirements, such as the retention period, has a big impact on your decisions about tooling, and, eventually, on the cost of the solution.

Visualization

In "User Interactions" on page 718, you learned about dashboards as a user-interaction solution offering visualization of the network's operational state. Dashboards are the most common way to present observed data to end users. The data is queried from the storage layer and rendered as defined.

When selecting a visualization tool, you should consider three key aspects:

- Correlating multiple observability data sources in one tool
- Having the flexibility to customize dashboards
- Including data from the SoT to use as a reference

Figure 14-10 shows an example that brings this all together. This dashboard (from Grafana) comes with custom panels for different types of data (metrics and logs), and the data from the SoT adds contextual information. Combining enriched metrics and logs (vertical dotted lines) in the same panel allows you to make more educated guesses about why a metric changes the value (i.e., because of a BGP session change). Also, notice that the BGP state metric (originally a number) is translated to something easier to understand: Idle or Established.

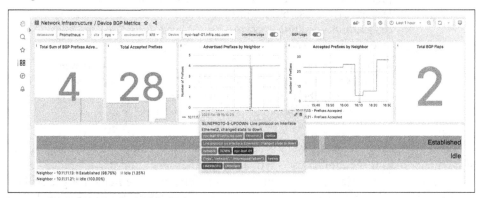

Figure 14-10. Network dashboard

The visualization tool should be flexible enough to create custom dashboards for several use cases. For instance, you might want to visualize the network topology with links colored based on the BGP state or to show the utilization of the links in a network topology.

Even though visualization is a key component of observability, it is not the only one. In the next section, you will see how to use the observed state to trigger actions.

Alerting

The other *consumer* of the observed state is the alerting component. Its main goal is to raise awareness (an event) of any deviation from the normal. This event can then be used for multiple purposes, like sending a notification to the on-call engineer or triggering an orchestration action.

In alerting, the most important point is to define what is *normal*. This can be a reference value (a threshold), taken from the SoT (e.g., an SLA defining 0.5% of packet loss), or can be *deduced* from previous behavior. In this second case, this deduction can arise from simple math like comparing the 95th percentile to the actual data or advanced machine learning solutions that automatically deduce what is not normal.

Artificial intelligence and machine learning (AI/ML) can provide educated *suggestions*, improving the criteria that decide when to alarm or not. AI/ML can dynamically process a huge amount of data to produce outcomes. For instance, as network engineers helping with capacity management, we may have reviewed traffic graphs to identify when an interface may hit its limit in the future. With AI/ML, you could get similar conclusions, but scaling the process to hundreds of thousands of interfaces. AI/ML is still incipient in networking, but its potential impact on network planning, design, and operations (aka AIOps) is huge as it can help with automating any type of decision (or help with suggestions).

AI/ML is a huge topic that we can't cover in this book, so we refer you to *Machine Learning for Network and Cloud Engineers* by Javier Antich (self-published) to better understand how these solutions are defined and *trained* to help in automating decisions.

Figure 14-11 depicts alerting system behavior. The alert engine is the heart of the system and takes three inputs: user-defined alert rules including the reference values coming from the SoT (e.g., the circuit SLA to understand whether a 1% packet loss is acceptable), silencing rules (to avoid unnecessary events), and the operational state data. The alert engine is also in charge of avoiding duplicating alerts by grouping them. Finally, it sends the alerts to various integrations, including instant messaging systems; email; incident management tools such as Opsgenie (*https://oreil.ly/rMgcQ*), Alerta (*https://alerta.io*), or PagerDuty (*https://www.pagerduty.com*); or orchestration endpoints ready to trigger automatic mitigation.

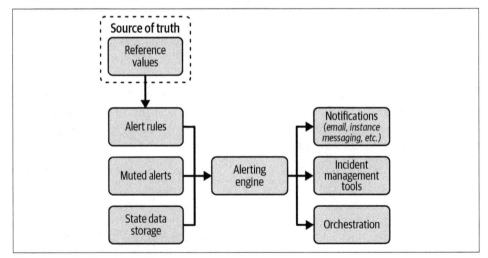

Figure 14-11. Alerting engine

To learn more about alerting, see *Site Reliability Engineering* by Betsy Beyer et al. (O'Reilly). Chapter 6 covers monitoring distributed systems (*https://oreil.ly/oJnOZ*).

Determining when an alert should be triggered is not trivial. It should come at the right time (expired events are useless to act on) and be relevant to avoid false-positive and nonactionable alerts. Nonactionable alerts (following an "alert on all the things" behavior) will inevitably be ignored because of oversaturation and on-call exhaustion.

The criteria used to trigger alerts, and their severity, should be based on the impact on the service and the capacity to act. One common rule for anomaly detection is to use *standard deviation* as a reference to see whether values are deviating from the *normal* ones. Imagine that an interface usually running at 10% of utilization jumps to 40%; this 4× increment could raise an alert, not for the value but for the increment.

 Don't forget to *watch the watcher*. Applying the concept of the *deadman switch*, the alerting system should alert when an expected metric isn't available. There are different ways to mitigate this alerting gap. You could pre-initialize all your metrics, ensuring that all your applications initialize them on start (with the consequent increase of storage cost). Alternatively, you could use the SoT as a reference, so if you *know* that there is an active switch in the inventory, but no related metrics, you'll know something is wrong with the state of the device.

Finally, to complete the architecture walk-through, it's time to focus on how we can connect the dots between its components.

Orchestration

Each component in the architecture has a purpose in the overall strategy. But, like a symphonic orchestra, a *director* is required for coordination. This analogy represents the role of *orchestration* in a network automation solution. Of course, for simple solutions, you may decide to omit orchestration, but when several steps are involved, its role is principal. Naturally, orchestration can be overarching or focused on certain processes.

As we noted before, network automation translates manual network operation workflows into automated ones; most of the repetitive work is performed by computers instead of humans. The orchestration solution should allow concatenating these tasks according to the desired flow, gluing all the tasks together.

As you can read between the lines, this is a precious skill for any network engineer evolving into a network automation engineer. You have to learn how to identify the current operational workflows to convert them into automated ones. Often this is not an easy task, because of the lack of procedures or the number of steps and interactions required.

Our recommendation is to apply a top-down iterative process. You start with understanding the global workflow, and iteratively break it into more detailed steps:

1. Identify how the step is kicked off and by whom.

2. Understanding this step as a black box, determine the required input and output data (i.e., external interactions, APIs, or humans). At this point, evaluate whether this step is necessary, so it could be omitted or consolidated in other tasks.

3. Normalize the data into structured data; minimize the required fields, and define the corresponding data validation schema to validate it before and after the workflow stage.

4. Determine whether it makes sense to break this step into smaller ones that require repeating the process.

> Approach this discovery process with an open mindset, ready to look for unknown data. Even if you are already familiar with the workflow, you may find surprises.

In the early stages of network automation adoption, workflow management may be seen as not so important. However, as you try to solve more complex operations, the orchestration becomes necessary, and workflow engines become your allies.

Workflow automation is a very open space where multiple products may do the job. Any solution that allows an *if this, then that* logic can implement some workflow orchestration. So, in its essence, a simple script with an `if/else` statement could handle the job. Indeed, the *gitops* approach, which checks changes in Git to trigger other tasks, uses this approach. However, some tools provide several features to facilitate implementing complex workflows. We could split this overall group into two main subgroups:

- Automation pipelines, such as Jenkins (*https://oreil.ly/bT8Ej*), GitHub Actions (*https://oreil.ly/E7cKT*), and GitLab CI/CD (*https://oreil.ly/G8Z1V*).

- Workflow engines, including AWX (*https://oreil.ly/0BN1-*), Rundeck (*https://oreil.ly/V_i9w*), Prefect (*https://oreil.ly/6YSEr*), and StackStorm (*https://oreil.ly/KmtkO*).

Having so many options, these are our recommended factors when evaluating these solutions (in addition to common software topics like scalability):

- How can a workflow be defined? Which language is used to define the workflow?
- How does a user interact with it (e.g., CLI or UI)? Is it customizable?
- How many integrations are available? Is it easier to extend them with new ones?
- How are events received or created? Maybe using webhooks, publish/subscribe mechanisms, or scheduler triggers?

Closely connected to orchestration, there is a subtopic worth mentioning: *event-driven automation*. We cover it in the next section.

Event-driven automation

The *event-driven* approach is a popular topic in network automation. The idea behind it is to establish a closed-loop solution that receives events and determines the appropriate response. These events can come from external integrations or any other of the architecture components—for instance, a webhook triggered from the SoT when an object is modified or an alert raised by the telemetry and observability stack. In both cases, the event-driven solution should have a related action to apply (or default to a fallback one).

The core of any event-driven solution is the *mapping* between the events and the follow-up actions without involving manual human intervention. This approach speeds up response to any event coming from the network and its mitigation or, at least, the gathering of information to help with troubleshooting. Some open source projects used for event-driven network automation use cases are StackStorm (*https://oreil.ly/HJovy*), Salt (*https://oreil.ly/nmocP*), and Ansible (*https://oreil.ly/8dOxW*).

> StackStorm and Salt are not explicitly covered in this edition of the book, but we have made the content from previous versions available at *https://oreilly-npa-book.github.io*.

Figure 14-12 describes a potential workflow for event-driven automation on top of the proposed architecture.

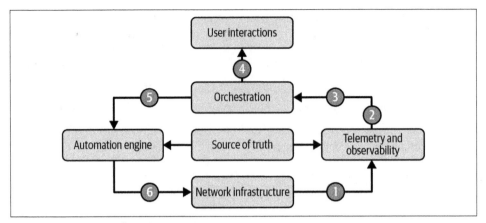

Figure 14-12. Event-driven automation

Here are the six steps of the workflow:

1. The network operational state changes.

2. After evaluating the new status versus the intended status (from the SoT), a new event is generated.

3. The event is received by the orchestration system, which triggers a new workflow execution.

4. Notifications are sent to inform users of the ongoing event.

5. The task to remediate the state is triggered in the automation engine that uses the intended state to determine the appropriate action.

6. The network infrastructure returns to the expected operational state, so no more events will follow.

To illustrate the practical benefits of event-driven network automation, suppose the current network OS has a known bug: a specific syslog message indicates an unrecoverable error, requiring a module to be rebooted. Upgrading the affected modules might require several weeks, and a solution is needed in the interim. Traditionally, this might be handled by paging an on-call network engineer in the middle of the night, who then logs into the network devices and manually reboots the module. With a workflow engine in place, you can write a rule to watch for a specific syslog message and, upon receipt, automatically schedule the run of a Python function or an Ansible playbook to reboot the module at a specific, less consequential time.

This section completes the walk-through of the architecture's components. Now that you've gained a good understanding of them, it's time to see how everything comes together with an example.

Understanding the Architecture with an Example

The goal of this example is to provide you with a mental reference to better comprehend how to approach building a network automation solution with the proposed architecture. Take it as a high-level overview of the process you would apply, in much more detail, when you face building your own solutions.

For this example, we have chosen a common network operational task: firewall rule management. Figure 14-13 illustrates an (extremely) simplified hybrid network setup, with on-premises and cloud network infrastructure. Our goal is to design an automated solution to provision the necessary firewall rules between two *applications*.

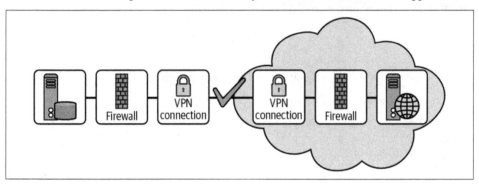

Figure 14-13. Firewall rule automation example

This scenario doesn't provide relevant details such as *what* will be the user's interface, *which* data will the user provide, or even *how* an application is defined. Sometimes you get part of this information, but more often you will obtain the responses throughout the design process. This vague context leads us to the first step in the process: *understanding* what the process/workflow looks like or should look like.

Determine the Operation's Workflow

To automate something, you must first understand it. Thus, you should gather information about the process in place today, to establish the minimum expected outcome of the automated version. This information may be in the form of documentation (e.g., diagrams or checklists) or tribal knowledge. Nevertheless, even unknown unknowns can be discovered through low-level detailed conversations.

As recommended in "Orchestration" on page 771, you could use a structured approach to understand the process from various perspectives and roles (e.g., network engineers and network users), and from multiple individuals in the same role (as each engineer may do things slightly differently). For instance, in the example, it would be especially relevant to understand the requirements of the security team that defines the security policy, but also the steps followed by the engineer to decide how to implement the security policy.

 Humans are creative by nature. Therefore, following checklists for common operations could incorporate some deviations. Take this into account in your analysis!

At this point, automation is not the main concern. You should focus on capturing, step by step, what happens in the current workflow. In our firewall automation example, steps could look like this:

1. An application owner notifies the network team about the source and destination IPs and ports.

2. A network operator checks whether the policy matches the security policy rules.

3. If so, they run some traceroutes to determine which devices must be updated.

4. The network engineer prepares the required configuration updates (using a diagram and previous examples of configuration snippets), and a change window to apply them is defined.

5. On the time window, a network engineer connects to the devices, one after the other, updating the configuration as planned.

6. Once the configurations are updated, the network engineer sends a notification to the requester with information about the change.

A lot of details and alternative flows have been omitted, but you can grasp what the current workflow looks like. This is the starting point, the minimum requirements the automation should address. Documenting this process is key to later understanding whether something is missing or is not accurate enough.

With this reference in place, you have to translate it into a workflow that utilizes the benefits of automation.

Translate the Workflow Steps to Automated Tasks

The first step in transforming a manual workflow into an automated one is to simplify user interactions and remove manual interactions. The first improves the UX and decreases the data validation effort, and the second speeds up processes and increases reliability.

Starting from the previous workflow definition, you could propose some changes or improvements (highlighted in the following list):

1. An application owner *creates a request* defining *the application names.*

2. The requested communication flow is *validated against the security policy automatically.*

3. If the communication is *accepted,* an *analytical path discovery* is calculated to determine the devices in the path (using the IP data from the application definition).

4. A *scheduled task* is created to trigger an *automatic render of the configuration* that is *pre-validated* before moving forward.

5. When the scheduled time comes, *the automation engine deploys the configuration* to the different network infrastructure, and a *post-validation check validates that the operational state is correct.*

6. Once the configurations are pushed, *an automated notification with all the relevant information is sent* to the application owner, who can *use a dashboard to observe* the outcomes of the change.

In this proposed workflow, the user needs to define only the application name, hiding the complexity of IP addresses and ports, making the user input easier to validate (the application definition is an omitted step that happens before this workflow). Moreover, if desired, no further human intervention in the process is necessary. This process simplification allows adding new steps (e.g., post-validation), which adds more value without significantly slowing the delivery time.

> When automating a workflow, don't worry about automating all the steps at once. Sometimes the effort needed to automate a task could block progress on easier ones. Delaying complex tasks until your automation journey is ready could be a smart decision.

Now that you have a clear plan of what the automation solution has to implement, it's time to map it to the network automation architecture.

Map the Automated Tasks to Architecture Components

With the steps defined, you will start noticing synergies among them, which will help group some of them. Then these groupings will map to various architectural components. As we mentioned in "Orchestration" on page 771, every task should be small enough to fit in one block. If that's not the case, choose the one that better aligns with the task's goal.

Figure 14-14 depicts the automated workflow in a sequence diagram; the *objects* are the architecture components.

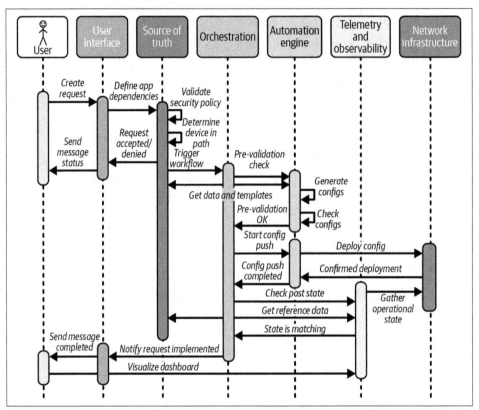

Figure 14-14. Automated workflow in a sequence diagram

In this diagram, you can observe how the tasks are related to the architecture components. This classification is important to understand the requirements needed in each block. As a high-level summary, we can summarize the requirements of each component in this scenario as follows:

User interactions
Offer a bidirectional communication channel to submit requests and get notifications of the process updates. Also, they allow direct access to visualize the dashboards representing the state of firewall operations.

Source of truth

Normalizes and validates the data received from the user, and performs extra data processing, including verifying the policy against the reference security policy, and discovering the devices that will be in the path of the communication flow. It also stores the *application* definition or provides a dynamic update of the servers registered for this *application* (i.e., a dynamic application service). Finally, it exposes the data and templates to generate the configuration artifacts, and, afterward, validates the operational state.

Orchestration

Coordinates the automation process either via a manual trigger from the user or scheduled after the changes in the SoT. Even though this sequence diagram shows only the *golden path*, it would handle any decision path to, in the end, communicate back to the user, via *user interactions*.

Automation engine

Uses the data and templates (defining the intent) to generate the configuration artifacts, pre-validates them to check whether they would provide the expected operational state, and then deploys the configuration to the network platforms.

Telemetry and observability

Gathers operational state continuously, and comparing to the intended one, it offers a post-validation check, besides providing access to relevant data (e.g., network flows or metrics) for visualization.

Once you understand what is expected from each component, you are ready to move to the next step, where you pick the tools to implement these functionalities.

> Keep in mind that, in a real-life scenario, you would gather more low-level information to better determine the requirements of each task.

Choose the Tools to Implement Each Component's Tasks

The first question to answer when approaching this phase, is the *build versus buy* dilemma. If you don't have really special requirements, you likely won't need to reinvent the wheel and build a complete solution from scratch. In this chapter, we have shared many open source solutions for each component, but many more options are available, both commercial and open source. Thus, you should evaluate which tools make more sense in your own environment regarding support, features, and extensibility.

Another key factor to consider here is your current tech stack and your team skills. If tools are already in place that can implement the new requirements, it seems reasonable to reuse them, if possible.

> As a rule of thumb, look for other options only when you identify a key requirement that can't be fulfilled with the current stack.

Resuming with the example, we propose a set of open source tools that could implement the automated workflow depicted in Figure 14-14. Consider this one of the many ways to solve the proposed example and not as any kind of recommendation:

User interaction
Mattermost (*https://oreil.ly/kpIZB*) is an instant messaging application to allow user interaction, and Grafana (*https://oreil.ly/ztVwv*) offers dashboards for network metrics visualization.

Source of truth
Nautobot (*https://oreil.ly/-M6RM*) defines the network inventory and the related models for application definition and firewall rules using the Firewall Models (*https://oreil.ly/Hrv1A*) app. It also allows integration with Git repositories (*https://git-scm.com*) to keep track of the Jinja templates for CLI-based firewalls, and HashiCorp Consul (*https://oreil.ly/zK1g5*) provides a dynamic mapping of application to IP addresses and ports.

Orchestration
AWX (*https://oreil.ly/IBMH1*) manages the workflow execution. It can be triggered manually by a network operator or via a webhook from Nautobot (*https://oreil.ly/-M6RM*) when a new firewall rule is created, updated, or deleted.

Automation engine
Batfish (*https://oreil.ly/96QMA*) provides pre-validation of network configurations rendered by Ansible (*https://oreil.ly/nbGmd*), using the data from the SoT. Ansible configures the on-premises firewalls too. For cloud services, Terraform (*https://oreil.ly/bqBlD*) is used to provision/update the services, also using the data from the SoT.

Telemetry and observability
The Telegraf (*https://oreil.ly/MwBF9*) collector retrieves network data metrics from the firewall services and stores them in Prometheus (*https://oreil.ly/Ux0ig*) for later consumption in a post-validation script, or via Grafana (*https://oreil.ly/DNFmi*) dashboards.

This high-level design is just the beginning of the story. It serves as a reference to start implementing the automation solution, but you should always be open to new requirements or improvement ideas that may impact the initial decision process. As we pointed out before, it's a good practice to document your architecture decisions, in order to make reviewing them later an easier task for you and others. And, trust us, you will eventually need to review them. Maybe some changes to the original workflow will appear or a new workflow will be implemented in parallel. With well-documented decisions, you will be able to either choose to reuse (and extend) the tooling in place or replace it with a new one.

Because so many tools are available, choosing one over another could be overwhelming. But don't get blocked by the *premature optimization* trap, spending too much time now on solving a future issue (that may not even happen). Using the proposed architecture, you will be able to replace any tool with a new one when the necessity arises.

Hopefully, this section helped you get into the network automation *mindset* and consolidate the content of this chapter.

Summary

This chapter had the ambitious goal of proposing an architectural approach to guide the design of network automation solutions. Technological knowledge that you learned throughout the book is an important foundation, but things get more complicated when you have to glue all these technologies (and tooling) together.

Our proposed network automation architecture gives you an easy-to-understand framework to map the functionalities of an operational workflow to a few components that summarize the main roles of a network automation solution (which is also mostly reusable for other IT infrastructure). Each architecture component has its role and relevance, but we stressed the importance of shifting to an intended approach where data drives the rest of the tasks, and integrations allow creation of complete solutions that can be adapted as needed.

Luckily, a lot of useful tools are out there to help you build solutions without having to start from scratch—but remember that automation is not about tooling, and you should never start your design with the tool. First, you need to make sure you understand the requirements and the expected outcomes. Then you can start mapping the features to the architecture and select which implementation fits your environment (better leaving the door open for future revisions).

We hope this architecture will help you get started building your first network automation solutions or improving your already implemented ones. This chapter closes the book, but this is only the beginning of your network automation journey. We encourage you to keep learning and exploring new technologies and tools to improve your automation skills. This book is a good starting point, but the network automation world is constantly evolving, and you should keep up with the latest trends and best practices while trying to apply them to your own projects.

Index

About the Authors

Matt Oswalt is a software engineer with a specific focus on distributed systems and internet/web protocols. He enjoys the challenge of working with large systems that require efficient, resilient design—both at scale and close to the metal. You can find him writing about his latest explorations at *oswalt.dev*.

Christian Adell is a network software engineer who has played multiple roles related to networking and IT automation. Currently, as principal architect at Network to Code, he is focused on building network automation solutions for diverse use cases, with great emphasis on open source software. He is passionate about learning and helping others to be happier, but also has more hobbies than hours in the day, so working remotely from Barcelona gives him the time and the space to achieve his dreams. He can be found on Twitter as *@chadell0*.

Scott S. Lowe works on the Developer Relations team at Pulumi Corporation. He currently focuses on cloud computing and IaC after having spent a number of years specializing in compute and network virtualization. Scott has authored several technical books over the course of his career, and shares technical content regularly on his blog at *blog.scottlowe.org*. He lives with his wife in Denver, Colorado, but they dream of living somewhere with white sand beaches and crystal clear water.

Jason Edelman is the founder and CTO at Network to Code, a leading network automation solutions provider. He founded Network to Code in 2014. Observing how DevOps was radically changing the IT operational models for systems administrators and developers, Jason saw an opportunity to combine existing technologies from the worlds of DevOps and software development within the networking infrastructure domain to create holistic network automation solutions. Prior to Network to Code, Jason spent a career in technical sales at Presidio, BlueWater, and Cisco, developing and architecting network solutions. He is a former CCIE and has a BE in computer engineering from Stevens Institute of Technology. You can find Jason on Twitter at *@jedelman8*.

Colophon

The animal on the cover of *Network Programmability and Automation* is a gavial crocodile (*Gavialis gangeticus*). This reptile can be found in two countries: India, along the Chambal, Girwa, and Son Rivers; and Nepal, along the Narayani River. The gavial's name originated from the knob of tissue that grows on the tip of the male's snout called a *ghara*, the Hindi word for *pot*.

The gavial is easily distinguishable from other crocodiles because of its long, slender snout and narrow, sharp teeth. It feeds primarily on small fish and crustaceans. It herds fish toward the shore and stuns them using an underwater jaw clap. It does not chew its prey but swallows it whole. This species rarely attacks humans, but with 110 interdigitated teeth, you don't want to get too close.

This crocodile is very long, measuring 13–20 ft (4–6 m). The color ranges from olive green to brown-gray with a light underside. It reaches maturity at 8–12 years. Males use their gharas to vocalize and blow bubbles during mating displays. Females make nests in the sand banks and guard the eggs for 83–94 days, then tend to the hatchlings for several months.

The preferred habitat of the gavial is high-banked rivers with clear, fast-flowing water and deep pools. Since the mid-1900s, the gavial's numbers have declined as much as 98 percent because of hunting for traditional medicine and drastic changes to their freshwater habitats.

Many of the animals on O'Reilly covers are endangered; all of them are important to the world.

The cover illustration is by Karen Montgomery, based on an antique engraving from *Braukhaus Lexicon*. The cover fonts are Gilroy Semibold and Guardian Sans. The text font is Adobe Minion Pro; the heading font is Adobe Myriad Condensed; and the code font is Dalton Maag's Ubuntu Mono.

Printed in the USA
CPSIA information can be obtained
at www.ICGtesting.com
JSHW052046080923
48116JS00006B/32

9 781098 110833